Themes
in American and
World Literature

HENRY I. CHRIST

AMSCO

AMSCO SCHOOL PUBLICATIONS, INC.
315 Hudson Street, New York, N. Y. 10013

Henry I. Christ has had a long and distinguished career as writer, editor, teacher, and supervisor. A specialist in language, literature, and composition, he has written more than a hundred textbooks, many of which are published by Amsco. For nearly ten years, he was the editor of the magazine **High Points**. He has been active in professional organizations and has held office at the local, state, and national levels. A frequent speaker at conventions and workshops, he has also lectured on educational television and frequently participated in curriculum development and evaluation.

Marie E. Christ has worked with Henry I. Christ as a partner throughout his writing career. She has provided many practical suggestions and usable materials. As always, her good judgment, common sense, and hard work played a major role in the development and preparation of this book.

Cover Photo: © MICHAEL KRASOWITZ/FPG International Corp.

When ordering this book, please specify:
either **R 478 P** or **THEMES IN AMERICAN AND WORLD LITERATURE**

ISBN 1-56765-042-2
NYC Item 56765-042-1

Printed in the United States of America

4 5 6 7 8 9 10   03 02 01

Contents

UNIT THREE | Can It Be Love?

UNIT SIX The Power of Poetry

UNIT SEVEN   Actions and Motivations

UNIT EIGHT | The World Over

To the Student

Themes in American and World Literature is an anthology of stories, plays, articles, essays, and poetry. All of these can be read for themselves alone, but enrichment material has been included to deepen appreciation and expand horizons.

The book has been divided into eight units, each with a special theme. Each unit has an introduction, with an appropriate quotation. The selections within the unit relate to the various themes. Each selection has a "teaser" to entice you to read the story. An introduction provides a helpful lead-in to each selection.

For deeper understanding and sharper reading skills, each selection has reading questions at the end. These focus on key reading skills like finding the main idea, identifying details, and drawing correct inferences. Words listed at grade 12 difficulty or above are tested. These are followed by questions designed to help you think about what you have just read. The section concludes with a "Language in Action" section that provides useful, lively information about language.

At the end of each unit, elements are tied together by questions that examine the selections with relation to each other. The Writing Portfolio helps you to gain valuable practice in writing, usually with relation to the selections you have just read. Then the section called "Other Areas of Communication" invites you to meet various creative challenges. The end-of-unit section concludes with a review of "Language in Action."

A glossary of words at the very end of the book provides additional information about the words tested in the text. An index of language items enables you to find a specific area of language that might interest you especially.

Themes in American and World Literature draws upon American sources, but also searches the world for stories from many countries: Third World countries as well as industrialized nations. The anthology reinforces the feeling that in a real sense, we belong to one world. The emotions of a disappointed young Syrian couple will be as completely understandable to you as those of an American teenager in love with an older man.

You will find a range of human emotions well represented in the selections that follow. Don't overlook the first goal: reading the selections for sheer enjoyment.

Acknowledgments

Grateful acknowledgment is made to the following sources for permission to reprint copyrighted materials. Every effort has been made to obtain permission to use previously published material; any errors or omissions are unintentional.

"All Summer in a Day," by Ray Bradbury. Reprinted by permission of Don Congdon Associates, Inc. Copyright © 1954, renewed 1982 by Ray Bradbury.

"The Day the Dam Broke," by James Thurber. Copyright © 1933, 1961 James Thurber. From MY LIFE AND HARD TIMES, published by HarperCollins.

"Nikishka's Secrets." From ARCTURUS THE HUNTING HOUND AND OTHER STORIES by Yuri Kazakov, translated by Anne Terry White. Translation copyright © 1968 by Anne Terry White. Used by permission of Doubleday, a division of Bantam Doubleday Dell Publishing Group, Inc.

"The Golden Kite, The Silver Wind," by Ray Bradbury. Reprinted by permission of Don Congdon Associates, Inc. Copyright © 1953, renewed 1981 by Ray Bradbury.

Tales from THE BEST-LOVED STORIES TOLD AT THE NATIONAL STORY-TELLING FESTIVAL. Copyright © 1991 by the National Association for the Preservation and Perpetuation of Storytelling. "Cindy Ellie," by Mary Carter Smith. Reprinted by permission of the author. "A Fisherman and His Wife," by Carol L. Birch. Reprinted by permission of the author. "Could This Be Paradise?" by Steve Sanfield. Reprinted by permission of the author.

"The Foghorn," from THE FOGHORN by Gertrude Atherton. Copyright 1934 by Gertrude Atherton. Copyright © renewed 1961 by Muriel Atherton Russel. Reprinted by permission of Houghton Mifflin Co. All rights reserved.

"The Girl on the Bus." From COLLECTED STORIES OF WILLIAM SANSOM by William Sansom. Copyright © 1950, 1953 by William Sansom. By permission of Little, Brown and Company.

"Dream Power Video," by Vicki Grove. Reprinted by permission of the author. Ted Moorhead provided valuable help in securing this permission.

"Fifteen, Summer" ("Mr. Cornelius, I Love You") from CRESS DELAHANTY, copyright 1952 and renewed 1980 by Jessamyn West, reprinted by permission of Harcourt Brace & Company.

"Feuille d'Album." From THE SHORT STORIES OF KATHERINE MANSFIELD by Katherine Mansfield. Copyright © 1920 by Alfred A. Knopf, Inc., and renewed 1948 by John Middleton Murry. Reprinted by permission of the publisher.

"The Sojourner." From THE BALLAD OF THE SAD CAFE AND COLLECTED SHORT STORIES by Carson McCullers. Copyright 1936, 1941, 1942, 1950, © 1955 by Carson McCullers, © renewed 1979 by Floria V. Lasky. Reprinted by permission of Houghton Mifflin Co. All rights reserved.

"A Cap for Steve," Copyright © 1952, renewed 1980 by Morley Callaghan, reprinted by permission of the Estate of Morley Callaghan.

"Here's to You," by Daniel Asa Rose. Copyright © 1995 by The New York Times Company. Reprinted by permission.

"Man in Hiding," by Vincent Starrett, copyright © 1964 by Davis Publications, Inc., © renewed, reprinted by permission of Dell Magazines, Inc.

"The Crime in Nobody's Room," by John Dickson Carr. Reprinted by permission of Harold Ober Associates, Inc. Copyright © 1940 by William Morrow & Co. Inc. Renewed 1968 by John Dickson Carr.

"The Case of the Rich Woman," by Agatha Christie. Reprinted by permission of Harold Ober Associates Incorporated. Copyright © 1932, 1933, 1934 by Agatha Christie. Renewed 1959, 1960, 1961 by Agatha Christie Mallowan.

"Deja Vu," by Mary Barrett. Reprinted by permission of the author.

Excerpt from "Kiddie-Kar Travel" from INSIDE BENCHLEY and DRAWINGS BY GLUYAS WILLIAMS. Copyright 1921, 1922, 1925, 1927, 1928, 1942 by Harper & Brothers. Copyright renewed © 1970 by Gertrude D. Benchley. Reprinted by permission of HarperCollins Publishers, Inc.

"You Can't Find It? Forget It. Your Loss Is the Place's Gain," by Minna Morse, from SMITHSONIAN Magazine, October 1993. Reprinted by permission of the author.

"Paradiso . . . Inferno?" Copyright 1995 by David J. Baker. Reprinted from May 1995 OPERA NEWS, by permission.

"Flurry at the Sheep Dog Trial." Reprinted by permission of Curtis Brown, Ltd. Copyright © 1942 by Eric Knight, renewed in 1966 by Ruth Jere Knight. First appeared in THE FLYING YORKSHIREMAN. Published by Harper.

Company, Inc., renewed © 1960 by M. D. Herter Norton and Mora Purtscher-Wydenbruck. Reprinted by permission of W. W. Norton & Company, Inc.

"Never," from COUNTRY TALES, by H. E. Bates. Reprinted by permission of Robinson Publishing, Laurence Pollinger Ltd., and the Estate of H. E. Bates.

"My Lord, the Baby," from HUNGRY STONES AND OTHER STORIES by Rabindranath Tagore (New York, Macmillan Publishing Co., 1916). Reprinted by permission of Simon & Schuster.

"Benediction," by Lu Hsun, translated by Edgar Snow. Reprinted by permission of Lois Snow.

"Bontshe the Silent," by Isaac Peretz. Translated from the Yiddish by Dr. Angelo S. Rappaport. Copyright © 1927 by Stanley Paul and Co., Ltd.

Photo-credits

All unit-opening photos supplied by
© THE STOCK MARKET

Unit 1   Trees in Forest
Unit 2   Boy Looking at Clouds
Unit 3   Couple on Bridge
Unit 4   Shadow of Man on Floor
Unit 5   Crowds, Boys and Girls
Unit 6   Greek Temple
Unit 7   Hand on Gate
Unit 8   Globe with Flags

UNIT ONE

Life Is an Adventure

Life is either a daring adventure or nothing. To keep our faces toward change and behave like free spirits in the presence of fate is strength undefeatable.

Helen Keller

"The game is afoot!" With this cry, Sherlock Holmes rallied his friend Dr. Watson to action and new adventures. The stories in this unit deal with adventure, but in each a different kind of adventure is displayed. "The Horse of the Sword," for example, is a romantic, wish-fulfillment story, always popular in books and movies.

Quite different is the realistic "Love of Life," Jack London's description of a harrowing escape in northern Canada. Also realistic, but in a low-key way, "Nikishka's Secrets" takes the reader on a magical journey with a young traveler.

The adventure in "The Day the Dam Broke" is all too real. The danger is threatening, but the author looks at the disaster with humor and warmth. The adventure in "All Summer in a Day" takes place on an alien planet, where sunshine is a rare and beautiful experience. "The Sorrel Colt" sensitively describes the adventure of a young child with a beloved colt.

All six stories deal in some way with adventure, but the adventure is not altogether physical.

The Horse of the Sword

Manuel Buaken

Filipino

MoroGlory had always obeyed me. He always responded to my lightest touch. But this time my sharp pull at the bridle brought no response. He had the bit between his teeth. Whip or no whip, he would not break his stride.

This unit begins and ends with a horse story. There are similarities and differences. Both were written by non-English writers: Buaken, a Filipino, educated in American universities, and Benito Lynch, a native Argentinian.

MoroGlory was called a bandit's horse. Unmanageable, he was given up as worthless until Maning, the narrator of the story, recognized in this fiery animal a kindred spirit and a true champion. This is the story of how MoroGlory changed from a mangy, disreputable, unkempt reject to a sparkling racer, filled with pride as well as strength.

At the Olympic Games, the equestrian events are grueling and sometimes terrifying. There is always the danger of a severe spill, like the kind that paralyzed Christopher Reeve. To avoid disaster, horse and rider must form a bond. If the rider lacks confidence, the horse will refuse to jump. But when horse and rider are in perfect harmony, the results are electrifying.

"The Horse of the Sword" tells of such a bonding.

The Horse of the Sword

"BOY, GET RID OF THAT HORSE," said one of the wise old men from Abra where the racing horses thrive on the good Bermuda grass of Luzon uplands. "That's a bandit's horse. See that Sign of Evil on him. Something tragic will happen to you if you keep him."

But another one of the old horse traders who had gathered at that auction declared: "That's a good omen. The Sword he bears on his shoulder means leadership and power. He's a true mount for a chieftain. He's a free man's fighting horse."

As for me, I knew this gray colt was a wonder horse the moment I saw him. These other people were blind. They only saw that this gray, shaggy horse bore the marks of many whips, that his ribs almost stuck through his mangy hide, that his great eyes rolled in defiance and fear as the auctioneer approached him. They couldn't see the meaning of that Sword he bore—a marking not in the color, which was a uniform gray, but in the way that the hair had arranged itself permanently: it was parted to form an outline of a sword that was broad on his neck and tapered to a fine point on his shoulder.

Father, too, was blind against this horse. He argued with me and scolded: "Maning, when I promised you a pony as a reward for good work in high school English, I thought you'd use good judgment in choosing. It is true, this horse has good blood, for he came from the Santiago stables—they have raised many fine racers, but this colt has always been worthless. He is bad-tempered, would never allow himself to be bathed and curried, and no one has ever been able to ride him. Now, that black over there is well trained—"

"Father, you promised I could choose for myself," I insisted. "I choose this horse. None of them can tame him, but I can. He's wild because his mouth is very tender—see how it is bled. That's his terrible secret."

My father always kept his promises, so he paid the few *pesos* they asked for this outlaw colt and made arrangements to have the animal driven, herded, up to our summer home in the hills.

"I used to play, but now I have work to do," I told Father. "I'll show you and everybody else what a mistake you made about my horse."

Father agreed with me solemnly, and smiled over my head at

5

Mother, but she wasn't agreeing at all. "Don't you go near that bad horse your father foolishly let you buy. You know he has kicked so many people."

It hurt me to disobey Mother, and I consoled myself with the thought she'd change her mind when I had tamed my Horse of the Sword.

But could I win where all others, smart grown men, had failed? I could, if I was right. So early in the morning I slipped off to the meadow. The Horse of the Sword was cropping the grass industriously, but defiantly, alert for any whips. He snorted a warning at me, and backed away skittishly as I approached. "What a body you have," I said, talking to accustom him to my voice and to assure him of my peaceful intentions. "Wide between the shoulders—that's for strength and endurance. Long legs for speed, and a proud arched neck, that's some Arabian aristocracy you have in you, Sword Horse."

I kept walking slowly toward him and talking softly, until he stopped backing away. He neighed defiance at me, and his eyes rolled angrily, those big eyes that were so human in their dare and their appeal. He didn't move now as I inched closer, but I could see his muscles twitch. Very softly and gently I put my hand on his shoulder. He jumped away. I spoke softly and again put my hand on the Sword of his shoulder. This time he stood. I kept my hand on his shaggy shoulder. Then slowly I slipped it up to his head, then down again to his shoulder, down his legs to his fetlocks. It was a major victory.

That very day I began grooming him, currying his coat, getting out the collection of insects that had burrowed into his skin. He sometimes jumped away, but he never kicked at me. And next day I was able to lead my gray horse across the meadow to the spring, with my hand on his mane as his only guide—this "untamable outlaw" responded to my light touch. It was the simple truth—his mouth was too tender for a jerking bridle bit. The pain just drove him wild; that's all that had made him an outlaw. Gentle handling, no loud shouts, no jerks on his tender mouth, good food and a cleaned skin—these spelled health and contentment. Kindness had conquered. In a few days the gaunt hollows filled out with firm flesh to give the gray horse beauty. Reckless spirit he always had.

Every morning I slipped off to the meadow—Mother was anxious to have the house quiet so Father could write his pamphlet on the language and Christianization of the Tinggians, so I had a free hand. It didn't take more than a month to change my find from a raging outlaw to a miracle of glossy horseflesh. But was his taming complete? Could I ride him? Was he an outlaw at heart?

In the cool of a late afternoon, I mounted to his back. If he threw me I should be alone in my defeat and my fall would be cushioned by the grass. He trembled a little as I leaped to his back. But he stood quiet. He turned his head, his big eyes questioning me. Then, obedient to my "*Kiph*"—"Go"—he trotted slowly away.

I knew a thrill then, the thrill of mastery and of fleet motion on the back of this steed whose stride was so smooth, so much like flying. He ran about the meadow eagerly, and I turned him into the mountain lane. "I know how a butterfly feels as he skims along," I crowed delightedly. Down the lane where the trees made dappled shade around our high-roofed bungalow we flew along. Mother stood beside her cherished flame tree, watching sister Dominga as she pounded the rice.

The Horse of the Sword pranced into the yard. Mother gasped in amazement. "Mother, I disobeyed you," I blurted out quickly. "I'm sorry, but I had to show you, and you were wrong, everybody was wrong about this horse."

Mother tried to be severe with me, but soon her smile warmed me, and she said, "Yes, I was wrong, Maning. What have you named your new horse?"

"A new name for a new horse, that's a good idea. Mother, you must name him."

Mother's imagination was always alive. It gave her the name at once. "Glory, that's his name. *MoroGlorioso*. Gray Glory." So MoroGlory it was.

Too soon, vacation was over and I had to go back to school. But MoroGlory went with me. "You take better care of that horse than you do of yourself," Father complained. "If you don't stop neglecting your lessons, I'll have the horse taken up to the mountain pasture again."

"Oh, no, Father, you can't do that," I exclaimed. "MoroGlory must be here for his lessons too. Every day I teach him and give him practice so that next spring, at the Feria, he is going to show his heels to all those fine horses they boast about so much."

Father knew what I meant. Those boasts had been mosquito bites in his mind too; for our barrio was known to be horse-crazy.

For instance, it was almost a scandal the way the Priest, Father Anastacio, petted his horse Tango. Tango ate food that was better than the priest's, they said. He was a beauty, nobody denied that, but the good Father's boasts were a little hard to take, especially for the Presidente.

The Presidente had said in public, "My Bandirado Boyo is a horse whose blood lines are known back to an Arabian stallion imported by the Conquistadores—these others are mere plow animals."

But the horse that really set the tongues wagging in Santa Lucia and in Candon was Allahsan, a gleaming sorrel who belonged to Bishop Aglipay and was said to share the Bishop's magic power. There were magic wings on his hooves, it was said, that let him carry the Bishop from Manila to Candon in one flying night.

Another boaster was the Municipal Treasurer—the Tesero, who

had recently acquired a silver-white horse, Purao, the horse with the speed and power of the foam-capped waves.

The Chief of Police hung his head in shame now. His Castano had once been the pride of Santa Lucia, had beaten Katarman—the black satin horse from the near-by barrio of Katarman who had so often humbled Santa Lucia's pride. Much as the horses of Santa Lucia set their owners to boasting against one another, all united against Katarman. Katarman, so the tale went, was so enraged if another horse challenged him that he ran until the muscles of his broad withers parted and blood spattered from him upon his rider, but he never faltered till his race was won.

These were the boasts and boasters I had set out to dust with defeat.

Winter was soon gone, the rice harvested and the sugar cane milled. Graduation from high school approached. At last came the Feria day, and people gathered, the ladies in sheer flowing gowns of many colors, the men in loose flowing shirts over cool white trousers. Excitement was a wild thing in the wind at the Feria, for the news of the challenge of the wonder horse MoroGlory had spread. I could hear many people shouting "*Caballo a Bintuangin*—The Horse of the Sword." These people were glad to see the once despised outlaw colt turn by magic change into the barrio's pride. They were cheering for my horse, but the riders of the other horses weren't cheering. I was a boy, riding an untried and yet feared horse. They didn't want me there, so they raised the entrance fee. But Father had fighting blood also, and he borrowed the money for the extra fee.

As we paraded past the laughing, shouting crowds in the Plaza, the peddlers who shouted "Sinuman—Delicious Cascarones" stopped selling these coconut sweets and began to shout the praises of their favorite. I heard them calling: "Allahsan for me. Allahsan has magic hooves." The people of Katarman's village were very loud. They cried out: "Katarman will win. Katarman has the muscles of the carabao.* Katarman has the speed of the deer."

The race was to be a long-distance trial of speed and endurance—run on the Provincial Road for a racetrack. A mile down to the river, then back to the Judge's stand in the Plaza.

MoroGlory looked them over, all the big-name horses. I think he measured his speed against them and knew they didn't have enough. I looked them over too. I was so excited, yet I knew I must be on guard as the man who walks where the big snakes hide. These riders were experienced; so were their horses. MoroGlory had my teaching only. I had run him this same course many times. MoroGlory must not spend his strength on the first mile; he must save his speed for a sprint. In the

---

*water buffalo

high school, I had made the track team. An American coach had taught me, and I held this teaching in my head now.

The starter gave his signal and the race began. Allahsan led out at a furious pace; the other horses set themselves to overtake him. It hurt my pride to eat the dust of all the others—all the way out the first mile. I knew it must be done. "Oomh, Easy," I commanded, and MoroGlory obeyed me as always. We were last, but MoroGlory ran that mile feather-light on his feet.

At the river's bank all the horses turned quickly to begin the fateful last mile. The Flagman said, "Too late, Boy," but I knew Moro-Glory.

I loosened the grip I held and he spurted ahead in flying leaps. In a few space-eating strides he overtook the tiring Allahsan. The pace-setter was breathing in great gasps. "Where are your magic wings?" I jeered as we passed.

"Kiph," I urged MoroGlory. I had no whip. I spoke to my horse and knew he would do his best. I saw the other riders lashing their mounts. Only MoroGlory ran as he willed.

Oh, it was a thrill, the way MoroGlory sped along, flew along, his hooves hardly seeming to touch the ground. The wind whipped at my face and I yelled just for pleasure. MoroGlory thought I was commanding more speed and he gave it. He flattened himself closer to the ground as his long legs reached forward for more and more. Up, and up. Past the strong horses from Abra, past the bright Tango. Bandirado Boyo was next in line. "How the Presidente's daughter will cry to see her Bandirado Boyo come trailing home, his banner tail in the dust," I said to myself as MoroGlory surged past him. The Tesero's Purao yielded his place without a struggle.

Now there was only Katarman, the black thunder horse ahead, but several lengths ahead. Could MoroGlory make up this handicap in this short distance, for we were at the Big Mango tree—this was the final quarter.

"Here it is, MoroGlory. This is the big test." I shouted. "Show Katarman how your Sword conquers him."

Oh, yes, MoroGlory could do it. And he did. He ran shoulder to shoulder with Katarman.

I saw that Katarman's rider was swinging his whip wide. I saw it came near to MoroGlory's head. I shouted to the man and the wind brought his answering curse at me. I must decide now—decide between Moro-Glory's danger and the winning of the race. That whip might blind him. I knew no winning was worth that. I pulled against him, giving up the race.

MoroGlory had always obeyed me. He always responded to my lightest touch. But this time my sharp pull at his bridle brought no response. He had the bit between his teeth. Whip or no whip, he would not break his stride. And so he pulled ahead of Katarman.

"MoroGlory—The Horse of the Sword," the crowd cheered as the gray horse swept past the judges, a winner by two lengths.

I leaped from his back and caught his head. Blood streamed down the side of his head, but his eyes were unharmed. The Sword on his shoulder was touched with a few drops of his own blood.

Men also leaped at Katarman, dragged his rider off and punished him before the Judges could interfere. The winner's wreath and bright ribbon went to MoroGlory, and we paraded in great glory. I was so proud. The Horse of the Sword had run free, without a whip, without spurs. He had proved his leadership and power. He had proved himself a "true mount for a chieftain, a free man's fighting horse," as the old Wise Man had said.

Golden days followed for MoroGlorioso. Again and again we raced,—in Vigan, in Abra, and always MoroGlory won.

Then came the day when my Father said, "The time has come for you, my son, to prove your Sword, as MoroGlory proved his. You must learn to be a leader," Father said.

And so I sailed away to America, to let the world know my will. As MoroGlory had proved himself, so must I.

Reading for Understanding

Main Idea

1. A major point made in the story can best be expressed in which of the following expressions?
   (a) An ounce of prevention is worth a pound of cure.
   (b) None so blind as those that will not see.
   (c) Appearances can be deceiving.
   (d) Good fences make good neighbors.

Details

2. Some of the men considered the horse's mark, the Sword, (a) a religious symbol (b) an ownership mark (c) a sign of evil (d) an indication of a meek temperament.

3. At Maning's first approach, the Horse of the Sword was (a) untroubled (b) vicious (c) indifferent (d) nervous.

4. In the race, the last horse to beat was (a) Tango (b) Bandirado Boyo (c) Allahsan (d) Katarman.

5. At the end of the race, MoroGlory (a) showed whip marks (b) dropped from exhaustion (c) turned on his master (d) broke away and raced off.

Inferences

6. MoroGlory was a raging outlaw because of (a) a tender mouth (b) Maning's cruelty (c) his defeat by Purao (d) bad bloodlines.

7. *Moro* is a word for (a) *Moor* (b) *bandit* (c) *gray* (d) *speed*.

8. The riders of the other horses were especially annoyed because (a) the Horse of the Sword wasn't a thoroughbred (b) they didn't want to lose to a boy (c) someone raised the entrance fee (d) Maning's father was a peasant.

9. The story emphasizes the importance of (a) having enough money for a good horse (b) having a horse with a long pedigree (c) using the whip skilfully (d) kindness and patience.

Order of Events

10. Arrange the items in the order in which they occurred. Use letters only.
    A. Allahsan goes out in front of the race.
    B. Maning leaves for America.
    C. Maning first approaches MoroGlory.
    D. MoroGlory pulls ahead of Tango.
    E. Father argues against buying MoroGlory.

Words in Context

1. "Down the lane where the trees made *dappled* shade around our high-roofed bungalow we flew along." **Dappled** (7) means marked with (a) small spots or patches (b) stripes running across the back (c) four or five different colors (d) brands or ownership marks.

2. "The horse that really set the tongues wagging was Allahsan, a gleaming *sorrel* who belonged to Bishop Aglipay. A **sorrel** (7) is

generally (a) jet black (b) wholly white with a black tail (c) light brown (d) high-spirited.

Thinking Critically about the Selection

1. Why was the father able to buy the horse for just "a few pesos"? How did this purchase show his love for his son?

2. True story: Snowman, a famous jumper, was destined for slaughter when he was picked up for a small sum. The new owner wanted a safe horse for his children to ride. Snowman proved to be no ordinary horse. He soon began to jump fences on his own. He was entered in competition and proved to be a constant winner. How does the real story of Snowman match the events in this story? What conclusion can be drawn about the treatment of animals?

3. What does the following sentence mean? "Those boasts had been mosquito bites in his mind too. (7)" *Mosquito bites* is a metaphor here (150). What is the comparison suggested?

4. The author has provided brief character sketches of various people: Father, Mother, Father Anastacio, the Presidente, Bishop Anglipay, the Tesero, the Chief of Police. How is each one distinguished from the others?

5. How does Maning tame the Horse of the Sword? Point out the slow steps he takes to win the horse's confidence.

6. How does the author build suspense in describing the race?

7. Would you have preferred or accepted an unhappy ending—perhaps a bad fall by MoroGlory or at least the loss of the race? Why or why not? See also "Other Areas of Communication," item 4 on page 81.

8. What is the appeal of racing—horse racing, auto racing, trotting · racing? Why do spectators get so caught up in the action, even if they have no personal stake in the outcome? Why are sports fans physically depressed if their teams lose? The win or loss doesn't affect their personal wellbeing.

9. The setting of the story is the Philippines. Do any elements show that this is in a special place? Is the plot possible anywhere? Explain.

10. Why did the author leave for America? After all, he had just had the peak experience of his life.

Language in Action

The Apostrophe

> The winner's wreath and bright ribbon went to MoroGlory, and we paraded in great glory.

You probably have little trouble with the apostrophe to show possession—if the word is singular. You correctly write *Nancy's ingenuity, the book's torn cover,* and *my sister-in-law's baby shower.* The rule is simple: to form the possessive singular of a noun, add *'s.*

The possessive plural sometimes provides difficulties. To form the possessive plural of a noun, first write the plural. If the plural ends in *s,* add an apostrophe. Boys' swim meet. If the plural does not end in *s,* and *'s: children's* toys. If you follow this simple rule, you'll never incorrectly write *mens'.* The plural of *man* is *men.* It doesn't end in *s;* therefore it takes *'s.*

Although names ending in *s* may take the apostrophe only (*Thomas*), you will also be correct if you add *'s* (*Thomas's*).

To show joint possession, use only one apostrophe: *Essie and Doug's mineral collection.*

Never use the apostrophe to form the possessive of a personal pronoun: *This is its stable. The camera is ours.*

The apostrophe has another important function: in contractions. An apostrophe indicates one or more missing letters:

It's time. (The apostrophe takes the place of a missing letter *i: it is.*)

Perry couldn't make it. (Missing *o*)

I'm satisfied. (Missing *a*)

Sometimes the apostrophe takes the place of more than one letter:

Where'd you put the tickets? (Missing *di*)

Sam should've called. (Missing *ha*)

How'd you like to eat early? (Missing letters *oul*)

There is an exception:

Janet won't get here on time. (Contraction for *will not*)

When using contractions, don't confuse these pairs:

you're—your　　they're—their

it's—its　　　　there's—theirs

All Summer in a Day

Ray Bradbury
American

> **The sun came out.**
> **It was the color of flaming bronze and it was very large.**
> **And the sky around it was a blazing blue tile color. And the**
> **jungle burned with sunlight as the children, released from**
> **their spell, rushed out, yelling, into the springtime.**

Suppose you lived in a land where the sun shone on only one day in seven years. How would you look forward to that magnificent sight that we all take for granted?

"All Summer in a Day" is set on Venus—not the barren, unlivable planet of recent knowledge, but a land of perennial rain forests and violent storms. Earth pioneers have settled this drenched land and live underground away from the turbulence of the surface. Most children cannot recall ever seeing the sun. One Earth-born child remembers from her childhood and lives for the moment when she can see the sun once more.

This is a science-fiction story, a work of the creative imagination (87), but it is also a study of how people behave. A recognizable classroom is contrasted with the exotic external setting. The events are all so strange . . . and so familiar.

14

All Summer in a Day

"READY?"

"Ready."

"Now?"

"Soon."

"Do the scientists really know? Will it happen today, will it?"

"Look, look; see for yourself!"

The children pressed to each other like so many roses, so many weeds, intermixed, peering out for a look at the hidden sun.

It rained.

It had been raining for seven years; thousands upon thousands of days compounded and filled from one end to the other with rain, with the drum and gush of water, with the sweet crystal fall of showers and the concussion of storms so heavy they were tidal waves come over the islands. A thousand forests had been crushed under the rain and grown up a thousand times to be crushed again. And this was the way life was forever on the planet Venus, and this was the schoolroom of the children of the rocket men and women who had come to a raining world to set up civilization and live out their lives.

"It's stopping, it's stopping!"

"Yes, yes!"

Margot stood apart from them, from these children who could never remember a time when there wasn't rain and rain and rain. They were all nine years old, and if there had been a day, seven years ago, when the sun came out for an hour and showed its face to the stunned world, they could not recall. Sometimes, at night, she heard them stir, in remembrance, and she knew they were dreaming and remembering gold or a yellow crayon or a coin large enough to buy the world with. She knew they thought they remembered a warmness, like a blushing in the face, in the body, in the arms and legs and trembling hands. But then they always awoke to the tatting drum, the endless shaking down of clear bead necklaces upon the roof, the walk, the gardens, the forests, and their dreams were gone.

All day yesterday they had read in class about the sun. About how like a lemon it was, and how hot. And they had written small stories or essays or poems about it:

I think the sun is a flower,
That blooms for just one hour.

That was Margot's poem, read in a quiet voice in the still classroom while the rain was falling outside.

"Aw, you didn't write that!" protested one of the boys.

"I did," said Margot. "I *did*."

"William!" said the teacher.

But that was yesterday. Now the rain was slackening, and the children were crushed in the great thick windows.

"Where's teacher?"

"She'll be back."

"She'd better hurry, we'll miss it!"

They turned on themselves, like a feverish wheel, all tumbling spokes.

Margot stood alone. She was a very frail girl who looked as if she had been lost in the rain for years and the rain had washed out the blue from her eyes and the red from her mouth and the yellow from her hair. She was an old photograph dusted from an album, whitened away, and if she spoke at all her voice would be a ghost. Now she stood, separate, staring at the rain and the loud wet world beyond the huge glass.

"What're *you* looking at?" said William.

Margot said nothing.

"Speak when you're spoken to." He gave her a shove. But she did not move; rather she let herself be moved only by him and nothing else.

They edged away from her, they would not look at her. She felt them go away. And this was because she would play no games with them in the echoing tunnels of the underground city. If they tagged her and ran, she stood blinking after them and did not follow. When the class sang songs about happiness and life and games her lips barely moved. Only when they sang about the sun and the summer did her lips move as she watched the drenched windows.

And then, of course, the biggest crime of all was that she had come here only five years ago from Earth, and she remembered the sun and the way the sun was and the sky was when she was four in Ohio. And they, they had been on Venus all their lives, and they had been only two years old when last the sun came out and had long since forgotten the color and heat of it and the way it really was. But Margot remembered.

"It's like a penny," she said once, eyes closed.

"No it's not!" the children cried.

"It's like a fire," she said, "in the stove."

"You're lying, you don't remember!" cried the children.

But she remembered and stood quietly apart from all of them and watched the patterning windows. And once, a month ago, she had refused to shower in the school shower rooms, had clutched her hands to her ears and over her head, screaming the water mustn't touch her head. So after that, dimly, dimly, she sensed it, she was different and they knew her difference and kept away.

There was talk that her father and mother were taking her back to Earth next year; it seemed vital to her that they do so, though it would mean the loss of thousands of dollars to her family. And so, the children hated her for all these reasons of big and little consequence. They hated her pale snow face, her waiting silence, her thinness, and her possible future.

"Get away!" The boy gave her another push. "What're you waiting for?"

Then, for the first time, she turned and looked at him. And what she was waiting for was in her eyes.

"Well, don't wait around here!" cried the boy savagely. "You won't see nothing!"

Her lips moved.

"Nothing!" he cried. "It was all a joke, wasn't it?" He turned to the other children. "Nothing's happening today. *Is* it?"

They all blinked at him and then, understanding, laughed and shook their heads. "Nothing, nothing!"

"Oh, but," Margot whispered, her eyes helpless. "But this is the day, the scientists predict, they say, they *know*, the sun . . . "

"All a joke!" said the boy, and seized her roughly. "Hey, everyone, let's put her in a closet before teacher comes!"

"No," said Margot, falling back.

They surged about her, caught her up and bore her, protesting, and then pleading, and then crying, back into a tunnel, a room, a closet, where they slammed and locked the door. They stood looking at the door and saw it tremble from her beating and throwing herself against it. They heard her muffled cries. Then, smiling, they turned and went out and back down the tunnel, just as the teacher arrived.

"Ready, children?" She glanced at her watch.

"Yes!" said everyone.

"Are we all here?"

"Yes!"

The rain slackened still more.

They crowded to the huge door.

The rain stopped.

It was as if, in the midst of a film concerning an avalanche, a tornado, a hurricane, a volcanic eruption, something had, first, gone wrong with the sound apparatus, thus muffling and finally cutting off all noise, all of the blasts and repercussions and thunders, and then, second, ripped the film from the projector and inserted in its place a peaceful tropical slide which did not move or tremor. The world ground to a standstill. The silence was so immense and unbelievable that you felt your ears had been stuffed or you had lost your hearing altogether. The children put their hands to their ears. They stood apart. The door slid back and the smell of the silent, waiting world came in to them.

The sun came out.

It was the color of flaming bronze and it was very large. And the sky around it was a blazing blue tile color. And the jungle burned with sunlight as the children, released from their spell, rushed out, yelling, into the springtime.

"Now, don't go too far," called the teacher after them. "You've only two hours, you know. You wouldn't want to get caught out!"

But they were running and turning their faces up to the sky and feeling the sun on their cheeks like a warm iron; they were taking off their jackets and letting the sun burn their arms.

"Oh, it's better than the sun lamps, isn't it?"

"Much, much better!"

They stopped running and stood in the great jungle that covered Venus, that grew and never stopped growing, tumultuously, even as you watched it. It was a nest of octopi, clustering up great arms of fleshlike weed, wavering, flowering in this brief spring. It was the color of rubber and ash, this jungle, from the many years without sun. It was the color of stones and white cheeses and ink, and it was the color of the moon.

The children lay out, laughing, on the jungle mattress, and heard it sigh and squeak under them, resilient and alive. They ran among the trees, they slipped and fell, they pushed each other, they played hide-and-seek and tag, but most of all they squinted at the sun until tears ran down their faces, they put their hands up to that yellowness and that amazing blueness and they breathed of the fresh, fresh air and listened and listened to the silence which suspended them in a blessed sea of no sound and no motion. They looked at everything and savored everything. Then, wildly, like animals escaped from their caves, they ran and ran in shouting circles. They ran for an hour and did not stop running.

And then—

In the midst of their running one of the girls wailed.

Everyone stopped.

The girl, standing in the open, held out her hand.

"Oh, look, look," she said, trembling.

They came slowly to look at her opened palm.

In the center of it, cupped and huge, was a single raindrop.

She began to cry, looking at it.

They glanced quietly at the sky.

"Oh. Oh."

A few cold drops fell on their noses and their cheeks and their mouths. The sun faded behind a stir of mist. A wind blew cool around them. They turned and started to walk back toward the underground house, their hands at their sides, their smiles vanishing away.

A boom of thunder startled them and like leaves before a new hurricane, they tumbled upon each other and ran. Lightning struck ten miles away, five miles away, a mile, a half mile. The sky darkened into midnight in a flash.

They stood in the doorway of the underground for a moment until it was raining hard. Then they closed the door and heard the gigantic sound of the rain falling in tons and avalanches, everywhere and forever.

"Will it be seven more years?"

"Yes. Seven."

Then one of them gave a little cry.

"Margot!"

"What?"

"She's still in the closet where we locked her."

"Margot."

They stood as if someone had driven them, like so many stakes, into the floor. They looked at each other and then looked away. They glanced out at the world that was raining now and raining and raining steadily. They could not meet each other's glances. Their faces were solemn and pale. They looked at their hands and feet, their faces down.

"Margot."

One of the girls said, "Well . . . ?"

No one moved.

"Go on," whispered the girl.

They walked slowly down the hall in the sound of cold rain. They turned through the doorway to the room in the sound of the storm and thunder, lightning on their faces, blue and terrible. They walked over to the closet door slowly and stood by it.

Behind the closet door was only silence.

They unlocked the door, even more slowly, and let Margot out.

Reading for Understanding

Main Idea

1. A main idea of the story is that (a) childhood cruelty can blast the life of a classmate (b) Venus is actually too uninhabitable to be colonized from Earth (c) children everywhere love sunlight (d) the storms of Venus are beneficial, supporting life.

Details

2. The children (a) dreamed about the sun (b) were proud that they had locked Margot up (c) hated their teacher (d) were born on Earth and transported to Venus.

3. To the children, the rain was (a) deadly (b) joyous (c) a fact of life (d) the basis of their songs.

4. The first sad sight in the open was (a) a crushed flower (b) a fallen tree (c) an injured classmate (d) a single raindrop.

Inferences

5. A child asks, "Will it happen today?" *It* refers to (a) Margot's release from the closet (b) the arrival of a spaceship from Earth (c) a surprise (d) sunshine.

6. "They edged away from her" (16) because Margot was (a) partially paralyzed (b) different (c) mean-spirited (d) teacher's pet.

7. The children tell Margot it's not the day because (a) the teacher told them to (b) they're being mean (c) Margot has lied to them (d) it isn't the day.

8. One color missing from the vegetation of Venus was (a) ash (b) white (c) green (d) ink.

Outcomes

9. When Margot is released from the closet, she'll probably be (a) happy (b) curious (c) pathetic (d) talkative.

Fact or Opinion

Tell whether the following is a fact or an opinion.

10. The children were justified in teaching Margot a lesson.

Words in Context

1. "It was as if, in the midst of a film concerning an avalanche, a tornado, a hurricane, a volcanic eruption, something had, first, gone

wrong with the sound apparatus, thus muffling and finally cutting off all noise, all of the blasts and *repercussions* and thunders." **Repercussions** (17) are sounds which are (a) noisy (b) repeated (c) wearying (d) frightening.

2. "They stopped running and stood in the great jungle that covered Venus, that grew and never stopped growing, *tumultuously,* even as you watched." **Tumultuously** (18) means (a) steadily (b) unexpectedly (c) frighteningly (d) violently.

Thinking Critically about the Story

1. There are two main aspects of this story: the alien setting and the thoughtless cruelty of children. Would this story have been as effective if set on some cloud-shrouded area on earth? Why or why not?

2. Is it a human characteristic to take for granted all the blessings of life? Can we consciously train ourselves to appreciate what we have? How?

3. In an article in *Psychology Today,* Robin Westen says, "Kids' gossip is decidedly different from adults'; it's more innocent and more cruel. Children will gossip in front of the kids they're talking about." How can children be both "more innocent and more cruel"? Were Margot's classmates both innocent and cruel? Explain.

4. What was the root of Margot's inability to relate to her classmates? What experiences set her apart? How old was she when she last saw the sun? How old were her classmates?

5. How did the author contrast the ominous rainy setting with the vision of the brilliant sun? Point out examples of good description.

6. What is the significance of this line: "Behind the closet door was only silence"?

7. What effect will the experience probably have upon Margot?

8. Why did the author choose the title "All Summer in a Day"? Is it an appropriate title? Does the word *summer* have good connotations (323)?

9. What picture does the following line paint for you? "They turned on themselves, like a feverish wheel, all tumbling spokes."

Language in Action

Simile

> "It's like a penny," she said once, eyes closed.
> "It's like a fire in the stove."

Figurative language (459) depends heavily upon comparison. The most obvious comparison device is the simile, which generally uses *like* or *as* to make the comparison. The metaphor (150) omits these words.

An effective simile can be powerful. Samuel Taylor Coleridge created a vivid picture with "as idle as a painted ship upon a painted ocean." Jim Bishop described people "chattering like excited birds pulling at a conversational worm." William T. Polk described "a baby waving its arms and legs like a capsized beetle." Elizabeth Bishop said, "Think of a storm roaming the sky uneasily like a dog looking for a place to sleep in."

These are literary similes, but folk language is also filled with imaginative similes. A visitor to the South Islands of the Chesapeake Bay heard many expressions that go all the way back to Elizabethan English. When a native met the visitor's son, he commented, "Why I can see the muscles a 'swellin' under that young skin like yeast in the bakin' pan."

One trouble with similes, as with any expression, is the loss of effectiveness with overuse. The person who first created the following similes made a contribution to language: *dry as dust, red as a rose, teeth like pearls, quiet as a mouse.* When it was first created, the following extended simile was especially effective: *March came in like a lion and went out like a lamb.* Though it is still used occasionally to suggest March's unpredictable weather, the comparison has lost some of its freshness.

By all means, use similes to make your writing more colorful, but try to be original. If you want to suggest nervousness, for example, you might find *nervous as a candle flame* more effective than *as a student taking a test.*

The Day the Dam Broke

James Thurber
American

Two thousand people were abruptly in full flight. "Go east!" was the cry that arose—east away from the river, east to safety. "Go east! Go east! Go east!"

For many years, James Thurber wrote humorous pieces for the **New Yorker** magazine and produced some marvelous and distinctive cartoons. His was a special kind of humor, a blend of realistic detail and humorous exaggeration. His characters are impulsive, reckless, rash, but in all of them we can discover a little corner of ourselves. In this little sketch, you will meet the lieutenant-colonel, Aunt Edith Taylor, Dr. Mallory, and above all Grandfather, who had to be encouraged with an ironing board!

Underneath the hilarious account of a wholly imaginary threat, there is a serious commentary about human behavior, about how panic can overcome even the calmest individual.

The Day the Dam Broke

My MEMORIES of what my family and I went through during the 1913 flood in Ohio I would gladly forget. And yet neither the hardships we endured nor the turmoil and confusion we experienced can alter my feeling toward my native state and city. I am having a fine time now and wish Columbus were here, but if anyone ever wished a city was in hell it was during that frightful and perilous afternoon in 1913 when the dam broke, or, to be more exact, when everybody in town thought that the dam broke. We were both ennobled and demoralized by the experience. Grandfather especially rose to magnificent heights which can never lose their splendor for me, even though his reactions to the flood were based upon a profound misconception; namely, that Nathan Bedford Forrest's cavalry was the menace we were called upon to face. The only possible means of escape for us was to flee the house, a step which grandfather sternly forbade, brandishing his old army sabre in his hand. "Let the sons——come!" he roared. Meanwhile hundreds of people were streaming by our house in wild panic, screaming "Go east! Go east!" We had to stun grandfather with the ironing board. Impeded as we were by the inert form of the old gentleman—he was taller than six feet and weighed almost a hundred and seventy pounds—we were passed, in the first half-mile, by practically everybody else in the city. Had grandfather not come to, at the corner of Parsons Avenue and Town Street, we would unquestionably have been overtaken and engulfed by the roaring waters—that is, if there had *been* any roaring waters. Later, when the panic had died down and people had gone rather sheepishly back to their homes and their offices, minimizing the distances they had run and offering various reasons for running, city engineers pointed out that even if the dam had broken, the water level would not have risen more than two additional inches in the West Side. The West Side was, at the time of the dam scare, under thirty feet of water—as, indeed, were all Ohio river towns during the great spring floods of twenty years ago. The East Side (where we lived and where all the running occurred) had never been in any danger at all. Only a rise of some ninety-five feet could have caused the flood waters to flow over High Street—the thoroughfare that divided the east side of town from the west—and engulf the East Side.

The fact that we were all as safe as kittens under a cookstove did not, however, assuage in the least the fine despair and the grotesque desperation which seized upon the residents of the East Side when the cry spread like a grass fire that the dam had given way. Some of the most dignified, staid, cynical, and clear-thinking men in town abandoned their wives, stenographers, homes, and offices and ran east. There are few alarms in the world more terrifying than "The dam has broken!" There are few persons capable of stopping to reason when that clarion cry strikes upon their ears, even persons who live in towns no nearer than five hundred miles to a dam.

The Columbus, Ohio, broken-dam rumor began, as I recall it, about noon of March 12, 1913. High Street, the main canyon of trade, was loud with the placid hum of business and the buzzing of placid businessmen arguing, computing, wheedling, offering, refusing, compromising. Darius Conningway, one of the foremost corporation lawyers in the Middle-West, was telling the Public Utilities Commission in the language of Julius Caesar that they might as well try to move the Northern star as to move him. Other men were making their little boasts and their little gestures. Suddenly somebody began to run. It may be that he had simply remembered, all of a moment, an engagement to meet his wife, for which he was now frightfully late. Whatever it was, he ran east on Broad Street (probably toward the Maramor Restaurant, a favorite place for a man to meet his wife). Somebody else began to run, perhaps a newsboy in high spirits. Another man, a portly gentleman of affairs, broke into a trot. Inside of ten minutes, everybody on High Street, from the Union Depot to the Courthouse was running. A loud mumble gradually crystallized into the dread word "dam." "The dam has broke!" The fear was put into words by a little old lady in an electric, or by a traffic cop, or by a small boy: nobody knows who, nor does it now really matter. Two thousand people were abruptly in full flight. "Go east!," was the cry that arose—east away from the river, east to safety. "Go east! Go east! Go east!"

Black streams of people flowed eastward down all the streets leading in that direction; these streams, whose headwaters were in the drygoods stores, office buildings, harness shops, movie theatres, were fed by trickles of housewives, children, cripples, servants, dogs, and cats, slipping out of the houses past which the main streams flowed, shouting and screaming. People ran out leaving fires burning and food cooking and doors wide open. I remember, however, that my mother turned out all the fires and that she took with her a dozen eggs and two loaves of bread. It was her plan to make Memorial Hall, just two blocks away, and take refuge somewhere in the top of it, in one of the dusty rooms where war veterans met and where old battle flags and stage scenery were stored. But the seething throngs, shouting "Go east!" drew her along and the rest of us with her. When grandfather regained full consciousness, at

Parsons Avenue, he turned upon the retreating mob like a vengeful prophet and exhorted the men to form ranks and stand off the Rebel dogs, but at length he, too, got the idea that the dam had broken and, roaring "Go east!" in his powerful voice, he caught up in one arm a small child and in the other a slight clerkish man of perhaps forty-two and we slowly began to gain on those ahead of us.

A scattering of firemen, policemen, and army officers in dress uniforms—there had been a review at Fort Hayes, in the northern part of town—added color to the surging billows of people. "Go east!" cried a little child in a piping voice, as she ran past a porch on which drowsed a lieutenant-colonel of infantry. Used to quick decisions, trained to immediate obedience, the officer bounded off the porch and, running at full tilt, soon passed the child, bawling "Go east!" The two of them emptied rapidly the houses of the little street they were on. "What is it? What is it?" demanded a fat, waddling man who intercepted the colonel. The officer dropped behind and asked the little child what it was. "The dam has broke!" gasped the girl. "The dam has broke!" roared the colonel. "Go east! Go east! Go east!" He was soon leading, with the exhausted child in his arms, a fleeing company of three hundred persons who had gathered around him from living rooms, shops, garages, backyards, and basements.

Nobody has ever been able to compute with any exactness how many people took part in the great rout of 1913, for the panic, which extended from the Winslow Bottling Works in the south end to Clintonville, six miles north, ended as abruptly as it began and the bobtail and ragtag and velvet-gowned groups of refugees melted away and slunk home, leaving the streets peaceful and deserted. The shouting, weeping, tangled evacuation of the city lasted not more than two hours in all. Some few people got as far east as Reynoldsburg, twelve miles away; fifty or more reached the Country Club, eight miles away; most of the others gave up, exhausted, or climbed trees in Franklin Park, four miles out. Order was restored and fear dispelled finally by means of militiamen riding about in motor lorries bawling through megaphones: "The dam has *not* broken!" At first this tended only to add to the confusion and increase the panic, for many stampeders thought the soldiers were bellowing "The dam has now broken!," thus setting an official seal of authentication on the calamity.

All the time, the sun shone quietly and there was nowhere any sign of oncoming waters. A visitor in an airplane, looking down on the straggling, agitated masses of people below, would have been hard put to it to divine a reason for the phenomenon. It must have inspired, in such an observer, a peculiar kind of terror, like the sight of the *Marie Celeste,* abandoned at sea, its galley fires peacefully burning, its tranquil decks bright in the sunlight.

An aunt of mine, Aunt Edith Taylor, was in a movie theatre on High Street when, over and above the sound of the piano in the pit (a W. S. Hart picture was being shown), there rose the steadily increasing tromp of running feet. Persistent shouts rose above the tromping. An elderly man, sitting near my aunt, mumbled something, got out of his seat, and went up the aisle at a dogtrot. This started everybody. In an instant the audience was jamming the aisles. "Fire!" shouted a woman who always expected to be burned up in a theatre; but now the shouts outside were louder and coherent. "The dam has broke!" cried somebody. "Go east!" screamed a small woman in front of my aunt. And east they went, pushing and shoving and clawing, knocking women and children down, emerging finally into the street, torn and sprawling. Inside the theatre, Bill Hart was calmly calling some desperado's bluff and the brave girl at the piano played "Row! Row! Row!" loudly and then "In My Harem." Outside, men were streaming across the Statehouse yard, others were climbing trees, a woman managed to get up onto the "These Are My Jewels" statue, whose bronze figures of Sherman, Stanton, Grant, and Sheridan watched with cold unconcern the going to pieces of the capital city.

"I ran south to State Street, east on State to Third, south on Third to Town, and out east on Town," my Aunt Edith has written me. "A tall spare woman with grim eyes and a determined chin ran past me down the middle of the street. I was still uncertain as to what was the matter, in spite of all the shouting. I drew up alongside the woman with some effort, for although she was in her late fifties, she had a beautiful easy running form and seemed to be in excellent condition. 'What is it?' I puffed. She gave me a quick glance and then looked ahead again, stepping up her pace a trifle. 'Don't ask me, ask God!' she said.

"When I reached Grant Avenue, I was so spent that Dr. H. R. Mallory—you remember Dr. Mallory, the man with the white beard who looks like Robert Browning?—well, Dr. Mallory, whom I had drawn away from at the corner of Fifth and Town, passed me. 'It's got us!' he shouted, and I felt sure that whatever it was *did* have us, for you know what conviction Dr. Mallory's statements always carried. I didn't know at the time what he meant, but I found out later. There was a boy behind him on roller-skates, and Dr. Mallory mistook the swishing of the skates for the sound of rushing water. He eventually reached the Columbus School for Girls, at the corner of Parsons Avenue and Town Street, where he collapsed, expecting the cold frothing waters of the Scioto to sweep him into oblivion. The boy on the skates swirled past him and Dr. Mallory realized for the first time what he had been running from. Looking back up the street, he could see no signs of water, but nevertheless, after resting a few minutes, he jogged on east again. He caught up with me at Ohio Avenue, where we rested together. I should say that about seven hundred people passed us. A funny thing was that all of them were on foot. Nobody seemed to have had the courage to stop and start his car; but as I remember it, all cars had to be cranked in those days, which is probably the reason."

The next day, the city went about its business as if nothing had happened, but there was no joking. It was two years or more before you dared treat the breaking of the dam lightly. And even now, twenty years after, there are a few persons, like Dr. Mallory, who will shut up like a clam if you mention the Afternoon of the Great Run.

Reading for Understanding

Main Idea

1. The main idea is best expressed by which of the following statements?
    (a) A broken dam is a terrible tragedy.
    (b) Panic destroys judgment.
    (c) Heroism conquers fear.
    (d) A friend in need is a friend indeed.

Details

2. The High Street was (a) under water (b) incorrectly named (c) a dividing line (d) where the author's house was situated.
3. Darius Conningway was (a) the first to run (b) a lieutenant-colonel (c) the author's grandfather (d) a lawyer.
4. A portion of the story is told by (a) Aunt Edith Taylor (b) Dr. Mallory (c) a fireman (d) the mayor of Columbus.
5. The furthest the mob ran was to (a) the country club (b) Clintonville (c) the Winslow Bottling Works (d) Reynoldsburg.

Inferences

6. The panic was started (a) by accident (b) as an evil prank (c) when some water poured down High Street (d) after a confused announcement by a boy selling newspapers.

7. Grandfather's prowess as a carrier of people was (a) understated (b) applauded (c) the result of a hearty breakfast (d) terrifying.

8. Columbus residents didn't speak of the great dam incident because they were (a) brainwashed (b) still frightened (c) embarrassed (d) legally bound not to.

9. When Dr. Mallory shouted "It's got us!" *it* was actually (a) a terrified mongrel (b) the sound of rollerskates (c) the first water from the dam (d) a policeman's shouted command.

Fact or Opinion

Tell whether the following is a fact or an opinion.

10. The dam had not broken.

Words in Context

1.,2. "We were both *ennobled* and *demoralized* by the experience." **Ennobled** (24) means (a) uplifted (b) criticized (c) depressed (d) soured. **Demoralized** (24) means (a) made purer (b) aroused (c) made more evil (d) discouraged.

3. "His reactions to the flood were based upon a profound *misconception.*" A **misconception** (24) is a(n) (a) improper advertising (b) study (c) mistake (d) physical injury.

4.,5. "The fact that we were all as safe as kittens under a cookstove did not, however, *assuage* in the least the fine despair and the *grotesque* desperation which seized upon the residents of the East Side when the cry spread like a grass fire that the dam had given way." **Assuage** (25) means (a) relieve (b) increase (c) bypass (d) remember. **Grotesque** (25) means (a) violent (b) expected (c) shrill (d) monstrous.

6. "There are few persons capable to stopping to reason when that *clarion* cry strikes upon their ears, even persons who live in towns no nearer than five hundred miles to a dam." **Clarion** (25) means (a) intense though muted (b) loud and clear (c) anguished and sorrowful (d) tentative and uncertain.

7. "High Street, the main canyon of trade, was loud with the *placid* hum of business." **Placid** (25) means (a) monotonous (b) boisterous (c) usual (d) calm.

8. "Another man, a *portly* gentleman of affairs, broke into a trot." **Portly** (25) means (a) handsome (b) slender (c) stout (d) undignified.

9. "But the *seething* throngs, shouting 'Go east!' drew her along and the rest of us with her." **Seething** (25) means (a) rushing (b) striding (c) shouting (d) disciplined.

Thinking Critically about the Story

1. A dictionary describes panic as "a sudden overpowering fright; esp: a sudden unreasoning terror often accompanied by mass flight." Panic can be a killer, causing persons to be trampled to death when a calm exit would have saved all lives. How does Thurber take the serious event, panic in Columbus, and make it humorous?

2. How does Thurber describe Grandfather? What was his delusion?

3. How did the panic start? Why was the beginning ironic (264)?

4. Did some people join the rush without knowing what had supposedly happened? What comment does this make about the nature of panic?

5. Thurber writes, "The next day, the city went about its business as if nothing had happened, but there was no joking." The event had its comic side. Why did the people want no jokes about it?

6. Thurber uses a vivid simile (22): "We were all as safe as kittens under a cookstove." Do you find this an effective comparison?

Language in Action

Words and Reality

The fact that we were all as safe as kittens under a cookstove did not, however, assuage in the least the fine despair and the grotesque desperation which seized upon the residents of the East Side when the cry spread like a grass fire that the dam had given way.

Words don't always correspond to reality. Thurber's neighbors were, in reality, perfectly safe, but the words "the dam has given way" produced unnecessary panic. We are often ruled by words rather than the reality they try to capture. In naming floors, many hotels skip the thirteenth, going from the 12th to the 14th. Are superstitious visitors who find themselves on the "fourteenth floor" relaxed and happy even though they are actually on the *thirteenth* floor?

The following anecdote humorously points out the absurdity of confusing words with reality.

> One lion at the zoo received a regular meal of meat, while the other got only avocados, mangos, bananas, and other fruits. One day the undernourished lion called the keeper aside and complained, "Say, what goes on here? Every day I get overripe fruit while my friend over there lives like a king!"
>
> "Sssh," cautioned the keeper nervously. "The budget has been cut, and the new budget allows for only one lion. You're being carried on our books as a monkey."

Nikishka's Secrets

Yuri Kazakov
Russian

**"They are little fools, don't listen to them. They are mis-
chievous boys, everything is mischief with them; you are cleverer than all of them."**

"That's because I think a lot."

**"But don't think a lot and don't think a little but like this:
if you want to—think; if you don't want to, don't think."**

This is a low-key story. Nothing obviously dramatic happens.
The drama all occurs within the mind of a young boy. This is a maturing
experience for him.

The young hero undertakes a solitary trip of eight miles to his
father's fishing cabin. He rides a horse that acquires a distinct personality for the reader. He reaches his father and is given a fishing lesson.
They talk of the future.

This is a story to be savored. The descriptions of the Russian
wilderness bring the setting to life. Nikishka and his father are sympathetically revealed. The similarities and contrasts add interest to the
telling. There are no horrible experiences like that told in "Love of Life"
(49). There are no car chases or explosions. The story provides a quiet,
reflective look at another kind of life in a different kind of place.

Nikishka's Secrets

1

THE CABINS RAN out of the forest, ran out on the shore, and had nowhere else to run—they stopped, frightened, bunched up, and looked out, bewitched, at the sea. . . . The village stood all in a knot! In the narrow alleys wooden bridges resonantly echoed every step. When someone walked—you could hear it far away. The old women pressed to the windows, looked, and listened: was somebody carrying salmon, or going to the forest with a hunting bag, or just like that? . . . At night, in the strange white night, if a chap hurried after a girl, again everything was heard, and everybody knew who hurried after whom.

The village cabins with their high sheds were sensitive. They were strongly built, and each had a long life—they remembered everything, they knew everything. If a Pomor went away on a sailboat and it ran over the waves, the village saw the broad dark sail and knew: he was going to his fishery. If fishermen came in a motorboat from deep-sea fishing, the village knew about them—what they brought and how the fishing was. If an old man died, they prayed for him in their own fashion, read out of ancient books, laid him in the gloomy, sandy cemetery, and again the village saw everything and sensitively accepted the weeping of the wives.

Everybody in the village loved Nikishka. Somehow he wasn't like the rest—he was quiet and gentle, whereas all the children in the village who helped the fishermen were lively and mischievous. He was about eight years old, with a blond forelock, a pale, freckled face, big ears, limp and thin, and eyes that didn't match: the left one was yellowish, the right one turquoise. Sometimes he looked at you—and he was a silly baby; he fixed his eyes on you another time—and he looked like a wise old man.

Quiet and thoughtful was Nikishka. He kept away from children, didn't play, liked to listen to conversation, spoke seldom and then with questions: "And what's this?" "And why is that?" He was talkative only with his father and mother. His voice was delicate and pleasant, like a reed pipe, but he laughed in a deep voice like a person who is dumb: "Hui-hui-hui!" The children teased him. The least thing and they'd run and shout: "Nikishka-the-Silent! Silent One, laugh!" Then Nikishka would be angry and feel hurt. He would hide in the shed, sit there alone, rock his body, and whisper something. But it was nice in the shed: it was dark, nobody went in there, you could think about different things, and there was a strong smell of hay, and tar, and dry seaweed.

A horse stood saddled by Nikishka's porch. He was gnawing

the wattle fence, chipping it with his big yellow teeth; he got tired of it, closed his eyes, hung his head, slumped down, bent one hind foot under, sighed deeply every other breath, and opened his nostrils wide. The horse stood, dozed, and the village already knew: Nikishka was going to his father at the fishery, eight miles away, along the shore, past mountains and forest.

Nikishka came out on the stoop with his mother. Over his shoulder was a sealskin knapsack, on his feet boots, on his head a cap, and around his thin neck a scarf: it was already cold—October outside.

"Keep going along the shore, all the way along the shore. Don't turn off to the side. You'll have mountains on the way. You'll pass those mountains, and then the path itself will show you. It's near from there. Don't lose your way. Look well . . . It's only eight miles; it's near!"

Nikishka stood mute, puffing softly, not listening very well to his mother. He climbed on the horse, got into the saddle, put his feet in the stirrups, and frowned:

"Giddap!"

The horse started off. On the way he woke up and put his ears back—he wanted to understand what kind of rider he had on him now. The cabins rocked past. "Tuk-tuk," the horse's shoes clattered on the bridge. The huts came to an end, and the bathhouses poured out to meet them. There were many bathhouses, every courtyard had its own—and all were different: if the master of the house was a good one, the bathhouse was good; if he was a poor master, the bathhouse was not so good. But now the bathhouses came to an end, too, the gardens of oats passed by, and the sea glistened on the left.

The horse crunched along the sand, over the damp seaweed. He looked askance at the sea, and his eyes rolled—he didn't like the sea—he wanted to go farther to the right, as far from the water as possible. But Nikishka knowingly jerked the left rein and kicked the horse with his heels. The horse submitted but went along on the very edge of the water, bending his neck and snorting.

Not far from the shore were stones. There were many of them, exposed by the ebb tide; they were black and wet. Over by the stones the waves broke into foam, boiled up into white surf, and rumbled impotently. Here, near the shore, it was altogether still—you could see the bright bottom where sparks of mother-of-pearl shells blazed up and disappeared. A transparent wave was licking the sand. Sea gulls sat on the stones and looked sleepily at the sea. When Nikishka rode up, they flew off quietly, glided headlong just over the water and suddenly—wings up, tail like a fan—they sat down on the water. The low sun shone brightly, the sea beneath glistened and seemed to bulge. Long capes of land floated in a blue haze, as if they hung over the sea.

Nikishka looked around. His unmatched eyes were radiant; he let his lips spread in a smile. He looked at the sun, at the bulging, fiery sea, and laughed:

"Hui-hui-hui! . . . "

Sandpipers were flying over the shore, calling sadly, clear as glass. They teetered on their tall legs beside the sea and ran right up to the water: the wave retreated—and they went after it along the wet; the wave returned—and they went back.

"Kuli-kuli . . . " murmured Nikishka. He stopped the horse and looked at how choice they were with their beaks like an awl.

And what will you not find in the sand by the sea! There were wet red jellyfish, left behind by the ebb tide, looking like bloody liver, and other kinds of jellyfish—with four little violet rings in the middle. There were starfish with purplish, twisted rays, and there were also the tracks of sea gulls, long and tangled, and right there, too, their lilac-and-white droppings. Seaweed lay in piles, touched by decay, giving out a heavy, damp smell. And the track of bare feet, too, stretched along right by the water, turned off to the forest, and trampled near a curious dark snag grown into the sand. Who walked there? Where did he go and what for?

Nikishka was enjoying himself. The horse kept crunching with his hoofs and snorting. Sometimes he stepped by chance on a jellyfish, and it would splatter over the sand like precious stones. It was empty in front, empty behind, empty to the left, empty to the right. On the left was the sea, on the right the forest. And what was in the forest? In the forest there was heather, and there were crooked pines, little ones, wicked ones, and the same kind of birches. There were also berries in the forest, sweet ones: cowberries and bilberries. And mushrooms: sticky boletus, firm saffron milkcaps, russulas with a little film and with pine needles sticking up on their caps. Bears walked in the forest and other animals, but there were no birds at all, only hazel hens calling delicately to one another. Grandfather Sozon said: "The birds have flown away for some reason. Time was you'd go to the forest with a hunting bag and you'd shoot a whole bag full. But now the birds have flown away for some reason, God be with them, they have gone away completely."

Rivers ran out of the forest to the sea, big ones and little ones. Over the big rivers wooden bridges had been built. The horse sniffed the logs and listened to the water sounding below. He would take a step, bend his neck, and look back.

"Giddap!" Nikishka would say quietly.

The horse would take another step. But the sound on such bridges is hollow, and the water below is dark as strong tea. All the rivers run from the marshes. There is no pure water, all of it is dark, and the sea near the river mouths casts yellow foam upon the sand.

That black thing grown into the sand over there was either a snag or maybe a dark, uneven stone. The horse would notice it from afar, prick up his ears, raise his head high, and try his best to get to the side—he was afraid.

"Don't you try and dive to the side," Nikishka said to the horse. "That's nothing. That's just a tree that was growing, and it rotted and got stuck in the sand. See, it's a snag? That's what it is, it's nothing to hurt you."

The horse listened carefully, quivered his hide, snorted, and carried Nikishka on, ever on and on. He listened to Nikishka. All the animals listened to him.

Now the mountains began. High and black, they fell in a sheer wall to the sea. Small pines and birches clung to the precipices—they looked at the sea and waited for trouble. And down below was stony scree*: the stones were crawling down to the water to drink. There were many stones, piled one upon another. The horse walked more cautiously, sniffing, picking out where to put his feet. He walked and walked, got stubborn, stopped, and would go neither forward, nor back, nor to the side. Nowhere. Nikishka got down, took the horse by the bridle, and strode over the wet stones. The horse stretched out his neck, pressed his ears close, and stumbled after Nikishka, then cowered, shoes clicking, legs trembling. And the waves rolled noisily under his feet. "Shshshoo!" they ran up. "Ssss!" they ran back. "Shshshoo!" they ran up again.

No, the horse couldn't go on. It seemed to him that a watery abyss yawned on the left and that the sea was flowing in. It was making a lot of noise, while under his hoofs were stones—you couldn't escape, you couldn't run away! He stopped in terror, snorted, and showed his yellow teeth. Nikishka got angry. He jerked and pulled the bridle with all his strength. "Giddap!" he cried. The horse wouldn't go—he looked at Nikishka with quivering smoky violet eyes. Nikishka felt ashamed, came up, stroked the horse on the cheek, and whispered something gentle and caressing. The horse listened to Nikishka's whispering. He listened to the sound of the sea. He breathed heavily and swayed his sides. Where could he go? On the left was the sea, on the right the mountains, and there were stones before and behind. The horse gathered resolution, stumbled forward, and his shoes clicked anew.

At last they got out of the screes. Nikishka led the horse to a big stone, climbed into the saddle, and again the hoofs crunched along the sand and over the seaweed. And the land ahead kept putting capes out into the sea, like long, greedy fingers. Nikishka rode on—before him was a far-off blue cape. He rode up to it—interesting: and what lay over there, behind it? Behind it was another cape, extending still farther into the sea, and another, and another, and so on without end.

An imperceptible path was beginning, and the horse turned into it

---

*loose stones

of his own accord. Nikishka fell to thinking. He looked around and wanted to understand this mystery, wanted everything he saw to reveal itself to him all at once. If you didn't understand this mystery, all you could do was look with longing, drink it in with your eyes, listen with your ears, and smell. And Nikishka looked around enchanted, lost in thought, while the path went ever farther from the sea and on through the forest. It grew still and golden. Under the horse's feet there were tongues—yellow, red, and orange. It smelled of moss. Everywhere there were mushrooms—saffron milkcaps and ruddy milkcaps. The whole forest was burning. Only the fir trees were green, and heather spread in flat little islands. The forest was clad in all its beauty, while from under the earth peered mossgrown stones, dark and brown, and standing separately were gray, disfigured, twisted firs and birches, looking strangely like apple trees.

If only he would meet someone! But nobody came; Nikishka was alone in the silent forest. Would he come to the dwelling soon? There was no one to ask, the pines and firs kept still, the stones looked mysteriously at Nikishka from under the ground. And suddenly in the midst of this speechlessness, of this dead silence and the sounds of inanimate things, there came a song. And you could hear someone tapping with an ax and could smell smoke. With ears perked up, the horse neighed loudly and trotted ahead. He smelled a dwelling. Nikishka rode out of the forest. Before him was a little cabin—his father's fishery. Everything was new, everything strong and in good order; smoke poured from the chimney; on a long barge-pole an antenna huddled; nets were drying on racks; it smelled of fish; and a sailboat lay on rollers, its black side greasy. On the stoop sat his father, tapping with an ax. He was making a stern oar and singing a song.

2

His father saw Nikishka and got up—a huge bearded man in high boots and tarpaulin tunic with a knife at his belt. His hands were red, his face brown, his beard fair, while his eyes under their heavy brows were sharp and intent.

"My little son has come!" the father said joyfully. "That's the dream I was dreaming . . . Well, how are things at home there? Everybody alive?"

"Alive!" answered Nikishka. He got off the horse, swayed, and stamped his feet. "The chairman gave the horse to Uncle Ivan, mamma sent me, and I went . . . I rode and rode, I got all worn out, and my back hurts."

"Ah, you're my fine lad!" the father said and caressed Nikishka, stroking his flaxen hair with his large hand. "I heard stamping but couldn't figure out who it was. And there was Nikishka! You weren't afraid to come?"

"No, it was all right. I saw birds, I saw mushrooms, and I talked to the horse. It's an intelligent horse. Here, this is for you—mamma put it on me," and Nikishka took off the knapsack. "But why did the stones look at me? Do they think, too? Doubtless those that lie in an awkward position roll over at night—your side can get all tired lying the whole day."

"Stones?" the father said and fell to thinking. "You have to suppose that stones are alive too. Everything is alive!"

"And do you understand what the birches talk about?"

"Why, doubtless they talk in their own language, birch language. You have to know their language. Else how can you understand!"

"But where is Uncle Ivan?"

"Uncle Ivan went to a neighboring fishery, to Kerzhenka. Recently some fishermen were going there in a motor sailboat, and they took him along—they've got a bathhouse there. We haven't any here, so that's why Uncle Ivan went."

"And when will he go to the village?"

"Tomorrow he'll go to the village, to get medical treatment. His legs, you see, are all broken down. He'll go on the horse, along the shore."

"And how will I go?"

"You will stay with me. You'll stay? We'll go salmon fishing."

"I'll stay!"

"Well, now! I'll go and unsaddle the horse."

The father went, caught the horse, and unsaddled him. Then he brought out a rope and tied the horse to a birch so he shouldn't go off to the forest. Nikishka went into the cabin: there was a strong smell of fish, the coals in the stove were smoldering, there was bread on the table and some bowls and spoons. The walls were pasted over with posters, and up on a shelf was a pile of newspapers. It was clean in the cabin, swept up. Gauntlets hung on a rope, foot-cloths and trousers were drying. Nikishka went out, walked all around the cabin and looked in the barn. The barn was open, it was never locked—there was nobody to lock out. Nikishka was about to go into the barn and sit there awhile and think about the day's happenings, when suddenly something alive showed up in the barn, something dark red, like a dim flame. Its eyes shone, a reddish gleam blazed in its eyes, like the sun before setting. A dog! A big, shaggy . . .

Nikishka squatted down and, all eyes, looked at the dog, then glanced around—his father couldn't see. Nikishka started talking to the dog:

"Adya . . . Ooorr! Hoo-hoorrr . . . hum!"

The dog was silent, sniffed and put his head to one side. One ear up, the other down, he thrashed his tail—he liked Nikishka. When

Nikishka had had his fill of talking, he came out of the barn, and the dog ran behind him as if he had known him for ages. Nikishka looked at his father—how big and handsome he was, lit up by the sun, like a forest czar.

"Well, little son," his father said gaily, "we'll go after salmon right away! Just wait till I finish making the oar."

Nikishka went off a little and lay down on the warm sand. The dog ran up and lay down beside him, breathing fast. Nikishka closed his eyes. It seemed to him that he was still being rocked—that he was riding on the horse and that the sea gulls were endlessly flying over the sea, while the mountains and the forest went by. And someone was lightly singing a song, the voice now swelled, now died away. It was singing him to sleep, and the sun shone, while the sea kept saying: "Shshshoo!" as it rolled in, and "Ssss!" as it went back. The rotting seaweed smelled strong, it stupefied him, while clear as glass the sandpipers called: "Pee-peee! Pee-peee!"

Nikishka lay, neither sleeping nor dozing . . . The sand was warm, the dog was warm. He looked at Nikishka with fiery eyes and said: "Let's go to the forest, Nikishka!" "I'm going on the sea to watch for salmon!" Nikishka replied. But the dog kept on: "Let's go to the forest, I'll show you secrets. We'll hear what the birches whisper about, we'll find out what the stones think." Nikishka was curious about them. He was uncertain now whether to go on the sea or to the forest, but his father came up just at that moment with the new oar in his hand:

"Get up, little son, we'll go!"

Nikishka got up and went to the shore with his father. And the sea was glad: it blazed up, began to play, became blue, and seemed to beckon to them and spread out. The father leaned his chest against the sailboat and pushed it into the water. He seated Nikishka in the stern while he himself thumped along the water with his boots. But now he climbed into the sailboat, settled down between the oars, gave Nikishka a scull,* and they pulled away from the shore and unfurled the sail. The shore rocked, the dog on the shore rocked . . . But the father rowed well, the waves slapped at the sailboat's ribs and flew up in spray. They sailed cautiously up to the trap, tied the sailboat to the pole, and the father rose and looked intently below, into the inmost recess—nothing there!

"Empty," the father whispered and sat down quite at peace.

Nikishka looked around. It was quiet roundabout, not a sound. A light breeze blew steadily, the sun shone, the sea blinded the eyes, the shore was far away, dark, going to either side. And it seemed to Nikishka that he had been here, had sat long ago, for years, watching for salmon and thinking about something. Or did he dream that?

---

*oar

"The tide has begun," said the father. "The water went away, and now it is coming back."

"It's fair weather," quietly answered Nikishka. "It's nice! You can see the bottom . . . "

"Of course! The salmon likes a bright bottom. It doesn't need stones or seaweed. It likes to move on the bottom, in the mid-tide. High water or low tide—that doesn't suit it, it doesn't like that, but moves, I say, in the mid-tide."

"And that's the beetle?"

"That? That's the beetle, little son. To beat the salmon with. It is big and strong, so you can't pull it out, you'll get in a sweat. So we beat it with the beetle."

"And what if the salmon jumps out?"

"Why, no. We've got a trap for that. You see that cloth? That's a net. Those are walls on necklaces with drawstrings, and down below . . . Take a look, take a look!"

Nikishka leaned over the side, shaded his unmatched eyes with his hands, looked into the water, into the depths, and saw greenish patches of light on the bottom, saw the meshes of the net.

"You see? Look, down below there's a net, too—that's the bottom—that's the trap now, and over there are two gates, over there where the two poles stick up side by side, the gates are there . . . The salmon goes along, enters the gates—and into the trap, and in the trap we beat it. When it goes through the gates, the way is barred, we lift up the bottom and we beat the fish."

"I know," said Nikishka, remembering something.

"That's what I say, too—you know," agreed the father. "You know everything."

"But why do the boys tease me?"

"They are little fools, don't listen to them. They are mischievous boys, everything is mischief with them, but you are a good boy, quiet and intelligent, so they tease you. Don't listen to them, you are cleverer than all of them."

"That's because I think a lot."

"But don't think a lot and don't think a little, but like this: if you want to—think; if you don't want to—don't think."

"But now here's what I am thinking: where does this water in the sea go to and afterwards flows back? The rivers—they run into the sea, but where does the sea run into?"

"The sea? Hm!" the father scratched his beard, looked to the horizon and imagined. "The sea, we have to think, goes into the throat, into the Arctic Ocean. And from the ocean it pours into other oceans."

"And are there lots of other oceans?"

"Lots of them, little son. And there are many countries on earth."

"And were you there?"

"I was! In Italy and France I've been, and in Norway when I was a sailor."

"And what's Italy like?"

"Italy? Italy, little son, is a nice country. It's warm there, lots of sun, all kinds of fruits grow there, sweet and delicious. Everybody there is suntanned, they go around undressed, and there's no winter at all."

"How—no winter?"

"Like that. There's no snow, no frost, nothing. Sun the year around."

"Nice!" sighed Nikishka. "I'd like to go there!"

"And you will," said the father. "You'll grow up, study to be a captain, they'll give you a big ship in Arkhangelsk, and you'll go past Norway, around the earth, right into the Mediterranean Sea."

"And were you a captain?"

"No, I was a sailor. I've been everything: woodcutter, hunter, fisherman, trapper . . . "

"Oh, look there, what's that?"

"Where?"

"Over there it seems . . . "

"Ah! That's a seal. A seal, little son, swam up to take a look at us."

"I know. But where does he live?"

"He lives in the sea. In the daytime he earns his living catching fish, and at night he swims to the shore and sleeps on the stones in remote places."

"And why do they kill him? People don't eat him, you know."

"His pelt is a good one and he has lots of fat. He's easy to kill, he's stupid; they steal up and shoot him with a rifle. And we go after him in all sorts of ways: sometimes on sailboats, sometimes on icebreakers. Now more and more on icebreakers."

"But if the weather is bad, is it scary on a sailboat?"

"Oh, it's scary. You'll grow up and then I'll take you hunting animals—in time you'll get to know our little northern sea. Over there where the sparkles are," the father said, pointing with his hand, "where the sun is, there's a nice little island, Zhizhgin it's called. The seals herd there. On this Zhizhgin, the Pomors always earn a living. There's a little cabin on remote rocks. The Pomors go there in their sailboats, live there, eat there, wait for the wind, for good weather, that is. In good weather they put out to sea, shoot seals, and at night sleep on an ice floe. Sometimes in bad weather they get carried so fast, so fast—you shout with all your might and say good-by to your life. If a man is lucky, it will let go of him soon, the wind will change, it will calm down. But him whom it carries into the throat, past Kanin's Nose, and into the ocean . . . there, only if they spot him from an airplane will they save him, otherwise . . . "

"Salmon!" Nakishka whispered suddenly.

"Let's go!" The father moved to the nose, got down on his knees, and leaned over the trap. "And it's true! Well, heaven bless us, I'm going to lift the bottom, and you hold the beetle . . . "

Quickly the father untied the sailboat and rowed sideways around the trap to the gates. The gates came in from the sides; the father leaned down and put his hands in the water. Nikishka held onto his perch. And in the depths something was silently rushing around—something big, strong, and alive—the poles quivered, the guy-ropes vibrated like the strings of a harp. The nylon net rustled, and the father drew it to the sailboat. Nikishka stretched out his neck and looked down. Now there was less and less room for the salmon. Twice already it had lashed the surface. The father held the bottom he had picked up in one hand; with the other he felt around for the beetle. He found it, raised his hand, and waited for the moment to strike, while the salmon fought ever more violently, ever harder, struck noisily against the bottom of the sailboat, would not yield, and doused the fishermen with water. Now the fish was in full view, as if in a bowl of foam. If the salmon could cry out, it would cry out in terror. The father struck it with all his might on the head, and at once everything was cut short—the salmon became limp and flopped on its side. The father seized the fish by the gills, with an effort drew it into the sailboat, and the salmon shuffled down under Nikishka's feet. Nikishka looked at it with steadfast gaze, but it was still alive, its gills still quivered, its scales still contracted—a huge silvery fish with dark back, with lower jaw bent upward, and with large smoke-colored eyes.

The father let the bottom drop, got the sailboat away from the trap, wiped his face on his sleeve, wiped his hands, smelling of fish, on his trousers, and looked merrily at the salmon and at Nikishka.

"That's how we got her!"

Nikishka was pale, amazed, and could not collect himself. And again the sailboat was tied to the pole and rocked up and down on the wave. The father was silent. Laying his powerful red hands on his knees, he rested. As for Nikishka, now that he had become a little used to the salmon, he brought to mind his father's words about seals.

"No, I'd rather be a captain! I don't want to kill seals: they don't bother anybody . . . "

"You could be a captain," agreed the father and looked at the sky: "Take a look, clouds are drawing over the sky, hiding the sun. We'll go home soon . . . You can be a captain or you can also be an engineer . . . "

"An engineer? What for?"

"What do you mean—what for? You'll build something, that's a business, too. Even for us, you know: you could build an asphalt road along the shore, construct landings, lights will burn, machines will whirr . . . "

Nikishka sank into thought. He looked at the distant shore: how dark it was, how uninhabited. . . .

"All right," he decided. "I'll be an engineer."

"Well, now. We'll sit a little longer—and then home. I've got some fish there. Recently in the morning I was examining the net on the seashore, and many little fish had got caught. We'll make a fish soup and boil up some tea—it'll be nice to sleep, too. But now let's be quiet . . . We have to watch for salmon."

Everything was still, the sea kept still, the sailboat rocked noiselessly, the shore kept still, not a sound was borne from there. The low sun had already disappeared in the clouds; everything roundabout had grown dark and sad. And there was nobody anywhere! Everywhere it was empty, uninhabited. Occasional sea gulls flew, hazel hens hid in the forest on the shore, and the two fishermen in the sailboat rocked, and with them rocked the sleeping salmon.

3

The stove droned and crackled. It was warm in the cabin, twilight outside. The father lit the lamp and set a pail of water between his feet—he was scaling small spotted cod and thin navaga for a fish soup. And Nikishka dozed. He had had his fill of talking for the day, his fill of looking, listening, and rocking. He was tired—he was dozing and thinking goodness-knows-what.

The weather was changing sharply. An up-river dinner wind was blowing, you could hear the noise of the sea, in the west the sky grew greener and greener, a bluish tint showed, and the air became glassy: an evening of unusual purity began to come on, with stars and a lackluster heavenly light.

The red-haired dog was lying by the stove, sleeping and quivering in his sleep. Nikishka started up and listened with half an ear—his father was talking about something peaceful, long familiar, close: he was talking about fish, about the sea, about boats, about the village, about winds—midnight wind, shore wind, prankster wind, dinner wind . . . His father was big; he was bending low over the pail; his hair, flaxen like Nikishka's, hung down over his eyes; his beard was fluffed up. He himself was motionless, only his hands moved. The knife glittered, the fish fell in the pail with a splash, and his father's shadow on the wall gave a start. His father talked on and on in a low voice. Nikishka closed his eyes and saw his native land with its sea, its forests and its lakes, saw the sun, the silent birds, the strange animals. It seemed to him that he was just on the verge of learning some secret known to nobody else, that he would utter a mysterious word and the silence would be broken, and everything would start talking to Nikishka, and everything would all at once become comprehensible to him. But the word didn't come; the secret was not revealed. Nikishka heard his father's even voice and heard and saw much more besides.

He saw what the red-haired dog was dreaming about. He was dreaming about the forest, about terrible, unknown beasts who were attacking him from all sides. The dog ran and barked with fear, his only rescue was Nikishka. Nikishka heard—the stones beginning to whisper, the sea resounding, the trees in the forest rustling, someone about to call out . . . He saw—his father rocking on an ice floe in a storm and shouting; he saw, besides, a huge, angry salmon approaching the shore, swimming on the bottom, on the clear bottom, while behind it were others—they were looking for the hiding place of fathers.

The wood in the stove droned and crackled . . . Nikishka's father went out of the cabin to pour water from the pail; you could hear him walking behind the wall, getting wood, then entering the cabin. The wood dropped with a crash by the stove. The red-haired dog jumped up. Nikishka gave a start and opened his eyes.

"Are you asleep, little son?" his father said, bending over him. "Did you see what's going on in the open? Such a clear night! Take a look, go take a look . . . "

Nikishka went out—it was dark, cold, and a raw wind was blowing. The sun had long set, the forest couldn't be seen, but up above, among the stars, an oblong-shaped spot shone like a gem. It was as if a little cloud was floating at a terrible height, lit up by the last light of the sun. But now the little cloud slowly and uncertainly drew out in length, puffed up in the middle, and bent like a rainbow arch between west and east. Nikishka looked, his head tossed back. The door slammed, the dog ran up to Nikishka, and after the dog the father came out and also lifted up his head.

Vague shadows began to pass over the cloud. The colors kept changing, getting bluer, deeper—from milky to blue. It seemed to Nikishka that the cloud was straining, was trying to burn with a ruby-colored flame, trying to take over the place of the vanished sun. Stronger and stronger glimmered the colors, more and more light poured from above. But its efforts were vain: everything faded, and again great vague shadows moved sadly over the arch of light.

Nikishka looked; his father looked and was silent; the dog looked and was also silent; the horse was silent—he had fallen asleep by the birch. Everything was silent. Only the sea was brightened by the heavenly fire and sounded and resounded.

Now the light went out entirely. Nikishka went into the warm cabin and got on the bed, feet and all. The dog lay down by the stove. The father set the fish soup on the fire and put on the tea kettle.

Presently Nikishka would go to bed and dream extraordinary dreams. The village would stand around him, the cabins with their window-eyes and the forest would come close, the stones and mountains, the horse and the red-haired dog would appear, the sea gulls would come flying, the sandpipers would run together on their thin legs, the salmon would rise out of the sea—all of them would come to Nikishka. They would begin to look at him and wait silently for Nikishka's hidden word—so they could reveal to him all together the secrets of their dumb souls.

Reading for Understanding

Main Idea

1. The central point of the story is (a) a sensitive boy's reactions to the sights and sounds of the forest and the sea (b) the rigors of salmon fishing in northern Russia (c) the thoughtless cruelty to animals (d) the way in which a dog and its master bond.

Details

2. All the following describe Nikishka EXCEPT (a) freckled face (b) big ears (c) unmatched eyes (d) slight limp.

3. The month of the story is (a) September (b) October (c) November (d) December.

4. Nikishka finds all the following at the shore EXCEPT (a) jellyfish (b) starfish (c) crabs (d) seaweed.

5. Uncle Ivan is (a) the village mayor (b) a fisherman (c) the person who first greets Nikishka (d) a role model for Nikishka.

Inferences

6. The boys poked fun at Nikishka because (a) he had a blond forelock (b) his father was a fisherman (c) he was sensitive (d) he never listened.

7. Nikishka got the horse over a difficult spot by (a) pulling sharply on

the reins (b) speaking gently (c) going across and waiting for the horse (d) pausing for several hours.

8. We can assume that the Pomors' occupation (41) is (a) extremely hazardous (b) shut down in bad weather (c) devoted to the preservation of seals (d) disapproved of by Nikishka's father.

9. Nikishka was most upset by (a) the shadows in the forest (b) the long trip on horseback (c) the story of seal hunting (d) the behavior of his dog.

Order of Events

10. Arrange the items in the order in which they occurred. Use letters only.
    A. Nikishka reaches his father's cabin.
    B. Nikishka decides to be an engineer.
    C. Nikishka sets out for his father's cabin.
    D. The horse is afraid to go on.
    E. Nikishka and his father go fishing for salmon.

Words in Context

1. "He looked *askance* at the sea, and his eyes rolled." **Askance** (34) means (a) with distrust (b) backwards (c) with anticipation (d) keenly.

2. "Over by the stones the waves broke into little foam, boiled up into white surf, and rumbled *impotently*." **Impotently** (34) means (a) significantly (b) viciously (c) noisily (d) powerlessly.

3. "It seemed to him that a watery *abyss* yawned on the left and that the sea was flowing in." An **abyss** (36) is (a) deep pit (b) whirlpool (c) wave (d) waterspout.

4. "An *imperceptible* path was beginning, and the horse turned into it of his own accord." **Imperceptible** (36) means (a) difficult to see (b) well-marked (c) turning off to the right (d) well-traveled.

5. "And suddenly in the midst of this speechlessness, of this dead silence and the sounds of *inanimate* things, there came a song." **Inanimate**

(37) means (a) silent (b) without life (c) lively (d) commonplace. (See also "Personification," page 000.)

6. "Nikishka looked at it with *steadfast* gaze." **Steadfast** (42) means (a) uneasy (b) unwavering (c) solemn (d) curious.

Thinking Critically about the Story

1. "He looked around and wanted to understand this mystery, wanted everything he saw to reveal itself to him all at once." (37) What is it that Nikishka sought? Was this his "secret"? Does Nikishka ever find the answer in this story? Is there an answer?

2. How would you characterize Nikishka's father? Sympathetic? Sensitive? A good father? Give examples.

3. Why do young children harass other children who are different from them? Why did they pick on Nikishka? See also "All Summer in a Day," (15–19).

4. Environmentalists and workers often clash. Environmentalists want to save the precious heritage of irreplaceable giant trees. Loggers want to cut them down for their livelihood. Environmentalists protest the slaughter of seal pups. Trappers defend their actions by saying their livelihood depend on their actions. How can these conflicting needs be resolved?

5. Pick out good examples of description as Nikishka makes his way to his father's cabin.

6. Have you ever ridden a horse? Does the description of the horse's behavior ring true?

7. How does the father show that he knows and appreciates the fact that Nikishka is different from other boys?

8. How is the following statement a subtle comment on the father's personality?

" 'Empty,' the father whispered and sat down quite at peace." (39)

9. Is this the answer to question #1 above?

"It seemed to him that he was on the verge of learning some secret known to nobody else, that he would utter a mysterious word and the silence would be broken, and everything would start talking to Nikishka, and everything would all at once become comprehensible to him. But the word didn't come; the secret was not revealed."

Language in Action

Personification

> The cabins ran out of the forest, ran out on the shore, and had nowhere else to run—they stopped, frightened, bunched up, and looked out, bewitched, at the sea.

Cabins running? Being frightened? Looking at the sea? What's going on here! For effect, the author is using a common device of figurative language (459): personification.

Personification gives human traits to things not human. It may give life to inanimate objects, like the cabins in our example. Or we might say, "The saxophones wailed, and the violins cried." It can also give life to abstract ideas.

> Truth crushed to earth shall rise again.
> When Duty whispers low, "Thou must,"
>   The Youth replies, "I can."
> Love laughs at locksmiths.
> When cruelty stalks into a home, happiness flees.
> Justice is sometimes blind.

Perhaps it's a human trait to ascribe human traits to inanimate objects. If we stub our toe on a chair, we may primitively feel that the chair is out to get us. When a chest drawer sticks, the contest between the victim and the drawer is almost personal!

Personification is a common device, usually easy to identify.

Love of Life

"I say, Bill, I've sprained my ankle,"

Bill staggered on through the milky water. He did not look around. The man watched him go, and though his face was as expressionless as ever, his eyes were like the eyes of a wounded deer.

The other man limped up the farther bank and continued straight on without looking back.

Literature broadens your experiences, allowing you to live many lives in one. You identify yourself with the characters and thus live vicariously—through others. You can walk on the moon with Neil Armstrong. or even be Neil Armstrong. With imaginative participation, you expand your own horizons and enrich your experiences.

"Love of Life" provides the perfect example of a vicarious experience. In the warmth and comfort of your own room, you can share the terrifying suffering of the unnamed narrator. From the sprained ankle through the long trek to safety, you can sympathetically endure the incredible hardships of a cold, bleak, and unforgiving land.

Jack London knew the Far North through personal experience. In 1897, he joined the gold rush, seeking fortune in the Klondike. His mining efforts were unsuccessful, but they turned into pure gold when he mined the experiences and set some of his best stories in the Far North. Perhaps his most famous story is **Call of the Wild**, but he wrote a great many more novels and short stories.

Jack London was a born storyteller. He had the writer's gift of bringing actions, setting, and characters to life. You will find every slight detail in the following story a model of keen observation. You will find some of the details horrifying, but you will marvel at the strength of the human spirit.

For an adventure you won't soon forget, join Bill's deserted comrade as he struggles just to keep alive.

Love of Life

"This out of all will remain—
They have lived and have tossed:
So much of the game will be gain,
Though the gold of the dice has been lost."

They limped painfully down the bank, and once the foremost of the two men staggered among the rough-strewn rocks. They were tired and weak, and their faces had the drawn expression of patience which comes of hardship long endured. They were heavily burdened with blanket packs which were strapped to their shoulders. Head-straps, passing across the forehead, helped support these packs. Each man carried a rifle. They walked in a stooped posture, the shoulders well forward, the head still farther forward, the eyes bent upon the ground.

"I wish we had just about two of them cartridges that's layin' in that cache of ourn," said the second man.

His voice was utterly and drearily expressionless. He spoke without enthusiasm; and the first man, limping into the milky stream that foamed over the rocks, vouchsafed no reply.

The other man followed at his heels. They did not remove their footgear, though the water was icy cold—so cold that their ankles ached and their feet went numb. In places the water dashed against their knees, and both men staggered for footing.

The man who followed slipped on a smooth boulder, nearly fell, but recovered himself with a violent effort, at the same time uttering a sharp exclamation of pain. He seemed faint and dizzy and put out his free hand while he reeled, as though seeking support against the air. When he had steadied himself he stepped forward, but reeled again and nearly fell. Then he stood still and looked at the other man, who had never turned his head.

The man stood still for fully a minute, as though debating with himself. Then he called out:

"I say, Bill, I've sprained my ankle."

50

Bill staggered on through the milky water. He did not look around. The man watched him go, and though his face was expressionless as ever, his eyes were like the eyes of a wounded deer.

The other man limped up the farther bank and continued straight on without looking back. The man in the stream watched him. His lips trembled a little, so that the rough thatch of brown hair which covered them was visibly agitated. His tongue even strayed out to moisten them.

"Bill!" he cried out.

It was the pleading cry of a strong man in distress, but Bill's head did not turn. The man watched him go, limping grotesquely and lurching forward with stammering gait up the slow slope toward the soft sky-line of the low-lying hill. He watched him go till he passed over the crest and disappeared. Then he turned his gaze and slowly took in the circle of the world that remained to him now that Bill was gone.

Near the horizon the sun was smouldering dimly, almost obscured by formless mists and vapors, which gave an impression of mass and density without outline or tangibility. The man pulled out his watch, the while resting his weight on one leg. It was four o'clock, and as the season was near the last of July or first of August,—he did not know the precise date within a week or two,—he knew that the sun roughly marked the northwest. He looked to the south and knew that somewhere beyond those bleak hills lay the Great Bear Lake; also, he knew that in that direction the Arctic Circle cut its forbidding way across the Canadian Barrens. This stream in which he stood was a feeder to the Coppermine River, which in turn flowed north and emptied into Coronation Gulf and the Arctic Ocean. He had never been there, but he had seen it, once, on a Hudson Bay Company chart.

Again his gaze completed the circle of the world about him. It was not a heartening spectacle. Everywhere was soft sky-line. The hills were all low-lying. There were no trees, no shrubs, no grasses—naught but a tremendous and terrible desolation that sent fear swiftly dawning into his eyes.

"Bill!" he whispered, once and twice; "Bill!"

He cowered in the midst of the milky water, as though the vastness were pressing in upon him with overwhelming force, brutally crushing him with its complacent awfulness. He began to shake as with a fever, till the gun fell from his hand with a splash. This served to rouse him. He fought with his fear and pulled himself together, groping in the water and recovering the weapon. He hitched his pack farther over on his left shoulder, so as to take a portion of its weight from off the injured ankle. Then he proceeded, slowly and carefully, wincing with pain, to the bank.

He did not stop. With a desperation that was madness, unmindful of the pain, he hurried up the slope to the crest of the hill over which his comrade had disappeared—more grotesque and comical by far than that limping, jerking comrade. But at the crest he saw a shallow valley, empty of life. He fought with his fear again, overcame it, hitched the pack still farther over on his left shoulder, and lurched on down the slope.

The bottom of the valley was soggy with water, which the thick moss held, spongelike, close to the surface. This water squirted out from under his feet at every step, and each time he lifted a foot the action culminated in a sucking sound as the wet moss reluctantly released its grip. He picked his way from muskeg* to muskeg, and followed the other man's footsteps along and across the rocky ledges which thrust like islets through the sea of moss.

Though alone, he was not lost. Farther on he knew he would come to where dead spruce and fir, very small and withered, bordered the shore of a little lake, the *titchin-nichilie,* in the tongue of the country, the "land of little sticks." And into that lake flowed a small stream, the water of which was not milky. There was rush-grass on that stream—this he remembered well—but no timber, and he would follow it till its first trickle ceased at a divide. He would cross this divide to the first trickle of another stream, flowing to the west, which he would follow until it emptied into the river Dease, and here he would find a cache under an upturned canoe and piled over with many rocks. And in this cache would be ammunition for his empty gun, fish-hooks and lines, a small net—all the utilities for the killing and snaring of food. Also, he would find flour,—not much,—a piece of bacon, and some beans.

Bill would be waiting for him there, and they would paddle away south down the Dease to the Great Bear Lake. And south across the lake they would go, ever south, till they gained the Mackenzie. And south, still south, they would go, while the winter raced vainly after them, and the ice formed in the eddies, and the days grew chill and crisp, south to some warm Hudson Bay Company post, where timber grew tall and generous and there was grub without end.

These were the thoughts of the man as he strove onward. But hard as he strove with his body, he strove equally hard with his mind, trying to think that Bill had not deserted him, that Bill would surely wait for him at the cache. He was compelled to think this thought, or else there would not be any use to strive, and he would have lain down and died. And as the dim ball of the sun sank slowly into the northwest he covered every inch—and many times—of his and Bill's flight south before the downcoming winter. And he conned the grub of the cache and the grub of the Hudson Bay Company post over and over again. He had not eaten for two days; for a far longer time he had not had all he wanted to eat. Often he stooped and picked pale muskeg berries, put them into his mouth, and chewed and swallowed them. A muskeg berry is a bit of seed

---

*bog

enclosed in a bit of water. In the mouth the water melts away and the seed chews sharp and bitter. The man knew there was no nourishment in the berries, but he chewed them patiently with a hope greater than knowledge and defying experience.

At nine o'clock he stubbed his toe on a rocky ledge, and from sheer weariness and weakness staggered and fell. He lay for some time, without movement, on his side. Then he slipped out of the pack-straps and clumsily dragged himself into a sitting posture. It was not yet dark, and in the lingering twilight he groped about among the rocks for shreds of dry moss. When he had gathered a heap he built a fire,—a smouldering, smudgy fire,—and put a tin pot of water on to boil.

He unwrapped his pack and the first thing he did was to count his matches. There were sixty-seven. He counted them three times to make sure. He divided them into several portions, wrapping them in oil paper, disposing of one bunch in his empty tobacco pouch, of another bunch in the inside band of his battered hat, of a third bunch under his shirt on the chest. This accomplished, a panic came upon him, and he unwrapped them all and counted them again. There were still sixty-seven.

He dried his wet foot-gear by the fire. The moccasins were in soggy shreds. The blanket socks were worn through in places, and his feet were raw and bleeding. His ankle was throbbing, and he gave it an examination. It had swollen to the size of his knee. He tore a long strip from one of his two blankets and bound the ankle tightly. He tore other strips and bound them about his feet to serve for both moccasins and socks. Then he drank the pot of water, steaming hot, wound his watch, and crawled between his blankets.

He slept like a dead man. The brief darkness around midnight came and went. The sun arose in the northeast—at least the day dawned in that quarter, for the sun was hidden by gray clouds.

At six o'clock he awoke, quietly lying on his back. He gazed straight up into the gray sky and knew that he was hungry. As he rolled over on his elbow he was startled by a loud snort, and saw a bull caribou regarding him with alert curiosity. The animal was not more than fifty feet away, and instantly into the man's mind leaped the vision and the savor of a caribou steak sizzling and frying over a fire. Mechanically he reached for the empty gun, drew a bead, and pulled the trigger. The bull snorted and leaped away, his hoofs rattling and clattering as he fled across the ledges.

The man cursed and flung the empty gun from him. He groaned aloud as he started to drag himself to his feet. It was a slow and arduous task. His joints were like rusty hinges. They worked harshly in their sockets, with much friction, and each bending or unbending was accomplished only through a sheer exertion of will. When he finally gained his feet, another minute or so was consumed in straightening up, so that he could stand erect as a man should stand.

He crawled up a small knoll and surveyed the prospect. There were no trees, no bushes, nothing but a gray sea of moss scarcely diversified by gray rocks, gray lakelets, and gray streamlets. The sky was gray. There was no sun nor hint of sun. He had no idea of north, and he had forgotten the way he had come to this spot the night before. But he was not lost. He knew that. Soon he would come to the land of the little sticks. He felt that it lay off to the left somewhere, not far—possibly just over the next low hill.

He went back to put his pack into shape for travelling. He assured himself of the existence of his three separate parcels of matches, though he did not stop to count them. But he did linger, debating, over a squat moose-hide sack. It was not large. He could hide it under his two hands. He knew that it weighed fifteen pounds,—as much as all the rest of the pack,—and it worried him. He finally set it to one side and proceeded to roll the pack. He paused to gaze at the squat moose-hide sack. He picked it up hastily with a defiant glance about him, as though the desolation were trying to rob him of it; and when he rose to his feet to stagger on into the day, it was included in the pack on his back.

He bore away to the left, stopping now and again to eat muskeg berries. His ankle had stiffened, his limp was more pronounced, but the pain of it was as nothing compared with the pain of his stomach. The hunger pangs were sharp. They gnawed and gnawed until he could not keep his mind steady on the course he must pursue to gain the land of little sticks. The muskeg berries did not allay this gnawing, while they made his tongue and the roof of his mouth sore with their irritating bite.

He came upon a valley where rock ptarmigan rose on whirring wings from the ledges and muskegs. Ker—ker—ker was the cry they made. He threw stones at them, but could not hit them. He placed his pack on the ground and stalked them as a cat stalks a sparrow. The sharp rocks cut through his pants' legs till his knees left a trail of blood; but the hurt was lost in the hurt of his hunger. He squirmed over the wet moss, saturating his clothes and chilling his body; but he was not aware of it, so great was his fever for food. And always the ptarmigan rose, whirring, before him, till their ker—ker—ker became a mock to him, and he cursed them and cried aloud at them with their own cry.

Once he crawled upon one that must have been asleep. He did not see it till it shot up in his face from its rocky nook. He made a clutch as startled as was the rise of the ptarmigan, and there remained in his hand three tail-feathers. As he watched its flight he hated it, as though it had done him some terrible wrong. Then he returned and shouldered his pack.

As the day wore along he came into valleys or swales where game was more plentiful. A band of caribou passed by, twenty and odd animals, tantalizingly within rifle range. He felt a wild desire to run after them, a certitude that he could run them down. A black fox came toward him, carrying a ptarmigan in his mouth. The man shouted. It was a fearful cry, but the fox, leaping away in fright, did not drop the ptarmigan.

Late in the afternoon he followed a stream, milky with lime, which ran through sparse patches of rush-grass. Grasping these rushes firmly near the root, he pulled up what resembled a young onion-sprout no larger than a shingle-nail. It was tender, and his teeth sank into it with a crunch that promised deliciously of food. But its fibers were tough. It was composed of stringy filaments saturated with water, like the berries, and devoid of nourishment. He threw off his pack and went into the rush-grass on hands and knees, crunching and munching, like some bovine creature.

He was very weary and often wished to rest—to lie down and sleep; but he was continually driven on—not so much by his desire to gain the land of little sticks as by his hunger. He searched little ponds for frogs and dug up the earth with his nails for worms, though he knew in spite that neither frogs nor worms existed so far north.

He looked into every pool of water vainly, until, as the long twilight came on, he discovered a solitary fish, the size of a minnow, in such a pool. He plunged his arm in up to the shoulder, but it eluded him. He reached for it with both hands and stirred up the milky mud at the bottom. In his excitement he fell in, wetting himself to the waist. Then the water was too muddy to admit of his seeing the fish, and he was compelled to wait until the sediment had settled.

The pursuit was renewed, till the water was again muddied. But he could not wait. He unstrapped the tin bucket and began to bale the pool. He baled wildly at first, splashing himself and flinging the water so short a distance that it ran back into the pool. He worked more carefully, striving to be cool, though his heart was pounding against his chest and his hands were trembling. At the end of half an hour the pool was nearly dry. Not a cupful of water remained. And there was no fish. He found a hidden crevice among the stones through which it had escaped to the adjoining and larger pool—a pool which he could not empty in a night and a day. Had he known of the crevice, he could have closed it with a rock at the beginning and the fish would have been his.

Thus he thought, and crumpled up and sank down upon the wet earth. At first he cried softly to himself, then he cried loudly to the pitiless desolation that ringed him around; and for a long time after he was shaken by great dry sobs.

He built a fire and warmed himself by drinking quarts of hot water, and made camp on a rocky ledge in the same fashion he had the night before. The last thing he did was to see that his matches were dry and to wind his watch. The blankets were wet and clammy. His ankle pulsed with pain. But he knew only that he was hungry, and through his restless sleep he dreamed of feasts and banquets and of food served and spread in all imaginable ways.

He awoke chilled and sick. There was no sun. The gray of earth and sky had become deeper, more profound. A raw wind was blowing, and the first flurries of snow were whitening the hilltops. The air about him thickened and grew white while he made a fire and boiled more water. It was wet snow, half rain, and the flakes were large and soggy. At first they melted as soon as they came in contact with the earth, but ever more fell, covering the ground, putting out the fire, spoiling his supply of moss-fuel.

This was a signal for him to strap on his pack and stumble onward, he knew not where. He was not concerned with the land of little sticks, nor with Bill and the cache under the upturned canoe by the river Dease. He was mastered by the verb "to eat." He was hunger-mad. He took no heed of the course he pursued, so long as that course led him through the swale bottoms. He felt his way through the wet snow to the watery muskeg berries, and went by feel as he pulled up the rush-grass by the roots. But it was tasteless stuff and did not satisfy. He found a weed that tasted sour and he ate all he could find of it, which was not much, for it was a creeping growth, easily hidden under the several inches of snow.

He had no fire that night, nor hot water, and crawled under his blanket to sleep the broken hunger-sleep. The snow turned into a cold rain. He awakened many times to feel it falling on his upturned face. Day came—a gray day and no sun. It had ceased raining. The keenness of his hunger had departed. Sensibility, as far as concerned the yearning for food, had been exhausted. There was a dull, heavy ache in his stomach, but it did not bother him so much. He was more rational, and once more he was chiefly interested in the land of little sticks and the cache by the river Dease.

He ripped the remnant of one of his blankets into strips and bound his bleeding feet. Also, he rewrapped the injured ankle and prepared himself for a day of travel. When he came to his pack, he paused long over the squat moose-hide sack, but in the end it went with him.

The snow had melted under the rain, and only the hilltops showed white. The sun came out, and he succeeded in locating the points of the compass, though he knew now that he was lost. Perhaps, in his previous days' wanderings, he had edged away too far to the left. He now bore off to the right to counteract the possible deviation from his true course.

Though the hunger pangs were no longer so exquisite, he realized that he was weak. He was compelled to pause for frequent rests, when he attacked the muskeg berries and rush-grass patches. His tongue felt dry and large, as though covered with a fine hairy growth, and it tasted bitter in his mouth. His heart gave him a great deal of trouble. When he had travelled a few minutes it would begin a remorseless thump, thump, thump, and then leap up and away in a painful flutter of beats that choked him and made him go faint and dizzy.

In the middle of the day he found two minnows in a large pool. It was impossible to bale it, but he was calmer now and managed to catch them in his tin bucket. They were no longer than his little finger, but he was not particularly hungry. The dull ache in his stomach had been growing duller and fainter. It seemed almost that his stomach was dozing. He ate the fish raw, chewing with painstaking care, for the eating was an act of pure reason. While he had no desire to eat, he knew that he must eat to live.

In the evening he caught three more minnows, eating two and saving the third for breakfast. The sun had dried stray shreds of moss, and he was able to warm himself with hot water. He had not covered more than ten miles that day; and the next day, travelling whenever his heart permitted him, he covered no more than five miles. But his stomach did not give him the slightest uneasiness. It had gone to sleep. He was in a strange country, too, and the caribou were growing more plentiful, also the wolves. Often their yelps drifted across the desolation, and once he saw three of them slinking away before his path.

Another night; and in the morning, being more rational, he untied the leather string that fastened the squat moose-hide sack. From its open mouth poured a yellow stream of coarse gold-dust and nuggets. He roughly divided the gold in halves, caching one half on a prominent ledge, wrapped in a piece of blanket, and returning the other half to the sack. He also began to use strips of the one remaining blanket for his feet. He still clung to his gun, for there were cartridges in that cache by the river Dease.

This was a day of fog, and this day hunger awoke in him again. He was very weak and was afflicted with a giddiness which at times blinded him. It was no uncommon thing now for him to stumble and fall; and stumbling once, he fell squarely into a ptarmigan nest. There were four newly hatched chicks, a day old—little specks of pulsating life no more than a mouthful; and he ate them ravenously, thrusting them alive into his mouth and crunching them like egg-shells between his teeth. The mother ptarmigan beat about him with great outcry. He used his gun as a club with which to knock her over, but she dodged out of reach. He threw stones at her and with one chance shot broke a wing. Then she fluttered away, running, trailing the broken wing, with him in pursuit.

The little chicks had no more than whetted his appetite. He hopped and bobbed clumsily along on his injured ankle, throwing stones and screaming hoarsely at times; at other times hopping and bobbing silently along, picking himself up grimly and patiently when he fell, or rubbing his eyes with his hand when the giddiness threatened to overpower him.

The chase led him across swampy ground in the bottom of the valley, and he came upon footprints in the soggy moss. They were not his own—he could see that. They must be Bill's. But he could not stop, for the mother ptarmigan was running on. He would catch her first, then he would return and investigate.

He exhausted the mother ptarmigan; but he exhausted himself. She lay panting on her side. He lay panting on his side, a dozen feet away, unable to crawl to her. And as he recovered she recovered, fluttering out of reach as his hungry hand went out to her. The chase was resumed. Night settled down and she escaped. He stumbled from weakness and pitched head foremost on his face, cutting his cheek, his pack upon his back. He did not move for a long while; then he rolled over on his side, wound his watch, and lay there until morning.

Another day of fog. Half of his last blanket had gone into foot-wrappings. He failed to pick up Bill's trail. It did not matter. His hunger was driving him too compellingly—only—only he wondered if Bill, too, were lost. By midday the irk of his pack became too oppressive. Again he divided the gold, this time merely spilling half of it on the ground. In the afternoon he threw the rest of it away, there remaining to him only the half-blanket, the tin bucket, and the rifle.

An hallucination began to trouble him. He felt confident that one cartridge remained to him. It was in the chamber of the rifle and he had overlooked it. On the other hand, he knew all the time that the chamber was empty. But the hallucination persisted. He fought it off for hours, then threw his rifle open and was confronted with emptiness. The disappointment was as bitter as though he had really expected to find the cartridge.

He plodded on for half an hour, when the hallucination arose again. Again he fought it, and still it persisted, till for very relief he opened his rifle to unconvince himself. At times his mind wandered farther afield, and he plodded on, a mere automaton, strange conceits and whimsicalities gnawing at his brain like worms. But these excursions out of the real were of brief duration, for ever the pangs of the hunger-bite called him back. He was jerked back abruptly once from such an excursion by a sight that caused him nearly to faint. He reeled and swayed, doddering like a drunken man to keep from falling. Before him stood a horse. A horse! He could not believe his eyes. A thick mist was in them, intershot with sparkling points of light. He rubbed his eyes savagely to clear his vision, and beheld, not a horse, but a great brown bear. The animal was studying him with bellicose curiosity.

The man had brought his gun halfway to his shoulder before he realized. He lowered it and drew his hunting-knife from its beaded sheath at his hip. Before him was meat and life. He ran his thumb along the edge of his knife. It was sharp. The point was sharp. He would fling himself upon the bear and kill it. But his heart began its warning thump, thump, thump. Then followed the wild upward leap and tattoo of flutters, the pressing as of an iron band about his forehead, the creeping of the dizziness into his brain.

His desperate courage was evicted by a great surge of fear. In his weakness, what if the animal attacked him? He drew himself up to his most imposing stature, gripping the knife and staring hard at the bear. The bear advanced clumsily a couple of steps, reared up, and gave vent to a tentative growl. If the man ran, he would run after him; but the man did not run. He was animated now with the courage of fear. He, too, growled, savagely, terribly, voicing the fear that is to life germane and that lies twisted about life's deepest roots.

The bear edged away to one side, growling menacingly, himself appalled by this mysterious creature that appeared upright and unafraid. But the man did not move. He stood like a statue till the danger was past, when he yielded to a fit of trembling and sank down into the wet moss.

He pulled himself together and went on, afraid now in a new way. It was not the fear that he should die passively from lack of food, but that he should be destroyed violently before starvation had exhausted the last particle of the endeavor in him that made toward surviving. There were the wolves. Back and forth across the desolation drifted their howls, weaving the very air into a fabric of menace that was so tangible that he found himself, arms in the air, pressing it back from him as it might be the walls of a wind-blown tent.

Now and again the wolves, in packs of two and three, crossed his path. But they sheered clear of him. They were not in sufficient numbers, and besides they were hunting the caribou, which did not battle, while this strange creature that walked erect might scratch and bite.

In the late afternoon he came upon scattered bones where the wolves had made a kill. The débris had been a caribou calf an hour before, squawking and running and very much alive. He contemplated the bones, clean-picked and polished, pink with the cell-life in them which had not yet died. Could it possibly be that he might be that ere the day was done! Such was life, eh? A vain and fleeting thing. It was only life that pained. There was no hurt in death. To die was to sleep. It meant cessation, rest. Then why was he not content to die?

But he did not moralize long. He was squatting in the moss, a bone in his mouth, sucking at the shreds of life that still dyed it faintly pink. The sweet meaty taste, thin and elusive almost as a memory, maddened him. He closed his jaws on the bones and crunched. Sometimes it was the bone that broke, sometimes his teeth. Then he crushed the bones between rocks, pounded them to a pulp, and swallowed them.

He pounded his fingers, too, in his haste, and yet found a moment in which to feel surprise at the fact that his fingers did not hurt much when caught under the descending rock.

Came frightful days of snow and rain. He did not know when he made camp, when he broke camp. He travelled in the night as much as in the day. He rested wherever he fell, crawled on whenever the dying life in him flickered up and burned less dimly. He, as a man, no longer strove. It was the life in him, unwilling to die, that drove him on. He did not suffer. His nerves had become blunted, numb, while his mind was filled with weird visions and delicious dreams.

But ever he sucked and chewed on the crushed bones of the caribou calf, the least remnants of which he had gathered up and carried with him. He crossed no more hills or divides, but automatically followed a large stream which flowed through a wide and shallow valley. He did not see this stream nor this valley. He saw nothing save visions. Soul and body walked or crawled side by side, yet apart, so slender was the thread that bound them.

He awoke in his right mind, lying on his back on a rocky ledge. The sun was shining bright and warm. Afar off he heard the squawking of caribou calves. He was aware of vague memories of rain and wind and snow, but whether he had been beaten by the storm for two days or two weeks he did not know.

For some time he lay without movement, the genial sunshine pouring upon him and saturating his miserable body with its warmth. A fine day, he thought. Perhaps he could manage to locate himself. By a painful effort he rolled over on his side. Below him flowed a wide and sluggish river. Its unfamiliarity puzzled him. Slowly he followed it with his eyes, winding in wide sweeps among the bleak, bare hills, bleaker and barer and lower-lying than any hills he had yet encountered. Slowly, deliberately, without excitement or more than the most casual interest, he followed the course of the strange stream toward the skyline and saw it emptying into a bright and shining sea. He was still unexcited. Most unusual, he thought, a vision or a mirage—more likely a vision, a trick of his disordered mind. He was confirmed in this by sight of a ship lying at anchor in the midst of the shining sea. He closed his eyes for a while, then opened them. Strange how the vision persisted! Yet not strange. He knew there were no seas or ships in the heart of the barren lands, just as he had known there was no cartridge in the empty rifle.

He heard a snuffle behind him—a half-choking gasp or cough. Very slowly, because of his exceeding weakness and stiffness, he rolled over on his other side. He could see nothing near at hand, but he waited patiently. Again came the snuffle and cough, and outlined between two jagged rocks not a score of feet away he made out the gray head of a wolf. The sharp ears were not pricked so sharply as he had seen them on other wolves; the eyes were bleared and bloodshot, the head seemed to droop limply and forlornly. The animal blinked continually in the sunshine. It seemed sick. As he looked it snuffled and coughed again.

This, at least, was real, he thought, and turned on the other side so that he might see the reality of the world which had been veiled from him before by the vision. But the sea still shone in the distance and the ship was plainly discernible. Was it reality, after all? He closed his eyes for a long while and thought, and then it came to him. He had been making north by east, away from the Dease Divide and into the Coppermine Valley. This wide and sluggish river was the Coppermine. That shining sea was the Arctic Ocean. That ship was a whaler, strayed east, far east, from the mouth of the Mackenzie, and it was lying at anchor in Coronation Gulf. He remembered the Hudson Bay Company chart he had seen long ago, and it was all clear and reasonable to him.

He sat up and turned his attention to immediate affairs. He had worn through the blanket-wrappings, and his feet were shapeless lumps of raw meat. His last blanket was gone. Rifle and knife were both missing. He had lost his hat somewhere, with the bunch of matches in the band, but the matches against his chest were safe and dry inside the tobacco pouch and oil paper. He looked at his watch. It marked eleven o'clock and was still running. Evidently he had kept it wound.

He was calm and collected. Though extremely weak, he had no sensation of pain. He was not hungry. The thought of food was not even pleasant to him, and whatever he did was done by his reason alone. He slipped off his pants' legs to the knees and bound them about his feet. Somehow he had succeeded in retaining the tin bucket. He would have some hot water before he began what he foresaw was to be a terrible journey to the ship.

His movements were slow. He shook as with a palsy. When he started to collect dry moss, he found he could not rise to his feet. He tried again and again, then contented himself with crawling about on hands and knees. Once he crawled near to the sick wolf. The animal dragged itself reluctantly out of his way, licking its chops with a tongue which seemed hardly to have the strength to curl. The man noticed that the tongue was not the customary healthy red. It was a yellowish brown and seemed coated with a rough and half-dry mucus.

After he had drunk a quart of hot water the man found he was able to stand, and even to walk as well as a dying man might be supposed to walk. Every minute or so he was compelled to rest. His steps were feeble and uncertain, just as the wolf's that trailed him were feeble and uncertain; and that night, when the shining sea was blotted out by blackness, he knew he was nearer to it by no more than four miles.

Throughout the night he heard the cough of the sick wolf, and now and then the squawking of the caribou calves. There was life all around him, but it was strong life, very much alive and well, and he knew the sick wolf clung to the sick man's trail in the hope that the man would be first. In the morning, on opening his eyes, he beheld it regarding him with a wistful and hungry stare. It stood crouched, with tail between its legs, like a miserable and woe-begone dog. It shivered in the still morning wind, and grinned dispiritedly when the man spoke to it in a voice that achieved no more than a hoarse whisper.

The sun rose brightly, and all morning the man tottered and fell toward the ship on the shining sea. The weather was perfect. It was the brief Indian Summer of the high latitudes. It might last a week. Tomorrow or next day it might be gone.

In the afternoon the man came upon a trail. It was of another man, who did not walk, but who dragged himself on all fours. The man thought it might be Bill, but he thought in a dull, uninterested way. He had no curiosity. In fact, sensation and emotion had left him. He was no longer susceptible to pain. Stomach and nerves had gone to sleep. Yet the life that was in him drove him on. He was very weary, but it refused to die. It was because it refused to die that he still ate muskeg berries and minnows, drank his hot water, and kept a wary eye on the sick wolf.

He followed the trail of the other man who dragged himself along, and soon came to the end of it—a few fresh-picked bones where the soggy moss was marked by the foot-pads of many wolves. He saw a squat moose-hide sack, mate to his own, which had been torn by sharp teeth. He picked it up, though its weight was almost too much for his feeble fingers. Bill had carried it to the last. Ha! ha! He would have the laugh on Bill. He would survive and carry it to the ship in the shining sea. His mirth was hoarse and ghastly, like a raven's croak, and the sick wolf joined him, howling lugubriously. The man ceased suddenly. How could he have the laugh on Bill if that were Bill; if those bones, so pinky-white and clean, were Bill?

He turned away. Well, Bill had deserted him; but he would not take the gold, nor would he suck Bill's bones. Bill would have, though, had it been the other way around, he mused as he staggered on.

He came to a pool of water. Stooping over in quest of minnows, he jerked his head back as though he had been stung. He had caught sight of his reflected face. So horrible was it that sensibility awoke long enough to be shocked. There were three minnows in the pool, which was too large to drain; and after several ineffectual attempts to catch them in the tin bucket he forbore. He was afraid, because of his great weakness, that he might fall in and drown. It was for this reason that he did not trust himself to the river astride one of the many drift-logs which lined its sand-spits.

That day he decreased the distance between him and the ship by three miles; the next day by two—for he was crawling now as Bill had crawled; and the end of the fifth day found the ship still seven miles away and him unable to make even a mile a day. Still the Indian Summer held on, and he continued to crawl and faint, turn and turn about; and even the sick wolf coughed and wheezed at his heels. His knees had become raw meat like his feet, and though he padded them with the shirt from his back it was a red track he left behind him on the moss and stones. Once, glancing back, he saw the wolf licking hungrily his bleeding trail, and he saw sharply what his own end might be—unless—unless he could get the wolf. Then began as grim a tragedy of existence as was ever played—a sick man that crawled, a sick wolf that limped, two creatures dragging their dying carcasses across the desolation and hunting each other's lives.

Had it been a well wolf, it would not have mattered so much to the man; but the thought of going to feed the maw of that loathsome and all but dead thing was repugnant to him. He was finicky. His mind had begun to wander again, and to be perplexed by hallucinations, while his lucid intervals grew rarer and shorter.

He was awakened once from a faint by a wheeze close in his ear. The wolf leaped lamely back, losing its footing and falling in its weakness. It was ludicrous, but he was not amused. Nor was he even afraid. He was too far gone for that. But his mind was for the moment clear, and he lay and considered. The ship was no more than four miles away. He could see it quite distinctly when he rubbed the mists out of his eyes, and he could see the white sail of a small boat cutting the water of the shining sea. But he could never crawl those four miles. He knew that, and was very calm in the knowledge. He knew that he could not crawl half a mile. And yet he wanted to live. It was unreasonable that he should die after all he had undergone. Fate asked too much of him. And, dying, he declined to die. It was stark madness, perhaps, but in the very grip of Death he defied Death and refused to die.

He closed his eyes and composed himself with infinite precaution. He steeled himself to keep above the suffocating languor that lapped like a rising tide through all the wells of his being. It was very like a sea, this deadly languor, that rose and rose and drowned his consciousness bit by bit. Sometimes he was all but submerged, swimming through oblivion with a faltering stroke; and again, by some strange alchemy of soul, he would find another shred of will and strike out more strongly.

Without movement he lay on his back, and he could hear, slowly drawing near and nearer, the wheezing intake and output of the sick wolf's breath. It drew closer, ever closer, through an infinitude of time, and he did not move. It was at his ear. The harsh dry tongue grated like sandpaper against his cheek. His hands shot out—or at least he willed them to shoot out. The fingers were curved like talons, but they closed on empty air. Swiftness and certitude require strength, and the man had not this strength.

The patience of the wolf was terrible. The man's patience was no less terrible. For half a day he lay motionless, fighting off unconsciousness and waiting for the thing that was to feed upon him and upon which he wished to feed. Sometimes the languid sea rose over him and he dreamed long dreams; but ever through it all, waking and dreaming, he waited for the wheezing breath and the harsh caress of the tongue.

He did not hear the breath, and he slipped slowly from some dream to the feel of the tongue along his hand. He waited. The fangs pressed softly; the pressure increased; the wolf was exerting its last strength in an effort to sink teeth in the food for which it had waited so long. But the man had waited long, and the lacerated hand closed on the jaw. Slowly, while the wolf struggled feebly and the hand clutched feebly, the other hand crept across to a grip. Five minutes later the whole weight of the man's body was on top of the wolf. The hands had not sufficient strength to choke the wolf, but the face of the man was pressed close to the throat of the wolf and the mouth of the man was full of hair. At the end of half an hour the man was aware of a warm trickle in his throat. It was not pleasant. It was like molten lead being forced into his stomach, and it was forced by his will alone. Later the man rolled over on his back and slept.

There were some members of a scientific expedition on the whale-ship *Bedford*. From the deck they remarked a strange object on the shore. It was moving down the beach toward the water. They were unable to classify it, and, being scientific men, they climbed into the whale-boat alongside and went ashore to see. And they saw something that was alive but which could hardly be called a man. It was blind, unconscious. It squirmed along the ground like some monstrous worm. Most of its efforts were ineffectual, but it was persistent, and it writhed and twisted and went ahead perhaps a score of feet an hour.

Three weeks afterward the man lay in a bunk on the whale-ship *Bedford*, and with tears streaming down his wasted cheeks told who he was and what he had undergone. He also babbled incoherently of his mother, of sunny Southern California, and a home among the orange groves and flowers.

The days were not many after that when he sat at table with the scientific men and ship's officers. He gloated over the spectacle of so much food, watching it anxiously as it went into the mouths of others. With the disappearance of each mouthful an expression of deep regret came into his eyes. He was quite sane, yet he hated those men at mealtime. He was haunted by a fear that the food would not last. He inquired of the cook, the cabin-boy, the captain, concerning the food stores. They reassured him countless times; but he could not believe them, and pried cunningly about the storeroom to see with his own eyes.

It was noticed that the man was getting fat. He grew stouter with each day. The scientific men shook their heads and theorized. They limited the man at his meals, but still his girth increased and he swelled prodigiously under his shirt.

The sailors grinned. They knew. And when the scientific men set a watch on the man, they knew too. They saw him slouch for'ard after breakfast, and, like a mendicant, with outstretched palm, accost a sailor. The sailor grinned and passed him a fragment of sea biscuit. He clutched it avariciously, looked at it as a miser looks at gold, and thrust it into his shirt bosom. Similar were the donations from other grinning sailors.

The scientific men were discreet. They let him alone. But they secretly examined his bunk. It was lined with hardtack; the mattress was stuffed with hardtack; every nook and cranny was filled with hardtack. Yet he was sane. He was taking precautions against another possible famine—that was all. He would recover from it, the scientific men said; and he did, ere the *Bedford's* anchor rumbled down in San Francisco Bay.

Reading for Understanding

Main Idea

1. Which of trhe following expressions best sums up the main idea of the story?
   (a) Never fry a fish till it's caught.
   (b) Never leave till tomorrow what you can do today.
   (c) A burnt child dreads the fire.
   (d) Never say die.

Details

2. Bill (a) sprained his ankle (b) abandoned his companion (c) came back for his companion (d) was in excellent shape.

3. The muskeg berries (a) were delicious (b) grew in dry country (c) were not nutritious (d) satisfied the hungry man's appetite.

4. The moose-hide sack contained (a) gold (b) food (c) ammunition (d) maps.

5. A ptarmigan is obviously a kind of (a) fish (b) small mammal (c) insect (d) bird.

6. What the man thought was a horse proved to be a (a) moose (b) wolf (c) deer (d) bear.

7. The caribou calf had been (a) killed by wolves (b) seen following its mother (d) mixed with a band of elk (d) able to elude its attackers.

8. The ship was lying in (a) Hudson Bay (b) Coronation Gulf (c) the Mackenzie (d) the Dease Divide.

9. The ship that saved him was a(n) (a) steamship out of Vancouver (b) Eskimo canoe (c) whaler (d) fur-trader.

Inferences

10. At the start of the story, the season was (a) spring (b) summer (c) autumn (d) winter.

11. The two men had obviously been in the Far North to (a) trap bear (b) fish for salmon (c) find gold (d) survey the territory for the government.

12. The fear that remained with the man after he had been rescued was the fear of (a) freezing (b) getting lost (c) starvation (d) criticism by the sailors.

13. Bill probably (a) made it to the cache (b) came back looking for his partner (c) was rescued by an earlier ship (d) died.

Outcome

14. After the events in the story, the survivor probably (a) outfitted another expedition to the north country (b) set up a memorial for Bill (c) never returned (d) sought a position with the ship that had rescued him.

Fact or Opinion

Tell whether the following is a fact or an opinion.

15. If Bill and his partner had stayed together, they would both have survived.

Words in Context

1. "The first man, limping into the milky stream that foamed over the rocks, *vouchsafed* no reply" **Vouchsafed** (50) means (a) granted (b) rejected (c) confirmed (d) disregarded.

2. "The man watched him go, limping grotesquely and *lurching* forward with stammering gait up the slow slope toward the soft skyline

of the low-lying hill." **Lurching** (51) means (a) hastening (b) staggering (c) crawling (d) traveling.

3. "Near the horizon the sun was smouldering dimly, almost *obscured* by formless mists and vapors." **Obscured** (51) means (a) accentuated (b) vividly colored (c) shadowed (d) concealed.

4. "He cowered in the midst of the milky water, as though the vastness were pressing in upon him with overwhelming force, brutally crushing him with its *complacent* awfulness." **Complacent** (51) means (a) hideous (b) obvious (c) unconcerned (d) repeated.

5. "Then he proceeded, slowly and carefully, *wincing* with pain, to the bank." **Wincing** (51) means (a) walking (b) flinching (c) succeeding (d) stopping.

6. "Here he would find a *cache* under an upturned canoe and piled over with many rocks." A **cache** (52) is a (a) metal safe (b) moose-hide sack (c) pile of gold (d) hiding place.

7. "It was a slow and *arduous* task." **Arduous** (53) means (a) important (b) repeated, (c) strenuous (d) enjoyable.

8. "He was compelled to wait until the *sediment* had settled." A **sediment** (55) is a (a) deposit (b) moss (c) wave (d) stone.

9. "*Sensibility*, as far as concerned the yearning for food, had been exhausted." **Sensibility** (56) means (a) sensitivity (b) worry (c) determination (d) curiosity.

10. "He now bore off to the right to counteract the possible *deviation* from his true course. **Deviation** (56) means (a) acute angle (b) compass reading (c) departure (d) poorly marked trail.

11. "There were four newly hatched chicks, a day old—little specks of *pulsating* life." **Pulsating** (57) means (a) joyous (b) throbbing (c) fragile (d) recently born.

12. "At times his mind wandered farther afield, and he plodded on, a mere automaton, strange *conceits* and *whimsicalities* gnawing at his brain." **Conceits** and **whimsicalities** (58) are (a) fanciful ideas (b) bitter disappointments (c) happy memories (d) headaches.

13. "The animal was studying him with *bellicose* curiosity." **Bellicose** (58) means (a) mild (b) aggressive (c) concealed (d) sympathetic.

14. "He, too, growled, savagely, terribly, voicing the fear that is to life *germane* and that lies twisted about life's deepest roots." **Germane** (59) means (a) foreign (b) a puzzle (c) closely related (d) disconnected.

15. "But the sea still shone in the distance and the ship was plainly *discernible*." **Discernible** (61) means (a) recognizable (b) at rest in in the harbor (c) reachable (d) in distress.

16. "In the morning, on opening his eyes, he beheld it regarding him with a *wistful* and hungry stare." **Wistful** (62) means (a) aggressive and impatient (b) keen and unchanging (c) warm and sympathetic (d) sad and thoughtful.

17. "His mirth was hoarse and ghostly, like a raven's croak, and the sick wolf joined him, howling *lugubriously.*" **Lugubriously** (62) means (a) noisily (b) mournfully (c) joyously (d) uninterruptedly.

18, 19. "After several *ineffectual* attempts to catch them in the tin bucket, he *forbore.*" **Ineffectual** (62) means (a) futile (b) continuing (c) repeated (d) partially successful. **Forbore** (62) means (a) wept (b) made a last attempt (c) gave up (d) slept.

20, 21. "The thought of going to feed the maw of that *loathsome* and all but dead thing was *repugnant* to him." **Loathsome** (63) means (a) covered with hair (b) cruel (c) hateful (d) watchful. **Repugnant** (63) means (a) revolting (b) alarming (c) absurd (d) meaningful.

22. "It was *ludicrous,* but he was not amused." **Ludicrous** (63) means (a) surprising (b) reasonable (c) thought-provoking (d) laughable.

23. "But the man had waited long, and the *lacerated* hand closed on the jaw." **Lacerated** (64) means (a) powerful (b) lightly scratched (c) mangled (d) impatient.

24. "He also babbled *incoherently* of his mother, of sunny Southern California, and a home among the orange groves and flowers." **Incoherently** (64) means (a) joyfully (b) wildly (c) enthusiastically (d) tearfully.

25. "They saw him slouch for'ard after breakfast, and like a *mendicant,* with outstretched palm, accost a sailor." A **mendicant** (65) is a (a) seaman (b) friar (c) beggar (d) police officer.

26. He clutched it *avariciously,* looked at it as a miser looks at gold, and thrust it into his shirt bosom." **Avariciously** (65) means (a) slyly (b) angrily (c) swiftly (d)greedily.

Thinking Critically about the Story

1. The title applies to the wolf as well as to the man. Why does London show the wolf to be a parallel sufferer? What is gained by this subtle comparison? Did you feel any sympathy for the wolf? Did London expect that?

2. What motivates Bill to leave his partner behind? What clues does London provide to explain in some way, if not excuse, Bill's apparent treachery?

3. Would Bill probably have survived if he had stayed with his partner, instead of abandoning him? Explain.

4. In the ancient story of King Midas, everything he touches turns to gold, but the gold almost destroys him. How does that story apply to "Love of Life"?

5. The word *panic,* from the Greek forest god Pan, was coined to suggest the anxiety that overcomes a traveler lost in the woods, not knowing which way to turn. Have you ever been lost, even momentarily, in the woods? Can you suggest the terror you felt?

6. Why was the survivor so abnormal in his attitude toward food?

7. How is the fate of the moose-hide pack a barometer of the man's changing attitude toward gold?

8. Of the many harrowing experiences, which seemed to you the bleakest, most horrifying?

Language in Action

Noah Webster and American Spelling

> He went back to put his pack into shape for travelling.

If you check the spelling of *traveling* in an American dictionary, you'll find the single-*l* spelling first. The second spelling, with two *l*'s as above tends to be used in England. There are many differences between English and American English. Someone once humorously called England and America "Two countries separated by a common language!"

Differences in spelling can often be traced to the efforts of one man: Noah Webster. During the early years of the United States. Webster was a scholar, a compiler of dictionaries and spelling books. Indeed, his name is often used as a prestige name for a dictionary. After Webster's death in 1843, George and Charles Merriam took on the task of keeping the dictionaries up to date. The flow of new words into the language requires frequent updating.

Webster's influence upon American English is deep and extensive. In his famous *Spelling Book,* he eliminated the *u* from almost every *our* word: *ardor, favor,* and *honor.* He substituted single consonants for un-necessarily doubled consonants. *Jeweller* became *jeweler. Frolick* became *frolic. Waggon* became *wagon.* Webster used a single instead of a double consonant in words like *kidnaped* (British *kidnapped*) and *traveler* (*traveller*). Many of the rejected spellings are still retained in British English.

The list goes on and on. Many *ce* words were spelled *se. Offence, defence,* and *suspence* became *offense, defense,* and *suspense. Re* words became *er* words, as *theater, center,* and *caliber.*

Further drastic change in American spelling has been urged for centuries. Why not make English phonetic? Why not change *head* to *hed, thumb* to *thum, women* to *wimmen,* and *tongue* to *tung?* Webster tried but failed. Americans will accept some simplification, but reject a spelling that looks "too strange" to them. Massive efforts have been made to change *night* to *nite,* for example, but except for a few unsuccessful attempts, *night* retains its old spelling.

Changes like these destroy the language!" the critics cry. Proponents say, "Think of all the time lost to misspellings due to nonphonetic spelling." What do you think?

The Sorrel Colt

Benito Lynch
Argentine

> "Now you're in for it! his mother said very excitedly. "Yes, you'll catch it now! Have you seen your colt?"
> Mario turned red, then pale.
> "What's wrong? What's happened, Mama?"
> "Your colt is running loose in the garden and he has damaged lots of things."

How many children have dreamed of owning a pony or a colt of their own! This most universal of children's daydreams comes true for Mario. He is given a beautiful sorrel (light brown) colt that captures his heart. Unfortunately, the colt is a headstrong animal, not easily tamed. As the story progresses, we begin to sense why its original owner had gladly given it away.

The author, the Argentinian Benito Lynch, has looked into the heart of a boy and provided a convincing picture for his readers. Mario is an ordinary boy, interested in the normal things of childhood like taunting his little brother. But the arrival of the colt changes Mario from a carefree eight-year-old into a concerned colt owner—with reason for concern. For Mario, however, the balance clearly tilts toward the joy of owning the free-spirited, independent colt.

The Sorrel Colt

MARIO WAS TIRED OF "Tiger," a game of his own invention, played by pursuing through the tree-tops his brother Leo who was supposed to defend himself bravely by using green figs as projectiles. So Mario strolled to the backyard gate behind the vegetable and flower garden. Under the noon sun, leaning against one of the old posts, he looked up and down the street, waiting patiently in the hope that his little brother, still eager to continue the fight up there on the highest branch of the fig-tree, would get tired in his turn of taunting him with shouts of "stupid carrot" and "obstinate mule." Suddenly an unexpected sight filled him with happy surprise.

Turning the corner of the garden, a man was entering the lane and slowly approaching. He was mounted on a big-bellied mare which was followed by a tiny colt.

"Say!"

And Mario, his eyes wide open and his face flushed, walked over to the edge of the path to get a better view of the procession.

A colt! To understand his emotion, one must figure out what a colt meant to Mario at this time in his life, what it meant to have a colt of his own, that is to say a real horse proportioned to his size.

It was his hobby, his passion, his constant dream. But unfortunately, he knew from experience that his parents didn't want animals in the garden because they ate plants and scraped the bark off the trees.

Way off on the Ranch, they said he could have anything he wanted, that is to say, some docile little pony, but here in the garden, back of the house, no animals were permitted!

That's why Mario was going to be a good boy, as usual, just watching with suppressed desire the passing of that little miracle. But unexpectedly something extraordinary happened.

When he reached Mario, without stopping his trotting mare and hardly turning his head, the strapping rider with sullen face under his red beret let fly at Mario a stupendous offer.

"Say, kid! If you want this colt, you can have it! I'm taking it to the field to kill it!"

As he listened, Mario felt the ground heaving under his feet. His eyes grew misty, all his blood rushed to his head. But alas! He knew all the laws of his home with such finality that he didn't hesitate a second. Red as a tomato, he refused, shame-faced.

"No! Thanks! No!"

The robust young fellow shrugged his shoulders slightly and without adding a word continued along under the sunlight that filled the street. He whisked away with him, following the weary pace of the mare, that gem of a sorrel colt which trotted gracefully after. With its fluffy light-colored tail it flicked the flies off as if it were a big horse.

"Mama!"

Mario rushed headlong toward the house like a colt, without speaking to his brother who, unaware of anything new and still mounted on his fig-tree, took advantage of his brother's hasty passing to pelt him with some figs. Mario arrived under the arbor, blurting out, "Oh, Mama! Oh, Mama!"

The mother, busy at her sewing, seated in an armchair under the young vines, got up startled.

"Holy Virgin! What's the matter, son?"

"Nothing, Mama, nothing—just that a man—"

"Well what, son, what is it?"

"A man passed with a wonderful little colt and he wanted to give it to me!"

"What a scare you gave me!" The mother smiled with relief; but he, excited, continued without listening to her.

"A wonderful colt, Mama, a sorrel colt, small, this high—and the man said he was going to kill him, Mama!"

And now another amazing thing happened. Contrary to all logic and to what would seem normal, Mario heard his mother say to him in a grieved tone, "Really? Good Heavens! Why didn't you accept? Silly boy! We shall soon be going to the Ranch!"

In the face of that extraordinary, unexpected and astounding remark, the boy opened his mouth wide. But he was so crazy about the colt that he didn't stop for questions. With an "I'll call him, then!"—as excited and resonant as a neigh, the boy darted for the door.

"Be careful, son!" shouted the mother.

Careful my eye! Mario was running so fast that his brother couldn't hit him with a single fig as he flashed by.

When he dashed out into the street, the glare of the sun dazzled him. No colt, no mare, no man to be seen anywhere! But presently his straining eyes made out over there in the distance the red beret dancing to the rhythm of a trot in the midst of a cloud of dust.

The clods of dry mud made him stumble and fall several times, his emotion almost choked him, the hateful yapping dogs of the laundress got in his way, but nothing mattered. Nothing, nobody could stop Mario in his mad race.

Before he had covered a few hundred yards, he managed to reach with his voice the ears of that supreme master of his joy, who was going along dejectedly on his humble big-bellied mare.

"Ss! Ss!—Man! Man!"

On hearing him, the strapping young fellow stopped his nag and waited for Mario, frowning.

"Well, what do you want?"

"The colt—I want the colt," blurted Mario almost choking, and at the same time he stretched out both arms toward the animal as if he expected them to receive it like a store package.

The man's face wore an uncertain expression.

"Fine," he said, "lead him off, then." And he added quickly, looking at the boy's hands, "Didn't you bring a halter, or anything?"

Once more Mario flushed.

"No, I didn't."

And puzzled, he gazed all around him as if he expected to find halters hidden among the weeds.

"Well, you sure are dumb as a sausage!"

The man dismounted and twisted off a bit of wire that happened to be swinging free by the thorn-hedge. In the meantime, the child watched him in excitement but without any regret, for if a great king once offered his kingdom for a horse, certainly Mario could, without loss of face, accept an insult in exchange for a colt.

Only Mario could realize what this sorrel colt meant to him, although he did damage plants, he bit, he kicked, and he refused to go when it suited him. Once he even yanked a lock of hair from the boy's head with one bite, thinking no doubt that it was hay. But how nicely he ate sugar out of his hand and neighed when he saw him in the distance!

This colt was his love, his worry, his aim in life, his light of the spirit—so much so that his parents had acquired the habit of using the animal as a means of controlling the youngster and making him behave.

"If you don't do your lessons, you can't go out this afternoon on the colt. If you act like that, we'll take away your colt. If you do this or if you fail to do that . . . "

Always the colt standing watch over the misconduct of Mario like the flaming banner of an invincible army in the midst of battle! But at the same time the colt was a delight, so gentle, so fond, so cunning!

The horse-breaker of the Ranch, a skillful leather braider, had made him a marvelous halter. Little by little, the other ranch hands, because they were fond of Mario or wanted to outrival one another, had made all the other equipment, till now the boy had a pretty riding outfit that aroused everyone's admiration.

For Mario, he was the finest of all colts and the handsomest creature in the whole world who some day would be a great race horse. His conviction of this was so firm that when his brother Leo joked and

called the sorrel "little donkey" and other complimentary names of the
sort, these sounded like true blasphemies to Mario.

On the other hand, when the Ranch foreman said, after squinting
at the colt, "In my opinion, he is going to grow up into a beauty," Mario
found the foreman the most understanding and intelligent man around.

Mario's father had decided to plant a garden in the grounds near
the house. But it happened that this "hateful colt"—that is what some
were calling him now, even Mama, perhaps because he stepped on some
new chicks—this creature seemed opposed to the idea of a garden. This
could be gathered from the determination with which he attacked tender
little plants each time he was let loose, so that Mario had been officially
notified that it was a rule never to leave him untethered at night. Still
Mario forgot, had, in fact, forgotten a number of times, so that finally,
one morning, his exasperated father said to him, shaking his index finger
a lot and emphasizing by that rhythm the gravity of his warning, "The
first day that darned colt ever again damages a single plant, that same day
we'll turn him loose in the open country."

"Oh! Oh!" In the open country! Turn him loose! Could Mario's
father possibly know what such a threat meant to his boy?

One would have to be eight years old like him, think the way he
does and love his sorrel colt just as he loved him, to estimate the enormity
of such a menace.

The open country! Turn him loose! The open country was for
Mario something infinite, unfathomable; and to send his colt out into
that vastness seemed as atrocious and inhuman as throwing a new born
babe into the sea.

It was not surprising therefore that Mario had stopped being
careless, and a whole long week now had passed without the infliction by
the colt of the slightest hurt to the tiniest flower.

Outside, a radiant February morning was dawning. Mario, lying across
his bed with his feet against the wall, was confiding to his brother Leo
some of his plans for the brilliant future of his sorrel colt. Unexpectedly
his mother came into the bedroom.

"Now you're in for it!" she said very excitedly. "Yes, you'll catch
it now! Have you seen your colt?"

Mario turned red, then pale.

"What's wrong? What's happened, Mama?"

"Your colt is running loose in the garden and he has damaged
lots of things!"

The whole world was tumbling down on Mario.

"But how can that be?" he managed to say. "How?"

"I don't know how," his mother answered, "but you can't say I
didn't warn you till I was blue in the face! Now your father . . . "

"But I tied him up! I tied him up!"

And while he hastily put on some clothes with trembling hands, everything about him seemed murky as if the room had filled with smoke.

It was an awful disaster. Never before had the colt managed to create so much devastation. This time he had not only trampled the lawn but had even carried his mischief to the flower-bed. Here, apparently scraping with his hoof, he had torn up by the roots a number of the rare carnations set out carefully in a graceful diamond pattern.

"My goodness, what you've done! What you've done, baby!"

And as in a dream and not knowing what he was doing, Mario knelt down on the moist earth and started feverishly to set the carnations upright, while "Baby" or "The Rascal" stood by motionless, his head lowered, the halter slipped off his muzzle, and an expression of cynical indifference in his whole attitude.

Like a sleep-walker, as if he were stepping in a soft wool-stuffed mattress, Mario led the colt by the halter along the wide way with its border of poplars. At its end yonder was the large cattle gate with its white posts, and outside extended the terrible open country in its desolate immensity.

The poor boy's head throbbed with the rush of blood to his brain and he saw things hazily through a cloud. He still heard ringing in his ears the catastrophic admonition of his father.

"Take that colt and turn him loose in the open!"

Mario did not weep because he couldn't shed tears. But he walked along like a mechanical toy; he walked in such a very queer way that his mother watched anxiously from the garden.

The fact was that for Mario, the other side of that cattle gate with its white posts was the end of everything. It was the vortex into which, in a few more seconds, all his being was going to tumble, his very existence swallowed up with his sorrel colt.

When Mario had covered half the distance, his mother could not bear it any longer and she moaned, nervously pressing the father's arm, "That's enough, John! That's enough!"

"All right! Call him back!"

But just then Leo rushed off quickly, the mother uttered a piercing scream and the father ran desperately in Mario's direction.

There, close to the cattle gate, Mario in his canvas smock had collapsed on the turf like a bird winged by a bullet.

A few days later when Mario could finally sit up in his bed, his parents, smiling, but with eyelids red and faces pale with so much anxious wakefulness, forced the sorrel colt into the bedroom, one tugging at the halter and the other pushing hard behind his rump.

Reading for Understanding

Main Idea

1. The central theme of the story is (a) the difficulty of training a colt
   (b) the love of a boy for his colt (c) a father's strictness (d) a mother's
   love.

Details

2. "Tiger" was (a) the name of the sorrel colt (b) Mario's nickname for
   his brother (c) a game (d) the name of Mario's cat

3. Mario saved the colt from (a) starvation (b) cruelty (c) neglect (d)
   death.

4. The man called Mario "dumb" because (a) he didn't have a halter
   (b) he couldn't make up his mind immediately (c) he had never
   ridden a horse (d) he didn't offer to pay for the colt.

5. For the parents the last straw was (a) Mario's insolence (b) the
   destruction of the garden (c) the colt's tendency to run away (d)
   Mario's destruction of the carnations.

6. The halter was made by (a) the foreman (b) Mario's father (c) the
   horse-breaker (d) the original owner.

Inferences

7. The story is set in Argentina in the season of (a) spring (b) summer
   (c) autumn (d) winter.

8. The threat of punishment was finally overcome by (a) the colt's
   sudden change for the better (b) Leo's pleading (c) Mario's promise
   to repair the garden (d) the parents' love.

9. In the future the colt would probably be (a) tied up more securely
   (b) given to Leo instead of Mario (c) turned loose (d) sold.

Fact or Opinion

Tell whether the following is a fact or an opinion.

10. The colt could be tamed.

Words in Context

1. Mario "waiting patiently in the hope that his little brother . . . would get tired in his turn of *taunting* him with shouts of 'stupid carrot' and 'obstinate mule.'" **Taunting** (72) means (a) getting his attention (b) calling (c) prodding (d) mocking (See also *taunt-taut,* 585).

2. "Way off on the Ranch, they said he could have anything he wanted, that is to say, some *docile* little pony, but here in the garden, back of the house, no animals were permitted!" **Docile** (72) means (a) obedient (b) multicolored (c) inexpensive (d) spirited.

3. Mario's brother "took advantage of his brother's hasty passing to *pelt* him with some figs." **Pelt** (73) means (a) bombard (b) arouse (c) confuse (d) insult.

4. "With an' I'll call him then!—as excited and *resonant* as a neigh, the boy darted for the door." **Resonant** (73) means (a) echoing (b) irritating (c) terrifying (d) pleasing.

5. "Always the colt standing watch over the misconduct of Mario like the flaming banner of an *invincible* army in the midst of battle!" **Invincible** (74) means (a) crusading (b) unconquerable (c) enemy (d) retreating.

6. "One would have to be eight years old like him, think the way he does, and love his sorrel colt just as he loved him, to estimate the *enormity* of such a menace." **Enormity** (75) means (a) measured result (b) threatening nature (c) approach (d) pleasing proportions.

7,8. "The open country was for Mario something infinite, *unfathomable;* and to send his colt out into that vastness seems as *atrocious* and inhuman as throwing a newborn babe into the sea." **Unfathomable** (75) means not (a) manageable (b) workable (c) understandable (d) likable. **Atrocious** (75) means extremely (a) unexpected (b) unreasonable (c) wicked (d) thoughtless.

9. "Everything about him seemed *murky* as if the room had filled with smoke." **Murky** (76) means (a) moist (b) unpleasant (c) odorous (d) hazy.

10. "Never before had the colt managed to create so much *devastation.*" **Devastation** (76) means (a) destruction (b) inconvenience (c) change (d) rearrangement.

11. "It was the *vortex* into which, in a few more seconds, all his being

was going to tumble, his very existence swallowed up by his sorrel colt." A **vortex** (76) is a (a) reflex (b) whirlpool (c) surf (d) haven.

Thinking Critically about the Story

1. What is the significance of the last line, with the colt being *forced* into the room? What does this suggest about the future?
2. Why did the young man want to get rid of the sorrel colt? What clues in the story provide a possible answer?
3. What suggests that Mario was a normal boy before the colt came into his life? How did the colt bring adventure into Mario's life?
4. Were Mario's parents good parents? Give examples to prove your point. Are the two different in their reactions to Mario?
5. Have you ever wanted something with all your heart? Did you get it? Was it what you expected?
6. Were you able to answer question 7 on page 77? What was the clue to the correct answer? (Hint: seasons in the southern hemisphere are different from ours.)
7. In addition to the gift of the colt, what act of kindness did the colt's original owner show toward Mario?
8. Mario's parents use the colt as a means of getting Mario to behave. How? Are such parental tactics fair? Explain.

Language in Action

Our Boxing Skills

Only Mario could realize what this sorrel colt meant to him, although he did damage plants, he bit, he kicked, and he refused to go when it suited him . . . The colt was his love, his worry, his aim in life, his light of the spirit.

The real world is overwhelming. To exercise some control, we put things into mental boxes. When we can put a certain plant into a mental box called *poison ivy,* we can avoid painful rashes in the future.

Tree, table, basketball, snake, computer, automobile—these are all convenient boxes. There may be little dispute about them, but trouble arises
when boxes are abstract like *truth, liberty, beauty,* and *evil.*

Your boxes are not exactly *mine.* When *you* visualize a chair, *you*
may see a kitchen chair; *I* may see a recliner. When you visualize a snake,
you may see a poisonous rattler about to strike; I may see a harmless
garter snake, a household pet. No two boxes are precisely the same, but
we manage to communicate fairly well anyway—a miracle. It's those
abstract classifications that cause most trouble.

Mario's classification of the colt was different from his parents'.
To Mario, the colt was a wonderful, lovable thing of beauty. To his
parents, the colt was a major nuisance, destructive and unmanageable.
Which classification is right? The colt fits into both boxes! In reality,
apparent contradictions sometimes disappear. (See also Paradox 284).

Life Is an Adventure

ACTIVITIES

Thinking Critically about the Stories

1. The writer Helen Keller was blind and deaf; yet she managed to live a rich and full life, even managing to speak in a strange and singsong way. What does her quotation on page 3 mean to you? How do you personally feel about the quotation?

2. Of the two stories in which a horse plays a major role ("The Horse of the Sword" and "The Sorrel Colt"), which did you prefer? Why?

3. "Nikishka's Secret" also features a horse. Is Nikishka's horse described as accurately as Maning's and Mario's? Give examples.

4. "All Summer in a Day" has a sad ending. "The Horse of the Sword" has a happy ending. Do you prefer stories or movies with happy endings?

5. "The Horse of the Sword" features an intensely competitive race. How do you feel about competition? Do you enjoy a good contest in which you must pit your skills against those of others? Explain.

6. Readers tend to identify with characters they read about. With which character did you identify most closely? Why?

The Writing Portfolio

Writing Good Sentences

A writing portfolio is a helpful guide for you right now, for college preparation, and for the years beyond secondary school. A writing portfolio provides direction, helps you take charge of your writing, collect it with a purpose, and refer to it over and over. Your writing reflects you. Though the process is challenging and sometimes formidable, the results are rewarding.

A portfolio is a collection of your accomplishments, principally your writing. An applicant for a job may take a portfolio of descriptions of school or work experiences to the personnel manager to suggest the range of the applicant's abilities. A photographer may carry a portfolio of his pictures to display his skills. An advertiser may take a portfolio of his ads to a prospective client to stimulate interest in the advertiser's ideas.

Throughout this book you will be gathering materials for your own portfolio. It will suggest who you are, what your interests and talents are. The units in this book will provide writing activities to include in your portfolio, but you are encouraged to add personal items to this collection, too—for example, observations of people, bits of dialogue, descriptions of memorable experiences. This course of action enriches your life and opens your ears and eyes.

Decide upon the format and container for your material. Stationery stores sell useful folders. Look beyond this book. Continue the portfolio after the book has become a memory. The portfolio will become one of your treasured possessions.

Now let's begin. Most of the questions, as well as those at the end of later units, are based upon reading experiences. Do not be limited by these, however. The more writing you do, the more relaxed and skillful you become.

The heart of writing is the sentence. All kinds of writing depend on the single sentence. Henry David Thoreau once wrote, "A sentence should read as if its author, had he held a plough instead of a pen, could have drawn a furrow deep and straight to the end." Good sentences don't ramble. They waste no words. They come to the point swiftly and directly. They allow the reader to follow the thought without confusion. "Haste makes waste" is a better sentence than "Impetuous and rash actions often result in extravagant expenditure of energy."

Now try your hand at writing thoughtful, clear English sentences.

1. Each evening for a week, write a single sentence presenting some idea you had during the day.

   Example

   Monday—I wonder why the old bank building is being torn down.

   Tuesday—That roaming terrier shouldn't be allowed loose on a busy street.

   Wednesday—I think I'll take Creative Writing next semester.

2. Write a follow-up sentence to this one: "I have planned the ideal vacation."

3. Pick up an object such as a ballpoint pen or a wallet. Touch it as though you could not see it. Pretend you picked it up in the dark. How would you describe it? Write a sentence describing it in such a

way that your fellow students will be able to identify it. Try to appeal only to the sense of touch.

4. Boil down the following sentence into the original simple proverb. "It's best not to cry when for some reason or other the milk has been carelessly spilled."

5. Complete the following sentence:

   A crowded city street is like . . .

   Rain on the roof sounds like . . .

   Biting into ice cream is like . . .

6. Write a sentence summing up the character of the narrator of "Love of Life."

7. Write a sentence explaining what you think one of Nikishka's secrets was (45).

8. Write a sentence comparing or contrasting the two horses in "The Horse of the Sword" and "The Sorrel Colt."

9. Write a sentence giving your own opinion of another science fiction story like "All Summer in a Day."

10. Write a single sentence identifying the nature of James Thurber's humor. (Exaggeration? Understatement? Absurdity?)

Other Areas of Communication

1. Here are two quotations somewhat at odds in their central messages:

   (a) On every side of us are men who hunt for their personal Northwest Passage, too often sacrificing health, strength, and life itself in the search, and who shall say they are happier in their vain but hopeful quest than wiser, duller folks who sit at home, venturing nothing and, with sour laughs, deriding the seekers for their fabled thoroughfare.

   —Kenneth Roberts

   (b) Men will search for starlings in foreign lands and pay no heed to the lark at home.

   —Dagobert D. Runes

   Appoint one student to present the Roberts point of view and another the Runes point of view. Half the class will take one side and half the other. Then decide if, in any sense, both are right.

2. In the essay "On Running After One's Hat," G. K. Chesterton

suggests that adventure depends on your point of view. If your hat blows off in the wind, and you run after it in a state of anger and vexation, you are taking the wrong attitude. Look on it as an adventure, not an irritation. An irritation may be only an adventure improperly considered. Set up a class discussion on that theme. Have different class members take opposing points of view.

3. Set up a panel discussion on the topic "Wit vs. Humor." Panel topics might include the following:

The Difference Between Wit and Humor
James Thurber—Humorist or Wit?
My Favorite Sitcom—Witty or Humorous?
What Makes a Situation Funny?
What Is a Sense of Humor?

4. Each of the following quotations comments about adventure. After you have read them, appoint a class leader who will lead the discussion of such questions as these:

(a) Which seems the best description?
(b) How would you apply one of the quotations to a story in this unit?
(c) What is your own personal definition of adventure?

Adventure is something you seek for pleasure, or even for profit, like a gold rush or invading a country; for the illusion of being more alive than ordinarily, the thing you *will* to occur; experience is what really happens to you in the long run; the truth that finally overtakes you.

—Katherine Anne Porter

The greatest adventures are experience in the soul of men, not across oceans or deserts.

—Dagobert D. Runes

5. "All Summer in a Day" is a representative Ray Bradbury science-fiction story. Another story of his, "The Golden Kite, the Silver Wind," appears on page 89. Read still another Bradbury story or a story by another science-fiction author and prepare to report to the class. If you wish, compare your story with one of the many *Star Trek* episodes.

Language in Action—a Review

You may refer to the preceding pages to answer these questions.

1. The incorrect use of the apostrophe is found in (a) ladies' sneakers

(b) childrens' department (c) Gladys's performance (d) Robin and Tom's arrival.

2. The apostrophe is NOT used in the possessive of (a) proper names (b) names of cities (c) personal pronouns (d) abstract nouns.

3. Each of the following sentences contains a simile EXCEPT:

   (a) "But my heart is all a-flutter like the washing on the line."
   —Nathalia Crane

   (b) "The road was a ribbon of moonlight over the purple moor."
   —Alfred Noyes, "The Highwayman"

   (c) "Deep in the shady sadness of a vale sat gray-haired Saturn, quiet as a stone."
   —John Keats, "Hyperion"

   (d) "April is like a child that smiles in waking."
   —Nathalia Crane

4. "It's amazing how astronomers have discovered so much about stars, but how did they ever discover the stars' names?" This is an example of (a) the confusion of words and reality (b) excellent critical thinking (c) the application of common sense to a scientific challenge (d) a condemnation of a loose scientific method.

5. Each of the following is an example of personification EXCEPT

   (a) "The gale howled outside, but we were snug in our log cabin."
   (b) "The rain-soaked sky scowled at the bedraggled athletes."
   (c) "A cold moon looked down on the deserted village."
   (d) "Sam and Harry continued to disagree heatedly."

6. Each of the following is a phonetic spelling EXCEPT (a) favor (b) ardor (c) traveler (d) women.

7. One of Noah Webster's spelling changes survives in (a) jeweller (b) theatre (c) kidnaped (d) tongue.

8. A basic element in all language is (a) simplified spelling (b) classification (c) phonetic spelling (d) eager acceptance of new words.

9. In simile the basic element is (a) comparison (b) criticism (c) personification (d) action verbs.

10. A major obstacle in the way of simplified spelling is (a) computers (b) inadequate printing presses (c) conservatism (d) the heavy hand of Noah Webster.

UNIT TWO

The Creative Imagination

Imagination is more important than knowledge

Albert Einstein

In one sense, **neoteny** (nee-OT-e-nee) is not a new word. It is used when an insect retains in maturity some of the characteristics of its larval state. In recent years, the word has extended its meaning to human activities and personalities. **Neoteny** can be applied when an adult human being retains some of the desirable qualities of childhood: a creative imagination, a sense of awe and wonder, an openness to new things and ideas.

The poet William Wordsworth tried to capture that childhood joy in these lines:

There was a time when meadow, grove, and

stream,

The earth and every common sight,

To me did seem

Apparelled in celestial light,

The glory and the freshness of a dream.

Then he adds wistfully:

It is not now an it hath been of yore.

Why not? What has happened? Where has that "celestial light" gone?

87

Growing up is a difficult challenge. When you were a child, all things were possible. Every new day was a new experience. Alas, as you grow, you discover limitations, some of them necessary. You learned that you can't fly by jumping off a barn roof! But the real limitations tended to create imagined ones. "I'll never be able to pass math." "I'm giving up the clarinet. It's too hard for me." "I can't . . . I can't . . . I can't." You may not become an antarctic explorer, an astronaut, or a movie star, but there are still thousands of options open to you, if you keep the alertness and imagination of childhood.

The positive childhood qualities are especially visible in creative adults. Inventors, artists, writers, research scientists, composers—all of these exemplify the childhood sense of wonder, of adventure, of ever searching for new horizons. Were you surprised to read above that Albert Einstein valued imagination above knowledge?

The stories that follow demonstrate imagination in many forms. Ray Bradbury departs from science fiction to tell an amazing parable, a tale with a moral. Seumas O'Kelly tells a wondrous Irish tale, where things are upside down and the unexpected becomes the expected. Carol L. Birch and Steve Sanfield tell folk stories with imaginative details. Mary Carter Smith charms with a warm retelling of the Cinderella story. Douglas Hyde carries the Irish sense of the absurd to a wild conclusion. Gertrude Atherton tells a story that will surprise and, perhaps, shock you a little.

The Golden Kite, The Silver Wind

Ray Bradbury
American

**One without the other is nothing. Together, all will be
beauty and cooperation and a long and enduring life.**

There is an old childhood saying: "Sticks and stones may break
my bones, but words can never hurt me." Like some folk wisdom, this
statement is sadly untrue. Words **can** hurt. Indeed, much of the pain
in the world is caused by words, not actual deeds. Hurtful words
shouted in an argument do inflict lasting harm.

Words are symbols (96–97). Like words, symbols influence
our lives. Some symbols like the Star of David, the Cross, and the
Crescent may have positive effects on worshipers. Other symbols, like
the swastika of Nazi Germany, may lead to disastrous results. Mickey
Mouse is a happy symbol of Disneyland. The skull and crossbones is
a warning symbol of poison. Symbols can run us or ruin us.

In this story, Ray Bradbury imagines neighboring cities that get
into a catastrophic competition for the silliest of reasons. The rulers
are obsessed by symbols, not reality. They almost destroy their lands
because mere symbols, not they, are the masters of their fate. This is
a parable, a story with a moral. What message is Bradbury trying to
convey to us?

The Golden Kite, The Silver Wind

In the shape of a *pig?*" cried the Mandarin.

"In the shape of a pig," said the messenger, and departed.

"Oh, what an evil day in an evil year," cried the Mandarin. "The town of Kwan-Si, beyond the hill, was very small in my childhood. Now it has grown so large that at last they are building a wall."

"But why should a wall two miles away make my good father sad and angry all within the hour?" asked his daughter quietly.

"They build their wall," said the Mandarin, "in the shape of a pig! Do you see? Our own city wall is built in the shape of an orange. That pig will devour us, greedily!"

"Ah."

They both sat thinking.

Life was full of symbols and omens. Demons lurked everywhere, Death swam in the wetness of an eye, the turn of a gull's wing meant rain, a fan held *so*, the tilt of a roof, and, yes, even a city wall was of immense importance. Travelers and tourists, caravans, musicians, artists, coming upon these two towns, equally judging the portents, would say, "The city shaped like an orange? No! I will enter the city shaped like a pig and prosper, eating all, growing fat with good luck and prosperity!"

The Mandarin wept. "All is lost! These symbols and signs terrify. Our city will come on evil days."

"Then," said the daughter, "call in your stonemasons and temple builders. I will whisper from behind the silken screen and you will know the words."

The old man clapped his hands despairingly. "Ho, stonemasons! Ho, builders of towns and palaces!"

The men who knew marble and granite and onyx and quartz came quickly. The Mandarin faced them most uneasily, himself waiting for a whisper from the silken screen behind his throne. At last the whisper came.

"I have called you here," said the whisper.

"I have called you here," said the Mandarin aloud, "because our city is shaped like an orange, and the vile city of Kwan-Si has this day shaped theirs like a ravenous pig——"

Here the stonemasons groaned and wept. Death rattled his cane in the outer courtyard. Poverty made a sound like a wet cough in the shadows of the room.

"And so," said the whisper, said the Mandarin, "you raisers of walls must go bearing trowels and rocks and change the shape of *our* city!"

The architects and masons gasped. The Mandarin himself gasped at what he had said. The whisper whispered. The Mandarin went on: "And you will change our walls into a club which may beat the pig and drive it off!"

The stonemasons rose up, shouting. Even the Mandarin, delighted at the words from his mouth, applauded, stood down from his throne. "Quick!" he cried. "To work!"

When his men had gone, smiling and bustling, the Mandarin turned with great love to the silken screen. "Daughter," he whispered, "I will embrace you." There was no reply. He stepped around the screen, and she was gone.

Such modesty, he thought. She has slipped away and left me with a triumph, as if it were mine.

The news spread through the city; the Mandarin was acclaimed. Everyone carried stone to the walls. Fireworks were set off and the demons of death and poverty did not linger, as all worked together. At the end of the month the wall had been changed. It was now a mighty bludgeon with which to drive pigs, boars, even lions, far away. The Mandarin slept like a happy fox every night.

"I would like to see the Mandarin of Kwan-Si when the news is learned. Such pandemonium and hysteria; he will likely throw himself from a mountain! A little more of that wine, oh Daughter-who-thinks-like-a-son."

But the pleasure was like a winter flower; it died swiftly. That very afternoon the messenger rushed into the courtroom. "Oh, Mandarin, disease, early sorrow, avalanches, grasshopper plagues, and poisoned well water!"

The Mandarin trembled.

"The town of Kwan-Si," said the messenger, "which was built like a pig and which animal we drove away by changing our walls to a mighty stick, has now turned triumph to winter ashes. They have built their city's walls like a great bonfire to burn our stick!"

"The Mandarin's heart sickened within him, like an autumn fruit upon an ancient tree. "Oh, gods! Travelers will spurn us. Tradesmen, reading the symbols, will turn from the stick, so easily destroyed, to the fire, which conquers all!"

"No," said a whisper like a snowflake from behind the silken screen.

"No," said the startled Mandarin.

"Tell my stonemasons," said the whisper that was a falling drop of rain, "to build our walls in the shape of a shining lake."

The Mandarin said this aloud, his heart warmed.

"And with this lake of water," said the whisper and the old man, "we will quench the fire and put it out forever!"

The city turned out in joy to learn that once again they had been saved by the magnificent Emperor of ideas. They ran to the walls and built them nearer to this new vision, singing, not as loudly as before, of course, for they were tired, and not as quickly, for since it had taken a month to rebuild the wall the first time, they had had to neglect business and crops and therefore were somewhat weaker and poorer.

There then followed a succession of horrible and wonderful days, one in another like a nest of frightening boxes.

"Oh, Emperor," cried the messenger, "Kwan-Si has rebuilt their walls to resemble a mouth with which to drink all our lake!"

"Then," said the Emperor, standing very close to his silken screen, "build our walls like a needle to sew up that mouth!"

"Emperor!" screamed the messenger. "They make their walls like a sword to break your needle!"

The Emperor held, trembling, to the silken screen. "Then shift the stones to form a scabbard to sheathe that sword!"

"Mercy," wept the messenger the following morn, "they have worked all night and shaped their walls like lightning which will explode and destroy that sheath!"

Sickness spread in the city like a pack of evil dogs. Shops closed. The population, working now steadily for endless months upon the changing of the walls, resembled Death himself, clattering his white bones like musical instruments in the wind. Funerals began to appear in the streets, though it was the middle of summer, a time when all should be tending and harvesting. The Mandarin fell so ill that he had his bed drawn up by the silken screen and there he lay, miserably giving his architectural orders. The voice behind the screen was weak now, too, and faint, like the wind in the eaves.

"Kwan-Si is an eagle. Then our walls must be a net for that eagle. They are a sun to burn our net. Then we build a moon to eclipse their sun!"

Like a rusted machine, the city ground to a halt.

At last the whisper behind the screen cried out:

"In the name of the gods, send for Kwan-Si!"

Upon the last day of summer the Mandarin Kwan-Si, very ill and withered away, was carried into our Mandarin's courtroom by four starving footmen. The two mandarins were propped up, facing each other. Their breaths fluttered like winter winds in their mouths. A voice said:

"Let us put an end to this."

The old men nodded.

"This cannot go on," said the faint voice. "Our people do nothing but rebuild our cities to a different shape every day, every hour. They have no time to hunt, to fish, to love, to be good to their ancestors and their ancestors' children."

"This I admit," said the mandarins of the towns of the Cage, the Moon, the Spear, the Fire, the Sword and this, that, and other things.

"Carry us into the sunlight," said the voice.

The old men were borne out under the sun and up a little hill. In the late summer breeze a few very thin children were flying dragon kites in all the colors of the sun, and frogs and grass, the color of the sea and the color of coins and wheat.

The first Mandarin's daughter stood by his bed.

"See," she said.

"Those are nothing but kites," said the two old men.

"But what is a kite on the ground?" she said. "It is nothing. What does it need to sustain it and make it beautiful and truly spiritual?"

"The wind, of course!" said the others.

"And what do the sky and the wind need to make *them* beautiful?"

"A kite, of course—many kites, to break the monotony, the sameness of the sky. Colored kites, flying!"

"So," said the Mandarin's daughter. "You, Kwan-Si, will make a last rebuilding of your town to resemble nothing more nor less than the wind. And we shall build like a golden kite. The wind will beautify the kite and carry it to wondrous heights. And the kite will break the sameness of the wind's existence and give it purpose and meaning. One without the other is nothing. Together, all will be beauty and cooperation and a long and enduring life."

Whereupon the two mandarins were so overjoyed that they took their first nourishment in days, momentarily were given strength, embraced, and lavished praise upon each other, called the Mandarin's daughter a boy, a man, a stone pillar, a warrior, and a true and unforgettable son. Almost immediately they parted and hurried to their towns, calling out and singing, weakly but happily.

And so, in time, the towns became the Town of the Golden Kite and the Town of the Silver Wind. And harvestings were harvested and business tended again, and the flesh returned, and disease ran off like a frightened jackal. And on every night of the year the inhabitants in the Town of the Kite could hear the good clear wind sustaining them. And those in the Town of the Wind could hear the kite singing, whispering, rising, and beautifying them.

"So be it," said the Mandarin in front of his silken screen.

Reading for Understanding

Main Idea

1. The main idea of the story is (a) how vain men make mistakes (b) the importance of kite flying in Imperial China (c) the wisdom of women (d) how symbols can disguise reality.

Details

2. The town of Kwan-Si at first built the walls in the shape of (a) an orange (b) a bludgeon (c) a pig (d) a bonfire.
3. The whisper from behind the silken screen came from (a) the Mandarin (b) the stonemason (c) the daughter (d) the messenger.
4. The shape built to counteract the lake was (a) a mouth (b) an orange (c) a bludgeon (c) a golden kite.
5. The problem was finally resolved by (a) the daughter (b) the son (c) the prime minister (d) the Mandarin Kwan-Si.

Inferences

6. The Mandarin considered the orange (a) a last resort (b) an unlucky symbol (c) the mainstay of the economy (d) the principal color of the Mandarin's coat of arms.
7. The Mandarin Kwan-Si was (a) a stronger leader than the Mandarin of the neighboring city (b) a cruel leader who rose to power on deception (c) as silly as his neighbor (d) a suitor to the Mandarin's daughter.
8. The people "have no time to hunt, to fish" because they (a) are off to war (b) are constantly building walls (c) are too much involved in the affairs of state (d) have incurred the wrath of Kwan-Si.

Author's Tone

9. The author's tone is one of (a) unquenched hilarity (b) unrelieved gloom (c) studied indifference (d) tolerant affection.

Order of Events

10. Arrange the items in the order in which they occurred. Use letters only.
    A. The kite
    B. The pig
    C. The bludgeon
    D. The orange
    E. The lake

Words in Context

1. "The news spread through the city; the Mandarin was *acclaimed*." **Acclaimed** (91) means (a) blamed (b) summoned (c) applauded (d) terrified.

2. "It was now a mighty *bludgeon* with which to drive pigs, boars, even lions, far away." A **bludgeon** (91) is a (a) sword (b) stick (c) gun (d) loud noise.

3. " 'Such *pandemonium* and hysteria; he will likely throw himself from a mountain.' " **Pandemonium** (91) means (a) uproar (b) weeping (c) joy (d) confrontation.

Thinking Critically about the Story

1. The person who finally turned things around had done everything possible to help her father. What would have happened if she hadn't stepped in at the end?

2. It isn't the symbol that governs people's lives. It's the meaning applied to the symbols that has an effect. How could the problem have been solved at any moment by giving a different interpretation to the symbols. Here's a hint: why not interpret the lake and the bonfire cooperatively? Sometimes water is needed to douse a bonfire. Sometimes a bonfire is needed to provide warmth, heat water, and cook food.

3. There are many fine descriptive touches in the story—for example,

"Poverty made a sound like a wet cough in the shadows of the room." Find other examples.

4. How could the moral of the story be applied to other human activities—for example, racial hatred, ethnic cleansing, religious intolerance?

5. List five other symbols that play a role in human affairs. Do not use the symbols listed below.

6. How does superstition play a role in our lives even though this is supposedly a reasonable, sane society?

7. Is rivalry between countries good, bad, a little of both? Explain.

8. At the Olympic Games, the avowed purpose is the appreciation of individual achievement. Yet the media always emphasize the nationalism, listing how many medals each participating country has received. Should the national totals be eliminated? Why or why not?

9. Why is the title "The Golden Kite, The Silver Wind" instead of "The Lake and The Mouth"?

Language in Action

Symbols

"They build their wall," said the Mandarin, "in the shape of a pig! Do you see? Our own city wall is built in the shape of an orange. That pig will devour us, greedily."
Life was full of symbols and omens.

"How ridiculous," you rightly say. "How could the shape of the two cities have anything to do with the deteriorating relations?"

The story demonstrates in an amusing and somewhat exaggerated way the power of symbols in our lives. The American flag, a preeminent symbol, stirs the heart of all Americans. Symbols *stand for* things and ideas, but they *are not* the things or ideas. Other symbols include punctuation marks, the + sign, the judge's robe, an Olympic medal, a wedding ring, a graduation diploma, a traffic sign.

You recognize that a wedding ring is not the marriage; it stands for the marriage. You sometimes fail to realize, though, that words are symbols, not reality. If the word *snake,* gives you a queasy feeling, you are being affected by a symbol, not by the real thing. If your mouth waters when you hear *a steak smothered with onions,* you are reacting to the symbols.

Here are two examples revealing the symbolic nature of language.

(a) "Your house is not legally in Minnesota. This survey puts it 20 yards over the Wisconsin line." "Really? That's wonderful. Now I won't have any more of those cold Minnesota winters!"

(b) A century ago a Hungarian scholar decided that Hungarian must be the original language because the Hungarian word for scissors, *ollo*, actually looks like a pair of scissors.

The Shoemaker

Seumas O'Kelly
Irish

"Oh, indeed they do, swallows wear shoes. Twice a year swallows wear shoes. They wear them in the spring and again at the fall of the year. They wear them when they fly from one world to another. And they cross the Dead Sea. Did you ever hear tell of the Dead Sea? You did. Well, well!"

If you think "swallows wear shoes" is a strange bit of news, wait a moment. The master storyteller will tell you how to find out what color hair your future wife will have, how electricity was first discovered, why we have rain. The shoemaker may look like a careworn artisan, but he has the soul of a poet and the eloquence of an orator.

The Irish sense of humor is legendary, with its wonderful sense of the absurd. It survived centuries of problems and still brings laughter. Many comedians, like Hal Roach, tap this rich vein. An example of that typically sly humor is the **Irish bull**. It is an upside-down, contradictory statement like this: "It was hereditary in his family to have no children," Or "He's the kind of person who looks you straight in the eye while he's stabbing you in the back.".

There is a central contradiction in this story, too. All around Gobstown, absentee landlords were raising rents and evicting tenants. At Gobstown, however, the landlord lowered rents until he was as poor as his tenants. How could he be so mean! The shoemaker blames the good man for his becoming a lowly shoemaker. How that explanation makes "sense" is the burden of the story. Welcome to the upside-down world of Irish humor.

The Shoemaker

I. Obeying a domestic mandate, Padna wrapped a pair of boots in paper and took them to the shoemaker, who operated behind a window in a quiet street.

The shoemaker seemed to Padna a melancholy man. He wore great spectacles, had a white patch of forehead, and two great bumps upon it. Padna concluded that the bumps had been encouraged by the professional necessity of constantly hanging his head over his knees.

The shoemaker invited Padna to sit down in his workshop, which he did. Padna thought it must be very dreary to sit there all day among old and new boots, pieces of leather, boxes of brass eyelets, awls, knives, and punchers. No wonder the shoemaker was a melancholy-looking man.

Padna maintained a discreet silence while the shoemaker turned his critical glasses upon the boots he had brought him for repair. Suddenly the great glasses were turned upon Padna himself, and the shoemaker addressed him in a voice of amazing pleasantness.

"When did you hear the cuckoo?" he asked.

Padna, at first startled, pulled himself together. "Yesterday," he replied.

"Did you look at the sole of your boot when you heard him?" the shoemaker asked.

"No," said Padna.

"Well," said the shoemaker, "whenever you hear the cuckoo for the first time in the spring, always look at the sole of your right boot. There you will find a hair. And that hair will tell you the kind of a wife you will get."

The shoemaker picked a long hair from the sole of Padna's boot and held it up in the light of the window.

"You'll be married to a brown-haired woman," he said. Padna looked at the hair without fear, favor, or affection, and said nothing.

The shoemaker took his place on his bench, selected a half-made shoe, got it between his knees, and began to stitch with great gusto. Padna admired the skilful manner in which he made the holes with his awl and drew the wax-end with rapid strokes. Padna abandoned the impression that the shoemaker was a melancholy man. He thought he never sat near a man so optimistic, so mentally emancipated, so detached from the indignity of his occupation.

"These are very small shoes you are stitching," said Padna, making himself agreeable.

"They are," said the shoemaker. "But do you know who makes the smallest shoes in the world? You don't? Well, well!—The smallest shoes in the world are made by the clurichaun, a cousin of the leprechaun. If you creep up on the west side of a fairy fort after the sun has set and put your ear to the grass, you'll hear the tapping of his hammer. And do you know who the clurichaun makes shoes for? You don't? Well, well!—He makes shoes for the swallows. Oh, indeed they do, swallows wear shoes. Twice a year swallows wear shoes. They wear them in the spring, and again at the fall of the year. They wear them when they fly from one world to another. And they cross the Dead Sea. Did you ever hear tell of the Dead Sea? You did. Well, well!—No bird ever yet flew across the Dead Sea. Any of them that tried it dropped and sank like a stone. So the swallows, when they come to the Dead Sea, get down on the bank, and there the clurichauns have millions of shoes waiting for them. The swallows put on their shoes and walk across the Dead Sea, stepping on bright yellow and black stepping-stones that shine across the water like a lovely carpet. And do you know what the stepping-stones across the Dead Sea are? They are the backs of sleeping frogs. And when the swallows are all safe across, the frogs waken up and begin to sing, for then it is known the summer will come. Did you never hear that before? No? Well, well!"

A cat, friendly as the shoemaker himself, leapt on to Padna's lap. The shoemaker shifted the shoe he was stitching between his knees, putting the heel where the toe had been.

"Do you know where they first discovered electricity?" he asked.

"In America," Padna ventured.

"No. In the back of a cat. He was a big buck Chinese cat. Every hair on him was seven inches long, in color gold, and thick as copper wire. He was the only cat who ever looked on the face of the Empress of China without blinking, and when the Emperor saw that, he called him over and stroked him on the back. No sooner did the Emperor of China stroke the buck cat than back he fell on his plush throne, as dead as his ancestors. So they called in seven wise doctors from the seven wise countries of the East to find out what it was killed the Emperor. And after seven years they discovered electricity in the backbone of the cat, and signed a proclamation that it was from the shock of it the Emperor had died. When the Americans read the proclamation, they decided to do whatever killing had to be done as the cat had killed the Emperor of China. The Americans are like that—all for imitating royal families."

"Has this cat any electricity in her?" Padna asked.

"She has," said the shoemaker, drawing his wax-end. "But she's a civilized cat, not like the vulgar fellow in China, and civilized cats hide their electricity much as civilized people hide their feelings. But one day last summer I saw her showing her electricity. A monstrous black rat came prowling from the brewery, a bald patch on his head and a piece missing from his left haunch. To see that fellow coming up out of a gullet and stepping up the street, in the middle of the broad daylight, you'd imagine he was the county inspector of police."

"And did she fight the rat?" Padna asked.

The shoemaker put the shoe on a last and began to tap with his hammer. "She did fight him," he said. "She went out to him twirling her moustaches. He lay down on his back. She lay down on her side. They kept grinning and sparring at each other like that for half an hour. At last the monstrous rat got up in a fury and come at her, the fangs stripped. She swung round the yard, doubled in two, making circles like a Catherine wheel about him until the old blackguard was mesmerized. And if you were to see the bulk of her tail then, all her electricity gone into it! She caught him with a blow of it under the jowl, and he fell in a swoon. She stood over him, her back like the bend of a hoop, the tail beating about her, and a smile on the side of her face. And that was the end of the monstrous brewery rat."

Padna said nothing, but put the cat down on the floor. When she made some effort to regain his lap, he surreptitiously suggested, with the tip of his boot, that their entente was at an end.

A few drops of rain beat on the window, and the shoemaker looked up, his glasses shining, the bumps on his forehead gleaming. "Do you know the reason God makes it rain?" he asked.

Padna, who had been listening to the conversation of two farmers the evening before, replied, "I do. To make turnips grow."

"Nonsense!" said the shoemaker, reaching out for an awl. "God makes it rain to remind us of the Deluge. And I don't mean the Deluge that was at all at all. I mean the Deluge that is to come. The world will be drowned again. The belly-band of the sky will give, for that's what the rainbow is, and it only made of colors. Did you never know until now what the rainbow was? No? Well, well!—As I was saying, when the belly-band of the sky bursts the Deluge will come. In one minute all the valleys of the earth will be filled up. In the second minute the mountains will be topped. In the third minute the sky will be emptied and its skin gone, and the earth will be no more. There will be no ark, no Noah, and no dove. There will be nothing only one great waste of grey water and in the middle of it one green leaf. The green leaf will be a sign that God has gone to sleep, the trouble of the world banished from His mind. So whenever it rains remember my words."

Padna said he would, and then went home.

II. When Padna called on the shoemaker for the boots that had been left for repair, they were almost ready. The tips only remained to be put on the heels. Padna sat down in the little workshop, and under the agreeable influence of the place he made bold to ask the shoemaker if he had grown up to be a shoemaker as the geranium had grown up to be a geranium in its pot on the window.

"What!" exclaimed the shoemaker. "Did you never hear tell that I was found in the country under a head of cabbage? No! Well, well! What do they talk to you at home about at all?"

"The most thing they tell me," said Padna, "is to go to bed and get up in the morning. What is the name of the place in the country where they found you?"

"Gobstown," said the shoemaker. "It was the most miserable place within the ring of Ireland. It lay under the blight of a good landlord, no better. That was its misfortune, and especially my misfortune. If the Gobstown landlord was not such a good landlord it's driving on the box of an empire I would be today instead of whacking tips on the heels of your boots. How could that be? I'll tell you that.

"In Gobstown the tenants rose up and demanded a reduction of rent; the good landlord gave it to them. They rose up again and demanded another reduction of rent; he gave it to them. They went on rising up, asking reductions, and getting them, until there was no rent left for anyone to reduce. The landlord was as good and as poor as our best.

"And while all this was going on Gobstown was surrounded by estates where there were the most ferocious landlords—rack-renting, absentee, evicting landlords, landlords as wild as tigers. And these tiger landlords were leaping at their tenants and their tenants slashing back at them as best they could. Nothing, my dear, but blood and the music of grapeshot and shouts in the night from the jungle. In Gobstown we had to sit down and look on, pretending, moryah, that we were as happy as the day was long.

"Not a scalp was ever brought into Gobstown. No man of us ever went out on an adventure which might bring him home again through the mouth of the county jail. Not a secret enterprise that might become a great public excitement was ever hatched, not to speak of being launched. We had not as much as a fife-and-drum band. We did not know how to play a tin whistle or beat upon the tintinnabulum. We never waved a green flag. We had not a branch of any kind of a league. We had no men of skill to draft a resolution, indite a threatening letter, draw a coffin, skull, and crossbones, fight a policeman, or even make a speech. We were never a delegate at a convention, an envoy to America, a divisional executive, a deputation, or a demonstration. We were nothing. We wilted under the blight of our good landlord as the green stalk wilts under the frost of the black night—Hand me that knife. The one with the wooden handle.

"In desperation we used rouse ourselves and march into the demonstrations on other estates. We were a small and an unknown tribe.

The Gobstown contingent always brought up the rear of the procession—a gawky, straggling, bad-stepping, hay-foot, straw-foot lot! The onlookers hardly glanced at us. We stood for nothing. We had no name. Once we rigged up a banner with the words on it, 'Gobstown to the Front!' but still we were put to the back, and when we walked through this town, the servant girls came out of their kitchens, laughed at us, and called out, 'Gobstown to the Back of the Front!'

"The fighting men came to us, took us aside, and asked us what we were doing in Gobstown. We had no case to make. We offered to bring forward our good landlord as a shining example, to lead our lamb forward in order that he might show up the man-eaters on the other estates. The organizers were all hostile. They would not allow us into the processions any more. If we could bring forward some sort of roaring black devil, we would be more than welcome. Shining examples were not in favor. We were sent home in disgrace and broke up. As the preachers say, our last state was worse than our first.

"We became sullen and drowsy and fat and dull. We got to hate the sight of each other, so much so that we began to pay our rents behind each other's backs, at first the reduced rents, then, gale day by gale day, we got back to the original rent, and kept on paying it. Our good landlord took his rents and said nothing. Gobstown became the most accursed place in all Ireland. Brother could not trust brother. And there were our neighbors going from one sensation to another. They were as lively as trout, as enterprising as goats, as intelligent as Corkmen. They were thin and eager and good-tempered. They ate very little, drank water, slept well, men with hard knuckles, clean bowels, and pale eyes. Anything they hit went down. They were always ready to go to the gallows for each other.

"I had a famous cousin on one of these estates, and I suppose you heard of him? You didn't! What are they teaching you at school at all? Latin grammar? Well, well!—My cousin was a clumsy fellow with only a little of middling kind of brains, but a bit of fight in him. Yet look at the way he got on, and look at me, shodding little boys like yourself! I was born under a lucky star but my cousin was born under a lucky landlord—a ferocious fellow who got into a garret in London and kept roaring across at Ireland for more and more blood. Every time I thought of that old skin of a man howling in the London garret I said to myself, 'He'll be the making of my cousin.' And so, indeed, he was. Three agents were brought down on my cousin's estate. State trials were running like great plays in the courthouse. Blood was always up. They had six fife-and-drum bands and one brass band. They had green and gold banners with harps and streamers, and mottoes in yellow lettering, that took four hardy men to carry on a windy day. The heads of the Peelers* were hardly ever

*police

out of their helmets. The resident magistrate rose one day in the bosom of his family, his eyes closed, to say grace before meals, and from dint of habit he was chanting the Riot Act over the table until his wife flew at him with, 'How dare you, George! The mutton is quite all right!' Little boys no bigger than yourself walking along the roads to school in that splendid estate could jump up on the ditch and make good speeches."

"My cousin's minute books—he was secretary of everything —would stock a bookshop, and were noted for beautiful expressions. He was the author of ten styles of resolution construction. An enemy christened him Resolving Kavanagh. Every time he resolved to stand where he always stood he resolved. Everybody put up at his house. He was seen in more torchlight processions than Bryan O'Lynn. A room in his house was decorated in a beautiful scheme of illuminated addresses with border designs from the Book of Kells. The homes of the people were full of the stumps of burned-down candles, the remains of great illuminations for my cousin whenever he came out of prison. I tell you no lie when I say that that clumsy cousin of mine became clever and polished, all through pure practice. He had the best of tutors. The skin of a landlord in the London garret, his agents, their understrappers, removable magistrates, judges, Crown solicitors, county inspectors of police, sergeants, constables, secret service men—all drove him from fame to fame until in the end they chased him out the only gap that was left open to the like of him—the English Parliament. Think of the streak of that man's career! And there was I, a man of capacity and brains, born with the golden spoon of talent in my mouth, dead to the world in Gobstown! I was rotting like a turnip under the best and the most accursed of landlords. In the end I could not stand it—no man of spirit could.

"One day I took down my ashplant, spat on my fist, and set out for my cousin's place. He gave me no welcome. I informed him as to how the land lay in Gobstown. I said we must be allowed to make a name for ourselves as the producers of a shining example of a landlord. My cousin let his head lie over a little to one side and then said. 'In this country shining examples ought only be used with the greatest moderation.' He looked out through the window and after some time said, 'That Gobstown landlord is the most dangerous lunatic in all Ireland.' 'How is that?' said I. 'Because,' said my famous cousin, 'he has a perfect heart.' He put his head over to the other side, looked at me and said, 'If Gobstown does not do something, he may be the means of destroying us all.' 'How?' said I. 'He may become contagious,' said my cousin. 'Only think of his example being followed and Ireland turned into one vast tract of Gobstowns! Would not any fate at all be better than that?' I who knew said, 'God knows it would.'

"My cousin sighed heavily. He turned from me, leaving me standing there in the kitchen, and I saw him moving with a ladder to the loft overhead. This be mounted and disappeared in the black rafters. I could hear him fumbling somewhere under the thatch. Presently down he came the ladder, a gun in one hand, and a fistful of cartridges in the other. He spoke no word, and I spoke no word. He came to me and put the gun in my hand and the handful of cartridges in my pocket. He walked to the fire and stood there with his back turned. I stood where I was, a Gobstown mohawk, with the gun in my hand. At last I said, 'What is this for?' and grounded the gun a little on the floor. My cousin did not answer at once. At last he said without moving, 'It's for stirring your tea, what else?' I looked at him and he remained as he was and, the sweat breaking out on the back of my neck, I left the house and made across the fields for home, the cartridges rattling in my pocket every ditch I leapt, the feel of the gun in my hand becoming more familiar and more friendly.

"At last I came to the summit of a little green hill overlooking Gobstown, and there I sat me down. The sight of Gobstown rose the gorge* in me. Nothing came out of it but weak puffs of turf smoke from the chimneys—little pallid thin streaks that wobbled in the wind. There, says I, is the height of Gobstown. And no sound came up out of it except the cackle of geese, and then the bawl of an old ass in the bog. There, says I, is the depth of Gobstown. And rising up from the green hill I made up my mind to save Ireland from Gobstown even if I lost my own soul. I would put a bullet in the perfect heart of our good landlord.

"That night I lay behind a certain ditch. The moon shone on the nape of my neck. The good landlord passed me by on the road, he and his good wife, chattering and happy as a pair of lovers. I groped for the gun. The queerest feeling came over me. I did not even raise it. I had no nerve. I quaked behind the ditch. His footsteps and her footsteps were like cracks of this hammer on my head. I knew, then, in that minute, that I was no good, and that Gobstown was for ever lost—What happened me? Who can say that for certain? Many a time have I wondered what came over me in that hour. I can only guess.—Nobody belonging to me had ever been rack-rented.** I had never seen any of my own people evicted. No great judge of assize had ever looked down on me from his bench to the dock and addressed to me stern words. I had never heard the clang behind me of a prison door. No royal hand of an Irish constabularyman had ever brought a baton down on my head. No carbine had ever butted the soft places of my body. I had no scars that might redden with memories. The memories I had and that might give me courage were not memories of landlords. There was nothing of anger in my heart for the Gobstown landlord, and he went by. I dragged my legs out of the ditch and drowned my cousin's gun in a boghole. After it I dropped in

*made me angry
**paid excessive rent

the handful of cartridges. They made a little gurgle in the dark water like blood in a shot man's throat. And that same night I went home, put a few things in a red handkerchief, and stole out of Gobstown like a thief. I walked along the roads until I came to this town, learned my trade, became a respectable shoemaker, and—tell your mother I never use anything only the best leather. There are your boots, Padna, tips and all—half-a-crown. Thanks, and well wear!"

Reading for Understanding

Main Idea

1. The main idea of this story is best expressed in which of the following?
   (a) Time waits for no man.
   (b) You never can tell.
   (c) The shoemaker's children go shoeless.
   (d) It's a long road that has no turning.

Details

2. According to the shoemaker, a man's future wife's hair color can be found by (a) checking the sole of the right boot (b) hearing the wakening frogs in spring (c) studying the actions of a cat (d) listening to the song of a nightingale.

3. The clurichaun is (a) an Irish stringed instrument (b) a magistrate in an Irish district court (c) a villainous highwayman (d) a leprechaun's cousin.

4. The shoemaker's cat (a) destroyed a vicious dog (b) was an unfriendly beast (c) carried an electric charge (d) was responsible for the shoemaker's staying put.

5. The shoemaker's cousin was (a) the Gobstown landlord (b) Padna (c) Resolving Kavanagh (d) Brian O'Lynn.

Inferences

6. This story is written with (a) hatred for cowards (b) a dislike of the shoemaker (c) tongue in cheek (d) a serious but concealed message.

7. The shoemaker is a master at (a) his craft (b) the tall story (c) hating the Gobstown landlord (d) straight talk.

8. The story shows the Irish capacity for (a) laughing at themselves (b) disliking honorable men (c) learning a craft (d) enjoying prosperity.

Tone of the Story

9. The tone of the story is (a) bitter (b) solemn (c) melancholy (d) light.

Outcomes

10. At the conclusion of the story, the shoemaker (a) kept on repairing shoes (b) returned to Gobstown (c) joined a neighboring protest group (d) decided to kill the Gobstown landlord.

Words in Context

1. "Obeying a domestic *mandate,* Padna wrapped a pair of boots in paper and took them to the shoemaker, who operated behind a window in a quiet street." A **mandate** (99) is a (a) query (b) suggestion (c) command (d) comment.

2. "Padna maintained a *discreet* silence while the shoemaker turned his critical glasses upon the boots he had brought him for repair." **Discreet** (99) means (a) pained (b) sensible (c) unexpected (d) glum.

3. "The shoemaker . . . began to stitch with great *gusto.*" **Gusto** (99) means (a) enthusiasm (b) skill (c) directness (d) great stitches.

4., 5. "He thought he never sat near a man so optimistic, so mentally *emancipated,* so detached from the *indignity* of his occupation." **Emancipated** (99) means (a) liberated (b) unbalanced (c) cheerful (d) tied down. **Indignity** (99) means (a) monotony (b) reputation (c) uncertainty (d) humiliation.

6., 7. "He *surreptitiously* suggested, with the tip of his boot, that their *entente* was at an end." **Surreptitiously** (101) means (a) slyly (b) forcefully (c) angrily (d) excitedly. **Entente** (101) means (a) disagreement (b) understanding (c) employment (d) storytelling.

8. "We were never a delegate at a convention, an envoy to America, a divisional executive, a *deputation,* or a demonstration." A **deputation** (102) is a (a) law-enforcement group (b) gathering of judges (c) visiting committee (d) branch of government.

Thinking Critically about the Story

1. The author introduces subtle touches that show a sly sense of humor. One such is the "domestic mandate" in the first line. Apparently it was Padna's wife who said, "Padna, get those boots repaired!" Point out other examples of sly humor.

2. The shoemaker is ready to weave a tall tale out of a customer's question or comment. Point out how he cleverly introduces the swallows' shoes, the electric cat, and the flood. Note how cleverly he makes the transition to his own story from the customer's comments.

3. By the shoemaker's odd logic, his life in Gobstown prevented him from becoming a famous man. Explain how he reached that conclusion.

4. O'Kelly delights in character sketches. How did Resolving Kavanagh earn his name?

5. The landlord has never done an evil thing. He and his wife are a happy, though poor, pair of lovers. Why is the shoemaker so angry?

6. What do you suppose the shoemaker's early life was really like?

7. The shoemaker says, "I had a famous cousin on one of these estates, I suppose you heard of him? You didn't! What are they teaching you at school at all? Latin grammar? Well, well!" Could Padna have reasonably been expected to know the "famous cousin"? Why does the shoemaker ask what they teach at school? What comment is he making about education?

Language in Action

Polar Thinking

> "Gobstown," said the shoemaker. "It was the most miserable place within the ring of Ireland."

Most miserable reveals a tendency in communication: to support one extreme or the other. This habit, sometimes called *polar thinking* or *two-value judgments,* avoids the more likely middle ground. "You're either with me or against me!" Actually, I may be with you in some respects, opposed in others. "Choose between me or Frances." Why do I have to choose? I may like you both.

The child's world is simple. Children's literature emphasizes the division between good and bad, hero and villain. Cinderella is beautiful and kind, without a flaw. Her stepmother is thoroughly evil, without a redeeming quality. While it is true that some people, like Adolf Hitler, seem to be entirely evil, most people are combinations of many different qualities, some admirable, some less than admirable.

Adult fiction and movies tend to show complexity. In *The Idylls of the King,* Alfred Lord Tennyson wrote

"He is all fault who hath no fault at all,
For who loves me must have a touch of earth."

Two-value judgments surface strongly in politics. To some Republicans, all Democrats are evil villains, practically sprouting horns. To some Democrats, Republicans are monstrous scoundrels. The reality is that both groups have special strengths and weaknesses.

Keep in mind the intervening words between extremes. Between *beautiful* and *ugly,* for example, there are many transitional words: *lovely, pretty, attractive, plain, unattractive, homely.* Also keep in mind that all these words are judgment words (118) that may tell more about you than the object of the description.

Cindy Ellie

Mary Carter Smith
American

"Something mighty strange happened tonight. As the clock at City Hall began to strike 12, that African princess began to run like crazy. She ran so fast, she ran right out of one of her golden sandals. The mayor's son found it and kept it. He's really upset over that sister.

The Cinderella folktale is one of the world's oldest. It has been traced all the way back to the ninth century in China. There are more than 500 European versions of the tale, but the best-known is by Charles Perrault in 1669. Rossini made it into the opera **La Cenerentola**. Prokoviev created a ballet. Walt Disney made it into an animated film. In addition, there are various movie versions, some with **Cinderella** in the title. There is something universally satisfying about a rags-to-riches story, especially one in which the downtrodden heroine gives her tormentors their comeuppance.

Mary Carter Smith, the author of "Cindy Ellie," is the official griot of the state of Maryland. A griot is a hereditary storyteller in West Africa whose function is to keep an oral history of the tribe or village, entertaining with stories, poems, songs, and dances. Ms. Smith is also co-founder of the Association of Black Storytellers. Her imagination has added a charming tale to the ever-growing **Cinderella** treasure trove.

Why another version of the Cinderella story? This is a special retelling, warm and delightful. Though it is written in colorful language, with some substandard English, "Cindy Ellie" is warmhearted, humorous, and recognizably human. Though varying from other versions in details, it retains the spirit and outline of the traditional folktale down to the "fairy godmother." Indeed, the new and different details provide many of the chuckles you'll experience

Cindy Ellie

Once upon a time, over in East Baltimore, there lived a happy family: Sam Johnson, his wife, Lula, and their daughter, Ellie. Lula was good and kind—a quiet, church-going woman—but mighty puny and sickly. One day Lula called Ellie to her bedside and said, "Child, Mama ain't feeling so well. One of these days I might leave you."

"Oh, Mama, don't say that," Ellie said, with tears in her eyes. "Don't cry, child," her mama answered. "All of us go sometime, and I'd rather it be me than you. So there are a few things I want to tell you. Always mind your daddy. Stay in church, go to school, and learn that book. Remember what I'm telling you."

"All right, Mama, I'll remember."

One day not long after that, the poor woman just up and died, real peaceful-like and quiet.

Honey, let me tell you, she had a beautiful funeral. Sam sure put her away nice. The Senior Choir turned out full force. The Junior Choir was there. And the Gospel Chorus just sang their hearts out. The church was *crowded*. Folks all on the outside too, with loudspeakers going. Lula's lodge sisters was there in their white dresses and them purple sashes all edged in gold. Ellie was on the front row beside her daddy, just as cute as she could be in a white dress and her hair in a fine bush. Ellie was one purty young black sister, with skin like black velvet.

Child, let me tell you, that poor woman's body wasn't hardly cold before them church sisters was after Sam Johnson like flies after honey! 'Cause he had a good job down Sparrow's Point, with lots of seniority. And they had just paid for one of them big pretty houses on Broadway, with them pretty white marble steps.

That poor man, like so many good men, was weak for a pretty face and big legs and big hips. One hussy, the boldest of 'em all, had a heart as hard as a rock. The milk of human kindness had curdled in her breast. But she did have a pretty face, big legs, and great big hips. Ooh-wee! She could put on! Made like she loved Ellie so and was always bringing barbecued ribs, collard greens, cracklin' bread, and jelly layer-cake to Ellie and Sam. Well, that man fell right into her trap. She had him cornered and married before you could say Jackie Robinson.

Then bless my soul. You ain't never seen such a change in nobody. First off, that woman went down to South Car'lina to get her two big-footed ugly gals that her mama'd been keeping. Brought them back to Baltimore, put poor Ellie out of her pretty room with the canopied bed, and let her ugly gals sleep in that pretty room. Made poor little Ellie sleep on a pallet in the cellar.

Now, Ellie's mama had been wise. When everybody else was converting their furnaces to oil and gas, she said, "Uh uh. One day they gon' be hard to get." She had kept her coal furnace. Poor little Ellie had to do all the cooking, cleaning, washing, and ironing. She had to scrub them marble steps twice a day too and wait on them ugly gals hand and foot. Not only that, but in the winter she had to keep the fire going and clean out the ashes and cinders. So they got to calling her Cindy Ellie.

Tell you the truth, I believe that woman had put some roots on that man. 'Cause no matter how she mistreated Cindy Ellie, he never said a word—he was just crazy 'bout that big-legged woman.

That November the good white folks, the good Asian folks, and the good black folks all turned out and voted for a good black brother who was running for mayor, and he won the election by a landslide. He was going to have his inauguration ball down at the Convention Center, and so many folks had voted for him that they had to hold it for two nights running. The mayor's son had come home from Harvard to go to the ball.

Oh, them stepsisters was primping and buying designer gowns to go to the ball. Poor Cindy Ellie had to give one of 'em a perm, the other a jheri curl, and both of them facials—not that it helped much. Honey, them gals was ugly from the inside out.

"Cindy Ellie, don't you wish you could go to the ball?" they teased.

"Oh, you're making fun of me," Cindy Ellie said.

So Cindy Ellie's daddy, her stepmother, and them two ugly gals all went to the ball and left poor Cindy Ellie at home. Now, Cindy Ellie had a godmama. She had been her dear mama's best friend, and she still had a key to the house. She came to the house that night, as she often did, to sneak food to poor Cindy Ellie and found the child lying on her hard pallet, just crying her heart out.

"Why are you crying, child?" she asked her.

"Be-because I want to go to the ball."

Now, this godmama had been born with a veil over her face, down in New Orleans. She knew a thing or two about voodoo and hoodoo. Besides that, she had a High John the Conqueror root that she always used for good. The godmama told Cindy Ellie, "Go upstairs to the kitchen, child. Look in the kitchen-cabinet drawer, and bring me the biggest white onion you can find." Cindy Ellie was an obedient child, so she didn't ask why. She just did what her godmama told her to do. Cindy Ellie brought the onion to her godmama. Then the two of them went out in the back yard. The godmama lay that onion on the ground, and then she stepped back and waved that root over it. And right before their eyes that onion turned into a long white Cadillac that parked itself in the back alley.

"Cindy Ellie, go up to the third floor, and bring me that mouse trap." Cindy Ellie brought it down. In its cage were two little black mice. The godmama told Cindy Ellie to open the cage door, and them mice started out. But that godmama waved that root over them, and they turned into two six-foot-tall black chauffeurs dressed in shining white uniforms with fancy white caps. They had on tall black boots, and they was bowing and scraping. "All right, Cindy Ellie, you can go to the ball now."

"But Godmama, look at me. I'm clean, but I'm ragged."

"Don't worry 'bout it," her godmama said. Then she stepped back and waved that root over Cindy Ellie. Her rags turned into a dazzling dress of pink African lace. Her hair was braided into a hundred shining braids, and on the end of each braid were beads of pure gold. Her eyes were beautifully shaded, and her skin shone like polished ebony. On each ear hung five small diamond earrings. On her tiny feet were dainty golden scandals encrusted with dazzling jewels. Cindy Ellie was laid back!

As one of the chauffeurs helped her into the white Cadillac, her godmama told her, "Be sure you leave before midnight, or you'll be as you was. Your Cadillac will turn back into an onion, your chauffeurs into mice, and your clothes into rags." Cindy Ellie promised that she would leave before midnight. And away she went, as happy as could be.

At the ball, not long afterward, the mayor's son heard that a beautiful girl who looked like an African princess had arrived. He came out to see her and said to himself, "This sure is one fine fox." He asked her, "May I escort you into the ballroom?" Cindy Ellie replied in tones soft and low, "I don't mind if you do." He helped her out of her limousine and escorted her into the ballroom and to the head table.

Every eye was on Cindy Ellie. You could have heard a pin drop. Then voices could be heard, whispering, "Gorgeous," "Lovely," "Devastating," "Elegant." Even the mayor himself could not take his eyes off her. His wife agreed that she was indeed a charming young woman. The other ladies were looking at her clothes and wishing their own gowns were half as beautiful as Cindy Ellie's.

Although the table was loaded with sumptuous food, Toussaint, the mayor's son, couldn't eat a bite—he was too busy looking at Cindy Ellie. Then the band started to play, and Cindy Ellie and Toussaint danced as if they had been dancing together all their lives. Cindy Ellie was friendly and courteous to everyone she met. She even sat beside her stepsisters, who had no idea who she was, and invited them to come back the next night. For Toussaint had begged Cindy Ellie to return for the second night of the ball.

Then Cindy Ellie heard the clock strike 11:45. She murmured to Toussaint, "Really, I must be getting home," and rushed out as fast as she could go. As soon as she was home, Cindy Ellie called her godmama and thanked her for such a splendid time. Then the doorbell rang, and she heard her stepsisters' voices: "Hurry, stupid! Open the door!"

Cindy Ellie came out, yawning and rubbing her eyes as if she'd been asleep. "Did you have a good time?" she asked. "Oh, it was all right, but we didn't get to dance with the mayor's son. He danced only with some new girl nobody had ever seen before. She had on some ol' African clothes. But on her they did look good. She had the good sense to recognize what quality people we are, and she asked the mayor's son to invite all of us to come tomorrow night."

"What was her name?" asked Cindy Ellie.

"No one knows. The mayor's son is dying to find out who she is."

Cindy Ellie said, "You don't mean it. Oh, how I wish I could go to the ball tomorrow night. Lillie, won't you lend me your old blue gown so I can go too?" The sisters almost split their sides laughing. "You, with your ragged self, go to the inauguration ball? Wouldn't that be something else! Of course not. Come and help us get undressed and turn back the covers on the bed so we can go to sleep."

And the next night, as on the night before, poor little Cindy Ellie was left behind while the rest of them went to the ball again. Her godmama came in and heard the child crying again. "Why you crying, child? You want to go to that ball again?"

"Yes, ma'am."

"I thought so. You've been a good child all your life, and you always respect your elders. So don't worry. You can go to the ball again. Now dry your eyes, and get your face together. Look in that kitchen-cabinet drawer, and bring me the biggest yellow onion you can find." Cindy Ellie came back with the biggest yellow onion you ever laid eyes on. Then the two of them went out in the back yard. The godmama laid that onion on the ground, and then she stepped back and waved the root over it. And right before their eyes, that onion turned into a solid gold Mercedes-Benz about half a block long and parked itself in the back alley.

"Cindy Ellie, go up on the third floor, and bring me that rat trap," said her godmama. Cindy Ellie brought it down, and in its cage were two big white rats. You see, the family lived so close to Johns Hopkins Hospital that mice and rats from the laboratories up there used to escape and get into the house. They took that cage out in the back yard, and the godmama stood back and waved that High John the

Conqueror root over them, and they turned into two seven-foot-tall white chauffeurs dressed in shining gold uniforms with fancy gold caps. They had on long white boots, and they was bowing and scraping.

"All right, Cindy Ellie, you can go to the ball now."

"But Godmama, look at me. I'm clean, but I'm ragged."

"Don't worry 'bout it," her godmama said. Then she stepped back and waved that root over Cindy Ellie. Her rags turned into a dress made of pure silk kente, the royal cloth from Ghana, and worth thousands of dollars. On her head was a headdress of the rarest taffeta, standing tall and just gorgeous. Her big pretty eyes were beautifully shaded, and her skin was shining like polished ebony. Golden bracelets covered her arms clean up to her shoulders. On each ear hung five small diamond earrings. On her tiny feet were dainty golden sandals encrusted with dazzling jewels. She was cool!

As one of the chauffeurs helped her into that gold Mercedes-Benz, her godmama told her, "Be sure you leave before midnight, or you'll be as you was. That Mercedes-Benz will turn back into an onion, your chauffeurs into rats, and your clothes into rags." Cindy Ellie promised that she would leave before midnight. Away she went, as happy as could be.

As they drove up, Toussaint was waiting for her. She went into the ballroom draped on his arm. Oh, they was having such a good time, laughing and talking and waltzing and boogieing. That poor child forgot all about the time. Then she heard the clock as it began to strike 12. She ran out of there as fast as her legs could carry her—so fast that she ran out of one of her sandals. Toussaint ran behind her, but he couldn't see where she had gone. He picked up the golden sandal.

He asked the security people, "Did you see an African princess run by you?"

"No," they said. "We did see a girl dressed in rags run out of the door. We thought she had stole something. But that chick was gone!"

That night when the family came home from the ball, they told Cindy Ellie, "Something mighty strange happened tonight. As the clock at City Hall began to strike 12, that African princess began to run like crazy. She ran so fast, she ran right out of one of her golden sandals. The mayor's son found it and kept it. He's really upset over that sister."

Child, the next day the mayor's son came on television, came on the radio, and announced to every paper in Baltimore that he would marry the girl whose foot fit that sandal he had picked up. Now, a lot of folks who had supported the mayor lived in the places surrounding Baltimore. So first all them sorority girls and debutantes and folks like that tried to fit their foot in that sandal. Wouldn't fit none of them girls in Columbia, Cockeysville, Randallstown, and all the places like that. Then they went to them rich folks' houses up on Cadillac Row. Wouldn't fit none of them girls neither. Then they went to all them condominiums downtown by the Inner Harbor and them fancy townhouses. Wouldn't fit none of them neither. Finally they come to East Baltimore.

Length and long they came to Broadway and knocked at the Johnson's residence. The mayor's men came in with that golden sandal on a red velvet pillow. Them two stepsisters tried their best to put on that shoe. They pushed, and they jugged, but their big feet would not get into that shoe. No way, José!

"May I try?" asked Cindy Ellie.

"No, stupid. It's not for the likes of you," the sisters said.

"Yes, you may try on the sandal," the mayor's representative said. "For the proclamation issued by the mayor said that any girl in Baltimore and surrounding areas may try." He spoke kindly to Cindy Ellie. "Sit down, miss, and see if it fits you." And do you know, that sandal just slid on Cindy Ellie's little foot as smooth as silk. Then she pulled the other sandal from the pocket in her clean but ragged dress.

As soon as she put it on her foot, right there before their very eyes, Cindy Ellie was transformed into the African princess they had seen the two nights before. Them sisters had a fit.

"Oh, Cindy Ellie, we didn't mean you no harm! Oh, Cindy Ellie, please forgive us!" They was on the floor, rolling around and carrying on.

Cindy Ellie told them, "Get up off that floor, and stop all that whooping and hollering. I forgive you."

Then Cindy Ellie was transported to the mayor's mansion in his private limousine. Toussaint was there, waiting to welcome her with open arms. Cindy Ellie was true to her word. For she forgave her stepsisters not only in word but also in deed: she found them two ugly councilmen for husbands. Toussaint and Cindy Ellie were married in the biggest Baptist church in East Baltimore, and the reception was held in the Convention Center. And they lived happily, happily, forever after.

Reading for Understanding

Main Idea

1. The main idea can best be expressed by which of the following sayings?
   (a) Where there's smoke there's fire.
   (b) Once bitten, twice shy.
   (c) Virtue will triumph.
   (d) The proof of the pudding is in the eating.

Details

2. Lula was (a) one of the stepsisters (b) the wife of Sam Johnson (c) the stepmother (d) Cindy Ellie's godmama.

3. The stepsisters had been staying (a) in North Carolina (b) with their father (c) with their grandma (d) next door to Cindy Ellie's family.

4. The godmama had been born in (a) East Baltimore (b) Sparrow's Point (c) South Carolina (d) New Orleans.

5. The mayor's son went to (a) Columbia (b) Harvard (c) Princeton (d) Temple.

Inferences

6. Ellie's father (a) failed in his responsibility for Ellie (b) was a respected member of the city council (c) was sought after only by the stepmother (d) arranged for the mayor's son to meet his daughter.

7. Ellie's mother's choice of heating (a) was no help to Ellie (b) failed to heat the house (c) was a last-minute idea (d) was objected to by her husband.

8. Apparently, being born with a veil over the face (a) prophesied a life of hard work (b) conferred certain magical powers on the owner (c) was fairly common in some areas of the country (d) was bad luck.

Author's Style

9. The style of "Cindy Ellie" is (a) warm and relaxed (b) nervous and upsetting (c) argumentative and wordy (d) serious and sober.

Fact or Opinion

Tell whether the following is a fact or an opinion.

10. Cindy Ellie was the most beautiful girl in East Baltimore.

Word in Context

"Made poor little Ellie sleep on a *pallet* in the cellar." A pallet (112) is a (a) kind of hammock (b) foldaway mattress (c) overstuffed sofa (d) crude bed.

Thinking Critically about the Story

1. Does the manner of telling the story satisfy you? Did you find the street language helpful to the story? Explain.
2. How many parallels to the usual version of *Cinderella* can you find in the story—for example, the coach and the Cadillac?
3. This version replaces the glass slippers with golden. Which do you prefer?
4. Mary Carter Smith, the author, introduced this story with a comment: "I tell 'Cindy Ellie' because of my desire to give urban audiences stories they can relate to." Has she succeeded? Explain.
5. The author adds, "The tale incorporates satire, humor, and African-American traditions and encourages voting, cleanliness, and forgiveness." Point out examples of each quality she mentions.
6. "Ethnic, cultural, and racial diversity is a source of America's strength." How do you feel about the quotation?
7. If this story were converted into a television sitcom episode, what qualities would inevitably be lost? Does the written word still have some advantages over the powers of television?

Language in Action

Judgment Words

> "Every eye was on Cindy Ellie. You could hear a pin drop. Then voices could be heard, whispering, "Gorgeous," "Lovely," "Devastating," "Elegant.""

What wonderful words to describe the heroine of "Cindy Ellie"! They help us to visualize the radiant dancer as she was observed by the assembled guests. Words like these enrich our lives and imaginations, but they present some pitfalls, too. Above all, we must realize that the words are not tied forever with Cindy Ellie. They are judgment words that exist only in the minds of the speakers and the listeners.

Some labels are more verifiable than others. If we say, "Tiffany was a member of the relay team," the statement is verifiable. If we say

"Tiffany was egotistical," we use a judgment word that cannot be checked.

The flavor or connotation (323) of a word is individual. To some voters, the word *liberal* is a red flag, arousing strong negative feelings. To other voters, the same word is an acceptable label for their own beliefs.

Judgment words are individual. *Lazy, bungling, incompetent, stupid,* and *reckless* are negative words that may be applied to individuals who are rated *energetic, steady, competent, wise,* and *careful* by others. How can that be? The words exist in the brain, not "out there."

When you listen to the next political debate or campaign speech, notice how many words are judgment words, expressing only the *opinions* of the speakers.

Leeam O'Rooney's Burial

Douglas Hyde
Irish

The priest went in, and began driving out the pig, when Leeam rose up out of the straw and said: "Where are you going with my pig, Father Patrick"?

When the priest saw Leeam, off and away with him, and he crying out: "In the name of God, I order you back to your grave, William O'Rooney."

Imagine: a woman's husband, Leeam O'Rooney, goes off to sell a wagon load of wheat. When he comes back, he sickens and dies. She buries the man with all the needed rites and then looks around for a younger man. Rather hastily, she decides to marry the servant boy. After a "decent" interval of a week, the wife does remarry, but there is no honeymoon.

The complications begin. A man calling himself **Leeam O'Rooney** shows up and demands to be let in the house. What happens thereafter is the heart of this folktale translated and retold by Douglas Hyde. As in "The Shoemaker" (98), this tale retains the wit and liveliness we come to associate with Irish humor. Though the subject is superficially tragic, the telling relishes the absurdity.

Prepare to meet Leeam O'Rooney, the liveliest corpse in folklore.

Leeam O'Rooney's Burial

In the olden time there was once a man named William O'Rooney, living near Clare-Galway. He was a farmer. One day the landlord came to him and said: "I have three years' rent on you, and unless you have it for me within a week, I'll throw you out on the side of the road."

"I'm going to Galway with a load of wheat tomorrow, said Leeam (William), "and when I get the price of it I'll pay you."

Next morning he put a load of wheat on the cart, and was going to Galway with it. When he was gone a couple of miles from the house, a gentleman met him and asked him: "Is it wheat you've got on the cart?"

"It is," says Leeam; "I'm going to sell it to pay my rent."

"How much is there in it?" said the gentleman.

"There's a ton, honest, in it," said Leeam.

"I'll buy it from you," said the gentleman, "and I'll give you the biggest price that's going in the market. When you'll go as far as the cart *boreen* (little road) that's on your left hand, turn down, and be going till you come to a big house in the valley. I'll be before you there to give you your money."

When Leeam came to the *boreen* he turned in, and was going until he came as far as the big house. Leeam wondered when he came as far as the big house, for he was born and raised in the neighbourhood, and yet he had never seen the big house before, though he thought he knew every house within five miles of him.

When Leeam came near the barn that was close to the big house, a little lad came out and said: "A hundred thousand welcomes to you, William O'Rooney," put a sack on his back and went in with it. Another little lad came out and welcomed Leeam, put a sack on his back, and went in with it. Lads were coming welcoming Leeam, and putting the sacks on their backs and carrying them in, until the ton of wheat was all gone. Then the whole of the lads came round him, and Leeam said; "Ye all know me, and I don't know ye!" Then they said to him: "Go in and eat your dinner; the master's waiting for you."

Leeam went in and sat down at table; but he had not the second mouthful taken till a heavy sleep came on him, and he fell down under the table. Then the enchanter made a false man like William, and sent him home to William's wife with the horse and cart.

When the false man came to Leeam's house, he went into the room, lay down on the bed and died.

It was not long till the cry went out that Leeam O'Rooney was dead. The wife put down water, and when it was hot, she washed the body and put it over the board (*i.e.*, laid it out). The neighbours came, and they keened sorrowfully over the body, and there was great pity for the poor wife, but there was not much grief on herself, for Leeam was old and she was young. The day on the morrow the body was buried, and there was no more remembrance of Leeam.

Leeam's wife had a servant boy, and she said to him: "You ought to marry me and to take Leeam's place."

"It's too early yet, after there being a death in the house," said the boy; "wait till Leeam is a week buried."

When Leeam was seven days and seven nights asleep, a little boy came to him and awoke him, and said: "You've been asleep for a week; but we sent your horse and cart home. Here's your money, and go."

Leeam came home, and as it was late at night nobody saw him. On the morning of that same day Leeam's wife and the servant lad went to the priest and asked him to marry them.

"Have you the marriage money?" said the priest.

"No," said the wife; "but I have a *sturk* of a pig at home, and you can have her in place of money."

The priest married them, and said: "I'll send for the pig tomorrow."

When Leeam came to his own door, he struck a blow on it. The wife and the servant boy were going to bed, and they asked: "Who's there?"

"It's I," said Leeam; "open the door for me."

When they heard the voice, they knew that it was Leeam who was in it, and the wife said: "I can't let you in, and it's a great shame, you to be coming back again, after being seven days in your grave."

"Is it mad you are?" said Leeam.

"I'm not mad," said the wife; "doesn't every person in the parish know that you are dead, and that I buried you decently. Go back to your grave, and I'll have a mass read for your poor soul tomorrow."

"Wait till daylight comes," said Leeam, "and I'll give you the price of your joking!"

Then he went into the stable, where his horse and the pig were, stretched himself in the straw, and fell asleep.

Early on the morning of the next day, the priest said to a little lad that he had: "Get up, and go to Leeam O'Rooney's house, and the woman that I married yesterday will give you a pig to bring home with you."

The boy came to the door of the house, and began knocking at it with a stick. The wife was afraid to open the door, but she asked: "Who's there?"

"I," said the boy; "the priest sent me to get a pig from you."

"She's out in the stable," said the wife; "you can get her for yourself, and drive her back with you."

The lad went into the stable, and began driving out the pig, when Leeam rose up and said: "Where are you going with my pig?"

When the boy saw Leeam, he never stopped to look again, but out with him as hard as he could, and he never stopped till he came back to the priest, and his heart coming out of his mouth with terror.

"What's on you?" says the priest.

The lad told him that Leeam O'Rooney was in the stable, and would not let him drive out the pig.

"Hold your tongue, you liar!" said the priest; "Leeam O'Rooney's dead and in the grave this week."

"If he was in the grave this seven years, I saw him in the stable two moments ago; and if you don't believe me, come yourself, and you'll see him."

The priest and the boy then went together to the door of the stable, and the priest said: "Go in and turn me out that pig."

"I wouldn't go in for all ever you're worth," said the boy.

The priest went in, and began driving out the pig, when Leeam rose up out of the straw and said: "Where are you going with my pig, Father Patrick?"

When the priest saw Leeam, off and away with him, and he crying out: "In the name of God, I order you back to your grave, William O'Rooney."

Leeam began running after the priest, and saying, "Father Patrick, Father Patrick, are you mad? Wait and speak to me."

The priest would not wait for him, but made off home as fast as his feet could carry him, and when he got into the house, he shut the door. Leeam was knocking at the door till he was tired, but the priest would not let him in. At last, he put his head out of a window in the top of the house, and said: "William O'Rooney, go back to your grave."

"You're mad, Father Patrick! I'm not dead, and never was in a grave since I was born," said Leeam.

"I saw you dead," said the priest; "you died suddenly, and I was present when you were put into the grave, and made a fine sermon over you."

"The devil from me, but, as sure as I'm alive, you're mad!" said Leeam.

"Go out of my sight now," said the priest, "and I'll read a mass for you, tomorrow."

Leeam went home then, and knocked at his own door, but his wife would not let him in. Then he said to himself: "I may as well go and pay my rent now." On his way to the landlord's house, everyone who saw

Leeam was running before him, for they thought he was dead. When the landlord heard that Leeam O'Rooney was coming, he shut the doors and would not let him in. Leeam began knocking at the hall door till the lord thought he'd break it in. He came to a window in the top of the house, put out his head, and asked: "What are you wanting?"

"I'm come to pay my rent like an honest man," said Leeam.

"Go back to your grave, and I'll forgive you your rent," said the lord.

"I won't leave this," said Leeam, "till I get a writing from you that I'm paid up clean till next May."

The lord gave him the writing, and he came home and knocked at his own door, but the wife would not let him in. She said that Leeam O'Rooney was dead and buried, and that the man at the door was only a deceiver.

"I'm no deceiver," said William; "I'm after paying my master three years' rent, and I'll have possession of my own house, or else I'll know why."

He went to the barn and got a big bar of iron, and it wasn't long till he broke in the door. There was great fear on the wife, and the newly married husband. They thought they were in the time of the General Resurrection, and that the end of the world was coming.

"Why did you think I was dead?" said Leeam.

"Doesn't everybody in the parish know you're dead?" said the wife.

"Your body from the devil," said Leeam, "you're hum-bugging me long enough, and get me something to eat."

The poor woman was greatly afraid, and she dressed him some meat, and when she saw him eating and drinking, she said: "It's a miracle."

Then Leeam told her his story from first to last, and she told him each thing that happened, and then he said: "I'll go to the grave tomorrow, till I see the *behoonuch** ye buried in my place."

The day on the morrow Leeam brought a lot of men with him to the churchyard, and they dug open the grave, and were lifting up the coffin, when a big black dog jumped out of it, and made off, and Leeam and the men after it. They were following it till they saw it going into the house in which Leeam had been asleep, and then the ground opened, and the house went down, and nobody ever saw it from that out; but the big hole is to be seen till this day.

When Leeam and the men went home, they told everything to the priest of the parish, and he dissolved the marriage that was between Leeam's wife and the servant boy.

---

*Gaelic *bitheamhnach*, "thief, rascal"

Leeam lived for years after that, and he left great wealth behind him, and they remember him in Clare-Galway still, and will remember him if this story goes down from the old people to the young.

Reading for Understanding

Main Idea

1. Which of the following quotations from Mark Twain best represents the central idea of this story?
   (a) Put all your eggs in the one basket and watch that basket.
   (b) One of the most striking differences between a cat and a lie is that a cat has only nine lives.
   (c) Always do right. This will gratify some people, and astonish the rest.
   (d) The reports of my death are greatly exaggerated.

Details

2. The oddity about the big house was that (a) Leeam had never seen it before (b) it was painted a different color from the rest of the houses (c) it had no barn (d) it had a huge porch.

3. Leeam's cart held (a) corn (b) rice (c) wheat (d) potatoes.

4. Leeam awakened (a) after a day of untroubled sleep (b) on his wife's wedding day (c) in time to punish the enchanter (d) with a headache.

5. The false man turned out to be a (a) dog (b) ghost (c) neighbor (d) former friend.

Inferences

6. As far as his wife was concerned, the main problem with Leeam was his (a) drinking (b) gambling (c) appearance (d) age.

7. A contribution to Leeam's prosperity was (a) his wife's business skills (b) the rent that had been forgiven (c) a return visit from the enchanter (d) discovery of gold on his property.

8. Upon his return home, Leeam was (a) welcomed by his wife (b) blessed by the priest (c) baffled by events (d) fearful for his life.

9. We may assume that on Leeam's return (a) the wife was not happy (b) Leeam sought another wife (c) Leeam's fortunes went downhill (d) his cart was stolen.

Order of Events

10. Arrange the items in the order in which they occurred. Use letters only.
    A. His wife marries the servant boy.
    B. Leeam digs up his coffin.
    C. Leeam sets out with his wheat to sell.
    D. The false Leeam dies.
    E. The priest gets a scare.

Thinking Critically about the Story

1. Why is it important for the story that Leeam be a straightforward, unimaginative man? Note the commonplace details.
2. Point out the sly humor involving the wife, the servant boy, and the date set for the wedding. What is the significance of these lines: "there was no more remembrance of Leean"?
3. Can you suggest a reason for the enchanter's putting Leeam to sleep for a week and sending a magical substitute?
4. What proof do the townspeople suggest for the big house's mysterious disappearance?
5. What benefits did Leeam get from his "death" and "rebirth"?

Language in Action

Intonation and the Exclamation Point

"The devil from me, but, as sure as I'm alive, you're mad!" said Leeam.

The words are a good clue to the manner in which Leeam is speaking, but the exclamation point adds an extra direction. Exclamation points are useful for expressing strong and sudden feelings, as in the quotation above. But an overuse of the exclamation point deadens writing:

> I was so tired! I went to bed! I slept eleven hours! In the morning I was as exhausted as ever!

Intonation is defined as "the rise and fall in pitch of the voice in speech." In Chinese, pitch may distinguish one word from another. In English, pitch drastically affects meaning in vocal communication.

> "Tim came in first in the track meet."
> "Oh, really."

In reading the reply, can you suggest enthusiasm, indifference, disappointment, anger, sarcasm? Would an exclamation point be helpful for some the intonations?

Here's one of the best examples of how crucial intonation can be:

> "We've been told that two negatives can make a positive, but two positives can never make a negative."
> "Yeah, right!"

If the reply is said sarcastically, two positives do indeed make a negative, but the reply can also be taken as agreeing with the original comment. How would you read aloud each possibility?

A Fisherman and His Wife

Carol L. Birch
American

Could This Be Paradise?

Steve Sanfield
American

"What do you wish?" the fish inquired. "Oh, my wish is not so simple. I want my wife and me to find contentment, and I do not know where it is." "Go in peace," said the fish. "Your wish has come true." Then the fish disappeared, never to be seen again.

In **Man and Superman**, the playwright George Bernard Shaw said, "There are two tragedies in life. One is to lose your heart's desire. The other is to gain it." These two stories support Shaw's comment.

The tales have been paired because they have similar themes. In both, there is dissatisfaction with ordinary life. In both, characters attempt to remedy the problem, to find a newer and better way of life. How they fare is the subject of both folktales.

Though superficially similar, the stories are different, as you will see. The end of one is clearcut, with a strong moral. The end of the other is left hanging. You, the reader, must decide if it is a happy ending or not. How you decide may be a reflection of your own philosophy of life.

Both Carol L. Birch and Steve Sanfield are famous storytellers. They have discovered engaging folktales and have retold them charmingly for modern readers and listeners. Anyone who has ever heard a skilled storyteller weave a yarn can remember the experience with pleasure.

A Fisherman and His Wife

Once upon a time there was a fisherman named Jacques, who lived with his wife, Monique, in the south of France, where days are warm and nights are balmy. From Jacques they had fresh fish to eat, and from Monique's garden there were fresh vegetables on their table. Fragrant herbs and wildflowers of every hue grew in sweet profusion around their cottage.

But they were not happy. They could not enjoy what they had because they were so bitterly aware of what they did not have. Try as they might, they could not get ahead, so they greeted each day with fear and anxiety. Fear narrowed their vision, and anxiety left them with a bitter taste in their mouths.

One day Jacques caught a magic fish who promised three wishes over a year and a day, and they believed that they would finally know true contentment in their lives. Monique and Jacques talked late into the night, and the next morning at dawn Jacques went down to the sea and called out as he had been instructed:

Fishy, fishy in the sea,
Prithee cometh unto me.
Monique and her husband, Jacques,
Have a wish for you to grant.

The fish leaped above the dazzling sea and asked. "What do you wish?" "My wife and I wish to be prosperous vineyard owners!" replied Jacques. "Go in peace," called out the fish. "It is just as you wish."

Jacques ran down the road, past the small cottage that had once been home, eagerly searching for Monique. He saw her in the distance, pacing, wearing a nervous smile and a lovely gown. Together they gave the laborers in the fields and the servants in their new mansion the day off so that the two could revel privately in their new-found luxuries.

The next day Jacques began the life of a prosperous vineyard owner. He had known such cold from his days at sea that he looked forward to working on warm and dry land. And at first he was happy. He said the chill was finally gone from his bones. But soon the dust of the earth filled his eyes and mouth. The sun seemed to beat relentlessly upon his back. Eventually, he became more miserable than he had ever been as a fisherman.

Now, Monique was also happy with her new life—at first. But she had never managed servants before, and she was uncertain in her role. Worst of all, the women in town would not receive her, while the wives of the fishermen were suspicious of her new wealth and ways.

After six months of this life the dissatisfied couple decided to use their second wish. and Jacques once again called on the magic fish at the break of day:

> *Fishy, fishy in the sea,*
> *Prithee cometh unto me.*
> *Monique and her husband, Jacques,*
> *Have a wish for you to grant.*

"Are you happy?" asked the fish. "No, my wife and I wish that I would be the mayor of the village." "Go in peace," said the fish. "Your wish is granted."

Jacques passed their small cottage and looked at it longingly. As he passed the vineyard, he spat on the ground. About a mile from town he saw a crowd of people waiting . . . for him? One wanted to know what he intended to do about a land dispute, another demanded an appointment in private, and a third shrieked at him for failing to find more water for the town.

Jacques and Monique had dreams of what their lives would now be like. Which dreams came true? Oh, they seemed to be treated less suspiciously, but behind their backs the gossiping went on relentlessly. Now the women in town had to receive Monique, but they did not accept her. As for Jacques, he was free from the chill of the sea and the dust of the land, but his office brought unforeseen demands. He wanted to be a good mayor, so he spent hours hearing disputes and still longer hours considering them. When he wasn't at work, he was thinking of work. It seemed that someone was always unhappy. And most often it was his wife.

Feeling more and more isolated, Monique began visiting the small cottage where she and Jacques had lived. She transplanted wildflowers and herbs from the hills to their yard. She twined wild roses about the door. She enjoyed the labors that she had abhorred—hoeing the garden, whitewashing the cottage, weaving covers and curtains and carpets. If she just sat in the mayor's residence, the hours dragged on. At the cottage, while she worked, the time flew. But her thoughts always went back to the final wish that dangled enticingly before her. She wondered what would release them from their fear and anxiety, which had only deepened.

After just three months Monique suggested a final wish. "Go to the fish, and ask to be the King of France! You'll have councilors for all the tiresome duties, and we'll have parties. When you have to work, I will have the theater, the opera, and ballets to attend. No one will dare to talk against us!"

Because Jacques did not oppose her, Monique thought he agreed with her. The next day Jacques called out a final time:

Fishy, fishy in the sea,
Prithee cometh unto me.
Monique and her husband, Jacques,
Have a wish for you to grant.

"Are you happy?" asked the fish. "No," said Jacques sorrowfully, "this is not the life for us." "What do you seek?" the fish called out above the swelling sea. "Well, my wife wants me to be the King of France, but I do not think I am any better suited to that life." "What do you wish?" the fish inquired. "Oh, my wish is not so simple. I want my wife and me to find contentment, and I do not know where it is." "Go in peace," said the fish. "Your wish has come true." Then the fish disappeared, never to be seen again.

Jacques walked slowly back toward town. When he came to the small cottage where he and Monique had lived, he saw her there with her back bent over the garden. Once again she wore an old and shabby dress. But when Monique looked up, her smile was radiant. She ran to Jacques, and they kissed and kissed again. "Oh, Husband, you wished well! I had forgotten all that we had."

So Jacques and Monique began to live their old lives anew. They enjoyed living in the south of France, where the days are warm and the nights are balmy. They savored the fresh fish and vegetables on their table. They reveled in the fragrant herbs and wildflowers of every hue that grew in sweet profusion around their cottage. And, oh, they lived contentedly and much more happily ever after.

Could This Be Paradise?

There was once a man who was unhappy with his life. Nothing seemed to be right. He had to work much too hard for far too little. Neither his friends nor his neighbors gave him the respect he felt he deserved. His wife was always complaining, and his children were never satisfied.

Despite his hopes, his condition did not improve, so he spent most of his time dreaming about Paradise. Whether he was alone or with others, whether at work or at rest, the idea of Paradise filled his head. "Someday," he kept telling himself, "someday I'm going to go to Paradise."

And one day—no different from any other—he decided that this was the day he was going to set off for Paradise.

Rising from his morning table, without saying a word to his wife and his two children, he went out the front door, past the gate with the broken latch, and through the open fields, until he came to the edge of the marketplace. He already knew which women would buy what goods from which merchants at what price and what they would argue about. He passed a bakery opposite a butcher shop, went on through the center of town with its synagogue and town hall, and continued out through another set of fields to the base of a long, steep hill.

He climbed the hill until he reached the beginning of a broad plateau. There he paused and took one last look at his village below. He was sure he would never see it again. He was a man bound for Paradise.

All day he walked along that plateau, and when the sun was setting in the west, he decided to take shelter under a tall pine tree. Before going to sleep, he removed his shoes and pointed them in the direction he was sure Paradise lay.

But how was he to know that in the darkest hour of the night a demon, an imp, would come and—either to punish him or to save him or to teach him a lesson or maybe just to play a joke on him—take his shoes and turn them around? No way for the man to know that.

The next morning the man rose early, said his prayers, and stepped into his shoes, certain that they would lead him to Paradise. Off he went, his head filled with dreams. Suddenly, there he was at the edge of the plateau, and just below him, Paradise. He had arrived.

Strange, he thought, *it's not much bigger than my own village. Oh well.*

He descended the hill and walked through the fields to the center of town. Here in Paradise there were also a synagogue and a town hall. As he stood there looking at them, the man thought, *They've been lying to me all these years—or at least exaggerating. They said that everything in Paradise would shine and gleam, but these buildings, why, they're almost as shabby as those in my own village.*

He passed a bakery that stood opposite a butcher shop. He began to suspect that when he entered the marketplace, he would know which women would buy what goods from which merchants at what price and what they would argue about—and he did.

Now more sad than angry, he was sure that if he continued through the fields in front of him, he would come to a gate with a broken latch—and he did.

As he stood there pondering his situation, he heard a whining voice from the house. "Come in and eat your food."

It was enough to drive a man mad. It sounded just like his own wife. But never having said no to his wife and being a bit hungry, he went into the house. He sat down, ate some black bread and some herring, and had a cup of coffee.

Two children came running up to him and jumped into his lap. Playing with his beard, the youngest one asked, "You'll stay with us this time, won't you, Papa?"

Not wanting to say no to the children, he agreed.

And to this very day, that man sits at that table every morning, drinking his coffee, trying to figure out whether he's in Paradise.

Reading for Understanding

Main Idea

1. Which proverb best summarizes a main point of both selections?

   (a) Habit, if not resisted, becomes necessity.
   (b) All happiness is in the mind.
   (c) Never trouble trouble till trouble troubles you.
   (d) The wise are too smart to deny their own ignorance.

Details

2. The first wish of Monique and Jacques was to (a) become celebrities (b) go the Paris (c) own a vineyard (d) own a large ship.

3. A major problem of Monique's was (a) learning to be a gardener (b)

her negative feelings toward Jacques (c) managing servants (d) trying to enjoy fishing.

4. The suggestion about becoming King of France was (a) the fish's (b) Jacques' (c) the mayor's (d) Monique's.

5. The item of clothing that turned the man around was (a) a pair of shoes (b) a hunting cap (c) a woolen coat (d) a shirt embroidered by his wife.

6. The gate with the broken latch stood (a) at the butcher's (b) at the entrance to Paradise (c) on the plateau (d) at his own house.

Inferences

7. If Jacques had been given the original third wish (a) he'd have been miserable (b) the fish would have congratulated him (c) Monique would have divorced him (d) he might have been given three others.

8. The paradise seeker's actions toward his wife and children were (a) protective (b) inconsiderate (c) intentionally cruel (d) merited.

9. The one who knew best after all was (a) Monique (b) Jacques (c) the fish (d) the mayor.

Fact or Opinion

Tell whether the following is a fact or an opinion.

10. By the end of "Could This Be Paradise?" the seeker had found his goal.

Words in Context

1. "Fragrant herbs and wildflowers of every *hue* grew in sweet profusion around their cottage." **Hue** (129) means (a) shape (b) kind (c) color (d) taste.

2. "Together they gave the laborers in the fields and the servants in their new mansion the day off so that the two could *revel* privately in their new-found luxuries." **Revel** (130) means (a) celebrate (b) take stock (c) discover anew (d) think about.

3. "The sun seemed to beat *relentlessly* upon his back." **Relentlessly**

(130) means (a) warmly (b) unpityingly (c) humidly (d) at regular intervals.

Thinking Critically about the Stories

1. Though the stories have been paired for their similar theme, there are many differences. Point these out.

2. Folktales arise from the folk, the people. As *The Standard Dictionary of Folklore* has put it, "Folklore materials thrive in a society in which there are people of considerable native intelligence, artistic appreciation, memory, imagination, and creative urge, who can comprehend, value, remember, and recreate their native folklore and thus propagate it as living tradition." What elements in the two stories suggest that these tales did originate with the people, not with a famous author?

    For example, the story of three wishes appears over and over again in folklore. It reflects a common human daydream. The lure of instant wealth sustains state lotteries. The advertising for the lotteries stresses the theme of wish fulfilment and appeals to a universal human longing.

3. Proverbs like those on page 133 express folk wisdom. They express in a single sentence a generalization that makes a point about people and life. They have their limitations, of course. Life is far too complicated to sum up in a sentence. Then, too, proverbs sometimes give conflicting advice:

Look before you leap.

He who hesitates is lost.

What other one-sentence message, other than the answer on page 131, can you supply as a bit of folk wisdom to take with you after you've finished the stories?

4. In *The Blue Bird,* Maurice Maeterlinck also suggests a search for happiness. Two children, Tyltyl and Mytyl, go on a quest to find the Blue Bird of Happiness. They fail and then discover that the Blue Bird has been in their garden all along. At the end of Voltaire's *Candide,* the hero, after many adventures, declares, "We must cultivate our garden." Which of the two folk stories most closely resembles the two just mentioned? Explain.

5. "The grass is always greener in the next man's yard." What contrib-

utes to this human failing? How do the characters in these stories display those failings?

6. The perennial Christmas movie *It's a Wonderful Life* shows us a man like the seeker in "Can This Be Paradise?" How does he learn a lesson that is also similar to a lesson learned by Monique and Jacques?

7. The title "Can This Be Paradise?" states the central question of the story. Has the man found Paradise? Explain.

8. English writer Somerset Maugham tells a fable about a Baghdad merchant whose servant came home trembling from the market-place.

> "Master," cried the servant, "just now when I was in the market-place I was jostled by a woman in the crowd and when I turned I saw it was Death that jostled me. She looked at me and made a threatening gesture."
>
> Terrified the servant asked the master for a horse to escape Death. After the servant had ridden off to Samarra, the merchant became annoyed at losing the services of his servant. He went down to the market place to question Death and complain.
>
> Death explained that the gesture was not a threat but rather an expression of surprise. "I was astonished to see him in Baghdad, for I had an appointment with him tonight in Samarra."

What similarity is there between the anecdote and "Can This Be Paradise?"

Language in Action

Generalizations

> Neither his friends nor his neighbors gave him the respect he felt he deserved. His wife was always complaining, and his children were never satisfied.

Generalizations can be useful if we keep in mind their limitations. "All poison ivy plants should be avoided" is a pretty useful generalization, as is "Never drive a car with faulty brakes." But generalizations can be hazardous, too.

Sound advice is to use absolute words sparingly. Words like *all, always, every, never,* and *entirely* should carry red flags to alert you to their frequent misuse. "All participants had a chance to speak" is a sound comment. "Real-estate agents are never interested in the buyer's needs" is unfair. It's certain that the wife of "Could This Be Paradise" was not *always* complaining. His children were *sometimes* satisfied. It's easy to fall into the *always, never* trap.

Hasty generalizations can lead to errors in thinking. "Six of the boys in the class refused to try out for track. All the boys in that class have no class spirit." Perhaps they show class spirit in other ways.

Here are some typical generalizations:

Every girl in the senior class is stuck-up (*stuck-up* is an idiom, 436).

All Irishmen (Spaniards, Englishmen, whatever) are alike.

Every man has his price.

Nobody is ever nice to me.

The Foghorn

Gertrude Atherton
American

**That foghorn. What was it trying to tell her? A boat . . . fog
. . . why was it so hard to remember? So hard to awaken? Ellen must have given her an overdose.**

"The Foghorn" is constructed like a mystery story. A young
woman daydreams about many things. She catalogues elements of
her physical beauty. She reviews recent events. She especially dwells
upon her special love . . . for a married man. Something is wrong,
though. The author cleverly suggests some baffling elements in her
memory. And through it all there is the sound of the foghorn.

There was a time when Gertrude Atherton was one of the most
successful American novelists. Her novel, **Black Oxen,** published in
1923 was a runaway hit. Fiction tends to date, though. Best-selling
authors are soon left behind. The sensation of one decade is often
forgotten in the next. A glance at old best-seller lists is a melancholy
reminder of how fickle fame is. There are exceptions, of course, like
John Steinbeck, Thomas Wolfe, and Ernest Hemingway. These have
become landmarks in the history of American literature, but most
novels find their way to the shelves of remainder booksellers and then
disappear altogether. Dr. Samuel Johnson, eighteenth-century essay-
ist, expressed it best: "No place affords a more striking conviction of
the vanity of human hopes than a public library."

Though only a short story, "The Foghorn" has survived better
than lengthier and more ambitious works. After you have finished the
story, you'll realize why.

The Foghorn

WHAT AN ABSURD vanity to sleep on a hard pillow and forego that last luxurious burrowing into the very depths of a mass of baby pillows! . . . her back was already as straight as—a chimney? . . . who was the Frenchman that said one must reject the worn counters? . . . but this morning she would have liked that sensuous burrowing, and the pillow had never seemed so hard, so flat . . . yet how difficult it was to wake up! She had had the same experience once before when the doctor had given her medicine for insomnia . . . could Ellen, good creature, have put a tablet in the cup of broth she took last thing at night: 'as a wise precaution,' the doctor had said genially. What a curse insomnia was! But she had a congenital fear of drugs and had told no one of this renewal of sleeplessness, knowing it would pass.

And, after all, she didn't mind lying awake in the dark; she could think, oh, pleasant lovely thoughts, despite this inner perturbation—so cleverly concealed. How thankful she was to be tall enough to carry off the new fashion in sleeves! If trains would only come in again, she would dress her hair high some night (just for fun) and look—not like her beloved Mary Stuart, for Mary was almost ugly if one analyzed her too critically. Charm? How much more charm counted than mere beauty, and she herself had it 'full measure and running over,' as that rather fresh admirer had announced when drinking her health at her coming-out party . . . what was his name? . . . six years ago. He was only a college boy . . . how could one remember? There had been so many since.

Ninon de l'Enclos? She was passable in her portraits, but famous mainly for keeping young . . . Diane de Poictiers? She must have needed charm double-distilled if she looked anything like an original portrait of her hung at a loan exhibition in Paris: flaxen hair, thin and straight, drawn severely from a bulging brow above insufferably sensual eyes—far too obvious and 'easy' for the fastidious male of today—a flaxen complexion, no high lights; not very intelligent. Interesting contrast in taste centuries apart—perhaps.

Madame Récamier? Better-looking than most of the historic beauties: hair piled high—but then she wore a slip of an Empire gown . . . well, never mind. . . .

She ranked as a beauty herself, although perhaps charm had something to do with it. Her mouth was rather wide, but her teeth were exquisite. Something rather obscure was the matter in that region of brilliant enamel this morning. A toothache? She had never had a toothache. Well, there was no pain . . . what matter? . . . something wrong, though; she'd go to the dentist during the day. Her nose was a trifle tip-tilted, but very thin and straight, and anyhow the tilt suited the way she carried her head, 'flung in the air.' Her complexion and hair and eyes were beyond all cavil . . . she was nothing so commonplace as a down-right blonde or brunette . . . how she should hate being catalogued! The warm, bright waving masses of her hair had never been cut since her second birthday. They, too, were made for burrowing.

Her mother's wedding dress had a long train. But the delicate ivory of the satin had waxed with time to a sickly yellow. Her mother hadn't pressed the matter when she was engaged to John St. Rogers, but she had always expressed a wish that each of her daughters should wear the dress to the altar. Well, she had refused outright, but had consented to have her own gown trimmed with the lace: yards and yards of *point d'Alençon*—and a veil that reached halfway down the train. What a way to spend money! Who cared for lace now? Not the young, anyhow. But Mother was rather a dear, and she could afford to be quite unselfish for once, as it certainly would be becoming. When the engagement was broken, they told the poor old darling that she cried because she would have another long wait before watching all that lace move up the aisle on a long slender figure that made her think pridefully of the graceful skeleton hidden within one hundred and seventy resented pounds.

Well, she would never wear that lace—nor any wedding gown. If she were lucky enough to marry at all, the less publicity the better . . . a mere announcement (San Francisco papers please copy) . . . a quiet return from Europe . . . a year or two in one of those impersonal New York apartment-houses where no one knew the name of his next-door neighbor.

How strange that she of all girls should have fallen in love with a married man—or, at all events, accepted the dire consequences. With a father that had taken to drugs and then run off with another woman—luckily before Mother had come in for Granddad's for-tune—and . . . what was it Uncle Ben had once said, queer twists in this family since 'way back.' It had made her more conventional than her natural instincts would have prompted; but, no, let her do herself justice: she had cultivated a high standard of character and planted her mind with flowers both sturdy and fair—that must have been the reason she had fallen in love at last, after so many futile attempts. No need for her to conceal from him the awful truth that she read the Greek and Latin classics in the original text, attended morning classes over at the Univer-sity . . . odd, how men didn't mind if you 'adored' music and pictures, but if they suspected you of being intellectual, they either despised or feared you, and faded away. . . .

Fog on the Bay. Since childhood she had loved to hear that

long-drawn-out, almost-human moan of the foghorn as she lay warm and
sheltered in bed. It was on a night of fog they had spoken for the first
time, although they had nodded at three or four formal dinners given to
the newcomers who had brought letters to the elect. Bostonians were
always popular in San Francisco; they had good manners and their
formality was only skin-deep. The men were very smart; some of the
women, too; but as a rule they lacked the meticulous grooming and
well-set-up appearance of their men. She had been impressed the first
time she had met him: six feet (she herself was five feet six), somewhere
in the thirties, very spare, said to be a first-rate tennis player, and had
ranked as an all-round athlete at Harvard; had inherited a piece of
property in San Francisco which was involving him in litigation, but he
was in no haste to leave, even before they met.

That had been at the Jeppers', and as the house commanded a
fine view of the Bay, and she was tired of being torn from some man every
time they circled the ballroom, she had managed to slip away and had
hidden behind the curtains of the deep bow window at the end of the
hall. In a moment she was aware that someone had followed her, and
oddly enough she knew who it was, although she didn't turn her head;
and they stood in silence and gazed together at the sharp dark outlines
of the mountains on the far side of the Bay; the glittering spheroids of
golden light that were ferryboats, the islands with their firm, bold outlines, now almost visibly drooping in slumber . . . although there always
seemed to her to be an atmosphere of unrest about Alcatraz, psychic
emanation of imprisoned men under rigid military rule, and officials no
doubt as resentful in that dull monotonous existence on a barren rock .
. . A light flickered along a line of barred upper windows; doubtless a
guard on his round . . .

The band of pulsing light on the eastern side of the Bay: music
made visible . . . stars as yellow and bright above, defying the thin silver
of the moon . . . lights twinkling on Sausalito opposite, standing out
boldly from the black mass of Tamalpias high-flung above. Her roving
eyes moved to the Golden Gate, narrow entrance between two crouching
forts, separating that harbor of arrogant beauty from the gray waste of
the Pacific—ponderous, rather stupid old ocean . . .

For the first time he spoke: 'The fog! Chief of San Francisco's
many beauties.'

She had nodded, making no other reply, watching that dense yet
imponderable white mass push its way through the Golden Gate like a
laboring ship . . . then riding the waters more lightly, rolling a little,
writhing, whiffs breaking from the bulk of that ghostly ship to explore
the hollows of the hills, resting there like puffs of white smoke. Then,
over the cliffs and heights on the northern side of the Bay, a swifter, more
formless, but still lovely white visitant that swirled down and over the

inland waters, enshrouding the islands, Sausalito, where so many English-men lived, but a low fog—the moon and stars still visible . . . the foghorns, one after another, sending forth their long-drawn-out moans of utter desolation. . . .

With nothing more to look at, they had seated themselves on a small sofa, placed there for reticent couples, and talked for an hour—a desultory exploring conversation. She recalled none of it. A few mornings later they had met on the Berkeley ferryboat, accidentally no doubt, and he had gone on with her in the train and as far as the campus . . . Once again. . . . After that, when the lecture was over, in the Greek Theatre . . . wonderful hours . . . how easy to imagine themselves in Greece of the fifth century B.C., alone in that vast gray amphitheater, the slim, straight trees above quivering with the melody of birds!

Never a word of love—not for months. This novel and exciting companionship was enough . . . depths of personality to explore—in glimpses! Sometimes they roamed over the hills, gay and carefree. They never met anyone they knew.

Winter. Weeks of pouring rain. They met in picture galleries, remote corners of the Public Library, obscure restaurants of Little Italy under the shadow of Telegraph Hill. Again they were unseen, undiscovered.

He never came to the house. Since her mother's death and the early marriages of the girls, Uncle Ben had come to live with her in the old house on Russian Hill; the boys were East at school; she was free of all family restrictions, but her old servants were intimate with all the other servants on the Hill. She barely knew his wife. He never spoke of her.

Spring. A house-party in the country, warm and dry after the last of the rains. After dinner they had sat about on the terraces, listening to a group singing within, admiring the 'ruins' of a Roman temple at the foot of the lawn lit by a blazing moon.

He and she had wandered off the terrace, and up an almost perpendicular flight of steps on the side of the mountain that rose behind the house . . . dim aisles of redwoods, born when the earth was young, whose long trunks never swayed, whose high branches rarely sang in the wind—unfriendly trees, but protective, sentinel-like, shutting out the modern world; reminiscent were those closely planted aisles of ancient races . . . forgotten races . . . god-like races, perhaps.

Well, they had felt like gods that night. How senseless to try to stave off a declaration of love . . . to fear . . . to wonder . . . to worry . . . How inevitable . . . natural . . . when it came! Hour of hours. . . .

They had met the next day in a corner of their favorite little restaurant, over a dish of spaghetti, which she refused to eat as it had liver in it, and talked the matter out. No, she would not enter upon a secret intrigue; meeting him in some shady quarter of the town, where no questions were asked, in some horrible room which had sheltered thousands of furtive 'lovers' before them . . . she would far rather never see him again. . . . He had smiled at the flight taken by an untrained imagination, but nodded. . . . No, but she knew the alternative. He had no intention of giving her up. No hope of a divorce. He had sounded his wife; tentatively at first, then told her outright he loved another woman. She had replied that he could expect no legal release from her. It was her chance for revenge and she would take it. . . . A week or two and his business in San Francisco would be settled . . . he had an independent fortune . . . would she run away with him? Elope in good old style? Could she stand the gaff? All Europe for a perpetual honeymoon—unless his wife were persuaded by her family later on to divorce him. Then he would return and work at something. He was not a born idler.

She had consented, of course, having made up her mind before they met. She had had six years of 'the world.' She knew what she wanted. One might 'love' many times, but not more than once find completion, that solidarity which makes two as one against the malignant forces of life. She had no one to consider but herself. Her mother was dead. Her sisters, protected by husbands, wealth, position, would merely be 'thrilled.' The boys and Uncle Ben, of course, would be furious. Men were so hopelessly conservative.

For the rest of the world she cared exactly nothing.

That foghorn. What was it trying to tell her? A boat . . . fog . . . why was it so hard to remember? So hard to awaken? Ellen must have given her an overdose. Fragmentary pictures . . . slipping down the dark hill to the wharf . . . her low delighted laugh echoed back to her as he helped her into the boat . . . one more secret lark before they flung down the gage . . . How magnificently he rowed . . . long, sweeping, easy strokes as he smiled possessively into her eyes and talked of the future. . . . No moon, but millions of stars that shed a misty golden light . . . rows of light on the steep hillsides of the city. The houses dark and silent . . . a burst of music from Fort Mason . . .

Out through the Golden Gate, still daring . . . riding that oily swell . . . his chuckle as she had dared him to row straight across to China . . . Her sharp anxious cry as she half-rose from her seat and pointed to a racing mountain of snow-white mist.

He had swept about at once and made for the beach below Sutro Heights. Too late. Almost as he turned, they were engulfed. Even an old fisherman would have lost his sense of direction.

And then the foghorns began their warnings. The low, menacing roar from Point Bonito. The wailing siren on Alcatraz. Sausalito's throaty bass. The deep-toned bell on Angel Island. She knew them all, but they seemed to come from new directions.

A second . . . a moment . . . an hour . . . later . . . a foreign but unmistakable note. Ships—two of them. . . . Blast and counterblast. . . . She could barely see his white rigid face through the mist as he thrust his head this way and that trying to locate those sounds. . . . Another abrupt swerve . . . crash . . . shouts . . . her own voice shrieking as she saw his head almost severed—the very fog turned red. . . .

She could hear herself screaming yet. It seemed to her that she had been screaming since the beginning of time.

She sat up in bed, clasping her head between her hands, and rocked to and fro. This bare small room, just visible in the gray dawn. . . . She was in a hospital, of course. Was it last night or the night before they had brought her here? She wondered vaguely that she felt no inclination to scream any more, now that she had struggled to full consciousness. . . . Too tired, perhaps . . . the indifference of exhaustion. . . . Even her eyes felt singularly dry, as if they had been baked in a hot oven. She recalled a line, the only memorable line, in Edwin Arnold's 'Light of Asia,' 'Eyepits red with rust of ancient tears.' . . . Did her eyes look like that? But she did not remember crying . . . only screaming. . . .

Odd that she should be left alone like this. Uncle Ben and the girls must have been summoned. If they had gone home, tired out, they should have left a nurse in constant attendance . . . and surely they might have found her a better room. . . . Or had she been carried into some emergency hospital? . . . Well, she could go home today.

Her hands were still clasping her head when another leaf of awareness turned over, rattling like parchment. Hair. Her lovely abundant hair. . . . She held her breath as her hands moved exploringly over her head. Harsh short bristles almost scratched them.

She had had brain fever, then. Ill a long time . . . weeks . . . months, perhaps. . . . No wonder she felt weak and spent and indifferent! But she must be out of danger, or they would not leave her like this. . . . Would she suffer later, with renewed mocking strength? Or could love be burnt out, devoured by fever germs? A short time before, while not yet fully conscious, she had relived all the old hopes, fears, dreams, ecstasies; reached out triumphantly to a wondrous future, arrogantly sure of herself and the man, contemptuous of the world and its makeshift conventions. . . . And now she felt nothing. . . .

But when she was well again? Twenty-four! Forty, fifty, years more; they were a long-lived family. Her mother had been killed at a railroad crossing. . . . Well, she had always prided herself on her strength. She would worry through the years somehow.

Had the town rung with the scandal when the newspapers flared forth next morning? No girl goes rowing at night with a married man unless there is something between them. Had his wife babbled? Were the self-righteous getting off the orthodoxies of their kind? Punished for their sin. Retributive justice meted out to a girl who would break up a home and take a married man for her lover.

Retributive justice! As if there were any such thing in life as justice. All helpless victims of the law of cause and effect. Futile, aspiring, stupidly confident links in the inexorable chain of Circumstance. . . . Commonplace minds croaking, 'Like father like daughter'. . . .

How she hated, hated, *hated*, self-righteousness, smug hypocrisy . . . illogical minds—one sheep bleating like another sheep—not one of them with the imagination to guess that she never would have stooped to a low secret intrigue. . . .

She had been pounding her knee with her fist in a sudden access of energy. As it sputtered out and she felt on the verge of collapse, her hand unfolded and lay palm down on the quilt. . . . She felt her eyes bulging. . . . She uttered her first sound: a low almost inarticulate cry.

Her hand? That large-veined, skinny thing? She had beautiful long white hands, with skin as smooth as the breast of a dove. Of no one of her beauty's many parts had she been prouder, not even when she stood now and then before the glass and looked critically, and admiringly, at the smooth, white, rounded perfection of her body. She had given them a golden manicure set on one of their birthdays, a just tribute; and they were exquisitely kept, although she hated conspicuous nails. . . .

A delusion? A nightmare? She spread the other hand beside it . . . side by side the two on the dingy counterpane . . . old hands . . . Shorn hair will grow again . . . but hands . . .

Mumbling. Why mumbling? She raised one of those withered yellow hands to her mouth. It was empty.

Brain fever! The sun had risen. She looked up at the high barred window. She understood.

Voices at the door. She dropped back on the pillow and closed her eyes and lay still. The door was unlocked, and a man and woman entered: doctor and nurse, as was immediately evident. The doctor's voice was brisk and business-like and deeply mature; the woman's, young and deferential.

'Do you think she'll wake again, doctor?'

'Probably not. I thought she would be gone by now, but she is still breathing.' He clasped the emaciated wrist with his strong fingers. 'Very feeble. It won't be long now.'

'Is it true, doctor, that sometimes, just before death, reason is restored and they remember and talk quite rationally?'

'Sometimes. But not for this case. Too many years. Look in every hour, and when it is over, ring me up. There are relatives to be notified. Quite important people, I believe.'

'What are they like?'

'Never seen them. The law firm in charge of her estate pays the bills. Why should they come here? Couldn't do her any good, and nothing is so depressing as these melancholia cases. It's a long time now since she was stark raving. That was before my time. Come along. Six wards after this one . . . Don't forget to look in. Good little girl. I know you never forget.'

They went out and locked the door.

Reading for Understanding

Main Idea

1. A central point of the story is best expressed in which of the following?
   (a) A burnt child fears the fire.
   (b) A murderer returns to the scene of the crime.
   (c) Time devours all things.
   (d) Fear is the father of cruelty.

Details

2. Diane de Poictiers (a) was pictured in a portrait (b) was Madame Recamie's cousin (c) looked like Mary Stuart (d) was a debutante.

3. John St. Rogers was (a) a doctor (b) a married man (c) the family lawyer (d) a former fiance.

4. The "barren rock" with prisoners was (a) Sausalito (b) Alcatraz (c) Point Bonito (d) Fort Mason.

5. The central character was proudest of her (a) knowledge of Greek and Latin (b) hands (c) teeth (d) rowing skill.

Inferences

6. Ellen was probably (a) a sister (b) Ben's wife (c) a servant (d) a doctor.

7. The first indication of trouble was (a) the hard pillow (b) her mouth (c) the doctor's conversation (d) her hands.

8. The boatride into the harbor can best be characterized as (a) well thought out (b) unwise (c) promising (d) admirable.

9. Before the accident, the main character had decided to (a) give up her love (b) ask the wife to divorce her lover (c) sign away her fortune (d) forget about her reputation.

10. After the end of the story, the main character (a) makes a remarkable recovery (b) lingers for several more years (c) dies (d) calls in the doctor for further consultation.

Words in Context

1. "This morning she would have liked that *sensuous* burrowing, and the pillow had never seemed so hard, so flat." **Sensuous** (139) means (a) warm (b) electric (c) trouble-free (d) luxurious.

2. "She had a *congenital* fear of drugs and had told no one of this renewal of sleeplessness, knowing it would pass." **Congenital** (139) means (a) existing from birth (b) all-absorbing (c) little understood (d) reasonable.

3. "She could think, oh, pleasant lovely thoughts, despite this inner *perturbation*—so cleverly concealed." **Perturbation** (139) means (a) wishy-washiness (b) agitation (c) balance (d) self-deceit,

4. "Flaxen hair, thin and straight, drawn severely from a bulging brow above insufferably sensual eyes—far too obvious and 'easy' for the *fastidious* male of today." **Fastidious** (139) means (a) strong (b) finicky (c) effeminate (d) unsympathetic.

5. "Her complexion and hair and eyes were beyond all *cavil*." **Cavil** (140) means (a) reason (b) comparison (c) faultfinding (d) regret.

6. "How strange that she of all girls should have fallen in love with a married man—or, at all events, accepted the *dire* consequences." **Dire** (140) means (a) usual (b) rewarding (c) inevitable (d) dreadful.

7. "The men were very smart; some of the women, too; but as a rule they lacked the *meticulous* grooming and well-set-up appearance of their men." **Meticulous** (141) means (a) careful (b) superficial (c) lively (d) complicated.

8., 9. "There always seemed to her to be an atmosphere of unrest about Alcatraz, *psychic emanation* of imprisoned men under rigid military rule." **Psychic** (141) means (a) bitter (b) dreary (c) spiritual (d) visible. **Emanation** (141) means (a) riddle (b) outflow (c) advertisement (d) jailbreak.

10. "Her eyes moved to the Golden Gate, narrow entrance between two crouching forts, separating that harbor of arrogant beauty from the gray waste of the Pacific—*ponderous,* rather stupid old ocean . . . " **Ponderous** (141) means (a) picturesque (b) unpredictable (c) hospitable (d) massive.

11. "Then, over the cliffs and heights on the northern side of the Bay, a swifter, more formless, but still lovely white visitant that swirled down and over the inland waters, *enshrouding* the islands . . . " **Enshrouding** (142) means (a) revealing (b) missing (c) emphasizing (d) enclosing.

12., 13. "With nothing more to look at, they had seated themselves on a small sofa, placed there for *reticent* couples, and talked for an hour—a *desultory,* exploring conversation." **Reticent** (142) means (a) quiet (b) newly acquainted (c) expressive (d) quarreling. **Desultory** (142) means (a) rambling (b) rapid (c) intense (d) argumentative.

14. "No, she would not enter upon a secret intrigue; meeting him in some horrible room which had sheltered thousands of *furtive* lovers before them." **Furtive** (143) means (a) anxious (b) secret (c) romantic (d) false.

15. "One might find 'love' many times, but not more than once find completion, that solidarity which makes two as one against the *malignant* forces of life." **Malignant** (143) means (a) unexpected (b) nourishing (c) unavoidable (d) hostile.

16. "*Retributive* justice meted out to a girl who would break up a home and take a married man for her lover." **Retributive** (145) means (a) cruel (b) unfair (c) deserved (d) surprising.

17., 18. "*Futile,* aspiring, stupidly confident links in the *inexorable* chain of Circumstance." **Futile** (145) means (a) useless (b) hopeful (c) planned (d) pitiful. **Inexorable** (145) means (a) unbroken (b) merciless (c) unbiased (d) commonplace.

19. "She uttered her first sound: a low almost *inarticulate* cry." **Inarticulate** (145) means (a) shrill (b) pleading (c) unintentional (d) soundless.

20. "The doctor's voice was brisk and business-like and deeply mature; the woman's, young and *deferential.*" **Deferential** (145) means (a) audible (b) melodious (c) respectful (d) hesitant.

21. "He clasped the *emaciated* wrist with his strong fingers." **Emaciated** (145) means (a) withered (b) shapeless (c) bent (d) fleshy.

Thinking Critically about the Story

1. In 1996, a Florida woman awakened from a coma that had kept her near death for two years. The article reporting the event said, "The 40-year-old Orlando woman's story highlights the mysterious nature of comas, the unconscious states that can trap some brain-injured persons in slumber until death—while mercifully releasing others." The lady in question made great progress, but she was lucky. Apparently the patient in our story had sunk into a coma. At what point did you begin to suspect that this was going to have a tragic ending?

2. Was the principal character vain? What clues suggest this failing?

3. "Odd, how men didn't mind if you 'adored' music and pictures, but if they suspected you of being intellectual, they either despised you or feared you, and faded away . . . " Why do people try to conceal their intelligence in an effort to be average? Is this concealment courageous, stupid? How does peer pressure (516) play a role?

4. Why did the principal character decide to break all rules and run away with a married man?

5. Since the principal character tells almost the entire story, she has no reason to name herself. Yet at the very end, the doctor or nurse could have given the patient a name. Why didn't the author name the character?

6. How does the doctor's bored, unconcerned conversation with the nurse further emphasize the tragedy of the poor sufferer?

7. Every now and then a case is brought to court to determine whether or not a life-support system should be removed from an apparently hopelessly ill comatose patient. How do you feel about such decisions?

8. What does the foghorn symbolize (96–97)?

9. "Spaghetti, which she refused to eat as it had liver in it." Why does the author introduce this bit of trivia?

10. Point out the steps that lead to the patient's final awareness of the truth.

Language in Action

Metaphor

> Would she suffer later, with renewed mocking strength? Or could love be burnt out, devoured by fever germs?"

In the two sentences above metaphor plays a strong role. *Mocking, burnt,* and *devoured* are not to be taken literally (459). Love wasn't physically incinerated. *Devoured* is usually reserved for the eating habits of larger animals. *Mocking* may also be considered personification (48).

Like simile (22), metaphor involves a comparison of two unlike things or ideas. If we say, "Zoe is a lot like Alicia," we are making a simple comparison, not a metaphor. But if we say, "Zoe is a walking encyclopedia," we are comparing Zoe with an encyclopedia, two obviously unlike items.

Metaphor is not just an adornment of poetry (450). It is also embedded in the language of everyday life. Note the metaphors in this dialogue between two high school students:

> "Ouch, that test really threw me. Were you as bowled over as I was?"
>
> "No, I think I aced it, except for question three. That was a shocker."
>
> "You're a lucky dog! But then you were always a brain."
>
> "Hey, at last you're able to see through my wild playboy masquerade!"

If you listen to conversations, you'll find that metaphors abound.

The Creative Imagination

ACTIVITIES

Thinking Critically about the Stories

1. How did Albert Einstein's life prove that imagination is more important that knowledge (87)?
2. Joseph Joubert said, "He who has imagination without learning has wings and no feet." Does this contradict the Einstein quotation (87), or does it supplement it?
3. Read each of the following definitions of imagination and decide with which of these you agree.

> The lunatic, the lover, and the poet
> Are of imagination all compact.
>
> —William Shakespeare

> If the greatest philosopher in the world found himself upon a plank wider than actually necessary, but hanging over a precipice his imagination would prevail, though his reason convinces him of his safety.
>
> —Blaise Pascal

> Man consists of body, mind, and imagination. His body is faulty, his mind is untrustworthy, but his imagination has made his life on this planet an intense practice of all the lovelier energies.
>
> —John Masefield

> Memory is the mother of invention, reason, and skill.
>
> —Mark Van Doren

4. What do the two Irish stories ("Leeam O'Rooney's Burial" and "The Shoemaker") have in common? Give examples.
5. Which of the stories seems to you to be most imaginative? Justify your choice.
6. Three of the stories were written by women; four by men. Is there a difference in the style and emotional content? Do women tend to write differently, or are the supposed differences a myth?

The Writing Portfolio

The Paragraph

Often in writing, the hardest part is beginning. How do you start the juices flowing? How do you overcome indecision and distraction? Writing is a lot like eating peanuts. Once you start, it's easy to keep going. Like the first peanut, the first sentence can lead the way to more sentences.

Experienced writers know that there are two strategies. The first method is to jot down at random any and all ideas that come. This method, called brainstorming, may lead to an outline. The second method is just to begin, realizing that later you'll want to revise the first draft.

In Unit One, you had practice creating single, effective sentences. The next step is the paragraph. In writing a theme, when do you begin a new paragraph?

1. In an explanation—when you go to a new step or idea.
2. In a description—when you change the mood, setting, or point of view.
3. In a narrative—when you change the time, the place of the action.
4. In written conversation—when you change the speaker.

Many paragraphs may consist of a sentence or two, as in writing dialogue. Other paragraphs, especially explanatory or expository paragraphs, may consist of a number of sentences that stick to one topic. Often the topic is announced at the beginning of the paragraph. This topic sentence is a signpost telling the reader what to expect. An effective paragraph often includes a clincher, which sums up the topic.

These are some common ways of developing a paragraph:

1. Giving examples
2. Providing details
3. Comparing and contrasting
4. Giving reasons
5. Defining

Choose those activities (153) that you are most interested in. The topic sentence has been provided. For each topic sentence you choose, write a solid paragraph developing the topic suggested.

1. When I choose a subject to take in school, I usually have a good reason.

2. By the time I graduate from high school, there is one skill I hope to develop.

3. Though similar in many ways, the stories by Hyde and O'Kelly reveal some differences.

4. "Could This Be Paradise?" confirms the old proverb that the grass is always greener on the other side of the fence.

5. Though different in details, "Cindy Ellie" caught the spirit of the traditional Cinderella story.

6. One story in this unit affected me strongly.

7. In some ways, a folktale is like a country ballad.

8. A bitter truth may be more acceptable if told in a fable or folktale.

9. My room at home is a treasure house of objects I love.

Other Areas of Communication

1. Check the computer (or card-index file) in your local library and find out how many books by Ray Bradbury are available. Borrow one and report to the class on both the computer results and the book you chose.

2. Seven students, each choosing a different story, will present its special qualities and solicit votes for calling it the best story in the unit. After all have been presented, the class will take a vote and crown the winning story.

3. If possible, borrow the opera *La Cenerentola* from the library or a video store. Screen it at home and prepare to play portions in class. Then compare it with "Cindy Ellie." It certainly differs in details, but is it similar in spirit? Explain.

4. Study the following quotation.

   Michelangelo's famous statue of David was fashioned from a block of marble that had been spoiled in the quarrying and cast away as of no value. The great creative artist used his imagination; first he built up in his mind's eyes a vision of what could be done with that spoiled block of marble. Working patiently over a long period of time he brought into existence the beauty and wonder that he had built up in his mind.

   —Jacob M. Braude

Read the biographical entry on Michelangelo in a good encyclopedia and report to the class. If possible, bring to class a book of Michelangelo's sculptures.

5. Select from *TV Guide* or a newspaper summary of a week's programs a program that strikes you as possibly imaginative. Watch it and then report to the class. Did it show the kind of imagination that we have been reading about? Did it justify the time you spent on it?

Language in Action—a Review

1. You may refer to the preceding sections to answer these questions. The oak tree is often used as a symbol of (a) flexibility (b) strength (c) family life (d) faithlessness.

2. Polar thinking is best exemplified by the expression (a) *waste not, want not* (b) *too many cooks* (c) *a stitch in time* (d) *either-or.*

3. The following series is arranged from hot to cold: hot sultry warm moderate . . . chilly cold. The missing word is (a) *frigid* (b) *scalding* (c) *humid* (d) *cool.*

4. The best example of a judgment word is (a) coward (b) president (c) driver (d) pitcher.

5. Which of the following might justify the use of an exclamation point:
   (a)   A sherbet is a chilled dessert.
   (b)   A liter is slightly more than a quart.
   (c)   I shouted to the inattentive pedestrian, "Look out."
   (d)   Come to tonight's showing of *Pride and Prejudice.*

6. Intonation may be directly affected by (a) pitch (b) speed (c) volume (d) spelling.

7. "Harriet and Barb passed me in the hall without saying *hello.* The whole stage crew is made up of snobs." This is best considered an example of (a) hasty generalization (b) false comparison (c) bandwagon (d) learning by doing.

8. All the following may be considered absolute words EXCEPT (a) *always* (b) *possibly* (c) *everyone* (d) *all.*

9. In the following group, which one contains a metaphor?
   (a)   That's as cool as the other side of the pillow.
   (b)   In manufacturing chlorophyll, the leaf is a sun-trap.
   (c)   Scrooge was as pitiless as the driving sleet.

    (d)   Elaine was as graceful as a gazelle.

10. Each of the following is a metaphor EXCEPT

    (a)   The trees were two sentinels against the sky.
    (b)   Janice is secretary of the junior class.
    (c)   Jeremy's thinking was muddy.
    (d)   The scientist stumbled upon the discovery.

UNIT THREE

Can It Be Love?

Four of the most difficult words to define are **life** (452), **humor** (357), **poetry** (446), and **love**. This book cannot provide the final answer for each, but it does provide some food for thought. Each of the following is a valiant attempt to define **love**. No single definition can capture all the facets of love, but the definitions below may set you thinking.

Life has taught us that love does not consist of gazing at each other but in looking outward together in the same direction.

Antoine de Saint-Exupéry

Love is the child of freedom, never that of domination.

Erich Fromm

Love that has been given to you is too sacred a thing to be talked of to anyone . . . except just to the person who is like part of you and who will feel it as you do.

Olive Schreiner

157

We receive love—from our children as well as others—not in proportion to our demands or sacrifices or needs, but roughly in proportion to our own capacity to love.

Rollo May

We find rest in those we love, and we provide a resting place in ourselves for those who love us.

Saint Bernard of Clairvaux

Love is the way it is.

Thaddeus Golas

Love is like butter; it goes well with bread.

Yiddish Proverb

How bold one gets when one is sure of being loved.

Sigmund Freud

The selections that follow show a surprising range, from the yearning of a young man for a beautiful stranger to the belated love of a husband for his ex-father-in-law. The stories involve people of all ages, from the young California girls to the brokenhearted Norwegian farmer. Love brings forth tears and laughter. There are many faces of love. This unit will provide samples.

The Girl on the Bus

William Sansom
British

He knew that he would never see the girl again. However, she had sent his spirits up . . . but soon, it was apparent, too far. For once outside the park, her park, the world proclaimed itself again.

Books and movies are filled with brief encounters. Potential young lovers pass by, meet briefly, and then disappear from each others' lives. In "Maud Muller," the American poet John Greenleaf Whittier described such a brief encounter that came to nothing. The poem concludes with these lines:

For of all sad words of tongue or pen
The saddest are these: "It might have been!"

This is the story of a strong infatuatiion, kindled by one disappointment after another. Will Harry ever meet the beautiful girl he yearns for?

The Girl on the Bus

SINCE to love is better than to be loved, unrequited love may be the finest love of all. If this is so, then the less requited the finer. And it follows that the most refined passion possible for us must finally be for those to whom we have never even spoken, whom we have never met. The passing face, the anguish of a vision of a face, a face sitting alone in

159

front of you so endearing and so moving and so beautiful that you are torn and sick inside with hope and despair, instant despair . . . for it is hopelessly plain that no word can ever be spoken, those eyes will never greet yours, in a few minutes the bell will ring, the bus will shudder to a stop, and down some impersonal side street she will be gone. Never to be seen again. Gone even is the pain of listening to where she will book for—a fourpenny, or a three-halfpence ticket?

It is due to such an encounter that I find engaging the story of my friend Harry. Only Harry's girl was not on a bus, she passed on skis.

It was one late January afternoon when Harry was walking out at Haga. The snow lay thick, and everywhere over the fine rolling park groups of Stockholmers had sought out the best slopes for an afternoon's skiing. The sun was already low and yellow over the firs, it sent a cold tired dusk across the snow—and one could feel the pleasantly weary, flushed trudge of the skiers making their last climb before nightfall. Harry walked about tasting this air of a winter's day ending, enjoying the rich smell of birchwood burning, watching the first yellow lights square in the cream-colored palace, tasting his own frosted breath. Up on the highest ridge stood the line of cavalry barracks, the fantastic line of false medieval war-tents—their great carved wooden folds were draped to the snow, a last glint of the sun flashed the gold emblems on their snow-domed roofs. From such an elegant extravagance it must have been fine to see the blue-cloaked cavalry ride forth steaming and jangling onto snowy hills. But now it was a ghost-house: and as if in evocation of its ghosts, every so often through the tall erect firs black-crouched skiers would glide, swift as shadows, like trees themselves flickering downward home.

It was some time then, in this bright half-light, that Harry turned and saw on the path behind him the figure of a girl trudging up on skis. He walked down toward her, enjoying the precision of her slender erect shape slide-stepping along towards him. Skiers walk with a beautifully controlled motion, feet always close together on the long hickory, pressing so lightly forward in long strides, pausing it seems invisibly between each forward motion, listening to a music playing somewhere in their shoulders—and always in firm endeavor, as on some enviable purposed unhurried quest pondering seriously forward.

Harry was looking down at her skis as she came up, taking pleasure from the movement and the slimness of her stride. So that not until she was nearly parallel with him and about to pass did he glance up at her face.

What he saw then took his breath away, he drew in a deep astounded breath and this then disappeared, so that there was nothing inside him at all.

Poor Harry did not have even a bus-ride's worth, not a three-ha'pence worth. He had the length of two long ski-strides' worth. But that, he said, was in its expanded way enough. Not as much as he

wanted—that would have amounted to a lifetime—but enough to provoke the indelible impression such passing visions may leave for a lifetime.

It would be useless to describe her. When Harry told me he
talked of "beauty" and of a color of hair and a grace of cheek-bone and
an expression of lips. But what he said did not amount to a concrete
image, and particularly she did not necessarily fit the blueprint of my own
imagined vision, should such a one ever chance to pass. Each to his own.
Suffice it that this woman's face and manner and whatever she evoked
was for Harry perfection: was beyond what he thought might be perfection: was absolute.

He was so shocked he nearly stopped, he certainly hesitated and
half turned his body—heavily coated and thus making what must have
been a most noticeable movement—to follow his wide-eyed worshiping
glance. But in the same short time, perhaps on her second stride forward,
she suddenly turned her face to him. Terrified, he looked away. He never
knew whether she saw him staring, or saw him at all, or looked past or
through him—he only felt a surge of embarrassment out of all proportion
to the occasion. He felt small, despairing, hopeless, and above all horrified
that she might have caught his eye and thought it the eye of an intruder.

She passed. It was a long time before Harry could bring himself
to turn around. But by then she was a black speck among others in the
lengthening snow, she was irretrievable.

For the next minutes Harry walked on and out of the park, elated
in spite of his distress. He was elated in the way a man is when he has
suddenly come face to face with a giddying good work of art. The feeling
was universal—it made to say: "Good, good—so there are still such things
in the world!" It was a feeling of hope.

But of no practical hope. He knew that he would never see the
girl again. However, she had sent his spirits up . . . but soon, it was
apparent, too far. For once outside the park, her park, the world proclaimed itself again. And it looked exceedingly bare and dull. The tram-
ride home, among skiers now wet and drab in the electric light, was
lowering. His hotel, white-walled as a sanatorium, primed with red
corridor lights and reticent switches, appalled him with its sterile gloom.
He took a glass of aquavit and telephoned a friend for dinner.

They went to a large old-fashioned restaurant. There were many
hundreds of people, an orchestra of twenty players blared music to the
farthest microphoned corner, waiters bobbed and slid like black dolphins
in the white sea of tablecloth, and all around and up to the roof, high as
an exhibition hall, the gilded ornament twisted and plushly glittered.
There were palms, flowers, flags and chandeliers.

But here also Strindberg had kept his private dining-room: and it
was with something of the same pessimist eye that Harry now allowed his
spirits to sink below the level of the nightfaring populace about. A tarnish

shadowed the gilt, a dull propriety seemed to stuff the people. The band played ballad music of the 'nineties—and he felt no nostalgia, but a vehement disgust at the stuffed rose-love-garden pomp the song pictured for him. The diners, sitting too erect and quiet and uncomfortably unlaughing, began to look like the awkward guests at a staff-dinner. Two Salvation Army lasses, in fur bonnets, threaded their way through the tables. When the band began suddenly to play a gay Spanish march it was no better, it sounded too slow. And there were too many fiddles.

Now if you knew Harry as I know Harry, you would know that Harry then began to worry. He began to theorize. "The sight of that girl," he told himself, "has colored my whole life. By a hundredth chance I was in Stockholm, by a hundredth chance I went to Haga, by another hundredth I happened to be passing that path at that moment—and I had to see *her*. Now forever I am left with a standard of beauty which my world will always slightly fail. My relationships with women will never seem quite so keen, all other pursuits will seem henceforth without quite so much purpose. Of course, I shall enjoy myself in degree. But perfection has been trifled with. This kind of thing goes deeper than one thinks . . . Oh why in hell did I go to Haga? And it is not as if I was as young as I was."

He was still considering her on the train next morning at Malmö: "The woman was always destined to be unattainable—and it is significant that I am leaving the city today. I suppose this will result in a fixation on Stockholm for the rest of my life. God knows how many superior contracts in other towns I shall discard for the subconscious opportunity of getting back to this blasted place."

The train drew into Norrköping and lunch was served. It was difficult, sitting wedged with three other men, to know how much of each small dish to take for himself, so he took too little of each. But rather much of the one he liked most. In guilty despondence, he looked out at the short orange trams circling the Norrköping neatnesses. How plain life could be! And these men eating in front and to the side of him were so large and well-conditioned! He felt himself smaller against their giant, businessy, gray-suited size. None of them spoke. They exchanged the dishes with little bows, and then relapsed into their erect selves. But as the train drew slowly out of Norrköping a group of children waved from behind railings. As one man, the three leaned slightly forward and made small flutterings with their white heavy hands. And without a word readdressed themselves to their food.

Hell, thought Harry, looking down at his own hand and seeing that it had not even the initiative to join in such a dull nice action. Hell, he thought, I shall have to wake myself up. And it was then that he decided on a new course of life, a disciplined course of self-indulgence. He would drink more, seek out more people, spend more money and work less.

The lowlands of Sweden rolled by. The sky hung gray and wet, the mossy turf with its scattering of huge time-smoothed boulders looked very ancient. Sometimes these boulders had been rolled to the edge of a field, but often they were too heavy to be moved, and lay still in the center proclaiming their great, icy age. It was very difficult for Harry, wedged in now with his coffee, to see how to start on his new program. It would have been ostentatious, he felt, to order a few brandies. But when one of the men asked for an after-dinner sherry, he did the same. One of these was enough. He felt slightly sick. The businessmen, in their hard girth and with their large pale faces, began to look very like boulders.

But at Malmö a difference charged the air. At first this might have passed for the ambrosia of arrival—a search for luggage, the disturbing sea-air, the genial sheds and asphalt of docks. The delight of safe danger. But no—once aboard the ferry what had come upon people was evident. A glance into the smoke-room told much of the tale. Already, five minutes after the train had arrived, they were singing in the smoke-room. Tables were already massing empty bottles. The three silent, kind, well-conditioned, Swedish businessmen were laughing together and sitting spread and easy. But it was not only a matter of alcohol—although the free dispensation of this, after a severely restricted country, proved in every way intoxicating. It was a broader sense of freedom. A shedding of propriety, of reserve—a change of manners, not from good to bad, but from good to good of another kind. Geniality and tolerance warmed the air.

Waiters hurried up with plates of enormous Danish sandwiches. In the very sandwiches there could be felt the difference between the two countries parted by a mile of water. Gone were the elegant and excellent Swedish confections, here were thick slabs of appetizing meat and fish piled hugely helter-skelter on a token of bread: Smörgåsbord had become Smørrebrød. And when they landed and he walked about the Danish train, Harry noticed immediately how the people had lost height and gained thickness: and how the porters wore dirtier, easier clothes. And standing in the street there was a beggar.

But although at first Harry responded to this interesting new brightness, he soon found he was the only one on the train who had no reason to be elated. He sank into greater gloom. He tried to revive his spirits with a fine meal and a night out in Copenhagen. But even when friendly Copenhageners, seeing him sitting alone, asked him to sit with them, plied him with food and drink, joked and prompted him in every way to enjoy himself—his mood remained. He felt nervous, frustrated, dull.

The next day, a little freshened by the morning, he boarded a midday boat train for Esbjærg and England. After all, he felt, things might be better. He was a fool to have taken a passing emotion so seriously. In fact, it was only an emotion and as such ephemeral and replaceable.

So that when they came to the Great Belt, and the train trundled aboard the ferry that was to take it across that wide flat water—Harry took to regarding his fellow-passengers with more interest. There is always an excitement when a compartmented train turns out its passengers to walk about and make a deckful. One has grown used and even loyal to one's own compartment: one knows the number of the carriage, it seems to be the best number of all! one even feels a sympathetic acquaintanceship with people seen through the glass of adjoining compartments and with those in the corridor. But there, on the boat, one must face a rival world—the world of other carriages. One resents their apparent assumption of equality—yet, inimical or not, it is a source of wonder that here are so many fellow-travelers of whose existence one was ignorant. One notes them with interest. One must watch and sniff.

Almost the first person Harry noted was the girl from Haga.

It could not be, it could, it was. Harry's heart jumped and his stomach sank. He turned furtively away.

He walked twenty yards down the deck, took out a cigarette and pretended that it was necessary to turn to light this against the wind. Then he backed against the cabin wall and, thus hidden, watched her. His emotion beat so strong that he imagined every passenger on the boat must recognize it, there would be a conspiracy aboard to smile about him. And consequently, though in the past days he had reproved himself for not having taken more courageous action at their first encounter—he had imagined all kinds of calm, forceful gallantry—his instinct now was for instant flight. However, common sense and a suspicion of the ridiculous strengthened him. And he was able to compromise by watching her from a distance.

She stood for a few minutes on deck, not watching the wide gray water but engrossed in her bag and some process of putting her coat and scarf and hat in order. These affairs she conducted with a tranquil efficiency. She was detached and sure, removed from all the others. She never raised her eyes to look at other people.

Then she turned and walked along to the luncheon saloon. Carefully, Harry followed, pausing and looking away as if in search of somebody or something else, and chose a table about three away from hers. There he munched his enormous pork cutlet and kept her surveyed. Every time he dared to look at her it seemed a stolen, intrusive moment. But he congratulated himself on his discretion. He told himself there was time, she must be going aboard for the Harwich boat. There, with a day and a night to stroll about the large saloons, opportunity would present itself. He stole another glance. With horror he found her looking straight at him, frowning a little. She knew!

He left, and went down the steel staircase to where the train, strangely tall and of such dark heavy metal, stood waiting. He sat smoking and unnerved, alone in the carriage. But in a few minutes the ferry docked, and soon the train was rumbling out onto Jutland and the last stretch to Esbjærg.

The ship, white and clean and smiling with stewardesses, welcomed them from the smoke and cramp of the train. But the weather was beginning to blow, a freshness of pounding black waves echoed in from the North Sea and storm clouds raced ragged across a dark sky. Harry hurried aboard, established his cabin, and went up to watch the other passengers come up the gangway. He waited for half an hour, watched the last arrivals drift in from the lighted sheds across the gritty dark quay. But he had missed her. In some panic, and in her absence growing more self-assured each moment, he searched the ship. Up and down the steep stairways, in and out of strange saloons, into the second class and once, daring all, by intentional mistake into the ladies' rest room. But she was nowhere. And the ship sailed.

Harry saw how he had missed his second chance. He looked back at that hour on the ferry and cursed his ineptitude. He despised himself, as he saw himself independent and adult and assured yet balking at the evident chance. He swore that if ever again . . . but when she appeared in the lounge after dinner he plunged his hand out for a colored engineering gazette. All his fears returned. One does not necessarily learn from experience.

The smoking-room was large and furnished with fresh, modern, leather arm-chairs. The tables were ridged: and on that evening the ridges were necessary, and then not always high enough—for it was a very stormy night, and the ship was rolling badly. Glasses and cups slid slowly about like motivated chessmen, and more than once the ship gave a great shuddering lurch that threw everything smashing to the floor. Harry, behind his gazette, prayed that his coffee would not be shot off clownishly across the saloon. He did not think then what a good excuse that might make to smile at her. He only prayed not to look a fool.

For her part, she sat serenely writing a letter. For some reason her glass of brandy never slid an inch. It seemed to borrow composure from her. Harry concentrated on an advertisement for dozers. And, curiously, this calmed him. It seemed so absurd, it showed up the moment: life is so very various, nothing has quite such a unique importance as we give it.

The storm grew in force. High waves smashed themselves with animal force against the windows, and the ship rolled more thunderously than ever. Stewards staggered, the arm-chairs tugged at their floor-chains. Perhaps the smoke-room was half-full when coffee began: but now it was emptying, people who had resisted so far began to feel sick, and for others it had become difficult to read or to talk or, among those tilting tables, to think. As they went swaying and skidding through the doors some laughed like people at a funfair: others dared not open their mouths. And so there came a moment, in spite of the drumming sea-noises outside, when Harry noticed a distinct quiet in the room. He looked round and saw that the room was nearly empty. There had descended the well-kept void dullness, the perceptible silence of a waiting-room. Two business-men sat apart reading. Their smallest movement in that polished quiet attracted attention. The girl wrote calmly on. The panic rose again in Harry's chest. It would be so easy to go over and pick a magazine from the case at her side. There were even magazines lying on her own table! With no possibility of offence he could ask her permission to read one.

He knew it was then or never. He began instantly to invent excuses. For the first time he tried to reason. There, Harry said to himself, is this girl whose appearance has knocked me silly. But I know that a hundred to one her personality will never match this illusory loveliness. How do I know she won't be an utter fool? A bitch? A moron? . . . And then I'll have spoiled this—he could almost sigh with romantic detach-ment—beautiful experience. I have sipped—and that is forever more satisfying than the gross full draught. Then he looked at her again, and the detachment left him.

All right, he groaned, then at least there is the curse of classifica-tion. That has not yet disappeared. Suppose she answered me too gen-teelly? Or too broadly? Or in this accent or that—he heard in his ears those for which he held a deep, illogical apathy. Then he remembered she was Swedish. It would not happen.

He looked back at the dozers. He saw they were described in refined lettering as "earth-moving equipment." He flung the magazine aside and in pale apprehension rose to his feet. The ship gave a lurch. He steadied himself. And then with great difficulty moved toward her.

Halfway across, exactly opposite the door, he who never did began to feel sea-sick. It was as if the paleness he had felt come over his face was spreading through him, and now with every roll of the ship a physical quease turned his stomach. It may have begun as a sickness of apprehension, but it took on all the symptoms of a sickness of sea. He felt weak, wretched and unsure of what next. He turned out through the door and balanced down the stairway to his cabin. In the lower bunk his cabin-companion lay pale and retching. The room smelled richly of sick. Harry added to it.

But only a little later, weak and having forgotten all about the girl, he fell into a deep, unmolested sleep. Twice in the night he woke—once when his heavy suitcase slid thudding from one end of the cabin to the other, once when he himself was nearly rolled out of the bunk. But he was no longer sick.

He woke late, feeling well and hungry. The ship was still pitching as heavily as before. He shaved with difficulty, watching his face swing in and out of the mirror, chasing with his razor the water that rolled in the opposite direction to that chosen by the ship. Then upstairs to breakfast. The whole ship was deserted. Harry looked at his watch, wondering whether he had misread the time and if it was perhaps still early—but his watch and the purser's clock made it already eleven o'clock. The notion smiled through him that the company had taken to the boats in the night, he was in a well-equipped ghost-ship with steam up. And indeed, walking through the deserted saloons, it felt like that. But in the dining-room three waiters were sitting.

During a breakfast that he could only eat by holding his cup in one hand and both cutting and forking his ham with the other, a waiter told him they were having one of the worst crossings he had ever known. Waves, even in such a great modern ship, had smashed plate-glass in the night. A settee had broken its chains, raced across the smoking-lounge and had run over a steward, breaking his leg. Of course, it was quite safe, but the ship would be about six hours late. They had made no headway at all during the night, they had simply sat rolling in the middle of the North Sea.

Harry wandered out along the passages and into the smoke-room. It was vexing to be so late. He was in no exact hurry, but an empty ship in stormy weather is a most tedious ordeal, and the long tossing day stretched out gray and eventless. One cannot easily write, it is difficult even to read, getting drunk is simpler but as aimless as the crashing glasses. To be sick is dreadful, but to spend a day lurching among lurching things, with never a level moment, is, if not unendurable, of the deepest, most troublesome tedium.

For a while Harry watched the waves. Some seemed higher than the ship itself, it seemed impossible not to be capsized. A sudden wet wall of gray running water would erect itself high as a housefront over the valley of the smoke-room window: then at the last moment up would go the ship on another unseen wave. All blew cold gray, but there was no mist—a gale wind whipped spray from the waves and tore the dishcloth smoke to pieces. Low clouds scudded too fast to notice the ship, the horizon was no more than a jagged encampment of near waves. Not a bird, not a ship in sight.

Harry's thoughts naturally centered on what was still at the back of his mind. Breakfast over, he brought her foremost. And found to his surprise that he was no longer apprehensive of her. He welcomed the probability of her appearance, he welcomed the emptiness of the ship. She was obviously not the seasick type, she was likely to appear. And with an empty ship there would be more opportunity to speak—and at the same time nobody to smile behind his back if she snubbed him. It seemed that his sickness of the night before had proved in all ways cathartic.

He welcomed the luncheon gong, and in his expectant joy remembered with a smile the Swedish word for this: *gonggong*. But she did not appear at luncheon. And gradually, his spirits falling and his stomach swelling, Harry ploughed in these difficult seas through the enormous and exquisite Danish meal.

The afternoon was terrible. Nothing, nothing happened. A few odd men came lurching through. Two young Danish fellows sat for a long time laughing over their drinks. Harry went down to pack, but was forced by the state of his companion to complete this as quickly as possible.

An hour before the ship was due in people began to come up exhausted or rested from the sanctuary of their cabins. The ship was steaming close against the English littoral,* and the seas were much calmer. Disconsolate, Harry rose from his arm-chair, threw aside the paper on which he had been reduced to writing lists of all the vegetables he knew beginning with the letter "p," and walked round to the little bar for a drink. There she was, bright as a bad penny, perched up on a stool between those two laughing young men.

His heart sank, but he went grimly to the other end of the bar and, with his back turned, ordered a dobbeltsnaps. He could not hear what was said, for between high laughter they spoke in the low intimate voices of people telling anecdotes: but he could watch them in a slice of mirror. And. . . . So there! What had he told himself? Hadn't he been right? She was just an ordinary flirt! She hadn't talked to these men until five minutes before, and now she was going it hell-for-leather! Easy as pie, pie-in-the-sky! He might have known it! Hell, he *had* known it! And that's why (subconsciously of course) he hadn't gone up to her. . . . But through this Harry knew deeply and quite consciously that he envied the young men and deprecated his own driveling loutish cowardice. He turned and took one last look at her. She was wonderful . . . yes, she was wonderful.

He went downstairs and made ready to leave. In a while the ship docked. He took his bags and shuffled down among the line of passengers to the rail-lined dock. It was a curious relief to feel the land under one's feet, it brought what felt like a light unheard buzzing to the ears. Then the familiar smells and a further shuffle through the customs.

Suddenly, going through the doorway to the platform, he saw her again. She was clutching the arm of a large ugly elderly man. She was stroking this man. Together the two, the elegant fresh young girl and that obscene old figure, passed through the door. Harry believed his eyes and he was disgusted.

He had to pass them. They stood in the wan light of the old-fashioned station, she fingering about in her bag and at every moment

---

*coast

flashing her eyes up at him, he bloated, gloat-eyed, mumbling heaven-knew-what salivary intimacies. It crossed Harry's mind how strange was the phenomenon of these shipboard passengers one never sees until the last moment, these cabined mysteries—and it struck him again horribly how this applied to those two, the old slug lying down there in the comfortable depths of the ship with his fair, fresh girl . . . .

The girl looked up and met Harry's eyes. She immediately smiled, it seemed in relief, and came up to him. She spoke excitedly, apologetically in Swedish:

—Oh, please do excuse me . . . but it's funny I remember distinctly I once saw you in Haga, you speak Swedish? You see, my father and I—we've lost our seat reservations. Could you tell me what is best to do? . . . We're new here . . . .

Harry's heart leapt. The lights in the station seemed to turn up, it was suddenly almost sunny. With delight he showed them to the end of the train where he knew there were empty carriages. Together they traveled to London and never stopped talking. He insisted on driving them to their hotel.

Harry and his lady have now been married some seven years. He has never, as far as can be known, regretted the requital.

Reading for Understanding

Main Idea

1. A major point to be derived from this story is that (a) infatuations are silly (b) travel by sea is a risky business (c) first impressions may be reliable (d) skiing is a good way for a young man to meet girls.

Details

2. Harry first saw the girl (a) in a bus (b) on a ship (c) on skis (d) in a train.

3. Norrköping is (a) in Sweden (b) a ski park (c) a suburb of Haga (d) a Danish delicacy.

4. The mood of the passengers seemed to grow lighter (a) between Stockholm and Malmö (b) on the ferry (c) in England (d) at the ski park.

5. The ship to England had to cross (a) the English Channel (b) the strait between Denmark and Sweden (c) an open section of the Atlantic Ocean (d) the North Sea.

6. While the ship was pitching wildly, the girl (a) wrote calmly (b) asked Harry for help (c) became seasick (d) cried out in terror.

7. The girl asked for assistance (a) to steady her father's walk (b) on the ski slope (c) in Danish (d) in Swedish.

8. At one point, Harry's resolve to speak to the girl was thwarted by (a) two young men from England (b) seasickness (c) the girl's father (d) a blizzard.

Inferences

9. Harry found himself in Sweden (a) on a business trip (b) to meet a girl (c) on vacation (d) by accident.

10. Haga is apparently a (a) bus station (b) restaurant (c) park (d) Danish city.

11. In reality, the girl (a) was unaware of Harry's feelings about her (b) disliked Harry on first sight (c) rejected Harry after all (d) was self-centered.

Author's Attitude

12. The author of the story (a) is irritated by Harry's actions (b) thinks the girl doesn't merit Harry's attentions (c) is antagonistic toward brief encounters (d) is pleasantly amused by Harry's story.

Outcomes

13. Harry probably (a) regretted his hasty decision (b) told his wife about his early crush on her (c) went to Sweden every year on vacation (d) asked the author to use an assumed name in telling the story.

Order of Events

14. Arrange the items in the order in which they occurred. Use letters only.

A. The girl addresses Harry.
B. Harry becomes seasick.
C. Harry sees the girl on the ski slope.
D. The girl begins to write a letter on shipboard.
E. Harry takes a train to the ferry.

Fact or Opinion

Tell whether the following is a fact or an opinion.
15. The girl was the most beautiful skier on the slope.

Words in Context

1. "Since to love is better than to be loved, *unrequited* love may be the finest of all." **Unrequited** (159) means not (a) understood (b) enthusiastic (c) wise (d) returned.
2. "Suffice it is that this woman's face and manner and whatever she *evoked* was for Harry perfection." **Evoked** (161) means (a) brought out (b) discounted (c) reflected (d) called upon.
3. "He was *elated* in the way a man is when he has suddenly comes face to face with a giddying good work of art." **Elated** (161) means (a) amazed (b) curious (c) joyful (d) thoughtful.
4. "The band played ballad music of the 'nineties—and he felt no *nostalgia*." **Nostalgia** (162) is a longing for (a) companionship (b) the past (c) stimulation (d) the impossible.
5. "In guilty *despondence*, he looked out at the short orange trams circling the Norrköping neatnesses." **Despondence** (162) means (a) anticipating (b) depression (c) renewed interest (d) curiosity.
6. "It would have been *ostentatious*, he thought, to order a few brandies." **Ostentatious** (163) means, (a) showy (b) discreet (c) counterproductive (d) tactful.
7. "The businessmen, in their hard *girth* and with their large pale faces, began to look very like boulders." **Girth** (163) refers to (a) attitude (b) selfishness (c) appearance (d) size.
8. "At first this might have passed for the *ambrosia* of arrival." **Ambro-**

sia (163) is used here to suggest (a) excitement (b) demands (c) indifference (d) disappointment.

9. "In fact, it was only an emotion and as such *ephemeral* and replaceable." **Ephemeral** (163) means (a) notable (b) uncomfortable (c) temporary (d) unsatisfactory.

10. "One resents their apparent assumption of equality—yet *inimical* or not it is a source of wonder that there are so many fellow-travelers of whose existence one was ignorant." **Inimical** (164) means (a) surprising (b) unfriendly (c) uncomfortable (d) unexpected.

11. "He turned *furtively* away." **Furtively** (164) means (a) sadly (b) quickly (c) reluctantly (d) secretly.

12. "She stood for a few minutes on deck, not watching the wide gray water but *engrossed* in her bag and some process of putting her coat and scarf and hat in order." **Engrossed** (164) means (a) challenged (b) nonchalant (c) distracted (d) absorbed.

13. "Every time he dared to look at her it seemed a stolen, *intrusive* moment." **Intrusive** (164) means (a) meddling (b) precious (c) inspiring (d) elusive.

14. "He looked back at that hour on the ferry and cursed his *ineptitude*." **Ineptitude** (165) means (a) misfortune (b) shyness (c) incompetence (d) lack of restraint.

15. "It seemed to borrow *composure* from her." **Composure** (165) means (a) fragility (b) calm (c) beauty (d) restlessness.

16. "There had descended the well-kept void dullness, the *perceptible* silence of a waiting-room." **Perceptible** (166) means able to be (a) written about (b) communicated (c) resented (d) felt.

17. "I knew that a hundred to one her personality will never match this *illusory* loveliness." **Illusory** (166) means (a) obvious (b) deceptive (c) extreme (d) enviable.

18. He "found to his surprise that he was no longer *apprehensive of* her." **Apprehensive of** (167) means (a) angry with (b) in communication with (c) concerned about (d) indifferent about.

19. "*Disconsolate,* Harry rose from his arm chair." **Disconsolate** (168) means (a) heavy-hearted (b) energized (c) deep in thought (d) determined.

20. "Through this Harry knew deeply and quite consciously that he envied the young men and *deprecated* his own driveling loutish cowardice." **Deprecated** (168) means (a) reviewed (b) evaluated (c) examined (d) disapproved.

21. "Together the two, the elegant fresh young girl and that *obscene* old figure, passed through the door." **Obscene** (168) means (a) stocky (b) flushed (c) indecent (d) sympathetic.

Thinking Critically about the Story

1. Were you surprised by the title? Should the story have been titled "The Girl on Skis"? Why did the author choose to use *bus* instead of *skis?* Note paragraph 2.

2. Is love at first sight really love? Did Harry truly love the girl before he actually met her?

3. How does the author skilfully build up Harry's seemingly hopeless attraction? Point out the situations in which Harry looks longingly at the girl.

4. In a humorous reply to the sentiments of John Greenleaf Whittier (159), Bret Harte wrote:

   More sad are those we daily see:
   It is, but hadn't ought to be.

   How does "The Girl on the Bus" seem to belie both sentiments, Whittier's and Harte's?

5. The song "Some Enchanted Evening" from *South Pacific* is a tribute to spontaneous love. Can you recall a television program or movie in which a similar situation was shown?

6. Obsession, a disturbing and overwhelming feeling for another, often characterizes a one-sided infatuation. Obsession is often dangerous. Does Harry fit the description of a man with a dangerous obsession? Why or why not?

7. This is a miniature travel account. Point out the author's use of scenery to suggest Harry's changes of moods.

8. The Marilyn Monroe movie *The Seven-Year Itch* suggests the seventh year as a crisis year in marriage. Harry had been married seven years. What are the prospects for a long and happy marriage? What does the narrator think?

9. In the opening two sentences, the author attempts a bit of humor. If we accept that it is better to love than to be loved (a debatable

sentiment), then it follows that the less returned love is, the better. With that logic, it would have been better had Harry not succeeded. This is topsy-turvy humor, of course. How does the author acknowledge his "error" in the last sentence of the story?

Language in Action

Point of View

A story is always told from a certain point of view. If told in the first person with *I* as the narrator, the story has a sense of directness. The readers feel closer to the action, but there are limitations. A sentence like the following is unusable in a first person narrative: "When I mentioned California, Ruby thought about her early days in Sacramento." How could the narrator know Ruby's innermost thoughts?

A way around this problem is the omniscient (all-knowing) third-person point of view. This is a common method of storytelling because the writer can look into the hearts of every character. In this unit, "Mr. Cornelius, I Love You" (186–197) is told from the omniscient third-person point of view.

A variation of that point of view is the limited third-person. A story is told from the point of view of a character in the story, so that the reader knows and sees only what that character knows and sees. This is a favorite technique in detective stories. It combines some of the directness of the first-person narrative with the greater freedom of the third-person narrative. Yet it doesn't give the mystery away since the main character is puzzled along with the reader. "The Crime in Nobody's Room" (266–280) uses the limited third-person technique.

"The Girl on the Bus" uses an interesting combination of techniques. The first two paragraphs are in the first person. Then the author tells the story in the third person, not from a limited point of view but from the omniscient. He reports how Harry thinks and feels. We must assume that Harry has told the narrator or implied how he felt. The author takes it from there.

Dream Power Video

Vicki Grove
American

> "Hey, aren't you the girl Mr. Lowry always calls on?" he
> asked cheerfully, sticking his hands deep in the pockets of his
> letter jacket. "Nan, right?"
> I was shocked that he knew my name, and I forced myself
> to look up at him and smile, "Right! Well! Hi there." Stupid.

Teenagers often underestimate themselves. They worry about
their appearance, develop an inferiority complex, dismiss their real
virtues as unimportant. Part of the problem lies with the media and
their preoccupation with impossibly beautiful women and incredibly
handsome men. Models, who represent a tiny fraction of the population, become ridiculous role models. Since becoming as physically
attractive as the models is out of the question for most teenagers,
much unnecessary anguish results.

It is not uncommon to see a handsome husband and ordinary-
looking wife happily married. The reverse is true. The partners looked
below the surface and saw qualities that would survive the challenges
of life. An old Pennsylvania Dutch saying, "Kisses don't last, but
cooking do," is a humorous way of saying that physical appeal is not
enough for the long road ahead. Besides, beauty is indeed in the eye
of the beholder.

Nan, intelligent but not a raving beauty, finds that compatibility
with a boy goes deeper than the surface.

Dream Power Video

When my Aunt Sissy opened her video rental store and offered me an after-school, part-time job as her assistant, she thought the first thing we needed was a cute name and a gimmicky slogan to go with it.

"You know," she explained, gesturing with her hands in that perky way she has. "To make us different from other video places in town. So people will want to come to our little shop instead of going to one of those big, glitzy places."

I frowned and pushed my glasses up.

"Okay, let's approach this logically," I said. "Why do people rent movies? Ask yourself that question."

"Anything you say, Professor," she teased. But then she leaned forward onto the counter, her chin in her hands. "To escape from reality for a couple of hours, I guess."

I ignored that "professor" thing. It was just sort of a nickname a few people had for me. "Yes, but more than that," I told her. "I mean, you can escape from reality by taking a nap or studying for a physics exam. I say people rent movies because they need dreams in their lives. Romance and happy endings. Action, adventure."

Sissy looked totally shocked. Then she jerked up straight, smiling. "You known, Nan, you surprise me sometimes. That was the last thing I expected from you, but I'll bet you're right on track!"

Sissy meant she didn't expect me to think in terms of dreams and romance. But actually, most shy, quiet people are probably experts on dreams, if you stop and think about it logically. For one thing, we have more time on our hands for dreaming.

Sissy did a happy little dance right there in the middle of the shop, her shoulders moving up and down, her long red hair swishing into her face as she snapped her fingers. I looked uneasily toward the window, but no one, luckily, was passing by.

"Dream Power Video!" she squealed, grabbing me, trying to pull me into her dance. I stiffened, and she let go. "Perfect! Oh, Nan, I knew you'd come up with something!"

She hugged me then. I couldn't keep the frames of my glasses from jabbing into her neck. She didn't seem to care.

"We still need a slogan, remember?" I told her in a muffled, squeezed voice, and she let me go and chewed her bottom lip, tapping her chin with her bright red thumbnail.

I gave her a couple of minutes to come up with the obvious

slogan herself. Then I gave up. "How about this—'Your Dreams Are Our Business.' "

"Oh, Nan, that's just so perfect!" she bubbled. "I mean, I just know this is going to work! People are going to start relying on us to help them pick the perfect dream escape. Just like they rely on beauticians to help them pick hairstyles and salespeople to help them pick shoes!"

I bent quickly to begin carrying some boxes into their little slots in the storage shelves. Yes, I decided, I could see myself picking dreams for other people. Like I said, I was an expert on dreams, like I guess most people are who spend quite a bit of time alone.

When I came to work after school the next afternoon, we stenciled our slogan onto the big plate glass window out front and decorated it with fluffy cotton clouds. We stuck out a "Grand Opening" sign too, and by the end of the week, the place was doing a good business. So good that Sissy hired her friend, Liza, to help us part-time.

The three of us—Sissy, Liza and I—quickly began to believe in our own gimmick. I mean, it sounds a little strange, but when people came in, smiling sheepishly, and asked if we were the place they'd heard about that could cater to people's dreams, we told them that we could. We assured them that we could figure out and make anybody's two-hour video dream come true. Then we made a game of directing them toward the section of the store where they looked like they most belonged.

Sissy was the best at this. She really got into it.

"Let's see, now," she would say, standing thoughtfully with her hands on her hips and sizing up three sweaty-looking junior high school boys. "Don't tell me, let me guess! I'll just bet you want the back section with the sports flicks. We have a new one about some guys whose team starts out in last place and goes on to win the pennant. Twice!"

"Yes!" the three guys said, punching the air, then following her happily toward that section.

Word got around that we were dream guessers, and soon everybody wanted us to look at them and guess their dreams. It got to be a game, for us and our customers. With most people, it was surprisingly easy.

Of course, not everybody fit the dreams we guessed for them, and they were quick to tell us so. But you would be surprised how often we were right.

The afternoon B.J. Tarpley walked in, I was working alone. Sissy had gone to eat, and Liza wasn't due till the evening rush, a couple of hours later. Ever since I'd started working, I'd worried about what would happen if somebody from school came in, and I had to be the one to wait on them. I had sort of a plan for it if that happened. I'd just keep my head ducked so my hair covered most of my face, and I'd pretend to be reading the announcements of new videos. Not that most people in the junior class would probably really recognize me anyway, or know who I actually was. Raytown South is a big school. I mean, to most people, I would just be "that girl in chess club," or "that girl Mr. Lowry calls on when nobody else knows the equation." So it was no big deal if my hair didn't hide me, I kept telling myself.

Still, I totally got flustered when suddenly there was B.J., swinging through the double doors as easily as he swung through the halls at school. And he didn't ignore me and go over to the shelves like he was supposed to. He headed straight for the counter, where I was ducking my head for all I was worth, trying to keep track of him through my bangs while my heart jumped around.

"Hey, aren't you the girl Mr. Lowry always calls on?" he asked cheerfully, sticking his hands deep in the pockets of his letter jacket. "Nan, right?"

I was shocked that he knew my name, and I forced myself to look up at him and smile. "Right! Well! Hi there!" Stupid!

"Hi," he said, still grinning. "So go ahead. Guess my dream."

Of all the obvious dreams we'd encountered in the three weeks of running the store, this was far and away the most obvious. He belonged in the section of the store with the He-man stuff. Take-charge guys. Robo-hunks.

"Uh," I forced out, "Well, let's see. If you approach this logically . . . ," I took a deep breath and glanced toward a huge cut-out of Sylvester Stallone by the action/adventure section. He followed my gaze.

"You think I dream of being him?" he asked. I could feel a burning behind my eye sockets. I was that flustered. "Like I said, if you approach this logically—," I began again, then stopped and swallowed hard. He was captain of the soccer team, popular as anything. So why was he putting me through this, when it was so obvious? Couldn't he just go away? Just then Sissy and Liza came breezing in, gabbing a mile a minute about some sale they'd been to.

Sissy got a few feet from me, noticed B.J., got exactly the wrong idea and immediately became supercharged. This humiliating reaction happens whenever a member of my family catches me within shouting distance of a member of the opposite sex.

"Well, who's this?" she gushed, fixing on B.J. with a laserbeam smile. "A friend from school? I don't get to meet many of your friends, Nan."

"Customer," I said through clenched teeth. "He's a customer, Sissy."

"With a Raytown South jacket, which makes him a classmate, right?" she said with a giggle, hitting me on the shoulder like I was teasing her. Then she leaned forward across the counter to read the name embroidered above the big R on B.J.'s jacket. "Ben," she said. "Nice to meet you, Ben!"

"I'm going back to organize the storeroom," I forced out, turning and blindly groping for the doorway that would lead me to where I could die of embarrassment in peace.

"Wait!" Sissy persisted in a sweet, joking voice.

"Go get a burger! That's an order. Go, go, go!" I held my breath, my blood roaring in my ears. Sure enough, the worst was yet to come. "Hey, maybe Ben hasn't eaten yet!" Sissy went on. "Sure, I could eat," said B.J.

"Great!" Sissy put both hands on my shoulders and actually shoved me through the opening of the counter, practically into B.J.'s face. "See? This is perfect. Stay out as long as you want. Liza's here early, so no problem. Right, Liza?"

"No problem!" Liza echoed, grinning innocently, ear to ear. "I'm really sorry," I croaked when we were outside the store. I collapsed back against the plate glass window, and it waffled dangerously. B.J. pressed both hands against the glass to stabilize it, as I jumped clumsily out of the way, making the window wobble even more.

"You okay?" he asked, looking at me, not the swaying glass.

I made my hands into fists and shoved them into my pockets, but it was no use. They wouldn't stay there. Seconds later, my nervous fingers were groping through my hair, shoving it behind my ears, pulling it around my face, shoving it back again. My left thumb found the hangnail on my pinky and began digging at it.

"Listen, you can just go now," I whispered desperately. "I mean, that lady, Sissy, well, she's the owner of this place, and she's my aunt, so I guess in a way, it's only logical that she would be . . . worried. About me. Still, she goes way overboard."

B.J. shrugged. "Food's important. Nutrition and all that stuff. Energy."

Did he really not get it, not know how foolish and humiliated someone like me felt trapping someone like him into spending time with her like this?

"Like I said, you can go now!" I pleaded. "Food's important! I couldn't agree more. So you can go eat, okay? I've got stuff to do, so I'll just like, uh, do it."

A car full of kids drove by and honked. "Beej!" someone yelled, and B.J. waved brightly. Someone in the car laughed, a female laugh. Because I was near him? Was that the joke?

I couldn't stand this another minute. "So goodby!" I pretty much yelled and took off at a run. I heard him call something behind me, then told myself to get real. He was probably calling out to those kids who had passed us. Thank goodness the sidewalks were clogged with people at that time of day. I felt relief as I was lost in the crowd. After three or four blocks, I cut sharply left and headed toward the back entrance to the video store.

The back door opened into the storeroom, and I figured I'd work back there the rest of the night. I didn't want to see anybody-especially not Sissy. The storeroom was quiet and gloomy this time of evening, a good place for hiding, for recovering from massive, near lethal humiliation. And there was lots to do back there.

But I'd barely closed the outside door and entered the comforting shadows of the storeroom when the other door, the one leading from the storeroom into the shop, burst open, letting in an explosion of bright, frantic light and sound.

"Yoo-hoo? Nanette? You back here, kiddo?"

Sissy leaned in my direction, squinting into the shadows, her shape a dark silhouette framed in the bright doorway.

"Leave me alone," I whimpered. "Oh, sweetheart, it'll be okay," Sissy whispered, hurrying toward my voice with her arms held out in hug mode. "You'll see—it will! He's already . . . "

He's already history, I finished mentally for her. I ducked away and grabbed a stack of videos I had left in the storeroom when I'd come to work that day. The videos were some of my favorite Hitchcock thrillers and Woody Allen movies that I'd borrowed for about the tenth time. No one but me ever seemed to check them out, but still they needed to be reshelved in the classics section, and I had to get away from Sissy's sympathy.

"Aunt Sissy, I love you, but not all of us can be open, and dazzling, and—and spontaneous like you. You shouldn't have forced me on B.J. like that! Guys like him are only interested in flashy, beautiful girls. Dream girls. Girls with everything going for them."

"You have everything going for you," Sissy said.

I just rolled my eyes. Why was she pretending she didn't know what I was talking about? My throat throbbed so much, I suddenly couldn't speak, and there wasn't anything left to say anyhow. Clutching those great old videos for dear life, I squeezed past her and made a beeline into the shop and toward the classics section in the far back corner.

No one was ever back there, which was why when I rounded the corner and ran right into B.J., the videos I was holding flew from my arms like popcorn.

"Hey, steady," he said, grabbing my shoulders. "You okay?"

I could only nod, numbly, in shock. He smiled, then bent to pick up the plastic boxes. "Just like I suspected. You're the reason *Sleeper* and *Vertigo* are never here when I look for them, right? And I'll just bet you've got *Annie Hall* too."

"Still at home," I whispered. "I planned on—on watching it tonight—again."

B.J. turned and began gently placing the videos on the shelf above the little tags with their names. "You sort of hurt my feelings today, you know," he said, then cleared his throat. "I came in here hoping you would guess my dream. But you stereotyped me, just like everybody else does. I thought, well, I hoped you would have a better read on me than that."

He turned around, looked right into my eyes. "I want to go to film school someday. I love photography. But people box you in to categories, expect you to be like you've always been since junior high. The Jock."

The Egghead, I thought. Then I decided to take a huge chance. "I know. The Egghead," I whispered.

"I always knew there was more to you than that," B.J. said, looking straight into my eyes.

"You—you did?" I asked, blinking.

"Do you think I would have come in here looking for you if I didn't?" he fired back.

"Do you mean you came in here looking for me?" I couldn't believe my ears.

B.J. smiled and touched the back of my hand with his left index finger.

"So, would you mind some company while you watch *Annie Hall* tonight?" he asked, moving that finger slowly up toward my wrist, where a vein to my heart throbbed happily, dizzily, and not the least bit logically.

Reading for Understanding

Main Idea

1. The main idea of the story is that (a) videos provide a wholesome form of recreation (b) sometimes people hurt when they think they are helping (c) school athletes tend to like ordinary-looking girls (d) physical beauty may not be the most important element in a relationship.

Details

2. The person who actually created the name "Dream Power Video" was (a) Nan (b) Sissy (c) Liza (d) B.J.

3. The person who actually created the slogan "Your Dreams Are Our Buinesss" was (a) Nan (b) Sissy (c) Liza (d) B.J.

4. Nan particularly liked the films of (a) Alfred Hitchcock and John Wayne (b) Woody Allen and John Wayne (c) Alfred Hitchcock and Woody Allen (d) Woody Allen and Sylvester Stallone.

5. For escape, Nan chose (a) the storeroom (b) the video sports section (c) the hamburger restaurant (d) her aunt's apartment.

Inferences

6. Aunt Sissy's personality is (a) quiet (b) lighthearted (c) grim (d) unpleasant.

7. B.J. was apparently looking for a girl (a) who flattered him (b) who excelled in sports (c) with similar interests (d) with extraordinary beauty.

8. It seems fair to assert that (a) the video store could use another helper (b) Aunt Sissy intended to be a bothersome busybody (c) Nan under-estimated herself (d) B.J. was insincere in playing up to Nan.

Order of Events

9. Arrange the items in the order in which they occurred. Use the letters only.
   A. Nan runs into B.J. and drops some tapes.
   B. B.J. says that he had come in to the shop to meet Nan.
   C. The video store has a grand opening.
   D. B.J. first speaks to Nan.
   E. Sissy suggests that B.J. and Nan go to lunch.

Fact or Opinion

Tell whether the following is a fact or opinion.

10. B.J. says that his interests are similar to Nan's.

Word in Context

"But you *stereotyped* me, just like everybody else does." **Stereotyped** (181) means (a) classified (b) criticized (c) praised (d) disregarded.

Thinking Critically about the Story

1. Do you agree with the introduction that advertising, television, and the movies provide impossible goals for young people? How should a teenager avoid the glittering traps of the media?
2. What attracted B.J. to Nan? Is this attraction a realistic possibility, or a fiction writer's dream? Explain.
3. Are similarities of interest important even in teen dating? Explain.
4. A guide in India explained that her marriage had been arranged by parents. When Americans on the tour were shocked, the guide said, "Compare your divorce rate with ours." Why do such arranged marriages seem, on average, to last longer than Western romantic marriages? Does that mean that American marriages should be arranged, too?
5. For the first time in history, VCR owners have on video most of the world's movie treasures. Have you taken advantage of this wealth? Do you sometimes rent old movies? If so, why?
6. Do you have a movie favorite that you have rented more than once? Tell what the appeal is.
7. Aunt Sissy is a natural matchmaker. Does bringing two people together in hopes of finding a match usually fail? If so, why?

Language in Action

Stereotypes

B.J. is convinced that Joan has stereotyped him, as indeed she has. The word *stereotype* derives from an earlier day, before modern methods of printing. A stereotype was a metal plate cast from metal type. Once cast, the plate could not easily be changed.

A *stereotype* is also a fixed mental image representing an oversimplified, uncritical judgment.

All groups have been victims of the stereotype. Because some teenagers are immature, cartoons, television skits, and the movies often picture the typical teenager as giddy, emotionally unbalanced, and downright silly. Some other typical stereotypes include the bride who can't cook, the humorless Englishman, the kindly grandfather, the thrifty

Scotsman, the absent-minded professor, the meddling mother-in-law (658), the impractical poet, the jolly Irishman. . . . The list goes on and on. Think of the current sitcoms and realize how many stereotypes fill the screen.

Some stereotypes are foolish but probably harmless. Other stereotypes can hurt and do damage. Racial, national, and ethnic stereotypes often destroy friendships and cause grievous harm.

Mr. Cornelius, I Love You

Jessamyn West
American

> "What did I say?" Mr. Delahanty asked, "To cause all that?"
> Mrs. Delahanty continued without speaking to shake bits
> of food from the flowers. "Gertrude, did what I said sound
> cruel and hateful to you?"
> "No, John, not to me," she answered. "But then I'm not in
> love with Mr. Cornelius."

All the stories in this unit deal with love in one form or other; yet this is the only story with **love** in the title. Despite this, there will be some who say, "The love demonstrated in this chapter isn't really love, at all, merely a girlhood crush." You can decide for yourself. Cress Delahanty's adoration of Mr. Cornelius is totally absorbing . . . and extremely vulnerable, but is it love?

Cress's feelings, are, she thinks, little understood or appreciated by her parents or friends. They come at a critical time in her development. Ruthlessly destroyed, this deep affection could cause her pain and hinder her ability to love later in life. Fortunately, there is a key person who sees the love for what it is, understands it, and brings Cress in as a partner in the task of helping Mr. Cornelius to recover.

What seems like a pointless obsession is a step in the growing maturity of a young woman.

Mr. Cornelius, I Love You

MR. AND MRS. DELAHANTY, Cress, and Cress's friends, Jo Grogan and Bernadine Deevers, sat down to the Delahanty dinner table on Wednesday evening. The table was round with a white cloth that dipped at its four corners to the floor, so that in the dusk of the dining room the cloth seemed actually to be supporting the table. Mrs. Delahanty, who hadn't even expected Cress home for dinner, let alone Jo and Bernadine, felt apologetic about the food which, besides being rather uninviting, was skimpy in amount: a small salmon loaf, Harvard beets, mashed potatoes, and for dessert a cabinet pudding which did nothing to redeem the meal that had gone before. But the girls didn't seem to know or care what they put in their mouths and she decided that strawberries and fresh asparagus would have been wasted on them.

A mockingbird was singing in the orange grove outside the opened windows and the girls listened, a spoonful of cabinet pudding lifted to their opened lips—then, as the song ceased, put the spoons down without having tasted a bite. Mr. and Mrs. Delahanty had given up trying to carry on a conversation with them and treated them as so many portraits ranged round their dining room—"Girls at Dusk," or "Reveries of Youth." They talked their own talk and let the girls dream their dreams, wrap their feet around the rungs of their chairs, and listen (mouths open, eyes closed) to the bird song.

"I saw Doc Mendenhall in town today," Mr. Delahanty said.

Mrs. Delahanty said "Yes?" waiting for whatever it was that made this fact worth reporting, but Bernadine interrupted his train of thought, if he had one, by extending her long arms toward the darkening windows and singing very softly, "Oh night of love, oh beauteous night." Bernadine was barefooted (it was the spring's great fad at high school) though she was eighteen, and wore an elaborate blue voile dress which drifted about her like a sky-stained cloud. Bernadine was to be married the day after school was out and sometimes, Mrs. Delahanty felt, overplayed her role of bride-to-be.

It was already, unbelievably, the last week of school which, in Southern California, is the second week in June, a time climatically as well as scholastically neither one thing nor another, neither spring nor summer, neither truly school nor truly vacation. Class routines had been

186

relaxed but not abandoned. Grade-wise, the feeling among the students was that the year was already water over the dam; still they couldn't be positive; some of the teachers were still going through the motions of setting down grades in their record books. Climatically the days started spring-like, damp and gray with threat even of one more unseasonal rain; at 1 P.M. exactly the day did an about-face, took on September inclinations. At that hour the overcast burned away and the tawny grasses, sun-bleached foothills, and smoldering flowers of full summer emerged. It was very confusing after getting up into a dripping cold which made sweaters and open fires necessary, to finish the day barefooted, hot-cheeked, and as naked as possible.

Cress and Jo both wore shorts and halters. Cress had shasta daisies tucked in the V of her halter and Jo Grogan, with those three flame-colored hibiscus in her short dark hair, might have been August itself on any calendar of girls. As the day darkened the white tablecloth grew silvery, the mockingbird retreated deeper into the orchard, and Mrs. Delahanty felt that the whole scene might be unreal, a mirage cast up into the present out of either the past or the future—that girls *had* sat in many a darkening room in years gone by and would so sit in the future; but that "now," the present minute, was unreal, only the past whisking by on its way to the future, or the future casting a long prophetic shadow to rearwards.

"Jo," she said briskly, "if you'll put some more custard on your pudding you might be able to eat it."

"I beg your pardon," said Jo. "Were you speaking to me?"

"Never mind," Mrs. Delahanty told her. "I was only urging you to eat."

"Oh food!" said Cress. "Food. Who cares about food?"

"I do," said Bernadine. "Howie adores puddings. Will you copy down this recipe for me, Mrs. Delahanty? I plan to serve Howie a different pudding every single night for thirty nights. I already have twenty-two recipes."

"Tapioca, jello, and bread," said Jo, sing-songing. "If puddings be the food of love, cook on."

The mockingbird had ceased to sing. The leaves of the bougain-villaea vine which clambered over the dining-room wall rustled faintly. Mrs. Delahanty began taking the spoons from the serving dishes.

Mr. Delahanty remarked in the voice of a man who has had the words in mind for some time, "Doc Mendenhall says that Frank Cornelius had a bad hemorrhage this morning."

Mrs. Delahanty laid the spoons down, clattering. "Oh John!" she said. "I understood he was getting better."

There was a note in her voice of condemnation, as if Mr. Cornelius had not tried hard enough, as if he were a turncoat, a traitor to his generation—and hers. When old people sickened and died, men and women in their seventies and eighties, that was to be expected. But thirty-eight! That was a direct threat to her and John.

"I don't think he's taken very good care of himself," Mr. Delahanty explained. "You can't throw off t.b. just by wishing. You've got to co-operate, rest, stay put. I've seen Cornelius about town off and on all spring. Baseball, things like that. Staggering around half-alive. I saw him yesterday, sitting along the road out by his place. Today, a hemorrhage. He was asking for . . . "

Cress sprang to her feet, interrupting her father. "You mustn't say that. You have no right to say that." She pulled the daisies from the neck of her halter and passed them from hand to hand distractedly. "You don't have any idea what it's like to be dying. Do you?" she insisted.

Mr. Delahanty agreed instantly. "No, I don't, Crescent. The worst I ever had was a touch of shingles."

"Don't be funny," Cress said, her chin quivering. "Don't be funny about death. How can you understand how terrible it is for Mr. Cornelius to think he may die, no matter how much he takes care of himself? And that if he doesn't go out and see the sunshine and people and trees today he may never see them again. Never, never. And you were never a great athlete like Mr. Cornelius, so it's a thousand times worse for him than it would be for you to stay in bed. And you blame him. You blame him for not giving in. You blame him—" She paused, trying to steady her voice. "I hate—I hate *people* who say cruel things like that." She looked at her father and Mr. Delahanty looked back. Then she dropped her daisies onto her plate amidst the uneaten salmon and beets and ran from the room.

Mrs. Delahanty, after the sound of the slammed door had stopped echoing, leaned over and began to gather up the daisies. The two girls excused themselves and left the room.

"What did I say?" Mr. Delahanty asked. "To cause all that?"

Mrs. Delahanty continued without speaking to shake bits of food from the flowers. "Gertrude, did what I said sound cruel and hateful to you?"

"No, John, not to me," she answered. "But then I'm not in love with Mr. Cornelius."

In her bedroom, Cress sat on the floor, her head on the window sill. When she felt an arm about her shoulders, Jo's by the weight and pressure, she said, "Go away, please go away and leave me alone." The arm remained where it was. Jo knew, and so did Bernadine. Not much, because there wasn't much to know, except that she had seen Mr. Cornelius three times to look at him and had spoken to him twice and that she loved him and would willingly die for him.

There was "not much to know" in what was called the outside world; but inside herself, in her dreams and imaginings there was nothing *but* Mr. Cornelius. She had decided out of her experience of loving Mr. Cornelius that the knowledge people had of one another, parents of children, anyway, was almost nothing. She could sit at the dinner table with her father and mother, answering their questions about school, but being in reality thousands of miles away in some hot dry land nursing Mr. Cornelius back to health; and her father and mother never noticed her absence in the least.

In her dreams she and Mr. Cornelius sometimes went away together, Mr. Cornelius saying, "Cress, without knowing it I have been searching for you all of my life. My sickness is no more than the sum of my disappointment, and without you I can never get well."

Sometimes in her dreams Mrs. Cornelius came to her and the gist of what she said was, "My life with Mr. Cornelius has been a failure. He has not many months to live. I do not want to stand between him and his happiness in the little time that is left. Go, with my blessing."

But for the most part Mrs. Cornelius and the Cornelius boys did not exist in her dreams; even the world, as she knew it in what was called "real life," was greatly altered; or, perhaps, simplified. Changed, anyway, so that it consisted of nothing but sunshine, a background of sand or water, and a grassy or sandy bank against which Mr. Cornelius reclined, getting well. And as he got well she waited on him, and talked to him. As a matter of fact, every thought in her mind had become part of an unending monologue directed toward the omnipresent mental image of Mr. Cornelius. Everything she saw immediately became words in a report to Mr. Cornelius; and if, by chance, some experience was so absorbing as to momentarily obscure his image, she made up for it by living the whole scene through once again just for him. Sometimes she imagined that Mr. Cornelius kissed her. She had to be careful about these imaginings however. She had never been kissed, family didn't count, of course, and since she supposed that when you were kissed by the man you loved, the sensations were near to swooning, swooning was what she nearly did whenever she had imaginings of this kind.

Most often she simply helped Mr. Cornelius as he reclined in the midst of the sunny simplified landscape, his thin beautiful face becoming tanned and fuller as his health improved; but not more beautiful. That was impossible. She doted on his hawk-nose and dark crest; she dismissed every other face she saw as pudgy and ill-shaped by comparison. In her dream she picked flowers for Mr. Cornelius, went to the library for him, read to him, smoothed his brow, sometimes kissed him and always, always gazed at him with enraptured eyes. But all the time she was imagining this life with Mr. Cornelius she suffered, because Mr. Cornelius was dying and there was nothing she could do about it; she suffered because she had feelings which she did not know how to express, suffered because she had put the core of her life outside its circumference.

She sat up, and Jo took her arm away. It was still light enough to see Bernadine on the floor leaning against the bed, and Jo by her side. The pitcher of white stock on her desk reflected what light there was, like a moon. The room was quiet and warm and full of misery.

"There is nothing you can do, Cress," Jo said. "You love him and he is dying. You can't do anything about either one. All you can do is to endure it."

"I can do something," Cress said.

"What?" Jo asked.

"I can go to Mr. Cornelius and tell him I love him."

"Oh no," Bernadine said, very shocked. "You can't do that."

"Why not?" Cress asked.

"You don't know whether he loves you or not."

"What does that have to do with it? I'm not going to him to ask him if he loves me. I'm going to tell him that I love him."

"Is that what you really want to do, Cress?" Jo asked.

"No—if you mean by want to, do I feel good about going. I feel awful about going. It makes me feel sick to my stomach to even think about it. It gives me the shakes."

Jo once again put an arm around Cress's shoulders. "It's a fact," she reported to Bernadine. "She's shaking like a leaf."

"Look, Cress," Bernadine said. "I'm almost married myself. It's just a matter of days. For all practical purposes I *am* married. You must think of Mr. Cornelius, Cress, and what he'd feel. I know if Howie was sick and maybe dying he wouldn't want some other woman coming to his sick bed and saying, 'I love you.' The first thing he'd do, I know, is say to me, 'Bernadine, throw this madwoman out.' And that's exactly what Mr. Cornelius is liable to say to you."

"I know it," Cress said bleakly.

"Well, then?" Bernadine asked, pride of reasoning in her voice. "Are you still going?"

Cress huddled silent, unanswering.

"It's probably not a very kind thing to do," Jo suggested in her deep, thoughtful voice. "Go to see him now when he's so sick."

"Oh I *know* that. If I just asked myself what was kind I would never do it. But what has kindness got to do with love? I'm not doing it to be kind to Mr. Cornelius. I'm doing it because I have to."

"Have to?" Jo reminded her, steadily. "You don't have to. Sit right here. Sit still. By morning everything will be different."

"By morning Mr. Cornelius may be dead."

"Well then," Bernadine said, "all your problems will be over. Mr. Cornelius will be dead and you'll be sad. But you won't have bothered him or made a fool of yourself."

"I don't care about making a fool of myself."

"You do care. You're still shaking. And think about Mrs. Cornelius. How's she going to feel about someone barging in on her sick husband, making passionate declarations of love?"

"It wouldn't be passionate. I would just say, very quietly, the minute I got there, 'I love you, Mr. Cornelius.' Then leave."

"Cress," Bernadine said, "what actually do you see yourself doing? You get there, the whole family is around the bed, and doctors and priests too, maybe. What are your plans? To say 'I beg your pardon but I've a little message for Mr. Cornelius'? Then push your way through them all to the bedside, drop on your knee, kiss his wasted hand and say, 'Mr. Cornelius, I love you.' Is that it?"

"Oh, don't heckle her, Bernadine," Jo said.

"What I see myself doing," said Cress, "is telling Mr. Cornelius something I have to tell him."

"How," asked Bernadine, "do you see yourself getting there?" Bernadine had Howie's car while he was in the army and she had driven the girls home from school. "Do you see yourself walking eight miles?"

"If I have to," Cress said.

"O.K.," Bernadine told her. "I'll drive you. And let's go right away and get it over with."

Mr. Cornelius was still living in the small one-room tent-house at the edge of the walnut grove in which his home stood. Here he was away from the noises of his family and was able to get the fresh air he needed. It was nine o'clock when Bernadine stopped the car in front of the Cornelius ranch. A dim light was burning inside the tent-house, but there was nothing to indicate the presence of the crowd of people she had prophesied. "Here we are," she said, turning off the engine.

Cress wished for any catastrophe, however great, which would prevent her from having to leave the car. She felt real hatred for Bernadine and Jo. Why, if they were convinced that she shouldn't come, hadn't they remained steadfast? What kind of friends were they, to give way to their better judgment so weakly? And what were her parents thinking about? Why had they permitted her to go riding off into the night? To tell a strange man she loved him? True, she hadn't told them where she was going nor that she loved a strange man. But what were parents for if not to understand without being told? She blamed them for her fright and unhappiness.

Still anything that *happened* would be better than continuing to live in a make-believe world in which she only dreamed that she told Mr. Cornelius she loved him. And she knew that if Bernadine were to start the car now she would jump out and run toward the tent-house and the declaration which would start her to living inside her dream. She opened the car door and stepped out into the night air which, after the warmth of the car, was damp and cold against her bare legs and arms.

"Cheerio," said Bernadine quite calmly as she was walking away from the car under the dark canopy of the big trees toward the dimly lighted room. Why was it so hard to do what she had set her heart on doing?

She stood at the screened door looking into the room as into a picture. Why did it seem like a picture? The small number of furnishings? Their neat arrangement, dresser balanced by table, chair by bed? The light falling from a bulb, shaded by blue paper, so that part of the room was in deep shadow? But most of all, was it picture-like because she had imagined the room and Mr. Cornelius for so long, that a frame had grown up about them in her mind? Now, would it be possible to break that frame? She opened the screen door, stepped into the room and became a part of the picture by that easy act.

Mr. Cornelius lay on a high narrow bed. He lay very straight, his head supported by three or four pillows and his hands folded across an ice pack which he held to his chest. His eyes were closed and his face, in spite of his illness, was warm with color. At the sight of him all of Cress's doubts left her. Oh Mr. Cornelius, she thought, I do truly love you and I have come at last to tell you.

Without opening his eyes Mr. Cornelius said, "Joyce, I think I'm going to be sick."

Joyce. Cress was surprised at the name. It seemed too gentle for the bus driver. "It's not Joyce, Mr. Cornelius," Cress said. "It's me."

Then Mr. Cornelius opened his eyes and Cress was enchanted all over again by the enormous blaze of being alive and searching and understanding which she saw there.

"It's Cress," he said, in a very low careful voice, "the track-meet girl." Then he closed his eyes. "I'm going to be sick," he said. "Hand me the basin."

The basin, Cress saw, was an enamel wash bowl on the night stand by the bed. She got it, put it on the bed beside Mr. Cornelius.

"Help me," Mr. Cornelius said and Cress helped him the way her mother had helped her when she was sick after her tonsils were out, by putting an arm around his shoulders and supporting him.

"Don't be scared," Mr. Cornelius whispered. "It's not a hemorrhage. I'm just going to lose my supper."

He did and afterwards he lay back against his pillows for a minute or two, then he reached up his hand and rang the bell which was suspended from the headboard of his bed.

"A glass of water," he told Cress, and Cress was holding it for him to rinse his mouth when Mrs. Cornelius arrived. Mrs. Cornelius paid no more attention to her than if she'd been some kind of device to help Mr. Cornelius—like the ice pack or the bell. She took the glass from Cress's hand, slipped her arm around her husband's shoulders and said,

"Frank, Frank. Oh thank God, Frank, no more blood. Just your supper and that doesn't matter. I made you eat too much. This was to be expected. If you can swallow a bite or two later I'll fix you another. How do you feel now, honey?"

Cress had backed away from the bed. Mrs. Cornelius was wearing a housecoat or dressing gown of deep red, lightened by wreaths of tiny yellow and white flowers. What she looked like now was not a General in the Russian army but Robert Louis Stevenson's wife, "trusty, dusky, vivid and true with eyes of gold and bramble dew." Her bosom, which had spoiled the lines of her chauffeur's coat, was exactly right for pillowing an invalid's head, and her chestnut hair, curled corkscrew crisp, said "Never give up," as plain as any words, said "Fight on," said "Defy the universe." And all the time she was cradling Mr. Cornelius in her arms, and helping him rinse his mouth she was pressing her cheek to his hair and speaking comforting words through which there ran a mixture of laughing and joking.

"Take this to the bathroom and empty it," she said to Cress when Mr. Cornelius had finished rinsing his mouth. She handed the basin to Cress and nodded toward a door at the back of the room. Cress, ordinarily too squeamish to pull off her own Band-Aids, marched away with it without a word.

When she returned Mr. Cornelius was once more against his pillows and Mrs. Cornelius was wiping his face with a damp cloth.

"Where'd you come from?" she asked Cress as she took the basin from her.

"From out there," Cress said, nodding toward the road. "The girls are waiting for me. In the car," she explained.

Mrs. Cornelius paused in her washing. "What did you come *for?*" she asked.

Cress welcomed the question. It was a wonderful help, like the upward spring of the diving board against her feet when she was reluctant to take off into deep water. Though she no longer had so great a need to say what she had come to say, some change had taken place in her since she had come into the room; what had been locked inside her and had been painful, because unsaid, had somehow, without a word being spoken, gotten itself partially expressed. She was not sure how. Nevertheless she had come to speak certain words. They were the answer to Mrs. Cornelius' question. They were *why* she had come.

So, louder than was necessary, and in a voice cracking with strain she said, "I came to tell Mr. Cornelius I loved him." Then she turned, resolutely, and said the words directly to Mr. Cornelius. "Mr. Cornelius, I love you."

At that Mrs. Cornelius laughed, not jeering, not angry, not unbelieving, but in the soft delighted way of a person who has received an unexpected gift, a pleasure never dreamed of but one come in the nick of time and most acceptable.

"Oh, Frankie," she said, running her hand through Mr. Cornelius' thick black hair, "look at what we've got here."

"What we've got," was what she'd said as if, Cress thought, I'd said I loved them both. And then, watching Mr. Cornelius reach for his wife's hand, she saw that there was nothing she could give to Mr. Cornelius without giving it also to Mrs. Cornelius. Because they were not two separated people. They were really one, the way the Bible said. It was an astounding discovery. It was almost too much for her. It held her motionless and speculating. She felt as if her mind, by an infusion of light and warmth, was being forced to expand to accommodate this new idea. And it was an idea which, contrary to all her expectations, she liked. It was exactly what she wanted. Not Mr. Cornelius alone on a stretch of desert sand and she kissing his wasted hand—in spite of her six months' dreaming. What she wanted was Mr. and Mrs. Cornelius. She was so happy for Mrs. Cornelius' presence she almost took and kissed *her* plump brown unwasted hand.

Mrs. Cornelius, however, was continuing her laughing murmur to her husband. "Frankie," she said, "oh Frankie, you old jackanapes. You old irresistible. What's all this talk about being on your last legs? Done for? Caved in? With school girls coming with professions of love? Pretty school girls. Boy, we're not cashing in our checks just yet. Not us. What's your name, dear?" she asked Cress.

Mr. Cornelius answered in his low half-whispering voice. "She's John Delahanty's daughter, Crescent. They call her Cress at school."

"Well," said Mrs. Cornelius. "I've heard the boys mention you. Where'd you see Frank?"

"At a track meet."

"I stared at her some," Mr. Cornelius said. "Reminded me of you at her age. So alive."

"Was I ever like that?" Mrs. Cornelius asked her husband.

"That's what *I* thought about Mr. Cornelius," Cress said.

"Alive?" asked Mrs. Cornelius.

"Oh yes. More than anyone there. More than the boys. I thought his eyes fed on the sights," she said, daring the poetry of her thoughts.

"Fed?" Mrs. Cornelius studied the word then accepted it. "I see what you mean. Now, Frank," she said, "will you lie still and take care of yourself? Unknown school girls loving you and wanting you to get well. You do, don't you?" she asked Cress.

"Oh yes," Cress said. "I was willing to die for him."

Her voice evidently convinced Mrs. Cornelius. "Oh, Frank," she said, "school girls willing to die for you and you not half trying."

"Mrs. Cornelius," Cress said, wanting, since even partial confession made her feel so much better, to tell everything, "I ought to tell you something else." She stumbled for words. "I ought to tell you what else I planned."

"I bet you planned to run away with Frank and nurse him back to health."

Cress was amazed. "Yes," she said, her face burning with guilt and foolishness, "yes I did. How did you know?"

"Oh Frank, don't it bring it all back to you? No wonder you were reminded of me. *I* was going to run away with the minister," she said, turning to Cress. "Save him from his wife and family. And he *was* the most beautiful man in the world, Frank. You can't hold a candle to your father—never could."

Cress wanted to say something, but she couldn't settle on what. She had too many emotions to express. Exhilaration at being released from the isolation of her dreaming; relief to find that other girls had loved secretly too, but most of all joy to have acted, to have made for herself a single undivided world in which to live.

"Oh Mrs. Cornelius," she said, "oh Mrs. Cornelius . . ."

"Cress," asked Mrs. Cornelius, "can you play cards? Or checkers?"

"Yes," Cress said, "I can. I like to."

"And read out loud? Of course you can do that, can't you? Why don't you come read to Frank? And play cards with him? It gets so darn lonesome for him. I work. The boys work, and besides they haven't got enough patience to sit still. And the good people come in and tell Frank how their uncles or mothers passed away with consumption and for him to be resigned. He needs somebody interested in living, not dying. Would you come?"

"Oh yes. If you want me—if he wants me. I could come every day all summer."

"O.K.," Mrs. Cornelius said, "we'll plan on it. Now you'd better run on. Frank's had a bad day. He's worn out."

Cress looked at Mr. Cornelius. His eyes were closed but he opened them at Mrs. Cornelius' words and made a good-by flicker with the lids.

"Good night," Cress said.

Mrs. Cornelius went to the door with her. "We'll count on you," she said once again and put a hand on Cress's shoulder and gave her a kind of humorous loving shake before she turned away.

Cress flew to the car propelled, it seemed, by the beat of her heart as a bird is propelled by the beat of its wings. The walnut leaves were alive and fluttering in the warm air and all about her mockingbirds were singing like nightingales. As she emerged from the grove she saw the June stars big and heavy-looking like June roses. This is the happiest hour of my life, she thought, and she yearned to do something lovely for the girls, something beautiful and memorable; but all she could think of was to ask them to go to town for milk shakes.

"I could stand some food," Bernadine said, "after all that waiting."

"He was sick," Cress explained, "and Mrs. Cornelius and I had to take care of him."

"Mrs. Cornelius? Did she come out?"

"Of course," Cress answered. "Wouldn't you, if Howie was sick?"

Bernadine had no answer to this. She started the car and after they had gone a mile or so Jo asked, "Did you tell him?"

"Of course."

"Does he love you?" Bernadine asked.

Cress felt sorry for Bernadine. "You're a fine one to be getting married," she said. "Of course he doesn't. He loves Joyce."

"Joyce? Who's Joyce?"

"Mrs. Cornelius. I remind him some of her. I adore Mrs. Cornelius. She is like Mrs. Robert Louis Stevenson and *they* are one person. Mr. and Mrs. Cornelius, I mean. They are truly married. I don't suppose you understand," she said, arrogant with new knowledge, "but what is for the one is for the other. I am going to help her take care of him this summer. Isn't that wonderful? Maybe I can really help him get well. Isn't this the most gloriously beautiful night? Oh, I think it's the most significant night of my life." The two girls were silent, but Cress was too full of her own emotions to notice.

When they went into the soda fountain, she looked at their reflection in the mirror and liked what she saw. The three of them had always been proud of one another. Bernadine had glamour, Jo character, and Cress personality; that was the division they made of themselves. "Look at Bernadine, listen to Cress, and let Jo act," someone had said. Oh, but I've broken through that, Cress thought, I can act, too. She searched for some understanding of the part Mrs. Cornelius had played in that breakthrough. If she had said, "You wicked girl," or made her feel that loving was a terrible thing, would she have been pushed back, fearful, into the narrowness of dreaming, and into dreaming's untruths? She didn't know. She couldn't hold her mind to such abstractions.

"What we want," she said to Lester Riggins, the boy at the fountain, "is simply the most stupendous, colossal, overpowering concoction you ever served."

"This is a special night?" Lester asked.

"Super-special."

"How come?"

"Bernadine's going to be married."

"Known that for six months."

"Jo's been accepted for Stanford. With special praise."

"Old stuff."

"Then there's me."

"What about you?"

"I'm alive."

"That's different," Lester said. "Why didn't you tell me in the first place? How do you like it?"

"Being alive? Fine," said Cress. "Better than shooting stars."

"O.K., O.K.," Lester said. "This obviously merits the Riggins' special. Expense any issue?"

"No issue," Cress said.

He brought them something shaped, roughly, like the Eiffel Tower, but more dramatically colored.

"Here it is, girls. Here's to being alive!"

They sank their spoons in it and ate it down, their appetites equal to the whole of it, color, size, sweetness and multiplicity of ingredients.

Reading for Understanding

Main Idea

1. The main idea of the story can best be summarized by which of the following?
   (a) Teenage girls spend too much time on futile daydreaming.
   (b) What begins as a superficial attraction can deepen into a more mature love.
   (c) Cress's mother fails to understand her deepest needs.
   (d) Life is a challenge, difficult at best.

Details

2. Cress first saw Mr. Cornelius (a) in a school play (b) in a math class (c) in a supermarket (d) at a track meet.

3. The about-to-be married person is (a) Jo (b) Cress (c) Bernardine (d) Joyce.

4. Howie is (a) a groom-to-be (b) Mr. Cornelius's best friend (c) related to Mrs. Delahanty (d) loved by Jo.

5. Before the visit, Cress had spoken to Mr. Cornelius (a) once (b) twice (c) three times (d) frequently.

6. Mrs. Cornelius (a) scolded Cress for her foolishness (b) tended to be pessimistic about her husband's illness (c) expected Cress's visit (d) put Cress to work.

7. Cress was driven to the Cornelius house by (a) Bernardine (b) Jo (c) Mr. Delahanty (d) Mrs. Delahanty.

Inferences

8. At the dinner table, the girls didn't take part in the adults' conversation because (a) they were totally absorbed in their own interests (b) they were all excited about the coming marriage (c) Jo and Bernardine had all the latest information about Mr. Cornelius's illness (d) the evening was hot and stifling.

9. The one who may have understood Cress best was (a) Jo (b) Bernardine (c) Mrs. Delahanty (d) Mr. Delahanty.

10. Mr. Delahanty made a tactical error in (a) not allowing Cress to drive (b) criticising the custard pudding (c) blaming Mr. Cornelius for his serious plight (d) urging the girls to eat.

11. Joyce was able to take matters in stride because of (a) Cress's reputation as a good nurse (b) Mr. Cornelius's request (c) her downbeat attitude toward Mr. Cornelius (d) the maturity of her love for her husband.

Author's Attitude

12. The attitude of the author toward Cress's love is one of (a) amazement (b) sympathy (c) criticism (d) indifference.

Outcome

13. After the events in the story, Cress probably (a) followed through on her promise (b) went away on vacation (c) decided not to attend the coming wedding (d) had a disagreement with Mrs. Cornelius.

Order of Events

14. Arrange the items in the order in which they occurred. Use letters only.
    A. Cress enters the Cornelius house.
    B. Cress promises to help all summer.
    C. Cress blows up at her father.

D. Mr. Delahanty mentions Mr. Cornelius's condition.

E. Cress decides to visit Mr. Cornelius.

Fact or Opinion

Tell whether the following is a fact or an opinion.

15. Cress's infatuation with Mr. Cornelius was immature.

Words in Context

1. "She pulled the daisies from the neck of her halter and passed them from hand to hand *distractedly*." **Distractedly** (188) means (a) absent-mindedly (b) anxiously (c) quickly (d) angrily.

2. "Sometimes in her dreams Mrs. Cornelius came to her and the *gist* of what she said was, 'My life with Mr. Cornelius has been a failure.' " **Gist** (189) means (a) substance (b) hope (c) heartbreak (d) disagreement.

3. "If, by chance, some experience was so absorbing as to momentarily *obscure* his image, she made up for it by living the whole scene through once again just for him." **Obscure** (189) means (a) enhance (b) replace (c) paint (d) conceal.

4. "She felt as if her mind, by an *infusion* of light and warmth, was being forced to expand to accommodate this new idea." **Infusion** (194) means (a) rejection (b) awareness (c) replacement (d) saturation.

5. "*Exhilaration* at being released from the isolation of her dreaming." **Exhilaration** (195) means (a) irritation (b) surprise (c) negative arousal (d) joy.

Thinking Critically about the Story

1. Coming-of-age is a commonplace expression. Sometimes it has a legal force: "Upon the person's coming-of-age, he/she will become heir to the . . . fortune." Sometimes, it has a less material force: a turning point, a moment that starts a person on the road to maturity. "Mr.

Cornelius, I Love You" is a story with a turning point. At the beginning of the story, Cress is a self-obsessed teenager, concerned only
with her own life and feelings. At the end, she is becoming a mature
young woman, realistically evaluating her own emotions and the emotions of those who surround her. The selfish self-centeredness has been
replaced by something finer. At what point does the turning point occur? Explain.

2. Who, in your opinion, is the hero or heroine of the story? Why did
   you choose this person?

3. Is the relationship between Cress and her parents realistically portrayed? Give examples to prove your point.

4. The girls are alike in many ways, but also profoundly different.
   Choose Bernardine, Jo, or Cress and provide a thumbnail sketch of
   the one you choose.

5. Do some people enjoy misery? Though in good health, they rarely
   smile or take an upbeat attitude. What satisfaction does a feeling of
   gloom provide for such people?

6. What is Mr. Cornelius's attitude toward Cress?

7. Does Cress show the same attitudes as a modern groupie who
   swoons for a singer or other celebrity?

8. Is puppy love between two young people different from the crush
   that young people sometimes develop toward an adult? Explain.

9. The role of mental attitude in the treatment of disease is an oft-ar-
   gued one. How do you feel? Is Mrs. Cornelius's approach to the
   illness a sound one? Explain.

10. "Cress was too full of her own emotions to notice." (196) Does this
    sentence suggest that Cress's road to maturity still stretches on? Is
    true maturity ever attained?

11. At one point, Jo says, "If puddings be the food of love, cook on."
    This is an adaptation of lines from Shakespeare's *Twelth Night*. Is Jo
    showing off or merely expressing momentary joy? Explain.

Language in Action

When Sound Fits the Sense

"Mrs. Cornelius, however, was continuing her laughing murmur
to her husband."

If you close your eyes and whisper *murmur*, you will notice that the sound of the word *murmur* fits its definition. An oft-quoted pair of lines by Tennyson is a prime example of the marriage of sound and sense:

> The moan of doves in immemorial elms,
> And murmuring of innumerable bees.

Mean, immemorial, murmuring, innumerable—all the words provide music as well as meaning.

Onomatopoeia is the use of words that by their sounds imitate or suggest their meaning. (See also page 471.) You use onomatopoeia every time you say that soda *fizzes*, fire *crackles*, dishes *clatter*, a fly *buzzes*. Here's a sampling of other onomatopoeic words you use: *bang, boom, blubber, bubble, clank, click, crash, honk, hum, purr, rattle, snap, squeak, thud, twitter, zip, zoom.*

For those poets who would use the language effectively, Alexander Pope, 18th-century poet, has the following advice:

> 'Tis not enough no harshness gives offense,
> The sound must seem an echo to the sense;
> Soft is the strain when Zephyr gently blows,
> And the smooth stream in smoother numbers flows;
> But when the loud surges lash the sounding shore,
> The hoarse, rough verse should like the torrent roar.

Contrast the soft, quiet tone of lines 3 and 4 with the roaring sound of lines 5 and 6.

Feuille d'Album

Katherine Mansfield
British

Don't let the title frighten you. It means **Album Leaf** or **Page** and suggests a series of snapshots. Here, the events center on Ian French, a desperately shy painter. Not unattractive, he arouses the interest of many women, but French is blind to their charms. Then, one day, he sees, across the way, **the** girl. Like Harry in "The Girl on the Bus," French romanticizes his neighbor and devises ways to meet her. Like Harry, he sometimes despairs, but he keeps hoping. Then one day he has an opportunity. How he chooses to meet the girl is one of the strangest meetings in literature.

Feuille d'Album

He really was an impossible person. Too shy altogether. With absolutely nothing to say for himself. And such a weight. Once he was in your studio he never knew when to go, but would sit on and on until you nearly screamed, and burned to throw something enormous after him when he did finally blush his way out—something like the tortoise stove. The strange thing was that at first sight he looked most interesting. Everybody agreed about that. You would drift into the café one evening and there you would see, sitting in a corner, with a glass of coffee in front of him, a thin, dark boy, wearing a blue jersey with a little grey flannel jacket buttoned over it. And somehow that blue jersey and the grey jacket with the sleeves that were too short gave him the air of a boy that has made up his mind to run away to sea. Who has run away, in fact, and will get up in a moment and sling a knotted handkerchief containing his nightshirt and his mother's picture on the end of a stick, and walk out into the night and be drowned. . . . Stumble over the wharf edge on his way to the ship, even. . . . He had black close-cropped hair, grey eyes with long lashes, white cheeks and a mouth pouting as though he were determined not to cry. . . . How could one resist him? Oh, one's heart was wrung at sight. And, as if that were not enough, there was his trick of blushing. . . . Whenever the waiter came near him he turned crimson—he might have been just out of prison and the waiter in the know. . . .

"Who is he, my dear? Do you know?"

"Yes. His name is Ian French. Painter. Awfully clever, they say. Someone started by giving him a mother's tender care. She asked him how often he heard from home, whether he had enough blankets on his bed, how much milk he drank a day. But when she went round to his studio to give an eye to his socks, she rang and rang, and though she could have sworn she heard someone breathing inside, the door was not answered. . . . Hopeless!"

Someone else decided that he ought to fall in love. She summoned him to her side, called him "boy," leaned over him so that he might smell the enchanting perfume of her hair, took his arm, told him how marvellous life could be if one only had the courage, and went round to his studio one evening and rang and rang. . . . Hopeless.

"What the poor boy really wants is thoroughly rousing," said a third. So off they went to cafés and cabarets, little dances, places where you drank something that tasted like tinned apricot juice, but cost twenty-seven shillings a bottle and was called champagne, other places, too thrilling for words, where you sat in the most awful gloom, and where some one had always been shot the night before. But he did not turn a hair. Only once he got very drunk, but instead of blossoming forth, there he sat, stony, with two spots of red on his cheeks, like, my dear, yes, the dead image of that ragtime thing they were playing, like a "Broken Doll." But when she took him back to his studio he had quite recovered, and said "good night" to her in the street below, as though they had walked home from church together. . . . Hopeless.

After heaven knows how many more attempts—for the spirit of kindness dies very hard in women—they gave him up. Of course, they were still perfectly charming, and asked him to their shows, and spoke to him in the cafe, but that was all. When one is an artist one has no time simply for people who won't respond. Has one?

"And besides I really think there must be something rather fishy somewhere . . . don't you? It can't all be as innocent as it looks! Why come to Paris if you want to be a daisy in the field? No, I'm not suspicious. But——"

He lived at the top of a tall mournful building overlooking the river. One of those buildings that look so romantic on rainy nights and moonlight nights, when the shutters are shut, and the heavy door, and the sign advertising "a little apartment to let immediately" gleams forlorn beyond words. One of those buildings that smell so unromantic all the year round, and where the concierge* lives in a glass cage on the ground floor, wrapped up in a filthy shawl, stirring something in a saucepan and ladling out tit-bits to the swollen old dog lolling on a bed cushion. . . . Perched up in the air the studio had a wonderful view. The two big windows faced the water; he could see the boats and the barges swinging up and down, and the fringe of an island planted with trees, like a round bouquet. The side window looked across to another house, shabbier still and smaller, and down below there was a flower market. You could see the tops of huge umbrellas, with frills of bright flowers escaping from them, booths covered with striped awning where they sold plants in boxes and clumps of wet gleaming palms in terra cotta jars. Among the flowers the old women scuttled from side to side like crabs. Really there was no need for him to go out. If he sat at the window until his white beard fell over the sill he still would have found something to draw . . . .

How surprised those tender women would have been if they had managed to force the door. For he kept his studio as neat as a pin. Everything was arranged to form a pattern, a little "still life" as it were—the saucepans with their lids on the wall behind the gas stove, the bowl of eggs, milk jug and teapot on the shelf, the books and the lamp with the crinkly paper shade on the table. An Indian curtain that had a fringe of red leopards marching round it covered his bed by day, and on the wall beside the bed on a level with your eyes when you were lying down there was a small neatly printed notice: GET UP AT ONCE.

Every day was much the same. While the light was good he slaved at his painting, then cooked his meals and tidied up the place. And in the evenings he went off to the café, or sat at home reading or making out the most complicated list of expenses headed: "What I ought to be able to do it on," and ending with a sworn statement . . . "I swear not to exceed this amount for next month. Signed, Ian French."

Nothing very fishy about this; but those far-seeing women were quite right. It wasn't all.

One evening he was sitting at the side window eating some prunes and throwing the stones on to the tops of the huge umbrellas in the deserted flower market. It had been raining—the first real spring rain of the year had fallen—a bright spangle hung on everything, and the air smelled of buds and moist earth. Many voices sounding languid and content rang out in the dusky air, and the people who had come to close their windows and fasten the shutters leaned out instead. Down below in the market the trees were peppered with new green. What kind of trees were they? he wondered. And now came the lamplighter. He stared at the

---

*building superintendent

house across the way, the small, shabby house, and suddenly, as if in answer to his gaze, two wings of windows opened and a girl came out on to the tiny balcony carrying a pot of daffodils. She was a strangely thin girl in a dark pinafore, with a pink handkerchief tied over her hair. Her sleeves were rolled up almost to her shoulders and her slender arms shone against the dark stuff.

"Yes, it is quite warm enough. It will do them good," she said, putting down the pot and turning to some one in the room inside. As she turned she put her hands up to the handkerchief and tucked away some wisps of hair. She looked down at the deserted market and up at the sky, but where he sat there might have been a hollow in the air. She simply did not see the house opposite. And then she disappeared.

His heart fell out of the side window of his studio, and down to the balcony of the house opposite—buried itself in the pot of daffodils under the half-opened buds and spears of green. . . . That room with the balcony was the sitting-room, and the one next door to it was the kitchen. He heard the clatter of the dishes as she washed up after supper, and then she came to the window, knocked a little mop against the ledge, and hung it on a nail to dry. She never sang or unbraided her hair, or held out her arms to the moon as young girls are supposed to do. And she always wore the same dark pinafore and the pink handkerchief over her hair. . . . Whom did she live with? Nobody else came to those two windows, and yet she was always talking to some one in the room. Her mother, he decided, was an invalid. They took in sewing. The father was dead. . . . He had been a journalist—very pale, with long moustaches, and a piece of black hair falling over his forehead.

By working all day they just made enough money to live on, but they never went out and they had no friends. Now when he sat down at his table he had to make an entirely new set of sworn statements. . . . Not to go to the side window before a certain hour: signed, Ian French. Not to think about her until he had put away his painting things for the day: signed, Ian French.

It was quite simple. She was the only person he really wanted to know, because she was, he decided, the only other person alive who was just his age. He couldn't stand giggling girls, and he had no use for grown-up women. . . . She was his age, she was—well, just like him. He sat in his dusky studio, tired, with one arm hanging over the back of his chair, staring in at her window and seeing himself in there with her. She had a violent temper; they quarrelled terribly at times, he and she. She had a way of stamping her foot and twisting her hands in her pinafore . . . furious. And she very rarely laughed. Only when she told him about an absurd little kitten she once had who used to roar and pretend to be a lion when it was given meat to eat. Things like that made her laugh. . . . But as a rule they sat together very quietly; he, just as he was sitting now, and she with her hands folded in her lap and her feet tucked under, talking in low tones, or silent and tired after the day's work. Of course, she never asked him about his pictures, and of course he made the most wonderful drawings of her which she hated, because he made her so thin and so dark. . . . But how could he get to know her? This might go on for years. . . .

Then he discovered that once a week, in the evenings, she went out shopping. On two successive Thursdays she came to the window wearing an old-fashioned cape over the pinafore, and carrying a basket. From where he sat he could not see the door of her house, but on the next Thursday evening at the same time he snatched up his cap and ran down the stairs. There was a lovely pink light over everything. He saw it glowing in the river, and the people walking towards him had pink faces and pink hands.

He leaned against the side of his house waiting for her and he had no idea of what he was going to do or say. "Here she comes," said a voice in his head. She walked very quickly, with small, light steps; with one hand she carried the basket, with the other she kept the cape together. . . . What could he do? He could only follow. . . . First she went into the grocer's and spent a long time in there, and then she went into the butcher's where she had to wait her turn. Then she was an age at the draper's matching something, and then she went to the fruit shop and bought a lemon. As he watched her he knew more surely than ever he must get to know her, now. Her composure, her seriousness and her loneliness, the very way she walked as though she was eager to be done with this world of grown-ups all was so natural to him and so inevitable.

"Yes, she is always like that," he thought proudly. "We have nothing to do with these people."

But now she was on her way home and he was as far off as ever. . . . She suddenly turned into the dairy and he saw her through the window buying an egg. She picked it out of the basket with such care—a brown one, a beautifully shaped one, the one he would have chosen. And when she came out of the dairy he went in after her. In a moment he was out again, and following her past his house across the flower market, dodging among the huge umbrellas and treading on the fallen flowers and the round marks where the pots had stood. . . . Through her door he crept, and up the stairs after, taking care to tread in time with her so that she should not notice. Finally, she stopped on the landing, and took the key out of her purse. As she put it into the door he ran up and faced her.

Blushing more crimson than ever, but looking at her severely he said, almost angrily: "Excuse me, Mademoiselle, you dropped this."

And he handed her an egg.

Reading for Understanding

Main Idea

1. The main thread of the story is (a) advice on how to meet new people (b) the place of art in determining a man's personality (c) a man's attempt to overcome a desperate shyness (d) the negative side of neatness.

Details

2. French's appearance in the cafe reminded some customers of a (a) successful writer (b) seaman (c) waiter (d) sculptor.

3. The major attraction of French's apartment was its (a) spaciousness (b) convenience (c) closeness to transportation (d) view.

4. French did his painting mostly (a) in the morning (b) after dinner (c) at the cafe (d) on weekends.

5. In his daydreams, the girl (a) had an invalid mother (b) took in laundry (c) was a journalist (d) lived with her grandparents.

6. The girl's shopping trips occurred (a) on Tuesdays (b) when she was out of cheese (c) once a week (d) when she knew French would be at the store.

Inferences

7. French's appearance was (a) careless and unattractive (b) frightening (c) strange enough to cause constant scorn (d) pleasant enough to attract women.

8. The terrible quarrels described on page 205 occurred (a) at a cafe (b) in a daydream (c) after French gave his gift (d) over the girl's unchanging outfit.

Outcome

9. After receiving the gift, the girl probably (a) hadn't realized she had dropped the egg (b) gasped in astonishment (c) thanked French warmly (d) told French she had wanted to meet him.

Fact or Opinion

Tell whether the following is a fact or an opinion.

10. French was ridiculous in his associations with women.

Words in Context

1. "Among the flowers the old women *scuttled* from side to side, like crabs." **Scuttled** (204) means (a) shuffled (b) swayed (c) dipped (d) plodded.

2. "Many voices sounding *languid,* and content rang out in the dusky air." **Languid** (204) means (a) forceful (b) bitter (c) loud (d) listless.

3. "Her *composure,* her seriousness and her loneliness, the very way she walked as though she was eager to be done with the world of grown-ups all was so natural to him and so inevitable." **Composure** (206) means (a) frailty (b) appearance (c) curiosity (d) poise.

Thinking Critically about the Story

1. What made various women show an interest in French? What killed that interest?

2. Probably, some of the women who took French under their wing were attractive, even beautiful. Yet the girl that French was attracted to was slender, plainly dressed, apparently not a great beauty. What was there about the girl that appealed to French? Are handsome men sometimes attracted to plain women? Are beautiful women sometimes attracted to plain men? How can such things be? Do movies and television sometimes present inaccurate pictures of man-woman relationships? Explain.

3. What might the girl think when presented with an egg she obviously hadn't dropped? Could the very absurdity have helped French's plan?

4. Does the egg gift suggest French's sense of humor or his desperation?

5. What does buying one egg suggest about the financial means of the girl?

6. What do French's daydreams about his hoped-for life with the girl tell about his personality?

7. Why did the author introduce such an absurd gift instead of a possible gift like a loaf of bread?

8. Sometimes people fall in love with their idea of a person, rather than with a person. Is French's image of the girl likely to reflect the real person? Explain.

Language in Action

The French Contribution

"Feuille d'Album" is French. *Feuille,* the French word for *leaf, page,* has many relatives and ancestors. It is descended from the Latin *folium,* also leaf. The Middle French of centuries ago coined the word *trefeuil,* "Three leafed." The word passed into English as *trefoil,* a three-leafed plant—for example *clover.*

Many *leaf* roots came to English directly from Latin and not through the French. *Foliage,* a combination of *leaves,* is a good example. *Folio,* for *page number,* is another. Note that even in English, a page may be called a *leaf.* We may "*leaf* through a book," turning the pages.

A great many words have come to us through French—for example, *camouflage, chaperon, depot, debutante, fiancée, resume,* and *role.* Language is forever interesting and unpredictable. English has borrowed both *chauffeur* and *garage* from the French. Americans and the British are amusingly different in their pronunciations of these words. Americans use an American pronunciation for *chauffeur* and a French pronunciation for *garage.* The British do the opposite, using a British pronunciation for *garage* and a French pronunciation for *chauffeur.*

See also "The Norman Conquest" (pages 397–398).

The Sojourner

Carson McCullers
American

Elizabeth answered; her familiar voice was a fresh shock to him. Twice he had to repeat his name, but when he was identified, she sounded glad. He explained that he was only in town for that day. They had a theater engagement, she said—but she wondered if he would come by for an early dinner. Ferris said he would be delighted.

The recipe for a successful romance has sometimes been abbreviated to "Boy meets girl. Boy loses girl. Boy gets girl back." Sometimes, though, the third stage is lacking. In this story, John Ferris seizes a moment to see his former wife in her new family situation. The visit is bittersweet.

The title is significant. A sojourner is a temporary resident, one who stays for a short time. Buried in the French origin of the word is the Latin **diurnum—day**. A sojourner "stays for a day" . . . or a brief time. The visit with his wife stirs feelings that John Ferris didn't realize he had, bringing a change in him that might be for the better.

The Sojourner

THE TWILIGHT BORDER between sleep and waking was a Roman one this morning: splashing fountains and arched, narrow streets, the golden lavish city of blossoms and age-soft stone. Sometimes in this semi-consciousness he sojourned again in Paris, or war German rubble, or Swiss skiing and a snow hotel. Sometimes, also, in a fallow Georgia field at hunting dawn. Rome it was this morning in the yearless region of dreams.

John Ferris awoke in a room in a New York hotel. He had the feeling that something unpleasant was awaiting him—what it was, he did not know. The feeling, submerged by matinal necessities, lingered even after he had dressed and gone downstairs. It was a cloudless autumn day and the pale sunlight sliced between the pastel skyscrapers. Ferris went into the next-door drugstore and sat at the end booth next to the window glass that overlooked the sidewalk. He ordered an American breakfast with scrambled eggs and sausage.

Ferris had come from Paris to his father's funeral which had taken place the week before in his home town in Georgia. The shock of death had made him aware of youth already passed. His hair was receding and the veins in his now naked temples were pulsing and prominent and his body was spare except for an incipient belly bulge. Ferris had loved his father and the bond between them had once been extraordinarily close—but the years had somehow unraveled this filial devotion; the death, expected for a long time, had left him with an unforseen dismay. He had stayed as long as possible to be near his mother and brothers at home. His plane for Paris was to leave the next morning.

Ferris pulled out his address book to verify a number. He turned the pages with growing attentiveness. Names and addresses from New York, the capitals of Europe, a few faint ones from his home state in the South. Faded, printed names, sprawled drunken ones. Betty Wills: a random love, married now. Charlie Williams: wounded in the Hürtgen Forest, unheard of since. Grand old Williams—did he live or die? Don Walker: a B.T.O. in television, getting rich. Henry Green: hit the skids after the war, in a sanitarium now, they say. Cozie Hall: he had heard that she was dead. Heedless, laughing Cozie—it was strange to think that she too, silly girl, could die. As Ferris closed the address book, he suffered a sense of hazard, transience, almost of fear.

It was then that his body jerked suddenly. He was staring out of the window when there, on the sidewalk, passing by, was his ex-wife. Elizabeth passed quite close to him, walking slowly. He could not understand the wild quiver of his heart, nor the following sense of recklessness and grace that lingered after she was gone.

Quickly Ferris paid his check and rushed out to the sidewalk. Elizabeth stood on the corner waiting to cross Fifth Avenue. He hurried toward her meaning to speak, but the lights changed and she crossed the street before he reached her. Ferris followed. On the other side he could easily have overtaken her, but he found himself lagging unaccountably. Her fair brown hair was plainly rolled, and as he watched her Ferris recalled that once his father had remarked that Elizabeth had a 'beautiful carriage.' She turned at the next corner and Ferris followed, although by now his intention to overtake her had disappeared. Ferris questioned the bodily disturbance that the sight of Elizabeth aroused in him, the dampness of his hands, the hard heartstrokes.

It was eight years since Ferris had last seen his ex-wife. He knew that long ago she had married again. And there were children. During recent years he had seldom thought of her. But at first, after the divorce, the loss had almost destroyed him. Then after the anodyne of time, he had loved again, and then again. Jeannine, she was now. Certainly his love for his ex-wife was long since past. So why the unhinged body, the shaken mind? He knew only that his clouded heart was oddly dissonant with the sunny, candid autumn day. Ferris wheeled suddenly and, walking with long strides, almost running, hurried back to the hotel.

Ferris poured himself a drink, although it was not yet eleven o'clock. He sprawled out in an armchair like a man exhausted, nursing his glass of bourbon and water. He had a full day ahead of him as he was leaving by plane the next morning for Paris. He checked over his obligations: take luggage to Air France, lunch with his boss, buy shoes and an overcoat. And something—wasn't there something else? Ferris finished his drink and opened the telephone directory.

His decision to call his ex-wife was impulsive. The number was under Bailey, the husband's name, and he called before he had much time for self-debate. He and Elizabeth had exchanged cards at Christmastime, and Ferris had sent a carving set when he received the announcement of her wedding. There was no reason *not* to call. But as he waited, listening to the ring at the other end, misgiving fretted him.

Elizabeth answered; her familiar voice was a fresh shock to him. Twice he had to repeat his name, but when he was identified, she sounded glad. He explained he was only in town for that day. They had a theater engagement, she said—but she wondered if he would come by for an early dinner. Ferris said he would be delighted.

As he went from one engagement to another, he was still bothered at odd moments by the feeling that something necessary was forgotten. Ferris bathed and changed in the late afternoon, often thinking about Jeannine: he would be with her the following night. 'Jeannine,' he would say, 'I happened to run into my ex-wife when I was in New York. Had dinner with her. And her husband, of course. It was strange seeing her after all these years.'

Elizabeth lived in the East Fifties, and as Ferris taxied uptown he glimpsed at intersections the lingering sunset, but by the time he reached his destination it was already autumn dark. The place was a building with a marquee and a doorman, and the apartment was on the seventh floor.

'Come in, Mr. Ferris.'

Braced for Elizabeth or even the unimagined husband, Ferris was astonished by the freckled red-haired child; he had known of the children, but his mind had failed somehow to acknowledge them. Surprise made him step back awkwardly.

'This is our apartment,' the child said politely. 'Aren't you Mr. Ferris? I'm Billy. Come in.'

In the living room beyond the hall, the husband provided another surprise; he too had not been acknowledged emotionally. Bailey was a lumbering red-haired man with a deliberate manner. He rose and extended a welcoming hand.

'I'm Bill Bailey. Glad to see you. Elizabeth will be in, in a minute. She's finishing dressing.'

The last words struck a gliding series of vibrations, memories of the other years. Fair Elizabeth, rosy and naked before her bath. Half-dressed before the mirror of her dressing table, brushing her fine, chestnut hair. Sweet, casual intimacy, the soft-fleshed loveliness indisputably possessed. Ferris shrank from the unbidden memories and compelled himself to meet Bill Bailey's gaze.

'Billy, will you please bring that tray of drinks from the kitchen table?'

The child obeyed promptly, and when he was gone Ferris remarked conversationally, 'Fine boy you have there.'

'We think so.'

Flat silence until the child returned with a tray of glasses and a cocktail shaker of Martinis. With the priming drinks they pumped up conversation: Russia, they spoke of, and the New York rain-making, and the apartment situation in Manhattan and Paris.

'Mr. Ferris is flying all the way across the ocean tomorrow,' Bailey said to the little boy who was perched on the arm of his chair, quiet and well behaved. 'I bet you would like to be a stowaway in his suitcase.'

Billy pushed back his limp bangs. 'I want to fly in an airplane and be a newspaperman like Mr. Ferris.' He added with sudden assurance, 'That's what I would like to do when I am big.'

Bailey said, 'I thought you wanted to be a doctor.'

'I do!' said Billy. 'I would like to be both. I want to be a atom-bomb scientist too.'

Elizabeth came in carrying in her arms a baby girl.

'Oh, John!' she said. She settled the baby in the father's lap. 'It's grand to see you. I'm awfully glad you could come.'

The little girl sat demurely on Bailey's knees. She wore a pale pink crepe de Chine frock, smocked around the yoke with rose, and a matching silk hair ribbon tying back her pale soft curls. Her skin was summer tanned and her brown eyes flecked with gold and laughing. When she reached up and fingered her father's horn-rimmed glasses, he took them off and let her look through them a moment. 'How's my old Candy?'

Elizabeth was very beautiful, more beautiful perhaps than he had ever realized. Her straight clean hair was shining. Her face was softer, glowing and serene. It was a madonna loveliness, dependent on the family ambiance.

'You've hardly changed at all,' Elizabeth said, 'but it has been a long time.'

'Eight years.' His hand touched his thinning hair self-conciously while further amenities were exchanged.

Ferris felt himself suddenly a spectator—an interloper among these Baileys. Why had he come? He suffered. His own life seemed so solitary, a fragile column supporting nothing amidst the wreckage of the years. He felt he could not bear much longer to stay in the family room.

He glanced at his watch. 'You're going to the theater?'

'It's a shame,' Elizabeth said, 'but we've had this engagement for more than a month. But surely, John, you'll be staying home one of these days before long. You're not going to be an expatriate, are you?'

'Expatriate,' Ferris repeated. 'I don't much like the word.'

'What's a better word?' she asked.

He thought for a moment. 'Sojourner might do.'

Ferris glanced again at his watch, and again Elizabeth apologized. 'If only we had known ahead of time—'

'I just had this day in town. I came home unexpectedly. You see, Papa died last week.'

'Papa Ferris is dead?'

'Yes, at Johns-Hopkins. He had been sick there nearly a year. The funeral was down home in Georgia.'

'Oh, I'm so sorry, John. Papa Ferris was always one of my favorite people.'

The little boy moved from behind the chair so that he could look into his mother's face. He asked, 'Who is dead?'

Ferris was oblivious to apprehension; he was thinking of his father's death. He saw again the outstretched body on the quilted silk within the coffin. The corpse flesh was bizarrely rouged and the familiar hands lay massive and joined above a spread of funeral roses. The memory closed and Ferris awakened to Elizabeth's calm voice.

'Mr. Ferris's father, Billy. A really grand person. Somebody you didn't know.'

'But why did you call him *Papa* Ferris?'

Bailey and Elizabeth exchanged a trapped look. It was Bailey who answered the questioning child. 'A long time ago,' he said, 'your mother and Mr. Ferris were once married. Before you were born—a long time ago.'

'Mr. Ferris?'

The little boy stared at Ferris, amazed and unbelieving. And Ferris's eyes, as he returned the gaze, were somehow unbelieving too.

Was it indeed true that at one time he had called this stranger, Elizabeth, Little Butterduck during nights of love, that they had lived together, shared perhaps a thousand days and nights and—finally—endured in the misery of sudden solitude the fiber by fiber (jealousy, alcohol and money quarrels) destruction of the fabric of married love.

Bailey said to the children, 'It's somebody's suppertime. Come on now.'

'But Daddy! Mama and Mr. Ferris—I—'

Billy's everlasting eyes—perplexed and with a glimmer of hostility—reminded Ferris of the gaze of another child. It was the young son of Jeannine—a boy of seven with a shadowed little face and knobby knees whom Ferris avoided and usually forgot.

'Quick march!' Bailey gently turned Billy toward the door. 'Say good night now, son.'

'Good night, Mr. Ferris.' He added resentfully, 'I thought I was staying up for the cake.'

'You can come in afterward for the cake,' Elizabeth said. 'Run along now with Daddy for your supper.'

Ferris and Elizabeth were alone. The weight of the situation descended on those first moments of silence. Ferris asked permission to pour himself another drink and Elizabeth set the cocktail shaker on the table at his side. He looked at the grand piano and noticed the music on the rack.

'Do you still play as beautifully as you used to?'

'I still enjoy it.'

'Please play, Elizabeth.'

Elizabeth arose immediately. Her readiness to perform when asked had always been one of her amiabilities; she never hung back, apologized. Now as she approached the piano there was the added readiness of relief.

She began with a Bach prelude and fugue. The prelude was as gaily iridescent as a prism in a morning room. The first voice of the fugue, an announcement pure and solitary, was repeated intermingling with a second voice, and again repeated within an elaborated frame, the multiple music, horizontal and serene, flowed with unhurried majesty. The principal melody was woven with two other voices, embellished with countless ingenuities—now dominant, again submerged, it had the sublimity of a single thing that does not fear surrender to the whole. Toward the end, the density of the material gathered for the last enriched insistence on the dominant first motif and with a chorded final statement the fugue ended. Ferris rested his head on the chair back and closed his eyes. In the following silence a clear, high voice came from the room down the hall.

'Daddy, how *could* Mama and Mr. Ferris—' A door was closed.

The piano began again—what was this music? Unplaced, familiar, the limpid melody had lain a long while dormant in his heart. Now it spoke to him of another time, another place—it was the music Elizabeth used to play. The delicate air summoned a wilderness of memory. Ferris was lost in the riot of past longings, conflicts, ambivalent desires. Strange that the music, catalyst* for this tumultuous anarchy, was so serene and clear. The singing melody was broken off by the appearance of the maid.

'Miz Bailey, dinner is out on the table now.'

Even after Ferris was seated at the table between his host and hostess, the unfinished music still overcast his mood. He was a little drunk.

'*L'improvisation de la vie humaine,*' he said. 'There's nothing that makes you so aware of the improvisation of human existence as a song unfinished. Or an old address book.'

'Address book?' repeated Bailey. Then he stopped, noncommittal and polite.

'You're still the same old boy, Johnny,' Elizabeth said with a trace of the old tenderness.

It was a Southern dinner that evening, and the dishes were his old favorites. They had fried chicken and corn pudding and rich, glazed candied sweet potatoes. During the meal Elizabeth kept alive a conversation when the silences were overlong. And it came about that Ferris was led to speak of Jeannine.

'I first knew Jeannine last autumn—about this time of the year—in Italy. She's a singer and she had an engagement in Rome. I expect we will be married soon.'

The words seemed so true, inevitable, that Ferris did not at first acknowledge to himself the lie. He and Jeannine had never in that year spoken of marriage. And indeed, she was still married—to a White Russian moneychanger in Paris from whom she had been separated for five years. But it was too late to correct the lie. Already Elizabeth was saying: 'This really makes me glad to know. Congratulations, Johnny.'

He tried to make amends with truth. 'The Roman autumn is so beautiful. Balmy and blossoming.' He added, 'Jeannine has a little boy of six. A curious trilingual** little fellow. We go to the Tuileries sometimes.'

A lie again. He had taken the boy once to the gardens. The sallow foreign child in shorts that bared his spindly legs had sailed his boat in the concrete pond and ridden the pony. The child had wanted to go in to the puppet show. But there was not time, for Ferris had an engagement at the Scribe Hotel. He had promised they would go to the guignol*** another afternoon. Only once had he taken Valentin to the Tuileries.

---

*agent for change
**speaking three languages
***puppet show

There was a stir. The maid brought in a white-frosted cake with pink candles. The children entered in their night clothes. Ferris still did not understand.

'Happy birthday, John,' Elizabeth said. 'Blow out the candles.'

Ferris recognized his birthday date. The candles blew out lingeringly and there was the smell of burning wax. Ferris was thirty-eight years old. The veins in his temples darkened and pulsed visibly.

'It's time you started for the theater.'

Ferris thanked Elizabeth for the birthday dinner and said the appropriate good-byes. The whole family saw him to the door.

A high, thin moon shone above the jagged, dark skyscrapers. The streets were windy, cold. Ferris hurried to Third Avenue and hailed a cab. He gazed at the nocturnal city with the deliberate attentiveness of departure and perhaps farewell. He was alone. He longed for flighttime and the coming journey.

The next day he looked down on the city from the air, burnished in sunlight, toylike, precise. Then America was left behind and there was only the Atlantic and the distant European shore. The ocean was milky pale and placid beneath the clouds. Ferris dozed most of the day. Toward dark he was thinking of Elizabeth and the visit of the previous evening. He thought of Elizabeth among her family with longing, gentle envy and inexplicable regret. He sought the melody, the unfinished air, that had so moved him. The cadence, some unrelated tones, were all that remained; the melody itself evaded him. He had found instead the first voice of the fugue that Elizabeth had played—it came to him, inverted mockingly and in a minor key. Suspended above the ocean the anxieties of transience and solitude no longer troubled him and he thought of his father's death with equanimity. During the dinner hour the plane reached the shore of France.

At midnight Ferris was in a taxi crossing Paris. It was a clouded night and mist wreathed the lights of the Place de la Concorde. The midnight bistros gleamed on the wet pavements. As always after a transocean flight the change of continents was too sudden. New York at morning, this midnight Paris. Ferris glimpsed the disorder of his life: the succession of cities, of transitory loves; and time, the sinister glissando* of the years, time always.

'*Vite! Vite!*'** he called in terror. '*Dépêchez-vous.*'

Valentin opened the door to him. The little boy wore pajamas and an outgrown red robe. His grey eyes were shadowed and, as Ferris passed into the flat, they flickered momentarily.

'*J'attends Maman.*'***

---

*glide up or down the musical scale
**quick, hurry
***I'm waiting for mama.

Jeannine was singing in a night club. She would not be home before another hour. Valentin returned to a drawing, squatting with his crayons over the paper on the floor. Ferris looked down at the drawing—it was a banjo player with notes and wavy lines inside a comic-strip balloon.

'We will go again to the Tuileries.'

The child looked up and Ferris drew him closer to his knees. The melody, the unfinished music that Elizabeth had played, came to him suddenly. Unsought, the load of memory jettisoned—this time bringing only recognition and sudden joy.

'Monsieur Jean,' the child said, 'did you see him?'

Confused, Ferris thought only of another child—the freckled, family-loved boy. 'See who, Valentin?'

'Your dead papa in Georgia.' The child added, 'Was he okay?'

Ferris spoke with rapid urgency: 'We will go often to the Tuileries. Ride the pony and we will go into the guignol. We will see the puppet show and never be in a hurry any more.'

'Monsieur Jean,' Valentin said. 'The guignol is now closed.'

Again, the terror the acknowledgment of wasted years and death. Valentin, responsive and confident, still nestled in his arms. His cheek touched the soft cheek and felt the brush of the delicate eyelashes. With inner desperation he pressed the child close—as though an emotion as protean as his love could dominate the pulse of time.

Reading for Understanding

Main Idea

1. A major theme of the story is that (a) ex-husbands and ex-wives cannot truly be friends (b) a return to the past can bring a spiritual change (c) divorces result in lasting unhappiness for both parties (d) children are not truly appreciated.

Details

2. John Ferris was in New York (a) on business (b) to meet his ex-wife (c) after a funeral (d) for a Thanksgiving reunion.

3. Betty Wills is mentioned as (a) a friend of Elizabeth's (b) Bailey's sister (c) a close friend, now dead (d) a former love.

4. Ferris hadn't seen his ex-wife (a) since Christmas (b) since her visit to Paris (c) since her wedding (d) for eight years.

5. Jeannine is (a) Ferris's present love (b) the mother of Billy (c) Elizabeth's maid of honor (d) John's father's second wife.

6. To entertain Ferris, Elizabeth (a) played the piano (b) took out an old photo book (c) invited Ferris to join the theater party (d) told of a trip to Europe.

7. At the Baileys', Ferris was surprised by (a) an old diary (b) a birthday cake (c) a recitation by Billy (d) Bailey's rapid-fire quick wit.

Inferences

8. In later years, (a) Ferris's brother had ceased writing (b) Ferris's mother blamed him for her husband's illness (c) Ferris and his father had grown apart (d) Ferris had proposed marriage to several women.

9. The sight of Elizabeth (a) reinforced Ferris's original decision to divorce her (b) heightened Ferris's sense of loneliness (c) aroused feelings of antagonism toward Bill Bailey (d) made him resolve to win her back.

10. Billy was upset to learn that (a) his mother had been married before (b) Ferris was actually his father (c) Ferris was staying on for two more days (d) he couldn't go to the puppet show.

The Mood of the Story

11. The mood of the story is one of (a) well-earned joy (b) deep bitterness (c) gentle sadness (d) unsatisfied curiosity.

Cause and Effect

12. The break-up of the Ferris marriage many years ago can probably be traced to (a) a third person (b) a difference in their incomes (c) Ferris's desire to have children (d) unresolved quarrels.

Outcomes

13. As a result of his visit with the Baileys, Ferris will probably (a) change his attitude toward Valentin (b) break off with Jeannine (c) turn around and go back to New York (d) give up his U.S. citizenship.

Order of Events

14. Arrange the events in the order in which they occurred. Use letters only.
    A. Billy greets Ferris at the door.
    B. Ferris's father dies.
    C. Valentin tells Ferris the puppet show is closed.
    D. Ferris sees Elizabeth on the street.
    E. Elizabeth enters with a baby girl.

Fact or Opinion

Tell whether the following is a fact or an opinion.

15. In the past, Ferris has spent little time with Valentin.

Words in Context

1. "His body was spare except for an *incipient* belly bulge." **Incipient** (211) means (a) huge (b) displeasing (c) rounded (d) beginning.

2. "As Ferris closed the address book, he suffered a sense of hazard, *transience*, almost of fear." **Transience** (211) suggests a lack of (a) meaning (b) anger (c) permanence (d) forethought.

3. "Then, after the *anodyne* of time, he had loved again, and then again." **Anodyne** (212) means (a) memory (b) painkiller (c) passage (d) cruelties.

4. "He knew only that his clouded heart was oddly *dissonant* with the sunny, candid autumn day." **Dissonant** (212) means (a) out of tune (b) in harmony (c) unaffected (d) fully aware.

5. "It was a madonna loveliness, dependent on the family *ambiance*." **Ambiance** (214) means (a) history (b) atmosphere (c) gentleness (d) playfulness.

6. "His hand touched his thinning hair self-consciously while further *amenities* were exchanged." **Amenities** (214) are (a) gifts (b) inquiries (c) ideas (d) pleasantries.

7. "Ferris felt himself suddenly a spectator—an *interloper* among these Baileys." **Interloper** (214) means (a) intruder (b) unwanted relative (c) unhappy guest (d) associate.

8. " 'You're not going to be an *expatriate,* are you?' " An **expatriate** (214) (a) lives away from his native country (b) is unpatriotic (c) never stays in one place long (d) is a former politician on the run.

9. "Ferris was *oblivious to apprehension.*" **Oblivious to** (214) means (a) concerned about (b) attentive to (c) unaware of (d) accepting of. **Apprehension** (214) means (a) being arrested (b) understanding (c) worry (d) good cheer.

10. "Her readiness to perform when asked had always been one of her *amiabilities.*" **Amiabilities** (215) means (a) skills (b) pleasantnesses (c) annoyances (d) anxieties.

11. "The prelude was as gaily *iridescent* as a prism in a morning room." **Iridescent** (215) is used here in a special sense to mean (a) suitable (b) changeable (c) melodic (d) sparkling.

12. "The music, horizontal and *serene,* flowed with unhurried majesty." **Serene** (215) means (a) vertical (b) peaceful (c) colorful (d) animated.

13. "The principal melody was woven with two other voices, *embellished* with countless ingenuities." **Embellished** (215) means (a) decorated (b) repetitious (c) mindful of (d) defined.

14. "It had the *sublimity* of a single thing that does not fear surrender to the whole." **Sublimity** (215) means (a) appeal (b) challenge (c) nobility (d) appearance.

15. "Unplaced, familiar, the *limpid* melody had lain a long while dormant in his heart." **Limpid** (216) means (a) clear and simple (b) complicated and subtle (c) soft and fuzzy (d) loud but pleasant.

16. "Ferris was lost in the riot of past longings, conflicts, *ambivalent* desires." **Ambivalent** (216) means (a) pressing (b) dramatic (c) violent (d) conflicting.

17.,18. "Strange that the music, catalyst for this *tumultuous anarchy,* was so serene and clear." **Tumultuous** (216) means (a) unexpected (b) raging (c) satisfying (d) disagreeable. **Anarchy** (216) means (a) revelation (b) music (c) disorder (d) thoughtfulness.

19. "He gazed at the *nocturnal* city with the deliberate attentiveness of departure and perhaps farewell." **Nocturnal** (217) deals with (a) beauty (b) night (c) traffic (d) light.

20. "The next day he looked down on the city from the air, *burnished* in sunlight, toylike, precise." **Burnished** (217) means (a) reddened (b) outlined (c) polished (d) exposed.

21. "He thought of Elizabeth among her family with longing, gentle envy, and *inexplicable* regret." **Inexplicable** (217) means not able to be (a) explained (b) stated (c) discovered (d) tolerated.

22. "He thought of his father's death with *equanimity*." **Equanimity** (217) means (a) regret (b) sadness (c) happy memory (d) calmness.

23. "Ferris glimpsed the disorder of his life: the succession of cities, of *transitory* loves." **Transitory** (217) means (a) passionate (b) faithless (c) well-remembered (d) short-lived.

24. "Unsought, the load of memory *jettisoned*—this time bringing only recognition and sudden joy." **Jettisoned** (218) means (a) returned (b) discarded (c) pained (d) rejoiced.

25. "With inner desperation he pressed the child close—as though an emotion as *protean* as his love could dominate the pulse of time." **Protean** (218) means (a) sentimental (b) wholesome (c) unique (d) changeable.

Thinking Critically about the Story

1. In J.B. Priestley's play *Dangerous Corner,* the pleasant amiability of a group changes drastically because of one statement. Discord and disintegration follow. Then Priestley takes the readers or listeners back to a moment before the fateful comment, for a second chance. This time, the comment is not made, and the evening proceeds on its quiet, happy way. Priestley seems to say that momentous events sometimes turn on a seemingly innocent word or decision. Apply that idea to "The Sojourner." Suppose that Ferris had not given in to an impulse. Suppose he had not "turned that corner" and called his ex-wife. How would his later life have been different? Was Ferris better for his bittersweet visit to his wife and her new family? Explain.

2. Are there any clues that suggest one party might have been more guilty than the other in the divorce of Ferris and Elizabeth? Explain.

3. How do Ferris and Bailey differ? Why was Elizabeth probably seeking a different type the second time around?

4. "He was alone" (217). What significance does this statement have in the context of the story?

5. "Billy's everlasting eyes—perplexed and with a glimmer of hostility—reminded Ferris of the gaze of another child." Why the hostility? Who was the other child?

6. Why does the author bring in Elizabeth's music? What effect does it have on Ferris?

7. How has the name *sojourner* suited Ferris's life?

8. " 'Address book?' repeated Bailey (216). Then he stopped, noncommittal and polite." Why does Elizabeth understand while her husband does not?

9. Why does Ferris tell Valentin, "We'll never be in a hurry any more"?

10. *Jettison* (218) or *jetsam*, makes an interesting pair with *flotsam*. Look up both and be ready to distinguish between *flotsam* and *jetsam*.

Language in Action

Allusions

Dinosaur hunters search for clues that provide insight into the past. A giant tooth may suggest a Tyrannosaurus Rex. Language, too, is filled with hidden clues that reveal our past. A single word can suggest a mythology that has nourished the world's literature. A good example is *protean* (218). The dictionary and the context tell us it means *changeable*, but that's only part of the story. Proteus, the herdsman of Neptune, was a great prophet, but seekers couldn't catch him because he could assume different shapes.

Iridescence (215) suggests Iris, the Greek goddess of the rainbow. *Ocean* (213) comes from a Greek name for the river that supposedly circled the earth. There was also a Greek Titan, Oceanus, whose children were gods of all the world's rivers.

An allusion is an implied or indirect reference, like the allusion to Proteus concealed in *protean*. Many allusions come from mythology, a number of which are listed on page 218. Some are from other literature. The allusion may be obvious as in a *Romeo*, or concealed, as in *lilliputian* (tiny), from *Gulliver's Travels*.

Allusions may come from still other areas. *Bobby*, a familiar name for an English policeman, came from Sir Robert Peel, who organized the London police force. The Christmas flower, *poinsettia*, was brought to this country more than a century ago by Joel Poinsett, the ambassador to Mexico. *Silhouette* was named for Etienne de Silhouette, a French administrative official.

A Cap for Steve

Morley Callaghan
Canadian

The Father

Björnstjerne Björnson
Norwegian

"Well, here you are," Mr. Hudson said, and he put the two bills in Steve's hand. "It's a lot of money. But I guess you had a right to expect as much."

With a dazed, fixed smile, Steve handed the money slowly to his father, and his face was white.

These two stories are paired for obvious reasons: both deal with the relationship between a father and his son. There are similarities in relationships, but there are great dissimilarities too, in setting, mood, and plot.

"The Father" is told in a spare, direct style. The events speak for themselves, and the author doesn't inject his own thoughts. Where "The Father" is lean and spare, "A Cap for Steve" is emotional and detailed. We are taken into the lives and hearts of Steve and his father in a way quite different from the technique of "The Father."

Both stories reveal a deep love of a father for his son, but that love is demonstrated quite differently in each.

Since both stories were written in an earlier day, you will probably find the money amounts mentioned lower than you might expect today. The stories, though, are timeless.

A Cap for Steve

DAVE DIAMOND, a poor man, a carpenter's assistant, was a small, wiry, quick-tempered individual who had learned how to make every dollar count in his home. His wife, Anna, had been sick a lot, and his twelve-year-old son, Steve, had to be kept in school. Steve, a big-eyed, shy kid, ought to have known the value of money as well as Dave did. It had been ground into him.

But the boy was crazy about baseball, and after school, when he could have been working as a delivery boy or selling papers, he played ball with the kids. His failure to appreciate that the family needed a few extra dollars disgusted Dave. Around the house he wouldn't let Steve talk about baseball, and he scowled when he saw him hurrying off with his glove after dinner.

When the Phillies came to town to play an exhibition game with the home team and Steve pleaded to be taken to the ball park, Dave, of course, was outraged. Steve knew they couldn't afford it. But he had got his mother on his side. Finally Dave made a bargain with them. He said that if Steve came home after school and worked hard helping to make some kitchen shelves he would take him that night to the ball park.

Steve worked hard, but Dave was still resentful. They had to coax him to put on his good suit. When they started out Steve held aloof, feeling guilty, and they walked down the street like strangers; then Dave glanced at Steve's face and, half-ashamed, took his arm more cheerfully.

As the game went on, Dave had to listen to Steve's recitation of the batting average of every Philly that stepped up to the plate; the time the boy must have wasted learning these averages began to appal him. He showed it so plainly that Steve felt guilty again and was silent.

After the game Dave let Steve drag him onto the field to keep him company while he tried to get some autographs from the Philly players, who were being hemmed in by gangs of kids blocking the way to the club-house. But Steve, who was shy, let the other kids block him off from the players. Steve would push his way in, get blocked out, and come back to stand mournfully beside Dave. And Dave grew impatient. He was wasting valuable time. He wanted to get home; Steve knew it and was worried.

Then the big, blond Philly outfielder, Eddie Condon, who had been held up by a gang of kids tugging at his arm and thrusting their score cards at him, broke loose and made a run for the club-house. He was jostled, and his blue cap with the red peak, tilted far back on his head, fell off. It fell at Steve's feet, and Steve stooped quickly and grabbed it. "Okay, son," the outfielder called, turning back. But Steve, holding the hat in both hands, only stared at him.

"Give him his cap, Steve," Dave said, smiling apologetically at the big outfielder who towered over them. But Steve drew the hat closer to his chest. In an awed trance he looked up at big Eddie Condon. It was an embarrassing moment. All the other kids were watching. Some shouted. "Give him his cap."

"My cap, son," Eddie Condon said, his hand out.

"Hey, Steve," Dave said, and he gave him a shake. But he had to jerk the cap out of Steve's hands.

"Here you are," he said.

The outfielder, noticing Steve's white, worshipping face and pleading eyes, grinned and then shrugged. "Aw, let him keep it," he said.

"No, Mister Condon, you don't need to do that," Steve protested.

"It's happened before. Forget it," Eddie Condon said, and he trotted away to the club-house.

Dave handed the cap to Steve; envious kids circled around them and Steve said, "He said I could keep it, Dad. You heard him, didn't you?"

"Yeah, I heard him," Dave admitted. The wonder in Steve's face made him smile. He took the boy by the arm and they hurried off the field.

On the way home Dave couldn't get him to talk about the game; he couldn't get him to take his eyes off the cap. Steve could hardly believe in his own happiness. "See," he said suddenly, and he showed Dave that Eddie Condon's name was printed on the sweat-band. Then he went on dreaming. Finally he put the cap on his head and turned to Dave with a slow, proud smile. The cap was away too big for him; it fell down over his ears. "Never mind," Dave said. "You can get your mother to take a tuck in the back."

When they got home Dave was tired and his wife didn't understand the cap's importance, and they couldn't get Steve to go to bed. He swaggered around wearing the cap and looking in the mirror every ten minutes. He took the cap to bed with him.

Dave and his wife had a cup of coffee in the kitchen, and Dave told her again how they had got the cap. They agreed that their boy must have an attractive quality that showed in his face, and that Eddie Condon must have been drawn to him—why else would he have singled Steve out from all the kids?

But Dave got tired of the fuss Steve made over that cap and of the way he wore it from the time he got up in the morning until the time he went to bed. Some kid was always coming in, wanting to try on the cap. It was childish, Dave said, for Steve to go around assuming that the cap made him important in the neighbourhood, and to keep telling them how he had become a leader in the park a few blocks away where he played ball in the evenings. And Dave wouldn't stand for Steve's keeping the cap on while he was eating. He was always scolding his wife for accepting Steve's explanation that he'd forgotten he had it on. Just the same, it was remarkable what a little thing like a ball cap could do for a kid, Dave admitted to his wife as he smiled to himself.

One night Steve was late coming home from the park. Dave didn't realize how late it was until he put down his newspaper and watched his wife at the window. Her restlessness got on his nerves. "See what comes from encouraging the boy to hang around with those park loafers," he said. "I don't encourage him," she protested. "You do," he insisted irritably, for he was really worried now. A gang hung around the park until midnight. It was a bad park. It was true that on one side there was a good district with fine, expensive apartment houses, but the kids from that neighbourhood left the park to the kids from the poorer homes. When his wife went out and walked down to the corner it was his turn to wait and worry and watch at the open window. Each waiting moment tortured him. At last he heard his wife's voice and Steve's voice, and he relaxed and sighed; then he remembered his duty and rushed angrily to meet them.

"I'll fix you, Steve, once and for all," he said. "I'll show you you can't start coming into the house at midnight."

"Hold your horses, Dave," his wife said. "Can't you see the state he's in?" Steve looked utterly exhausted and beaten.

"What's the matter?" Dave asked quickly.

"I lost my cap," Steve whispered; he walked past his father and threw himself on the couch in the living-room and lay with his face hidden.

"Now, don't scold him, Dave," his wife said.

"Scold him. Who's scolding him?" Dave asked, indignantly. "It's his cap, not mine. If it's not worth his while to hang to it, why should I scold him?" But he was implying resentfully that he alone recognized the cap's value.

"So you are scolding him," his wife said. "It's his cap. Not yours. What happpened, Steve?"

Steve told them he had been playing ball and he found that when he ran the bases the cap fell off; it was still too big despite the tuck his mother had taken in the band. So the next time he came to bat he tucked the cap in his hip pocket. Someone had lifted it, he was sure.

"And he didn't even know whether it was still in his pocket," Dave said sarcastically.

"I wasn't careless, Dad," Steve said. For the last three hours he had been wandering around to the homes of the kids who had been in the park at the time; he wanted to go on, but he was too tired. Dave knew the boy was apologizing to him, but he didn't know why it made him angry.

"If he didn't hang on to it, it's not worth worrying about now," he said, and he sounded offended.

After that night they knew that Steve didn't go to the park to play ball; he went to look for the cap. It irritated Dave to see him sit around listlessly, or walk in circles, trying to force his memory to find a particular incident which would suddenly recall to him the moment when the cap had been taken. It was no attitude for a growing, healthy boy to take, Dave complained. He told Steve firmly once and for all that he didn't want to hear any more about the cap.

One night, two weeks later, Dave was walking home with Steve from the shoemaker's. It was a hot night. When they passed an ice-cream parlour Steve slowed down. "I guess I couldn't have a soda, could I?" Steve said. "Nothing doing," Dave said firmly. "Come on now," he added as Steve hung back, looking in the window.

"Dad, look!" Steve cried suddenly, pointing at the window. "My cap! There's my cap! He's coming out!"

A well-dressed boy was leaving the ice-cream parlour; he had on a blue ball cap with a red peak, just like Steve's cap. "Hey, you!" Steve cried, and he rushed at the boy, his small face fierce and his eyes wild. Before the boy could back away Steve had snatched the cap from his head. "That's my cap!" he shouted.

"What's this?" the bigger boy said. "Hey, give me my cap or I'll give you a poke on the nose."

Dave was surprised that his own shy boy did not back away. He watched him clutch the cap in his left hand, half crying with excitement as he put his head down and drew back his right fist: he was willing to fight. And Dave was proud of him.

"Wait, now," Dave said. "Take it easy, son," he said to the other boy, who refused to back away.

"My boy says it's his cap," Dave said.

"Well, he's crazy. It's my cap."

"I was with him when he got this cap. When the Phillies played here. It's a Philly cap."

"Eddie Condon gave it to me," Steve said. "And you stole it from me, you jerk."

"Don't call me a jerk, you little squirt. I never saw you before in my life."

"Look," Steve said, pointing to the printing on the cap's sweatband. "It's Eddie Condon's cap. See? See, Dad?"

"Yeah. You're right, Son. Ever see this boy before, Steve?" "No," Steve said reluctantly.

The other boy realized he might lose the cap. "I bought it from a guy," he said. "I paid him. My father knows I paid him." He said he got the cap at the ball park. He groped for some magically impressive words and suddenly found them. "You'll have to speak to my father," he said.

"Sure, I'll speak to your father," Dave said. "What's your name? Where do you live?"

"My name's Hudson. I live about ten minutes away on the other side of the park." The boy appraised Dave, who wasn't any bigger than he was and who wore a faded blue windbreaker and no tie. "My father is a lawyer," he said boldly. "He wouldn't let me keep the cap if he didn't think I should."

"Is that a fact?" Dave asked belligerently. "Well, we'll see. Come on. Let's go." And he got between the two boys and they walked along the street. They didn't talk to each other. Dave knew the Hudson boy was waiting to get to the protection of his home, and Steve knew it, too, and he looked up apprehensively at Dave. And Dave, reaching for his hand, squeezed it encouragingly and strode along, cocky and belligerent, knowing that Steve relied on him.

The Hudson boy lived in that row of fine apartment houses on the other side of the park. At the entrance to one of these houses Dave tried not to hang back and show he was impressed, because he could feel Steve hanging back. When they got into the small elevator Dave didn't know why he took off his hat. In the carpeted hall on the fourth floor the Hudson boy said, "Just a minute," and entered his own apartment. Dave and Steve were left alone in the corridor, knowing that the other boy was preparing his father for the encounter. Steve looked anxiously at his father, and Dave said, "Don't worry, Son," and he added resolutely, "No one's putting anything over on us."

A tall balding man in a brown velvet smoking-jacket suddenly opened the door. Dave had never seen a man wearing one of those jackets, although he had seen them in department-store windows. "Good evening," he said, making a deprecatory gesture at the cap Steve still clutched tightly in his left hand. "My boy didn't get your name. My name is Hudson."

"Mine's Diamond."

"Come on in," Mr. Hudson said, putting out his hand and laughing good-naturedly. He led Dave and Steve into his living-room. "What's this about that cap?" he asked. "The way kids can get excited about a cap. Well, it's understandable, isn't it?"

"So it is," Dave said, moving closer to Steve, who was awed by the broadloom rug and the fine furniture. He wanted to show Steve he was at ease himself, and he wished Mr. Hudson wouldn't be so polite. That meant Dave had to be polite and affable, too, and it was hard to manage when he was standing in the middle of the floor in his old windbreaker.

"Sit down, Mr. Diamond," Mr. Hudson said. Dave took Steve's arm and sat him down beside him on the chesterfield. The Hudson boy watched his father. And Dave looked at Steve and saw that he wouldn't face Mr. Hudson or the other boy; he kept looking up at Dave, putting all his faith in him.

"Well, Mr. Diamond, from what I gathered from my boy, you're able to prove this cap belonged to your boy."

"That's a fact," Dave said.

"Mr. Diamond, you'll have to believe my boy bought that cap from some kid in good faith."

"I don't doubt it," Dave said. "But no kid can sell something that doesn't belong to him. You know that's a fact, Mr. Hudson."

"Yes, that's a fact," Mr. Hudson agreed. "But that cap means a lot to my boy, Mr. Diamond."

"It means a lot to my boy, too, Mr. Hudson."

"Sure it does. But supposing we called in a policeman. You know what he'd say? He'd ask you if you were willing to pay my boy what he paid for the cap. That's usually the way it works out," Mr. Hudson said, friendly and smiling, as he eyed Dave shrewdly.

"But that's not right. It's not justice," Dave protested. "Not when it's my boy's cap."

"I know it isn't right. But that's what they do."

"All right. What did you say your boy paid for the cap?" Dave said reluctantly.

"Two dollars."

"Two dollars!" Dave repeated. Mr. Hudson's smile was still kindly, but his eyes were shrewd, and Dave knew the lawyer was counting on his not having the two dollars; Mr. Hudson thought he had Dave sized up; he had looked at him and decided he was broke. Dave's pride was hurt, and he turned to Steve. What he saw in Steve's face was more powerful than the hurt to his pride: it was the memory of how difficult it had been to get an extra nickel, the talk he heard about the cost of food, the worry in his mother's face as she tried to make ends meet, and the bewildered embarrassment that he was here in a rich man's home, forcing his father to confess that he couldn't afford to spend two dollars. Then Dave grew angry and reckless. "I'll give you the two dollars," he said.

Steve looked at the Hudson boy and grinned brightly. The Hudson boy watched his father.

"I suppose that's fair enough," Mr. Hudson said. "A cap like this can be worth a lot to a kid. You know how it is. Your boy might want to sell—I mean be satisfied. Would he take five dollars for it?"

"Five dollars?" Dave repeated. "Is it worth five dollars, Steve?" he asked uncertainly.

Steve shook his head and looked frightened.

"No, thanks, Mr. Hudson," Dave said firmly.

"I'll tell you what I'll do," Mr. Hudson said. "I'll give you ten dollars. The cap has a sentimental value for my boy, a Philly cap, a big-leaguer's cap. It's only worth about a buck and a half really," he added. But Dave shook his head again. Mr. Hudson frowned. He looked at his own boy with indulgent concern, but now he was embarrassed. "I'll tell you what I'll do," he said. "This cap—well, it's worth as much as a day at the circus to my boy. Your boy should be recompensed. I want to be fair. Here's twenty dollars," and he held out two ten-dollar bills to Dave.

That much money for a cap, Dave thought, and his eyes brightened. But he knew what the cap had meant to Steve; to deprive him of it now that it was within his reach would be unbearable. All the things he needed in his life gathered around him; his wife was there, saying he couldn't afford to reject the offer, he had no right to do it; and he turned to Steve to see if Steve thought it wonderful that the cap could bring them twenty dollars.

"What do you say, Steve?" he asked uneasily.

"I don't know," Steve said. He was in a trance. When Dave smiled, Steve smiled too, and Dave believed that Steve was as impressed as he was, only more bewildered, and maybe even more aware that they could not possibly turn away that much money for a ball cap.

"Well, here you are," Mr. Hudson said, and he put the two bills in Steve's hand. "It's a lot of money. But I guess you had a right to expect as much."

With a dazed, fixed smile Steve handed the money slowly to his father, and his face was white.

Laughing jovially, Mr. Hudson led them to the door. His own boy followed a few paces behind.

In the elevator Dave took the bills out of his pocket. "See, Stevie," he whispered eagerly. "That windbreaker you wanted! And ten dollars for your bank! Won't Mother be surprised?"

"Yeah," Steve whispered, the little smile still on his face. But Dave had to turn away quickly so their eyes wouldn't meet, for he saw that it was a scared smile.

Outside, Dave said, "Here, you carry the money home, Steve. You show it to your mother."

"No, you keep it," Steve said, and then there was nothing to say. They walked in silence.

"It's a lot of money," Dave said finally. When Steve didn't answer him, he added angrily, "I turned to you, Steve. I asked you, didn't I?"

"That man knew how much his boy wanted that cap," Steve said.

"Sure. But he recognized how much it was worth to us."

"No, you let him take it away from us," Steve blurted.

"That's unfair," Dave said. "Don't dare say that to me."

"I don't want to be like you," Steve muttered, and he darted across the road and walked along on the other side of the street.

"It's unfair," Dave said angrily, only now he didn't mean that Steve was unfair, he meant that what had happened in the prosperous Hudson home was unfair, and he didn't know quite why. He had been trapped, not just by Mr. Hudson, but by his own life. Across the road Steve was hurrying along with his head down, wanting to be alone. They walked most of the way home on opposite sides of the street, until Dave could stand it no longer. "Steve," he called, crossing the street. "It was very unfair. I mean, for you to say . . . " But Steve started to run. Dave walked as fast as he could and Steve was getting beyond him, and he felt enraged and suddenly he yelled, "Steve!" and he started to chase his son. He wanted to get hold of Steve and pound him, and he didn't know why. He gained on him, he gasped for breath and he almost got him by the shoulder. Turning, Steve saw his father's face in the street light and was terrified; he circled away, got to the house, and rushed in, yelling, "Mother!"

"Son, Son!" she cried, rushing from the kitchen. As soon as she threw her arms around Steve, shielding him, Dave's anger left him and he felt stupid. He walked past them into the kitchen.

"What happened?" she asked anxiously. "Have you both gone crazy? What did you do, Steve?"

"Nothing," he said sullenly.

"What did your father do?"

"We found the boy with my ball cap, and he let the boy's father take it from us."

"No, no," Dave protested. "Nobody pushed us around. The man didn't put anything over us." He felt tired and his face was burning. He told what had happened; then he slowly took the two ten-dollar bills out of his wallet and tossed them on the table and looked up guiltily at his wife.

It hurt him that she didn't pick up the money, and that she didn't rebuke him. "It is a lot of money, Son," she said slowly. "Your father was only trying to do what he knew was right, and it'll work out, and you'll understand." She was soothing Steve, but Dave knew she felt that she needed to be gentle with him, too, and he was ashamed.

When she went with Steve to his bedroom, Dave sat by himself. His son had contempt for him, he thought. His son, for the first time, had seen how easy it was for another man to handle him, and he had judged him and had wanted to walk alone on the other side of the street. He looked at the money and he hated the sight of it.

His wife returned to the kitchen, made a cup of tea, talked soothingly, and said it was incredible that he had forced the Hudson man to pay him twenty dollars for the cap, but all Dave could think of was Steve was scared of me.

Finally, he got up and went into Steve's room. The room was in darkness, but he could see the outline of Steve's body on the bed, and he sat down beside him and whispered, "Look, Son, it was a mistake. I know why. People like us—in circumstances where money can scare us. No, no," he said, feeling ashamed and shaking his head apologetically; he was taking the wrong way of showing the boy they were together; he was covering up his own failure. For the failure had been his, and it had come out of being so separated from his son that he had been blind to what was beyond the price in a boy's life. He longed now to show Steve he could be with him from day to day. His hand went out hesitantly to Steve's shoulder. "Steve, look," he said eagerly. "The trouble was I didn't realize how much I enjoyed it that night at the ball park. If I had watched you playing for your own team—the kids around here say you could be a great pitcher. We could take that money and buy a new pitcher's glove for you, and a catcher's mitt. Steve, Steve, are you listening? I could catch you, work with you in the lane. Maybe I could be your coach . . . watch you become a great pitcher." In the half-darkness he could see the boy's pale face turn to him.

Steve, who had never heard his father talk like this, was shy and wondering. All he knew was that his father, for the first time, wanted to be with him in his hopes and adventures. He said, "I guess you do know how important that cap was." His hand went out to his father's arm. "With that man the cap was—well it was just something he could buy, eh Dad?" Dave gripped his son's hand hard. The wonderful generosity of childhood—the price a boy was willing to pay to be able to count on his father's admiration and approval—made him feel humble, then strangely exalted.

The Father

THE MAN WHOSE STORY STORY is here to be told was the wealthiest and most influential person in his parish; his name was Thord Överaas. He appeared in the parson's study one day, tall and earnest.

"I have gotten a son," said he, "and I wish to present him for baptism."

"What shall his name be?"

"Finn—after my father."

"And the sponsors?"

They were mentioned, and proved to be the best men and women of Thord's relations in the parish.

"Is there anything else?" inquired the parson, and looked up. The peasant hesitated a little.

"I should like very much to have him baptized by himself," said he, finally.

"That is to say on a weekday?"

"Next Saturday, at twelve o'clock noon."

"Is there anything else?" inquired the parson.

"There is nothing else," and the peasant twirled his cap, as though he were about to go.

Then the parson rose. "There is yet this, however," said he, and walking toward Thord, he took him by the hand and looked gravely into his eyes: "God grant that the child may become a blessing to you!"

One day sixteen years later Thord stood once more in the parson's study.

"Really, you carry your age astonishingly well, Thord," said the parson, for he saw no change whatever in the man.

"That is because I have no troubles," replied Thord.

To this the parson said nothing, but after a while he asked: "What is your pleasure this evening?"

"I have come this evening about that son of mine who is to be confirmed tomorrow."

"He is a bright boy."

"I did not wish to pay the parson until I heard what number the boy would have when he takes his place in the church tomorrow."

"He will stand number one."

"So I have heard, and here are ten dollars for the parson."

"Is there anything else I can do for you?" inquired the parson, fixing his eyes on Thord.

"There is nothing else."

Thord went out.

Eight years more rolled by, and then one day a noise was heard outside of the parson's study, for many men were approaching; and at their head was Thord, who entered first.

The parson looked up and recognized him.

"You come well attended this evening, Thord," said he.

"I am here to request that the banns* may be published for my

---

*notice of a proposed marriage

son; he is about to marry Karen Storliden, daughter of Gudmund, who stands here beside me."

"Why, that is the richest girl in the parish."

"So they say," replied the peasant, stroking back his hair with one hand.

The parson sat awhile as if in deep thought, then entered the names in his book, without making any comments; and the men wrote their signatures underneath. Thord laid three dollars on the table.

"One is all I am to have," said the parson.

"I know that very well, but he is my only child; I want to do it handsomely."

The parson took the money.

"This is now the third time, Thord, that you have come here on your son's account."

"But now I am through with him," said Thord, and folding up his pocketbook he said farewell and walked away.

The men slowly followed him.

A fortnight later, the father and son were rowing across the lake, one calm, still day, to Storliden to make arrangements for the wedding.

"This thwart* is not secure," said the son, and stood up to straighten the seat on which he was sitting.

At the same moment the board he was standing on slipped from under him; he threw out his arms, uttered a shriek, and fell overboard.

"Take hold of the oar!" shouted the father, springing to his feet and holding out the oar.

But when the son had made a couple of efforts, he grew stiff.

"Wait a moment!" cried the father and began to row toward his son.

Then the son rolled over on his back, gave his father one long look, and sank.

Thord could scarcely believe it; he held the boat still and stared at the spot where his son had gone down, as though he must surely come to the surface again. There rose some bubbles, then some more, and finally one large one that burst; and the lake lay there as smooth and bright as a mirror again.

For three days and three nights people saw the father rowing round and round the spot, without taking either food or sleep; he was dragging the lake for the body of his son. And toward morning of the third day he found it and carried it in his arms up over the hills to his gard.**

It might have been about a year from that day when the parson, late one autumn evening, heard someone in the passage outside of the

---

*a rower's seat
**farm, our word *garden*

door, carefully trying to find the latch. The parson opened the door, and in walked a tall, thin man, with bowed form and white hair. The parson looked long at him before he recognized him. It was Thord.

"Are you out walking so late?" said the parson, and stood still in front of him.

"Ah, yes! It is late," said Thord, and took a seat.

The parson sat down also, as though waiting. A long, long silence followed. At last Thord said:

"I have something with me that I should like to give to the poor; I want it to be invested as a legacy in my son's name."

He rose, laid some money on the table, and sat down again. The parson counted it.

"It is a great deal of money," said he.

"It is half the price of my gard. I sold it today."

The parson sat long in silence. At last he asked, but gently:

"What do you propose to do now, Thord?"

"Something better."

They sat there for a while, Thord with downcast eyes, the parson with his eyes fixed on Thord. Presently the parson said, slowly and softly:

"I think your son has at last brought you a true blessing."

"Yes, I think so myself," said Thord, looking up, while two big tears coursed slowly down his cheeks.

Reading for Understanding

Main Idea

1. The main idea of both stories, though expressed differently, is (a) the uncertainties of life and fate (b) a father's love for his son (c) the lack of understanding between fathers and sons (d) the cruelty of some persons toward others.

Details

2. Eddie Condon is (a) related to Steve and Dave (b) the wealthy father (c) Dave's idol (d) a baseball player.

3. The boy with Steve's cap said that (a) it was his father's (b) a baseball player had given it to him (c) he had found it (d) he had bought it.

4. Mr. Hudson gave Steve (a) $2 (b) $10 (c) $20 (d) another cap in return.

5. Steve was impressed by Mr. Hudson's (a) smoking jacket (b) baseball skills (c) sleek automobile (d) angry manner.

6. The cap was eventually (a) lost a second time at the park by Steve (b) kept by the Hudson boy (c) returned to the baseball player (d) soon forgotten by Steve.

7. The tragedy that struck Thord was (a) loss of a fortune (b) disrespect by his son (c) an automobile accident (d) a drowning.

8. Gudmund was (a) Thord's brother (b) the son's father-in-law to-be (c) a close friend of the parson (d) the parson.

Inferences

9. At the beginning of the story, Dave (a) did not understand or sympathize with Steve (b) was a model parent unappreciated by his son (c) was a person too much concerned about his large fortune (d) had an interest in baseball that was transmitted to his son.

10. Throughout the bargaining incident, Mr. Hudson was (a) viciously cruel in defense of his son (b) more sympathetic to Steve than to his son (c) pleasant but superior in manner (d) amused by the difficulties over a hat.

11. Which of the following statements can be said about both stories? (a) Through difficulties, both Dave and Thord grew in understanding. (b) The sons in both stories were very similar. (c) Dave and Thord were similar in the way they handled their sons. (d) Children should be allowed to express their viewpoints.

12. The personality of Thord changes from (a) likable to unpleasant (b) gloomy to humorous (c) proud to humble (d) friendly to unfriendly.

Author's Purpose

13. The purpose of the author of "A Cap for Steve" was to show how (a) false values warp personality (b) children ought to obey their parents (c) dissension between husband and wife can influence a son (d) a stressful situation can result in positive growth.

Order of Events

14. Arrange the items in the order in which they occurred. Use letters only.

    A. Steve accepts the money.
    B. Steve acquires his precious cap.

    C. Dave reluctantly takes Steve to a ballgame.

    D. Steve sees his hat on another boy's head.

    E. Dave becomes close to Steve.

Fact or Opinion

    Tell whether the following is a fact or an opinion.

15. Steve should have refused the money for his hat.

Words in Context

1. "He *swaggered* around wearing the cap and looking in the mirror every ten minutes." **Swaggered** (226) suggests walking with a touch of (a) arrogance (b) uncertainty (c) humility (d) fierceness.

2. "He looked *apprehensively* at Dave." **Apprehensively** (229) means (a) understandingly (b) uneasily (c) reflectively (d) angrily.

3. " 'Good evening,' " he said, making a *deprecatory* gesture at the cap Steve still clutched tightly in his left hand." **Deprecatory** (229) means (a) wistful (b) sharp (c) apologetic (d) humorous.

4. "That meant Dave had to be polite and *affable*, too." **Affable** (229) means (a) gracious (b) uncompromising (c) jocular (d) affectionate.

5. "He looked at his own boy with *indulgent* concern, but now he was embarrassed." **Indulgent** (231) means (a) well-concealed (b) serious (c) fond (d) anxious.

6. "It hurt him that she didn't pick up the money, and that she didn't *rebuke* him." **Rebuke** (232) means (a) scold (b) praise (c) speak to (d) question.

7. "The wonderful generosity of childhood . . . made him feel humble, then strangely *exalted*." **Exalted** (233) means (a) freed of guilt (b) uplifted (c) confused (d) enlightened.

Thinking Critically about the Stories

1. How did the episode with the cap deepen the love and understanding between Steve and Dave?

2. Why was the cap so important to Steve? What did it represent to him?

3. What kind of person was Mr. Hudson? Was he fair in his solution to the cap problem?

4. How does the author contrast Dave and Mr. Hudson?

5. What role does Steve's mother play in the events? How does the author present her?

6. In "The Father," what is the attitude of the parson toward Thord? How does he react to Thord's various requests?

7. Irony (264) says one thing but suggests another. At one point, Thord explains his unchanged appearance by saying, "That is because I have no troubles." Why is this ironic in the light of the later events?

9. How does the tragedy make Thord a better person?

10. *Hubris* is defined as "excessive pride or self-confidence." The word is often used to express the fall of heroes in Greek tragedy. Does the word apply to Thord? Explain.

Language in Action

Subjective, Objective Writing

The two stories show an interesting difference in the writing. "The Father" illustrates objective writing. "A Cap for Steve" illustrates subjective writing. Each is effective in its own way.

Objective writing is a series of reports. It concentrates on the facts and doesn't try to interpret them. It lets the reader do the interpreting. "The Father," contains deep and personal emotion, a crushing anguish at the end. Yet it just reports the events, leaving to the reader the task of deciding how the characters feel. The parson, for example, does not entirely approve of Thord's pride, but the author doesn't label the disapproval. He shows it subtly by the parson's replies to Thord. He doesn't label Thor's arrogance, either. He shows it.

Subjective writing, on the other hand, provides the author's interpretation. It leaves less to the imagination and does more work for the reader. "A Cap for Steve" uses labeling words like *quick-tempered. resentful, half-ashamed, shy, envious.* These occur throughout the story. We don't have to infer that Dave is indignant in saying, "Who's scolding him." We are given the word itself.

Poetry tends to be subjective. Good news reporting tends to be objective. In some ways, objective writing is harder to master. Writers tend to choose a point of view (174) from which to tell a story. A story may be told from the first-person or third-person point of view (174) in either the subjective or objective mode.

Here's to You

Daniel Asa Rose
American

A self-portrait he did in his youth shows a dashing spirit: wind-blown, courageous and something else—mean. The man definitely had a mean streak.

Mother-in-law jokes are a staple of sitcoms. A tradition has persisted for generations that in-laws are to be tolerated, though seldom loved. The reality is different. In many marriages, the in-laws are a beloved part of the total family, respected and welcomed for the love and energy that they have invested in raising the married pair.

"Here's to You" tackles the in-law problem, too, though with a difference. Superficially, this is the old tired husband–father-in-law competition, with the two men barely tolerating each other. But this story has a deeper dimension. After years of separation, the two men come to a belated realization of what matters most in life and a keener appreciation of each other's sometimes-annoying qualities.

Here's to You

JUST BECAUSE YOU BREAK UP WITH A woman is no reason to break up with her dad. You still use the squash racquet he gave you one Christmas, after all. You still haven't quite got around to tossing out the bay rum after-shave he gave you during Reagan's first term. In my case, it's the front lawn that keeps me connected. Every time I mow the lawn, I remember when he drove cross-country to visit and defiantly parked his

Porsche center-grass, where he felt a driveway *should* be, rather than behind the house, where I had one paved. How can you break up with the people in your past, even when they happen to be your basic ex-father-in-law from hell?

For, in actual truth, Wesley and I had never got along. I took my cue from the father-daughter axis that was already in place when I got there. He bullied her, she cried; she baited him, he bit. They were perfect for each other. When I married Laura, they very courteously widened the dynamic to include me. Before long, I too was baiting and biting to beat the band, taking Laura's side to Wesley, taking the old man's side to my wife. Brandy in hand, I would stay up till 2 in the morning with Wes trying to explicate his daughter to him while he reduced sauces and took potshots at alleged lapses in my grammar; then I'd mount the stairs and get side-blasted by my wife for cozying up to the enemy. Bridegrooms take note: this is a thankless position to be in.

But what a worthy enemy he was. Just to call him a retired physicist who cooked gourmet is not to do justice to the full cantankerous hulk of the man. Barrel-chested and bull-headed, with enough vinegar to insure that he would live to be 100, he was also a robust and unrepentant womanizer, a bomber pilot who had once flown 35 missions over Germany, a man who believed he had been gypped out of due credit for electrifying the organ and a gifted oil painter on the side. A self-portrait he did in his youth shows a dashing spirit: wind-blown, courageous and something else—mean. The man definitely had a mean streak. He looked and acted a lot like Gene Hackman in "Unforgiven": genial-sadistic, with a snare-drum laugh that did not mind if it caused pain.

Laura, herself, was a match for her pop—glamorous and tough. Their fights were legion. Into this maelstrom I gallantly stepped, dancing the 2 A.M. fool's dance of defending each to the other. Soon neither would talk to me. Inevitably, all the bitterness Wes had amassed against his daughter was aimed in my direction. And Laura started treating me as she had always treated her father, revelling, even, as if it were I who had grounded her her entire senior year, I who had ripped off my dinner jacket and chased her hippie friends from her debutante ball with a butcher knife.

And so seven years after making both their rather colorful acquaintances, I courteously narrowed the dynamic by accepting my wife's divorce. They were left to themselves. It became no longer my business how many modifiers were allegedly left dangling. Contact with the father-in-law lapsed.

Five years passed.

And so it was that coming back from Tibet six months ago, I was told that Wes had been hospitalized. I was startled to find old-fashioned endearments spring to my mind: why the old war horse, the old coot, the old codger had been laid low at last. Everything was starting to go: his liver backed up, his hemorrhoids burned, his toes turned black. Though we hadn't spoken in five years, I sent him a batch of prayer beads I'd bartered for in Shigatse. "These are from the Dalai Lama to heal you back to health," I wrote. "The kids need a grandpa who keeps on ticking."

He rallied. He was home from the hospital, chasing the private nurse in his silk bathrobe. He was well enough to take up the pen in his crabbed hand. Four months after I sent him the beads, an envelope arrived: just my name and my town, no street, no zip code—definitive proof that the bull-headedness was intact. Unsealing the letter, I had to wonder why I was letting him park on my front lawn again. For here was the bitterness spewing forth unabated, as though the faucet had been stopped up these five years and now flooded forth to catalogue all my generation's ancient arrogance, our uppity impertinence, our lack of respect for our elders. He also enclosed a copy of "Strunk and White" in case my grammar was still remiss, ha ha. But then the tone softened. He was talking about something new. About *why* our youthful arrogance irked him, about how he himself had once had a hard time coming to grips with his place in the world and learning to respect *his* elders. The tone was better than fatherly: it was a sharing as equals. It ended with these incredible words: "Can we not forgive each other our faults?"

After a month, I at last discovered what to send him back. I packed up a tape of Siobhan McKenna singing various passages from "Finnegans Wake." "It may not be grammatical," I said, "but can we agree it's music?" I told him I regretted wasting those 2 A.M.'s sparring instead of learning his technique for reducing sauces. I asked him if he was planning to fly any more bombing missions over Germany. I spoke of how well my sons, his grandchildren, were doing and said I saluted him across the gene pool. "Here, here," I said, metaphorically raising one of the brandy glasses we used to share, "let's do forgive and celebrate. I toast your renewable good health."

So it's easy, is it not, to pick up where you left off? There is no earthly reason to stop communicating with a man just because you divorced his daughter, no reason in the world not to keep the dialogue going ad infinitum. Except one. For this bullying bruiser who was going to live to be 100 suddenly dropped, just like that. Before I could send off my package, this unstoppable man with his burly chest and nasty brilliance was cut down, the private nurse uncaught, the hurtful snare drum of a laugh shut down at last. I had meant to pick up where we left off; now we were just leaving off. Wesley Love died, and what was music and what was not would have to wait until some later debate.

Here's to you, ex-father-in-law. I'm sorry we never recognized each other for what we were. Probably you were not the ogre I thought, just a mortal straining to suck in your gut in your canary yellow Lacoste shirt. I was just a kid trying to lock horns with one of the big guys. Why didn't we know that then? Why aren't we all more gentle with each other now?

Reading for Understanding

Main Idea

1. The main idea of the story is best expressed in which of the following? (a) "Bridegrooms take note: this is a thankless position to be in." (b) "Can we not forgive each other our faults?" (c) "I told him I regretted wasting those 2 A.M.'s sparring instead of learning his technique for reducing sauces." (d) "So it's easy, is it not, to pick up where you left off?"

Details

2. Wesley is all of the following EXCEPT a (a) bomber pilot (b) gourmet cook (c) strict father (d) gentle person.
3. The author returned from a trip to (a) Tibet (b) Nepal (c) India (d) Bhutan.
4. The author's wife's name is (a) Siobhan (b) Jean (c) Laura (d) not mentioned.
5. In the father-daughter arguments, the author (a) always took his wife's side (b) always took his father-in-law's side (c) was in the middle (d) actually enjoyed the lively give-and-take.

Inferences

6. Underneath the outward hostility, it seems probable that (a) the wife was superior in arguments (b) both men respected the other (c) Wesley deeply disliked his own daughter (d) the author could never forgive.
7. The most unexpected event in the story was (a) Wesley's sudden serious illness (b) the author's trip (c) the divorce itself (d) the continuing split between the two men.
8. The author's wife (a) avoided serious disagreements with her father

(b) transferred her bitterness toward her father to her husband (c) was consistently an unappreciated peacemaker (d) was ready for remarriage after five years.

Tone of the Selection

9. The tone of the selection can best be characterized as (a) bitter (b) angry (c) hesitant (d) mellow.

Fact or Opinion

Tell whether the following is a fact or an opinion.

10. Wesley's final illness included his liver.

Words in Context

1. "I would stay up till 2 in the morning with Wes, trying to *explicate* his daughter to him." **Explicate** (242) means (a) blame (b) explain (c) poke fun at (d) introduce.

2. "Just to call him a retired physicist who cooked gourmet is not to do justice to the full *cantankerous* hulk of the man." **Cantankerous** (242) means (a) huge (b) underestimated (c) grumpy (d) disgusting.

3. "He looked and acted like Gene Hackman in *Unforgiven: genial-sadistic* with a snare-drum laugh that did not mind if it caused pain." **Genial-sadistic** (242) means (a) cheerful-helpful (b) violent-evil (c) casual-indifferent (d) pleasant-cruel.

4. "Into this *maelstrom* I gallantly stepped, dancing the 2 A.M. fool's dance of defending each to the other." A **maelstrom** (242) is a (a) kind of cereal (b) no man's land (c) tropical storm (d) whirlpool.

5., 6. For here was the bitterness *spewing* forth *unabated*." **Spewing** (243) means (a) spurting (b) inching (c) stammering (d) tearing. **Unabated** (243) means (a) unpleasant (b) unwelcome (c) undiminished (d) unexpected.

7. "Before I could send off my package, this unstoppable man with his *burly* chest and nasty brilliance was cut down." **Burly** (243) means (a) lean (b) poorly shaped (c) prominent (d) husky.

Thinking Critically about the Story

1. The poet/novelist George Meredith once wrote:

   No villain need be! Passions spin the plot:
   We are betrayed by what is false within.

   Is there a villain in this story? Explain.
2. The author paints his father-in-law with all his warts. Yet he includes some very positive comments. Point these out.
3. Do you know anyone who likes to argue just for the sake of arguing, taking either side in a debate just to keep the sparks flying? What prompts a person to do this?
4. It's easy to love the lovable. Is there any obligation to love the unlovable as well? Does the author ultimately love Wesley? Explain.
5. In some relationships, the two people play games. The games often substitute for reality, saving the participants from dealing with real issues. Do the characters in "Here's to You" play games? Explain.
6. There is a French expression: "Tout comprendre; tout pardonner." Or "to understand all is to forgive all." Does the expression apply to this story? How?
7. *Maelstrom* (242) is a word with a history. It is a famous whirlpool off Norway's west coast. The word derives from two Norwegian words meaning "grinding stream." A legend tells that two magic millstones aboard a vessel sank in this region. They had ground out so much salt the vessel foundered, but the millstones continued to grind out salt, keeping the waters forever "turbulent and salty." *Ogre* is another colorful word. What can you find out about its history?

Language in Action

Latin Phrases in English

Most words from Latin roots have become normal English words, but some few words and phrases still retain the form they have in Latin. *Ad infinitum* (243), "without end or limit," for example, is just such a phrase. Here are some of the more common.

carpe diem—pluck the day (enjoy the moment)
caveat emptor—let the buyer beware
Deo volente—God willing
ex libris—from the books of (used on bookplates)
mea culpa—my fault (an admission of personal fault)
mens sana in corpore sano—a sound mind in a sound body

One phrase deserves special mention: *post hoc, ergo propter hoc,* meaning "after this, therefore because of this." This is an argument that asserts because something happened after another event, it happened because of it. If I believe I failed a test because I broke a mirror, I may use that faulty argument. The truth may be that I didn't study!

Can It Be Love?

Thinking Critically about the Stories

1. Which definition of *love* on pages 157–158 seems most apt to you? Why?
2. How many different kinds of love are demonstrated in this unit—for example, the infatuation of a young man for a woman just glimpsed? Identify each. Do you think each qualifies as an example of love?
3. In the past, marriages were not usually based on romantic love. What is romantic love? Is it a good basis for a successful marriage? What else is needed?
4. Tell which story appealed to you most and suggest your reasons for the choice.
5. There are few marriages more romantic than those involving Hollywood stars. Why do so many Hollywood and other celebrity marriages fail?
6. Which stories provide examples of love realized too late? Why?
7. Which character in this unit appealed to you most? Why?
8. When we read fiction, we tend to identify with one of the characters. With which character did you identify most closely? Explain.

The Writing Portfolio

Writing the Longer Theme

After the single sentence and the paragraph, you are invited to try your hand at a longer challenge. The basic elements are still the sentence and the paragraph, but these must be welded together into a satisfactory whole.

To link your paragraphs, you will find connectives helpful. The strongest links are conjunctions. Coordinate conjunctions can connect words, phrases, and clauses of equal rank: *and, but, or, nor.*

> Sheila plays field hockey, but Laura prefers volleyball.

Other conjunctions connect a dependent clause with an independent clause. A sample of these helpful connectors: *after, as, because, since, though, unless,* and *until.*

> Though the dam hadn't really broken, the townspeople were panicked.

Other helpful connectors include words like these:

after this	therefore	afterward
a day later	otherwise	finally

Try to use some of these connectors in the writing assignments that follow.

Choose those questions you are most interested in. The lengths of your responses will vary. When asked how long a man's legs should be, Abraham Lincoln replied, "Long enough to reach the ground." Your responses should be "long enough to reach the end!" Use these writing activities as warm-ups for assignments to come.

1. As you look ahead, what do you see in your future? What are your goals?

2. How do you plan to follow through, to reach the goals you've set?

3. Now turning to "Can It Be Love?" write a brief narrative follow-up to one of the following stories: "Dream Power Video," "Feuille d'Album," or "The Sojourner."

4. In "Dream Power Video," B.J. and Nan met socially in a video store. Does your community provide enough opportunities for your people to meet in socially acceptable places? Write an editorial for your school newspaper presenting your own point of view.

5. "Dream Power Video" captures teenage dialogue. Try your hand at recording conversation between two teenagers on dating, avoiding drugs, choosing clothes, or another topic. Get the speakers' permission.

6. Write the letter that John Ferris might have written from Paris, thanking Elizabeth for her hospitality. ("The Sojourner")

7. If you were a casting director for "Dream Power Video," which actor and actress would you cast for B.J. and Nan? Write a paragraph for each, justifying your choice.

8. If you have access to a computer and the Internet, research the use of lotteries and list some of the states participating. Add your own commentary.

Other Areas of Communication

1. If you were producing "Dream Power Video," which actor and actress would you cast for B.J. and Nan? Prepare a short talk for each, explaining your selection.

2. Are blind dates sometimes acceptable? Set up a panel discussion for your class. Set up in advance the topics to be considered—for example, the advantages and disadvantages, promises and perils.

3. Select from the library a collection of Katherine Mansfield's short stories. Be ready to report to the class on one of the stories.

4. Would one of the stories provide enough material for adaptation as a television play? Present your viewpoint in a talk of 3–5 minutes.

5. Set up a panel discussion of six students on the topic "Character Development in Fiction." Each participant will select a story and present a three-minute talk on character development in that story. Each speaker will analyze the methods used: by what the character does, says, or thinks; by the reactions of other characters to him or her; by what other characters say about him or her; by the author's comments on the character.

Language in Action—a Review

You may refer to the preceding pages to answer these questions.

1. The point of view least used by authors of detective stories is (a) the first person (b) the first person unlimited (c) the limited third person (d) the omniscient third-person.

2. All the following are common stereotypes EXCEPT the (a) handsome star athlete (b) talkative taxi driver (c) coach (d) cruel stepmother.

3. *Garage* and *chauffeur* are cited in the text because of their (a)

spelling (b) pronunciation (c) Greek derivation (d) history before the 20th century.

4. The suiting of sound to sense is called (a) onomatopoeia (b) stereo-type (c) simile (d) word strategy.

5. The word derived from literature is (a) *poinsettia* (b) *lilliputian* (c) *silhouette* (d) *bobby*.

6. "The stadium began to tremble. The players stood still and looked at the stadium roof. Was this an earthquake?" This is an example of (a) fiction (b) subjective writing (c) objective writing (d) exaggera-tion.

7. The expression *ex libris* is used (a) on legal documents (b) as part of a marriage license (c) in testing weight scales (d) to state ownership.

8. Another word for allusion is (a) *reference* (b) *deceit* (c) *hallucination* (d) *illustration*.

9. *Caveat emptor* gives advice to (a) buyers (b) artists (c) elected offi-cials (d) sellers.

10. Objective writing is preferred in a (a) poem (b) personal essay (c) news report (d) diary.

UNIT FOUR

I Love a Mystery

The most beautiful thing we can experience is

the mysterious. It is the source of all true art and power.

Albert Einstein

Einstein was, of course, talking about the larger and more important mysteries than those solved by Sherlock Holmes, Hercule Poirot, or Father Brown. Still, even a modest detective story contains a hint of the mysterious, a puzzle that seems too difficult to solve.

When the word **mystery** is mentioned, most people think of the detective story, but the mystery shelf in the average library contains a wide variety of types. There are, most of all, stories with detectives of all kinds. Then there are crime stories without a detective, like "Man in Hiding" (255). James Bond finds his way to these shelves, too, as do other spy and international-intrigue stories. Still, the most famous subcategory is the detective story.

"Why **do** people read detective stories?" asks the author Gladys Mitchell. Above all, she says, they have a definite plot. She adds, "Their writers must tidy up the loose ends, must supply a logical solution to the problem they have posed, must also, to hold the reader's attention, combine the primitive lust and energy of the hunter with the cold logic of the scholarly mind."

This unit contains a sampling of various types of mysteries. "Man in Hiding" and "Deja Vu" are crime stories without detectives. Both provide an unusual twist to the crimes. They suggest that punishment may come from circumstances, not the police.

The other stories introduce us to four different detective types. The blustering Colonel March ("The Crime in Nobody's Room") overpowers the characters by his presence and insight,

Father Brown ("The Oracle of the Dog") is a quite different type, introspective and understated, with a keen sense of human folly. The Old Man in the Corner ("The Glasgow Mystery"), like Father Brown solves the case from a distance, but he is a different personality, excitable and combative. If "Man in Hiding" has a crime without a detective, "The Case of the Rich Woman" has a detective, Parker Pyne, without a crime.

This is a cross-section that will show you some possibilities within this popular literary type.

Man in Hiding

Vincent Starrett
American

Dr. Loxley closed the outer door behind him and almost ran for <u>M. Boggs, Antiques</u>. As he locked the door of the antique shop, still shaking, he was relieved to see that the corridor was empty. They would follow him, of course, in a matter of minutes. Every office in the building would be searched, every office in the vast Merchandise Exchange.

It <u>had</u> to be the chest!

Dr. B. Edward Loxley had committed the perfect murder. Secure in a new identity, he cultivates all new friendships and looks forward to a reunion in Paris with a young woman. He has planned the major strategy so flawlessly that nothing can harm him.

He hasn't anticipated a fatal flaw in himself, however. As you read this story, notice the clues suggesting that the good doctor is his own worst enemy. Notice the clever twist that ends the story. Then consider the many uses of irony, page 264.

Man in Hiding

Dr. B. Edward Loxley (jocularly called "Bedward" by the Chicago gossip columnists), the wife-murderer for whom hundreds of police had been scouring the city for three weeks, sat quietly at his desk in the great Merchandise Exchange reading his morning mail. The frosted glass door of his outer office read simply: *William Drayham, Rare Books. Hours by Appointment.* After three weeks of security he was beginning to feel a little complacent. For three weeks he had not left his hiding place in the huge business complex and he had no intention of leaving it for the time being—except feet first.

It had all been carefully thought out beforehand. The office of "William Drayham" had been rented two months prior to the killing of his wife, and Loxley had quietly taken possession and created his new personality as a dealer in rare books. He had been accepted by all his neighbors in the sixth-floor corridor. The elevator starter was getting to know him. He breakfasted, lunched, and dined at the several restaurants in the building, was shaved by a favorite barber, and was—he had every reason to believe—an accepted fixture. His neighbors were inoffensive and unimaginative workers who did not for a moment question his identity, and the words *Rare Books* on the door were formidable enough to frighten away casual visitors.

Lora Loxley, murdered by suffocation, had been buried for nearly three weeks and even the newspapers were beginning to play down the sensational story. The feeling was growing that Dr. Loxley himself might also have been murdered and a desultory search for his body continued whenever the police had nothing more urgent to occupy them. Since Loxley's office window overlooked the river where, in addition to the normal traffic, police boats occasionally plied, he was able to watch the activities on the river with amused appreciation. He had now spent two lonely Saturdays and Sundays watching the weekend traffic with a pair of binoculars, waiting for any active renewal of police attention. He was on excellent terms with the watchmen in his part of the giant building, and they were now accustomed to seeing him at the most unlikely hours.

The Merchandise Exchange was actually a city within a city. It contained everything a man in hiding needed—restaurants, laundries, barber shops, tobacconists, dentists, newsstands, banking facilities, a gymnasium, even a postal station. He was already known by name in the restaurants and barber shops. He bought all the newspapers, morning and evening. Occasionally he dictated a letter to one of the public stenographers, ordering or declining rare books. As William Drayham he had a sufficient banking account downstairs for all his immediate needs. The rest of his wealth, in cash, was waiting in Paris—as was Gloria.

His principal bogies had been the watchmen and the cleaning women. But both fears had vanished. The watchmen had proved friendly, and the cleaning women, a friendly trio who liked candy, readily agreed to visit his office while he was having a late dinner. His domestic arrangements were simple. He slept on a couch in his inner office, which also contained a vault to which he could retire in an emergency. To date there had been no emergency.

Dr. Loxley pushed the mail aside impatiently. It was too early to expect a large response to the small rare-book advertisement he was running in a Sunday book-review supplement. But it was not too early for the coffee that Miss Marivole Boggs was willing to serve at all hours. What luck to have found so admirable a neighbor in the same corridor, and even, it might be said, in the same line! Rare books and antiques went very well together. Miss Boggs had been responsible for most of his infrequent customers. He glanced at his expensive wristwatch and left William Drayham's rare books without a pang.

The owner of *M. Boggs, Antiques,* as she described herself on the show window of her small shop at the end of the corridor, looked up at his entrance.

"Hello," she said. "I was hoping you'd come in."

"I couldn't resist," he said. His brown eyes took in the familiar room, resting for a moment on the suit of ancient armor that dominated one corner of the shop and the old Spanish chest that was Miss Boggs's pride and joy. "Well, I see nobody has bought either of them yet." It was one of their standing jokes that someday, when the rare-book business was better, he would buy them himself.

As Marivole Boggs poured his coffee she said, "The newspapers stories about that doctor are getting shorter every day. I'm beginning to believe he really *was* murdered."

They often discussed the missing Dr. Loxley, as indeed the whole city was doing. At first it had been Miss Boggs's idea that the "society doctor" had murdered his wife in favor of a more glamorous patient who was now living in sin with him somewhere on the French or Italian Riviera.

Dr. Loxley had thought not. "Too romantic, Miss Boggs. I still think his body is in the river or floating on its way to the Gulf of Mexico. That scarf they found on the river bank looks like it."

"Anyway, the police seem to have stopped looking," said Miss Boggs.

"Anyway, this is good coffee, my dear. I hope you'll give me your special recipe. Do you still plan to leave this month?"

"At once," she said. "I'm flying to New York tomorrow, if I can get away. I want to be in London for the Exhibition; then on to Paris, Rome, and Zurich. I'm enormously relieved that you'll be here to keep an eye on things, Bill. Coffee at all hours, eh?"

"Morning, noon, and night," he agreed, rising to leave. Her change of plan had startled him for a moment; but he was quick to see a distinct advantage in it for himself. "Never fear, I'll be here waiting for you when you return."

Strolling back to his own shop, humming a jaunty air, he became aware of a man leaving the doorway of the office directly opposite his own. Something about the man's carriage seemed familiar. The man was heading toward the elevators and walking fast. In an instant they would meet.

And suddenly Dr. Loxley realized that the man was indeed familiar. He was his own brother-in-law, Lawrence Bridewell.

Loxley's first instinct was to turn and flee, his second to return to *M. Boggs, Antiques*. His final decision, made in a split second, was to see the encounter through. His disguise had fooled better men than Larry Bridewell, although none who knew him better. With his former neat beard and mustache now gone, and his blue eyes transformed by brown contact lenses, Dr. Loxley was, to all appearances, another man. After that first appalling moment of indecision, he fumbled for a cigarette, realizing that after three weeks of growingly complacent safety, he was about to face the supreme test.

He tried and failed to light the cigarette. Then the two men were face to face, glancing at each other as men do in passing—and suddenly the test was over.

Or was it? Bridewell continued on his way to the elevators, still walking fast, and Loxley stumbled to his own door.

Did he dare look back? Had Bridewell turned to look back at *him*? Moving casually, Loxley stole a glance down the corridor. There was no doubt about it—Larry *was* looking back. Perhaps he had merely been troubled by an imagined resemblance.

Dr. Loxley had some difficulty opening his own door, and just before he closed it the thought occurred to him to look at the name on the door of the office from which his brother-in-law had emerged. Actually he knew very well what he would find there: *Jackson & Fortworth, Attorneys-at-Law*—and, below, the significant words: *Private Investigations*.

He tried to take himself in hand and was annoyed to find that he was shaking. Experimentally he ventured a drink to see what it would do for him. It helped considerably. But the whole incident haunted him the rest of the day and gave him a bad night. In the morning, however, his fears had evaporated. He was his confident self again—until, a few hours later, a second incident shook his nerve.

Returning from the cigar stand in the lobby, he passed the DeLuxe Dog Salon in one of the street-level corridors and, as he had often done before, paused to look into the windows at the fashionable dogs being barbered and prettified. It had always been an amusing spectacle, but this time, as he turned away, an appalling thing happened.

A well dressed woman was approaching the salon with a haughty French poodle on a leash. The woman looked familiar: Good Lord, she *was* familiar! She was Mrs. Montgomery Hyde, an old patient of his! Loxley's heart seemed to stop beating. Would she recognize him?

It was the dog that recognized him. With a refined little yelp the poodle jerked the leash from the woman's hand and flung himself against the doctor's legs.

With an effort, Loxley recovered his balance and somehow managed to recover his poise. It was his worst moment since the murder. Automatically he disengaged himself from the poodle's attentions and pulled the black ears.

"There, there, fellow," he said to the excited animal in a voice that he hoped was not his own. "I beg your pardon, Madam. Your dog appears to have made a mistake."

To his intense relief, Mrs. Montgomery Hyde agreed.

"Do forgive Toto's impulsiveness," she begged, snatching up the leash. "He loves everybody."

Dr. Loxley left the scene in almost a hurry. She had not recognized him! It seemed to him a miracle; but again he was annoyed to find himself shaking. And yet, wasn't it really a good omen? If Mrs. Hyde and his own brother-in-law had failed to recognize him, was there anything for him to fear?

Immediately he began to feel better. But when he had returned to his office, William Drayham again treated himself to a stiff drink.

In a moment of alert intelligence, he realized that for three weeks he had permitted himself to become too complacent. His meeting with Mrs. Hyde had taught him something that was important for him to remember: he had almost spoken her name! In the first onslaught of panic, he might well have betrayed himself. If it was important for him not to be recognized, it was equally important that *he* must not recognize anyone else.

It was clear to him now that this cat-and-mouse existence could not go on indefinitely. He must remain in hiding only until it was safe for him to emerge and get out of the country. Then William Drayham would ostentatiously pack his books and remove to New York. After that, the world was wide, with his immediate destination—Paris and Gloria.

For several days the chastened doctor lived cautiously, visiting *M. Boggs, Antiques* at intervals for coffee and to admire the suit of armor and the Spanish chest, which continued to fascinate him. He had promised Miss Boggs, now on her travels, not to cut the price on either if a buyer should turn up.

Twice, returning from the antique shop, he again caught a glimpse of his brother-in-law—both times entering the law office of Jackson & Fortworth—and had hurried to lock himself in his own office before Larry could emerge. What the devil did the fellow want with a firm of private investigators anyway?

The visit of Jackson, the senior lawyer of the firm, to the bookshop one morning took the doctor completely by surprise, or he might have locked the door.

"I've been intending to look in on you for some time, Mr. Drayham," said the lawyer cordially. "I'm Jackson, just across from you. Rare books have always interested me. Mind if I look around? I think that browse is the word."

Loxley rose from his chair abruptly, knocking a book from his desk to the floor. An icy fear had entered his heart. Was this the showdown at last, he wondered?

He shook hands effusively. "Glad to meet you, Mr. Jackson. By all means, browse. Is there anything special I can show you?"

But Jackson was already browsing. When he had finished, he strolled to the window. "Nice view of the river you have," he said appreciatively. "*My* windows all face an inner court." He walked to the door. "Just wanted to meet you, Mr. Drayham. I'll come in again when I have more time."

"Any time at all," said Loxley with warm courtesy.

Dr. Loxley sat down at his desk and reached for the lower drawer. Another little drink wouldn't hurt. What had the fellow really wanted? What had he hoped to learn? Or was he really one of those strange people who collected rare books?

One thing, however, was undeniably clear. Any day now he might have to leave the building and the city. If he was suspected, the blow would fall swiftly. At any minute the door might open again, and this time Jackson might not be alone. Why not get out of this trap immediately? What was there to stop him? His stock—300-odd volumes of miscellaneous volumes bought at a storage house—could be left behind if necessary.

What stopped him was Gloria's cable from Paris: TROUBLE HERE. PHONING FRIDAY NIGHT.

This was Thursday. Whatever else happened, he must wait for Gloria's call. His hand moved toward the lower drawer, then withdrew. Coffee, not whiskey, was what he needed; and after luncheon he spent most of the afternoon with Miss Boggs's weird collection of antiques. There he had an unobstructed view of Jackson's door, and was not himself visible. If Larry Bridewell was among the lawyer's visitors, Loxley did not see him.

Exploring the antique shop he paused, as always, to admire his two star exhibits, the almost frightening suit of armor and the massive Spanish chest. In a pinch, either would do as an emergency hiding place—if there was time enough to hide.

That evening he was startled to find his picture in the newspaper again—the face of Dr. B. Edward Loxley as he had looked with the neat little beard and moustache before he had murdered his wife. It seemed he'd been arrested by an alert Seattle policeman, but had denied his identity.

Dr. Loxley drew a long breath of relief. After all, perhaps he was still safe in this city within a city. But what could Gloria have to say to him that required a call from Paris? Bad news of some kind. Bad for somebody.

In spite of all his new fears, he hated to leave the building that had been his refuge. It had been his hope to live there indefinitely, undetected—never again to venture into the streets until Dr. Loxley was as forgotten as Dr. Crippen.

Again he slept off his fears and spent an uninterrupted forenoon with his view of the river and the morning newspapers. He was beginning to feel almost at ease again—indeed, when the insufferable Jackson knocked on his locked door and called a hearty greeting he almost welcomed having a visitor. But there was somebody with the attorney. Through the frosted pane Loxley could make out the shadowy outline of another man.

"May we come in?" the lawyer called out. "I've got a couple of friends here who want to talk to you."

Loxley rose uncertainly to his feet and moved to the door. So it had come at last! He had been right about his damned brother-in-law and this sneaking lawyer. This was the showdown. And suddenly Loxley knew what he had to do.

He unlocked the door and threw it open. "Come in, gentlemen," he said without emotion. "What can I do for you?"

Jackson was beaming. "These are my friends, Sergeants Coughlin and Ripkin, from headquarters. They hope you will come quietly." The lawyer laughed heartily at his own witticism.

"Come in, gentlemen, and sit down." Loxley forced a smile—he was panicking fast. He seated himself at his desk, trembling, and addressed and stamped an envelope. Then he stood up, shakily. "I was just going to the mail chute with an important letter. I'll be back in a few moments."

"Sure," said one of the two cops genially. "Take your time, Mr. Drayham."

Was there just the slightest emphasis on the name "Drayham" or was he merely imagining it?

Dr. Loxley closed the outer door behind him and almost ran for *M. Boggs, Antiques.* As he locked the door of the antique shop, still shaking, he was relieved to see that the corridor was empty. They would follow him, of course, in a matter of minutes. Every office in the building would be searched, every office in the vast Merchandise Exchange.

It *had* to be the chest!

It stood open as always, and he squeezed inside—an uncomfortable fit—then lowered the heavy lid until only a thin crack remained for air. Faintly now he thought he could hear footsteps in the corridor. He drew a deep breath and closed the lid.

There was a sharp "click," then only intense darkness.

Ten minutes later, Sergeant Ripkin said to his partner, "Wonder what's keeping that guy. We've still got about fifty tickets to sell, Pete."

"Oh, leave some with me," said Jackson. "I'll see that you get your money. Drayham's a good fellow—he'll buy a batch of them, I'm sure."

The two policemen, who had been hoping to dispose of all their remaining tickets for a benefit baseball game, departed leisurely.

The disappearance of William Drayham, a "rare-book dealer" with an office in the Merchandise Exchange, attracted less attention than the disappearance of Dr. B. Edward Loxley, but for a few days it was a mild sensation.

Returning from Europe a month later, Miss Boggs wondered idly when Bill would drop in for a cup of coffee. He had told her he would be here when she returned.

She puttered happily among her treasures. Some fool, she noted, had automatically locked the chest by closing it. One of these days she'd have to unlock it and raise the lid.

Reading for Understanding

Main Idea

1. The main idea may be suggested by which of the following common sayings?
    (a) It's an ill wind that blows nobody good.
    (b) Murder will out.
    (c) Empty barrels make the most noise.
    (d) Never leave till tomorrow what you can do today.

Details

2. A key element of Loxley's disguise was (a) a change of laugh (b) a large shoe size (c) formal clothes (d) eye color.

3. Loxley feared he might be recognized by (a) his brother-in-law (b) Miss Boggs (c) his tailor (d) none of these.

4. Bridewell visited the offices of (a) Dr. Crippen (b) an antique dealer (c) a private investigator (d) William Drayham.

Inferences

5. The most crucial element in the story proved to be (a) Miss Boggs' trip abroad (b) Toto's recognition of Loxley (c) Mrs. Montgomery Hyde's comments to him (d) good news from Gloria.

6. It is probable that the rare books (a) cost Loxley a small fortune (b) were not especially valuable (c) contained the best writing by English writers of the detective story (d) were the immediate cause of Loxley's fall.

7. The end of the mystery will occur when (a) Bridewell goes to the police (b) Drayham goes to New York (c) Miss Boggs opens the trunk (d) the police charge Loxley with murder.

8. William Drayham was (a) a policeman (b) a private detective (c) the husband of Lora (d) in love with Miss Boggs.

Order of Events

9. Arrange the items in the order in which they occurred. Use letters only.
   A. Drayham meets Miss Boggs.
   B. Loxley rents a bookstore.
   C. Loxley meets Mrs. Hyde.
   D. Loxley meets two policemen.
   E. Loxley murders his wife.

Fact or Opinion

Tell whether the following is a fact or an opinion.

10. Loxley placed most of his money in Paris to be with Gloria.

Words in Context

1. "After three weeks of security he was beginning to feel a little *complacent*." **Complacent** (256) means (a) nervous (b) bored (c) irritated (d) self-satisfied.

2. "The words *Rare Books* on the door were *formidable* enough to

frighten away casual visitors." **Formidable** (256) means (a) enticing (b) curious (c) evil (d) menacing.

3. "A *desultory* search for his body continued whenever the police had nothing more urgent to occupy them." **Desultory** (256) means (a) sluggish (b) mammoth (c) uninterrupted (d) well-publicized.

4. "He shook hands *effusively*." **Effusively** (260) means (a) gingerly (b) enthusiastically (c) warily (d) reluctantly.

Thinking Critically about the Story

1. What was Loxley's weakness? How did it finally defeat him?
2. Why does the author mention Paris as one of Miss Boggs' destinations?
3. Had Loxley committed the perfect crime? Is there such a thing as a perfect crime? Explain.
4. Does Loxley have a guilty conscience, or is he concerned solely with his own survival? Explain
5. Have you ever read another story or seen a movie in which a criminal is defeated by his own weaknesses? Tell about it.
6. In S. Walter Scott's novel *Ivanhoe,* Robin Hood is referred to as Locksley. Do you think the author had some comparison in mind when he named the leading character Loxley?
7. When Miss Boggs leaves (257), Loxley says, "Never fear, I'll be here waiting for you when you return." How does his expectation differ from the reality? How is it similar? See *Irony,* below.

Language in Action

Irony

A passenger whose fear of flying caused him to cancel a flight and take a train instead was involved in a fatal train accident.

"How ironic!" people said. "The very search for safety was in the end a source of disaster."

This is an example of situational irony. When the astronaut John

Glenn returned from hazardous trips in space and injured himself in a bathroom fall, people exclaimed, "How ironic." **Irony** involves a clash between what is and what seems (or ought) to be. John Glenn's space trip should have been much more dangerous than the "safety" of home.

Irony prevails throughout "Man in Hiding." Loxley consistently misinterprets people's actions. Like guilty persons everywhere, he reads danger and disclosure all around him, even in the most unlikely circumstances. The reality is that returning to the police would have been safe. Entering the chest was fatal. How ironic!

Verbal irony is similar. When Antony kept saying at Julius Caesar's funeral that "Brutus is an honorable man," he meant quite the opposite. Irony says one thing and suggests another. On page 500, Sir Joseph Porter suggests, "Stick close to your desks and never go to sea and you all may be Rulers of the Queen's Navee." One would expect a "Ruler of the Queen's Navee" to be acquainted with the sea.

Sarcasm, satire, and verbal irony are members of the same family.

The Crime in Nobody's Room

Carter Dickson
American

**"It's nobody's room, sir," the porter answered simply.
"There's not a sitting room like that in the whole building."**

Detective stories feature mysterious disappearances. Important clues vanish. Corpses seem to rise and walk away. Crucial articles of clothing suddenly become invisible. But to lose an entire room requires a special kind of ingenuity. It takes the genius of a Colonel March to "find" the room again.

Carter Dickson is a pen name of John Dickson Carr. Like Agatha Christie (308), he has created several sleuths. Under the **Carter Dickson** name, he introduced Colonel March and "The Old Man," Sir Henry Merrivale. Under the **John Dickson Carr** name, he gave us Gideon Fell. Though March, Merrivale, and Fell are very much alike, Carr's fans don't mind the similarities.

Colonel March, the detective in this story, is head of the Department of Queer Complaints, the Ragbag Department or the "Crazy House." He tackles problems that the regular police force is unable or unwilling to meddle with. Colonel March stories are filled with the kinds of puzzles presented in our story.

Carr is the master of the locked-room murder-mystery. In one of his stories, he actually discusses all the ways a murder can be committed within a seemingly locked room. Many of his stories seem to include supernatural elements, which are logically explained at the end. Though Carr plays fair and includes clues for the perceptive reader, his ingenious cleverness foils most puzzle solvers. Try to match wits with Colonel March in "The Crime in Nobody's Room."

The Crime in Nobody's Room

BANDS WERE PLAYING and seven suns were shining; but this took place entirely in the head and heart of Mr. Ronald Denham. He beamed on the car-park attendant at the Regency Club, who assisted him into the taxi. He beamed on the taxidriver. He beamed on the night porter who helped him out at his flat in Sloane Street, and he felt an irresistible urge to hand banknotes to everyone in sight.

Now, Ronald Denham would have denied that he had taken too many drinks. It was true that he had attended an excellent bachelor party, to celebrate Jimmy Bellchester's wedding. But Denham would have maintained that he was upheld by spiritual things; and he had proved his exalted temperance by leaving the party at a time when many of the guests were still present.

As he had pointed out in a speech, it was only a month before his own wedding to Miss Anita Bruce. Anita, in fact, lived in the same block of flats and on the same floor as himself. This fact gave him great pleasure on the way home. Like most of us, Denham in this mood felt a strong urge to wake people up in the middle of the night and talk to them. He wondered whether he ought to wake up Anita. But in his reformed state he decided against it, and felt like a saint. He would not even wake up Tom Evans, who shared the flat with him—though that stern young business man usually worked so late at the office that Denham got in before he did.

At a few minutes short of midnight, then, Denham steered his way into the foyer of Medici Court. Pearson, the night porter, followed him to the automatic lift.

"Everything all right, sir?" inquired Pearson in a stage whisper. Denham assured him that it was, and that he was an excellent fellow.

"You—er—don't feel like singing, do you, sir?" asked Pearson with some anxiety.

"As a matter of fact," said Denham, who had not previously considered this, "I do. You are full of excellent ideas, Pearson. But let us sing nothing improper, Pearson. Let it be something of noble sentiment, like——"

"Honestly, sir," urged Pearson, "if it was me, I wouldn't do it. *He's* upstairs, you know. We thought he was going to Manchester this afternoon, to stay a week, but he changed his mind. He's upstairs now."

This terrible hint referred to the autocrat of Medici Court, Cellini Court, Bourbon Court, and half a dozen other great hives. Sir Rufus Armingdale, high khan of builders, not only filled London with furnished flats which really were the last word in luxury at a low price: he showed his pride in his own merchandise by living in them.

"No special quarters for me," he was quoted as saying, with fist upraised for emphasis. "No castle in Surrey or barracks in Park Lane. Just an ordinary flat; and not the most expensive of 'em either. That's where I'm most comfortable, and that's where you'll find me."

Considering all the good things provided in Armingdale's Furnished Flats, even his autocratic laws were not much resented. Nor could anyone resent the fact that all flats in a given building were furnished exactly alike, and that the furniture must be kept in the position Rufus Armingdale gave it. Medici Court was "Renaissance," as Bourbon Court was "Louis XV": a tower of rooms like luxurious cells, and only to be distinguished from each other by an ornament on a table or a picture on a wall.

But Sir Rufus's leases even discouraged pictures. Considering that he was something of an art collector himself, and had often been photographed in his own flat with his favourite Greuze or Corot, some annoyance was felt at this. Sir Rufus Armingdale did not care. You either leased one of his flats, or you didn't. He was that that sort of man.

Otherwise, of course, Ronald Denham's adventure could not have happened. He returned from the bachelor party; he took Pearson's advice about the singing; he went up in the automatic lift to the second floor; and he walked into what the champagne told him was his own flat.

That he went to the second floor is certain. Pearson saw him put his finger on the proper button in the lift. But nothing else is certain, since the hall upstairs was dark. Pushing open a door—either his key fitted it or the door was open—Denham congratulated himself on getting home.

Also, he was a little giddy. He found himself in the small foyer, where lights were on. After a short interval he must have moved into the sitting room, for he found himself sitting back in an armchair and contemplating familiar surroundings through a haze. Lights were turned on here as well: yellow-shaded lamps, one with a pattern like a dragon on the shade.

Something began to trouble him. There was something odd, he thought, about those lamp shades. After some study, it occurred to him that he and Tom Evans hadn't any lamp shades like that. They did not own any bronze book ends either. As for the curtains . . .

Then a picture on the wall swam out of oblivion, and he stared at it. It was a small dull-coloured picture over the sideboard. And it penetrated into his mind at last that he had got into the wrong flat.

Everything now showed itself to him as wrong: it was as though a blur had come into focus.

"Here, I'm sorry!" he said aloud, and got up.

There was no reply. The heinousness of his offence partly steadied him. Where in the name of sanity was he? There were only three other flats on the second floor. One of these was Anita Bruce's. Of the others, one was occupied by a brisk young newspaper man named Conyers, and the other by the formidable Sir Rufus Armingdale.

Complete panic caught him. He felt that at any moment a wrathful occupant might descend on him, to call him a thief at worst or a snooper at best. Turning round to scramble for the door, he almost ran into another visitor in the wrong flat.

This visitor sat quietly in a tall chair near the door. He was a thin, oldish, well-dressed man, wearing thick-lensed spectacles, and his head was bent forward as though in meditation. He wore a soft hat and a thin oilskin waterproof coloured green: a jaunty and bilious-looking coat for such a quiet figure. The quiet light made it gleam.

"Please excuse——" Denham began in a rush, and talked for some seconds before he realized that the man had not moved.

Denham stretched out his hand. The coat was one of those smooth, almost seamless American waterproofs, yellowish outside and green inside; and for some reason the man was now wearing it inside out. Denham was in the act of telling him this when the head lolled, the smooth oilskin gleamed again, and he saw that the man was dead.

Tom Evans, stepping out of the lift at a quarter past one, found the hall of the second floor in complete darkness. When he had turned on the lights from a switch beside the lift, he stopped short and swore.

Evans, lean and swarthy, with darkish eyebrows merging into a single line across his forehead, looked a little like a Norman baron in a romance. Some might have said a robber baron, for he carried a brief case and was a stern man of business despite his youth. But what he saw now made him momentarily forget his evening's work. The hall showed four doors, with their microscopic black numbers, set some distance apart. Near the door leading to Anita Bruce's flat, Ronald Denham sat hunched on an oak settle. There was a lump at the base of his skull, and he was breathing in a way Evans did not like.

It was five minutes more before Denham had been whacked and pounded into semi-consciousness; and to such a blinding headache that its pain helped to revive him. First he became aware of Tom's lean, hook-nosed face bending over him, and Tom's usual fluency at preaching.

"I don't mind you getting drunk," the voice came to him dimly. "In fact, I expected it. But at least you ought to be able to carry your liquor decently. What the devil have you been up to, anyway? Hoy!"

"He had his raincoat on inside out," was the first thing Denham said. Then memory came back to him like a new headache or a new explosion, and he began to pour out the story.

"——and I tell you there's a dead man in one of those flats! I think he's been murdered. Tom, I'm not drunk; I swear I'm not. Somebody sneaked up behind and bashed me over the back of the head just after I found him."

"Then how did you get out here?"

"Oh, God, how should I know? Don't argue; help me up. I suppose I must have been dragged out here. If you don't believe me, feel the back of my head. Just feel it."

Evans hesitated. He was always practical, and there could be no denying the bruise. He looked uncertainly up and down the hall.

"But who is this dead man?" he demanded. "And whose flat is he in?"

"I don't know. He was an oldish man with thick glasses and a green raincoat. I never saw him before. Looked a bit like an American, somehow."

"Nonsense! Nobody wears a green raincoat."

"I'm telling you, he was wearing it inside out. If you ask me why, I'm going to bat my head against the wall and go to sleep again." He wished he could do this, for he could not see straight and his head felt like a printing press in full blast. "We ought to be able to identify the flat easily enough. I can give a complete description of it——"

He paused, for two doors had opened simultaneously in the hall. Anita Bruce and Sir Rufus Armingdale came out, in different stages of anger or curiosity at the noise.

If Evans had been more of a psychologist, he might have anticipated the effect this would have on them. As it was, he stood looking from one to the other, thinking whatever thoughts you care to attribute to him. For he was an employee of Sir Rufus, as manager of the Sloane Square Office of Armingdale Flats, and he could risk no trouble.

Anita seemed to take in the situation at a glance. She was small, dark, plump, and fluffy-haired. She was wearing a négligé and smoking a cigarette. Seeing the expressions of the other three, she removed the cigarette from her mouth in order to smile. Sir Rufus Armingdale did not look so much formidable as fretful. He had one of those powerful faces whose features seem to have run together like a bull pup's. But the old dressing gown, fastened up at the throat as though he were cold, took away the suggestion of an autocrat and made him only a householder.

He breathed through his nose, rather helplessly, until he saw an employee. His confidence returned.

"Good morning, Evans," he said. "What's the meaning of this?"

Evans risked it. "I'm afraid it's trouble, sir. Mr. Denham—well, he's found a dead man in one of the flats."

"Ron!" cried Anita.

"A dead man," repeated Armingdale, without surprise. "Where?"

"In one of the flats. He doesn't know which."

"Oh? why doesn't he know which?"

"He's got a frightful bump on the back of his head," said Anita, exploring. She looked back over her shoulder and spoke swiftly. "It's quite all right, Tom. Don't get excited. He's d-r-u-n-k."

"I am not drunk," said Denham, with tense and sinister calmness. "May I also point out that I am able to read and write, and that I have not had words spelled out in front of me since I was four years old? Heaven give me s-t-r-e-n-g-t-h! I tell you, I can describe the place."

He did so. Afterwards there was a silence. Anita, her eyes shining curiously, dropped her cigarette on the autocrat's hardwood floor and ground it out. The autocrat seemed too abstracted to notice.

"Ron, old dear," Anita said, going over and sitting down beside him, "I'll believe you if you're as serious as all that. But you ought to know it isn't *my* flat."

"And I can tell you it isn't mine," grunted Armingdale. "There certainly isn't a dead man in it. I've just come from there, and I know."

If they had not known Armingdale's reputation so well, they might have suspected him of trying to make a joke. But his expression belied it as well. It was heavy and lowering, with more than a suggestion of the bull pup.

"This picture you say you saw," he began. "The one over the sideboard. Could you describe it?"

"Yes, I think so," said Denham desperately. "It was a rather small portrait of a little girl looking sideways over some roses, or flowers of some kind. Done in that greyish-brown stuff; I think they call it sepia."

Armingdale stared at him.

"Then I know it isn't mine," he said. "I never owned a sepia drawing in my life. If this young man is telling the truth, there's only one flat left. I think I shall just take the responsibility of knocking, and——"

His worried gaze moved down towards the door of the flat occupied by Mr. Hubert Conyers, of the *Daily Record*. But it was unnecessary to knock at the door. It opened with such celerity that Denham wondered whether anyone had been looking at them through the slot of the letter box; and Hubert Conyers stepped out briskly. He was an unobtrusive, sandy-haired little man, very different from Denham's idea of a journalist. His only extravagance was a taste for blended shadings in his clothes, from suit to shirt to necktie; though he usually contrived to look rumpled. He was always obliging, and as busy as a parlour clock. But his manner had a subdued persuasiveness which could worm him through narrower places than you might have imagined.

He came forward drawing on his coat, and with a deft gesture he got into the middle of the group.

"Sorry, sorry, sorry," he began, seeming to propitiate everyone at once. "I couldn't help overhearing, you know. Good evening, Sir Rufus. The fact is, it's not my flat either. Just now, the only ornaments in my sitting room are a lot of well-filled ashtrays and a bottle of milk. Come and see, if you like."

There was a silence, while Conyers looked anxious.

"But it's got to be somebody's flat!" snapped Sir Rufus Armingdale, with a no-nonsense air. "Stands to reason. A whole confounded sitting room can't vanish like smoke. Unless—stop a bit—unless Mr. Denham got off at some other floor."

"I don't know. I may have."

"And I don't mind admitting——" said Armingdale, hesitating as everyone looked at him curiously. The autocrat seemed worried. "Very well. The fact is, *I've* got a picture in my flat something like the one Mr. Denham described. It's Grueze's 'Young Girl with Primroses.' But mine's an oil painting, of course. Mr. Denham is talking about a sepia drawing. That is, if he really saw anything. Does this dead man exist at all?"

Denham's protestations were cut short by the hum of an ascending lift. But it was not the ordinary lift in front of them; it was the service lift at the end of the hall. The door was opened, and the cage grating pulled back, to show the frightened face of the night porter.

"Sir," said Pearson, addressing Armingdale as though he were beginning an oration. "I'm glad to see *you*, sir. You always tell us that if something serious happens we're to come straight to you instead of the manager. Well, I'm afraid this is serious. I—the fact is, I found something in this lift."

Denham felt that they were being haunted by that phrase, "the fact is." Everybody seemed to use it. He recalled a play in which it was maintained that anyone who began a sentence like this was usually telling a lie. But he had not time to think about this, for they had found the elusive dead man.

The unknown lay on his face in one corner of the lift. A light in the roof of the steel cage shone down on his grey felt hat, on an edge of his thick spectacles, and on his oilskin waterproof. But the coat was no longer green, for he was now wearing it right-side-out in the ordinary way.

Anita, who had come quietly round beside Denham, seized his arm. The night porter restrained Tom Evans as the latter bent forward.

"I shouldn't touch him, sir, if I was you. There's blood."

"Where?"

Pearson indicated a stain on the grey-rubber floor. "And if I'm any judge, sir, he died of a stab through the heart. I—I lifted him up a bit. But I don't see any kind of knife that could have done it."

"Is this the man you saw?" Armingdale asked Denham quietly. Denham nodded. Something tangible, something to weigh and handle, seemed to have brought the force back to Armingdale's personality.

"Except," Denham added, "that he's now wearing his raincoat right-side-out. Why? Will somebody tell me that? Why?"

"Never mind the raincoat," Anita said close to his ear. "Ron, you don't know him, do you? You'll swear you don't know him?"

He was startled. She had spoken without apparent urgency, and so low that the others might not have heard her. But Denham, who knew her so well, knew that there was urgency behind the unwinking serious-ness of her eyes. Unconsciously she was shaking his arm. His wits had begun to clear, despite the pain in his skull; and he wondered.

"No, of course I don't know him. Why should I?"

"Nothing! Nothing at all. Ss-t!"

"Well, I know him," said Hubert Conyers.

Conyers had been squatting down at the edge of the lift, and craning his neck to get a close view of the body without touching it. Now he straightened up. He seemed so excited that he could barely control himself, and his mild eye looked wicked.

"I interviewed him a couple of days ago," said Conyers. "Surely you know him, Sir Rufus?"

" 'Surely' is a large word, young man. No, I do not know him. Why?"

"That's Dan Randolph, the American real-estate king," said Conyers, keeping a watchful eye on Armingdale. "All of you will have heard of him: he's the fellow who always deals in spot cash, even if it's a million. I'd know those spectacles anywhere. He's as near-sighted as an owl. Er—am I correctly informed, Sir Rufus, that he was in England to do some business with you?"

Armingdale smiled bleakly. "You have no information, young man," he said. "And so far as I'm concerned you're not getting any. So that's Dan Randolph! I knew he was in England; but he's certainly not made any business proposition to me."

"Maybe he was coming to do it."

"Maybe he was," said Armingdale, with the same air of a parent to a child. He turned to Pearson. "You say you found him in that lift. When did you find him? And how did you come to find him?"

Pearson was voluble. "The lift was on the ground floor, sir. I just happened to glance through the little glass panel, and I see him lying there. So I thought I'd better run the lift up here and get you. As for putting him there——" He pointed to the recall button on the wall outside the lift. "Somebody on any floor, sir, could have shoved him in here, and pressed this button, and sent him downstairs. He certainly wasn't put in on the ground floor. Besides, I saw him come into the building to-night."

"Oh?" put in Conyers softly. "When was this?"

"Might have been eleven o'clock, sir."

"Whom was he coming to see?"

Pearson shook his head helplessly and with a certain impatience. "These ain't service flats, sir, where you telephone up about every visitor. You ought to know we're not to ask visitors anything unless they seem to need help, or unless it's somebody who has no business here. I don't know. He went up in the main lift, that's all I can tell you."

"Well, what floor did he go to?"

"I dunno." Pearson ran a finger under a tight collar. "But excuse me, sir, may I ask a question, if you please? What's wrong exactly?"

"We've lost a room," said Ronald Denham, with inspiration. "Maybe you can help. Look here, Pearson: you've been here in these flats a long time. You've been inside most of them—in the sitting rooms, for instance?"

"I think I can say I've been in all of 'em, sir."

"Good. Then we're looking for a room decorated like this," said Denham. For the third time he described what he had seen, and Pearson's expression grew to one of acute anguish. At the end of it he shook his head.

"It's nobody's room, sir," the porter answered simply. "There's not a sitting room like that in the whole building."

At three o'clock in the morning, a sombre group of people sat in Sir Rufus Armingdale's flat, and did not even look at each other. The police work was nearly done. A brisk divisional detective-inspector, accompanied by a sergeant, a photographer, and a large amiable man in a top hat, had taken a statement from each of those concerned. But the statements revealed nothing.

Denham, in fact, had received only one more mental jolt. Entering Armingdale's flat, he thought for a second that he had found the missing room. The usual chairs of stamped Spanish leather, the refectory table, the carved gewgaws, greeted him like a familiar nightmare. And over the sideboard hung a familiar picture—that of a small girl looking sideways over an armful of roses.

"That's not it?" said Anita quickly.

"It's the same subject, but it's not the same picture. That's in oils. What sort of game do you suppose is going on in this place?"

Anita glanced over her shoulder. She had dressed before the arrival of the police; and also, he thought, she had put on more make-up than was necessary.

"Quick, Ron; before the others get here. Were you telling the truth?"

"Certainly. You don't think——?"

"Oh, I don't know and I don't care; I just want you to tell me. Ron, you didn't kill him yourself?"

He had not even time to answer before she stopped him. Sir Rufus Armingdale, Conyers, and Evans came through from the foyer; and with them was the large amiable man who had accompanied Divisional Inspector Davidson. His name, it appeared, was Colonel March.

"You see," he explained, with a broad gesture, "I'm not here officially. I happened to be at the theatre, and I dropped in on Inspector Davidson for a talk, and he asked me to come along. So if you don't like any of my questions, just tell me to shut my head. But I do happen to be attached to the Yard——"

"I know you, Colonel," said Conyers, with a crooked grin. "You're the head of the Ragbag Department, D-3. Some call it the Crazy House."

Colonel March nodded seriously. He wore a dark overcoat, and had a top hat pushed back on his large head; this, with his florid complexion, sandy moustache, and bland blue eyes, gave him something of the look of a stout colonel in a comic paper. He was smoking a large-bowled pipe with the effect of seeming to sniff smoke from the bowl rather than draw it through the stem. He appeared to be enjoying himself.

"It's a compliment," he assured them. "After all, somebody has got to sift all the queer complaints. If somebody comes in and reports (say) that the Borough of Stepney is being terrorized by a blue pig, I've got to decide whether it's a piece of lunacy, or a mistake, or a hoax, or a serious crime. Otherwise good men would only waste their time. You'd be surprised how many such complaints there are. But I was thinking, and so was Inspector Davidson, that you had a very similar situation here. If you wouldn't mind a few extra questions——"

"As many as you like," said Sir Rufus Armingdale. "Provided somebody's got a hope of solving this damned——"

"As a matter of fact," said Colonel March, frowning, "Inspector Davidson has reason to believe that it is already solved. A good man, Davidson."

There was a silence. Something unintentionally sinister seemed to have gathered in Colonel March's affable tone. For a moment nobody dared to ask him what he meant.

"Already solved?" repeated Hubert Conyers.

"Suppose we begin with you, Sir Rufus," said March with great courtesy. "You have told the inspector that you did not know Daniel Randolph personally. But it seems to be common knowledge that he was in England to see you."

Armingdale hesitated. "I don't know his reasons. He may have been here to see me, among other things. Probably was. He wrote to me about it from America. But he hasn't approached me yet, and I didn't approach him first. It's bad business."

"What was the nature of this business, Sir Rufus?"

"He wanted to buy an option I held on some property in—never mind where. I'll tell you in private, if you insist."

"Was a large sum involved?"

Armingdale seemed to struggle with himself. "Four thousand, more or less."

"So it wasn't a major business deal. Were you going to sell?"

"Probably."

Colonel March's abstracted eye wandered to the picture over the sideboard. "Now, Sir Rufus, that Greuze, 'Young Girl with Primroses.' I think it was recently reproduced, in its natural size, as a full-page illustration in the *Metropolitan Illustrated News.*"

"Yes, it was," said Armingdale. He added, "In—sepia."

Something about this afterthought made them all move forward to look at him. It was like the puzzle of a half truth: nobody knew what it meant.

"Exactly. Just two more questions. I believe that each of these flats communicates with a fire escape leading down into the mews behind?"

"Yes. What of it?"

"Will the same key open the front door of each of the flats?"

"No, certainly not. All the lock patterns are different."

"Thank you. Now, Mr. Conyers—a question for you. Are you married?"

Hitherto Conyers had been regarding him with a look of watchful expectancy, like an urchin about to smash a window and run. Now he scowled.

"Married? No."

"And you don't keep a valet?"

"The answer to that, Colonel, is loud and prolonged laughter. Honestly, I don't like your 'social' manner. Beston, our crime news man, knows you. And it's always, 'Blast you, Beston, if you print one hint about the Thingummy case I'll have your hide.' What difference does it make whether I'm married or not, or whether I have a valet or not?"

"A great deal," said March seriously. "Now, Miss Bruce. What is your occupation, Miss Bruce?"

"I'm an interior decorator," answered Anita.

She began to laugh. It may have been with a tinge of hysteria; but she sat back in a tall chair and laughed until there were tears in her eyes.

"I'm terribly sorry," she went on, holding out her hand as though to stop them, "but don't you see? The murder was done by an interior decorator. That's the whole secret."

Colonel March cut short Armingdale's shocked protest.

"Go on," he said sharply.

"I thought of it first off. Of course there's no 'vanishing room.' Some sitting room has just been redecorated. All the actual furnishings, tables and chairs and sideboards, are just the same in every room. The only way you can tell them apart is by small movable things—pictures, lamp shades, book ends—which could be changed in a few minutes.

"Ron accidentally walked into the murderer's flat just after the murderer had killed that old man. That put the murderer in a pretty awful position. Unless he killed Ron too, he was caught with the body and Ron could identify his flat. But he thought of a better way. He sent that man's body down in the lift and dragged Ron out into the hall. Then he simply altered the decorations of his flat. Afterwards he could sit down and dare anyone to identify it as the place where the body had been."

Anita's face was flushed with either defiance or fear.

"Warm," said Colonel March. "Unquestionably warm. That is why I was wondering whether you couldn't tell us what really happened."

"I don't understand you."

"Well, there are objections to the redecoration. You've got to suppose that nobody had ever been in the flat before and seen the way it was originally decorated. You've also got to suppose that the murderer could find a new set of lamp shades, pictures, and book ends in the middle of the night.——Haven't you got it the wrong way round?"

"The wrong way round?"

"Somebody," said March, dropping his courtesy, "prepared a dummy room to begin with. He put in the new lamp shades, the book ends, the copy of a well-known picture, even a set of new curtains. He entertained Randolph in that dummy room. He killed Randolph there. Afterwards, of course, he simply removed the knick-knacks and set the place right again. But it was the dummy room into which Ronald Denham walked. That, Mr. Denham, was why you did not recognize——"

"Recognize what?" roared Denham. "Where was I?"

"In the sitting room of your own flat," said Colonel March gravely. "If you had been sober you might have made a mistake; but you were so full of champagne that your instinct brought you home after all."

There were two doors in the room, and the blue uniform of a policeman appeared in each. At March's signal, Inspector Davidson stepped forward. He said:

"Thomas Evans, I arrest you for the murder of Daniel Randolph. I have to warn you that anything you say will be taken down in writing and may be used in evidence at your trial."

"Oh, look here," protested Colonel March, when they met in Armingdale's flat next day, "the thing was simple enough. We had twice as much trouble over that kid in Bayswater, who pinched all the oranges. And you had all the facts.

"Evans, as one of Sir Rufus's most highly placed and trusted employees, was naturally in a position to know all about the projected business deal with Randolph. And so he planned an ingenious swindle. A swindle, I am certain, was all he intended.

"Now you, Sir Rufus, had intended to go to Manchester yesterday afternoon, and remain there for a week. (Mr. Denham heard that from the night porter, when he was advised against singing.) That would leave your flat empty. Evans telephoned to Randolph, posing as you. He asked Randolph to come round to your flat at eleven o'clock at night, and settle the deal. He added that you *might* be called away to Manchester; but, in that event, his secretary would have the necessary papers ready and signed.

"It would have been easy. Evans would get into your empty flat by way of the fire escape and the window. He would pose as your secretary. Randolph—who, remember, always paid spot cash even if it involved a million—would hand over a packet of banknotes for a forged document.

"Why should Randolph be suspicious of anything? He knew, as half the newspaper-reading world knows, that Sir Rufus lived on the second floor of Medici Court. He had seen photographs of Sir Rufus with his favourite Greuze over the sideboard. Even if he asked the hall porter for directions, he would be sent to the right flat. Even if the hall porter said Sir Rufus was in Manchester, the ground had been prepared and Randolph would ask for Sir Rufus's secretary.

"Unfortunately, a hitch occurred. Sir Rufus decided not to go to Manchester. He decided it yesterday afternoon, after all Evans's plans had been made and Randolph was due to arrive. But Evans needed that money; as we have discovered to-day, he needed it desperately. He wanted that four thousand pounds.

"So he hit on another plan. Sir Rufus would be at home and his flat could not be used. But, with all the rooms exactly alike except for decorations, why not an *imitation* of Sir Rufus's flat? The same plan would hold good, except that Randolph would be taken to the wrong place. He would come up in the lift at eleven. Evans would be waiting with the door of the flat open, and would take him to a place superficially resembling Sir Rufus's. The numbers on the doors are very small; and Randolph, as we know, was so near-sighted as to be almost blind. If Evans adopted some disguise, however clumsy, he could never afterwards be identified as the man who swindled Randolph. And he ran no risk in using the flat he shared with Denham."

Anita interposed. "Of course!" she said. "Ron was at a bachelor party, and ordinarily it would have kept him there whooping until two or three o'clock in the morning. But he reformed, and came home early."

Denham groaned. "But I still can't believe it," he insisted. "Tom Evans? A murderer?"

"He intended no murder," said Colonel March. "But, you see, Randolph suspected something. Randolph showed that he suspected. And Evans, as a practical man, had to kill him. You can guess why Randolph suspected?"

"Well?"

"Because Evans is colour-blind," said Colonel March.

"It's too bad," Colonel March went on sadly, "but the crime was from the first the work of a colour-blind man. Now, none of the rest of you could qualify for that deficiency. As for Sir Rufus, I can think of nothing more improbable than a colour-blind art collector—unless it is a colour-blind interior decorator. Mr. Conyers here shows by the blended hues of brown or blue in his suits, shirts, and ties that he has a fine eye for colour effect; and he possesses no wife or valet to choose them for him.

"But Evans? He is not only partially, but wholly colour-blind. You gave us a spirited account of it. Randolph's body was sent up in the lift by Pearson. When Evans stepped forward, Pearson warned him not to touch the body, saying that there was blood. Evans said, 'Where?'—though he was staring straight down in a small, brightly lighted lift at a red bloodstain on a grey-rubber floor. Red on any surface except green or yellow is absolutely invisible to colour-blind men.

"That was also the reason why Randolph's waterproof was put on inside out. Randolph had removed his hat and coat when he first came into the flat. After Evans had stabbed him with a clasp knife, Evans put the hat and coat back on the body previous to disposing of it. But he could not distinguish between the yellowish outside and the green inside of that seamless oilskin.

"You, Mr. Denham, let yourself into the flat with your own key: which in itself told us the location of the 'vanished' room, for no two keys are alike. I also think that Miss Bruce could have told us all along where the 'vanished' room was. I am inclined to suspect she saw Randolph going into your flat, and was afraid you might be concerned in the murder."

"Oh, well," said Anita philosophically.

"Anyway, you spoke to a corpse about his coat being inside-out; and Evans rectified the error before he put the body in the lift. He had to knock you out, of course. But he genuinely didn't want to hurt you. He left the building by way of the fire escape into the mews. He disposed of his stage properties, though he was foolish enough to keep the money and the clasp knife on his person, where they were found when we searched him. When he came back here, he used the main lift in the ordinary way as though he were returning from his office. And he was genuinely concerned when he found you still unconscious on the bench in the hall."

There was a silence, broken by Armingdale's snort.

"But colour blindness! What's that got to do with the solution? How did you come to think the murderer must have been colour-blind to begin with?"

Colonel March turned to stare at him. Then he shook his head, with a slow and dismal smile.

"Don't you see it even yet?" he asked. "That was the starting point. We suspected it for the same reason Randolph suspected an imposture. Poor old Randolph wasn't an art critic. Any sort of coloured daub, in the ordinary way, he would have swallowed as the original 'Young Girl with Primroses' he expected to see. But Evans didn't allow for the one thing even a near-sighted man does know: colour. In his effort to imitate the decorations of Sir Rufus's flat, the fool hung up as an oil painting nothing more than a sepia reproduction out of an illustrated weekly."

Reading for Understanding

Main Idea

1. The main idea can best be expressed by which of the following statements?

   (a) The race is to the swift.
   (b) First impressions are soundest.
   (c) Check your assumptions.
   (d) Never trust an eyewitness.

Details

2. All the following statements about Anita Bruce are accurate EXCEPT

   (a) Denham was to marry her in a month.
   (b) She lived on the same floor as Denham.
   (c) She worried at first that Denham might have committed the murder.
   (d) She had been in love with Tom Evans.

3. Tom Evans was (a) an employee of Armingdale (b) a frustrated interior designer (c) a journalist (d) a friend of Colonel March's.

4. The most important clue in the story was (a) the character of Dan

Randolph (b) Denham's drunkenness (c) the curiosity of Anita (d) color-blindness.

5. The murder was actually committed in the room of (a) Conyers (b) Denham (c) Armitage (d) Bruce.

6. The robbery was planned because Randolph (a) was American (b) disliked Armitage (c) scorned British hospitality (d) always paid cash.

Inferences

7. The "lost-room" trick was dependent on (a) Denham's entering the room early (b) small items that could be replaced quickly (c) Armingdale's unpleasant manner (d) Anita Bruce's trust in Denham.

8. The plan also counted on (a) Armingdale's absence for a week (b) Denham's being a guest at a bachelor party (c) Anita's skill as an interior designer (d) Conyers' fussiness.

Order of Events

9. Arrange the items in the order in which they occurred. Use letters only.
   A. Denham leaves the party.
   B. The porter discovers the body in the lift.
   C. Colonel March points out the murderer.
   D. Conyers identifies the body.
   E. Denham discovers the body in the room.

Fact or Opinion

Tell whether the following is a fact or an opinion.

10. Tom Evans struck the man who shared his flat.

Words in Context

1. "The *heinousness* of his offense partly steadied him." **Heinousness** (269) means (a) nastiness (b) real meaning (c) results (d) extent.

2. "Evans, lean and *swarthy*, with darkish eyebrows merging into a single line across his forehead, looked a little like a Norman baron in a romance." **Swarthy** (269) means (a) with imperfect skin (b) of a dark complexion (c) menacing (d) yellowish.

3., 4. "Sir Rufus Armingdale did not look so much *formidable* as *fretful*." **Formidable** (270) means (a) arousing fear (b) likely to disagree (c) strange looking (d) stimulating curiosity. **Fretful** (270) means (a) ill (b) violent (c) irritated (d) questioning.

5., 6. "The *autocrat* seemed too *abstracted* to notice." **Autocrat** (271) means (a) builder (b) banker (c) leader (d) tyrant. **Abstracted** (271) means (a) angry (b) inattentive (c) confused (d) thoughtless.

7. "His expression *belied* it as well." **Belied** (271) means (a) confirmed (b) represented (c) overlooked (d) contradicted.

8. "It was heavy and *lowering*, with more than a suggestion of the bull pup." **Lowering** (271) means (a) dropping (b) grinning (c) frowning (d) smirking.

9. "He was an *unobtrusive*, sandy-haired little man, very different from Denham's idea of a journalist." **Unobtrusive** (271) means (a) inconspicuous (b) unreliable (c) indecisive (d) unimportant.

10. " 'Sorry, sorry, sorry,' he began, seeming to *propitiate* everyone at once." **Propitiate** (272) means (a) arouse (b) catch the attention of (c) soothe (d) attract.

11. "Pearson was *voluble*. 'The lift was on the ground floor, sir.' " **Voluble** (273) means (a) excited (b) defensive (c) resentful (d) talkative.

12. "A brisk divisional detective-inspector, accompanied by a sergeant, a photographer, and a large *amiable* man in a top hat, had taken a statement from each of those concerned." **Amiable** (274) means (a) overweight (b) agreeable (c) menacing (d) busy.

13. "Something unintentionally sinister seemed to have gathered in Colonel March's *affable* tone." **Affable** (275) means (a) hesitant (b) friendly (c) softspoken (d) hostile.

14. "Hitherto Conyers had been regarding him with a look of watchful expectancy, like an *urchin* about to smash a window and run." An **urchin** (276) is a (a) hardened criminal (b) mischievous youngster (c) kind of messenger (d) leader of a club.

Thinking Critically about the Story

1. The traditional puzzle-type detective story requires the author to play fair with the reader. All needed clues should be presented but they may be concealed. "Red herring" possibilities may also be

presented. Does Carter Dickson play fair with the reader? Should you have guessed the murderer before March reveals him? The author has to make one, and only one, character the murderer. The proof must have three parts: A, B, and C. Study the following analysis and then decide for yourself whether this is a classic "play-fair" detective story.

A. *The murderer is color blind.*
   - (a) He put up a sepia picture, assuming it resembled the original oil.
   - (b) He got the raincoat on inside out.
   - (c) The near-sighted Mr. Randolph could tell whether a picture was in color or sepia, even if the murderer couldn't.

B. *All but one are innocent.*
   - (a) Conyers wasn't color-blind. He dressed colorfully, with no wife or valet to help.
   - (b) Anita Bruce was an interior decorator, certainly not color-blind.
   - (c) Armingdale was an art collector, certainly not color-blind.
   - (d) Denham had been struck and injured by the murderer.

C. *The murderer is Tom Evans.*
   - (a) He *was* color-blind as proved when he couldn't see the red blood against the gray floor.
   - (b) He had motivation (cash) and opportunity (Armingdale employee), access to his and Denham's flat.

Well, there you have it? Was it fair? Too tricky? Too ingenious?

2. Carter Dickson's detectives ask questions that seem to be unimportant, irrelevant. Yet, in the explanation, they turn out to be significant. What was the significance in asking Conyers if he were married or had a valet (276)?

3. Writers of detective stories try to make their detectives distinctive, different from others. Hercule Poirot, for example, constantly calls upon his "little gray cells." Sherlock Holmes has his rapid, incredibly accurate deductions from tiny clues. The Old Man in the Corner (334) solves mysteries from the corner table in a London tea room. Colonel March can be set apart by his physical appearance so unlike that of a typical fictional detective. What other characteristics does the author apply to March?

4. Is "The Crime in Nobody's Room" an effective title? Can you think of other possibilities?

5. Are the characters in the story well drawn or are they merely props to advance the plot? Explain.

Language in Action

Paradox

> "If you had been sober, you might have made a mistake; but you were so full of champagne that your instincts brought you home after all."

Colonel March's statement may be called a *paradox,* defined in one sense as "a statement seemingly contradictory or opposed to common sense but perhaps true." Another example is the advice sometimes offered to parents: "If you would hold onto your children, let them go." Religious teachings sometimes seem paradoxical. Zen, for example, suggests that the more you seek absolute safety and security, the less secure you feel.

Some paradoxical statements are humorous.

Apathy is our greatest problem—but who cares.

I'm sorry I keep apologizing.

I hate people who hate others.

One of the most famous is a mind-boggler.

All generalizations are untrue—including this one.

Some paradoxes are matters of definition.

What happens when an irresistible force meets an immovable body?

If there is an irresistible force, by definition there is no immovable object . . . and vice versa.

Here's a simpler form of an old classic.

I lie all the time.

If I lie all the time, then the statement that I lie all the time is false. Apply the lesson of the preceding example to solve this and the generalization example.

The Oracle of the Dog

G. K. Chesterton
British

Many mystery stories, about men murdered behind locked doors and windows, and murderers escaping without means of entrance and exit, have come true in the course of the extraordinary events at Cranston on the shores of Yorkshire, where Colonel Druce was found stabbed from behind by a dagger that has entirely disappeared from the scene, and apparently even from the neighborhood.

Murder in a locked room (266) has always been a favorite of detective-story writers. Readers like to have a touch of the impossible as a major ingredient. True, the summer house in "The Oracle of the Dog" is a different kind of locked room, but it presents the same haunting impossibilities.

Some story titles are amusing, like "Banana Popsicles Good for What Ails You" (426). Some informative, like "Flurry at the Sheep-Dog Trial." (414) Some help create a mood, like "The Rising of the Moon" (560). Few titles, however, are as essential to the core of a mystery as "The Oracle of the Dog." The title gets to the heart of the story, reveals the most important clue, and provides Father Brown with ample opportunity for commentary about the gullibility of people. Though a believer in his religion, Father Brown is a skeptic about many of the mindless beliefs that sweep the land.

Of all fictional detectives, Father Brown holds an honored place, in the very top rung of puzzle-solvers.

The Oracle of the Dog

"Yes," said Father Brown, "I always like a dog so long as he isn't spelt backwards."

Those who are quick in talking are not always quick in listening. Sometimes even their brilliancy produces a sort of stupidity. Father Brown's friend and companion was a young man with a stream of ideas and stories, an enthusiastic young man named Fiennes, with eager blue eyes and blonde hair that seemed to be brushed back, not merely with a hair-brush but with the wind of the world as he rushed through it. But he stopped in the torrent of his talk in a momentary bewilderment before he saw the priest's very simple meaning.

"You mean that people make too much of them?" he said. "Well, I don't know. They're marvellous creatures. Sometimes I think they know a lot more than we do."

Father Brown said nothing; but continued to stroke the head of the big retriever in a half-abstracted but apparently soothing fashion.

"Why," said Fiennes, warming again to his monologue, "there was a dog in the case I've come to see you about; what they call the 'Invisible Murder Case,' you know. It's a strange story, but from my point of view the dog is about the strangest thing in it. Of course, there's the mystery of the crime itself, and how old Druce can have been killed by somebody else when he was all alone in the summer-house—"

The hand stroking the dog stopped for a moment in its rhythmic movement; and Father Brown said calmly, "Oh, it was a summer-house, was it?"

"I thought you'd read all about it in the papers," answered Fiennes. "Stop a minute; I believe I've got a cutting that will give you all the particulars." He produced a strip of newspaper from his pocket and handed it to the priest, who began to read it, holding it close to his blinking eyes with one hand while the other continued its half-conscious caresses of the dog. It looked like the parable of a man not letting his right hand know what his left hand did.

"Many mystery stories, about men murdered behind locked doors and windows, and murderers escaping without means of entrance and exit, have come true in the course of the extraordinary events at Cranston on the coast of Yorkshire, where Colonel Druce was found stabbed from behind by a dagger that has entirely disappeared from the scene, and apparently even from the neighborhood.

"The summer-house in which he died was indeed accessible at

one entrance, the ordinary doorway which looked down the central walk of the garden towards the house. But by a combination of events almost to be called a coincidence, it appears that both the path and the entrance were watched during the crucial time, and there is a chain of witnesses who confirm each other. The summer-house stands at the extreme end of the garden, where there is no exit or entrance of any kind. The central garden path is a lane between two ranks of tall delphiniums, planted so close that any stray step off the path would leave its traces; and both path and plants run right up to the very mouth of the summerhouse, so that no straying from the straight path could fail to be observed, and no other mode of entrance can be imagined.

"Patrick Floyd, secretary of the murdered man, testified that he had been in a position to overlook the whole garden from the time when Colonel Druce last appeared alive in the doorway to the time when he was found dead; as he, Floyd, had been on the top of a step-ladder clipping the garden hedge. Janet Druce, the dead man's daughter, confirmed this, saying that she had sat on the terrace of the house throughout that time and had seen Floyd at his work. Touching some part of the time, this is again supported by Donald Druce, her brother, who overlooked the garden standing at his bedroom window in his dressing-gown, for he had risen late. Lastly the account is consistent with that given by Dr. Valentine, a neighbour, who called for a time to talk with Miss Druce on the terrace, and by the Colonel's solicitor, Mr. Aubrey Traill, who was apparently the last to see the murdered man alive—presumably with the exception of the murderer.

"All are agreed that the course of events was as follows: about half-past three in the afternoon, Miss Druce went down the path to ask her father when he would like tea; but he said he did not want any and was waiting to see Traill, his lawyer, who was to be sent to him in the summer-house. The girl then came away and met Traill coming down the path; she directed him to her father and he went in as directed. About half an hour afterwards he came out again, the Colonel coming with him to the door and showing himself to all appearance in health and even high spirits. He had been somewhat annoyed earlier in the day by his son's irregular hours, but seemed to recover his temper in a perfectly normal fashion, and had been rather markedly genial in receiving other visitors, including two of his nephews who came over for the day. But as these were out walking during the whole period of the tragedy, they had no evidence to give. It is said, indeed, that the Colonel was not on very good terms with Dr. Valentine, but that gentleman only had a brief interview with the daughter of the house, to whom he is supposed to be paying serious attentions.

"Traill, the solicitor, says he left the Colonel entirely alone in the summer-house, and this is confirmed by Floyd's bird's-eye view of the garden, which showed nobody else passing the only entrance. Ten minutes later Miss Druce again went down the garden and had not reached the end of the path when she saw her father, who was conspicuous by his white linen coat, lying in a heap on the floor. She uttered a scream which brought others to the spot, and on entering the place they found the Colonel lying dead beside his basket-chair, which was also upset. Dr. Valentine, who was still in the immediate neighbourhood, testified that the wound was made by some sort of stiletto, entering under the shoulder-blade and piercing the heart. The police have searched the neighbourhood for such a weapon, but no trace of it can be found."

"So Colonel Druce wore a white coat, did he?" said Father Brown as he put down the paper.

"Trick he learnt in the tropics," replied Fiennes with some wonder. "He'd had some queer adventures there, by his own account; and I fancy his dislike of Valentine was connected with the doctor coming from the tropics too. But it's all an infernal puzzle. The account there is pretty accurate; I didn't see the tragedy, in the sense of the discovery; I was out walking with the young nephews and the dog—the dog I wanted to tell you about. But I saw the stage set for it as described: the straight lane between the blue flowers right up to the dark entrance, and the lawyer going down it in his blacks and his silk hat, and the red head of the secretary showing high above the green hedge as he worked on it with his shears. Nobody could have mistaken that red head at any distance; and if people say they saw it there all the time, you may be sure they did. This red-haired secretary Floyd is quite a character; a breathless, bounding sort of fellow, always doing everybody's work as he was doing the gardener's. I think he is an American; he's certainly got the American view of life; what they call the view-point, bless 'em."

"What about the lawyer?" asked Father Brown.

There was a silence and then Fiennes spoke quite slowly for him. "Traill struck me as a singular man. In his fine black clothes he was almost foppish, yet you can hardly call him fashionable. For he wore a pair of long, luxuriant black whiskers such as haven't been seen since Victorian times. He had rather a fine grave face and a fine grave manner, but every now and then he seemed to remember to smile. And when he showed his white teeth he seemed to lose a little of his dignity and there was something faintly fawning about him. It may have been only embarrassment, for he would also fidget with his cravat and his tie-pin, which were at once handsome and unusual, like himself. If I could think of anybody—but what's the good, when the whole thing's impossible? Nobody knows who did it. Nobody knows how it could be done. At least there's only one exception I'd make, and that's why I really mentioned the whole thing. The dog knows."

Father Brown sighed and then said absently, "You were there as a friend of young Donald, weren't you? He didn't go on your walk with you?"

"No," replied Fiennes smiling. "The young scoundrel had gone to bed that morning and got up that afternoon. I went with his cousins, two young officers from India, and our conversation was trivial enough. I remember the elder, whose name I think is Herbert Druce and who is an authority on horse-breeding, talked about nothing but a mare he had bought and the moral character of the man who sold her; while his brother Harry seemed to be brooding on his bad luck at Monte Carlo. I only mention it to show you, in the light of what happened on our walk, that there was nothing psychic about us. The dog was the only mystic in our company."

"What sort of a dog was he?" asked the priest.

"Same breed as that one," answered Fiennes. "That's what started me off on the story, your saying you didn't believe in believing in a dog. He's a big black retriever named Nox, and a suggestive name too; for I think what he did a darker mystery than the murder. You know Druce's house and garden are by the sea; we walked about a mile from it along the sands and then turned back, going the other way. We passed a rather curious rock called the Rock of Fortune, famous in the neighbourhood because it's one of those examples of one stone barely balanced on another, so that a touch would knock it over. It is not really very high, but the hanging outline of it makes it look a little wild and sinister; at least it made it look so to me, for I don't imagine my jolly young companions were afflicted with the picturesque. But it may be that I was beginning to feel an atmosphere; for just then the question arose of whether it was time to go back to tea, and even then I think I had a premonition that time counted for a good deal in the business. Neither Herbert Druce nor I had a watch, so we called out to his brother, who was some paces behind, having stopped to light his pipe under the hedge. Hence it happened that he shouted out the hour, which was twenty past four, in his big voice through the growing twilight; and somehow the loudness of it made it sound like the proclamation of something tremendous. His unconsciousness seemed to make it all the more so; but that was always the way with omens; and particular ticks of the clock were really very ominous things that afternoon. According to Dr. Valentine's testimony, poor Druce had actually died just about half-past four.

"Well, they said we needn't go home for ten minutes and we walked a little farther along the sands, doing nothing in particular—throwing stones for the dog and throwing sticks into the sea for him to swim after. But to me the twilight seemed to grow oddly oppressive and the very shadow of the top-heavy Rock of Fortune lay on me like a load. And then the curious thing happened. Nox had just brought back Herbert's walking stick out of the sea and his brother had thrown his in also. The dog swam out again, but just about what must have been the stroke of the half-hour, he stopped swimming. He came back again on to the shore and stood in front of us. Then he suddenly threw up his head and sent up a howl or wail of woe, if ever I heard one in the world.

" 'What the devil's the matter with the dog?' asked Herbert; but none of us could answer. There was a long silence after the brute's wailing and whining died away on the desolate shore; and then the silence was broken. As I live, it was broken by a faint and far-off shriek, like the shriek of a woman from beyond the hedges inland. We didn't know what it was then; but we knew afterwards. It was the cry the girl gave when she first saw the body of her father."

"You went back, I suppose," said Father Brown patiently. "What happened then?"

"I'll tell you what happened then," said Fiennes with a grim emphasis. "When we got back into that garden the first thing we saw was Traill the lawyer; I can see him now with his black hat and black whiskers relieved against the perspective of the blue flowers stretching down to the summer-house, with the sunset and the strange outline of the Rock of Fortune in the distance. His face and figure were in shadow against the sunset; but I swear the white teeth were showing in his head and he was smiling.

"The moment Nox saw that man, the dog dashed forward and stood in the middle of the path barking at him madly, murderously, volleying out curses that were almost verbal in their dreadful distinctness of hatred. And the man doubled up and fled along the path between the flowers."

Father Brown sprang to his feet with a startling impatience.

"So the dog denounced him, did he?" he cried. "The oracle of the dog condemned him. Did you see what birds were flying, and are you sure whether they were on the right hand or the left? Did you consult the augurs about the sacrifices? Surely you didn't omit to cut open the dog and examine his entrails. That is the sort of scientific test you heathen humanitarians seem to trust, when you are thinking of taking away the life and honour of a man."

Fiennes sat gaping for an instant before he found breath to say, "Why, what's the matter with you? What have I done now?"

A sort of anxiety came back into the priest's eyes—the anxiety of a man who has run against a post in the dark and wonders for a moment whether he has hurt it.

"I'm most awfully sorry," he said with sincere distress. "I beg your pardon for being so rude; pray forgive me."

Fiennes looked at him curiously. "I sometimes think you are more of a mystery than any of the mysteries," he said. "But anyhow, if you don't believe in the mystery of the dog, at least you can't get over the mystery of the man. You can't deny that at the very moment when the beast came back from the sea and bellowed, his master's soul was driven out of his body by the blow of some unseen power that no mortal man can trace or even imagine. And as for the lawyer, I don't go only by the dog; there are other curious details too. He struck me as a smooth, smiling, equivocal sort of person; and one of his tricks seemed like a sort of hint. You know the doctor and the police were on the spot very quickly; Valentine was brought back when walking away from the house, and he telephoned instantly. That, with the secluded house, small numbers, and enclosed space, made it pretty possible to search everybody who could have been near; and everybody was thoroughly searched—for a weapon. The whole house, garden, and shore were combed for a weapon. The disappearance of the dagger is almost as crazy as the disappearance of the man."

"The disappearance of the dagger," said Father Brown, nodding. He seemed to have become suddenly attentive.

"Well," continued Fiennes, "I told you that man Traill had a trick of fidgeting with his tie and tie-pin—especially his tie-pin. His pin, like himself, was at once showy and old-fashioned. It had one of those stones with concentric coloured rings that look like an eye; and his own concentration on it got on my nerves, as if he had been a Cyclops with one eye in the middle of his body. But the pin was not only large but long; and it occurred to me that his anxiety about its adjustment was because it was even longer than it looked; as long as a stiletto in fact."

Father Brown nodded thoughtfully. "Was any other instrument ever suggested?" he asked.

"There was another suggestion," answered Fiennes, "from one of the young Druces—the cousins, I mean. Neither Herbert nor Harry Druce would have struck one at first as likely to be of assistance in scientific detection; but while Herbert was really the traditional type of heavy Dragoon, caring for nothing but horses and being an ornament to the Horse Guards, his younger brother Harry had been in the Indian Police and knew something about such things. Indeed in his own way he was quite clever; and I rather fancy he had been too clever; I mean he had left the police through breaking some red-tape regulations and taking some sort of risk and responsibility of his own. Anyhow, he was in some sense a detective out of work, and threw himself in this business with more than the ardour of an amateur. And it was with him that I had an argument about the weapon—an argument that led to something new. It began by his countering my description of the dog barking at Traill; and he said that a dog at his worst didn't bark, but growled."

"He was quite right there," observed the priest.

"This young fellow went on to say that, if it came to that, he'd heard Nox growling at other people before then; and among others at

Floyd the secretary. I retorted that his own argument answered itself; for the crime couldn't be brought home to two or three people, and least of all to Floyd, who was as innocent as a harum-scarum schoolboy, and had been seen by everybody all the time perched above the garden hedge with his fan of red hair as conspicuous as a scarlet cockatoo. 'I know there's difficulties anyhow,' said my colleague, 'but I wish you'd come with me down the garden a minute. I want to show you something I don't think anyone else has seen.' This was on the very day of the discovery, and the garden was just as it had been: the stepladder was still standing by the hedge, and just under the hedge my guide stooped and disentangled something from the deep grass. It was the shears used for clipping the hedge, and on the point of one of them was a smear of blood."

There was a short silence, and then Father Brown said suddenly, "What was the lawyer there for?"

"He told us the Colonel sent for him to alter his will," answered Fiennes. "And, by the way, there was another thing about the business of the will that I ought to mention. You see, the will wasn't actually signed in the summer-house that afternoon."

"I suppose not," said Father Brown, "there would have to be two witnesses."

"The lawyer actually came down the day before and it was signed then; but he was sent for again next day because the old man had a doubt about one of the witnesses and had to be reassured."

"Who were the witnesses?" asked Father Brown.

"That's just the point," replied his informant eagerly, "the witnesses were Floyd the secretary and this Dr. Valentine, the foreign sort of surgeon or whatever he is; and the two have a quarrel. Now I'm bound to say that the secretary is something of a busybody. He's one of those hot and headlong people whose warmth of temperament has unfortunately turned mostly to pugnacity and bristling suspicion; to distrusting people instead of to trusting them. That sort of red-haired red-hot fellow is always either universally credulous or universally incredulous; and sometimes both. He was not only a Jack of all trades, but he knew better than all tradesmen. He not only knew everything, but he warned everybody against everybody. All that must be taken into account in his suspicions about Valentine; but in that particular case there seems to have been something behind it. He said the name of Valentine was not really Valentine. He said he had seen him elsewhere known by the name of De Villon. He said it would invalidate the will; of course he was kind enough to explain to the lawyer what the law was on the point. They were both in a frightful wax."

Father Brown laughed. "People often are when they are to witness a will," he said. "For one thing it means that they can't have any legacy under it. But what did Dr. Valentine say? No doubt the universal secretary knew more about the doctor's name than the doctor did. But even the doctor might have some information about his own name."

Fiennes paused a moment before he replied.

"Dr. Valentine took it in a curious way. Dr. Valentine is a curious man. His appearance is rather striking but very foreign. He is young but wears a beard cut square; and his face is very pale, dreadfully pale and dreadfully serious. His eyes have a sort of ache in them, as if he ought to wear glasses or had given himself a headache with thinking; but he is quite handsome and always very formally dressed, with a top hat and a dark coat and a little red rosette. His manner is rather cold and haughty, and he has a way of staring at you which is very disconcerting. When thus charged with having changed his name, he merely stared like a sphinx and then said with a little laugh that he supposed Americans had no names to change. At that I think the Colonel also got into a fuss and said all sorts of angry things to the doctor; all the more angry because of the doctor's pretensions to a future place in his family. But I shouldn't have thought much of that but for a few words that I happened to hear later, early in the afternoon of the tragedy. I don't want to make a lot of them, for they weren't the sort of words on which one would like, in the ordinary way, to play the eavesdropper. As I was passing out towards the front gate with my two companions and the dog, I heard voices which told me that Dr. Valentine and Miss Druce had withdrawn for a moment into the shadow of the house, in an angle behind a row of flowering plants, and were talking to each other in passionate whisperings—sometimes almost like hissings; for it was something of a lovers' quarrel as well as a lovers' tryst. Nobody repeats the sorts of things they said for the most part; but in an unfortunate business like this I'm bound to say that there was repeated more than once a phrase about killing somebody. In fact, the girl seemed to be begging him not to kill somebody, or saying that no provocation could justify killing anybody; which seems an unusual sort of talk to address to a gentleman who has dropped in to tea."

"Do you know," asked the priest, "whether Dr. Valentine seemed to be very angry after the scene with the secretary and the Colonel—I mean about witnessing the will?"

"By all accounts," replied the other, "he wasn't half so angry as the secretary was. It was the secretary who went away raging after witnessing the will."

"And now," said Father Brown, "what about the will itself?"

"The Colonel was a very wealthy man, and his will was impor- tant. Traill wouldn't tell us the alteration at that stage, but I have since heard, only this morning in fact, that most of the money was transferred from the son to the daughter. I told you that Druce was wild with my friend Donald over his dissipated hours."

"The question of motive has been rather overshadowed by the

question of method," observed Father Brown thoughtfully. "At that moment, apparently, Miss Druce was the immediate gainer by the death."

"Good God! What a cold-blooded way for talking," cried Fiennes, staring at him. "You don't really mean to hint that she—"

"Is she going to marry that Dr. Valentine?" asked the other.

"Some people are against it," answered his friend. "But he is liked and respected in the place and is a skilled and devoted surgeon."

"So devoted a surgeon," said Father Brown, "that he had surgical instruments with him when he went to call on the young lady at tea-time. For he must have used a lance or something, and he never seems to have gone home."

Fiennes sprang to his feet and looked at him in a heat of inquiry. "You suggest he might have used the very same lancet—"

Father Brown shook his head. "All these suggestions are fancies just now," he said. "The problem is not who did it or what did it, but how it was done. We might find many men and even many tools—pins and shears and lancets. But how did a man get into the room? How did even a pin get into it?"

He was staring reflectively at the ceiling as he spoke, but as he said the last words his eye cocked in an alert fashion as if he had suddenly seen a curious fly on the ceiling.

"Well, what would you do about it?" asked the young man. "You have a lot of experience, what would you advise now?"

"I'm afraid I'm not much use," said Father Brown with a sigh. "I can't suggest very much without having ever been near the place or the people. For the moment you can only go on with local inquiries. I gather that your friend from the Indian police is more or less in charge of your inquiry down there. I should run down and see how he is getting on. See what he's been doing in the way of amateur detection. There may be news already."

As his guests, the biped and the quadruped, disappeared, Father Brown took up his pen and went back to his interrupted occupation of planning a course of lectures on the Encyclical *Rerum Novarum*. The subject was a large one and he had to recast it more than once, so that he was somewhat similarly employed some two days later when the big black dog again came bounding into the room and sprawled all over him with enthusiasm and excitement. The master who followed the dog shared the excitement if not the enthusiasm. He had been excited in a less pleasant fashion, for his blue eyes seemed to start from his head and his eager face was even a little pale.

"You told me," he said abruptly and without preface, "to find out what Harry Druce was doing. Do you know what he's done?"

The priest did not reply, and the young man went on in jerky tones:

"I'll tell you what he's done. He's killed himself."

Father Brown's lips moved only faintly, and there was nothing practical about what he was saying—nothing that has anything to do with this story or this world.

"You give me the creeps sometimes," said Fiennes. "Did you—did you expect this?"

"I thought is possible," said Father Brown; "that was why I asked you to go and see what he was doing. I hoped you might not be too late."

"It was I who found him," said Fiennes rather huskily. "It was the ugliest and most uncanny thing I ever knew. I went down that old garden again and I knew there was something new and unnatural about it besides the murder. The flowers still tossed about in blue masses on each side of the black entrance into the old grey summer-house; but to me the blue flowers looked like devils dancing before some dark cavern of the underworld. I looked all round; everything seemed to be in its ordinary place. But the queer notion grew on me that there was something wrong with the very shape of the sky. And then I saw what it was. The Rock of Fortune always rose in the background beyond the garden hedge and against the sea. And the Rock of Fortune was gone."

Father Brown had lifted his head and was listening intently.

"It was as if a mountain had walked away out of a landscape or a moon fallen from the sky; though I knew, of course, that a touch at any time would have tipped the thing over. Something possessed me and I rushed down that garden path like the wind and went crashing through the hedge as if it were a spider's web. It was a thin hedge really, though its undisturbed trimness had made it serve all the purposes of a wall. On the shore I found the loose rock fallen from its pedestal; and poor Harry Druce lay like a wreck underneath it. One arm was thrown round it in a sort of embrace as if he had pulled it down on himself; and on the broad brown sands beside it, in large crazy lettering he had scrawled the words, 'The Rock of Fortune falls on the Fool.' "

"It was the Colonel's will that did that," observed Father Brown. "The young man had staked everything on profiting himself by Donald's disgrace, especially when his uncle sent for him on the same day as the lawyer, and welcomed him with so much warmth. Otherwise he was done; he'd lost his police job; he was beggared at Monte Carlo. And he killed himself when he found he'd killed his kinsman for nothing."

"Here, stop a minute!" cried the staring Fiennes. "You're going too fast for me."

"Talking about the will, by the way," continued Father Brown calmly, "before I forget it, or we go on to bigger things, there was a simple explanation, I think, of all that business about the doctor's name. I rather fancy I have heard both names before somewhere. The doctor is really a French nobleman with the title of the Marquis de Villon. But he is also an ardent Republican and has abandoned his title and fallen back on the forgotten family surname. 'With your Citizen Riquetti you have puzzled Europe for ten days.' "

"What is that?" asked the young man blankly.

"Never mind," said the priest. "Nine times out of ten it is a rascally thing to change one's name; but this was a piece of fine fanaticism. That's the point of his sarcasm about Americans having no names—that is, no titles. Now in England the Marquis of Hartington is never called Mr. Hartington; but in France the Marquis de Villon is called M. de Villon. So it might well look like a change of name. As for the talk about killing, I fancy that also was a point of French etiquette. The doctor was talking about challenging Floyd to a duel, and the girl was trying to dissuade him."

"Oh, I *see*," cried Fiennes slowly. "Now I understand what she meant."

"And what is that about?" asked his companion smiling.

"Well," said the young man, "it was something that happened to me just before I found that poor fellow's body; only the catastrophe drove it out of my head. I suppose it's hard to remember a little romantic idyll when you've just come on top of a tragedy. But as I went down the lanes leading to the Colonel's old place, I met his daughter walking with Dr. Valentine. She was in mourning of course, and he always wore black as if he were going to a funeral; but I can't say that their faces were very funereal. Never have I seen two people looking in their own way more respectably radiant and cheerful. They stopped and saluted me and then she told me they were married and living in a little house on the outskirts of the town, where the doctor was continuing his practice. This rather surprised me, because I knew that her old father's will had left her his property; and I hinted at it delicately by saying I was going along to her father's old place and had half expected to meet her there. But she only laughed and said, 'Oh, we've given up all that. My husband doesn't like heiresses.' And I discovered with some astonishment they really had insisted on restoring the property to poor Donald; so I hope he's had a healthy shock and will treat it sensibly. There was never much really the matter with him; he was very young and his father was not very wise. But it was in connection with that she said something I didn't understand at the time; but now I'm sure it must be as you say. She said with a sort of sudden and splendid arrogance that was entirely altruistic:

" 'I hope it'll stop that red-haired fool from fussing any more about the will. Does he think my husband, who has given up a crest and a coronet as old as the Crusades for his principles, would kill an old man in a summer-house for a legacy like that' Then she laughed again and said, 'My husband isn't killing anybody except in the way of business. Why, he didn't even ask his friends to call on the secretary.' Now, of course, I see what she meant."

"I see part of what she meant, of course," said Father Brown. "What did she mean exactly by the secretary fussing about the will?"

Fiennes smiled as he answered: "I wish you knew the secretary, Father Brown. It would be a joy to you to watch him make things hum, as he calls it. He made the house of mourning hum. He filled the funeral with all the snap and zip of the brightest sporting event. There was no holding him, after something had really happened. I've told you how he used to oversee the gardener as he did the garden, and how he instructed the lawyer in the law. Needless to say, he also instructed the surgeon in the practice of surgery; and as the surgeon was Dr. Valentine, you may be sure it ended in accusing him of something worse than bad surgery. The secretary got it fixed in his red head that the doctor had committed the crime; and when the police arrived he was perfectly sublime. Need I say that he became on the spot the greatest of all amateur detectives? Sherlock Holmes never towered over Scotland Yard with more Titantic intellectual pride and scorn than Colonel Druce's private secretary over the police investigating Colonel Druce's death. I tell you it was a joy to see him. He strode about with an abstracted air, tossing his scarlet crest of hair and giving curt impatient replies. Of course it was his demeanour during these days that made Druce's daughter so wild with him. Of course he had a theory. It's just the sort of theory a man would have in a book; and Floyd is the sort of man who ought to be in a book. He'd be better fun and less bother in a book."

"What was his theory?" asked the other.

"Oh, it was full of pep," replied Fiennes gloomily. "It would have been glorious copy if it could have held together for ten minutes longer. He said the Colonel was still alive when they found him in the summer-house and the doctor killed him with the surgical instrument on pretence of cutting the clothes."

"I see," said the priest. "I suppose he was lying flat on his face on the mud floor as a form of siesta."

"It's wonderful what hustle will do," continued his informant. "I believe Floyd would have got his great theory into the papers at any rate, and perhaps had the doctor arrested, when all these things were blown sky high as if by dynamite by the discovery of that dead body lying under the Rock of Fortune. And that's what we come back to after all. I suppose the suicide is almost a confession. But nobody will ever know the whole story."

There was a silence, and then the priest said modestly, "I rather think I know the whole story."

Fiennes stared. "But look here," he cried, "how do you come to know the whole story, or to be sure it's the true story? You've been sitting here a hundred miles away writing a sermon; do you mean to tell me you really know what happened already? If you've really come to the end, where in the world do you begin? What started you off with your own story?"

Father Brown jumped up with a very unusual excitement and his first exclamation was like an explosion.

"The dog!" he cried. "The dog, of course! You had the whole story in your hands in the business of the dog on the beach, if you'd only noticed the dog properly."

Fiennes stared still more. "But you told me just now that my feelings about the dog were all nonsense, and the dog had nothing to do with it."

"The dog had everything to do with it," said Father Brown, "as you'd have found out, if you'd only treated the dog as a dog and not as God Almighty, judging the souls of men."

He paused in an embarrassed way for a moment, and then said, with a rather pathetic air of apology:

"The truth is, I happen to be awfully fond of dogs. And it seemed to me that in all this lurid halo of dog superstitions nobody was really thinking about the poor dog at all. To begin with a small point, about his barking at the lawyer or growling at the secretary. You asked how I could guess things a hundred miles away; but honestly it's mostly to your credit, for you described people so well that I know the types. A man like Traill who frowns usually and smiles suddenly, a man who fiddles with things, especially at his throat, is a nervous, easily embarrassed man. I shouldn't wonder if Floyd, the efficient secretary, is nervy and jumpy too; those Yankee hustlers often are. Otherwise he wouldn't have cut his fingers on the shears and dropped them when he heard Janet Druce scream.

"Now dogs hate nervous people. I don't know whether they make the dog nervous too; or whether, being after all a brute, he is a bit of a bully; or whether his canine vanity (which is colossal) is simply offended at not being liked. But anyhow there was nothing in poor Nox protesting against those people, except that he disliked them for being afraid of him. Now I know you're awfully clever, and nobody of sense sneers at cleverness. But I sometimes fancy, for instance, that you are too clever to understand animals. Sometimes you are too clever to understand men, especially when they act almost as simply as animals. Animals are very literal; they live in a world of truisms. Take this case; a dog barks at a man and a man runs away from a dog. Now you do not seem to be quite simple enough to see the fact; that the dog barked because he disliked the man and the man fled because he was frightened of the dog. They had no other motives and they needed none. But you must read psychological mysteries into it and suppose the dog had super-normal vision, and was a mysterious mouthpiece of doom. You must suppose the

man was running away, not from the dog but from the hangman. And
yet, if you come to think of it, all this deeper psychology is exceedingly
improbable. If the dog really could completely and consciously realize the
murderer of his master, he wouldn't stand yapping as he might at a curate
at a tea-party; he's much more likely to fly at his throat. And on the other
hand, do you really think a man who had hardened his heart to murder
an old friend and then walk about smiling at the old friend's family, under
the eyes of his old friend's daughter and post-mortem doctor—do you
think a man like that could be doubled up by mere remorse because a
dog barked? He might feel the tragic irony of it; it might shake his soul,
like any other tragic trifle. But he wouldn't rush madly the length of a
garden to escape from the only witness whom he knew to be unable to
talk. People have a panic like that when they are frightened, not of tragic
ironies, but of teeth. The whole thing is simpler than you can understand.
But when we come to that business by the seashore, things are much
more interesting. As you stated them, they were much more puzzling. I
didn't understand that tale of the dog going in and out of the water; it
didn't seem to me a doggy thing to do. If Nox had been very much upset
about something else, he might possibly have refused to go after the stick
at all. He'd probably go off nosing in whatever direction he suspected the
mischief. But when once a dog is actually chasing a thing, a stone or a
stick or a rabbit, my experience is that he won't stop for anything but the
most peremptory command, and not always for that. That he should turn
round because his mood changed seems to me unthinkable."

"But he did turn round," insisted Fiennes, "and came back
without the stick."

"He came back without the stick for the best reason in the
world," replied the priest. "He came back because he couldn't find it. He
whined because he couldn't find it. That's the sort of thing a dog really
does whine about. A dog is a devil of a ritualist. He is as particular about
the precise routine of a game as a child about the precise repetition of a
fairy-tale. In this case something had gone wrong with the game. He
came back to complain seriously of the conduct of the stick. Never had
such a thing happened before. Never had an eminent and distinguished
dog been so treated by a rotten old walking-stick."

"Why, what had the walking-stick done?" inquired the young
man.

"It had sunk," said Father Brown.

Fiennes said nothing, but continued to stare, and it was the priest
who continued:

"It had sunk because it was not really a stick, but a rod of steel
with a very thin shell of cane and a sharp point. In other words, it was a
sword-stick. I suppose a murderer never got rid of a bloody weapon so
oddly and yet so naturally as by throwing it into the sea for a retriever."

"I begin to see what you mean," admitted Fiennes; "but even if a sword-stick was used, I have no guess of how it was used."

"I had a sort of guess," said Father Brown, "right at the beginning when you said the word summer-house. And another when you said that Druce wore a white coat. As long as everybody was looking for a short dagger, nobody thought of it; but if we admit a rather long blade like a rapier, it's not so impossible."

He was leaning back, looking at the ceiling, and began like one going back to his own first thoughts and fundamentals.

"All that discussion about detective stories like the Yellow Room, about a man found dead in sealed chambers which no one could enter, does not apply to the present case, because it is a summer-house. When we talk of a Yellow Room, or any room, we imply walls that are really homogeneous and impenetrable. But a summer-house is not made like that; it is often made, as it was in this case, of closely interlaced but still separate boughs and strips of wood, in which there are chinks here and there. There was one of them just behind Druce's back as he sat in his chair up against the wall. But just as the room was a summer-house, so the chair was a basket-chair. That also was a lattice of loopholes. Lastly, the summer-house was close up under the hedge; and you have just told me that it was really a thin hedge. A man standing outside it could easily see, amid a network of twigs and branches and canes, one white spot of the Colonel's coat as plain as the white of a target.

"Now, you left the geography a little vague; but it was possible to put two and two together. You said the Rock of Fortune was not really high; but you also said it could be seen dominating the garden like a mountain-peak. In other words, it was very near the end of the garden, though your walk had taken you a long way round to it. Also, it isn't likely the young lady really howled so as to be heard half a mile. She gave an ordinary involuntary cry, and yet you heard it on the shore. And among other interesting things that you told me, may I remind you that you said Harry Druce had fallen behind to light his pipe under a hedge."

Fiennes shuddered slightly. "You mean he drew his blade there and sent it through the hedge at the white spot. But surely it was a very odd chance and a very sudden choice. Besides, he couldn't be certain the old man's money had passed to him, and as a fact it hadn't."

Father Brown's face became animated.

"You misunderstand the man's character," he said, as if he himself had known the man all his life. "A curious but not unknown type of character. If he had really *known* the money would come to him, I seriously believe he wouldn't have done it. He would have seen it as the dirty thing it was."

"Isn't that rather paradoxical?" asked the other.

"This man was a gambler," said the priest, "and a man in disgrace

for having taken risks and anticipated orders. It was probably for something pretty unscrupulous, for every imperial police is more like a Russian
secret police than we like to think. But he had gone beyond the line and
failed. Now, the temptation of that type of man is to do a mad thing
precisely because the risk will be wonderful in retrospect. He wants to say,
'Nobody but I could have seized that chance or seen that it was then or
never. What a wild and wonderful guess it was, when I put all those things
together; Donald in disgrace; and the lawyer being sent for; and Herbert
and I sent for at the same time—and then nothing more but the way the
old man grinned at me and shook hands. Anybody would say I was mad
to risk it; but that is how fortunes are made, by the man mad enough to
have a little foresight.' In short, it is the vanity of guessing. It is the
megalomania of the gambler. The more incongruous the coincidence, the
more instantaneous the decision, the more likely he is to snatch the
chance. The accident, the very triviality, of the white speck and the hole
in the hedge intoxicated him like a vision of the world's desire. Nobody
clever enough to see such a combination of accidents could be cowardly
enough not to use them! That is how the devil talks to the gambler. But
the devil himself would hardly have induced that unhappy man to go
down in a dull, deliberate way and kill an old uncle from whom he'd
always had expectations. It would be too respectable."

He paused a moment; and then went on with a certain quiet
emphasis.

"And now try to call up the scene, even as you saw it yourself. As
he stood there, dizzy with his diabolical opportunity, he looked up and
saw that strange outline that might have been the image of his own
tottering soul—the one great crag poised perilously on the other like a
pyramid on its point—and remembered that it was called the Rock of
Fortune. Can you guess how such a man at such a moment would read
such a signal? I think it strung him up to action and even to vigilance. He
who would be a tower must not fear to be a toppling tower. Anyhow he
acted; his next difficulty was to cover his tracks. To be found with a
sword-stick, let alone a blood-stained sword-stick, would be fatal in the
search that was certain to follow. If he left it anywhere, it would be found
and probably traced. Even if he threw it into the sea the action might be
noticed, and thought noticeable—unless indeed he could think of some
more natural way of covering the action. As you know, he did think of
one, and a very good one. Being the only one of you with a watch, he
told you it was not yet time to return, strolled a little farther and started
the game of throwing in sticks for the retriever. But how his eyes must
have rolled darkly over all that desolate seashore before they alighted on
the dog!"

Fiennes nodded, gazing thoughtfully into space. His mind
seemed to have drifted back to a less practical part of the narrative.

"It's queer," he said, "that the dog really was in the story after all."

"The dog could almost have told you the story, if he could talk," said the priest. "All I complain of is that because he couldn't talk, you made up his story for him, and made him talk with the tongues of men and angels. It's part of something I've noticed more and more in the modern world, appearing in all sorts of newspaper rumours and conversational catchwords; something that's arbitrary without being authoritative. People readily swallow the untested claims of this, that, or the other. It's drowning all your old rationalism and scepticism, it's coming in like a sea; and the name of it is superstition." He stood up abruptly, his face heavy with a sort of frown, and went on talking almost as if he were alone. "It's the first effect of not believing in God that you lose your common sense, and can't see things as they are. Anything that anybody talks about, and says there's a good deal in it, extends itself indefinitely like a vista in a nightmare. And a dog is an omen and a cat is a mystery and a pig is a mascot and a beetle is a scarab, calling up all the menagerie of polytheism from Egypt and old India; Dog Anubis and great green-eyed Pasht and all the holy howling Bulls of Bashan; reeling back to the bestial gods of the beginning, escaping into elephants and snakes and crocodiles; and all because you are frightened of four words: 'He was made Man.' "

The young man got up with a little embarrassment, almost as if he had overheard a soliloquy. He called to the dog and left the room with vague but breezy farewells. But he had to call the dog twice, for the dog had remained behind quite motionless for a moment, looking up steadily at Father Brown as the wolf looked at St. Francis.

Reading for Understanding

Author's Purpose

1. A major purpose of the author was to show that (a) dogs have a mysterious power to identify criminals (b) there is a great deal of good even in evil persons (c) people's superstitions often interfere with their reasoning (d) to solve a problem, the detective must be at the scene.

Details

2. One of the most puzzling aspects of the crime was that (a) the Colonel was going to change his will (b) the Colonel was grave and

worried before his death (c) the dog had witnessed the murder (d) the murder weapon had apparently disappeared.

3. The person who fidgeted with his tie-pin was (a) the lawyer Traill (b) Dr. Valentine (c) Harry Druce (d) Donald Druce.

4. The two who apparently didn't get along well were (a) Fiennes and Dr. Brown (b) Valentine and Colonel (c) Janet Druce and her father (d) Floyd and Janet Druce.

5. The Colonel's son was named (a) Harry (b) Herbert (c) Aubrey (d) Donald.

6. Janet Druce was actually in love with (a) Mr. Traill (b) Dr. Valentine (c) Mr. Floyd (d) the narrator, Fiennes.

Inferences

7. The fatal flaw in the murderer's character was his (a) gambling (b) indecisiveness (c) talkativeness (d) envious nature.

8. To cover his deed, the murderer (a) blamed Dr. Valentine (b) said that the dog pointed out the murderer (c) called out the wrong time (d) said that he was miles away at the time.

9. In the opening statement, Father Brown is really saying (a) not to give supernatural powers to a dog (b) that dogs *are* really godlike creatures (c) nothing that has anything to do with the case (d) that dogs sometimes get on his nerves.

Cause and Effect

10. The murderer committed suicide because he realized that (a) his love for Janet Druce was impossible (b) he had killed the Colonel for nothing (c) he would soon be caught (d) the dog really knew his crime.

Words in Context

1. " 'Why,' said Fiennes, warming again to his *monologue*, 'there was a dog in the case I've come to see you about.' " A **monologue** (286) is characterized by (a) concise expression (b) an argumentative point of view (c) a single speaker (d) a thoughtfully expressed philosophy.

2. "For he wore a pair of long, *luxuriant* black whiskers such as haven't

been seen since Victorian times." **Luxuriant** (288) means (a) straggly (b) dark (c) abundant (c) conspicuous.

3. "When he showed his white teeth he seemed to lose a little of his dignity, and there was something faintly *fawning* about him." **Fawning** (288) means (a) insincere (b) antagonistic (c) unresponsive (d) wearying.

4. "Anyhow, he was in some sense a detective out of work, and threw himself in this business with the *ardour* of an amateur." (The American spelling would be *ardor*.) **Ardor** (291) means (a) skill (b) curiosity (c) experience (d) intensity.

5. "I *retorted* that his own argument answered itself." **Retorted** (292) means (a) explained (b) replied (c) insisted (d) denied.

6. "He said it would *invalidate* the will." **Invalidate** (292) means (a) test (b) support (c) make void (d) send to probate.

7. "It was something of a lovers' quarrel as well as a lovers' *tryst*." A **tryst** (293) is a lovers' (a) engagement party (b) disagreement (c) promise (d) secret meeting.

8. "No *provocation* could justify killing anybody." A **provocation** (293) is something that (a) moves to action (b) seems reasonable and logical (c) provides an excuse (d) hinders activity.

9. "Druce was wild with my friend Donald over his *dissipated* hours." **Dissipated** (293) means (a) unexplained (b) thoughtless (c) unpleasant (d) wasted.

10. " 'Nine times out of ten it is a rascally thing to change one's name, but this was a piece of fine *fanaticism*.' " **Fanaticism** (296) is characterized by (a) unusual aggressiveness (b) creativity (c) weary boredom (d) excessive enthusiasm.

11. "She said with a sort of sudden and splendid arrogance that was entirely *altruistic*." **Altruistic** (296) means (a) out-of-place (b) unselfish (c) objectionable (d) unexpected.

12. " 'Does he think my husband, who has given up a crest and a coronet as old as the Crusades for his principles, would kill an old man in a summer-house for a *legacy* like that?' " **Legacy** (296) means (a) inheritance (b) principle (c) lark (d) argument.

13. "Of course it was his *demeanour* during these days that made Druce's daughter so wild with him." (*Demeanor* is the American spelling.) **Demeanour** (297) means (a) language (b) behavior (c) appetite (d) gloominess.

14. "Animals are very literal; they live in a world of *truisms*." A **truism** (298) is (a) instinctive (b) deceptive (c) self-evident (d) highly moral.

15. "When once a dog is actually chasing a thing, a stone or a stick or a rabbit, my experience is that he won't stop for anything but the most *peremptory* command, and not always for that." **Peremptory** (299) means (a) sympathetic (b) cruel (c) positive (d) bitter.

16. "A dog is a devil of a *ritualist*." A **ritualist** (299) is interested in (a) loud commands (b) a kind of prayer (c) set forms (d) authority.

17. "When we talk of a Yellow Room, or any room, we imply walls that are really *homogeneous* and impenetrable." **Homogeneous** (300) means (a) of one nature (b) pertaining to homicide (c) made of concrete (d) unsightly.

18. "'Isn't that rather *paradoxical?*'" asked the other." **Paradoxical** (300) means (a) humorous (b) impatient (c) contradictory (d) insulting. (See also *Paradox,* page 284.)

19. "As he stood there, dizzy with his *diabolical* opportunity, he looked up and saw that strange outline that might have been the image of his own tottering soul." **Diabolical** (301) means (a) unexpected (b) made-to-order (c) fortunate (d) devilish.

20. "But how his eyes must have rolled darkly over all that *desolate* seashore before they alighted on the dog!" **Desolate** (301) means (a) picturesque, (b) deserted (c) rocky (d) dramatic.

21. "A dog is an omen and a cat is a mystery and a pig is a mascot and a beetle is a scarab, calling up all the menagerie of *polytheism* from Egypt and old India." **Polytheism** (302) is a religion with (a) many gods (b) a nature god (c) a single, all-powerful god (d) a god for only one tribe.

Thinking Critically about the Story

1. What is the meaning of Father Brown's opening statement (286)? How does it apply to the story?

2. How do the following comments by Father Brown point toward the final solution?

"Oh, it was a summer house, was it?" (286)

"So Colonel Druce wore a white coat, did he?" said Father Brown as he put down the paper. (288)

"The disappearance of the dagger," said Father Brown, nodding. He seemed to have become suddenly attentive. (291)

"The problem is not who did it or what did it, but how it was done."
(294)

"The dog!" he cried. "The dog, of course! You had the whole story
in your hands in the business of the dog on the beach, if you'd only
noticed the dog properly." (298)

"All that discussion about detective stories like the Yellow Room, about
a man found dead in sealed chambers which no one could enter, does
not apply to the present case, because it is a summer house." (300)

3. Just as the author provides clues to Father Brown's thinking, as in
   #2 above, he also provides some red herrings to throw the reader off
   the track. The following, for example, are suspects.

   (a) Traill, the lawyer, smiled mysteriously (288), was an "equivocal"
       (doubtful) sort of person, "was always fiddling with a tie-pin."
   (b) Floyd, the secretary, not only witnessed the signing of the will
       but left in a rage.
   (c) Dr. Valentine had signed the will and possibly learned of an
       advantage to him, had argued with the Colonel, and had myste-
       riously changed his name.
   (d) Janet Druce stood to inherit from the will.

   Were you put off the scent by any of the author's tricks? Were you able
   to keep your eye on the basic problem?

4. What comments prove that G. K. Chesterton knew a great deal
   about dogs?

5. Like other stay-at-home detectives, Father Brown often solves crimes
   at a distance, as here. How does this feat make the stories more
   interesting?

6. Hundreds of common beliefs have never been proved by controlled
   experiment; yet they persist. What is your attitude toward the healing
   power of pyramids, the luck in finding a four-leaf clover, or magic
   numbers for winning the lottery? Can performers bend spoons by psychic power alone? How would Father Brown probably look upon such
   beliefs? What did he mean by such sarcastic comments as "Did you see
   what birds were flying?" (290) Reread the lines beginning "People
   readily swallow the untested claims of this, that, or the other." (302)

7. How does the title prove to be essential to the core of the mystery?
   How did the dog prove to be an oracle, but not in the mystical way
   that Fiennes had suggested.

8. Sarcasm, a relative of irony (264), stings in the comments of Father
   Brown about superstitions (302). Point out the sarcasm in the lines.

9. On page 288, Fiennes says, "The dog knows." True or false? Explain.

10. Chesterton wrote about superstitions more than 75 years ago. If our age is touted as the Age of Science, why do so many superstitions persist?

Language in Action

Reduplication

> The crime couldn't be brought home to two or three people, and least of all to Floyd, who was as innocent as a harum-scarum schoolboy.

Harum-scarum is an example of a whole class of interesting words. The process is known as *reduplication*. These words are related to baby-talk words like *teeny-weeny, choo-choo,* and *itsy-bitsy,* but they persist in adult speech. In English, they often have a humorous quality. The childish *Georgie-Porgie* is obviously lighthearted, but adult words like *fiddle-faddle* have a playful quality, too. In other languages, reduplication often plays a more serious role, indicating the duration of an action, a change of part of speech, or intensity.

English reduplication often changes a vowel, as in *flimflam, mishmash, flip-flop,* and *singsong.* Or it changes one or more consonants, as in *helter-skelter, hocus-pocus, willy-nilly,* and *ragtag.*

Occasionally both a vowel and consonants are changed, as in *topsy-turvy.* More rarely, a word or syllable is simply repeated as in *tomtom, tutu,* and *so-so.* Hawaiian seems to lend itself to such reduplications, as in *hula-hula.*

Here's a sampling of other reduplicated words.

claptrap	hurdy-gurdy	pitter-patter
hobnob	knickknack	razzle-dazzle
bubbub	mumbo-jumbo	telltale
hugger-mugger	namby-pamby	ticktock
humdrum	pell-mell	tutti-frutti

The Case of the Rich Woman

Agatha Christie
British

**When her eyes opened, it seemed to her that a long time
had passed. She remembered several things vaguely—strange,
impossible dreams; then a feeling of waking; then further
dreams. She remembered something about a car and the dark,
beautiful girl in nurse's uniform bending over her.**

If you had everything and were still bored and dissatisfied,
what would you do? Who could help you? Mrs. Abner Rymer finds
herself in that position and visits the mysterious Parker Pyne, detective.
Is he an honest man or a swindler? Does he have a solution?

Nearly everyone is familiar with the name **Agatha Christie**
because of her famous sleuth, the Belgian detective Hercule Poirot.
Second in popularity is Miss Marple, Agatha Christie's quiet, perceptive Englishwoman, quite different from Poirot. To find an outlet for
her amazing creativity, Christie created other detectives: Harley Quin
and Tuppence and Tommy, all different in style and mood. Still another
creation is Parker Pyne, the detective in this story. The differences
between Parker Pyne and Hercule Poirot are substantial. It's surprising
that they are both creations of the same writer.

Though Poirot and Pyne are indeed quite different, they are
alike in one respect: they generate an air of confidence. We somehow
believe that they will prevail, and they do.

The Case of the Rich Woman

THE NAME OF MRS. ABNER RYMER was brought to Mr. Parker Pyne. He knew the name and he raised his eyebrows.

Presently his client was shown into the room.

Mrs. Rymer was a tall woman, big-boned. Her figure was ungainly and the velvet dress and the heavy fur coat she wore did not disguise the fact. The knuckles of her large hands were pronounced. Her face was big and broad and highly colored. Her black hair was fashionably dressed, and there were many tips of curled ostrich in her hat.

She plumped herself down on a chair with a nod. "Good morning," she said. Her voice had a rough accent. "If you're any good at all you'll tell me how to spend my money!"

"Most original," murmured Mr. Parker Pyne. "Few ask that in these days. So you really find it difficult, Mrs. Rymer?"

"Yes, I do," said the lady bluntly. "I've got three fur coats, a lot of Paris dresses and such like. I've got a car and a house in Park Lane. I've had a yacht but I don't like the sea. I've got a lot of those high-class servants that look down their nose at you. I've traveled a bit and seen foreign parts. And I'm blessed if I can think of anything more to buy or do." She looked hopefully at Mr. Pyne.

"There are hospitals," he said.

"What? Give it away, you mean? No, that I won't do! That money was worked for, let me tell you, worked for hard. If you think I'm going to hand it out like so much dirt—well, you're mistaken. I want to spend it; spend it and get some good out of it. Now, if you've got any ideas that are worth while in that line, you can depend on a good fee."

"Your proposition interests me," said Mr. Pyne. "You do not mention a country house."

"I forgot it, but I've got one. Bores me to death."

"You must tell me more about yourself. Your problem is not easy to solve."

"I'll tell you and willing. I'm not ashamed of what I've come from. Worked in a farmhouse, I did, when I was a girl. Hard work it was, too. Then I took up with Abner—he was a workman in the mills near by. He courted me for eight years, and then we got married."

"And you were happy?" asked Mr. Pyne.

309

"I was. He was a good man to me, Abner. We had a hard struggle of it, though; he was out of a job twice, and children coming along. Four we had, three boys and a girl. And none of them lived to grow up. I dare say it would have been different if they had." Her face softened, looked suddenly younger.

"His chest was weak—Abner's was. They wouldn't take him for the war. He did well at home. He was made foreman. He was a clever fellow, Abner. He worked out a process. They treated him fair, I will say; gave him a good sum for it. He used that money for another idea of his. That brought in money hand over fist. He was a master now, employing his own workmen. He bought two concerns that were bankrupt and made them pay. The rest was easy. Money came in hand over fist. It's still coming in.

"Mind you, it was rare fun at first. Having a house and a tiptop bathroom and servants of one's own. No more cooking and scrubbing and washing to do. Just sit back on your silk cushions in the drawing-room and ring the bell for tea—like any countess might! Grand fun it was, and we enjoyed it. And then we came up to London. I went to swell dressmakers for my clothes. We went to Paris and the Riviera. Rare fun it was."

"And then?" said Mr. Parker Pyne.

"We got used to it, I suppose," said Mrs. Rymer. "After a bit it didn't seem so much fun. Why, there were days when we didn't even fancy our meals properly—us, with any dish we fancied to choose from! As for baths—well, in the end, one bath a day's enough for anyone. And Abner's health began to worry him. Paid good money to doctors, we did, but they couldn't do anything. They tried this and they tried that. But it was no use. He died." She paused. "He was a young man, only forty-three."

Mr. Pyne nodded sympathetically.

"That was five years ago. Money's still rolling in. It seems wasteful not to be able to do anything with it. But as I tell you, I can't think of anything else to buy that I haven't got already."

"In other words," said Mr. Pyne, "your life is dull. You are not enjoying it."

"I'm sick of it," said Mrs. Rymer gloomily. "I've no friends. The new lot only want subscriptions, and they laugh at me behind my back. The old lot won't have anything to do with me. My rolling up in a car makes them shy. Can you do anything, or suggest anything?"

"It is possible that I can," said Mr. Pyne slowly. "It will be difficult, but I believe there is a chance of success. I think it's possible I can give you back what you have lost—your interest in life."

"How?" demanded Mrs. Rymer curtly.

"That," said Mr. Parker Pyne, "is my professional secret. I never disclose my methods beforehand. The question is, will you take a chance? I do not guarantee success, but I do think there is a reasonable possibility of it."

"And how much will it cost?"

"I shall have to adopt unusual methods, and therefore it will be expensive. My charges will be one thousand pounds, payable in advance."

"You can open your mouth all right, can't you?" said Mrs. Rymer appreciatively. "Well, I'll risk it. I'm used to paying top price. Only when I pay for a thing, I take good care that I get it."

"You shall get it," said Mr. Parker Pyne. "Never fear."

"I'll send you the check this evening," said Mrs. Rymer, rising. "I'm sure I don't know why I should trust you. Fools and their money are soon parted, they say. I dare say I'm a fool. You've got nerve, to advertise in all the papers that you can make people happy!"

"Those advertisements cost me money," said Mr. Pyne. "If I could not make my words good, that money would be wasted. I *know* what causes unhappiness, and consequently I have a clear idea of how to produce an opposite condition."

Mrs. Rymer shook her head doubtfully and departed, leaving a cloud of expensive mixed essences behind her.

The handsome Claude Luttrell strolled into the office. "Something in my line?"

Mr. Pyne shook his head. "Nothing so simple," he said. "No, this is a difficult case. We must, I fear, take a few risks. We must attempt the unusual."

"Mrs. Oliver?"

Mr. Pyne smiled at the mention of the world-famous novelist. "Mrs. Oliver," he said, "is really the most conventional of all of us. I have in mind a bold and audacious coup. By the way, you might ring up Doctor Antrobus."

"Antrobus?"

"Yes. His services will be needed."

A week later Mrs. Rymer once more entered Mr. Parker Pyne's office. He rose to receive her.

"This delay, I assure you, has been necessary," he said. "Many things had to be arranged, and I had to secure the services of an unusual man who had to come half across Europe."

"Oh!" She said it suspiciously. It was constantly present in her mind that she had paid out a check for a thousand pounds and the check had been cashed.

Mr. Parker Pyne touched a buzzer. A young girl, dark, Oriental-looking, but dressed in white nurse's kit, answered it.

"Is everything ready, Nurse de Sara?"

"Yes. Doctor Constantine is waiting."

"What are you going to do?" asked Mrs. Rymer, with a touch of uneasiness.

"Introduce you to some Eastern magic, dear lady," said Mr. Parker Pyne.

Mrs. Rymer followed the nurse up to the next floor. Here she was ushered into a room that bore no relation to the rest of the house. Oriental embroideries covered the walls. There were divans with soft cushions and beautiful rugs on the floor. A man was bending over a coffeepot. He straightened as they entered.

"Doctor Constantine," said the nurse.

The doctor was dressed in European clothes, but his face was swarthy and his eyes were dark and oblique with a peculiarly piercing power in their glance.

"So this is my patient?" he said in a low, vibrant voice.

"I'm not a patient," said Mrs. Rymer.

"Your body is not sick," said the doctor, "but your soul is weary. We of the East know how to cure that disease. Sit down and drink a cup of coffee."

Mrs. Rymer sat down and accepted a tiny cup of the fragrant brew. As she sipped it the doctor talked.

"Here in the West, they treat only the body. A mistake. The body is only the instrument. A tune is played upon it. It may be a sad, weary tune. It may be a gay tune full of delight. That last is what we shall give you. You have money. You shall spend it and enjoy. Life shall be worth living again. It is easy—easy—so easy . . ."

A feeling of languor crept over Mrs. Rymer. The figures of the doctor and the nurse grew hazy. She felt blissfully happy and very sleepy. The doctor's figure grew bigger. The whole world was growing bigger.

The doctor was looking into her eyes. "Sleep," he was saying. "Sleep. Your eyelids are closing. Soon you will sleep. You will sleep . . ."

Mrs. Rymer's eyelids closed. She floated with a wonderful great big world . . . .

When her eyes opened it seemed to her that a long time had passed. She remembered several things vaguely—strange, impossible dreams; then a feeling of waking; then further dreams. She remembered something about a car and the dark, beautiful girl in nurse's uniform bending over her.

Anyway, she was properly awake now, and in her own bed.

At least, was it her own bed? It felt different. It lacked the delicious softness of her own bed. It was vaguely reminiscent of days almost forgotten. She moved, and it creaked. Mrs. Rymer's bed in Park Lane never creaked.

She looked round. Decidedly, this was not Park Lane. Was it a hospital? No, she decided, not a hospital. Nor was it a hotel. It was a bare room, the walls an uncertain shade of lilac. There was a deal washstand with a jug and basin upon it. There was a deal chest of drawers and a tin trunk. There were unfamiliar clothes hanging on pegs. There was the bed covered with a much-mended quilt and there was herself in it.

"Where *am* I?" said Mrs. Rymer.

The door opened and a plump little woman bustled in. She had red cheeks and a good-humored air. Her sleeves were rolled up and she wore an apron.

"There!" she exclaimed. "She's awake. Come in, doctor."

Mrs. Rymer opened her mouth to say several things—but they remained unsaid, for the man who followed the plump woman into the room was not in the least like the elegant, swarthy Doctor Constantine. He was a bent old man who peered through thick glasses.

"That's better," he said, advancing to the bed and taking up Mrs. Rymer's wrist. "You'll soon be better now, my dear."

"What's been the matter with me?" demanded Mrs. Rymer.

"You had a kind of seizure," said the doctor. "You've been unconscious for a day or two. Nothing to worry about."

"Gave us a fright, you did, Hannah," said the plump woman. "You've been raving, too, saying the oddest things."

"Yes, yes, Mrs. Gardner," said the doctor repressively. "But we mustn't excite the patient. You'll soon be up and about again, my dear."

"But don't you worry about the work, Hannah," said Mrs. Gardner. "Mrs. Roberts has been in to give me a hand and we've got on fine. Just lie still and get well, my dear."

"Why do you call me Hannah?" said Mrs. Rymer.

"Well, it's your name," said Mrs. Gardner, bewildered.

"No, it isn't. My name is Amelia. Amelia Rymer. Mrs. Abner Rymer."

The doctor and Mrs. Gardner exchanged glances.

"Well, just you lie still," said Mrs. Gardner.

"Yes, yes; no worry," said the doctor.

They withdrew. Mrs. Rymer lay puzzling. Why did they call her Hannah, and why had they exchanged that glance of amused incredulity when she had given them her name? Where was she, and what had happened?

She slipped out of bed. She felt a little uncertain on her legs, but she walked slowly to the small dormer window and looked out—on a farmyard! Completely mystified, she went back to bed. What was she doing in a farmhouse that she had never seen before?

Mrs. Gardner re-entered the room with a bowl of soup on a tray.

Mrs. Rymer began her questions. "What am I doing in this house?" she demanded. "Who brought me here?"

"Nobody brought you, my dear. It's your home. Leastways, you've lived here for the last five years—and me not suspecting once that you were liable to fits."

"*Lived* here? *Five* years?"

"That's right. Why, Hannah, you don't mean that you still don't remember?"

"I've never lived here! I've never seen you before."

"You see, you've had this illness and you've forgotten."

"I've never lived here."

"But you have, my dear." Suddenly Mrs. Gardner darted across to the chest of drawers and brought to Mrs. Rymer a faded photograph in a frame.

It represented a group of four persons: a bearded man, a plump woman (Mrs. Gardner), a tall, lank man with a pleasantly sheepish grin, and somebody in a print dress and apron—herself!

Stupefied, Mrs. Rymer gazed at the photograph. Mrs. Gardner put the soup down beside her and quietly left the room.

Mrs. Rymer sipped the soup mechanically. It was good soup, strong and hot. All the time her brain was in a whirl. Who was mad? Mrs. Gardner or herself? One of them must be! But there was the doctor, too.

"I'm Amelia Rymer," she said firmly. "I know I'm Amelia Rymer and nobody's going to tell me different."

She had finished the soup. She put the bowl back on the tray. A folded newspaper caught her eye and she picked it up and looked at the date on it, *October 19.* What day had she gone to Mr. Parker Pyne's office? Either the fifteenth or the sixteenth. Then she must have been ill for three days.

"That rascally doctor!" said Mrs. Rymer wrathfully.

All the same, she was a shade relieved. She had heard of cases where people had forgotten who they were for years at a time. She had been afraid some such thing had happened to her.

She began turning the pages of the paper, scanning the columns idly, when suddenly a paragraph caught her eye:

> Mrs. Abner Rymer, widow of Abner Rymer, the "button shank" king, was removed yesterday to a private home for mental cases. For the past two days she has persisted in declaring she was not herself, but a servant girl named Hannah Moorhouse.

"Hannah Moorhouse! So that's it," said Mrs. Rymer. "She's me, and I'm her. Kind of double, I suppose. Well, we can soon put *that* right! If that oily hypocrite of a Parker Pyne is up to some game or other—"

But at this minute her eye was caught by the name Constantine staring at her from the printed page. This time it was a headline.

DR. CONSTANTINE'S CLAIM

At a farewell lecture given last night on the eve of his departure for Japan, Dr. Claudius Constantine advanced some startling theories. He declared that it was possible to prove the existence of the soul by transferring a soul from one body to another. In the course of his experiments in the East he had, he claimed, successfully effected a double transfer—the soul of a hypothesized body A being transferred to a hypnotized body B and the soul of B to the body of A. On recovering from the hypnotic sleep, A declared herself to be B, and B thought herself to be A.

For the experiment to succeed, it was necessary to find two people with a great bodily resemblance. It was an undoubted fact that two people resembling each other were en rapport.* This was very noticeable in the case of twins, but two strangers, varying widely in social position but with a marked similarity of feature, were found to exhibit the same harmony of structure.

Mrs. Rymer cast the paper from her. "The scoundrel! The black scoundrel!"

She saw the whole thing now! It was a dastardly plot to get hold of her money. This Hannah Moorhouse was Mr. Pyne's tool—possibly an innocent one. He and that devil Constantine had brought off this fantastic coup.

But she'd expose him! She'd show him up! She'd have the law on him! She'd tell everyone—

Abruptly Mrs. Rymer came to a stop in the tide of her indignation. She remembered that first paragraph. Hannah Moorhouse had not been a docile tool. She had protested, had declared her individuality. And what had happened?

"Clapped into a lunatic asylum, poor girl," said Mrs. Rymer. A chill ran down her spine.

A lunatic asylum. They got you in there and they never let you get out. The more you said you were sane, the less they'd believe you. There you were and there you stayed. No, Mrs. Rymer wasn't going to run the risk of that.

The door opened and Mrs. Gardner came in.

"Ah, you've drunk your soup, my dear. That's good. You'll soon be better now."

"When was I taken ill?" demanded Mrs. Rymer.

"Let me see. It was three days ago—on Wednesday. That was the fifteenth. You were took bad about four o'clock."

"Ah!" The ejaculation was fraught with meaning. It had been just

---

*in harmony

about four o'clock when Mrs. Rymer had entered the presence of Doctor Constantine.

"You slipped down in your chair," said Mrs. Gardner. " 'Oh!' you says. 'Oh!' just like that. And then: 'I'm falling asleep,' you says in a dreamy voice. 'I'm falling asleep.' And fall asleep you did, and we put you to bed and sent for the doctor, and here you've been ever since."

"I suppose," Mrs. Rymer ventured, "there isn't any way you could know who I am—apart from my face, I mean."

"Well, that's a queer thing to say," said Mrs. Gardner. "What is there to go by better than a person's face, I'd like to know? There's your birthmark, though, if that satisfies you better."

"A birthmark?" said Mrs. Rymer, brightening. She had no such thing.

"Strawberry mark just under the right elbow," said Mrs. Gardner. "Look and see for yourself, my dear."

"This will prove it," said Mrs. Rymer to herself. She knew that she had no strawberry mark under the right elbow. She turned back the sleeve of her nightdress. The strawberry mark was there.

Mrs. Rymer burst into tears.

Four days later, Mrs. Rymer rose from her bed. She had thought out several plans of action and rejected them.

She might show the paragraph in the paper to Mrs. Gardner and the doctor and explain. Would they believe her? Mrs. Rymer was sure they would not.

She might go to the police. Would they believe her? Again she thought not.

She might go to Mr. Pyne's office. That idea undoubtedly pleased her best. For one thing, she would like to tell that oily scoundrel what she thought of him. She was debarred from putting this plan into operation by a vital obstacle. She was at present in Cornwall (so she had learned), and she had no money for the journey to London. Two and fourpence in a worn purse seemed to represent her financial position.

And so, after four days, Mrs. Rymer made a sporting decision. For the present she would accept things! She was Hannah Moorhouse. Very well, she would be Hannah Moorhouse. For the present she would accept that role, and later, when she had saved sufficient money, she would go to London and beard the swindler in his den.

And having thus decided, Mrs. Rymer accepted her role with perfect good temper, even with a kind of sardonic amusement. History was repeating itself indeed. This life here reminded her of her girlhood. How long ago that seemed!

The work was a bit hard after her years of soft living, but after the first week she found herself slipping into the ways of the farm.

Mrs. Gardner was a good-tempered, kindly woman. Her husband, a big, taciturn man, was kindly also. The lank, shambling man of the photograph had gone; another farmhand came in his stead, a good-humored giant of forty-five, slow of speech and thought, but a shy twinkle in his blue eyes.

The weeks went by. At last the day came when Mrs. Rymer had enough money to pay her fare to London. But she did not go. She put it off. Time enough, she thought. She wasn't easy in her mind about asylums yet. That scoundrel, Parker Pyne, was clever. He'd get a doctor to say she was mad and she'd be clapped away out of sight with no one knowing anything about it.

"Besides," said Mrs. Rymer, "a bit of a change does one good."

She rose early and worked hard. Joe Welsh, the new farmhand, was ill that winter, and she and Mrs. Gardner nursed him. The big man was pathetically dependent on them.

Spring came—lambing time; there were wild flowers in the hedges, a treacherous softness in the air. Joe Welsh gave Hannah a hand with her work. Hannah did Joe's mending.

Sometimes, on Sundays, they went for a walk together. Joe was a widower. His wife had died four years before. Since her death he had, he frankly confessed it, taken a drop too much.

He didn't go much to the Crown nowadays. He bought himself some new clothes. Mr. and Mrs. Gardner laughed.

Hannah made fun of Joe. She teased him about his clumsiness. Joe didn't mind. He looked bashful but happy.

After spring came summer—a good summer that year. Everyone worked hard.

Harvest was over. The leaves were red and golden on the trees.

It was October eighth when Hannah looked up one day from a cabbage she was cutting and saw Mr. Parker Pyne leaning over the fence.

"You!" said Hannah, alias Mrs. Rymer. "You . . ."

It was some time before she got it all out, and when she had said her say, she was out of breath.

Mr. Parker Pyne smiled blandly. "I quite agree with you," he said.

"A cheat and a liar, that's what you are!" said Mrs. Rymer, repeating herself. "You with your Constantines and your hypnotizing and that poor girl Hannah Moorhouse shut up with—loonies."

"No," said Mr. Parker Pyne, "there you misjudge me. Hannah Moorhouse is not in a lunatic asylum, because Hannah Moorhouse never existed."

"Indeed?" said Mrs. Rymer. "And what about the photograph of her that I saw with my own eyes?"

"Faked," said Mr. Pyne. "Quite a simple thing to manage."

"And the piece in the paper about her?"

"The whole paper was faked so as to include two items in a natural manner which would carry conviction. As it did."

"That rogue, Doctor Constantine!"

"An assumed name—assumed by a friend of mine with a talent for acting."

Mrs. Rymer snorted. "Ho! And I wasn't hypnotized either, I suppose?"

"As a matter of fact, you were not. You drank in your coffee a preparation of Indian hemp. After that, other drugs were administered and you were brought down here by car and allowed to recover consciousness."

"Then Mrs. Gardner has been in it all the time?" said Mrs. Rymer.

Mr. Parker Pyne nodded.

"Bribed by you, I suppose! Or filled up with a lot of lies!"

"Mrs. Gardner trusts me," said Mr. Pyne. "I once saved her only son from penal servitude."

Something in his manner silenced Mrs. Rymer on that tack. "What about the birthmark?" she demanded.

Mr. Pyne smiled. "It is already fading. In another six months it will have disappeared altogether."

"And what's the meaning of all this tomfoolery? Making a fool of me, sticking me down here as a servant—me with all that good money in the bank. But I suppose I needn't ask. You've been helping yourself to it, my fine fellow. That's the meaning of all this."

"It is true," said Mr. Parker Pyne, "that I did obtain from you, while you were under the influence of drugs, a power of attorney and that during your—er—absence, I have assumed control of your financial affairs, but I can assure you, my dear madam, that apart from that original thousand pounds, no money of yours has found its way into my pocket. As a matter of fact, by judicious investments your financial position is actually improved." He beamed at her.

"Then why—" began Mrs. Rymer.

"I am going to ask you a question, Mrs. Rymer," said Mr. Pyne. "You are an honest woman. You will answer me honestly, I know. I am going to ask you if you are happy."

"Happy! That's a pretty question! Steal a woman's money and ask her if she's happy. I like your impudence!"

"You are still angry," he said. "Most natural. But leave my misdeeds out of it for the moment. Mrs. Rymer, when you came to my office a year ago today, you were an unhappy woman. Will you tell me that you are unhappy now? If so, I apologize, and you are at liberty to take what steps you please against me. Moreover, I will refund you the thousand pounds you paid me. Come, Mrs. Rymer, are you an unhappy woman now?"

Mrs. Rymer looked at Mr. Parker Pyne, but she dropped her eyes when she spoke at last.

"No," she said. "I'm not unhappy." A tone of wonder crept into her voice. "You've got me there. I admit it. I've not been as happy as I am now since Abner died. I—I'm going to marry a man who works here—Joe Welsh. Our banns are going up next Sunday; that is, they *were* going up next Sunday."

"But now, of course," said Mr. Pyne, "everything is different."

Mrs. Rymer's face flamed. She took a step forward. "What do you mean—different? Do you think if I had all the money in the world it would make me a lady? I don't want to be a lady, thank you; a helpless, good-for-nothing lot they are. Joe's good enough for me and I'm good enough for him. We suit each other and we're going to be happy. As for you, Mr. Nosey Parker, you take yourself off and don't interfere with what doesn't concern you!"

Mr. Parker Pyne took a paper from his pocket and handed it to her. "The power of attorney," he said. "Shall I tear it up? You will assume control of your own fortune now, I take it."

A strange expression came over Mrs. Rymer's face. She thrust back the paper.

"Take it. I've said hard things to you—and some of them you deserved. You're a downy fellow, but all the same I trust you. Seven hundred pounds I'll have in the bank here—that'll buy us a farm we've got our eye on. The rest of it—well, let the hospitals have it."

"You cannot mean to hand over your entire fortune to hospitals?"

"That's just what I do mean. Joe's a dear, good fellow, but he's weak. Give him money and you'd ruin him. I've got him off the drink now, and I'll keep him off it. Thank God, I know my own mind. I'm not going to let money come between me and happiness."

"You are a remarkable woman," said Mr. Pyne slowly. "Only one woman in a thousand would act as you are doing."

"Then only one woman in a thousand's got sense," said Mrs. Rymer.

"I take off my hat to you," said Mr. Parker Pyne, and there was an unusual note in his voice. He raised his hat with solemnity and moved away.

"And Joe's never to know, mind!" Mrs. Rymer called after him.

She stood there with the dying sun behind her, a great blue-green cabbage in her hands, her head thrown back and her shoulders squared. A grand figure of a peasant woman, outlined against the setting sun.

Reading for Understanding

Main Idea

1. The main idea of the story can best be expressed in which of the following statements?
   (a) If you would be happy, have a goal in life.
   (b) Having "all that money can buy" solves problems.
   (c) If you have a problem, trust a stranger.
   (d) Acting on impulse may have grave consequences.

Details

2. Mrs. Rymer mentioned all the following possessions EXCEPT (a) a country house (b) fur coats (c) a yacht (d) a ruby necklace.

3. The price to be paid to Mr. Pyne was (a) 500 pounds (b) a thousand pounds (c) two thousand pounds (d) not mentioned.

4. Dr. Constantine (a) actually came from Japan (b) was a magician from the East (c) was an actor (d) performed minor miracles.

5. Mrs. Rymer had been taken to (a) London (b) Cornwall (c) Devon (d) Scotland.

6. The events in the story take about (a) two weeks (b) a month (c) a year (d) two years.

Inferences

7. When Mrs. Rymer had saved up enough money to go back to London, she delayed because (a) transportation was primitive (b) she was waiting for Parker Pyne to appear (c) she feared travel by herself (d) she really enjoyed her new life.

8. To convince Mrs. Rymer she was Hannah Moorhouse, Parker Pyne used all the following EXCEPT a (a) forged birth certificate (b) birthmark (c) newspaper article (d) photograph.

9. Throughout the story, Parker Pyne's manner was (a) deceitful and greedy (b) calm and unruffled (c) enthusiastic and excitable (d) reserved and unfriendly.

10. Although she didn't know it, Mrs. Rymer (a) needed a challenge (b)

loved money (c) liked Dr. Constantine (d) found peace in volunteer work.

11. A major change in Mrs. Rymer was (a) her attitude about giving money to hospitals (b) her yearning to return to the good old days (c) a complete lack of interest in living (d) a final dislike of Parker Pyne.

Cause and Effect

12. It is reasonable to say that Mrs. Rymer (a) could have achieved happiness without the meddling of Parker Pyne (b) needed a strong shock for her to change (c) would have met Joe Welsh without Mr. Pyne's actions (d) was weakened by her change of name.

Outcome

13. As a result of the events in the story, (a) Mrs. Rymer decided to go back to her luxuries (b) Parker Pyne gave up his detective business (c) Mrs. Rymer and Joe were married (d) Mrs. Rymer regretted her hasty decision.

Order of Events

14. Arrange the events in the order in which they occurred. Use letters only.
    A. Mrs. Rymer finds a birthmark.
    B. Mrs. Rymer sends Mr. Pyne away from the farm.
    C. Mr. Pyne agrees to take the case.
    D. Mrs. Rymer wakes up as Hannah Moorhouse.
    E. Mrs. Rymer sees the news items.

    Tell whether the following is a fact or an opinion.

15. Parker Pyne exceeded reasonableness in exposing Mrs. Rymer to so many changes.

Words in Context

1. "I have in mind a bold and *audacious* coup." **Audacious** (311) means (a) amusing (b) daring (c) many-sided (d) surprising.

2. "His face was *swarthy* and his eyes were dark and oblique with a peculiarly piercing power in their glance." **Swarthy** means (312) clean-shaven (b) sharp-featured (c) menacing, (d) dark.

3. "A feeling of *languor* crept over Mrs. Rymer." **Languor** (312) means (a) weariness (b) pleasure (c) uneasiness (d) expectation.

4. "Why had they exchanged that glance of amused *incredulity* when she had given them her name?" **Incredulity** (313) means (a) affection (b) irritation (c) unbelief (d) indifference.

5. "It was a *dastardly* plot to get hold of her money." **Dastardly** (315) means (a) underhanded (b) clever (c) unanticipated (d) vigorous.

6. "Hannah Moorhouse had not been a *docile* tool." **Docile** (315) means (a) outstanding (b) easily led (c) complaining (d) thoughtful.

7. "Her husband, a big *taciturn* man, was kindly also." **Taciturn** (317) means (a) powerfully built (b) uncommonly generous (c) sparing of words (d) sympathetic.

8. "I like your *impudence*." **Impudence** (318) means (a) independence (b) manner of speaking (c) thoughtfulness (d) boldness.

Thinking Critically about the Story

1. What tricks did Parker Pyne use to anticipate any problems with Mrs. Rymer's change of philosophy? Were they ethical? Did the end justify the means? Can the argument that the end justifies the means be used to justify obviously wrong actions? Explain.

2. After making a fortune, some people strive hard to make more and more unneeded money. Why?

3. Florida, like many other states, holds a state lottery. The prize usually starts around 7 million. If the prizes aren't won, the stakes keep increasing. The prize has reached 50 million dollars or more. At this point, the number of participants increases dramatically. Why? For daily living, is 50 million more necessary than 7?

4. State lotteries are a hot political topic in some states that have so far resisted the temptation. How do you feel about lotteries? Should state-run lotteries be abolished? Why or why not?

5. What was missing in Mrs. Rymer's wealthy life, something she found on the farm?

6. Was Mr. Pyne surprised by Mrs. Rymer's decision to stay and relinquish her money? What comment suggests his surprise?

7. A Doctor Antrobus is mentioned at the end of Mrs. Rymer's first visit to Parker Pyne. Does he appear later as the doctor who attended "Hannah Moorhouse"? Or is his name merely dropped in to impress Mrs. Rymer?

8. Why did Pyne prepare a newspaper article explaining Dr. Constantine's fake claim about transferring souls? How did Mrs. Rymer react to the article?

Language in Action

Connotation

Both *mother* and *mommy* have the same basic meaning, but there is a great difference. A word's dictionary definition is called its *denotation*. As words are used, they acquire extra meanings that may not be found in dictionaries. These extra meanings are called *connotation*. *Mother* is a general word for a female parent. It may be used for animals as well as for human beings. *Mommy* is a special word, an emotional word generally used by a child. The difference becomes apparent if we substitute one for another:

> I accept this prestigious Academy Award with humility. For her lifelong support, I want to pay special tribute to my mommy.

The meaning of *mommy* is clear, but the connotation is all wrong.

In our story, the phrase *lunatic asylum* is used. This is a remnant of an earlier day when mental deviation was looked upon with horror. Nowadays, we'd probably use the phrase *mental hospital,* which has a kinder connotation than *lunatic asylum.* Medical advances have improved our understanding of mental illness. All the strands that used to be lumped together as *lunacy* are now seen to be different problems with different treatments.

At one time, the mentally ill were neglected or actively mistreated. The word *bedlam,* meaning *uproar,* was taken from *St. Mary of Bethlehem Hospital* in London, a place where the mentally ill were cooped up in terrible conditions. The word *madhouse* retains the suggestion of uncontrollable commotion.

Whether a word has a favorable or unfavorable connotation sometimes depends on the individual. To utdoors people, *camping* has a pleasant connotation. Others may shudder at the word. For certain fans in the fall, *football* has wonderful connotations. To other members of the family, the associations may be negative.

Knowing dictionary definitions is a crucial skill. Knowing how connotations influence communication is another.

Déjà Vu

Mary Barrett
American

Mrs. Oliver's panic was now beginning to overwhelm her. There was only one gift left—the last one John had given her. She knew what it would mean if that one came back.

Déjà vu is a convenient French phrase that has become fairly common. Have you ever seen a place for the first time and had the strange feeling you'd seen it before? That's **déjà vu**—translated as "already seen." It's also applied to something heard or experienced.

In our story, Mrs. Oliver is experiencing a chilling case of **déjà vu**. She encounters a series of events that recall a series of events in the past. Though the gifts she receives should make her happy, they terrify her. There is a sense of mystery here, as in the other stories in the unit, but this provides a special shiver of horror.

Déjà Vu

Mrs. Oliver was puzzled. She always liked to pay cash, now that she could, and she no longer kept in touch with anyone out of town. Therefore she received almost no mail. The package which the mailman handed her was a surprise, and, like many surprises, unwelcome.

"There must be a mistake," Mrs. Oliver said uncertainly.

"No mistake, lady." And the mailman walked away.

Mrs. Oliver inspected the parcel. It was wrapped in brown paper and sealed with tape. Her name and address were clearly spelled out in neat block letters. The stamps were canceled with the local postmark.

She put the parcel down on the dining table. For some reason she was reluctant to open it. At the edge of awareness, the sensation gnawed at her that she had experienced this same event before. *Déjà vu.*

Don't be a fool, Mrs. Oliver said sternly to herself. She hoped that she wasn't getting eccentric, living alone as she had been since John died. Surely a package in the mail was nothing to be so upset about.

She pulled at the sealing tape. Under the paper was a plain white box bearing no identification. Its very impersonality somehow increased Mrs. Oliver's uneasiness.

The box was lined with white tissue paper. Lying in the center, like a cherished treasure, was a little music box with a dainty lady dancer on top.

Mrs. Oliver gasped. She picked up the box. She wound the little key. The lady dancer turned slowly, gracefully, and the music box tinkled "The Blue Danube Waltz."

It was impossible!

Mrs. Oliver sat down. Her hands were suddenly cold and her heart was beating fast.

It was the very first gift that John had sent to her. It came before they were married, when John was still courting her. The little Bavarian music box had arrived, then as now, in a parcel in the mail. Then, as now, it had been carefully wrapped and sealed. John was always a careful man.

She looked again at the address on the wrapping paper. It told her nothing. The printed words were impersonal, unrevealing.

Panic hit Mrs. Oliver like a sonic boom. She knew very well where she had last seen the music box—in Mr. Stover's store, where she had taken it to be sold.

She stood up shakily and forced herself into action.

"Mr. Stover, I would like to see the Bavarian music box which I sold to you."

Mr. Stover had been afraid of this. How much of the truth could he tell her? He looked at her closely. No, he decided, she was too agitated; even part of the truth would be too great a shock.

"I remember it," he said. "Had a little dancing girl, didn't it? That was sold some time ago."

Mrs. Oliver was uncertain whether to feel relief or apprehension.

"Do you remember who bought it?"

"No. I didn't know the man. He was a stranger who happened in. A young fellow. Didn't quibble about the price."

Mrs. Oliver felt dizzy. That would have been John's style.

"A young man, you said?"

"That's right. In his early thirties, I'd say."

Mrs. Oliver slept restlessly that night. She had distressing dreams from which she woke perspiring, her heart pounding, the thought of her dead husband vivid in her mind.

John. *He* was in his early thirties when they first met. He was handsome and ambitious, already a successful lawyer. It was inevitable that he would become an important man in state politics.

He was a good catch for any woman. And how persuasively he had courted her, showering her with attention and presents!

He had this house built for her, and had it furnished with the finest things. She appreciated all this. There was no passion on her part, but she couldn't, finally, resist him. Her family was an old one, far more distinguished than his, but their money had long ago trickled away. She could not afford not to marry for money. So it might as well be John.

If he was ever disappointed he was too gentlemanly to let it show.

She hid the music box in a drawer under the linen tablecloths and tried to forget it. It was not that simple. Whoever was manipulating Mrs. Oliver's state of mind was not only very clever but astonishingly well informed.

Only a week after the arrival of the music box another parcel was delivered. It, too, was carefully wrapped and sealed. The box was, again, disquieting in its impersonality.

Mrs. Oliver opened it and felt her knees go weak. Deep in tissue paper the box held the exquisite emerald brooch which John had given her on the day they were married. It was a lovely thing, of superb craftsmanship. Mr. Stover had given her a very good price for it. Now it lay in her hand, as sparkling as it was the day John had pinned it so tenderly on her bridal dress.

Mrs. Oliver tried to slow the beating of her heart. It wasn't good for her to be so upset. The doctor would be cross with her.

If this eerie procedure continued, she would receive many packages. John had been very generous with gifts. His practice brought in a great deal of money. To outside observers she seemed a very lucky woman. She had only to drop the smallest hint and John would buy her whatever she wanted.

Still, as time went by, she had felt more and more like a kept slave. She yearned for a little cash of her own. Not much. Just enough so that she could be free to buy some small things for herself. He never let her have a personal checking or bank account, and he gave her a minimum of pocket money.

"I would rather take care of you myself, dear," he said.

John overlooked nothing. He established charge accounts with the grocery store, the milkman, the dry cleaners. He bought all her clothes himself. In all the days of her marriage she never had more than a five-dollar bill of her own. Of course, John paid all the bills himself.

The packages continued to come. Mrs. Oliver lived in a state of constant agitation. The parcels arrived with no regularity, and she never knew on which day one would be delivered. There was, however, one thing she could be certain of ahead of time—the contents of each box. For the presents were coming back to her in the exact order John had given them to her.

Her birthday present, the diamond bracelet, was followed by the matching earrings John had given her for Christmas.

At first, when she was a new bride, she had been charmed by John's generosity. She had never owned beautiful things before, and the shower of extravagant gifts was like a dream come true. It was only in time that the longing for the illusion of financial independence came to sit on her soul like a lead weight; and in time the longing became an obsession.

John refused even to consider the possibility of her looking for a job.

"We're rich, dear," he said. "It would be ridiculous for you to work. You know that I'll get you anything you want."

As time passed, John's gifts brought her no joy. They seemed merely symbols of her bondage. She even had trouble pretending to be pleased.

Now, receiving them a second time, she felt even less pleasure. She felt only horror and repugnance. As each gift arrived she quickly hid it away.

His anniversary present of silver demitasse spoons came only shortly before the hand-blown crystal vase which John had brought back from a short trip out of town.

Mrs. Oliver's panic was now beginning to overwhelm her. There was only one gift left—the last one John had given her. She knew what it would mean if that one came back. And she knew with dreadful certainty that though it had been, in life, John's last gift, it would not now be. She knew that the final gift would come to her from the grave.

Mrs. Oliver, never a hardy woman, was not well. She hardly ever slept. When, finally, she did drop off, her dreams were terrifying, and she often woke up screaming.

She no longer had any appetite. She had lost so much weight that her dresses hung like bags. She hardly recognized herself in the mirror. Her eyes stared back at her from sunken sockets like glass globes in a skull.

The package came.

John's last gift.

She knew very well what the package contained even before she opened it. He had brought this gift on no special occasion—it had been a sudden whim. He had seen it in a store window and, on impulse, had gone in and bought it for her.

Her hands shook. She could hardly tear off the paper. Inside the white box lay the gift. It was a beautiful little emerald pillbox, made by an expert craftsman. It was truly a work of art. Mrs. Oliver put it out of sight as quickly as she could.

She tried to brace herself for what she knew was bound to come next. But what could she do? There was no way to anticipate how it would come, or in what form. There was no way to protect herself.

That night she went to bed early and lay there, wide-awake. Her eyes were open, staring unseeingly at the ceiling.

There was a knock at the door. It was not imperative—simply firm and sure.

Mrs. Oliver stepped into her bedroom slippers and put on her robe. She went silently down the stairs. She could no more have ignored that self-assured knock than she could have left the packages unopened. She was moved by an irresistible compulsion.

The knock sounded again—no louder than before, but still firm and self-confident.

Mrs. Oliver went to the door. She stood there, dizzy. Her hand was on the doorknob.

She was faint with panic and fatigue. Her body shook, out of control. She sank to the floor and her face pressed against the hard wood of the door.

Again the knock sounded.

There was a pounding in her ears. The hall seemed to tilt, first one way, then another.

"John," she whispered, "how did you know?"

It was John on the other side of the door. She was certain of that. And somehow he had learned the truth.

She had taken the poison out of the little enamel pillbox. She had put it in his demitasse. She was sure he hadn't seen her do it. She had sat there calmly and watched him drink the coffee, and die. And, finally, she had money of her own.

She should have known better, she thought fuzzily. She should have known she couldn't outwit John, that he would never stop giving her things.

She lay, a crumpled disorderly heap, on the floor of the hall. She was shrunken and unadorned. She looked old. She sighed, a long sigh, and then she died.

There was a final knock on the door, and then the sound of footsteps going away.

Mr. Stover was disappointed. He had waited until he had sent back all her lovely things, in the same order she had sold them, to tell her he loved her. Well, he would call again tomorrow.

Reading for Understanding

Central Idea

1. The central idea of the story is *best* expressed by which of the following quotations?

   (a) The only cure for grief is action.

   —G.H. Lewes

   (b) Every guilty person is his own hangman.

   —Seneca

   (c) Do not suppose opportunity will knock twice at your door.

   —Sebastien Chamfort

   (d) The mind grows by what it feeds on.

   —J.G. Holland

Details

2. Mrs. Oliver realized that the packages were mailed (a) a long time in the past (b) without a clear address (c) locally (d) by a friend.

3. The first gift she received was (a) a pillbox (b) an emerald brooch (c) a music box (d) none of these.

4. The gifts were actually (a) a labor of love (b) John's revenge (c) sent to the wrong address (d) those she had never seen before.

Inferences

5. Mrs. Oliver's death might be ascribed to (a) cancer (b) muscular dystrophy (c) pneumonia (d) heart failure.

6. Mr. Stover had (a) apparently saved the gifts to return to Mrs. Oliver (b) probably been asked by John to send the gifts to Mrs. Oliver (c) taken an extreme dislike to Mrs. Oliver (d) probably cheated Mrs. Oliver in buying the little treasures.

7. Mrs. Oliver objected most strenuously to John's (a) affairs with other women (b) need for control (c) physical cruelty and abuse (d) stinginess.

Cause and Effect

8. John's excessive generosity and love (a) pleased Mrs. Oliver throughout the marriage (b) aroused the jealousy of Mr. Stover (c) brought on his poisoning (d) almost bankrupted him.

Mood of the Story

9. The mood of the story is one of (a) joyous expectation (b) threatening disaster (c) alert curiosity (d) understated enthusiasm.

Fact or Opinion

Tell whether the following is a fact or an opinion.

10. Mrs. Oliver was responsible for the death of her husband John.

Words in Context

1. "Mrs. Oliver was uncertain whether to feel relief or *apprehension*." Apprehension (326) means (a) confusion (b) anxiety (c) understanding (d) jubilation.
2. "In time the longing became an *obsession*." Obsession (328) means (a) passing fancy (b) weird interpretation (c) something owned (d) fixed conviction.
3. "She felt only horror and *repugnance*." Repugnance (328) means (a) disgust (b) anger (c) fear (d) resistance.

Thinking Critically about the Story

1. This is a story that seems to bring in the supernatural. Were you taken in by the eerie suggestion? If not, at what point did you begin to suspect that the haunting was in Mrs. Oliver's head?

2. A great many stories that seem to tell of the supernatural have logical, reasonable endings. Others, however, leave the possibility in the air. Do you prefer your stories to have reasonable endings, or would you rather have an unexplained mystery? Explain.

3. What was Mr. Stover's strategy in sending the gifts to Mrs. Oliver? How did that strategy ultimately destroy Mrs. Oliver?

4. What kind of person was John? Pleasant? Loving? Generous? Obnoxious? Hateful? How do you see him?

5. Does true love seek to control? How would you have felt if you had been treated so generously but with so many restrictions?

6. Some authorities explain déjà vu by saying that it is caused by a brief time lapse between the first sighting and the feeling, "I've been here before." What do you think? Have you had an experience of déjà vu? Tell about it.

Language in Action

New Words

> Panic hit Mrs. Oliver like a sonic boom.

Your grandfather would have been puzzled by the words *sonic boom* . . . for good reason. A sonic boom did not exist before airplanes went faster than the speed of sound. The loud noise is a shock wave produced by the noise of an aircraft traveling at supersonic speeds. The Merriam-Webster *Collegiate Dictionary* lists the dates of the introduction of a word into the language. The date 1952 for *sonic boom* tells us about technology as well as about language.

English, unlike many other languages, is extremely receptive to new words. If there is a need and the need is met by a new word, English will adopt it freely. As the study of subatomic physics progressed, for example, English adopted many colorful new words for the various particles: *quark, meson, gluon, psion,* and *hadron.* As specialized words these are not in common use, but a great many new words *have* passed into everyday speech. When World War II ended, many mothers worked. A new occupation came into everyday life: staying with the baby while mother was at work. The word *baby-sitter* was coined to meet that need.

The world of computers has supplied a great many new words: *voice mail, internet, floppy disc, byte, printout, mainframe.* Some are old words used in new ways; for example, *mouse* for a small, movable device to control the cursor on a computer screen. Some expressions put together parts of other words, like *cyberspace* or *virtual reality*. *CD-ROM* is an abbreviation *for compact disc read-only memory*—for retrieval by a computer. *Nerd* was created by Dr. Seuss for a children's book in 1950. It's sometimes applied to any inept person, but when combined to make *computer nerd,* it may suggest a grudging respect for a person who has mastered the new technology.

As you read this, dozens of new words are clamoring to enter the language.

The Glasgow Mystery

Baroness E. Orczy
British

"No key or bolt was found on the inside of the door; the murderer, therefore, having accomplished his ghastly deed, must have locked his victim in, and probably taken the key away with him."

The Baroness Orczy is most famous as the author of **The Scarlet Pimpernel**, popular as a novel, a play, a film, and a television production. Besides her novels, she wrote a number of short stories with the Man in the Corner as the detective. Writing at the same time as A. Conan Doyle, she provides a special, old-fashioned flavor to her stories. In some ways, the Old Man resembles Sherlock Holmes in his method.

Like Father Brown (285), the Old Man solves crimes away from the scene, from his table in a London tearoom. "The Glasgow Mystery" provides another crime beyond the capacity of the police to solve. At the conclusion of an ideal mystery, the reader should say, "Oh, yes. I should have seen that!" Will you say that after you finish this story?

The Glasgow Mystery

I.

"It has often been declared," remarked the man in the corner, "that a murder—a successful murder, I mean—can never be committed single-handed in a busy city, and that on the other hand, once a murder *is* committed by more than one person, one of the accomplices is sure to betray the other, and that is the reason why comparatively so few crimes remain undetected. Now I must say I quite agree with this latter theory."

It was some few weeks after my first introduction to the man in the corner and the inevitable bit of string he always played with when unravelling his mysteries, and some time before he recounted to me his grim version of the tragedy in Percy-street, which I have already retold in the ROYAL.

Now I had made it a hard and fast rule whenever he made an assertion of that kind to disagree with it. This invariably irritated him; he became comically excited, produced his bit of string, and started off at rattling speed, after a few rude remarks directed at lady journalists in general and myself in particular, on one of his madly bewildering, true cock-and-bull stories.

"What about the Glasgow murder, then?" I remarked skeptically.

"Ah, the Glasgow murder," he repeated "Yes, what about the Glasgow murder? I see you are one of those people who, like the police, believe that Yardley was an accomplice to that murder, and you still continue to hope, as they do, that sooner or later he, and the other man, Upton, will meet, divide the spoils, and throw themselves into the expectant arms of the Glasgow police."

"Do you mean to tell me that you don't think Yardley had anything to do with that murder?"

"What does it matter what a humble amateur like myself thinks of that or any other case? Pshaw!" he added, breaking his bit of string between his bony fingers in his comical excitement. "Why, think a moment how simple is the whole thing! There was Mrs. Carmichael, the widow of a medical officer, young, good-looking, and fairly well-off, who for the sake of company, more than for actual profit-making, rents one of the fine houses in Woodbine Crescent with a view to taking in 'paying guests.' Her house is beautifully furnished—I told you she was fairly well-off. She has no difficulty in getting boarders.

"The house is soon full. At the time of which I am speaking she had ten or eleven 'guests'—mostly men out at business all day, also a married couple, an officer's widow with her daughter, and two journalists. At first she kept four female servants; then one day there was a complaint among the gentlemen boarders that their boots were insufficiently polished and their clothes very sketchily brushed. Chief among these complainants was Mr. Yardley, a young man who wrote verses for magazines, called himself a poet, and, in consequence, indulged in sundry eccentric habits which furnished food for gossip both in the kitchen and in the drawing-room over the coffee-cups.

"As I said before, it was he who was loudest in his complaint on the subject of his boots; it was he, again, who, when Mrs. Carmichael expressed herself willing to do anything to please her boarders, recommended her a quiet, respectable man named Upton to come in for a couple of hours daily, clean boots, knives, windows, and what-nots, and make himself 'generally useful'—I believe that is the technical expression. Upton, it appears, had been known to Mr. Yardley for some time, had often run errands and delivered messages for him, and had even been intrusted with valuable poetical MSS, to be left at various editorial offices.

"It was in July of last year, was it not, that Glasgow—honest, stodgy, busy Glasgow—was thrilled to its very marrow by the recital in its evening papers of one of the most ghastly and most dastardly crimes?

"At two o'clock that afternoon, namely, Mrs. Carmichael, of Woodbine Crescent, was found murdered in her room. Her safe had been opened, and all its contents—which were presumed to include a good deal of jewellery and money—had vanished. The evening papers had also added that the murderer was known to the police, and that no doubt was entertained as to his speedy arrest.

"It appears that in the household at Woodbine Crescent it was the duty of Mary, one of the maids, to take up a cup of tea to Mrs. Carmichael every morning at seven o'clock. The girl was not supposed to go into the room, but merely to knock at the door, wait for a response from her mistress, and then leave the tray outside on the mat.

"Usually Mrs. Carmichael took the tray in immediately, and was down to breakfast with her boarders at half-past eight. But on that eventful morning Mary seems to have been in a hurry. She could not positively state afterwards whether she had heard her mistress's answer to her knock or not; against that, she was quite sure that she had taken up the tray at seven o'clock precisely.

"When everybody went down to breakfast a couple of hours or so later, it was noticed that Mrs. Carmichael had not taken in her tea-tray as usual. A few anxious comments were made as to the genial hostess being unwell, and then the matter was dropped. The servants did not seem to have been really anxious about their mistress during the morning. Mary, who had been in the house two years, said that once before Mrs. Carmichael had stayed in bed with a bad headache until one o'clock.

"However, when the lunch hour came and went, Mrs. Tyrrell, one of the older lady boarders, became alarmed. She went up to her hostess's door and knocked at it loudly and repeatedly, but received no reply. The door, mind you, was locked or bolted, presumably, of course, from the inside. After consultation with her fellow boarders, Mrs. Tyrrell at last, feeling that something must be very wrong, took it upon herself to call in the police. Constable Rae came in; he too knocked and called, shook the door, and finally burst it open.

"It is not for me," continued the man in the corner, "to give you a description of that room as it appeared before the horrified eyes of the constable, the servants, and lady boarders; that lies more in your province than in mine.

"Suffice it to say that the unfortunate lady lay in her bed with her throat cut.

"No key or bolt was found on the inside of the door; the murderer, therefore, having accomplished his ghastly deed, must have locked his victim in, and probably taken the key away with him. Hardly had the terrible discovery been made than Emma the cook, half hysterical with fear and horror, rushed up to Constable Rae, and, clutching him wildly by the arm, whispered under her breath, 'Upton, Upton; he did it. I know . . . My poor mistress; he cut her throat with that fowl carver this morning. I saw it in his hand . . . It is him, constable!'

" 'Where is he?' asked the constable peremptorily. 'See that no one leaves the house. Who has seen this man?'

"But neither the constable, nor anyone else for that matter, was much surprised to find that on searching the house throughout, the man Upton had disappeared."

II.

"At first, of course, the case seemed simplicity itself. No doubt existed, either in the public mind or that of the police, as to Upton being the author of the grim and horrible tragedy. The only difficulty, so far, was the fact that Upton had managed not only to get away on the day of the murder, but also had contrived to evade the rigorous search instituted throughout the city after him by the police—a search, I assure you, in which many an amateur detective readily joined.

"The inquest had been put off for a day or two in the hope that Upton might be found before it occurred. However, three days had now elapsed, and it could not be put off any longer. Little did the public expect the sensational developments which the case suddenly began to assume.

"The medical evidence revealed nothing new. On the contrary, it added its usual quota of vague indefiniteness which so often helps to puzzle the police. The medical officer had been called in by Constable Rae, directly after his discovery of the murder. That was about two o'clock in the afternoon. Death had occurred a good many hours before that time, stated Dr. Dawlish—possibly nine or ten hours; but it might also have been eleven or twelve hours previously.

"Then Emma the cook was called. Her evidence was, of course, most important, as she had noticed and talked to the man Upton the very morning of the crime. He came as usual to his work, about a quarter to seven, but the cook immediately noticed that he seemed very strange and excited.

" 'What do you mean by strange?' asked the coroner.

" 'Well, it was strange of him, sir, to start first thing in the morning cleaning knives when we had as many knives as we wanted clean for breakfast.'

" 'Yes? He started cleaning knives, and then what did he do?'

" 'Oh, he turned and turned that there knife machine so as I told him he would be turning all the edges. Then he suddenly took up the fowl carver and said to me; "This fowl carver is awful blunt—where's the steel?" I says to him: "In the sideboard, of course, in the dining-room," and he goes off with the fowl carver in his hand, and that is the last I ever saw of that carver and of Upton himself.'

" 'Have you known Upton long?' asked the coroner.

" 'No, sir, he had only been in the house two days. Mr. Yardley gave him a character, and the mistress took him on, to clean boots and knives. His hours were half-past six to ten, but he used to turn up about a quarter to seven. He seemed obliging and willing, but not much up to his work, and didn't say much. But I hadn't seen him so funny except that morning when the poor missus was murdered.'

" 'Is this the carver you speak of?' asked the coroner, directing a constable to show one he held in his hand to the witness.

"With renewed hysterical weeping Emma identified the carver as the one she had last seen in Upton's hand. It appears that Detective McMurdoch had found the knife, together with the key of Mrs. Carmichael's bedroom door, under the hall mat. Sensational, wasn't it?" laughed the man in the corner; "quite in the style of the penny novelette—sensational, but not very mysterious.

"Then Mrs. Tyrrell had to be examined, as it was she who had first been alarmed about Mrs. Carmichael, and who had taken it upon herself to call in the police. Whether through spite or merely accidentally Mrs. Tyrrell insisted in her evidence on the fact that it was Mr. Yardley who was indirectly responsible for the awful tragedy, since it was he who had introduced the man Upton into the house.

"The coroner felt more interested. He thought he would like to put a few questions to Mr. Yardley. Now Mr. Yardley when called up did not certainly look prepossessing; and from the first most persons present were prejudiced against him. He was, as I think I said before, that *rara* *avis** a successful poet: he wrote dainty scraps for magazines and weekly journals.

"In appearance he was a short, sallow, thin man, with no body and long limbs, and carried his head so much to one side as to almost appear deformed. Here is a snapshot I got of him some time subsequently. He is no beauty, is he?

"Still his manner, his small shapely hands, and quiet voice undoubtedly proclaimed him a gentleman.

"It was very well known throughout the household that Mr. Yardley was very eccentric; being a poet he would enjoy the privilege with impunity. It appears that his most eccentric habit was to get up at unearthly hours in the morning—four o'clock sometimes—and wander about the streets of Glasgow.

" 'I have written my best pieces,' he stated in response to the coroner's astonished remark upon this strange custom of his, 'leaning against a lamp post in Sauchiehall Street at five o'clock in the morning. I spend my afternoons in the various public libraries, reading. I have only boarded and lodged in this house for two or three months, but, as the servants will tell you, I leave it long before they are up in the morning. I am never in to breakfast or luncheon, but always in to dinner. I go to bed early, naturally, as I require several hours sleep.'

"Mr. Yardley was then very closely questioned as to his knowledge of the man Upton.

" 'I first met the man,' replied Mr. Yardley, 'about a year ago. He was loafing in Buchanan Street, outside the *Herald* office, and spoke to me, telling me a most pitiable tale—namely, that he was an ex-compositor, had had to give up his work owing to failing eyesight, that he had striven for weeks and months to get some other kind of employment, spending in the meanwhile the hard-earned savings of many years' toil; that he had come to his last shilling two days ago, and had been reduced to begging, not for money, but for some kind of job—anything to earn a few honest coins.

" 'Well, I somehow liked the look of the man; moreover, as I just happened to want to send a message to the other end of the city, I sent Upton. Since then I have seen him almost every day. He takes my manuscripts for me to the editorial offices, and runs various errands. I have recommended him to one or two of my friends, and they have always found him honest and sober. He has eked out a very meagre livelihood in this way, and when Mrs. Carmichael thought of having a man in the house to do odd jobs, I thought I should be doing a kind act by recommending Upton to her. Little did I dream then what terrible consequences such a kind act would bring in its trail. I can only account for the man's awful crime by thinking that perhaps his mind had become suddenly unhinged.'

---

*rare bird

"All this seemed plain and straightforward enough. Mr. Yardley spoke quietly, without the slightest nervousness or agitation. The coroner and jury both pressed him with questions on the subject of Upton, but his attitude remained equally self-possessed throughout. Perhaps he felt, after a somewhat severe cross-examination on the part of the coroner, who prided himself on his talent in that direction, that a certain amount of doubt might lurk in the minds of the jury and consequently the public. Be that as it may, he certainly begged that two or three of the servants might be recalled in order to enable them to state definitely that he was out of the house, as usual, when they came downstairs that morning.

"One of the housemaids, recalled, fully corroborated that statement. Mr. Yardley's room, she said, was on the ground floor, next to the dining-room. She went into it soon after half-past six, turned down the bed, and began tidying it up generally.

"There was only one other witness of any importance to examine. One other boarder—Mr. James Lucas, a young journalist, employed on the editorial staff of the *Glasgow Banner*.

"The reason why he had been called specially was because he was well known to be one of the privileged guests of the house, and had been more intimate with the deceased than any of her other boarders. This privilege, it appears, chiefly consisted in being admitted to coffee, and possibly whiskey and soda after dinner, in Mrs. Carmichael's special private sitting-room. Moreover, there was a generally accepted theory among the other boarders that Mr. James Lucas entertained certain secret hopes with regard to his amiable hostess, and that, but for the fact that he was several years her junior, she might have encouraged these hopes.

"Now, Mr. James Lucas was the exact opposite of Mr. Yardley, the poet; tall, fair, athletic, his appearance would certainly prepossess everyone in his favour. He seemed very much upset, and recounted with much, evidently genuine, feeling, his last interview with the unfortunate lady—the evening before the murder.

" 'I spent about an hour with Mrs. Carmichael in her sitting-room,' he concluded, 'and parted from her about ten o'clock. I then went to my club, where I stayed pretty late, until closing time, in fact. After that I went for a stroll, and it was a quarter past two by my watch when I came in. I let myself in with my latch-key.

" 'It was pitch dark in the outer hall, and I was groping for my candle, when I heard the sound of a door opening and shutting on one of the floors above, and directly after someone coming down the stairs. As you have seen yourself, the outer hall is divided from the inner one by a glass door, which on this occasion stood open. In the inner hall there was a faint glimmer of light, which worked its way down from a skylight on one of the landings, and by this glimmer I saw Mr. Yardley descending the stairs, cross the hall, and go into his room. He did not see me, and I did not speak.'

"An extraordinary, almost breathless, hush had descended over all those assembled there. The coroner sat with his chin buried in his hand, his eyes resting searchingly on the witness who had just spoken. The jury had not uttered a sound. At last the coroner queried:

" 'Is the jury to understand, Mr. Lucas, that you can swear positively that at a quarter-past two in the morning, or thereabouts, you saw Mr. Yardley come down the stairs from one of the floors above and go into his own room, which is on the ground floor?'

" 'Positively.'

"That was enough. Mr. Lucas was dismissed and Mr. Yardley was recalled. As he once more stood before the coroner, his curious one-sided stoop, his sallowness, and length of limb seemed even more marked than before. Perhaps he was a shade or two paler, but certainly neither his hands nor his voice trembled in the slightest degree.

"Questioned by the coroner, he replied quietly:

" 'Mr. Lucas was obviously mistaken. At the hour he names I was in bed and asleep.'

"There had been excitement and breathless interest when Mr. James Lucas had made his statement, but that excitement and breathlessness was as nothing compared with the absolutely dumbfounded awe which fell over everyone there, as the sallow, half-deformed, little poet, gave the former witness so completely, so emphatically the lie.

"The coroner himself hardly knew how to keep up his professional dignity as he almost gasped the query:

" 'Then is the jury to understand that you can swear positively that at a quarter-past two o'clock on that particular morning you were in bed and asleep?'

" 'Positively.'

"It seemed as if Mr. Yardley had repeated purposely the other man's emphatic and laconic assertion. Certainly his voice was as steady, his eye as clear, his manner as calm as that of Mr. Lucas. The coroner and jury were silent, and Mr. Yardley turned to where young Lucas had retired in a further corner of the room. The eyes of the two met, almost like the swords of two duellists before the great attack; neither flinched. One or the other was telling a lie. A terrible lie since it might entail loss of honour, or life perhaps to the other, yet *neither* flinched. One was telling a lie, remember, and in everyone's mind there arose at once the great all absorbing queries 'Which?' and 'Wherefore!' "

III.

I HAD been so absorbed in listening to the thrilling narrative of that highly dramatic inquest that I really had not noticed until then that the man in the corner was recounting it as if he had been present at it himself.

"That is because I heard it all from an eye-witness," he suddenly replied with that eerie knack he seemed to possess of reading my thoughts, "but it must have been very dramatic, and, above all, terribly puzzling. You see there were two men swearing against one another, both in good positions, both educated men; it was impossible for any jury to take either evidence as absolutely convincing, and it could not be proved that either of them lied. Mr. Lucas might have done so from misapprehension. There was just a possibility that he had had more whiskey at his club than was good for him. Mr. Yardley, on the other hand, if he lied, lied because he had something to hide, something to hide in that case which might have been terrible.

"Of course Dr. Dawlish was recalled, and with wonderful learning and wonderful precision he repeated his vague medical statements:

" 'When I examined the body with my colleague, Dr. Swanton, death had evidently supervened several hours ago. Personally, I believe that it must have occurred certainly more like twelve hours ago than seven.

"More than that he could not say. After all, medical science has its limits.

"Then Emma, the cook, was again called. There was an important point which, oddly enough, had been overlooked up to this moment. The question, namely, of the doormat under which the knife (which, by the way, was blood-stained) and also the key of Mrs. Carmichael's bedroom door was found. Emma, however, could make a very clear and very definite statement on that point. She had cleaned the ball and shaken the mat at half-past six that morning. At that hour the housemaid was making Mr. Yardley's bed; he had left the house already. There certainly was neither key nor knife under the mat then.

"The balance of evidence, which perhaps for one brief moment had inclined oh, ever so slightly, against Mr. Yardley, returned to its original heavy weight against the man Upton. Of course there was practically nothing to implicate Mr. Yardley seriously The coroner made a résumé of the case before his jury worthy of a judge in the High Courts.

"He recapitulated all the evidence. It was very strong, undeniable, damning against Upton, and the jury could arrive but at one conclusion with regard to him. Then there was the medical evidence. That certainly favoured Upton a very little, if at all. Remember that both the medical gentlemen refused to make a positive statement as to the time; their evidence could not, therefore, be said to weigh either for or against anyone.

"There was then the strange and unaccountably conflicting evidence between two gentlemen of the house—Mr. Lucas and Mr. Yardley. That was a matter which for the present must rest between either of these gentlemen and their conscience. There was also the fact that the man Upton—the evident actual murderer—had been introduced into the house by Mr. Yardley. The jury knew best themselves if this fact should or should not weigh with them in their decision.

"That was the sum total of the evidence. The jury held but a very brief consultation. Their foreman pronounced their verdict of 'Wilful murder against Upton.' Not a word about Mr. Yardley. What could they have said? There was really no evidence against him—not enough, certainly, to taint his name for ever with so hideous a blight.

"In a case like that, remember, the jury are fully aware that the police would never for a moment lose sight of a man who had so narrowly escaped a warrant as Yardley had done. Relying on the certainty that very soon Upton would be arrested, it was not to be doubted for a moment but that he would betray his accomplice, if he had one. Criminals in such a plight nearly always do. In the meanwhile, every step of Yardley's would be dogged, unbeknown to himself, even if he attempted to leave the country. As for Upton——."

The man in the corner paused. He was eyeing me through his great bone-rimmed spectacles, watching with ironical delight my evident breathless interest in his narrative. I remembered that Glasgow murder so well. I remember the talks, the arguments, the quarrels that would arise in every household. Was Yardley an accomplice? Did he kill Mrs. Carmichael at two in the morning? Did he tell a lie? If so, why? Did Mr. James Lucas tell a lie? Many people, I remember, held this latter theory, more particularly as Mrs. Carmichael's will was proved some days later, and it was found that she had left all her money to him.

For a little while public opinion veered dead against him. Some people thought that if he were innocent he would refuse to touch a penny of her money; others, of a more practical turn of mind, did not see why he should not. He was a struggling young journalist; the lady had obviously been in love with him, and intended to marry him; she had a perfect right—as she had no children or any near relative—to leave her money to whom she choose, and it would indeed be hard on him, if, through the act of some miscreant, he should at one fell swoop be deprived both of wife and fortune.

Then, of course, there was Upton—Upton! Upton! whom the police could not find! who must be guilty, seeing that he so hid himself, who never would have acted the hideous comedy with the carver. Why should he have wilfully drawn attention to himself, and left, as it were, his visiting card on the scene of the murder?

Why? why? why?

"Ah, yes, why?" came as a funny, shrill echo from my eccentric *vis-a-vis.** "I see that in spite of my earnest endeavour to teach you to think out a case logically and clearly, you start off with a preconceived

---

*person opposite

notion, which naturally leads you astray *because* it is preconceived, just like any blundering detective in these benighted islands."

"Preconceived?" I retorted indignantly. "There is no question of preconception. Whether Mr. Yardley knew of the contemplated murder or not, whether he was an accomplice or Mr. Lucas, there is one thing very clear—namely, that Upton was not innocent in the matter."

"What makes you say that?" he asked blandly.

"Obviously, because if he were innocent he would not have acted the hideous tragic comedy with the carver; he would not, above all, have absolutely damned himself by disappearing out of the house and out of sight at the very moment when the discovery of Mrs. Carmichael's murdered body had become imminent."

"It never struck you, I suppose," retorted the man in the corner with quiet sarcasm, "how *very* damning Upton's actions were on that particular morning?"

"Of course they were *very* damning. That is just my contention."

"And you have never then studied my methods of reasoning sufficiently to understand that when a criminal—a clever criminal, mind you—appears to be damning himself in the most brainless fashion, that is the time to guard against the clever pitfalls he is laying up for the police?"

"Exactly. That is why I, as well as many people connected with journalism, believe that Upton was acting a comedy in order to save his accomplice. The question only remains as to who the accomplice was."

"He must have been singularly unselfish and self-sacrificing, then."

"How do you mean?"

"According to your argument, Upton heaped up every conceivable circumstantial evidence against himself in order to shield his accomplice. Firstly he acts the part of strange, unnatural excitement, he loudly proclaims the fact that he leaves the kitchen with the fowl carver in his hand, thirdly he deposits that same blood-stained knife and the key of Mrs. Carmichael's room under the mat a few moments before he leaves the house. You must own that the man must have been singularly unselfish since, if he is ever caught, nothing would save him from the gallows, whilst, unless a great deal more evidence can be brought up, his accomplice could continue to go free."

"Yes, that might be," I said thoughtfully; "it was of course a part of the given plan. Many people held that Upton and Yardley were great friends—they might have been brothers, who knows?"

"Yes, who knows?" he repeated scornfully, as getting more and more excited his long thin fingers wound and unwound his bit of string, making curious complicated knots, and then undoing them feverishly.

"Do brothers usually so dote on each other, that they are content to swing for one another? And have you never wondered why the police never found Upton? How did he get away? Where is he? Has the earth swallowed him up?

"Surely a clumsy brute like that, who gives himself hopelessly away on the very day when he commits a murder, cannot have brains enough to hide altogether away from the police—a man who before a witness selects the weapon with which he means to kill his victim, and who then deliberately leaves it blood-stained there where it is sure to be found at once? Why imagine such a consummate fool evading the police, not a day, not a week, not a month, but nearly two years now, which means altogether? Why, such a fool as you, the public, and the police have branded him would have fallen into a trap within twenty-four hours of his attempt at evasion; whereas the man who planned and accomplished that murder was a genius before he became a blackguard."

"That's just what I said. He was doing it to shield his accomplice."

"His accomplice!" gasped the funny creature, with ever increasing excitement. "Yes, the accomplice he loved and cherished above all—his brother you say, perhaps. No, someone he would love ten thousand times more than any brother."

"Then you mean——"

"*Himself,* of course! Didn't you see it all along? Lord bless my soul! The young man—poet or blackguard, what you will—who comes into a boarding-house, then realises that its mistress is wealthy. He studies the rules of the house, the habits of its mistress, finds out about her money, her safe, her jewels, and then makes his plans. Oh, they were magnificently laid! That man ought to have been a great diplomatist, a great general—he was only a great scoundrel.

"The sort of disguise he assumed is so easy to manage. Only remember one thing: When a fool wishes to sink his identity he does so *after* he has committed a crime and is wanted by the police; he is bound, therefore, for the best part of the remainder of his life, to keep up the disguise he has selected at all times, every hour, every minute of the day; to alter his voice, his walk, his manners. On the other hand, how does a clever man like Yardley proceed?

"He chooses his disguise and assumes it *before* the execution of his crime: it is then only a matter of a few days, and when all is over, the individual, the known criminal, disappears; and, mind you, he takes great care that the criminal shall be known. Now in this case Upton is introduced into the house; say he calls one evening on Mr. Yardley's recommendation; Mrs. Carmichael sees him in the hall for a few moments, arranges the question of work and wages, and after that he comes every morning, with a dirty face, towzled hair, false beard and moustache—the usual type of odd job man very much down in his luck—his work lies in the kitchen, no one sees him upstairs, whilst the cook and kitchen folk never see Mr. Yardley.

"After a little while something—carelessness perhaps—might reveal the trick, but the deception is only carried on two days. Then the murder is accomplished and Upton disappears. In the meanwhile Mr. Yardley continues his eccentric habits. He goes out at unearthly hours; he is a poet; he is out of the house while Upton carries on the comedy with the carving knife. He knows that there never will be any evidence against him as Yardley; he has taken every care that all should be against Upton, all; hopeless, complete, absolute, damning!

"Then he leaves the police to hunt for Upton. He 'lies low' for a time, after a little while he will go abroad, I dare say he has done so already. A jeweller in Vienna, or perhaps St. Petersburg, will buy some loose stones of him, the stones he has picked out of Mrs. Carmichael's brooches and rings, the gold he will melt down and sell, the notes he can cash at any foreign watering-place, without a single question being asked of him. English banknotes find a very ready market abroad, and 'no questions asked.'

"After that he will come back to his friends in Glasgow and write dainty bits of poetry for magazines; the only difference being that he will write them at more reasonable hours. And during all the time the police will hunt for Upton.

"It was clever, was it not? You have his photo? I gave it you just now. Clever-looking, isn't he? As Upton he wore a beard and dyed his hair very black; it must have been a great trouble every morning, mustn't it?"

Reading for Understanding

Central Point

1. The central point of the story is a question of (a) accuracy in reporting (b) police efficiency (c) identity (d) curiosity.

Details

2. Mrs. Carmichael (a) expected to marry Yardley (b) was old and feeble (c) was jilted by Upton (d) took in boarders.

3. The first one to suspect that something was wrong was (a) Emma (b) Mrs. Tyrell (c) Constable Rae (d) Mary.

4. Upton was introduced into the household by (a) Emma (b) Mary (c) Mr. Yardley (d) Mrs. Tyrell.

5. Mr. Yardley insisted that he was a (a) retired army officer (b) journalist (c) poet (d) relative of Upton's.

Inferences

6. One important clue to the solution of the mystery was that (a) Lucas had been a favorite of Mrs. Carmichael's (b) Upton and Yardley were never seen together (c) Emma and Mary knew much more than they told (d) Detective McMurdoch found the knife under the hall mat.

7. The murderer succeeded because (a) he knew the routines of the house (b) the police falsified evidence (c) Yardley was basically an honest, if naive, young man (d) Lucas covered up for Yardley.

8. Of the characters in the story, the liar was (a) Lucas (b) Yardley (c) Mary (d) the coroner

Order of Events

9. Arrange the items in the order in which they occurred. Use letters only.
   A. Upton disappears.
   B. Yardley recommends Upton.
   C. Mrs. Carmichael does not take in her tea tray.
   D. The Old Man identifies the murderer.
   E. The jury identifies Upton.

Author's Attitude

10. The author's attitude toward her creation, the Man in the Corner, is one of (a) unwitting scorn (b) ill-concealed embarrassment (c) girlish awe (d) affectionate respect.

Words in Context

1., 2. "It was in July of last year, was it not, that Glasgow—honest, *stodgy,* busy Glasgow—was thrilled to its very marrow by the recital in its evening papers of one of the most ghastly and *dastardly* crimes." **Stodgy** (336) means (a) boring (b) colorful (c) overworked (d) exciting. **Dastardly** (336) means (a) intriguing (b) puzzling (c) unexpected (d) cowardly.

3. "Where is he?" asked the constable *peremptorily*. **Peremptorily** (337) means (a) swiftly (b) arrogantly (c) cautiously (d) heartlessly.

4., 5., 6. "Upton had managed not only to get away on the day of the murder, but also had *contrived* to *evade* the *rigorous* search instituted throughout the city after him by the police." **Contrived** (337) means (a) planned ingeniously (b) deceived unintentionally (c) accidentally achieved (d) obviously attempted. **Evade** (337) means (a) follow (b) dodge (c) counteract (d) resist. **Rigorous** (337) means (a) relentless (b) casual (c) evil (d) requested.

7. Mr. Yardley when called up did not certainly look *prepossessing*. **Prepossessing** (338) means (a) attractive (b) gaudy (c) tiresome (d) greedy.

8. In appearance he was a short, *sallow*, thin man, with no body and long limbs." **Sallow** (339) means (a) stocky and muscular (b) pale and sickly (c) well tanned (d) disagreeable.

9. "Being a poet he would enjoy the privilege with *impunity*." **Impunity** (339) suggests a lack of (a) enthusiasm (b) attentiveness (c) vitality (d) punishment.

10. "Perhaps his mind had become suddenly *unhinged*." **Unhinged** (339) means (a) flabby (c) uncertain (c) unusually keen (d) confused.

11. "That excitement and breathlessness was as nothing compared with the absolutely *dumbfounded* awe which fell over everyone there." **Dumbfounded** (341) means (a) obvious (b) unwarranted (c) groundless (d) bewildered.

12. "It seemed as if Mr. Yardley had repeated purposely the other man's emphatic and *laconic* assertion." **Laconic** (341) means (a) vivid and memorable (b) extensive and meaningful (c) short and pointed (d) contradictory.

13. "The coroner made a *résumé* of the case before his jury worthy of a judge in the High Courts." A **résumé** (342) is a (a) critical review (b) summary (c) mockery (d) plea.

14. "He *recapitulated* all the evidence." **Recapitulated** (342) means (a) reviewed (b) challenged (c) glossed over (d) omitted.

15. "There was really no evidence against him—not enough, certainly, to taint his name for ever with so hideous a *blight*." A **blight** (343) is a kind of (a) illumination (b) disease (c) reputation (d) discovery.

16. "For a little while public opinion *veered* dead against him." **Veered**

(343) means (a) protested loudly (b) changed direction (c) followed the course (d) bumped along.

17. "It is preconceived, just like any blundering detective in these *benighted* islands." **Benighted** (344) means (a) unenlightened (b) blessed (c) spacious (d) repressed.

18. "You must own that the man must have been *singularly* unselfish since, if he is ever caught, nothing would save him from the gallows." **Singularly** (344) means (a) cleverly (b) thoughtfully (c) remarkably (d) wearily.

19. "Do brothers usually so *dote on* each other that they are content to swing for one another." **Dote on** (344) means (a) imitate closely (b) fear irrationally (c) question sharply (d) love excessively.

20. "Why imagine such a *consummate* fool evading the police?" **Consummate** (345) means (a) foolish (b) complete (c) eager (d) original.

21. "Such a fool as you, the public, and the police have branded him would have fallen into a trap within twenty-four hours of his attempt at *evasion*." **Evasion** (345) means (a) repetition (b) disclosure (c) escape (d) success.

Thinking Critically about the Story

1. What crucial clues helped the Man in the Corner to a solution of the mystery?

2. Why did Upton take such pains to make himself appear so guilty?

3. What possible motive for the slaying was given to Lucas? Was it misleading?

4. The Man in the Corner agreed that Upton had an accomplice . . . but who? Why?

5. Why was it crucial for the murderer to change his identity before the crime, not after?

6. What was Yardley's motive in complaining about the polishing of his boots?

7. Yardley was short; Lucas, tall. Did this difference play a role in the solution of the crime? Explain.

8. The title "The Glasgow Mystery" is rather commonplace. Can you think of a better?

Language in Action

Concealed Metaphors

> "It was very well known throughout the household that Mr. Yardley was very eccentric."

Metaphor (150) compares unlike objects and adds a touch of poetry to speech and writing. The flower name *foxglove* is, for example, particularly apt. Some metaphors are almost as colorful, even though they are concealed in their etymologies, or word histories. *Eccentric*, for example, derives from the root *center* and the prefix *ec; out, out of,* or *off.* Someone who is *eccentric* is "off center," a rather clever way of labeling a deviation from the normal.

Like most of the stories in this book, "The Glasgow Mystery" has a great many concealed metaphors.

An *amateur* is a "lover." someone who loves a hobby as a pastime, not a profession.

Humble comes from *humus, earth.* A humble person is literally "down to earth."

A *manuscript* was once written by hand. Now a manuscript may come in many forms.

A *constable* was once an *officer of the stable.*

Crescent means *growing.* The *crescent* moon is *growing* toward full. The shape of the crescent moon has been extended to streets.

Widow comes from a root *to divide, to separate,* a grim reminder of the loss of a spouse.

Gossip is *god-sibb,* a sponsor of a child at baptism. We may suspect that baptismal get-togethers provide an opportunity for talk about others, or *gossip.*

I Love a Mystery

Thinking Critically about the Stories

1. What do you think Albert Einstein had in mind (253) when he talked of the mysterious? Are there mysteries in life that are beyond the power of the human mind to comprehend? Comment.

2. What is the single common thread that links "Man in Hiding" and "Déjà Vu"?

3. Compare or contrast the three great detectives: Colonel March ("The Crime in Nobody's Room"), the Man in the Corner ("The Glasgow Mystery"), and Father Brown ("The Oracle of the Dog"). Do you have a favorite? Explain.

4. Do you like to match wits with the detective? Do you try to guess the murderer before the great revelation, or do you just sit back and enjoy the puzzle? Explain.

5. Which one of the stories had no murder? Did you find it equally interesting, however? Present your point of view.

6. Which of the stories came closest to satisfying your own taste in detective stories? Why?

The Writing Portfolio

Editing and Revising

Some of the writing in your portfolio may be for yourself alone: notes, bits of observation, diary entries. Other materials will be for the eyes of others. These should be edited and revised before "publishing" them.

A first draft gets the ideas on paper, suggests the general structure, and clarifies your thinking. Part of the job is checking technical matters like punctuation and spelling. Another part is checking your writing for clarity. Here's a helpful checklist:

1. Do you begin with an interest catcher and hold that interest?
2. Are your paragraphs forceful and complete?
3. Do you make it easy for your readers to follow? Do you use connecting words?
4. Are your sentences effective, clear and varied?
5. Is your ending satisfying?

As you write one or more of the following themes, go carefully over your first draft. Sometimes it's a good idea to write that first draft on alternate lines, leaving room for insertions and changes.

1. What kind of fiction do you prefer? Romances? Historical Novels? Science fiction? Mysteries? Stories of international intrigue? Choose a category and support your choice by citing examples.
2. A recent tendency in horror movies is to emphasize the blood. Alien creatures burst from chest cavities. Human beings are mutilated before the camera. Older methods relied on suggestion: a dark corridor, a moving drape, a shadow. Do you prefer your horror movies obvious or subtle? Explain, with examples.
3. Do you consider television or the movies a better medium for presenting horror movies? Explain.
4. Do you enjoy a sense of mystery in your own life? Do you prefer NOT to open a birthday gift until the actual day because you enjoy wondering about it? Would you like to know how a magician performs his tricks, or do you enjoy the sense of mystery he or she creates? Explain your point of view.
5. Agatha Christie, Carter Dickson, and G. K. Chesterton enjoy pulling surprises. In "The Oracle of the Dog," for example, Chesterton turns upside down the popular mythology that dogs are somehow mysteriously able to know things impossible to human beings. How do you feel about surprise endings? Are you annoyed or pleased by stories that end in a surprise? Explain.
6. Mrs. Rymer in "The Case of the Rich Woman" reclaimed happiness without her money. Obviously, money is needed to survive, but is an excessive amount of money a barrier to happiness? What do you think? Present your point of view.
7. Baroness E. Orczy wrote *The Scarlet Pimpernel* (334). If you have ever seen or read one of the versions, tell a bit about it and whether or not you enjoyed it.

Other Areas of Communication

1. Read another Father Brown short story, an Agatha Christie novel, or a Carter Dickson (John Dickson Carr) novel. Prepare to report to the class.

2. Which is your favorite television mystery (detective story, crime story, suspense, spy story, fantasy)? Be ready to tell why you enjoy it. Consider such things as plot, characterization, mood, dialogue, setting, and theme.

3. Watch a television program dealing with crime and law enforcement. Use these standards in judging the program.

   (a) Did the program refrain from making crime attractive, profitable, or even cute?

   (b) Was the story presented in a way so that the listener tends to identify himself with the forces of law and order?

   (c) Were the procedures used in solving the crime realistic and believable?

   (d) Were the characters complex and human or mere cardboard figures?

   Report to the class, giving your own opinion of the standards set up.

4. The selections in this unit have sections that lend themselves to dramatizations—for example, the revelation scene in "The Crime in Nobody's Room" or Mrs. Rymer's interview with Parker Pyne ("The Case of the Rich Widow"). With a classmate or classmates, select a scene and prepare to dramatize it for the class.

5. The power of television was demonstrated by a single small act. When Telly Savalas's television character Kojak sucked on a lollipop instead of a cigarette, lollipop sales worldwide increased 500%. Set up a panel discussion of 4–6 participants on the topic "How Television Influences Our Daily Lives." Consider such topics as fads, clothing styles, hair styles, popular expressions, commercials.

6. The number of television detectives grows with each year. Here is a representative listing of TV sleuths. Many of these programs are in syndication and possibly familiar to you. Set up a class discussion to consider questions like these. How many detectives can you recognize? What is the characteristic method used by each detective? How personable is the detective? What are the reasons for the program's success—or, possibly, ultimate failure? Is the mood of the program serious or light?

Father Brown	Matt Houston	McMillan and Wife
Amos Burke	Hunter	Petrocelli

Frank Cannon	Barnaby Jones	Ellery Queen
Charlie Chan	Kojak	Quincy
Columbo	Magnum, P.I.	Rockford
Adam Dalgliesh	Mannix	The Saint
Jessica Fletcher	Philip Marlowe	Spenser
Hart to Hart	Miss Marple	Remington Steele
Sherlock Holmes	Perry Mason	Lord Peter Whimsey
Matlock	McCloud	Nero Wolfe

Language in Action

A Review

You may refer to the preceding pages to answer these questions.

1. If I say, "I'm just too lucky" after sitting on a just-painted seat, I am using (a) metaphor (b) simile (c) irony (d) personification.
2. The following are all examples of reduplication EXCEPT (a) fiddle-de-dee (b) singsong (c) pell-mell (d) tutti-frutti.
3. The essence of paradox is (a) agreement (b) contradiction (c) drama (d) illness.
4. A word's connotation (a) may vary from individual to individual (b) is the same as denotation (c) is relatively unchanging (d) is easily spotted.
5. A word's connotations are generally (a) unpleasant (b) narrow in scope but rich in history (c) broader than its denotations (d) humorous.
6. In computer language, a *mouse* (a) moves a cursor (b) runs a floppy disc (c) makes voice mail possible (d) is a mistake in operation.
7. The word *nerd* was created (a) for the computer (b) in 1950 (c) to describe a subatomic physicist (d) within the last 20 years.
8. For information about when words entered the language, consult (a) Roget's Thesaurus (b) Samuel Johnson's *Dictionary of the English Language* (c) *Merriam-Webster's Collegiate Dictionary* (d) *Encyclopedia of Words and Phrases*.

9. *Eccentric* is an example of (a) flowery writing (b) poor definition (c) antagonistic reporting (d) concealed metaphor.

10. The basis of all metaphor is (a) comparison (b) irony (c) paradox (d) conflict.

UNIT FIVE

For the Fun of It

As for life, (452), poetry (446), and love (157), the following quotations provide food for thought, though not final answers. What is humor? What makes something funny? Why is something funny for one person and not for another? Here are some comments and attempts at definitions.

Men will confess to treason, murder, arson, false teeth, or a wig. How many of them will own up to a lack of humor?

Frank Moore Colby

Laughter is the shortest distance between two people.

Victor Borge

I think the next best thing to solving a problem is finding some humor in it.

Frank A. Clark

He who laughs, lasts.

Mary P. Poole

In telling jokes

If you can't remember them,

Don't dismember them.

Anthony J. Pettito

A sense of humor is a sense of proportion.

Kahlil Gibran

Here you will find examples of many types of humor. Mark Twain combines exaggeration with outrageous characterization. Saki takes an absurd situation and carries it to an absurd conclusion, logical if we accept the problem. James Thurber retells a funny episode from childhood and glorifies it with some keen but sympathetic insights. Stephen Leacock pokes fun at himself in the great tradition of comedians like Bill Cosby and Bob Newhart.

Eric Knight provides an excellent example of humor through characterization. George Bernard Shaw once said, "My way of joking is telling the truth. That is the funniest joke in the world." Eric Knight tells the truth and it is funny.

You will find other ways of achieving humor in the stories that follow.

My Financial Career

Stephen Leacock
Canadian

Kiddie-Kar Travel

Robert Benchley
American

In America there are two classes of travel—first class, and with children. Traveling with children corresponds roughly to traveling third-class in Bulgaria. They tell me there is nothing lower in the world than third-class Bulgarian travel.

These stories have been paired because they use a special kind of exaggeration: good-natured and gentle. Indeed, understatement is often used as well. They were written by two humorists who died a half-century ago within a year of each other.

"My Financial Career" is dated in many ways. The sum of money is trivial by today's standards. The innocence of the depositor is far-fetched in today's sophisticated age. The account is still funny, though, because the petty vanities and weaknesses of human nature don't change.

"Kiddie-Kar Travel" was written at a time when train travel was the principal means of transportation. Note, though, that except for a few details, the article might now apply to bus travel and air travel, as well. Children on airplanes are more restricted because of the special requirements of travel, but most seasoned air travelers have met more than one Roger on a flight.

Note how the authors bring characters to life: the clerk and the bank manager in "My Financial Career," and the lady in a black silk dress in "Kiddie-Kar Travel." The authors seem to be saying, "People are endlessly fascinating. Here's a sample."

My Financial Career

WHEN I go into a bank, I get rattled. The clerks rattle me; the wickets rattle me; the sight of the money rattles me; everything rattles me. The moment I cross the threshold of a bank I am a hesitating jay. If I attempt to transact business there, I become an irresponsible idiot.

I knew this beforehand; but when my salary was raised to fifty dollars a month, I felt that the bank was the only place for it. So I shambled in and looked timidly around at the clerks. I had an idea that a person about to open an account needed to consult the manager. I went up to a wicket marked "Accountant." The accountant was a tall, cool devil—the very sight of him rattled me. My voice was sepulchral.

"May I see the manager?" I said, and added solemnly, "Alone." I don't know why I said "alone."

"Certainly," said the accountant and fetched him. The manager was a grave, calm man. I held my fifty-six dollars clutched in a crumpled ball in my pocket.

"Are you the manager?" I said. Heaven knows I didn't doubt it.

"Yes," he said.

"May I see you?" I asked. "Alone?" I didn't want to say "alone" again, but without it my question seemed self-evident.

The manager looked at me in some alarm. He felt that I had a terrible secret to reveal.

"Come in here," he said, leading the way to a private room and turning the key.

"We are safe from interruption here," he said. "Sit down."

We both sat down and looked at one another. I found no voice to speak.

"You are a Pinkerton detective, I presume," he said.

He had gathered from my mysterious manner that I was a detective. I knew what he was thinking and felt all the worse.

"No, not from Pinkerton's," I said, seemingly to imply that I came from a rival agency. "To tell the truth," I went on, as if I *had* been prompted to lie about the matter, "I am not a detective at all. I have come to open an account. I intend to keep all my money in this bank."

The manager looked relieved, but still serious; he concluded now that I was a son of Baron Rothschild, or a young Gould.

"A very large account, I suppose," he said.

"Fairly large," I whispered. "I propose to deposit fifty-six dollars now, and fifty dollars a month regularly."

The manager got up and opened the door. He called to the accountant.

"Mr. Montgomery," he said, unkindly loud, "this gentleman is opening an account; he will deposit fifty-six dollars. Good-morning."

I rose. A big iron door stood open at the side of the room.

"Good morning," I said and stepped into the safe.

"Come out," said the manager coldly, showing me the other way.

I went up to the accountant's wicket and poked the ball of money at him with a quick, convulsive movement, as if I were doing a trick. My face was ghastly pale.

"Here," I said, "deposit it." The tone of the words seemed to mean, "Let us do this painful business while the fit is on us."

He took the money and gave it to another clerk. He made me write the sum on a slip and sign my name in a book. I no longer knew what I was doing. The bank swam before my eyes.

"Is it deposited?" I asked, in a hollow, vibrating voice.

"It is," said the accountant.

"Then I want to draw a check."

My idea was to draw out six dollars for present use. Someone gave me a checkbook through a wicket, and someone else began telling me how to write the check. The people in the bank had the impression that I was an invalid millionaire. I wrote something on the check and thrust it in at the clerk. He looked at it.

"What! Are you drawing it all out again?" he asked in surprise. Then I realized that I had written fifty-six instead of six. I was too far gone to reason now. I had a feeling that I could not explain my act. All the clerks had stopped writing to look at me.

Reckless with misery, I made a plunge.

"Yes, the whole thing."

"You withdraw your money from the bank!"

"Every cent of it."

"Are you not going to deposit any more?" said the clerk, astonished.

"Never!"

An idiot hope struck me that he might think someone had insulted me while I was writing the check and that I had changed my mind. I made a wretched attempt to look like a man with a fearfully quick temper.

The clerk prepared to pay the money.

"How will you have it?" he said.

"Oh." I caught his meaning and answered without even trying to think, "In fifties."

He gave me a fifty-dollar bill.

"And the six?" he asked dryly.

"In sixes," I said.

He gave me the money, and I rushed out. As the big doors swung behind me. I caught the echo of a roar of laughter that went up to the ceiling of the bank. Since then I bank no more. I keep my money in cash in my trousers pocket, and my savings in silver dollars in a sock.

Kiddie-Kar Travel

In America there are two classes of travel—first class, and with children. Traveling with children corresponds roughly to traveling third-class in Bulgaria. They tell me there is nothing lower in the world than third-class Bulgarian travel.

The actual physical discomfort of traveling with the kiddies is not so great, although you do emerge from it looking as if you had just moved the piano upstairs singlehanded. It is the mental wear and tear that tells and for a sensitive man there is only one thing worse, and that is a church wedding in which he is playing the leading comedy role.

There are several branches of the ordeal of Going on Choo-Choo, and it is difficult to tell which is the roughest. Those who have taken a very small baby on a train maintain that this ranks as pleasure along with having a nerve killed. On the other hand, those whose wee companions are in the romping stage, simply laugh at the claims of the first group. Sometimes you will find a man who has both an infant *and* a romper with him. Such a citizen should receive a salute of twenty-one guns every time he enters the city and should be allowed to wear the insignia of the Pater Dolorosa, giving him the right to solicit alms on the cathedral steps.

There is much to be said for those who maintain that rather should the race be allowed to die out than that babies should be taken from place to place along our national arteries of traffic. On the other hand, there *are* moments when babies are asleep. (Oh, yes, there are. There *must* be.) But it is practically a straight run of ten or a dozen hours for your child of four.

You may have a little trouble in getting the infant to doze off, especially as the train newsboy waits crouching in the vestibule until he sees signs of slumber on the child's face and then rushes in to yell, "Copy of *Life,* out to-day!" right by its pink, shell-like ear. But after it is asleep, your troubles are over except for wondering how you can shift your cramped arm to a new position without disturbing its precious burden.

If the child is of an age which denies the existence of sleep, however, preferring to run up and down the aisle of the car rather than sit in its chair (at least a baby can't get out of its chair unless it falls out and even then it can't go far), then every minute of the trip is full of fun. On the whole, having traveled with children of all the popular ages, I would be inclined to award the Hair Shirt to the man who successfully completes the ride with a boy of, let us say, three.

In the first place, you start with the pronounced ill will of two thirds of the rest of the occupants of the car. You see them as they come in, before the train starts, glancing at you and yours with little or no attempt to conceal the fact that they wish they had waited for the four o'clock. Across from you is perhaps a large man who, in his home town, has a reputation for eating little children. He wears a heavy gold watch chain and wants to read through a lot of reports on the trip. He is just about as glad to be opposite a small boy as he would be if it were a hurdy-gurdy.*

In back of you is a lady in a black silk dress who doesn't like the porter. Ladies in black silk dresses always seem to board the train with an aversion to the porter. The fact that the porter has to be in the same car with her makes her fussy to start with, and when she discovers that in front of her is a child of three who is already eating (you simply have to give him a lemon-drop to keep him quiet at least until the train starts) she decides that the best thing to do is simply to ignore him and not give him the slightest encouragement to become friendly. The child therefore picks her out immediately to be his buddy.

For a time after things get to going all you have to do is answer questions about the scenery. This is only what you must expect when you have children, and it happens no matter where you are. You can always say that you don't know who lives in that house or what that cow is doing. Sometimes you don't even have to look up when you say that you don't know. This part is comparatively easy.

It is when the migratory fit comes on that you will be put to the test. Suddenly you look and find the boy staggering down the aisle, peering into the faces of people as he passes them. "Here! Come back here, Roger!" you cry, lurching after him and landing across the knees of the young lady two seats down. Roger takes this as a signal for a game and starts to run, screaming with laughter. After four steps he falls and starts to cry.

---

*hand organ

On being carried kicking back to his seat, he is told that he mustn't run down the aisle again. This strikes even Roger as funny, because it is such a flat thing to say. Of course he is going to run down the aisle again and he knows it as well as you do. In the meantime, however, he is perfectly willing to spend a little time with the lady in the black silk dress.

"Here, Roger," you say, "don't bother the lady."

"Hello, little boy," the lady says, nervously, and tries to go back to her book. The interview is over as far as she is concerned. Roger, however, thinks that it would be just dandy to get up in her lap. This has to be stopped, and Roger has to be whispered to.

He then announces that it is about time that he went to the washroom. You march down the car, steering him by the shoulders and both lurching together as the train takes the curves and attracting wide attention to your very obvious excursion. Several kindly people smile knowingly at you as you pass and try to pat the boy on the head, but their advances are repelled, it being a rule of all children to look with disfavor on any attentions from strangers. The only people they want to play with are those who hate children.

On reaching the washroom you discover that the porter has just locked it and taken the key with him, simply to be nasty. This raises quite a problem. You explain the situation as well as possible, which turns out to be not well enough. There is every indication of loud crying and perhaps worse. You call attention to the Burrows Rustless Screen sign which you are just passing and stand in the passageway by the drinking cups, feverishly trying to find things in the landscape as it whirls by which will serve to take the mind off the tragedy of the moment. You become so engrossed in this important task that it is some time before you discover that you are completely blocking the passageway and the progress of some fifteen people who want to get off at Utica. There is nothing for you to do but head the procession and get off first.

Once out in the open, the pride and prop of your old age decides that the thing to do is pay the engineer a visit, and starts off up the platform at a terrific rate. This amuses the onlookers and gives you a little exercise after being cramped up in that old car all the morning. The imminent danger of the train's starting without you only adds to the fun. At that, there might be worse things than being left in Utica. One of them is getting back on the train again to face the old gentleman with the large watch chain.

The final phase of the ordeal, however, is still in store for you when you make your way (and Roger's way) into the diner. Here the plunging march down the aisle of the car is multiplied by six (the diner is never any nearer than six cars and usually is part of another train). On the way, Roger sees a box of animal crackers belonging to a little girl and commandeers it. The little girl, putting up a fight, is promptly pushed over, starting what promises to be a free-for-all fight between the two families. Lurching along after the apologies have been made, it is just a series of unwarranted attacks by Roger on sleeping travelers and equally unwarranted evasions by Roger of the kindly advances of very nice people who love children.

In the diner, it turns out that the nearest thing they have suited to Roger's customary diet is veal cutlets, and you hardly think that his mother would approve of those. Everything else has peppers or sardines in it. A curry of lamb across the way strikes the boy's fancy and he demands some of that. On being told that he has not the slightest chance in the world of getting it but how would he like a little crackers-and-milk, he becomes quite upset and threatens to throw a fork at the Episcopal clergyman sitting opposite. Pieces of toast are waved alluringly in front of him and he is asked to consider the advantages of preserved figs and cream, but it is curry of lamb or he gets off the train. He doesn't act like this at home. In fact, he is noted for his tractability. There seems to be something about the train that brings out all the worst that is in him, all the hidden traits that he has inherited from his mother's side of the family. There is nothing else to do but say firmly: "Very well, then, Roger. We'll go back *without* any nice dinner," and carry him protesting from the diner, apologizing to the head steward for the scene and considering dropping him overboard as you pass through each vestibule.

In fact, I had a cousin once who had to take three of his little ones on an all-day trip from Philadelphia to Boston. It was the hottest day of the year and my cousin had on a woolen suit. By the time he reached Hartford, people in the car noticed that he had only two children with him. At Worcester he had only one. No one knew what had become of the others and no one asked. It seemed better not to ask. He reached Boston alone and never explained what had become of the tiny tots. Anyone who has ever traveled with tiny tots of his own, however, can guess.

Reading for Understanding

Main Idea

1. The main point of "My Financial Career" is (a) the cruelty of bank managers (a) the incompetence of the narrator (c) the mercilessness of banks (d) the importance of financial planning.

2. A major point of "Kiddie-Kar Travel" is that (a) trains are no place for small children (b) train schedules are poorly constructed (c) a child is mean-spirited by nature (d) American trains are better than Bulgarian.

Details

3. Before depositing his money, the narrator (a) counted it in the bank (b) scolded the accountant (c) checked each clerk to find a kind one (d) asked to see the manager.

4. When withdrawing his money, the narrator (a) asked for fifties (b) joked with the clerk (c) thanked the manager (d) left a portion in is account.

5. The narrator of "Kiddie-Kar Travel" thinks the most difficult age for a child on a train is (a) one (b) two (c) three (d) four.

6. Roger had a fight over (a) a box of animal crackers (b) a man's watch chain (c) a lady's book (d) another little boy.

7. At the diner, Roger insisted on (a) crackers-and-milk (b) peppers (c) sardines (d) curry of lamb.

Inferences

8. The manager was respectful to the bank depositor at first because he thought the depositor was (a) a relative of the accountant (b) an inspector from the Treasury Department (c) a Pinkerton detective (d) a celebrity.

9. Despite his dismay at events on the train, the author realizes that (a) people on trains are all kindly (b) his child is a normal active child (c) dining room facilities are generally hopeless (d) the trip is really rather satisfying.

Fact or Opinion

Tell whether the following is a fact or an opinion.

10. In "Kiddie-Kar Travel," the lady in the black silk dress was probably unmarried with no children of her own.

Words in Context

1. "My voice was *sepulchral.*" **Sepulchral** (360) means (a) tinny (b) quivering (c) excited (d) somber.

2. "I went up to the accountant's wicket and poked the ball of money at him with a quick, *convulsive* movement, as if I were doing a trick."

Convulsive (361) means (a) frantic (b) steady (c) impulsive (d) proud.

3. "Ladies in black silk dresses always seem to board the train with an *aversion to* the porter." **Aversion to** (363) means (a) wave to (b) criticism for (c) dislike of (d) suggestion for.

4. "Here! Come back here, Roger!" you cry, *lurching* after him and landing across the knees of the young lady two seats down." **Lurching** (363) means (a) shouting (b) crawling (c) parading (d) staggering

5. "You become so *engrossed in* this important task that it is some time before you discover that you are completely blocking the passageway and progress of some fifteen people who want to get off at Utica." **Engrossed in** (364) means (a) excited by (b) aware of (c) perplexed by (d) absorbed in.

6. "The *imminent* danger of the train's starting without you only adds to the fun." **Imminent** (364) means (a) obvious (b) overlooked (c) threatening (d) postponed.

7., 8. "It is just a series of *unwarranted* attacks by Roger on sleeping travelers and equally unwarrented *evasions* by Roger of the kindly advances of very nice people who love children." **Unwarranted** (365) means (a) not justified (b) uncertain (c) not available (d) not understandable. **Evasions** (365) are (a) illusions (b) avoidances (c) attacks (d) conversations.

9. "In fact, he is noted for his *tractability*." **Tractability** (365) means (a) liveliness (b) weariness (c) curiosity (d) obedience.

Thinking Critically about the Selections

1. How does Stephen Leacock reveal his own weaknesses? Why do we laugh when people put themselves down in a gentle way?

2. How does the Leacock selection show that it was written in an earlier day?

3. The bank manager appears in a brief segment; yet he is sharply observed and effectively described. Point out the touches that reveal his personality.

4. One explanation of humor is that it shows us incongruities, contradictions, things that conflict. To see a tiny dog led on a leash by a seven-foot basketball player is funnier than seeing the same dog with

a six-year-old. How does Benchley use incongruities in describing the experiences of Roger on the train?

5. Robert Benchley once acted in humorous short films. In one of them, he goes to bed and places his slippers carefully so that he can step into them when he arises. During the night, the slippers turn around by themselves; thus, he's frustrated when he tried to slip them on in the morning without bending. He is demonstrating the "antihuman qualities of inanimate objects." Audiences found the movie hilarious. What was funny? Does Benchley use any of the same techniques in "Kiddie-Kar Travel"?

6. Have you ever traveled with a small child on a bus, train, or plane? Did your experiences resemble Benchley's in any way? How did you manage in an automobile? Did you yourself ever groan, "Are we there yet?" Why does transportation often bring out the worst in children, expecially traveling brothers and sisters?

Language in Action

Our English Heritage

> I rose. A big iron door stood open at the side of the room.
> "Good morning," I said.

There is nothing unusual or startling about the three quoted sentences, but they demonstrate one important aspect of our language. They contain only words of Anglo-Saxon, or Old English, derivation. By a dictionary count, words derived from Latin and Greek far outnumber the words that came down to us from Old English, but that fact disguises an important truth: a count of the words we use *in ordinary conversation* would show a great majority of Old English words. If all the words of Old English origin were suddenly eliminated from our language, we'd scarcely be able to say a complete sentence. If all Latin and Greek words disappeared, we'd be sorely handicapped, but we'd still be able to converse.

Everyday words like *man, woman, house, sun, moon, grass, good, child, sleep* and *stone* are of Old English origin, as are the common personal pronouns—*I, we, you, he, she, it.* The constantly used conjunctions and prepositions and the articles *a, an, the* are also of Old English extraction.

In unusual situations we rely on Old English:

Stay away from that stove. It's hot!

I love you.

Let's go to the beach today.

Don't ever ask me to go there again!

Where did you leave the tickets for tonight's meeting? We'll be late.

Old English is related to many other old tongues on the continent of Europe. It represents the strong Germanic basis of our language. The Romance words, especially from French and Latin, represent the other strand. English has both, a source of diversity and richness of synonyms. See also the Norman Conquest (397–398).

The Stolen White Elephant

Mark Twain
American

"Very well—as to men. At one meal—or, if you prefer, during one day—how many men will he eat, if fresh?"

"He would not care whether they were fresh or not; at a
single meal he would eat five ordinary men."

"Very good; five men, we will put that down. What nationalities would he prefer?"

"He is indifferent about nationalities. He prefers acquaintances, but is not prejudiced against strangers."

If someone were asked to provide an example of Mark Twain's
special comic style, the preceding conversation would do nicely. It
has the typical Mark Twain exaggeration concealed in sentences of
sweet reasonableness. It reveals the personalities of the two speakers,
both men of very limited intellect. "He prefers acquaintances" has an
insane kind of sense, as though the speakers were talking about a
preference for mashed potatoes. The entire story, with an elephant

out of science fiction, not reality, is a study in absurdity stemming from premises that seem logical to the two principal characters.

Peter Sellers, in the classic **Pink Panther** series, immortalized the bumbling, pretentious, puffed-up Inspector Clouseau. Detective Blunt precedes Clouseau by a century, but he seems almost a role model—and his detectives are not much better!

Mark Twain is best known for **Tom Sawyer** and **Huckleberry Finn**. Here he is in a delightful shorter work showing his abilities in exaggeration, satire, and caricature.

The Stolen White Elephant

I

THE FOLLOWING CURIOUS history was related to me by a chance railway acquaintance. He was a gentleman more than seventy years of age, and his thoroughly good and gentle face and earnest and sincere manner imprinted the unmistakable stamp of truth upon every statement which fell from his lips. He said:

You know in what reverence the royal white elephant of Siam* is held by the people of the country. You know it is sacred to kings, only kings may possess it, and that it is indeed in a measure even superior to kings, since it receives not merely honor but worship. Very well; five years ago, when the troubles concerning the frontier line arose between Great Britain and Siam, it was presently manifest that Siam had been in the wrong. Therefore every reparation was quickly made, and the British representative stated that he was satisfied and the past should be forgotten. This greatly relieved the King of Siam, and partly as a token of gratitude, but partly also, perhaps, to wipe out any little remaining vestige of unpleasantness which England might feel toward him, he wished to send the Queen a present—the sole sure way of propitiating an enemy, according to Oriental ideas. This present ought not only to be a royal one, but supremely royal. Wherefore, what offering could be so meet as

---
*now called Thailand

that of a white elephant? My position in the Indian civil service was such that I was deemed peculiarly worthy of the honor of conveying the present to Her Majesty. A ship was fitted out for me and my servants and the officers and attendants of the elephant, and in due time I arrived in new York harbor and placed my royal charge in admirable quarters in Jersey City. It was necessary to remain awhile in order to recruit the animal's health before resuming the voyage.

All went well during a fortnight; then my calamities began. The white elephant was stolen! I was called up at dead of night and informed of this fearful misfortune. For some moments I was beside myself with terror and anxiety; I was helpless. Then I grew calmer and collected my faculties. I soon saw my course—for indeed there was but the one course for an intelligent man to pursue. Late as it was, I flew to New York, and got a policeman to conduct me to the headquarters of the detective force. Fortunately I arrived in time, though the chief of the force, the celebrated Inspector Blunt, was just on the point of leaving for his home. He was a man of middle size and compact frame, and when he was thinking deeply he had a way of knitting his brows and tapping his forehead reflectively with his finger, which impressed you at once with the conviction that you stood in the presence of a person of no common order. The very sight of him gave me confidence and made me hopeful. I stated my errand. It did not flurry him in the least; it had no more visible effect upon his iron self-possession than if I had told him somebody had stolen my dog. He motioned me to a seat, and said calmly:

'Allow me to think a moment, please.'

So saying, he sat down at his office table and leaned his head upon his hand. Several clerks were at work at the other end of the room; the scratching of their pens was all the sound I heard during the next six or seven minutes. Meantime the inspector sat there, buried in thought. Finally he raised his head, and there was that in the firm lines of his face which showed me that his brain had done its work and his plan was made. Said he—and his voice was low and impressive—

'This is no ordinary case. Every step must be warily taken; each step must be made sure before the next is ventured. And secrecy must be observed—secrecy profound and absolute. Speak to no one about the matter, not even the reporters. I will take care of *them;* I will see that they get only what it may suit my ends to let them know.' He touched a bell; a youth appeared. 'Alaric, tell the reporters to remain for the present.' The boy retired. 'Now let us proceed to business—and systematically. Nothing can be accomplished in this trade of mine without strict and minute method.'

He took a pen and some paper. 'Now. Name of the elephant?'

'Hassan Ben Ali Ben Selim Abdallah Mohammed Moisé Alhammal Jamsetjejeebhoy Dhuleep Sultan Ebu Bhudpoor.'

'Very well. Given name?'

'Jumbo.'

'Very well. Place of birth?'

'The capital city of Siam.'

'Parents living?'

'No, dead.'

'Had they any other issue besides this one?'

'None. He was an only child.'

'Very well. These matters are sufficient under that head. Now please describe the elephant, and leave out no particular, however insignificant—that is, insignificant from *your* point of view. To me in my profession there *are* no insignificant particulars; they do not exist.'

I described, he wrote. When I was done, he said:

'Now listen. If I have made any mistakes, correct me.'

He read as follows:

'Height, 19 feet; length from apex of forehead to insertion of tail, 26 feet; length of trunk, 16 feet; length of tail, 6 feet; total length including trunk and tail, 48 feet; length of tusks 9½ feet; ears in keeping with these dimensions; footprint resembles the mark left when one up-ends a barrel in the snow; color of the elephant, a dull white; has a hole the size of a plate in each ear for the insertion of jewelry, and possesses the habit of a remarkable degree of squirting water upon spectators and of maltreating with his trunk not only such persons as he is acquainted with, but even entire strangers; limps slightly with his right hind leg, and has a small scar in his left armpit caused by a former boil; had on, when stolen, a castle containing seats for fifteen persons, and a gold-cloth saddle-blanket the size of an ordinary carpet.'

There were no mistakes. The inspector touched the bell, handed the description to Alaric, and said:

'Have fifty thousand copies of this printed at once and mailed to every detective office and pawnbroker's shop on the continent.' Alaric retired. 'There—so far, so good. Next, I must have a photograph of the property.'

I gave him one. He examined it critically, and said:

'It must do, since we can do no better; but he had his trunk curled up and tucked into his mouth. That is unfortunate, and is calculated to mislead, for of course he does not usually have it in that position.' He touched his bell.

'Alaric, have fifty thousand copies of this photograph made, the first thing in the morning, and mail them with the descriptive circulars.'

Alaric retired to execute his orders. The inspector said:

'It will be necessary to offer a reward, of course. Now as to the amount?'

'What sum would you suggest?'

'To *begin* with, I should say, well twenty-five thousand dollars. It is an intricate and difficult business; there are a thousand avenues of escape and opportunities of concealment. These thieves have friends and pals everywhere—'

'Bless me, do you know who they are?'

The wary face, practiced in concealing the thoughts and feelings within, gave me no token, nor yet the replying words, so quietly uttered.

'Never mind about that. I may, and I may not. We generally gather a pretty shrewd inkling of who our man is by the manner of his work and the size of the game he goes after. We are not dealing with a pickpocket or a hall thief, now, make up your mind to that. This property was not "lifted" by a novice. But, as I was saying, considering the amount of travel which will have to be done, and the diligence with which the thieves will cover up their traces as they move along, twenty-five thousand may be too small a sum to offer, yet I think it worth while to start with that.'

So we determined upon that figure, as a beginning. Then this man, whom nothing escaped which could by any possibility be made to serve as a clue said:

'There are cases in detective history to show that criminals have been detected through peculiarities in their appetites. Now, what does this elephant eat, and how much?'

'Well, as to *what* he eats, he will eat *anything*. He will eat a man, he will eat a Bible, he will eat anything *between* a man and a Bible.'

'Good, very good indeed, but too general. Details are necessary, details are the only valuable things in our trade. Very well—as to men. At one meal—or, if you prefer, during one day—how many men will he eat, if fresh?

'He would not care whether they were fresh or not; at a single meal he would eat five ordinary men.'

'Very good; five men; we will put that down. What nationalities would he prefer?'

'He is indifferent about nationalities. He prefers acquaintances, but is not prejudiced against strangers.'

'Very good. Now, as to Bibles. How many Bibles would he eat at a meal?'

'He would eat an entire edition.'

'It is hardly succinct enough. Do you mean the ordinary octavo,* or the family illustrated?'

'I think he would be indifferent to illustrations; that is, I think he would not value illustrations above simple letterpress.'

'No, you do not get my idea. I refer to bulk. The ordinary octavo Bible weighs about two pounds and a half, while the great quarto with

---

*a book page size

the illustrations weighs ten or twelve. How many Doré Bibles would he eat at a meal?'

'If you knew this elephant, you could not ask. He would take what they had.'

'Well, put it in dollars and cents, then. We must get at it somehow. The Doré costs a hundred dollars a copy, Russia leather, beveled.'

'He would require about fifty thousand dollars' worth—say an edition of five hundred copies.'

'Now that is more exact. I will put that down. Very well; he likes men and Bibles; so far, so good. What else will he eat? I want particulars.'

'He will leave Bibles to eat bricks, he will leave bricks to eat bottles, he will leave bottles to eat clothing, he will leave clothing to eat cats, he will leave cats to eat oysters, he will leave oysters to eat ham, he will leave ham to eat sugar, he will leave sugar to eat pie, he will leave pie to eat potatoes, he will leave potatoes to eat bran, he will leave bran to eat hay, he will leave hay to eat oats, he will leave oats to eat rice, for he was mainly raised on it. There is nothing whatever that he will not eat but European butter, and he would eat that if he could taste it.'

'Very good. General quantity at a meal—say about—'

'Well, anywhere from a quarter to half a ton.'

'And he drinks—'

'Everything that is fluid. Milk, water, whisky, molasses, castor oil, camphene, carbolic acid—it is no use to go into particulars; whatever fluid occurs to you set it down. He will drink anything that is fluid, except European coffee.'

'Very good. As to quantity?'

'Put it down five to fifteen barrels—his thirst varies; his other appetites do not.'

'These things are unusual. They ought to furnish quite good clues toward tracing him.'

He touched the bell.

'Alaric, summon Captain Burns.'

Burns appeared. Inspector Blunt unfolded the whole matter to him, detail by detail. Then he said in the clear, decisive tones of a man whose plans are clearly defined in his head, and who is accustomed to command:

'Captain Burns, detail Detectives Jones, Davis, Hasley, Bates and Hackett to shadow the elephant.'

'Yes, sir.'

'Detail Detectives Moses, Dakin, Murphy, Rogers, Tupper, Higgins, and Bartholomew to shadow the thieves.'

'Yes, sir.'

'Place a strong guard—a guard of thirty picked men, with a relief of thirty—over the place from whence the elephant was stolen, to keep strict watch there night and day, and allow none to approach—except reporters—without written authority from me.'

'Yes, sir.'

'Place detectives in plain clothes in the railway, steamship, and ferry depots, and upon all roadways leading out of Jersey City, with orders to search all suspicious persons.'

'Yes, sir.'

'Furnish all these men with photograph and accompanying descriptions of the elephant, and instruct them to search all trains and outgoing ferryboats and other vessels.'

'Yes, sir.'

'If the elephant should be found, let him be seized, and the information forwarded to me by telegraph.'

'Yes, sir.'

'Let me be informed at once if any clues should be found—footprints of the animals, or anything of that kind.'

'Yes, sir.'

'Get an order commanding the harbor police to patrol the frontages vigilantly.'

'Yes, sir.'

'Dispatch detectives in plain clothes over all the railways, north as far as Canada, west as far as Ohio, south as far as Washington.'

'Yes, sir.'

'Place experts in all the telegraph offices to listen to all messages; and let them require that all cipher dispatches be interpreted to them.'

'Yes, sir.'

'Let all these things be done with the utmost secrecy—mind, the most impenetrable secrecy.'

'Yes, sir.'

'Report to me promptly at the usual hour.'

'Yes, sir.'

'Go!'

'Yes, sir.'

He was gone.

Inspector Blunt was silent and thoughtful a moment, while the fire in his eye cooled down and faded out. The he turned to me and said in a placid voice:

'I am not given to boasting, it is not my habit; but—we shall find the elephant.'

I shook him warmly by the hand and thanked him; and I *felt* my thanks, too. The more I had seen of the man the more I liked him, and the more I admired him and marveled over the mysterious wonders of his profession. Then we parted for the night, and I went home with a far happier heart than I had carried with me to his office.

II

NEXT MORNING IT WAS all in the newspapers, in the minutest detail. It even had additions—consisting of Detective This, Detective That, and Detective The Other's 'Theory' as to how the robbery was done, who the robbers were, and whither they had flown with their booty. There were eleven of these theories, and they covered all the possibilities; and this single fact shows what independent thinkers detectives are. No two theories were alike or much resembled each other, save in one striking particular, and in that one all the eleven theories were absolutely agreed. That was, that although the rear of my building was torn out and the only door remained locked, the elephant had not been removed through the rent, but by some other (undiscovered) outlet. All agreed that the robber had made that rent only to mislead the detectives. That never would have occured to me or to any other layman, perhaps, but it had not deceived the detectives for a moment. Thus, what I had supposed was the only thing that had no mystery about it was in fact the very thing I had gone furthest astray in. The eleven theories all named the supposed robbers, but no two named the same robbers; the total number of suspected persons was thirty-seven. The various newspaper accounts all closed with the most important opinion of all—that of Chief Inspector Blunt. A portion of this statement read as follows:

> 'The Chief knows who the two principals are namely, "Brick" Duffy and "Red" McFadden. Ten days before the robbery was achieved he was already aware that it was to be attempted and had quietly proceeded to shadow these two noted villains; but unfortunately on the night in question their track was lost, and before it could be found again the bird was flown—that is the elephant.'
>
> 'Duffy and McFadden are the boldest scoundrels in the profession: the chief has reasons for believing that they are the men who stole the stove out of the detective headquarters on a bitter night last winter—in consequence of which the chief and every detective present were in the hands of the physicians before morning, some frozen feet, others with frozen fingers, ears, and other members.'

When I read the first half of that I was more astonished than ever at the wonderful sagacity of this strange man. He not only saw everything in the present with a clear eye, but even the future could not be hidden from him. I was soon at his office, and said I could not help wishing he had had those men arrested, and so prevented the trouble and loss; but his reply was simple and unanswerable.

'It is not our province to prevent crime, but to punish it. We cannot punish it until it is committed.'

I remarked that the secrecy with which we had begun had been marred by the newspapers; not only all our facts but all our plans and purposes had been revealed; even all the suspected persons had been named; these would doubtless disguise themselves now, or go into hiding.

'Let them. They will find that when I am ready for them my hand will descend upon them, in their secret places, as unerringly as the hand of fate. As to the newspapers, we *must* keep in with them. Fame, reputation, constant public mention—these are the detective's bread and butter. He must publish his facts, else he will be supposed to have none; he must publish his theory, for nothing is so strange or striking as a detective's theory, or brings him so much wondering respect; we must publish our plans, for these the journals insist upon having, and we could not deny them without offending. We must constantly show the public what we are doing, or they will believe we are doing nothing. It is much pleasanter to have a newspaper say, "Inspector Blunt's ingenious and extraordinary theory is as follows," than to have it say some harsh thing, or, worse still, some sarcastic one.'

'I see the force of what you say. But I noticed that in one part of your remarks in the papers this morning you refused to reveal your opinion upon a certain minor point.'

'Yes, we always do that; it has a good effect. Besides, I had not formed any opinion on that point, anyway.'

I deposited a considerable sum of money with the inspector, to meet current expenses, and sat down to wait for news. We were expecting the telegrams to begin to arrive at any moment now. Meantime I reread the newspapers and also our descriptive circular, and observed that our $25,000 reward seemed to be offered only to detectives. I said I thought it ought to be offered to anybody who would catch the elephant. The inspector said:

'It is the detectives who will find the elephant, hence the reward will go to the right place. If other people found the animal, it would only be by watching the detectives and taking advantage of clues and indications stolen from them, and that would entitle the detectives to the reward, after all. The proper office of a reward is to stimulate the men who deliver up their time and their trained sagacities to this sort of work, and not to confer benefits upon chance citizens who stumble upon a capture without having earned the benefits by their own merits and labors.'

This was reasonable enough, certainly. Now the telegraphic machine in the corner began to click, and the following dispatch was the result:

> FLOWER STATION, N. Y., 7:30 A.M.
>
> Have got a clue. Found a succession of deep tracks across a farm near here. Followed them two miles east without result; think elephant went west. Shall now shadow him in that direction.
>
> DARLEY, *Detective.*

'Darley's one of the best men on the force,' said the inspector. 'We shall hear from his again before long.'

Telegram No. 2 came:

> BARKER'S, N.J., 7:40 A.M.
>
> Just arrived. Glass factory broken open here during night, and eight hundred bottles taken. Only water in large quantity near here is five miles distant. Shall strike for there. Elephant will be thirsty. Bottles were empty.
>
> BAKER, *Detective*.

'That promises well, too,' said the inspector. 'I told you the creature's appetites would not be bad clues.'

Telegram No. 3:

> TAYLORVILLE., L.I., 8:15 A.M.
>
> A haystack near here disappeared during night. Probably eaten. Have got a clue, and am off.
>
> HUBBARD, *Detective*.

'How he does move around!' said the inspector. 'I knew we had a difficult job on hand, but we shall catch him yet.'

> FLOWER STATION, N.Y., 9 A.M.
>
> Shadowed the tracks three miles westward. Large, deep, and ragged. Have just met a farmer who says they are not elephant tracks. Says they are holes where he dug up saplings for shade trees when ground was frozen last winter. Give me orders how to proceed.
>
> DARLEY, *Detective*.

'Aha! a confederate of the thieves! The thing grow warm,' said the inspector.

He dictated the following telegram to Darley:

> Arrest the man and force him to name his pals. Continue to follow the tracks—to the Pacific, if necessary.
>
> CHIEF BLUNT.

Next telegram:

> CONEY POINT, PA. 8:45 A.M.
>
> Gas office broken open here during night and three months' unpaid gas bills taken. Have got a clue and am away.
>
> MURPHY, *Detective*.

'Heavens!' said the inspector; 'would he eat gas bills?'

'Through ignorance, yes; but they cannot support life. At least, unassisted.'

Now came this exciting telegram:

IRONVILLE, N.Y., 9:30 A.M.

Just arrived. This village in consternation. Elephant passed through here at five this morning. Some say he went east, some say west, some north, some south—but all say they did not wait to notice particularly. He killed a horse; have secured a piece of it for a clue. Killed it with his trunk; from style of blow, think he struck it left-handed. From position in which horse lies, think elephant traveled northward along line of Berkley railway. Has four and half hours' start, but I move on his track at once.

HAWES, *Detective.*

I uttered exclamations of joy. The inspector was as self-contained as a graven image. He calmly touched his bell.

'Alaric, send Captain Burns here.'

Burns appeared.

'How many men are ready for instant orders?'

'Ninety-six, sir.'

'Send them north at once. Let them concentrate along the line of the Berkley road north or Ironville.'

'Yes, sir.'

'Let them conduct their movements with the utmost secrecy. As fast as others are at liberty, hold them for orders.'

'Yes, sir.'

'Go!'

'Yes, sir,'

Presently came another telegram:

SAGE CORNERS, N.Y., 10:30.

Just arrived. Elephant passed through here at 8:15. All escaped from the town but a policeman. Apparently elephant did not strike at policeman, but at the lamp post. Got both. I have secured a portion of the policeman as clue.

STUMM, *Detective.*

'So the elephant has turned westward,' said the inspector. 'However, he will not escape, for my men are scattered all over that region.'

The next telegram said:

GLOVER'S, 11:15.

Just arrived. Village deserted, except sick and aged. Elephant passed through three quarters of an hour ago. The anti-temperance mass meeting was in session; he put his trunk in at a window and washed it out with water from cistern. Some swallowed it—since dead; several drowned. Detectives Cross and O'Shaughnessy were passing through town, but going south—so missed elephant. Whole region for many miles around in terror—people flying from their homes. Wherever they turn they meet elephant, and many are killed.

BRANT, *Detective.*

I could have shed tears, this havoc so distressed me. But the inspector only said:

'You see—we are closing in on him. He feels our presence; he has turned eastward again.'

Yet further troublous news was in store for us. The telegraph brought this:

> HOGANPORT, 12:19.
>
> Just arrived. Elephant passed through half an hour ago, creating wildest fright and excitement. Elephant raged around streets; two plumbers going by, killed one—other escaped. Regret general.
>
> O'FLAHERTY, *Detective.*

'Now he is right in the midst of my men,' said the inspector. 'Nothing can save him.'

A succession of telegrams came from detectives who were scattered through New Jersey and Pennsylvania, and who were following clues consisting of ravaged barns, factories, and Sunday school libraries, with high hopes—hopes amounting to certainties, indeed. The inspector said:

'I wish I could communicate with them and order them north, but that is impossible. A detective only visits a telegraph office to send his report; then he is off again, and you don't know where to put your hand on him.'

Now came this dispatch:

> BRIDGEPORT, CT., 12:15.
>
> Barnum offers rate of $4,000 a year for exclusive privilege of using elephant as traveling advertising medium from now till detectives find him. Wants to paste circus poster on him. Desires immediate answer.
>
> BOGGS, *Detective.*

'That is perfectly absurd!' I exclaimed.

'Of course it is,' said the inspector. 'Evidently Mr. Barnum, who thinks he is so sharp, does not know me—but I know him.'

Then he dictated this answer to the dispatch:

> Mr. Barnum's offer declined. Make it $7,000 or nothing.
>
> *Chief* BLUNT.

'There. We shall not have to wait long for an answer. Mr. Barnum is not at home; he is in the telegraph office—it is his way when he has business on hand. Inside of three—'

> DONE.—P. T. BARNUM.

So interrupted the clicking telegraphic instrument. Before I could make a comment upon this extraordinary episode, the following dispatch carried my thoughts into another and very distressing channel:

BOLIVIA, N.Y., 12:50.

Elephant arrived here from the south and passed through toward the forest at 11:50, dispersing a funeral on the way, and diminishing the mourners by two. Citizens fired some small cannon balls into him, and then fled. Detective Burke and I arrived ten minutes later, from the north, but mistook some excavations for footprints, and so lost a good deal of time; but at last we struck the right trail and followed it to the woods. We then got down on our hands and knees and continued to keep a sharp eye on the track, and so shadowed it into the brush. Burke was in advance. Unfortunately the animal had stopped to rest; therefore, Burke having his head down, intent upon the track, butted up against the elephant's hind legs before he was aware of his vicinity. Burke instantly rose to his feet, seized the tail, and exclaimed joyfully. 'I claim the re-' but got no further, for a single blow of the huge trunk laid the brave fellow's fragments low in death. I fled rearward, and the elephant turned and shadowed me to the edge of the wood, making tremendous speed, and I should inevitably have been lost, but that the remains of the funeral providentially intervened again and diverted his attention. I have just learned that nothing of that funeral is now left; but this is no loss, for there is an abundance of material for another. Meantime, the elephant has disappeared again.

MULROONERY, *Detective.*

We heard no news except from the diligent and confident detectives scattered about New Jersey, Pennsylvania, Delaware, and Virginia—who were all following fresh and encouraging clues—until shortly after 2 P.M., when this telegram came:

BAXTER CENTER, 2:15.

Elephant been here, plastered over with circus bills, and broke up a revival, striking down and damaging many who were on the point of entering upon a better life. Citizens penned him up, and established a guard. When Detective Brown and I arrived, some time after, we entered enclosure and proceeded to identify elephant by photograph and description. All marks tallied exactly except one, which we could not see—the boil scar under armpit. To make sure, Brown crept under to look, and was immediately brained—that is, head crushed and destroyed, though nothing issued from debris. All fled; so did elephant, striking right and left with much effect. Has escaped, but left bold blood track from cannon-wounds. Rediscovery certain. He broke southward, through a dense forest.

BRENT, *Detective.*

That was the last telegram. At nightfall a fog shut down which was so dense that objects but three feet away could not be discerned. This lasted all night. The ferry boats and even the omnibuses had to stop running.

III

NEXT MORNING THE papers were as full of detectives theories as before; they had all our tragic facts in detail also, and a great many more which they had received from their telegraphic correspondents. Column after column was occupied, a third of its way down, with glaring headlines, which it made my heart sick to read. Their general tone was like this:

'THE WHITE ELEPHANT AT LARGE! HE MOVES UPON HIS FATAL MARCH! WHOLE VILLAGES DESERTED BY THEIR FRIGHT-STRICKEN OCCUPANTS! PALE TERROR GOES BEFORE HIM, DEATH AND DEVASTATION FOLLOW AFTER! AFTER THESE, THE DETECTIVES. BARNS DESTROYED, FACTORIES GUTTED, HARVESTS DEVOURED, PUBLIC ASSEMBLAGES DISPERSED, ACCOMPANIED BY SCENES OF CARNAGE IMPOSSIBLE TO DESCRIBE! THEORIES OF THIRTY-FOUR OF THE MOST DISTINGUISHED DETECTIVES ON THE FORCE! THEORY OF CHIEF BLUNT!'

'There!' said Inspector Blunt, almost betrayed into excitement, 'this is magnificent! This is the greatest windfall that any detective organization ever had. The fame of it will travel to the ends of the earth, and endure to the end of time, and my name with it.'

But there was no joy for me. I felt as if I had committed all those red crimes, and that the elephant was only my irresponsible agent. And how the list had grown! In one place he had 'interfered with an election and killed five repeaters.' He had followed this act with the destruction of two poor fellows, named O'Donohue and McFlannigan, who had 'found a refuge in the home of the oppressed of all lands only the day before, and were in the act of exercising for the first time the noble right of American citizens at the polls, when stricken down by the relentless hand of the Scourge of Siam.' In another, he had 'found a crazy sensation-preacher preparing his next season's heroic attacks on the dance, the theater, and other things which can't strike back, and had stepped on him.' And in still another place he had 'killed a lightning-rod agent.' And so the list went on, growing redder and redder, and more and more heartbreaking. Sixty persons had been killed, and two hundred and forty wounded. All the accounts bore just testimony to the activity and devotion of the detectives, and all closed with the remark that 'three hundred thousand citizens and four detectives saw the dread creature, and two of the latter he destroyed.'

I dreaded to hear the telegraphic instrument begin to click again. By and by the messages began to pour in, but I was happily disappointed in their nature. It was soon apparent that all trace of the elephant was lost. The fog had enabled him to search out a good hiding place unobserved. Telegrams from the most absurdly distant points reported that a dim vast mass had been glimpsed there through the fog at such an hour, and was 'undoubtedly the elephant.' This dim vast mass had been glimpsed in

New Haven, in New Jersey, in Pennsylvania, in interior New York, in Brooklyn, and even in the city of New York itself! But in all cases the dim vast mass had vanished quickly and left no trace. Every detective of the large force scattered over this huge extent of country sent his hourly report, and each and every one of them had a clue, and was shadowing something, and was hot upon the heels of it.

But the day passed without other result.

The next day the same.

The next just the same.

The newspaper reports began to grow monotonous with facts that amounted to nothing, clues which led to nothing, and theories which had nearly exhausted the elements which surprise and delight and dazzle.

By advice of the inspector I doubled the reward.

Four more dull days followed. Then came a bitter blow to the poor, hardworking detectives—the journalists declined to print their theories, and coldly said, 'Give us a rest.'

Two weeks after the elephant's disappearance I raised the reward to $75,000 by the inspector's advice. It was a great sum, but I felt that I would rather sacrifice my whole private fortune than lose my credit with my government. Now that the detectives were in adversity, the newspapers turned upon them, and began to fling the most stinging sarcasms at them. This gave the minstrels an idea, and they dressed themselves as detectives and hunted the elephant on the stage in the most extravagant way. The caricaturists made pictures of detectives scanning the country with spyglasses, while the elephant, at their backs, stole apples out of their pockets. And they made all sorts of ridiculous pictures of the detective badge—you have seen that badge printed in gold on the back of detective novels, no doubt—it is a wide-staring eye, with the legend, 'WE NEVER SLEEP.' When detectives called for a drink, the would-be facetious barkeeper resurrected an obsolete form of expression and said, 'Will you have an eye-opener?' All the air was thick with sarcasms.

But there was one man who moved calm, untouched, unaffected, through it all. It was that heart of oak, the Chief Inspector. His brave eye never drooped, his serene confidence never wavered. He always said:

'Let them rail on; he laughs best who laughs last.'

My admiration for the man grew into a species of worship. I was at his side always. His office had become an unpleasant place to me, and now became daily more and more so. Yet if he could endure it I meant to do so also; at least, as long as I could. So I came regularly, and stayed—the only outsider who seemed to be capable of it. Everybody wondered how I could; and often it seemed to me that I must desert, but at such times I looked into that calm and apparently unconscious face, and held my ground.

About three weeks after the elephant's disappearance I was about to say, one morning, that I should *have* to strike my colors and retire, when the great detective arrested the thought by proposing one more superb and masterly move.

This was to compromise with the robbers. The fertility of this man's invention exceeded anything I have ever seen, and I have had a wide intercourse with the world's finest minds. He said he was confident he could compromise for $100,000 and recover the elephant. I said I believed I could scrape the amount together, but what would become of the poor detectives who had worked so faithfully? He said:

'In compromises they always get half.'

This removed my only objection. So the inspector wrote two notes, in this form:

> DEAR MADAM—Your husband can make a large sum of money (and be entirely protected from the law) by making an immediate appointment with me.
>
> *Chief* BLUNT.

He sent one of these by his confidential messenger to the 're-puted wife' of Brick Duffy, and the other to the reputed wife of Red McFadden.

Within the hour these offensive answers came:

> YE OWLD FOOL: brick McDuffey's bin ded 2 yere.
>
> BRIDGET MAHONEY.

> CHIEF BAT—Red McFadden is hung and in heving 18 month. Any Ass but a detective knose that.
>
> MARY O'HOOLIGAN.

'I had long suspected these facts,' said the inspector; 'this testimony proves the unerring accuracy of my instinct.'

The moment one resource failed him he was ready with another. He immediately wrote an advertisement for the morning papers, and I kept a copy of it.

> A.—xwblv.242 N. Tjnd—fz328wmlg. Ozpo—; 2 mo. ogw. Mum.

He said that if the thief was alive this would bring him to the usual rendezvous. He further explained that the usual rendezvous was a place where all business affairs between detectives and criminals were conducted. This meeting would take place at twelve the next night.

We could do nothing till then, and I lost no time in getting out of the office, and was grateful indeed for the privilege.

At 11 the next night I brought $100,000 in bank notes and put them into the chief's hands, and shortly afterward he took his leave, with the brave old undimmed confidence in his eye. An almost intolerable hour dragged to a close; then I heard his welcome tread, and rose gasping and tottered to meet him. How his fine eyes flamed with triumph! He said:

'We've compromised! The jokers will sing a different tune tomorrow! Follow me!'

He took a lighted candle and strode down into the vast vaulted basement where sixty detectives always slept, and where a score were now playing cards to while the time. I followed close after him. He walked swiftly down to the dim remote end of the place, and just as I succumbed to the pangs of suffocation and was swooning away he stumbled and fell over the outlying members of a mighty object, and I heard him exclaim as he went down:

'Our noble profession is vindicated. Here is your elephant!'

I was carried to the office above and restored with carbolic acid. The whole detective force swarmed in, and such another season of triumphant rejoicing ensued as I had never witnessed before. The reporters were called, baskets of champagne were opened, toasts were drunk, the handshakings and congratulations were continuous and enthusiastic. Naturally the chief was the hero of the hour, and his happiness was so complete and had been so patiently and worthily and bravely won that it made me happy to see it, though I stood there a homeless beggar, my priceless charge dead, and my position in my country's service lost to me through what would always seem my fatally careless execution of a great trust. Many an eloquent eye testified its deep admiration for the chief and many a detective's voice murmured, 'Look at him—just the king of the profession—only give him a clue, it's all he wants, and there ain't anything hid that he can't find.' The dividing of the $50,000 made great pleasure; when it was finished the chief made a little speech while he put his share in his pocket, in which he said, 'Enjoy it, boys, for you've earned it; and more than you've earned for the detective profession undying fame.'

A telegram arrived, which read:

> MONROE, MICH., 10 P.M.
> First time I've struck a telegraph office in over three weeks. Have followed those footprints, horseback, through the woods, a thousand miles to here, and they get stronger and bigger and fresher every day. Don't worry—inside of another week I'll have the elephant. This is dead sure.
>
> DARLEY, *Detective*.

The chief ordered three cheers for 'Darley, one of the finest minds on the force,' and then commanded that he be telegraphed to come home and receive his share of the reward.

So ended that marvelous episode of the stolen elephant. The newspapers were pleasant with praises once more, the next day, with one contemptible exception. This sheet said, 'Great is the detective! He may be a little slow in finding a little thing like a mislaid elephant—he may hunt him all day and sleep with his hot rotting carcass all night for three weeks, but he will find him at last—if he can get the man who mislaid him to show him the place!'

Poor Hassan was lost to me forever. The cannon shots had wounded him fatally, he had crept to that unfriendly place in the fog, and there, surrounded by his enemies and in constant danger of detection, he had wasted away with hunger and suffering till death gave him peace.

The compromise cost me $100,000; my detective expenses were $42,000 more; I never applied for a place again under my government; I am a ruined man and a wanderer in the earth—but my admiration for that man, whom I believe to be the greatest detective the world has ever produced, remains undimmed to this day, and will so remain unto the end.

Reading for Understanding

Main Idea

1. The main idea of the selection can be summed up in one word: (a) wisdom (b) incompetence (c) achievement (d) rewards.

Details

2. The elephant was stolen from (a) Siam (b) Taylorsville, N.J. (c) Jersey City (d) New York City.

3. The initial reward was set at (a) $25,000 (b) $50,000 (c) $75,000 (d) $100,000.

4. Duffy and MacFadden were (a) top detectives (b) ace reporters (c) skilled elephant handlers (d) bold scoundrels.

5. The elephant was finally found (a) on a farm near Monroe, Michigan (b) in P.T. Barnum's circus (c) in the police basement (d) in a cavern in Delaware.

Inferences

6. The information Detective Blunt printed about the elephant was essentially (a) important (b) contradicted by the narrator (c) commonplace (d) worthless.

7. The narrator's great faith in Detective Blunt was (a) misplaced (b) justified (c) wavering (d) embarrassing to Blunt.

8. The reports sent by the various detectives during the final three weeks proved to be (a) comforting (b) useless (c) irritating (d) helpful.

Tone of the Selection

9. The tone of the selection is one of (a) bitter denunciation (b) uncritical approval (c) satirical amusement (d) sorrowful disappointment.

Cause and Effect

10. The cannonballs fired in Bolivia, N.Y., eventually (a) made a hero of Detective Boggs (b) solved the case (c) were discarded as a rumor by Inspector Blunt (d) saved the storyteller's money.

Words in Context

1. "It was presently *manifest* that Siam had been in the wrong." **Manifest** (371) means (a) broadcast (b) uncertain (c) overlooked (d) obvious.

2. "He wished to send the Queen a present—the sole sure way of *propitiating* an enemy." **Propitiating** (371) means: (a) satisfying (b) annoying (c) arousing the curiosity of (d) identifying.

3. "Every step must be *warily* taken; each step must be sure before the next is ventured." **Warily** (372) means (a) smartly (b) carefully (c) repeatedly (d) admirably.

4. "This property was not 'lifted' by a *novice*." A **novice** (374) is a (a) beginner (b) thief (c) holy person (d) part-time detective.

5. "It is hardly *succinct* enough. Do you mean the ordinary octavo, or the family illustrated?" **Succinct** (374) means (a) elaborately described richly informative (c) brief and to the point (d) developed at length.

6. "Then he turned to me and said in a *placid* voice . . . " **Placid** (376) means (a) harsh (b) trembling (c) calm (d) weary.

7. "The elephant had not been removed through the *rent,* but by some other (undiscovered) outlet." A **rent** (377) is a (a) sum of money (b) hole (c) skylight (d) locked door.

8. "When I read the first half of that I was more astonished than ever at the wonderful *sagacity* of this strange man." **Sagacity** (377) means (a) confidence (b) curiosity (c) watchfulness (d) shrewdness.

9. "I could have shed tears, this *havoc* so distressed me." **Havoc** (381) means (a) disaster (b) news (c) wound (d) trial.

10. "A succession of telegrams came from detectives who were . . . following clues consisting of *ravaged* barns, factories, and Sunday school libraries, with high hopes—hopes amounting to certainties, indeed." **Ravaged** (381) means (a) ruined (b) recently visited (c) well marked (d) decaying.

11. "At nightfall a fog shut down which was so dense that objects but three feet away could not be *discerned.*" **Discerned** (382) means (a) reached (b) found (c) seen (d) approached.

12.,13. "Barns destroyed, factories gutted, harvests devoured, public assemblages *dispersed,* accompanied by scenes of *carnage* impossible to describe." **Dispersed** (383) means (a) arrested (b) covered by news media (c) warned (d) scattered. **Carnage** (383) means (a) executions (b) destruction (c) thievery (d) protests.

14. "Now that the detectives were in *adversity,* the newspapers turned upon them." **Adversity** (384) is (a) unemployment (b) prison (c) denial (d) misfortune.

15. "When detectives called for a drink, the would-be *facetious* barkeeper resurrected an obsolete form of expression." **Facetious** (384) means (a) engaged (b) humble (c) moody (d) humorous.

Thinking Critically about the Story

1. At what point did you begin to realize that Inspector Blunt was a pompous man of limited cleverness? Point out examples of his many weaknesses.

2. Incredibly, Blunt treats the stolen elephant as he'd treat other stolen goods. What pointless bits of information does he solicit from the narrator?

3. Mark Twain's humor is, at times, outrageous. At one point he writes of the funeral incident: "I have just learned that nothing of that

funeral is now left; but this is no loss, for there is an abundance of material for another." An abundance of material? What kind?

4. One of the most obvious points of exaggeration is the havoc wrought by the elephant. Point out three separate reports that are obviously exaggerated to the point of fantasy.

5. What is the final irony (264) in the "capture" of the elephant?

6. How does the last report, by Darley, Detective, neatly sum up the absurdity of the "Case of the Stolen White Elephant"?

7. Point out the humor in Blunt's confident attempt to bribe the "wives" of Brick Duffy and Red McFaddan. How does this episode add to our picture of Inspector Blunt?

8. How does the final sentence carry the fiction of the great detective to its ridiculous conclusion?

Language in Action

The Latin Contribution

There are cases in detective history to show that criminals have been detected through peculiarities in their appetites.

In the quoted sentence, these words are of Latin origin: *cases, detective, history, criminals, detected, peculiarities, appetites.* Although Old English (368) is still most common in everyday speech, Latin, whether directly or through French, plays a major role. Words of Latin origin account for more English words than any other group, perhaps as many as 50%. Some words of Latin origin have been in the language so long that they seem like Old English: *street, mile, wine, pound, temple, candle, spend.* Some words, like *animal, vacuum, superior, verbatim,* and *alibi,* have been borrowed without change. Others, like *exquisite, establish,* and *despair,* are clearly of Latin origin, though changed somewhat in form.

For building a vocabulary, knowing Latin roots can help. A sample of such roots would include *ali*—other, *aqu*—water, *aud*—hear, *brev*—short, *cred*—believe, *doc*—teach, and others too numerous for mention here.

Because of the Latin influence on Old English, we now have pairs of words with useful distinctions. In the following list, the first word is Old English; the second is the Latin origin. Can you distinguish between them?

eat, devour	small, diminutive
fall, collapse	stir, commotion
illness, disease	strike, collide
earner, student	tarnish, stain
scare, terrify	wise, intelligent

The influence of Latin upon the basic English tongue is far-reaching and continuing. Latin entered the language at many different periods . . . and is still active as a source of new words.

You Can't Find It? Forget It. Your Loss Is the Place's Gain

Minna Morse
American

We were coming out of the kitchen when I saw a blonde woman wandering about. She was my old roommate from college. I hadn't heard from her in years. "Oh, Lord," I said. It was my long lost friend Diana.

How many **single** socks or single earrings do you own? Where are the other members of those pairs? How many articles have disappeared within your very walls? How many times have you called out, in vain, "Has anyone seen my Chicago Bulls T-shirt" or something similar? Robert Benchley (368) always insisted that inanimate objects are out to get us, sometimes by just disappearing.

Wonder no more. You are about to discover the real reason for the mysterious vanishing. Your favorite cap, your inexpensive but beloved necklace—they're not in your house any more. Where have they gone? Somewhere there is a Place. . . .

Minna Morse has taken an experience common to all of us and provided a charming explanation. Now if you could only find that place!

You Can't Find It? Forget It. Your Loss Is the Place's Gain

In all our travels, Seth and I have yet to find the perfect hideaway, but not long ago we began to suspect that many of our belongings have discovered one of their own. A typical morning finds each of us frantically searching for articles of clothing, jewelry or other accessories. "Honey, where'd you put my gray argyles?" Seth bellows from the bedroom. "I didn't touch them!" I yell back. "Have you seen my watch?"

When it comes to losing things, we're pretty much like other couples. Unlike other couples, however, we don't eventually call to each other, "Never mind—I found it." Our lost things don't get found. My watch will not show up again. His left sock has vanished for good. Likewise an address book, a pair of summer sandals, a Tupperware lid, a dumbbell.

We have just enough room to accommodate everything we own. We do not have a pet that might be dragging our clothes and trinkets off to the doghouse or the litter box. There is no space under our bed for wayward items to collect.

We used to believe there was a logical explanation for these mysterious disappearances. But the day finally came when we had to face up to the truth: logic just doesn't apply. Now, whenever another hankie, hat or necktie joins the ranks of the *desaparecidos,** Seth and I assume that it has gone to "the Place."

The Place is a haven for lost stuff. We used to joke about it, but then we noticed that whenever we did, our possessions began to vanish at an increasing rate. Now we know the Place is real. We're convinced that it will continue to quietly suck property from our world into some other realm, where all the things that were ever lost repose, and to where all the things still to be lost will go.

Last week, on our way to a wedding, we took a wrong turn. By the time we realized what had happened, we'd driven completely off the map the bride had given us. We were lost.

---

*disappearing objects

It was an understandable mistake: it was very foggy. When the fog lifted, we found ourselves near two white stone cottages. Each had a sign with one of our names on it. We went into the cottage that said "Minna."

As soon as we stepped across the threshold, the door slammed shut behind us and locked. After a few futile lunges, we gave up and decided to look around. Passing through a strangely familiar nursery filled with pacifiers, we came to a tiny schoolroom. Pencils and pens were scattered everywhere. Covering a desktop were pages ripped from spiral notebooks and scrawled with writing that resembled my own: "Read p. 50–74, test Monday," "Science project due next Friday . . . ACK!"

Another room was packed with small pieces of paper. Seth plucked one from the pile. On it was the name and phone number of a woman I'd recently met at a conference. I reached in and grabbed another. The number of a man I'd gone out with—a long time ago. I quickly crumpled it up and tossed it back in.

"Let's go upstairs," I said. I realized that we'd found the Place—or *my* Place, at any rate. We spent what seemed like hours looking around—in a towering bureau packed with clothes; in a jewelry box overflowing with single earrings; in a kitchen full of appliance parts.

We were coming out of the kitchen when I saw a blonde woman wandering about. She was my old roommate from college. I hadn't heard from her in years. "Oh Lord," I said. It was my long-lost friend Diana. "Minna!" she exclaimed as she ran to greet us. "I am so sorry I haven't called, but you wouldn't believe what I've been through . . . " She looked around at the piles of junk. "Well, I guess you would, wouldn't you?"

Together, Seth, Diana and I explored, hoping to find an escape. "Did you ever lose a computer?" Seth asked me. "No," I answered, and went to the terminal where he was standing and called up the directory. I vaguely recognized the filenames, and then I understood—they were all the files I'd ever zapped.

Down in the basement we found a large freezer, with a sign that said "Lost Weight." "This could be gross," I warned the others as we peeked inside.

"That couldn't be more than 10 to 15 pounds," Seth said, sizing up what was there. "You said you'd lost tons over the years." Thinking back on a lifetime of yo-yo dieting, I wondered where all that weight had gone. Then the answer occurred to me.

"I've never weighed more than 10 or 15 pounds more than I weigh now," I said. "That's what's there."

"Where's the rest?" Diana asked.

I rested my hands on my hips. "It's back where it started. Do you know what that means?"

My companions looked confused.

"It means things don't always stay in the Place." I proclaimed. "It means there's a way out of here!"

Suddenly I felt like Nancy Drew. After probing the walls for secret doors, I spotted a black hole in the floor: "Maybe this is it."

It was. When we emerged, Diana was gone. I assume she went back to New York where she belongs. Seth and I got in the car and tried to find our way to the wedding.

"Are we almost there?" I asked him after a while.

"No," he said. He pulled over to the side of the road and fumbled with the papers on the seat between us. Then, with a sigh, he made a U-turn.

"Where are you going?" I asked.

"Back to the Place," he said. "I think it's got our directions."

Reading for Understanding

Main Idea

1. The main idea of the selection can best be expressed by which of the following?
   (a) A strange Experience
   (b) A Science Fiction Lesson
   (c) A Woman's Bad Daydream
   (d) Solved: the Mystery of Misplaced Items

Details

2. The author and her husband were lost (a) not far from home (b) on the way to a wedding (c) because the husband didn't listen to his wife (d) but found their way without incident.

3. Part of the problem was (a) a blizzard (b) bad roads (c) the fog (d) a misplaced road sign.

4. The jewelry box in the Place (a) was overflowing with single earrings (b) was encrusted with diamonds (c) was being held by Diana (d) belonged to the husband's mother.

5. A return visit to the Place would be needed for (a) those missing clothes (b) Diana (c) Minna's husband (d) the directions.

Inferences

6. The author and her husband found themselves in the Place because (a) they were lost (b) it was shelter from the weather (c) the author wanted to visit (d) Diana had asked them to come.

7. The author writes, "I quickly crumpled it up and tossed it back in." She crumpled it quickly because (a) Diana was closely observing her (b) she didn't want her husband to know (c) she was in a hurry to see what would come next (d) her husband tried to take it away from her.

8. Diana had appeared in the Place because (a) she, too, was attending the wedding (b) the author had "lost" her, too (c) the author's husband had once dated her (d) she was a journalist writing an article about the Place.

Mood of the Selection

9. The mood of the selection is one of (a) clever exaggeration (b) irritated frankness (c) intense deliberation (d) melancholy remembrance

Outcome

10. At the conclusion of the story, (a) the author and her husband decided to skip the wedding (b) more of the author's possessions will end up at the Place (c) the author and her husband will divorce (d) Diana will become a close friend again.

Thinking Critically about the Selection

1. Why does the author list in detail and in great variety all the things they have lost?

2. What makes the selection funny?

3. A major source of humor is poking fun at oneself. How does Minna reveal some of her own weaknesses?

4. "His left sock had vanished for good." Left sock? Aren't socks

generally useful for both feet? Why does she mention this point? (A few centuries ago, shoes were made for either foot.)

5. How did the author finally decide that there must be an exit to escape from the Place?

6. One problem with comedians is the occasional tendency to "break up," to laugh at the humor of the things the're doing or saying. It's a kind of "look how funny I am" weakness. Yet the situation is funnier if the participants *play* it straight, as Leslie Nielsen does in the *Police Squad* movies. Does the author "keep a straight face" throughout the selection? Does she report the events seriously?

Language in Action

The Norman Conquest

"It means things don't always stay in the Place," I proclaimed.

In 1066, William the Conqueror, from Normandy, defeated King Harold and placed himself on the English throne. The changes had far-reaching political results, but the changes in language were perhaps even more important in the long run. The invasion changed English from a relatively "pure" Germanic tongue, with close links to Northern Europe, to a mixed Germanic-Romance language. Though the Anglo-Saxon underclass deeply resented the arrival of their new overlords, they began, inevitably, to adopt some Norman-French words. These words were of Latin origin. The Norman invaders stayed on in their new home until through intermarriage they became part of the English people. The Norman language, like the Norman rulers, was absorbed into English.

In *Ivanhoe*, Sir Walter Scott points out how the new language emphasized class distinctions. The Old English words *sheep, deer, calf,* and *ox* dealt with animals on the hoof. The French eqivalents *mutton, veal, venison,* and *beef* dealt with meat on the table. Scott asked, "Who did the hard work?" The Old English *house*, suggesting a modest dwelling, was matched by the Norman French *mansion*, suggesting wealth and power. The Old English *ask* was matched by the Norman French *demand*.

Mario Pei, author of *The Story of Language*, makes an interesting point. Family names are part of a language's fundamental stock of words. *Mother, father, daughter, son, sister,* and *brother* come down straight from Old English. More distant relationships have come to us from the Norman Conquest: *uncle, aunt, nephew, niece,* and *cousin.* English combined the Norman *grand* with the Old English *father* to create *grandfather.* Of course, if we go far enough back into the past, both Germanic and Romance roots will turn out to be related. They are both part of the Indo-European family.

If it were not for the Norman invasion, *stay* and *place* in the quotation above would probably have been replaced by old Germanic equivalents like *abide* and *spot.* The union of the two major strands, Germanic and Romance, has enriched the language beyond all imagining.

Paradiso . . . Inferno?

David J. Baker
American

The Background

"Saki"
Scottish

"In every company, they pay you backstage. You have your heart in your mouth, they're giving you all this cash, you don't know what to do with it. I put it in my dresses—I always get fatter toward the third act!"

These paired selections provide a look at the arts, but with quite a difference of subject matter and style. David J. Baker gives us a view of the opera, especially as it is played in Italy. Italian audiences are quite unlike those anywhere else in the world. The title is a clue, suggesting the great Italian poet Dante: Paradiso . . . Inferno; Heaven . . . Hell. Apparently, playing opera in Italy is a mixed bag—filled with unexpected challenges and unrestrained extremes. The "demonic, occasionally angelic Italian audience" can be gloriously happy or bitterly miserable.

Saki (pen name of H.H. Munro) takes a different look at the arts—an absurdly funny fiction of one man's plight. The master tattoo artist Signor Andreas Pincini decorates the back of Henry Deplis with a magnificent scene from Greek mythology. You might think that Monsieur Deplis owns his back and the masterpiece so glowingly displayed on it. Alas, that work of art is declared a national treasure, and Deplis' life is changed forever.

Baker relishes human absurdity with real-life examples. Saki says, "What if . . ." and carries it to a farcical conclusion.

Paradiso . . . Inferno?

A popular joke a few years ago asked: How does a European know he has died and gone to heaven? Answer: All the cooks are French, the mechanics German, the policemen English, the bankers Swiss and the lovers Italian. And how does a European define hell? That's where all the cooks are English, the mechanics French, the policemen German, the bankers Italian and the lovers Swiss.

And what if all the opera houses were Italian? That would be Paradiso, wouldn't it? We asked a handful of singers, conductors, critics and others about their experiences in opera houses up and down the boot. How heavenly is opera in Italy?

Singing *Aida* at Milan's La Scala represents the ultimate dream for many a soprano. Yet Martina Arroyo, on reaching that pinnacle, found the rehearsals as memorable as the performances. "We were standing onstage rehearsing," Arroyo recalls, "when the chorus walked out on strike, and we were told to go home. I left after a lot of argument and screaming and carrying on from everybody. Then they called us back. So we finally go back to the rehearsal, and we're standing onstage. Plácido's there, Fiorenza Cossotto's there, we're all standing around, Cappuccilli's even there—and no orchestra. This time the orchestra struck."

Arroyo had other trying experiences, too. "There was that *Don Carlo* in Rome in '74 when Grace [Bumbry] and I were running back and forth to the theater because the taxis were striking. One day the theater didn't tell us the performance started at 5:00, rather than the usual 9:00 P.M.. We only got the news about 4:00. No taxis—we walked, or ran, to the theater. I went onstage for the first act with no makeup, no vocalizing. I just got into costume, ran on and sang."

But there's more. "One night in Verona we had to do one of those unusual entrances but were stuck under trapdoors that nobody had remembered to unlock. There was a hilarious *Aida* in Bologna, where the Ethiopians were dressed like little crickets, with green appendages. Radamés was brought in on something we called 'the royal throne.'"

The Italian press also caused Arroyo some headaches. "In Verona—I had come to see Ruggero Raimondi perform—they reported that I was his new girlfriend! My mother-in-law was *furious.*"

American conductor Steven Mercurio remembers a nightmarish experience during Rome Opera's 1994 production of Zemlinsky's *Der Geburtstag der Infantin.* "Two or three minutes into the prelude, general manager Gian Carlo Menotti jumps out onstage, waving for me to stop. There's an electricians' strike—we're without lighting. Somehow we struggled through, using only the fixed lights, but you're left with the unreal quality of it all—the eighty-year-old general manager interrupting the prelude, the singers onstage unable to hear what he's saying through the curtain, trying to make the best of things. Twenty minutes into the opera, the electricians figured they'd made their point, and the lights were restored."

Rico Saccani, another American conductor, had a famous Italian baritone refuse to enter the theater after seeing an American colleague enter wearing purple—an absolute bearer of bad luck. But after fifteen years living and working in Italy, Saccani has learned to put aside "our American work ethic," especially around holiday time, which can be almost any time. "Sorry, Maestro," he might be told, "today is Carnevale and half of the orchestra has children in the parade." Or, "Sorry, Maestro, but today is the Festa of Gnocchi and the ladies of the orchestra cook all day." Or the whole orchestra may disappear to buy groceries for a long weekend.

Strikes in Italy seem to come in all sizes, even in different colors. Rehearsing in Venice, soprano June Anderson experienced what is called a "white strike" or sitdown. Preparations for the city's first *La Sonnambula* in 150 years, in the dilapidated Teatro Malibran, were halted to protest a faulty heating system. "The orchestra players staged their white strike," she recalls, "just sitting silently in the pit. Now I would have understood if they had insisted on *leaving* and not playing. But that they would just *sit* there in the cold and not play—this I found bizarre." For Arroyo, "It was incidents like [the strikes] that made me say, thank you very much, *this* much fun I don't want. I'd rather work at Covent Garden or the Met or even Paris."

Labor disputes can seem inoffensive compared with Italian audiences and their violent mood swings. Soprano Kallen Esperian was reduced to tears, as a spectator, when the La Scala public hissed and booed Katia Ricciarelli during a slightly off night in *I Vespri Siciliani*. "All I could do was sit there in the box, crying. I was scheduled to follow her in that same production. When Ricciarelli canceled a few nights later, my debut was moved up. All day long before the performance, I kept breaking down and crying."

"I was scared to death!" soprano Diana Soviero recalls of her own La Scala debut. "During rehearsals, the stage manager kept leading me all over the stage. 'Diana,' he said to me, 'Diana, look, here's the exact spot where Callas did Medea, and over here Caruso sang "Celeste Aida," ' or whatever. Well. By the time I got to the premiere I could hardly walk on that stage. I was afraid they were going to throw bananas, tangerines, I didn't know what."

Robert Merrill's career was as its height at a time when foreigners found Italy less than welcoming. "When I was recording, they asked me if I wanted to come back to Milan and open the season in *Il Barbiere di Siviglia*. I was very touched and excited. I said, 'Yes, but how soon can you let me know?' Three or four weeks before the season started I got a telegram that said to make myself available. But by then I already had the Met, I already had concerts lined up. It was just very difficult back then to get together with them. You had to live in Europe to sing there."

Sherrill Milnes had a backstage visitor after his first date at La Scala, in 1978. "He stuck his hand out and said, 'Sono dal claque.' I thought that was his name—I didn't hear it as 'I'm from the claque.' I thought his name was Antonio Sono Dal Claque, and I shook his hand and said, 'Piacere' and then—I got it, 'I'm from the claque.' He didn't want my hand, he wanted to be paid." In more recent years the infamous practice of buying applause seems to have disappeared.

At RCA Victor's large recording studio on the outskirts of Rome, complete operas were taped each summer, with Richard Mohr producing. "One summer," Mohr recalls, "we arrived as usual and were told that the musicians would not perform unless they got an increase. We already had a three-year contract, with one year left to run. But they wanted an increase anyway, immediately. They had us over a barrel." The players got their raise, but at summer's end, RCA picked up and moved its studios to calmer London. "The Italians were wonderful. They played with complete knowledge of opera, and with real fire. But we found that a good English group could be turned into an Italian orchestra, given enough time with a good Italian conductor."

Certain American expatriates have made careers out of attending opera in Italy. But times change, or as the Italians say, "Tutto declina" (everything deteriorates). For most of these people, opera in Italy today is Paradise Lost. So they cherish their memories. Of Maria Callas, primarily. Translator and critic William Weaver recalls the diva's* *La Vestale* and *La Sonnambula* in the famous Visconti stagings, as well as other opening nights. He still enjoys La Scala performances under Riccardo Muti. "I don't know where the 'opera capital' is today," he adds, "but I get less

---

*prima donna

pleasure out of going to the opera now than I did years ago when Callas was singing."

Titlist/translator Sonya Haddad heard some of La Divina's final La Scala performances. A flubbed high note in the 1962 *Medea* unleashed terrifying boos from the house, "like the lions in the Colosseum ready to devour the Christians. Callas turned and glared out at the audience, and the next word in the text was '*Crudele!*' She turned and glared at the audience and spat the word out and continued singing. I think anyone else hearing the sound of that audience would have crumbled. She went on to finish in a blaze of glory. The house went wild. I think that is very typically Italian. You are instantly judged and instantly either booed or praised depending on that judgment. I've never heard anything like it since."

Verdi biographer Mary Jane Phillips-Matz' first impression of La Scala was "overwhelming. I'll never forget how I felt when that clock rolled around, up over the stage. They have that drum clock that rotates, and when it rolls to the appointed time the performance begins. It was just a stunning show—Vinay and Simionato in *Samson*. And I had never been anywhere where they turned the lights up in the boxes and the lights down in the theater. Always at La Scala, there's the sense of the past. So it was a spectacle matched with opera as grand as one probably ever could see it."

Along with its aura, La Scala has one famous spot onstage that commands the very best acoustics. "You can see where the floorboards are worn down in that precise area from centuries of use," confirms Esperian. "No matter what the staging is supposed to be, sooner or later the singers try to maneuver themselves into that position." Singers are reluctant, probably for superstitious reasons, to betray the exact location of this acoustical sanctuary on the vast La Scala stage. An observer can probably recognize it from performers' traffic patterns during any performance.

Above all, Phillips-Matz recalls "the down-home quality of opera in those places" years and decades ago. "I felt especially comfortable in Venice," she says. "La Fenice was like a family, a true family. There was never a moment when you didn't feel that you had walked into somebody's family home. My daughter Clare was in the children's chorus at the Fenice. After an evening performance, at twelve or one in the morning, she would walk home alone at night over the Accademia bridge and down to the Salute [church]."

It was the financial transactions at La Fenice that intrigued Robert Merrill, who made his Italian debut there, as Germont in *La Traviata*. "I was paid in lire—I don't know how many millions. And they brought it backstage after the second act, in a very large envelope. And there it was. Then I heard, 'Mr. Merrill, you're on,' so I left this envelope in my dressing room and went on. Well—mentally, it was not my best act. I couldn't wait to get back to my dressing room. And believe it or not, it was all there." "In every company," Soviero confirms, "they pay you backstage. You have your heart in your mouth, they're giving you all this cash, you don't know what to do with it. I put it in my dresses—I always get fatter toward the third act! Now I make every effort to have my money sent by wire. But then you have to be careful that it doesn't arrive seven years later."

Summertime opera has its devotees and its detractors. William Weaver prefers Pesaro to Spoleto, and he has entered the Arena at Verona exactly once. "It rained after the first act, so I heard Callas sing about four bars. Of which she later said to me, 'Oh yes, the easiest money I ever earned!' She wasn't the least bit sympathetic to my lament." For Saccani, "The opening each evening of Verona's Arena series is still a magical moment—the gong, the 20,000 spectators with candles, a full moon. For me it's still the mecca of summer opera. I love their custom of hurling the seat cushions onstage as a way of showing appreciation while the cast take their bows."

At Parma they hurl insults. On tape recordings of Parma performances, June Anderson has heard frequent outbursts during the singing, such as the voice from the audience yelling "Il maestro sta uccidendo *La Traviata*" (the conductor is killing *La Traviata*). Just how discriminating is the Parma public? "The fact is," says Weaver, "that was always something of a myth. The Parma audience really was only critical with the standard operas that they all knew by heart. I went to a performance of *Luisa Miller* years ago which, if it had been *Trovatore* or *Aida,* would have been booed off the stage. It was unfamiliar to the Parma audience, and the tenor managed to do a creditable job on the one aria that everyone knew, so they got by with it. Now, of course, Parma has become a much more sophisticated house, where you're just as likely to hear Janáček as Verdi."

After a decade's experience in Italy, Anderson wonders about some other myths surrounding the audiences. "We tend to think that all Italians go to opera. That's not at all true. It's more soccer [that attracts the vast public], and there are some opera houses where you think you're at a soccer game. Singing in Italy gives you a taste of what it must have been like in the nineteenth century when you didn't have the audience's total attention. We're spoiled today, because people [in America] usually are not walking in and out [during] performances, and they're not eating, whereas you still get a little of that in Italy. They're basically there for the arias. It's a funny audience. Most of them know the music, and they really are not interested in duets or trios. After a really strong duet there would just be a smattering of almost impolite applause, and then after the famous arias, everything would erupt."

Italian fans have commented to her on details like interpolated notes or optional cadenzas,* and Diana Soviero finds that they welcome a degree of artistic license, if exercised with imagination. "Alberto Cupido and I were doing *Manon,* in French, and in the Saint Sulpice scene, I sing, 'Oui, c'est moi, c'est moi' but I did it this way"—mimicking chest voice on "moi"—"and they were shouting 'Brava' in the middle of that line. I went 'Oui, c'est'—it wasn't at all *français,* but who cares, it was what I felt at that moment, and they appreciated every moment of it."

Non-Italians seem to experience opera in Italy as a hotbed of misbehavior. The best anecdotes practice an economy that spreads the blame: a diva walks out moments before the overture, and the disappointed fans tear out the seats. In a vintage story about a Verona Arena performance, everyone seemed to misbehave—a real lose-lose-lose situation: the tenor barely made it through "Nessun dorma," but the audience screamed for an encore; conductor Vittorio Gui left in a huff, halting the performance; management forced him to come back and repeat the aria; the tenor predictably cracked on the high note in the encore, and the audience in its fury nearly destroyed the 2,000-year-old Roman structure.

Just when Italy begins to sound like Opera Hell, a singer will suddenly soften. Arroyo reconsiders that strike-plagued Rome Opera season of 1974: "What was funny about it was when Grace and I refused to sing until they paid the workers in the house. We weren't asking for our money. We said they should at least pay the workers—they had not been paid in seventeen weeks. The report came back to the States that Grace and I had started a riot, which of course we had not. But when my mother heard it, she said, 'Now what are you making Grace do?' Imagining Grace without her makeup, running down the street, trying to get a taxi—those things *were* funny."

True connoisseurs relish the craziness of the Italian opera scene. Conductor Saccani: "Recently the dress rehearsal of *La Favorita* at Catania's Teatro Bellini, with an audience of 1,500, had to be interrupted for the fireworks celebrating the patron saint of the city, St. Agatha. Orchestra, chorus, cast and public all trekked out into the piazza in front of this spectacular opera house to share the thirty-minute display. Then everybody filed back in for Act IV."

During the 1990 Soccer World Cup Championships held in Italy, Saccani recalls, half of the 4,000-plus in attendance at an *Aida* in Cagliari's Roman arena were listening via transistor radio to a soccer match between Italy and an opposing team. Two thousand people, including the tenor himself, interrupted "Celeste Aida" with shouts of "GOAL!" to celebrate a moment of Italian sports history.

---

*brilliant passages

At some point, any list of Italy's operatic tastes, habits and differences turns to the practical question of money. For years, Italy spent more on opera than most other countries. Saccani sees coproduction, or production sharing, on the rise in Italy. "Gone are the days when each house would destroy the sets and costumes after one run of any opera, without any regard to expenses. This was truly unique in the opera world." Another sign of the times, for Weaver, is corporate sponsorship, which has changed the occupants in the boxes and other high-priced seats at premieres: "You see CEOs where you once saw dukes and princes."

Even without the financial cushion, many artists continue to find the birthplace of opera a congenial place to perform, partly because it's still an agreeable place to live. Saccani would advise foreign artists to "learn to trust in the Italian Miracle. If up to and including the dress rehearsal the quality is so bad you feel like canceling, so as not to jeopardize your name and reputation, *don't*. It will all be wonderful on opening night—somehow." Perhaps because of that audience—the demonic, occasionally angelic Italian audience.

The Background

"THAT WOMAN's art jargon tires me," said Clovis to his journalist friend. "She's so fond of talking of certain pictures as 'growing on one,' as though they were a sort of fungus."

"That reminds me," said the journalist, "of the story of Henri Deplis. Have I ever told it you?"

Clovis shook his head.

"Henri Deplis was by birth a native of the Grand Duchy of Luxembourg. On maturer reflection he became a commercial traveler. His business activities frequently took him beyond the limits of the Grand Duchy, and he was stopping in a small town of northern Italy when news reached him from home that a legacy from a distant and deceased relative had fallen to his share.

"It was not a large legacy, even from the modest standpoint of Henri Deplis, but it impelled him toward some seemingly harmless extravangances. In particular it led him to patronize local art as represented by the tattoo needles of Signor Andreas Pincini. Signor Pincini was, perhaps, the most brilliant master of tattoo craft that Italy had ever known, but his circumstances were decidedly impoverished, and for the sum of six hundred francs he gladly undertook to cover his client's back, from the collarbone down to the waistline, with a glowing representation of the Fall of Icarus. The design, when finally developed, was a slight disappointment to Monsieur Deplis, who had suspected Icarus of being a fortress taken by Wallenstein in the Thirty Years' War, but he was more than satisfied with the execution of the work, which was acclaimed by all who had the privilege of seeing it as Pincini's masterpiece.

"It was his greatest effort, and his last. Without even waiting to be paid, the illustrious craftsman departed this life, and was buried under an ornate tombstone, whose winged cherubs would have afforded singularly little scope for the exercise of his favorite art. There remained, however, the widow Pincini, to whom the six hundred francs were due. And thereupon arose the great crisis in the life of Henri Deplis, traveler of commerce. The legacy, under the stress of numerous little calls on its substance, had dwindled to very insignificant proportions, and when a pressing wine bill and sundry other current accounts had been paid there remained little more than 430 francs to offer to the widow. The lady was properly indignant, not wholly, as she volubly explained, on account of the suggested writing off of 170 francs, but also at the attempt to depreciate the value of her late husband's acknowledged masterpiece. In a week's time Deplis was obliged to reduce his offer to 405 francs, which circumstances fanned the widow's indignation into a fury. She canceled the sale of the work of art, and a few days later Deplis learned with a sense of consternation that she had presented it to the municipality of Bergamo, which had gratefully accepted it. He left the neighborhood as unobtrusively as possible, and was genuinely relieved when his business commands took him to Rome, where he hoped his identity and that of the famous picture might be lost sight of.

"But he bore on his back the burden of the dead man's genius. On presenting himself one day in the steaming corridor of a vapor bath, he was at once hustled back into his clothes by the proprietor, who was a North Italian, and who emphatically refused to allow the celebrated Fall of Icarus to be publicly on view without the permission of the municipality of Bergamo. Public interest and official vigilance increased as the matter became more widely known, and Deplis was unable to take a simple dip in the sea or river on the hottest afternoon unless clothed up to the collarbone in a substantial bathing garment. Later on the authorities of Bergamo conceived the idea that salt water might be injurious to the masterpiece, and a perpetual injunction was obtained which debarred the muchly harassed commercial traveler from sea bathing under any circumstances. Altogether, he was fervently thankful when his firm of employers found him a new range of activities in the neighborhood of Bordeaux. His thankfulness, however, ceased abruptly at the Franco-Italian frontier. An imposing array of official force barred his departure, and he was sternly reminded of the stringent law which forbids the exportation of Italian works of art.

"A diplomatic parley ensued between the Luxembourgian and Italian governments, and at one time the European situation became overcast with the possibilities of trouble. But the Italian government stood firm; it declined to concern itself in the least with the fortunes or even the existence of Henri Deplis, commercial traveler, but was immovable in its decision that the Fall of Icarus (by the late Pincini, Andreas), at present the property of the municipality of Bergamo, should not leave the country.

"The excitement died down in time, but the unfortunate Deplis, who was of a constitutionally retiring disposition, found himself a few months later once more the storm center of a furious controversy. A certain German art expert, who had obtained from the municipality of Bergamo permission to inspect the famous masterpiece, declared it to be a spurious Pincini, probably the work of some pupil whom he had employed in in his declining years. The evidence of Deplis on the subject was obviously worthless, as he had been under the influence of the customary narcotics during the long process of pricking in the design. The editor of an Italian art journal refuted the contentions of the German expert and undertook to prove that his private life did not conform to any modern standard of decency. The whole of Italy and Germany were drawn into the dispute, and the rest of Europe was soon involved in the quarrel. There were stormy scenes in the Spanish Parliament, and the University of Copenhagen bestowed a gold medal on the German expert (afterward sending a commission to examine his proofs on the spot), while two Polish schoolboys in Paris committed suicide to show what *they* thought of the matter.

"Meanwhile, the unhappy human background fared no better than before, and it was not surprising that he drifted into the ranks of Italian anarchists. Four times at least he was escorted to the frontier as a dangerous and undesirable foreigner, but he was always brought back as the Fall of Icarus (attributed to Pincini, Andreas, early twentieth century). And then one day, at an anarchist congress at Genoa, a fellow worker, in the heat of debate, broke a phial full of corrosive liquid over his back. The red shirt that he was wearing mitigated the effects, but the Icarus was ruined beyond recognition. His assailant was severely reprimanded for assaulting a fellow anarchist and received seven years' imprisonment for defacing a national art treasure. As soon as he was able to leave the hospital Henri Deplis was put across the frontier as an undesirable alien.

"In the quieter streets of Paris, especially in the neighborhood of the Ministry of Fine Arts, you may sometimes meet a depressed, anxious-looking man, who, if you pass him the time of day, will answer you with a slight Luxembourgian accent. He nurses the illusion that he is one of the lost arms of the Venus de Milo, and hopes that the French government may be persuaded to buy him. On all other subjects I believe he is tolerably sane."

Reading for Understanding

Main Idea

1. The main idea of "Pardiso . . . Inferno?" is (a) a comparison of French and Italian opera (b) labor strikes in La Scala (c) the ups and downs of playing to an Italian audience (d) ways in which opera stars control their audiences.

Details

2. An opera dress rehearsal in Catania was once interrupted by (a) a fireworks display (b) an electricians' strike (c) a prima donna's illness (c) a backstage fire.
3. When Maria Callas missed a high note in *Medea*, (a) she wept (b) the tenor covered for her (c) she started over (d) the audience booed.
4. A baritone once refused to enter the theater because (a) he had seen a black cat (b) a colleague was wearing purple (c) he had broken a mirror (d) he had laryngitis.
5. In "The Background," the amount promised Signor Pincini for his work was (a) 170 francs (b) 430 francs (c) 600 francs (d) paid in full.
6. Deplis was a native of (a) Italy (b) Denmark (c) Luxembourg (d) Germany.

Inferences

7. If an outdoor opera was rained out before its completion, (a) the manager apologized (b) the audience lost their money (c) the entire company moved indoors (d) rain checks were issued.
8. Apparently, a strong rival for opera in Italy was (a) television (b) movies (c) parades (d) soccer.

Tone of the Selection

9. The tone of "The Background" is (a) satirical (b) disagreeable (c) violent (d) melancholy.

Author's Attitude

10. The attitude of Baker toward Italians and Their Opera is one of (a) grim disapproval (b) unqualified praise (c) careless indifference (d) affectionate dismay.

Words in Context

1. "Yet Martina Arroyo, on reaching that *pinnacle*, found the rehearsals as memorable as the performances." **Pinnacle** (400) means (a) experience (b) high point (c) act of an opera (d) front of the stage.

2. "There was a hilarious *Aida* in Bologna, where the Ethiopians were dressed like little crickets, with green *appendages*." **Appendages** (400) can be (a) strange hats (b) walking sticks (c) colorful costumes (d) limbs.

3. "But that they would just sit there in the cold and not play—this I found *bizarre*." **Bizarre** (401) means (a) annoying (b) weird (c) unexpected (d) consistent.

4. "Certain American *expatriates* have made careers out of attending operas in Italy." **Expatriates** (402) (a) are basically unpatriotic (b) travel extensively (c) stay away from their native land (d) are fair-weather friends.

5. "Everything *deteriorates*." **Deteriorates** (402) means (a) declines (b) remains the same (c) surprises (d) repeats itself.

6. "Along with its *aura*, La Scala has one famous spot onstage that commands the very best acoustics." **Aura** (403) means (a) reputation (b) excellent location (c) famous history (d) atmosphere.

7. "Summertime opera has its *devotees* and detractors." **Devotees** (404) are (a) critics (b) supporters (c) lead singers (d) paid public relations people.

8. "They're basically there for the *arias*." **Arias** (404) are (a) stunning sets (b) conversations in song (c) solo performances (d) duets.'

9. "Italian fans have commented to her on details like *interpolated* notes of optional cadenzas." **Interpolated** (405) means (a) interpreted (b) high and shrill (c) slighted (d) inserted.

10. "True *connoisseurs* relish the craziness of the Italian opera scene." **Connoisseurs** (405) are (a) experts (b) occasional opera goers (c) music conductors (d) humorists.

11. "It was not a large *legacy*, even from the modest standpoint of Henry

Deplis." A **legacy** (406) is (a) an inheritance (b) a strongbox (c) a communication (d) an expectation.

12. "Signor Pincini was, perhaps, the most brilliant master of tattoo craft that Italy had ever known, but his circumstances were decidely *impoverished*." **Impoverished** (406) means (a) weary (b) disadvantaged (c) unexpected (d) poor.

13. "The illustrious craftsman departed this life and was buried under an *ornate* tombstone." **Ornate** (407) means (a) obviously neglected (b) showily decorated (c) solid granite (d) informative.

14. "When a pressing wine bill and *sundry* other current accounts had been paid off, there remained little more than 430 francs to offer to the widow." **Sundry** (407) means (a) demanding (b) wasteful (c) miscellaneous (d) overlooked.

15. "The lady was properly indignant, not wholly, as she *volubly* explained, on account of the suggested writing off of 170 francs." **Volubly** (407) means (a) talkatively (b) reasonably (c) sternly (d) cheerfully.

16. "A few days later Deplis learned with a sense of *consternation* that she had presented it to the municipality of Bergamo." **Consternation** (407) is (a) false courage (b) amazement (c) dismay (d) relief.

17. "Public interest and official *vigilance* increased as the matter became more widely known." **Vigilance** (407) means (a) interference (b) inactivity (c) willingness (d) watchfulness.

18. "He was sternly reminded of the *stringent* law which forbids the exportation of Italian works of art." **Stringent** (407) means (a) flexible (b) recently enacted (c) strict (d) sometimes overlooked.

19., 20. "The editor of an Italian art journal *refuted* the *contentions* of the German expert." **Refuted** (408) means (a) explored (b) disproved (c) supported (d) elaborated on. **Contentions** (408) means (a) pretenses (b) published letters (c) incorrect opinions (d) debating points.

21. "It was not surprising that he drifted into the ranks of Italian *anarchists*." **Anarchists** (408) (a) are secret royalists (b) rebel against all authority (c) believe in a strong central government (d) usually unite with Fascists.

Thinking Critically about the Selections

1. Murphy's Law states, "If things can go wrong, they will go wrong." Select three episodes from "Paradiso . . . Inferno?" to show that

things can indeed go wrong. How did the Italians involved in these problems accept the difficulties?

2. How do operas, operettas, and musical comedies differ from each other? Can you supply an example of each?

3. How does the matter-of-fact way in which David J. Baker tells the story of opera in Italy help the presentation?

4. What is the "Italian Miracle" mentioned in the last paragraph on page 406?

5. In his wonderful comedy routine, Victor Borge "creates an opera," gently poking fun at the form. If you've seen it, tell about it. Does the clever spoofing like this in any way damage opera? Explain.

6. Note that the central absurdity of "The Background" is a fantasy; yet the writer treats the subject with all seriousness, even to having the critics quarreling over Deplis' tattoo. How does his mock seriousness help the telling? See also page 397, item 6.

7. The most outrageous exaggeration is almost understated, as in "There were stormy scenes in the Spanish Parliament." What possible connection could there have been between Deplis' tattoo and the Spanish Parliament? Provide other examples of matter-of-fact exaggerations and absurdity.

8. The Italian government wouldn't let national treasures out of Italy. Other nations have belatedly tried to keep their treasures at home. Dozens of museums around the world are filled with treasures from Egypt, for example. Does the precious art belong in Cairo? In 1806, the Earl of Elgin brought sculptures to England from Greece, presumably to save them from destruction. In 1816, the Parthenon frieze and other sculptural elements were purchased by England and displayed in the British Museum. Now the Greek government wants them back. Should England relinquish the treasures known as the Elgin marbles? This is a knotty problem, not easily solved. Give your views. Consider questions like this: "Does art belong to the nation of origin or to the world?"

Language in Action

The Greek Contribution

His assailant was severely reprimanded for assaulting a fellow anarchist and received seven years' imprisonment for defacing a national treasure.

Anarchist, a word more used 75 years ago, than today, is a good introduction to the Greek contribution to English. It is derived from *an—no* and *archos—ruler.* An *anarchist* is one who believes in no governmental authority, no ruler. The word demonstrates a remarkable quality of Greek as a source of English words. The parts of the word join together easily and comfortably. The same negative prefix *an* appears in *anemia* (no blood), *anesthetic* (no feeling), *anonymous* (no name), and *anorexia* (no appetite). Without the *n*, the prefix gives us *amoral, apathy, asocial, aseptic,* and *asymmetrical. Arch,* in its turn, gives us *patriarch* (father as ruler), *matriarch* (mother as ruler), and *monarch* (single ruler).

Greek roots are incredibly useful. The Greek root for *write* gives us *autograph, biography, graphic,* and *telegraph.* The Greek root *cycl* gives us *bicycle, cyclone, cycle, encyclopedia, tricycle.* The Greek root *log* gives us all those ology words: *astrology, biology, geology, meteorology, psychology, zoology.* Science is especially indebted to Greek for the formation of English words: *atmosphere, barometer, cholorophyll, dynamite, electricity, hieroglyphic, hydrogen, phosphorus, planet, proton, telescope.*

It pays to know a few useful roots like *auto*—self, *demo*—people, *erg*—work, *hydr*—water, *lith*—stone, *morph*—form, *neo*—new, *nom*—law, *pan*—all, *phil*—love, *pod*—foot, *proto*—first, *soph*—wise, *tom*—cut, *trop*—turn, and *typ*—print.

Flurry at the Sheep-Dog Trial

Eric Knight
British

> **Flurry now had the handkerchief. She was walking to Sam, who stood, waiting triumphantly. Flurry came nearer to his feet and then began to circle round him.**
>
> **"She forgot," the men breathed. "She don't know what to do wi' it."**

The sheep dog Flurry was the pride of Yorkshire. In a critical contest, she was awarded second place. Then she was given a second challenge, a far more difficult one than any she could ever have had before. Could Flurry uphold the honor of Yorkshire against the best sheep dog in Lancashire?

This is a warm, humorous satisfying story about a sheep-dog trial, colorful characters, the sheep dog owner, and Flurry, the most incredible dog you're ever likely to meet in fiction or real life. The author uses dialect to recapture the mood and color of the good-natured contest. Try to say the sentences aloud, or silently, to capture the flavor of the piece.

This story is taken from Eric Knight's **The Flying Yorkshireman**. If you enjoyed meeting Sam Small and Flurry, you'll relish the complete book.

414

Flurry at the Sheep-Dog Trial

THE WIND came clear over the great flat part of the moor near Soderby. The gusts eddied, tearing away wisps of smell—the smell of men packed in knots, of sheep, of trampled heath grass. The size of the flatland made the noises small—the sharp barks of dogs, the voices of men speaking in deep dialect.

The men of the different sections stood in separate knots. Those from Polkingthorpe were ranged about Sam, their eyes on him trustingly, half fearfully, as if they were a little awed by what they had done, and the size of the bets they had made from village loyalty.

"Now, Sam," Gaffer Sitherthwick mumbled slowly, "tha's sure she can do it? For Ah've put up one pound again' two pound ten that she's the winner."

"Now hold up, Gaffer," Capper Wambley wavered. "Tha must remember she's never been really trained as a shepherd; but what Ah say is, the way Sam's trained her this past week she'll do owt he tells her best she can. And best ye can do is best, as any man'll agree."

"Thankee, Capper," Sam acknowledged. "Now, lads, if ye don't mind, Ah'd like to give her sort of secret instructions—and calm her down."

He led Flurry away from the knot of men, though she looked as though she needed no calming down. She was sedate and confident in her gait. At a distance, he knelt beside her and pretended to be brushing her coat.

"Now tha sees how it is, Flurry," he said. "There's t'four pens at each corner. In each is a sheep. Tha has to go to each one, take t'sheep out, and then put all four into t'middle pen. . . . Now thee watch this one—this is t'Lancashire entry, and she was champion last year. And she's no slouch."

They watched the black sheep dog from Lancashire, sailing across the field at a gallop, neatly collecting the sheep.

"See how t'shepherd holds his crook like to make a door for t'middle pen, Flurry? Now that's all Ah can do to help. Ah can point or signal, but Ah can nobbut make a sort of angle to help wi' t'sheep at t' middle pen."

There was a burst of applause, which meant that the Lancashire dog had set the record time for the trial.

"Come on, then, Miss Smartie," Sam said. "It'll be us."

Sam heard his name being announced. He walked with Flurry to the ring. He knelt beside her.

"Now remember—no biting sheep or tha'll lose points."

She gave him a look that should have withered him.

"Go," said the judge.

Away Flurry sailed, her belly almost flat to the ground. She went from pen to pen, chivvying the sheep into a compact knot. She brought them to the center pen, driving at them adeptly so that before they could stand, sheep-wise and stubborn, and wonder where they were going, they were safe in the center pen. Then she sat at the gate, her tongue lolling out, and a burst of applause said she had made good time.

Sam hurried over to his mate. He rushed to Capper Wambley, who owned, without doubt, the finest watch in the village.

"How about it, Capper?"

The old man cleared his throat importantly and stared at his watch.

"Well. T'road Ah make it—wi' varry exact computations—is that there ain't a split-second difference between thee and Lancashire. But mind ye—that's unofficial, o' course."

So the chums rocked in impatience as the last tests were run off, and then they stood in the common hush as the judge took off his hat and advanced.

"First place," he announced, "is a tie between Joe Pettigill's Black Tad and Sam Small's Flurry, as far as time is concerned. But the judges unanimously award first place, on the basis o' calmer conduct in handling t'sheep, to Pettigill's Black Tad fro' Lancashire."

Of course, Sam and his friends were quite put out about it, and Gaffer Sitherthwick almost had apoplexy as he thought of his lost pound. . . . Thus it might have been a black day in the history of Polkingthorpe Brig had not Pettigill decided to gloat a bit. He walked over past the chums and said triumphantly, "Why don't ye all coom over to Lancashire and learn reight how to handle a tyke?"

This was, of course, too, too much for any Yorkshireman to bear. So Sam came right back at him. "Oh, aye?" he said.

It wasn't a very good answer, but it was all he could think of at the moment.

"Oh, aye," echoed Pettigill . . . .

"Ah admit tha's got a fine bitch there, Pettigill, but ma tyke ain't used to sheep. But if it came, now, to a test o' real intelligence—well, here's five pounds even fro' me and ma mates says we'll win at any contest tha says."

"Then thy good money goes after thy bad," the Lancashire lad said.

So it was arranged that an extra test would be held, with each man picking his own test to show the intelligence of his dog. Mr. Watcliffe, a well-to-do sheep dealer who was one of the judges, agreed to make the decision as to which dog was best.

The moor rang with excited chatter as the news spread, and everyone scurried around to lay bets. The Polkingthorpe men all got side bets down—except the Gaffer. He declined, morosely, to bet any more. So the contest got under way. Pettigill and Sam drew straws to see which dog should show off first.

Pettigill got the short straw and had to start. "Now, lass," he said to his dog, "over there Ah've put a stick, a stone, ma cap, and a handkerchief. Will some sporting gentleman call out which one Ah should bid her bring first?"

"T'stick!" a voice called.

"Tad. Fotch me yon stick," Pettigill ordered.

Away raced the dog and brought it. One by one, as requested, the champion brought back the correct articles, dropping them at its owner's feet. The men burst into applause as it ended. Then up stepped Sam. He knelt beside Flurry and spoke so all could hear.

"Lying i' front o' Joe Pettigill," he announced, "is four articles. When Ah say 'Go!' ma tyke'll first take t'cap, go to the far sheep pen, and drop it inside there. Next she'll take t'stick, and drop it at the feet o' t'biggest lad on this moor. Third she'll take t'stone and drop it at t'feet o' t'second-best dog trainer on this moor. Finally, she'll take t'handkerchief—" and here Sam beamed floridly—"and drop it afore t'handsomest and knowingest man around these parts. Now ista ready?"

Sam looked at Flurry, who jumped to her feet and leaned forward as if held by an invisible leash. The crowd almost moaned in a sort of excitement, for they had never heard of a dog that could understand such a complicated set of commands.

"Go!" said Sam.

Away sailed Flurry, veering past Joe Pettigill's feet and snatching up the cap on the dead gallop without stopping. Going in the water-smooth racing stride of a collie, she went out to the far pen, dropped the cap, and streaked back. She snatched the stick and loped toward the crowd. The men parted to let her through. She quested about, until she saw Ian Cawper. She dropped it at his feet and the men moaned astonishment.

Back she went for the stone. She picked it up, and then stood, as if at a loss. The men drew in their breath.

But Flurry merely looked up at Joe Pettigill, walked forward one step and dropped the stone again.

The men roared in approval.

"That means Pettigill's second-best dog trainer," they said. "But now for Sam!"

Flurry now had the handkerchief. She was walking to Sam, who stood, waiting triumphantly. Flurry came nearer to his feet, and then began to circle round him.

"She forgot," the men breathed. "She don't know what to do wi' it."

Sam looked down, with a sort of agony in his eyes, for Flurry was trotting away from him—going away with the handkerchief in a hesitating sort of way. She was looking about her. She was walking to the center.

And then everyone saw what it was.

Flurry was going up to Mr. Watcliffe, the judge. She dropped the handkerchief at his feet, walked back to Sam, and sat properly at heel.

This time there was no cheering, for in that entire crowd it seemed as if a ghost had passed and lightly touched the back of every man's head, touching low down toward the neck where the short hairs grow, a touch that left a tingling sensation.

All one could hear was the voice of Mr. Watcliffe. "Why, bless my soul," he was saying. "Bless my very body and soul. She's almost human. Bless my soul."

Then he seemed to waken to his responsibility.

"Ah judge that the test has been won by Sam Small's tyke. If he will step forward, Ah'll give him the wager money."

This broke the spell. Sam went forward to collect, and the Polkingthorpe men went round with a roar to garner in the side bets they had made in the crowd. Everyone was in pocket except Gaffer Sitherthwick, which was also something to make that day a memorable one in Polkingthorpe's history. Seldom, if ever, did the Gaffer come out on the wrong side of money matters.

Together the chums all started home. Joe Pettigill stopped them and spoke like a true sport.

"That's a champion tyke tha has there, lad," he said.

"Thankee," said Sam, with the customary modesty. "We nobbut won by luck."

"But how about ma cap up there?" the Lancashireman asked.

"Nay, Ah nobbut said she'd tak' it," Sam pointed out. "It'll cost thee another five pound to have her bring it back."

Pettigill frowned, then grinned in appreciation.

"Here, Tad," he said. "Go up and get ma cap." And away sailed his own fine dog.

Away, too, went Sam, with all the men slapping him on the back, applauding his wit, skill, acumen, and perspicacity. They streamed over the moor toward Polkingthorpe Brig to tell the story of their mighty triumph.

Reading for Understanding

Main Idea

1. The main point of the story is (a) a sheep-dog's incredible performance (b) the folly of betting on sheep-dog trials (c) the hatred of two
   dogs toward each other (d) the limited obedience displayed by some
   sheep-dogs.

Details

2. The person who had the finest watch was (a) Capper Wambley (b)
   Joe Pettigill (c) Gaffer Sitherthwick (d) Mr. Watcliffe.
3. Black Tad was a (a) sheep-dog owner (b) judge (c) sheep dealer (d)
   dog.
4. The first object retrieved by Pettigill's dog was a (a) stone (b) cap (c)
   handkerchief (d) stick.
5. Flurry dropped the handkerchief at the feet of (a) Ian Cawper (b)
   Mr. Watcliffe (c) Sam Small (d) Joe Pettigill.

Inference

6. Flurry lost the first contest because (a) Sam was a very poor trainer
   (b) she wasn't used to sheep (c) Joe was dishonest (d) the judge was
   prejudiced.
7. Flurry's mood at every turn was one of (a) confidence (b) uncertainty (c) anger (d) confusion.
8. Flurry won by (a) following instructions (b) exactly following Sam's
   plan (c) flattering the owner of the other dog (d) never wavering in
   hesitation.

Mood of the Story

9. The mood of the story is one of (a) hostility (b) irritation (c) sadness
   (d) good humor.

Fact or Opinion

Tell whether the following is a fact or an opinion.

10. Sam looked down when Flurry turned away from him with the handkerchief.

Words in Context

1. "The guests *eddied,* tearing away wisps of smell." **Eddied** (415) means (a) lessened (b) roared (c) swirled (d) returned.
2. "She was *sedate* and confident in her gait." *Sedate* (415) means (a) handsome (b) conceited (c) unruffled (d) nervous.
3. "Gaffer Sitherthwick almost had *apoplexy* as he thought of his lost pound." **Apoplexy** (416) is a (a) stroke (b) nervous cough (c) loud disagreement (d) fight.
4. "Sam beamed *floridly.*" **Floridly** (417) suggests (a) a flower's bloom (b) an opponent's anger (c) a competitor's anxiety (d) a judge's certainty.
5. "The Polkingthorpe men went round with a roar to *garner* in the side bets they had made in the crowd." **Garner** (418) means (a) make a list (b) rejoice (b) talk about (d) gather.
6.,7. "Away, too, went Sam, with all the men slapping him on the back, applauding his wit, skill, *acumen,* and *perspicacity.*" **Acumen** (418) means (a) sense of humor (b) shrewdness (c) confidence (d) acute hearing. **Perspicacity** (418) means (a) hard work (b) likability (c) good sense (d) sense of loyalty.

Thinking Critically about the Story

1. How does the author paint a sympathetic picture of Flurry? Of Sam?
2. How do the little character sketches provide color and flavor? Point out examples.
3. How do you feel about the dialect? Do you think it improves the story? Explain.
4. Is this really a tall tale? Could a dog make the judgments that Flurry did? Does it matter? Explain.

5. In the final part of the test, how did Flurry prove to be smarter than Sam?

6. How did Pettigill prove to be a good sport?

7. Do you enjoy animal stories? If you have read "The Horse of the Sword" (4), compare it with "Flurry at the Sheep-Dog Trials." Are MoroGlory and Flurry somewhat alike? How similar are the two endings?

Language in Action

The Important Lowly Hyphen

"That means Pettigill's second-best dog trainer," they said.

The hyphen, often neglected or misused, can play an important role in communication. It is an aid to clarity. In the sentence above, the hyphen links *second* and *best*, forming *second-best*. If the hyphen had been placed between *best* and *dog*, the meaning would have been drastically affected:

"That means Pettigill's second best-dog trainer," they said.

An amusing example of a phrase needing a hyphen appeared on a police vehicle in Hendersonville, North Carolina. On the side was neatly labeled "Sheriff's Victims Services." A hyphen would have avoided a quick second reading: *Sheriff's Victim-Services*. But suppose a hyphen had been misplaced: *Sheriff's-Victims Services!*

The hyphen appears in many compound adjectives like *middle-aged, old-fashioned*, and *good-natured*. In some situations, whether or not a hyphen is used depends on placement in the sentence.

Allen wore a *dark-blue* jacket. (Hyphen)

Allen's jacket was *dark blue*. (No hyphen)

The hyphen appears in compound numbers from *twenty-one* to *ninety-nine*. It also shows family relationships: *son-in-law, great-uncle, great-great grandfather*.

When the first part of the compound noun is the main word, the plural form is usually used: *sisters-in-law, men-at-arms, attorneys-at-law*. In the first compound, for example, *law* isn't being pluralized; *sister* is.

Yes, the hyphen is a do-it-yourself-and-make-the-meaning-clearer kind of mark.

Remember: Bills Are People, Too

Mike Royko
American

Parents Should Choose Riskier Names for Babies

Bill Tammeus
American

Banana Popsicles Are Good for You

Benny Smith
American

It is my experience that guys named George and Bill are as solid and reliable and unassuming as a Labrador retriever. And you wear brown. About 70% of all brown suits, topcoats, and shoes are bought by guys named George or Bill. The rest by guys named Ed or Joe.

What's in a name indeed! Mike Royko explores the impact of a name on lifestyles and experiences. Bill Tammeus calls for greater creativity in naming babies.

Benny Smith doesn't bother with names but writes a gentle, bittersweet account of his experience with grandparents and banana popsicles. His low-key but effective tribute stirs our own childhood memories.

These three selections have been grouped together because they are all feature columns from the daily newspaper. All three were written under the pressure of a deadline; yet all three bear rereading. Some cheerful prose has come from the typewriters of exhausted columnists. Perhaps a certain amount of tension spurs creativity.

Remember: Bills Are People, Too

The man across the counter in the coffee shop politely said: "Excuse me, but I'd like to chat with you about names and sensitivity."

I hope your name isn't John.

"No," he said, with a chuckle. "I am not a John of any kind."

Good, I've heard from more angry Johns than I can count since I innocently described a men's room as a john.

"Yes, I noticed that," the man said.

Then my guess is that you are a George or a Bill.

"Why do you say that?"

Because you are a solid, reliable, unassuming and friendly looking person. It is my experience that guys named George and Bill are as solid and reliable and unassuming as a Labrador retriever. And you wear brown. About 70 percent of all brown suits, topcoats and shoes are bought by guys named George or Bill. The rest by guys named Ed or Joe.

"Amazing," he said. "You're right. My name is Bill."

Of course. There was no way you could be a Vic or a Nick or a Rick because you aren't wearing a gold chain. And you are too old to be a Kevin or a Shawn. Nor could you have been a Tyrone, a Leroy or a Jawon.

"Yep," he said, as guys named Bill are inclined to do, "I'm just plain Bill."

There is a song by that name, you know. Just Plain Bill. I believe it is the only song written about you Bills.

"No, there is also, 'Won't You Come Home, Bill Bailey,' in which a guilt-laden woman tries to reach out to the man she mistreated. But as wild guys go, Bill Bailey was kind of straight, since all his woman promised to do was wash the dishes and cook his meals. That's really all that we Bills need to live the good life."

Yes, solid, reliable, unassuming. If every man in America was named Bill, this would be Norway.

"I guess that's a compliment."

Whatever. So, I suppose you wanted to talk about how comforting it is to be a Bill, a handle nobody mocks or takes in vain.

"No," he said, becoming somber, as Bills will do whenever the opportunity arises. "Being a Bill isn't without its moments of pain. I think every Bill would tell you that, if we weren't so darned unassuming, pardon my French."

I wasn't aware of that.

"Oh, yes, because of my name, I have psychological wounds that go all the way back to my childhood."

Those are the worst kind.

"Yes, I was a mere lad when one day the mail came and I heard my mother shout: "Bills, bills, nothing but lousy bills. I hate bills."

And you misunderstood?

"Of course. I was a stunned and heartbroken little tyke. And it got worse when my father said, 'Everybody hates bills, but we're stuck with them. And then my mother said, 'I'd like to tear every bill to shreds.' Then I was not only stunned and heartbroken, but I was terrified."

I can imagine. I hope you asked your parents why they hated you.

"No, being a Bill, I was too unassuming to do that. So I just grew morose until a teacher asked me why I wrote so many suicide notes as my English essays. And I told her that my parents hated me and wanted to tear me to shreds."

I hope that this led to understanding.

"No, they sent a social worker to our house. And my parents agreed to take me to see a psychologist."

Good. All's well that ends well.

"But I just thought you might want to tell people that they might give some thought before they talk negatively or venomously about bills. That kind of talk can cause pain and suffering for those of us named Bill, and can even make us wince."

I can understand that and I'll pass your thoughts along. By the way, Bill, what do you do for a living?

"I'm a bill collector. Isn't that a coincidence?"

Parents Should Choose Riskier Names for Babies

Names, it is clear, go in and out of fashion.

Which explains why it's been at least six months—and probably much longer—since you've heard of anyone naming a baby Bertha or Wilbur.

I do not pick those hopelessly out-of-fashion names out of the empty air utterly at random. It turns out my late father's name was Wilbur and my mother's name is Bertha. Oh, the ignominy of it.

By the 1950s, when I did most of my growing up, they had become as embarrassing a set of parental names as a child was likely to get stuck with. It's hard to imagine a similarly awful thing for a child of the '90s, unless, perhaps, it's a father who still wears burgundy double-knit polyester pants with a white belt or a mother who goes to the store with spoolies in her hair. (Spoolies—you could ask someone over 40.)

I've just read another of those periodic stories about popular names for babies. At the moment, it says, the world is rapidly filling up with crumb-snatchers named Ashley, Austin, Brittany, Caitlyn, Dillon, Michael, Thomas, Brandon and Zachary. Other names on the rise seem to be Hannah, Morgan, (I know at least one of each), Makayla, Justin, Daniel and James.

By the way, the reporter who wrote the story to which I refer is named Stasia, which, in terms of popularity, is either in the early stages of coming or the late stages of going. Stasia works for a Redding, Calif., newspaper with a name as unfamous as the name Stasia—the *Record-Searchlight*.

Which brings me closer to what I'm trying to say about all of this, which is that I think parents should take more risks naming their kids. There are way too many Jennifers, Jasons and whatnot. But, as far as I know, there's not one kid named Record-Searchlight, even though such a name would stand out powerfully throughout a child's life.

Still, even I might acknowledge that naming a kid Record-Searchlight would be too eccentric. And what I mean by taking more risks in naming kids isn't that. It's more that there are perfectly good names out there that have been abandoned for inexplicable reasons. At least I can't explic them.

For instance, what's wrong with Gertrude? It served Gertrude Stein well, not hindering her advancement in the world a bit. Or what's wrong with Olive? Or Hortense? Or Mildred?

And is there something socially putrid about the name Orville? One of the Wright Brothers slid right through life named Orville, and it didn't clip his wings, so to speak. And can you think of any good reason today very few parents are naming children Ralph or Harvey or Earl or Perkins?

I admire the tendency of African-Americans and other ethnic minorities to come up with fresh and unique names for their babies. This is different than reclaiming abandoned names, but at least they've got the right spirit. Most fully assimilated white Americans haven't loosened up enough to do that.

Which is too bad. It would be a better world with more Violas and Archibalds. For one thing, like Bertha and Wilbur, they'd probably deserve each other.

Banana Popsicles Are Good for You

Six months ago I wrote a column about my grandparents which appeared on this page.

It gave me a chance to look back on what they taught me and how important their teachings were to my everyday life.

I am glad I wrote that column because, within those six months, I have lost two of my three grandparents. Fortunately, they got to read that column before their deaths.

But there is one thing I forgot to share with you—the story of the Banana Popsicle.

My grandfather, Benny Smith Sr., was an independent man who

loved his family. Sometime in the late 1970s, my two siblings and I went to live with him and my grandmother after my parents divorced.

For most children, divorce can have a major impact. I think living with my grandparents made it a little less traumatic for us.

Of course, my brother, sister and I would have rather stayed with our parents but, because that situation was not working out, staying with grandparents was the next best thing.

Even though my grandparents did not have the space in their two-bedroom home, they took us in without any hesitation.

I remember a lot of things about those early days staying in their Greenville, S.C., home, but what comes to mind most is the silver refrigerator.

To anyone else, it may have seemed like just another appliance, but to me—even now—it means something much greater.

For inside the freezer part of the two-door appliance was always a freshly stocked pile of banana popsicles. Some people say that garlic is a remedy to a lot of physical ailments, but to me a banana popsicle was the remedy to all of my problems.

Of course on hot summer days after I played with the neighboring kids in the park or in the street, the popsicle was a source of relief. It helped to cool me down after playing in 90-degree temperatures.

When I would fall and bruise my knee, my grandparents would use "old timey" remedies, a hug and,—yes—they'd give me a banana popsicle to help ease the pain.

When I would be disciplined by my grandfather, he used to always make me feel bad, but you could always guarantee about 15 minutes later he would say: "Now go on in dere and get you a popsicle."

Even though I would sometimes get mad at him for scolding me, I would gladly jump at his invitation.

Then several years passed. I was in college and was no longer living with my grandparents but would visit them on every opportunity I had.

Many times I knocked on the wooden screen door to their home and one of them would ask, "Who is it?"

"Me," I would answer.

One of them would unlatch the screen door and greet me with a smile and kiss. It always felt so good to sit in the living room, talk with them, and catch up on how people in the community were doing.

"You just come down?" my grandfather would ask.

"Yep and ya'll are my first stop," I would reply.

"You hungry?" he'd ask.

"Well, not really. I ate before I came."

"Why don't you go in dere and get you a popsicle."

That would always do it for me, because I would jump at the chance.

A chapter in the popsicle saga ended in May when my grandfather died. It was very weird to walk into the house and not see him sitting on the couch, looking at television. And believe it or not, it was very different to no longer have anyone to ask me that question that I had heard for at least 20 years: "Do you want a popsicle?"

But I decided that even though he was gone, I had something special that I had shared with him—something that other people never have the opportunity to share with their grandparents. So I just try to remember those times and, when I am down, know that in addition to God there is something else that can help ease my troubles—a banana popsicle.

Reading for Understanding

Main Idea

1. The main idea of the three selections (a) can be found in the first paragraph of each selection (b) are expressed in their titles (c) are essentially the same (d) are totally contradictory.

Details

2. A way to identify people named *Bill* is by (a) their quarrelsome natures (b) asking about childhood experiences (c) noticing their way of speaking (d) their favorite color, brown.

3. The name linked with *Bill* is (a) *Vic* (b) *Rick* (c) *George* (d) *Kevin*.

4. A name praised by Bill Tammeus is (a) Gertrude (b) Brittany (c) Dillon (d) Michael.

5. *Record-Searchlight* is (a) briefly mentioned as a child's name (b) a newspaper from Dearborn, Michigan (c) the newspaper for which Bill Tammeus writes a column (d) a book about naming babies.

6. Benny Smith (a) lived with his divorced mother (b) loves to eat orange popsicles (c) was brought up by grandparents (d) was bitter toward his father.

Inferences

7. Benny Smith's grandfather was (a) not actually related by blood (b) generally cruel to Benny (c) a newspaperman like Benny (d) a kindhearted man.

8. When Royko says, "This would be Norway," he is (a) assuming all the men would be solid, reliable, unassuming (b) paying tribute to Norwegian fashions (c) gently criticizing Europe (d) implying that we've had enough *Bills* already.

9. Tammeus suggests that (a) parents get into a rut in naming babies (b) *Brandon* is a better name than *Wilbur* (c) it's easy to become too weird in naming babies (d) *Bill* is really the perfect name.

Tone of the Selection

10. The tone of "Remember: Bills Are People, Too" is generally (a) serious (b) glum (c) lighthearted (d) smug.

Words in Context

1. "Because you are a solid, reliable, *unassuming* and friendly-looking person." **Unassuming** (423) means (a) unquestioning (b) modest (c) colorful (d) exciting.

2. "So I just grew *morose* until a teacher asked me why I wrote so many suicide notes as my English essays." **Morose** (424) means (a) quiet (b) gloomy (c) high-strung (d) offensive.

3. "That kind of talk . . . can even make us *wince.*" **Wince** (424) means (a) stammer (b) rebel (c) agree (d) flinch.

4. "Oh, the *ignominy* of it." **Ignominy** (425) means (a) surprise (b) attractiveness (c) disgrace (d) wonder.

5. "There are perfectly good names out there that have been abandoned for *inexplicable* reasons." **Inexplicable** (426) reasons (a) cannot be explained (b) stimulate curiosity (c) drive a hard bargain (d) do not remain unclear.

6. "My two *siblings* and I went to live with him and my grandmother." **Siblings** (427) are (a) first cousins (b) children with a common parent (c) stepchildren (d) close friends.

7. "For most children, divorce can have a major *impact*." **Impact** (427) means (a) attempt (b) compromise (c) success (d) shock.

Thinking Critically about the Selections

1. An essay has been defined as a "literary composition usually dealing with its subject from a limited or *personal* point of view." An article, by contrast, tends to be factual and *impersonal*. An article may explain the greenhouse effect, plead for an environmental cause, or support a political candidate. How would you classify the three selections? Why?

2. Which of the three selections was your favorite? Why?

3. In Shakespeare's *Romeo and Juliet,* Juliet says, "What's in a name? That which we call a rose, by any other name would smell as sweet." Do you agree? Does the name given a child play a part in his life? Provide examples.

4. Can you think of two or three names that especially appeal to you? Can you tell why?

5. Why do some names run in cycles of popularity? Do celebrity names often influence the naming of children? Is this wise, unwise, or unimportant?

6. Is Tammeus right? Are exotic names for babies better than more common ones? Can girls' names afford to be more unusual than boys' names? Why or why not?

7. Benny Smith recalls with relish a childhood treat that symbolized a happy home for him. Do you have a favorite dish, dessert, or candy bar that still delights you as much as it did when you were younger? Tell about it.

8. How does Benny Smith reveal the character of his grandfather?

Language in Action

Idioms

Names, it is clear, go in and out of fashion.

"Go in and out of fashion" is an example of an idiom, which has been defined as "a phrase in which the meaning of the whole expression is different from the total meanings of the words of which it is composed." Idioms vary from language to language. Indeed the root of the word is Greek suggesting the *individual*.

As idioms go, the one in the quotation above is fairly clear. But consider one like "the fat's in the fire." It means that a moment of decision has arrived, but the meaning cannot be derived by looking at the parts of the idiom. One plus one doesn't equal two.

Consider many of our formal idioms like "How do you do?" The speaker isn't really inquiring about the other's health or his activities. If you "keep it under your hat," you may not actually own a hat. When Gwen throws "cold water" on the picnic suggestion, she's nowhere near a water fountain. If Jeanne "cannot hold a candle to Sue," she needn't light a match. When you "draw the line" at a suggested activity, you needn't use chalk.

Here's a real-life example of how confusing an idiom can be to a non-native speaker. A parkway sign near an airport carried the following message:

"Give the grass a break."

Foreign visitors looked at the sign and scratched their heads. The English meaning "Stay off the grass" was lost on the newcomers.

The Night the Ghost Got In

James Thurber
American

"What is it?" he asked me.

"It's an old zither our guinea pig used to sleep on," I said.
It was true that a pet guinea pig we once had would never
sleep anywhere except on the zither, but I should never have
said so. Joe and the other cop looked at me a long time. They
put the zither back on a shelf.

A guinea pig that would sleep nowhere else but on a zither?
In James Thurber's world, anything can happen. A false rumor can
make idiots of an entire town (23). A ghost can run around a dining
room and start up the steps, only to disappear. A grandfather can relive
episodes of the Civil War, to the great discomfort of a startled
policeman. A mother can throw a shoe through a neighbor's closed
window to attract attention.

Thurber has the uncanny ability to capture a character in a
sentence or two: the narrator, Herman, Mother, the Bodwells, Joe,
Grandfather. Outrageous events are told with an understated, dead-
pan sincerity that enriches the events themselves. The matter-of-fact
style contrasts with the wild experiences of the author and his unusual
family.

Was there really a ghost? Who cares!

The Night the Ghost Got In

THE GHOST that got into our house on the night of November 17, 1915, raised such a hullabaloo of misunderstandings that I am sorry I didn't just let it keep on walking, and go to bed. Its advent caused my mother to throw a shoe through a window of the house next door and ended up with my grandfather shooting a patrolman. I am sorry, therefore, as I have said, that I ever paid any attention to the footsteps.

They began about a quarter past one o'clock in the morning, a rhythmic, quick-cadenced walking around the dining-room table. My mother was asleep in one room upstairs, my brother Herman in another; grandfather was in the attic, in the old walnut bed which, as you will remember, once fell on my father. I had just stepped out of the bathtub and was busily rubbing myself with a towel when I heard the steps. They were the steps of a man walking rapidly around the dining-room table downstairs. The light from the bathroom shone down the back steps, which dropped directly into the dining-room; I could see the faint shine of plates on the plate-rail; I couldn't see the table. The steps kept going round and round the table; at regular intervals a board creaked, when it was trod upon. I supposed at first that it was my father or my brother Roy, who had gone to Indianapolis but were expected home at any time. I suspected next that it was a burglar. It did not enter my mind until later that it was a ghost.

After the walking had gone on for perhaps three minutes, I tiptoed to Herman's room. "Psst!" I hissed, in the dark, shaking him. "Awp," he said, in the low, hopeless tone of a despondent beagle—he always half suspected that something would "get him" in the night. I told him who I was. "There's something downstairs!" I said. He got up and followed me to the head of the back staircase. We listened together. There was no sound. The steps had ceased. Herman looked at me in some alarm: I had only the bath towel around my waist. He wanted to go back to bed, but I gripped his arm. "There's something down there!" I said. Instantly the steps began again, circled the dining-room table like a man running, and started up the stairs toward us, heavily, two at a time. The light still shone palely down the stairs; we saw nothing coming; we only heard the steps. Herman rushed to his room and slammed the door. I slammed shut the door at the stairs top and held my knee against it. After a long minute, I slowly opened it again. There was nothing there. There was no sound. None of us ever heard the ghost again.

The slamming of the doors had aroused mother: she peered out of her room. "What on earth are you boys doing?" she demanded. Herman ventured out of his room. "Nothing," he said, gruffly, but he was, in color, a light green. "What was all that running around downstairs?" said mother. So she had heard the steps, too! We just looked at her. "Burglars!" she shouted intuitively. I tried to quiet her by starting lightly downstairs.

"Come on, Herman," I said.

"I'll stay with mother," he said. "She's all excited."

I stepped back onto the landing.

"Don't either of you go a step," said mother. "We'll call the police." Since the phone was downstairs, I didn't see how we were going to call the police—nor did I want the police—but mother made one of her quick, incomparable decisions. She flung up a window of her bedroom which faced the bedroom windows of the house of a neighbor, picked up a shoe, and whammed it through a pane of glass across the narrow space that separated the two houses. Glass tinkled into the bedroom occupied by a retired engraver named Bodwell and his wife. Bodwell had been for some years in rather a bad way and was subject to mild "attacks." Most everybody we knew or lived near had *some* kind of attacks.

It was now about two o'clock of a moonless night; clouds hung black and low. Bodwell was at the window in a minute, shouting, frothing a little, shaking his fist. "We'll sell the house and go back to Peoria," we could hear Mrs. Bodwell saying. It was some time before mother "got through" to Bodwell. "Burglars!" she shouted. "Burglars in the house!" Herman and I hadn't dared to tell her that it was not burglars but ghosts, for she was even more afraid of ghosts than of burglars. Bodwell at first thought that she meant there were burglars in his house, but finally he quieted down and called the police for us over an extension phone by his bed. After he had disappeared from the window, mother suddenly made as if to throw another shoe, not because there was further need of it but, as she later explained, because the thrill of heaving a shoe through a window glass had enormously taken her fancy. I prevented her.

The police were on hand in a commendably short time: a Ford sedan full of them, two on motorcycles, and a patrol wagon with about eight in it and a few reporters. They began banging at our front door. Flashlights shot streaks of gleam up and down the walls, across the yard, down the walk between our house and Bodwell's. "Open up!" cried a hoarse voice. "We're men from Headquarters!" I wanted to go down and let them in, since there they were, but mother wouldn't hear of it. "You haven't a stitch on," she pointed out. "You'd catch your death." I wound the towel around me again. Finally the cops put their shoulders to our big heavy front door with its thick beveled glass and broke it in: I could hear a rending of wood and a splash of glass on the floor of the hall. Their lights played all over the living-room and crisscrossed nervously in the dining-room, stabbed into hall-ways, shot up the front stairs and finally up the back. They caught me standing in my towel at the top. A heavy policeman bounded up the steps. "Who are you?" he demanded. "I live here," I said. "Well, whattsa matta, ya hot?" he asked. It was, as a matter of fact, cold; I went to my room and pulled on some trousers. On my way out, a cop stuck a gun into my ribs. "Whatta you doin' here?" he demanded. "I live here," I said.

The officer in charge reported to mother. "No sign of nobody, lady," he said. "Musta got away—whatt'd he look like?" "There were two or three of them," mother said, "whooping and carrying on and slam-ming doors." "Funny," said the cop. "All ya windows and doors was locked on the inside tight as a tick."

Downstairs, we could hear the tromping of the other police. Police were all over the place; doors were yanked open, drawers were yanked open, windows were shot up and pulled down, furniture fell with dull thumps. A half-dozen policemen emerged out of the darkness of the front hallway upstairs. They began to ransack the floor: pulled beds away from walls, tore clothes off hooks in the closets, pulled suitcases and boxes off shelves. One of them found an old zither that Roy had won in a pool tournament. "Looky here, Joe," he said, strumming it with a big paw. The cop named Joe took it and turned it over. "What is it?" he asked me. "It's an old zither our guinea pig used to sleep on," I said. It was true that a pet guinea pig we once had would never sleep anywhere except on the zither, but I should never have said so. Joe and the other cop looked at me a long time. They put the zither back on a shelf.

"No sign o' nuthin'," said the cop who had first spoken to mother. "This guy," he explained to the others, jerking a thumb at me, "was nekked. The lady seems historical." They all nodded, but said nothing; just looked at me. In the small silence we all heard a creaking in the attic. Grandfather was turning over in bed. "What's 'at?" snapped Joe. Five or six cops sprang for the attic door before I could intervene or explain. I realized that it would be bad if they burst in on grandfather unannounced, or even announced. He was going through a phase in which he believed that General Meade's men, under steady hammering by Stonewall Jackson, were beginning to retreat and even desert.

When I got to the attic, things were pretty confused. Grandfather had evidently jumped to the conclusion that the police were deserters from Meade's army, trying to hide away in his attic. He bounded out of bed wearing a long flannel nightgown over long woolen underwear, a nightcap, and a leather jacket around his chest. The cops must have realized at once that the indignant white-haired old man belonged in the house, but they had no chance to say so. "Back, ye cowardly dogs!"

roared grandfather. "Back t' the lines, ye blasted lily-livered cattle!" With that, he fetched the officer who found the zither a flat-handed smack alongside his head that sent him sprawling. The others beat a retreat, but not fast enough; grandfather grabbed Zither's gun from its holster and let fly. The report seemed to crack the rafters; smoke filled the attic. A cop cursed and shot his hand to his shoulder. Somehow, we all finally got downstairs again and locked the door against the old gentleman. He fired once or twice more in the darkness and then went back to bed. "That was grandfather," I explained to Joe, out of breath. "He thinks you're deserters." "I'll say he does," said Joe.

The cops were reluctant to leave without getting their hands on somebody besides grandfather; the night had been distinctly a defeat for them. Furthermore, they obviously didn't like the "layout;" something looked—and I can see their viewpoint—phony. They began to poke into things again. A reporter, a thin-faced, wispy man, came up to me. I had put on one of mother's blouses, not being able to find anything else. The reporter looked at me with mingled suspicion and interest. "Just what the hell is the real lowdown here, Bud?" he asked. I decided to be frank with him. "We had ghosts," I said. He gazed at me a long time as if I were a slot machine into which he had, without results, dropped a nickel. Then he walked away. The cops followed him, the one grandfather shot holding his now-bandaged arm, cursing and blaspheming. "I'm gonna get my gun back from that old bird," said the zither-cop. "Yeh," said Joe. "You—and who else?" I told them I would bring it to the station house the next day.

"What was the matter with that one policeman?" mother asked, after they had gone. "Grandfather shot him," I said. "What for?" she demanded. I told her he was a deserter. "Of all things!" said mother. "He was such a nice-looking young man."

Grandfather was fresh as a daisy and full of jokes at breakfast next morning. We thought at first he had forgotten all about what had happened, but he hadn't. Over his third cup of coffee, he glared at Herman and me. "What was the idee of all them cops tarryhootin' round the house last night?" he demanded. He had us there.

Reading for Understanding

Main Idea

1. The word that best defines the events in this story is (a) courage (b) intelligence (c) cruelty (d) confusion.

Details

2. When the narrator heard the noise, he first awakened (a) mother (b) grandfather (c) Herman (d) Joe.
3. Grandfather thought he was (a) a member of Stonewall Jackson's army (b) attacking deserters from Meade's army (c) a member of General Lee's staff (d) a messenger behind Union lines.
4. The one with just a towel around him was (a) the narrator (b) grandfather (c) Herman (d) Joe.

Inferences

5. When Herman said, "I'll stay with mother," he was (a) looking out for grandfather (b) extraordinarily brave (c) really scared (d) hoping to trap the ghost.
6. Mrs. Bodwell said, "We'll sell the house and go back to Peoria" because (a) of her neighbors (b) her husband had a new job (c) she needed a larger house (d) of her fear of the ghost.
7. Thurber's attitude toward the police in his house was one of (a) uncritical admiration (b) barely controlled anger (c) good-natured amusement (d) bitter contempt.
8. To say the least, grandfather is (a) a heroic veteran (b) a true family man (c) a friend of the police (d) subject to delusions.

Author's Attitude

9. The author's attitude toward his family is one of (a) justifiable irritation (b) affectionate tolerance (c) studied indifference (d) bitter remembrance.

Order of Events

10. Arrange the items in the order in which they occurred. Use letters only.
    A. Mother throws the shoe.
    B. Grandfather says, "What was the idee of all them cops tarry-hootin' round the house last night?"
    C. The narrator hears footsteps on the stairs.
    D. The police find the zither.
    E. Grandfather shoots a policeman.

Words in Context

1. " 'Awp,' he said, in the low, hopeless tone of a *despondent* beagle."
   Despondent (433) means (a) depressed (b) multicolored (c) vicious
   (d) spirited.
2. " 'Burglars!' she shouted *intuitively*." **Intuitively** (434) means (a)
   expressively (b) instinctively (c) excitedly (d) fearfully.
3. "The police were on hand in a *commendably* short time." **Commendably** (434) means (a) surprisingly (b) measurably (c) suspiciously (d) admirably.

Thinking Critically about the Selection

1. Thurber's language is colorful. Herman wakes up with an "Awp" in
   "the low, hopeless tone of a despondent beagle." Why a beagle and
   not a poodle or an Irish setter? Point out other examples of Thurber's vivid pictures.
2. Ordinarily, writers start a new paragraph for each new speaker, but
   Thurber runs several bits of conversation together in the same paragraph. Do you approve of this technique? Is anything gained?
3. What kind of person is grandfather? How does the last paragraph
   contradict our earlier picture of him?
4. If you've ever seen the Keystone cops in old silent movies, you know
   that they are depicted as comic figures, frantically rushing about,
   often with hilarious results. Are the policemen in this story like
   Keystone Cops? Why does Thurber describe them as he does?
5. What is the reaction of the police and the reporter to the inhabitants
   of the Thurber household? Are their reactions justified?

Language in Action

Malapropisms

"This guy," he explained to the others, jerking a thumb at me, "was
nekkid. The lady seems historical."

The misuse of *historical* for *hysterical* is labeled a *malapropism*. The name derives from Mrs. Malaprop, a character in Richard Brinsley Sheridan's play *The Rivals*. Sheridan coined the name from the French *mal a' propos*—"out of place." Mrs. Malaprop loved to use big words. Unfortunately, she tended to misuse them: *contagious* for *contiguous*, *allegory* for *alligator, delusions* for *allusions, felicity* for *facility, prejudice* for *precipice, reprehend* for *apprehend. Howler* and *boner* are other names for ridiculous blunders in language.

Every area of life is blessed with these humorous errors. A student wrote, "The Constitution of the United States was established to insure domestic hostility." Another wrote, "Emphasis is putting more distress on one word than another." A third, "Louis XVI was gelatined during the French Revolution." A young party hostess suggested that each arriving guest "mangle with the crowd."

Samuel Goldwyn, famous Hollywood producer, was known for his malapropisms, called *Goldwynisms*. Here's a sample. "The man was poised on the brink of an abscess."

Headlines sometimes provide choice examples:

Infant abdicated from hospital table

Court escapee still on the lamb

Philadelphia aims at illitracy

And some newspaper reports:

Kurt Beiner won the Middle School's spelling bee after correctly spelling *desicrate*.

Is your back tired? Are your mussels sore?

The sailor was admired by his piers.

When planting, water the seeds before sewing.

He is recovering from a near-fatal accident that sent him into a comma.

Keep your eye out. Those malapropisms are out there!

For the Fun of It

ACTIVITIES

Thinking Critically about the Selections

1. Madame de Stael wrote, "Wit consists in knowing the resemblance of things that differ, and the difference of things that are alike" What does this quotation mean to you? Do you agree with the point made? (See also page 84, item 3.)

2. Leigh Hunt wrote, "Wit is the clash and reconcilement of incongruities, the meeting of extremes around a corner." Is this a superior definition? Explain.

3. In science fiction, once you accept the basic idea or premise, things fall into place logically. In "All Summer in a Day" (14), for example, once you accept the basic concept—sunshine once in seven years—the story follows logically. Similarly, in "The Stolen White Elephant," once you accept the basic premise of a wild and savage elephant being tracked by a supremely confident, but incompetent detective, everything falls into place. Choose another selection in this unit. Point out the basic premise and point out how all the rest flows logically from it.

4. The poet William Wordsworth wrote, "Poetry is emotion recollected in tranquility." James Thurber wrote, "Humor is emotional chaos remembered in tranquility." How does the Thurber story show that Thurber practiced what he preached?

5. Which story especially appealed to your own sense of humor? Why? What kinds of comedy do you especially enjoy?

6. Don Herold wrote, "A humorist is a man who feels bad but who feels good about it." What do you suppose the writer meant?

7. H. L. Mencken wrote, "Human life is basically a comedy. Even the tragedies often seem comic to the spectator, and not infrequently they actually have comic touches for the victim. Happiness probably consists largely in the capacity to detect and relish them." Does this unusual quotation seem reasonable to you? What do you think Mencken had in mind?

The Writing Portfolio

Purposes of Writing

Writing may be classified by the purpose of the writer. Writing tends to demonstrate one of the following purposes:

1. Writing to inform (directions, explanations, reports)
2. Writing to persuade (editorials, letters to the editor, argumentative essays)
3. Writing to entertain (narrative, description, character sketch)
4. Writing to express oneself (diary, autobiography, poem, personal experience)
5. Writing to remember (notes, summaries, outlines, research papers)

As you look over the following suggestions, choose those you are most interested in.

1. The first chapter of Charles Dickens's *David Copperfield* has the title "I Am Born." Then it begins: "Whether I shall turn out to be the hero of my own life, or whether that station will be held by anybody else, these pages must show."

   Taking a cue from David Copperfield, begin an autobiography that you might complete some day.

2. Write a letter to the editor of your school newspaper suggesting a change of procedure in the lunchroom or some other area of school life.

3. Write a character sketch of Thurber's grandfather ("The Night the Ghost Got In.") Make up any traits needed to round out a picture of that colorful character.

4. Pretend that you have somehow found the Place (393). Write a humorous sketch of your experiences there, with emphasis on what you found there.

5. Do you agree that parents should choose riskier names for babies (425)? Write a light essay with the title "What's in a Name?"

6. Summarize the theme of "Paradiso . . . Inferno?" Where possible avoid using quotations and sentences from the text.

7. How does Mark Twain achieve his comic effects? Point out specific examples and give your opinion of his methods.

8. Benny Smith (426) pays tribute to his beloved grandfather. Is there an older member of your own family who has played a major role in your life? Share your experiences and feelings with others.

Other Areas of Communication

1. If you enjoyed Leacock and Benchley, you may enjoy a book by another humorist of their generation. From the library, borrow a book by Clarence Day, Corey Ford, Jean Kerr, Ring Lardner, S. J. Perelman, Ruth McKenney, Alexander Woollcott, or E. B. White. Report to the class. Consider whether the topics chosen by these writers are different from those chosen by modern-day humorists.

2. *Comic* and *comedian* have sometimes been distinguished by definition. One says funny things; the other says things which are funny. Which is which? Choose a favorite funny person or program on television and decide which definition fits the central character. Compare your choices with other students'.

3. Tape a sitcom and prepare to show it in class. Ask the class to critique it, pointing out good and bad points. What is the source of the humor? Slapstick? Characterization? Witty lines?

4. From your local video store, rent a silent-movie tape, starring Charlie Chaplin, Harold Lloyd, Laurel and Hardy, Buster Keaton, or some other comedian of the period. Be prepared to discuss ways in which the humor of the silent screen differs from that of the talkies. Which do you think requires the greater skill?

5. Before movies and television, opera, along with the stage, had to satisfy people's yearning for stories entertainingly told. Opera has had a fascinating history. Research the topic and prepare to report to class.

6. An Englishman returning to his country once said this about American musical comedies: "Nobody can sing . . . and everybody does!" If you have not seen an actual stage production of an American musical, you may have seen movie versions—for example, *My Fair Lady, Music Man, South Pacific,* and *The King and I;* in your opinion, was the criticism fair?

7. The stories of Saki make for good oral reading. Find "The Open Window" or another Saki story and prepare to read it aloud to the class. Or choose another Thurber story, perhaps from *My Life and Hard Times.*

Language in Action—a Review

You may refer to the preceding sections to answer these questions.

1. By actual count of words in conversation, the majority of words come originally from (a) Latin (b) Greek (c) French (d) Old English.

2. "Let's all go to the matinee today and meet Sally and Fred there." The word that is probably not of Old English origin is (a) *all* (b) *go* (c) *matinee* (d) *meet*.

3. Two words of Latin origin are (a) *collide—collapse* (b) *strike—terrify* (c) *scare—fall* (d) *strike—fall*.

4. Norman-French words were basically (a) Old English (b) Latin (c) Italian (d) Germanic.

5. After the Norman Invasion, Norman words tended to (a) show who held the power (b) destroy all traces of Old English (c) have little influence on the language (d) disappear.

6. The common root of *autograph, biography, telegraph,* and *graphic* means (a) sound (b) write (c) person (d) life.

7. The major function of the hyphen is to (a) separate words in series (b) make quotations clearer (c) join parts of a compound sentence (d) link words.

8. The idioms of a language (a) mean the same in other languages (b) are especially difficult for a foreigner (c) can be understood by studying each word individually (d) play a tiny role in communication.

9. Of the following examples, idiom is best illustrated by (a) The Andersons are well off. (b) I own a Yorkshire terrier. (c) The math test is tomorrow (d) Terry is going to Toledo tomorrow.

10. Of the following, the one that does NOT contain a malapropism is (a) Bruce won the tennis tourniquet (b) Julius Seized was assassinated on the steps of the capitol. (c) Three counter fitters were arrested for passing money obviously not genuine. (d) Our cat Spots is canny, crafty, and demanding.

UNIT SIX

The Power of Poetry

Carlyle once said of Tennyson: "Alfred is always carrying a bit of chaos around with him, and turning it into a cosmos." Well, that is poetry's job, and it is amazingly like the enterprise of life.

John Livingstone Lowes

The rituals of the earliest people seem to be in a form we might label **poetry**. Primitive chants as well as modern hymns have a special quality that might be called **poetic**. Like Samuel Johnson on page 449, a student once said, "I know what poetry is until you ask me. Then I'm not sure just what it means."

When you hear something you particularly enjoy, you might say, "That's poetry." Just what the quality is that makes it poetry is difficult to explain. Poetry has meant different things to different people.

In this unit, you'll meet different kinds of poetry: narrative, dramatic, lyric, and humorous. There will be some overlapping, since all classifications are matters of convenience and not written in stone. You will also read an opening essay: "Poetry . . . What Is It?" After you have finished the unit, you may have a better idea of how selections may be classified as poetry. You will also meet some poems that will amuse you, entertain you, and touch you.

Poetry . . . What Is It?

The most beautiful, impressive, and widely effective mode of saying things.

—Matthew Arnold

Robert Frost, Emily Dickinson, Walt Whitman, and Alfred, Lord Tennyson are considered great poets. Are they? Why? What is poetry anyway? How can you tell? Would you like to decide for yourself?

Six Selections

Here are six selections. Are they all poetry? Some? Which?

1. A flea and fly in a flue
   Were imprisoned, so what could they do?
   "Let us fly," said the flea.
   Said the fly, "Let us flee."
   So they flew through a flaw in the flue.
2. This goodly frame, the earth, seems to me a sterile promontory.
   This most excellent canopy, the air, look you, this brave
   o'erhanging firmament, this majestical roof fretted with
   golden fire, why it appears no other thing to me than a foul
   and pestilent congregation of vapors.
3. The pedigree of honey
   Does not concern the bee;

A clover, any time, to him
is aristocracy.

4. Now you will feel no rain
For each of you will be shelter to the other.
Now you will feel no cold
For each of you will be warmth to the other.
Now there is no loneliness. Now there is no loneliness.
Now you are two persons but there is but one life before you.
Go now to your dwelling place
To enter into the days of your togetherness
And may your days be good and long upon the earth.

5. Snow
        in the northern hills . . .
Rain
        in the coastal valleys . . .
Fog
        along the
                shores . . .
Today.

6.   Peonies scattering,
    two or three petals
        lie on one another.

Poetry . . . or Not?

Well, what did you think? How do you rate these as poetry? Let's
identify them and find out whether you change your rating after you
discover who wrote them. Does a selection become a poem because a
famous poet wrote it?

The first is a limerick that has come down to us from an uncertain
source and authorship. The second is a quotation from Shakespeare's
Hamlet. It is written in the form of prose, but it is often considered
"poetic." The third is a brief poem written by Emily Dickinson. The
fourth is an Apache wedding blessing. The fifth is a weather report taken
from the newspaper and arranged in "poetic" form. The sixth is a haiku
by the famous Japanese poet, Buson.

Are all of these poetry? Any of them? How can you tell? There is, in truth, no final answer. There is no one in a position to say, for example, "The second selection is true poetry, but selection six is not."

Defining Poetry

To make such a statement, we must first define *poetry*, but no one has yet succeeded in doing that successfully. There have been many attempts, as we shall see below, but there has never been precise agreement on what constitutes poetry. Even if we were able to arrive at such an agreement, we'd soon find that the application would present problems. We might, for example, arbitrarily define poetry as "a selection composed of four-line stanzas, with alternating lines of four feet and three feet. In each stanza, lines 2 and 4 must rhyme." We have, in fact, actually defined the *ballad* (466).

So far so good, but such a narrow, mechanical definition of poetry would not satisfy most people. They would consider such a definition too rigid. They might suggest that there must be an emotional content, use of visual imagery, clever use of sound effect.

Note the following attempts at a definition of poetry.

(a) "Poetry is . . . the spontaneous overflow of powerful emotions recollected in tranquillity."

—William Wordsworth

(b) "Poetry is at bottom a biography, the life of a man."

—Thomas Carlyle

(c) Poetry is "the language of feeling."

—Benedetto Croce

(d) "Prose is words in their best order; poetry, the best words in the best order."

—Samuel Taylor Coleridge

(e) "Poetry is the lava of imagination, whose eruption prevents the earthquake."

—Lord Byron

(f) "Poetry is not a science, it is an act of faith."

—Robert Graves

(g) "A poem should not mean
But be."

—Archibald MacLeish

(h) "Like a piece of ice on a hot stove, the poem must ride on its own melting."

—Robert Frost

 (i) "If poetry comes not as naturally as the leaves to a tree, it had better not come at all."

—John Keats

 (j) Poetry is "imaginary gardens with real toads in them."

—Marianne Moore

(k) "Every poem says much in little. It packs into the fewest possible words—by means of their sound, their sense, and their companionship—a wide or rare experience."

—Walter de la Mare

The preceding definitions are but a sample of descriptions of poetry that have come down to us through the years. A. E. Housman suggested, "Poetry seems to me more physical than intellectual." Robert Frost seemed to agree when he said a poem begins "as a lump in the throat, a sense of wrong, a homesickness, a lovesickness." Emily Dickinson said, "If I read a book and it makes my whole body so cold no fire can warm me, I know that is poetry."

Samuel Johnson said, "What is poetry? Why, Sir, it is much easier to say what it is not. We all know what light is, but it is not easy to tell what it is."

A student reacting to the weather report on page 447 said, "That must be poetry. It turns me on." Perhaps that is as good a definition as any. In this unit, you'll find many selections that have been classified as poetry. Perhaps some of these may turn you on.

The Four Ingredients

Perhaps when you were young, you thought that poetry had to have rhyme because so many poems for children do rhyme. Then you learned that the poetry in Shakespeare's plays rarely does rhyme. Or perhaps you felt that poems ought to have a definite rhythm. Then you came across the free verse of Walt Whitman, poetry without a regular rhythm. Whenever one ingredient is suggested as an essential part of poetry, you come upon a perfectly respectable poem without it.

There are, however, four basic ingredients which seem to be a part of most works classified as poetry. These ingredients can be remembered easily by recalling the key word TIME. Each letter refers to an important ingredient.

Thought

Imagery

Music

Emotion

Thought refers to the intellectual content of a poem, the idea that the poet seeks to present. *Imagery* refers to the figures of speech and to the appeals to the senses frequently used in poetry. *Music* refers to the poet's use of sound to gain an effect. Rhythm, rhyme, and onomatopoeia (use of words to suggest the sounds themselves) are some of the "musical" devices that poets call upon. *Emotion* is often the driving force behind the poem. Indignation, grief, and the joy of living are often portrayed in poetry. Picasso once said, "The artist is a receptacle for emotions that come from everywhere: from the sky, from the earth, from a scrap of paper, from a spider's web."

There is a fifth element, compression, which is usually characteristic of poetry. Poems condense experience. An old ballad like "Lord Randal" (466) tells a tragedy that could fill a volume—and it tells the tale in a handful of stanzas. Notice the compression in Emily Dickinson's poem on pedigrees (446). In four lines she ridicules snobbish claims to extra worth because of illustrious ancestors. Note, too, that she uses a comparison—the honey and the bee—to make her point.

Poetry and Everyday Life

The poet uses words in special ways, but such skill is not confined to the poet. Everyday speech is filled with touches of poetry. Think of these flower names: *baby's breath, Lady's slipper orchid, foxglove, love-in-a-mist, butter-and-eggs, forget-me-not, crown of thorns, adder's tongue, birdfoot violet, bluebonnet, Dutchman's breeches.* Some names may conceal the poetic meanings. *Dandelion* means "lion's tooth." A *daisy* is "the day's eye." An *aster* is "a star."

Two Ways of Writing a Poem

Compare the following two selections:

(a) Flower in the crannied wall,
  I pluck you out of the crannies:—

Hold you here, root and all, in my hand,
Little flower—but if I could understand
What you are, root and all, and all in all,
I should know what God and Man is.

—Alfred, Lord Tennyson
British

(b)   When I looked under the hedge—
the little grass called a shepherd's purse
was flowering.

—Basho
Japanese

The first is by one of the greatest English poets, Alfred, Lord Tennyson, once Poet Laureate of England. The second is by Basho, a great seventeenth-century Japanese poet. He perfected the haiku, a Japanese poem with seventeen syllables. You'll find more examples on pages 483–484.

The most striking similarity is the setting of the poems. In both, the poet sees a flower, and in both he tries to capture the scene for us. In both, the flower itself is inconspicuous. There is a gentle quiet mood in both poems.

There the similarities end, however, and the differences appear. There is an obvious difference in the length: three lines by Basho and six by Tennyson. The central difference is the attitude of the poet toward the flower. Basho notes it and captures it in a few syllables. He doesn't philosophize about it. He usually avoids philosophizing about life or seeking deeper meanings in symbols. In one haiku, he says,

How admirable:
to see lightning and not think
life is fleeting.

He seems to say, "Get away from excessive reliance on symbols. Life is life, not a flash of lightning, a pathless wood, or a great sea." His approach cuts through many of the symbolic devices that poets have relied upon. Basho's flower is a flower, not a symbol of the puzzle of life.

Tennyson, by contrast, uses the flower as a reason for commenting upon the mystery of life. Basho doesn't touch the flower. Tennyson uproots it. Basho doesn't exert domination over nature. Tennyson does. Nature is secondary to his musing about the meaning of life.

Which is the greater poem? As we have already seen, such a question is almost meaningless. Which do you prefer? That, at least, is a question that can be answered.

Even if we could define *better*, there would be little point in trying to decide which is better, since they are so different in style and approach. They demonstrate two altogether different approaches to poetry and, as such, deserve our attention.

Basho's approach tends to be more characteristic of some Eastern poetry, particularly of the haiku. Even in Japanese haiku, however, philosophy sometimes appears. And there are many touches in most Western poets that remind us of Basho's writing and of the Japanese haiku.

Note how the following lines from Shakespeare's *A Midsummer Night's Dream* resemble the haiku in the direct observation of flowers without pondering what they might mean.

> I know a bank where the wild thyme blows,
> Where oxlips and the nodding violet grows
> Quite over-canopied with luscious woodbine,
> With sweet musk-roses, and with eglantine.

The most famous haiku, possibly one of the most famous poems in the world, is by Basho.

> The old pond—
> a frog jumps in,
> sound of water.

If you've ever had the experience, these few syllables will bring it back to you.

That's Life

As we have seen, poets have two quite different ways of presenting an experience. They also have two distinguishable ways of reacting to life itself. They may accept life as it is, without attempting to judge, bless, criticize, or praise it. Or they may seek to evaluate life, to appraise it, put it into manageable boxes. The approach is often dictated by culture rather than conscious choice.

Some Eastern philosophies, notably Taoism and Zen, accept life and avoid making judgments and generalizations. Most Western philosophies seek to discover "the meaning of life" and to relate people to themselves, their fellows, their society, and the universe. Most Westerners agree with Socrates, who said, "An unexamined life is not worth living."

Western philosophies often stress action, doing. Eastern philosophies often stress quiet awareness and meditation. Westerners have a way of saying, "Don't just stand there; do something." Eastern philosophies may suggest, "Don't just do something; stand there." These different philosophies are reflected in the poetry in this unit.

Poets vary in their approach to the problems of life just as they vary in their re-creation of vivid experiences.

For Longfellow (*American*):

Life is real! Life is earnest!
    And the grave is not its goal;
Dust thou are, to dust returnest,
    Was not spoken of the soul.

For Shelley (*British*):

Life, like a dome of many-colored glass,
Stains the white radiance of Eternity,
Until Death tramples it to fragments.

For Issa (*Japanese*):

The world of dew
is the world of dew,
    And yet, and yet—

Even a writer of haiku dealing with simple observations allows himself an occasional comment about life's brevity. This haiku of Issa's is sometimes translated as "Dew evaporates, and all our world is dew."

How have the writers defined life? Samuel Butler said, "Life is playing a violin solo in public and learning the instrument as one goes on." Life has been called a "disease" (Alexander Pope), a "vapor that appeareth for a little time, and then vanisheth away" (James 4:14), a "march" (John Fletcher), a "winter's day" (Francis Quarles), a flight of a sparrow (the Venerable Bede), a "jest" (John Gay), a "fatal complaint" (O.W. Holmes), "a long lesson in humility" (J. M. Barrie), a "long headache" (John Masefield), a "gleam of time between two eternities" (Thomas Carlyle), a "fairy tale" (Hans Christian Andersen), a "series of surprises" (R. W. Emerson), the "art of avoiding pain" (Thomas Jefferson), a "game that must be played" (E. A. Robinson).

The musical *Fiddler on the Roof* has a memorable song, "L'chayim," "To life!" Poets have been singing this song since the dawn of history.

Understanding a Challenging Poem

The haiku are simple, easily understandable, but not superficial. They capture a moment in time like a three-dimensional snapshot. But they don't require some hard thinking to ferret out their meanings. Occasionally a poem is more difficult, more complex. Part of the pleasure lies in digging out the meaning. A poem that is perhaps most often misunderstood or only partially understood is Shelley's "Ozymandias."

> I met a traveler from an antique land
> Who said: "Two vast and trunkless legs of stone
> Stand in the desert . . . Near them, on the sand,
> Half sunk, a shattered visage lies, whose frown,
> And wrinkled lip, and sneer of cold command 5
> Tell that its sculptor well those passions read
> Which yet survive, stamped on these lifeless things,
> The hand that mocked them, and the heart that fed;
> And on the pedestal these words appear;
> 'My name is Ozymandias, king of kings; 10
> Look on my works, ye Mighty, and despair!'
> Nothing beside remains. Round the decay
> Of that colossal wreck, boundless and bare
> The lone and level sands stretch far away."

Most readers understand the theme of the poem without difficulty: the futility of earthly ambition in the setting of eternity. Great Ozymandias, despite his boast, is all but forgotten. His empire has disappeared and his fame is a mockery. His fallen statue symbolizes his lost wealth, power and fame.

Most readers are content to stop here, but if they do, they miss a delightful story concealed in lines 3–8. There is a little human drama revealed there for us—of a domineering, powerful king and an unimportant artist, but in the end the artist has the last word. The story is all there. It's a kind of puzzle. After you have studied lines 3–8 to your own satisfaction, consider these questions:

1. Whose hand and whose heart are mentioned in line 8?

2. Who did the sneering and who did the mocking? What was the sculptor's attitude toward the king?

3. What has survived (line 7)? What is the object of *survive*?

4. What was "stamped on these lifeless things"? What are the "lifeless things"? Who did the stamping?

5. How does the word *well* (line 6) tell us that the sculptor has psychological insight?

6. What passions are referred to in line 6?

7. What is the subject of *survive,* line 7?

How well did you understand lines 3–8? Now consider these possible answers to the questions.

1. It was the sculptor's hand and the king's heart.

2. Ozymandias did the sneering, and the sculptor did the mocking. The sculptor obviously disliked the king.

3. The passions have survived. They have survived both "the hand that mocked them" (the sculptor's) and "the heart that fed [them]" (the king's). They have survived because they have been stamped on stone.

4. The passions have been stamped on stone ("lifeless things") by the sculptor.

5. He "read those passions well," that is, with keen insight, for he was able to reproduce the passions in stone by means of the "frown," the "wrinkled lip," and the "sneer of cold command."

6. The passions are those of self-indulgence, a sense of power and one's own importance, an arrogant way of dealing with subordinates.

7. The subject is *which.* The antecedent of *which* is *passions.*

These questions and answers have illuminated the scene, with its two characters: the cruel king and the irreverent sculptor. Though the king has used his power to force the sculptor to do his bidding, the sculptor has made a lasting comment about the king. He has captured the king's worst qualities in stone. It is these that have survived.

Understanding this little scene within the poem deepens the irony of the poem. Not only do we learn that the king's fame, power, wealth, and empire have disappeared, but we also learn that something personal *has* survived after all. And what is that legacy to posterity? The artist's rendering of the tyrant's true character—frown, wrinkled lip, and sneer of cold command! Any interpretation of "Ozymandias" which overlooks the subtle irony of the sculptor's victory over temporal power misses half the enjoyment of the poem. Some poems, like the humorous poems on pages 494–507, can be enjoyed on the first reading. Others, like "My Last Duchess" (pages 464–465), call for closer reading. The poems that follow in this unit will provide a cross-section of poetic types. For convenience, the labels *Poem* and *Poetry* will be used throughout the unit.

Reading for Understanding

Main Idea

1. A major idea of this essay is that (a) all poetry, however varied in content, has the same style (b) the haiku is a verse form that is superior to the ballad (c) poetry defies an exact definition (d) a selection needs to have a strong rhythm to qualify as poetry.

Details

2. Two Shakespearean quotations mentioned in the essay are from (a) *Hamlet* and *Julius Caesar* (b) "*Ozymandias*" and *A Midsummer Night's Dream* (c) *Julius Caesar* and "*Ozymandias*" (d) *Hamlet* and *A Midsummer Night's Dream*.

3. The flower poem was written by (a) Tennyson (b) Shelley (c) Keats (d) Dickinson.

4. The person who called poetry "imaginary gardens with real toads in them" is (a) Robert Frost (b) Marianne Moore (c) Lord Byron (d) Thomas Carlyle.

5. All the following are mentioned as creators of haiku except (a) Basho (b) Buson (c) Onitsura (d) Issa.

Inferences

6. If we judge by the example on page 446, a limerick tends to be (a) humorous (b) intense (c) unrhymed (d) serious.

7. According to Housman, Frost, and Dickinson (449), poetry leads to (a) unquestioned joy (b) a physical reaction (c) an extreme curiosity (d) a mellow sadness.

8. Picasso's quotation (450) (a) applies only to painters (b) reflects a narrow point of view (c) is too far-fetched to be taken seriously (d) explains a source of poetry.

Author's Purpose

9. The author's purpose in providing the six selections on pages 446–447 is to (a) show the difference between poetry and mere verse (b) introduce readers to a beautiful Apache blessing (c) challenge readers to consider their ideas of poetry (d) compare Dickinson and Shakespeare.

Fact or Opinion

Tell whether the following is a fact or an opinion.

10. The most satisfying poetry uses rhyme for a special effect.

Words in Context

1. "We might, for example, *arbitrarily* define poetry as a 'selection composed of four-line stanzas, with alternating lines of four feet and three feet.'" *Arbitrarily* (448) means (a) high-handedly (b) unintentionally (c) accurately (d) humorously.

2. "Flower in the crannied wall, I pluck you out of the *crannies.*" *Crannies* (450) are (a) pockets of earth (b) cracks (c) stone faces (d) varieties of vegetation.

3. "Even a writer of haiku dealing with simple observations allows himself an occasional comment about life's *brevity.*" *Brevity* (453) means (a) bitterness (b) confusion (c) briefness (d) challenge.

4. "Life is 'a long lesson in humility.'" *Humility* (453) means (a) patience (b) love (c) disappointment (d) humbleness.

5. "The haiku are simple, easily understandable, but not *superficial.*" *Superficial* (454) means (a) intentionally confusing (b) shallow (c) imitative (d) obscure.

6. "The passions are those of *self-indulgence,* a sense of power and one's own importance, an arrogant way of dealing with subordinates." *Self-indulgence* (455) is opposed to (a) self-control (b) self-criticism (c) self-satisfaction (d) selfishness.

Thinking Critically about the Essay

1. If it is difficult to define poetry exactly and finally, what is the point of using the label *poetry* at all?

2. If you were asked to apply a label to each of the six selections on pages 446–447, to which ones would you apply the label poetry? Why?

3. If you compare the Tennyson poem and the Basho haiku on pages 450–451, which appeals to you more? Why? How does your choice suggest your own philosophy of life?

4. How does Lord Byron's definition of poetry (*c* on page 448) differ from Robert Frost's (*h* on page 449)? What point of similarity is there?

5. *Colossal* (454) comes from the Greek legend of the Colossus of Rhodes, a giant statue at the entrance to the harbor. How did the word acquire its present meaning? What other legends are suggested in the following words. Choose four to look up. A good dictionary will supply the answers.

atlas	hygiene	mercurial	stentorian
aurora	iridescent	music	tantalize
cereal	January	odyssey	Thursday
echo	jovial	panic	titanic
Friday	labyrinth	protean	Tuesday
helium	martial	saturnine	volcano
hyacinth	mausoleum	siren	Wednesday

See also Allusions (223).

6. How do you rate Matthew Arnold's definition of poetry (446) with those listed on page 448? If you had to choose one, which would you choose?

7. Another famous Basho haiku is the following:

>   A crow
>   has settled on a bare branch—
>   autumn evening.

What picture does this suggest to you? What is the mood of the selection? What words suggest that mood?

8. Many flower names are metaphors (150). Parts of the body also suggest metaphors; for example, a *leg* of the chair, a *head* of cabbage. How many more can you suggest?

9. "I was embarrassed" is a literal expression. "I nearly died from embarrassment" is figurative (22). *Literally* and *figuratively* are sometimes used incorrectly. Point out the absurdity of the following expression:

> When Bud tried to fill Dad's ears with a lame excuse, Dad's eyes popped, his cheeks flamed, and he literally hit the ceiling.

Language in Action

Figures of Speech (Figurative Language)

If we call a football lineman a *tiger*, we know that he's not a tiger, merely being compared with a tiger. The list of poetic flower word names on page 450 suggests many comparisons. An implied comparison like these is called a *metaphor*. Metaphors are common in everyday speech. A bowler *runs up* a score. We hate to *catch* a cold. He *caught* her warning glance.

A *simile* is also a comparison, but it is more obvious, using *like* or *as*. Ted is *like a bulldog* when he sets his mind on something. (Note also the metaphor *sets*.)

Personification gives human traits to things not human, animate or inanimate. Duty *calls*. Injustice *cries out*.

Metonymy substitutes one word for another closely associated with it. The kettle *boils*. (The water in the kettle boils, not the kettle itself.)

Synecdoche substitutes a part for the whole or a whole for the part. The Adamses have 40 *head* of cattle. (They own the cattle as well as the heads!) Kentucky defeated Syracuse. (The basketball teams, not the universities, won and lost.)

Though the names may fade away, keep in mind that figurative language is a major thread in all communication. Figurative language says "It is what it isn't," and we all enjoy using it.

Narrative and Dramatic Poetry

I gave commands
Then all smiles stopped together.

—Robert Browning

This, one of the most chilling quotations in all of poetry, suggests some of the range of poetry. In later chapters, you'll meet lyric and humorous poetry. Here, poetry tells a story, sometimes a dark one, as in "My Last Duchess;" sometimes a light one, as in "The Passionate Shepherd" and "The Nymph's Reply." Poetry, because of its compression, can say much in little. Sometimes mere suggestion can tell volumes.

Narrative poetry is ancient. The urge to tell a story before enchanted listeners inspired bards to tell and retell great legends. Sometimes these narratives flowered in the great epics:

Gilgamesh—Sumer

Beowulf—England (and Northern Europe)

The Odyssey and the Iliad of Homer—Ancient Greece

The Aeneid—Rome

The line between narrative and dramatic poetry blurs. There are dramatic elements in the epics. The confrontation between Hector and Achilles, for example, is filled with the elements of strong characterization, sharp dialogue, potential action. The **Iliad** is filled with other dramatic encounters. Similarly, there are narrative elements in dramatic poetry. The story of the Duke of Ferrara and his "last duchess" has a plot, motivation, conflict, and resolution. The high point of dramatic poetry, according to many critics, is the poetry of Shakespeare's plays, as in the quotation on page 446.

Old ballads are often cast in dramatic form. "Lord Randal" (466) is presented simply as a dialogue between a son and his mother. There are no extraneous elements, no opinions, no interpretations. The story is presented as simply and directly as it's possible to do. The simplicity intensifies the impact.

In addition to the dramatic poems, this section contains a sampling of narrative poems. Here the story is the important element, but compression is still the essential characteristic.

The Passionate Shepherd to His Love

Christopher Marlowe
British

The Nymph's Reply to the Shepherd

Attributed to Sir Walter Raleigh
British

Why So Pale and Wan, Fond Lover?

Sir John Suckling
British

In the long history of poetry, few poems interlock with each other as the first two do. In a spirit of romantic enthusiasm, Christopher Marlowe pens an invitation that is as contemporary as a personal computer. Why not give in to pleasure, taking no thought of tomorrow? Why not indulge every impulse? Why not?

Why not, indeed! Sir Walter Raleigh bends a hard and skeptical eye on the invitation. He matches a realistic probability with every inviting inducement in the first poem. These were written four hundred years ago, but the sentiments and humor speak to us across the centuries. It also has a bit of advice for modern nymphs!

To balance the advice to young women, Sir John Suckling provides some practical advice to a lovelorn young man. Here, *fond* means foolish. The three poems suggest that love and infatuation haven't changed in those 400 years!

The Passionate Shepherd to His Love

Come live with me and be my love,
And we will all the pleasures prove
That hills and valleys, dales and fields,
Or woods or steepy mountain yields.

And we will sit upon the rocks   5
And see the shepherds feed their flocks
By shallow rivers, to whose falls
Melodious birds sing madrigals.*

And I will make thee beds of roses
And a thousand fragrant posies;   10
A cap of flowers, and a kirtle*
Embroidered all with leaves of myrtle;

A gown made of the finest wool
Which from our pretty lambs we pull;
Fair-linèd slippers for the cold,   15
With buckles of the purest gold;

A belt of straw and ivy buds
With coral clasps and amber studs—
And if these pleasures may thee move,
Come live with me and be my love.   20

The shepherd swains* shall dance and sing
For thy delight each May morning—
If these delights thy mind may move,
Then live with me and be my love.

The Nymph's Reply to the Shepherd

If all the world and love were young,
And truth in every shepherd's tongue,
These pretty pleasures might me move,
To live with thee and be thy love.

*madrigals: lyrics adapted to a musical setting   kirtle: gown   swains: young gallants

But time drives flocks from field to fold,   5
When rivers rage, and rocks grow cold;
And Philomel* becometh dumb;
The rest complains of cares to come.

The flowers do fade, and wanton* fields
To wayward winter reckoning yields;
A honey tongue, a heart of gall,*   10
Is fancy's spring, but sorrow's fall.

Thy gowns, thy shoes, thy beds of roses,
Thy cap, thy kirtle, and thy posies,
Soon break, soon wither, soon forgotten,   15
In folly ripe, in reason rotten.

Thy belt of straw and ivy buds,
Thy coral clasps and amber studs,
All these in me no means can move,
To come to thee and be thy love.   20

But could youth last, and love still breed,
Had joys no date,* nor age no need,
Then these delights my mind might move,
To live with thee and be thy love.

Why So Pale and Wan, Fond Lover?

Why so pale and wan, fond lover?
  Prithee, why so pale?
Will, when looking well can't move her,
  Looking ill prevail?
  Prithee, why so pale?

Why so dull and mute, young sinner?
  Prithee, why so mute?
Will, when speaking well can't win her,
  Saying nothing do't?
  Prithee, why so mute?

Quit, quit, for shame; this will not move,
  This cannot take her.
If of herself she will not love,
  Nothing can make her:
  The devil take her!

---

*Philomel: the nightingale   wanton: merry, gay   gall: bitterness   date: end

My Last Duchess

Robert Browning
British

The previous poems were light and humorous, but this poem is quite the opposite. Put in the form of a dramatic monologue, the poem tells the story of an arrogant duke and his unfortunate wife. In a dramatic monologue, we must imagine a dialogue, but we hear only one speaker. It's much like listening to someone receiving a telephone call. From the one speaker we can hear, we must construct the conversation and the setting. In a play, a soliloquy involves a character speaking directly to the audience, thinking out loud. A dramatic monologue, on the other hand, suggests a listener, here an emissary to the Duke from a neighboring Count.

Imagine the two men walking along admiring the Duke's works of art. Perhaps the emissary sees a beautiful painting on the wall. The Duke replies, "That's my last Duchess painted on the wall." The poem takes off from there.

As you read, note that the Duke monopolizes the conversation. In his own mind, he is a man of good taste and fine sensibility, but the poem reveals him as a monster. Look for clues.

My Last Duchess

Scene: Ferrara

That's my last Duchess painted on the wall,
Looking as if she were alive. I call
That piece a wonder, now: Frà Pandolf's* hands
Worked busily a day, and there she stands.
Will't please you sit and look at her? I said   5
"Frà Pandolf" by design, for never read
Strangers like you that pictured countenance,
The depth and passion of its earnest glance,
But to myself they turned (since none puts by
The curtain I have drawn for you, but I)   10
And seemed as they would ask me, if they durst,
How such a glance came there; so, not the first
Are you to turn and ask thus. Sir, 'twas not
Her husband's presence only, called that spot

Frà Pandolf: a fictitious painter and monk of the Italian Renaissance. "Frà" means "Brother."

Of joy into the Duchess' cheek: perhaps   15
Frà Pandolf chanced to say, "Her mantle laps
Over my Lady's wrist too much," or "Paint
Must never hope to reproduce the faint
Half-flush that dies along her throat"; such stuff
Was courtesy, she thought, and cause enough   20
For calling up that spot of joy. She had
A heart—how shall I say?—too soon made glad,
Too easily impressed; she liked whate'er
She looked on, and her looks went everywhere.
Sir, 'twas all one! My favor* at her breast,   25
The dropping of the daylight in the West,
The bough of cherries some officious fool
Broke in the orchard for her, the white mule
She rode with round the terrace—all and each
Would draw from her alike the approving speech,   30
Or blush, at least. She thanked men—good; but thanked
Somehow—I know not how—as if she ranked
My gift of a nine-hundred-years-old name
With anybody's gift. Who'd stoop to blame
This sort of trifling? Even had you skill   35
In speech (which I have not) to make your will
Quite clear to such an one, and say, "Just this
Or that in you disgusts me; here you miss,
Or there exceed the mark"—and if she let
Herself be lessoned so, nor plainly set   40
Her wits to yours, forsooth, and made excuse
—E'en then would be some stooping, and I choose
Never to stoop. Oh sir, she smiled, no doubt,
Whene'er I passed her; but who passed without
Much the same smile? This grew; I gave commands;   45
Then all smiles stopped together. There she stands
As if alive. Will 't please you rise? We'll meet
The company below, then. I repeat,
The Count your master's known munificence
Is ample warrant that no just pretense   50
Of mine for dowry will be disallowed;
Though his fair daughter's self, as I avowed
At starting, is my object. Nay, we'll go
Together down, sir. Notice Neptune, though,
Taming a sea horse, thought a rarity,   55
Which Claus of Innsbruck cast in bronze for me!

*jewelry

Lord Randal

Anonymous
English Ballad

For incredible compression, few poems can match folk ballads. These wonderful little poems have come down to us from the past without ascribed authorship. Each one tells a story. Sometimes the tale is humorous like that wifely victory in "Get Up and Bar the Door" (498). Sometimes, though, the story is a dark and violent one, as in "Lord Randal."

The ballad is in the form of a dramatic dialogue between a young man and his mother. The first two lines of each stanza present the mother's questions. The second two lines present the son's answers. The first stanza is a neutral one. A young man is tired and seeks rest. But as the poem develops, we learn of foul play—first hinted at and then admitted. At what point does the mother begin to suspect foul play? How does the son finally tell of the plot against him, suggesting who his murderer is?

Note that the ballad implies much more than it says. The young man's deceptive calm conceals a horrible tragedy. Here we have enough material for a full-length motion picture, but it's all contained in five simple stanzas. We are left to ponder characterization and motive.

Lord Randal

15th Century

"O where hae ye been, Lord Randal, my son?
O where hae ye been, my handsome young man?"
"I hae been to the wild wood; mother, make my bed soon,
For I'm weary wi' hunting, and fain wald lie down."

"Where gat ye your dinner, Lord Randal, my son?   5
Where gat ye your dinner, my handsome young man?"
"I dined wi' my true love; mother, make my bed soon,
For I'm weary wi' hunting, and fain wald lie down."

"What gat ye to your dinner, Lord Randal, my son?
What gat ye to your dinner my handsome young man?"   10
"I gat eels boiled in broo;* mother, make my bed soon,
For I'm weary wi' hunting, and fain wald lie down."

---

*broo: broth

"What became of your bloodhounds, Lord Randal, my son?
What became of your bloodhounds, my handsome young
    man?"
"O they swelled and they died; mother, make my bed soon,   15
For I'm weary wi' hunting, and fain wald lie down."

"O I fear ye are poisoned, Lord Randal, my son!
O I fear ye are poisoned, my handsome young man!"
"O yes! I am poisoned; mother, make my bed soon,
For I'm sick at the heart, and I fain wald lie down."   20

Lochinvar

Sir Walter Scott
Scottish

The previous four poems all dealt with love or its counterfeit. "Lochinvar" is a true love story, complete with a young couple in love about to be thwarted by the young lady's father. Once again, poetry shows its skill in compression. There is a plot. There are well-drawn characters: fearless Lochinvar, his shy love, the unworthy groom-to-be, the overbearing father. There is a whirlwind narrative, as Lochinvar takes his fate in his own hands. A rollicking rhythm carries the story along. There is suspense as the lovers try to make their escape.

This seems the kind of story that belongs only to an age of romanticism when gallant young men dared everything for love. Actually, though, the same story line is used in Dustin Hoffman's early hit movie, *The Graduate*. Like Lochinvar, Hoffman steals the beautiful bride, Katharine Ross, from under the noses of the bride's family, at the altar.

Lochinvar

Oh, young Lochinvar is come out of the West,—
Through all the wide Border his steed was the best,
And, save his good broadsword, he weapon had none,—
He rode all unarmed, and he rode all alone.
So faithful in love, and so dauntless in war,
There never was knight like the young Lochinvar.

He stayed not for brake, and he stopped not for stone,
He swam the Eske river where ford there was none,
But, ere he alighted at Netherby gate,
The bride had consented, the gallant came late:
For a laggard in love, and a dastard in war,
Was to wed the fair Ellen of brave Lochinvar.

So boldly he entered the Netherby hall,
Among bridesmen, and kinsmen, and brothers, and all.
Then spoke the bride's father, his hand on his sword,
(For the poor craven bridegroom said never a word),
"Oh, come ye in peace here, or come ye in war,
Or to dance at our bridal, young Lord Lochinvar?"

"I long wooed your daughter, my suit you denied;—
Love swells like the Solway, but ebbs like its tide;—
And now am I come, with this lost love of mine,
To lead but one measure, drink one cup of wine.
There are maidens in Scotland more lovely by far,
That would gladly be bride to the young Lochinvar."

The bride kissed the goblet, the knight took it up,
He quaffed off the wine, and he threw down the cup.
She looked down to blush, and she looked up to sigh,
With a smile on her lips, and a tear in her eye.
He took her soft hand ere her mother could bar:
"Now tread we a measure," said young Lochinvar.

So stately his form, and so lovely her face,
That never a hall such a galliard did grace;
While her mother did fret, and her father did fume,
And the bridegroom stood dangling his bonnet and plume,
And the bridemaidens whispered, "'Twere better by far
To have matched our fair cousin with young Lochinvar."

One touch to her hand, and one word in her ear,
When they reached the hall-door, and the charger stood near;
So light to the croupe the fair lady he swung,
So light to the saddle before her he sprung!
"She is won! we are gone! over bank, bush, and scaur;*
They'll have fleet steeds that follow," quoth young Lochinvar.

---

*bare place on a mountainside

There was mounting 'mong Graemes of the Netherby clan;
Forsters, Fenwicks, and Musgraves, they rode and they ran;
There was racing and chasing on Cannobie Lee,
But the lost bride of Netherby ne'er did they see.
So daring in love, and so dauntless in war,
Have ye e'er heard of gallant like young Lochinvar?

The River Merchant's Wife: a Letter

A dramatic poem can take many forms, as we have seen. One of the most effective is a simple letter. The following poem has a dramatic setting. The husband of a young Chinese wife has gone away. We know something about her life through the descriptive opening stanzas. She has been faithful and loving, but her husband has suddenly left her.

The poem leaves us with many tantalizing questions. Why did the husband leave his young wife? What were his intentions in going? Will he ever return? Why did the husband drag his feet when he left? Now the mosses are growing by the gate. Do the mosses symbolize the wife's fate—to be abandoned?

This poem touches our emotions and leaves us with many tantalizing unanswered questions.

While my hair was still cut straight across my forehead
I played about the front gate, pulling flowers.
You came by on bamboo stilts, playing horse,
You walked about my seat, playing with blue plums.
We went on living in the village of Chokan:
Two small people, without dislike or suspicion.

At fourteen I married My Lord you.
I never laughed, being bashful.
Lowering my head, I looked at the wall.
Called to, a thousand times, I never looked back.

At fifteen I stopped scowling,
I desired my dust to be mingled with yours
Forever and forever and forever.
Why should I climb the look out?

At sixteen you departed,
You went into far Ku-to-yen, by the river of swirling eddies.
And you have been gone five months.
The monkeys make sorrowful noise overhead.

You dragged your feet when you went out.
By the gate now, the moss is grown, the different mosses,
Too deep to clear them away!
The leaves fall early this autumn, in wind.
The paired butterflies are already yellow with August
Over the grass in the West garden;
They hurt me. I grow older.
If you were coming down through the narrows of the river Kiang,
Please let me know beforehand,
And I will come out to meet you
  As far as Cho-fu-sa.

The Destruction of Sennacherib

Lord Byron
British

This poem shows another aspect of poetry: the ability to illuminate a Biblical incident in a handful of vivid lines. Sennacherib was a
powerful king of Assyria, conqueror of Babylon, scourge of his neighbors.
At one point, he mounted an attack on Jerusalem. The Biblical account
provides a bloody fate for the forces of Sennacherib: "The angel of the
Lord went out, and smote in the camp of the Assyrians an hundred
fourscore and five thousand."

Lord Byron took the spare description in *2 Kings* and *Isaiah* and
painted a picture of proud magnificence crushed in a night. Note the
contrast between the gorgeously attired attackers and the distorted bod-
ies after the terrible onslaught. Note, too, the galloping rhythm that
carries the poem along, much as it did the saga of Lochinvar (467). See
pages 475–476 for further comment about poetic rhythm.

The Destruction of Sennacherib

The Assyrian came down like the wolf on the fold,
And his cohorts* were gleaming in purple and gold,
And the sheen of their spears was like stars on the sea,
When the blue wave rolls nightly on deep Galilee.

Like the leaves of the forest when summer is green,
That host with their banners at sunset were seen:
Like the leaves of the forest when autumn hath blown,
That host on the morrow lay wither'd and strown.

For the Angel of Death spread his wings on the blast,
And breathed in the face of the foe as he pass'd
And the eyes of the sleepers wax'd deadly and chill,
And their hearts but once heaved, and forever grew still!

And there lay the steed with his nostril all wide,
But through it there roll'd not the breath of his pride;
And the foam of his gasping lay white on the turf,
And cold as the spray of the rock-beating surf.

And there lay the rider distorted and pale,
With the dew on his brow, and the rust on his mail:
And the tents were all silent, the banners alone,
The lances unlifted, the trumpet unblown.

And the widows of Ashur are loud in their wail,
And the idols are broke in the temple of Baal;
And the might of the Gentile, unsmote by the sword,
Hath melted like snow in the glance of the Lord!

Reading for Understanding

Main Idea

1. Which of the following best expresses the main idea?
   a. Dramatic poetry in purest form is preferable to simple narrative poetry.

---

*forces

b. Both dramatic and narrative poetry can present a story in compressed form.

c. Dramatic poetry tends to be downbeat and pessimistic, emphasizing the negative.

d. English ballads are superior to the poetry of named poets.

Details

2. All the following were mentioned as great epic poems EXCEPT (a) the *Aeneid* (b) *Beowulf* (c) *Gilgamesh* (d) *Paradise Lost.*

3. Lord Randal's mother notices that (a) the dogs are not with her son (b) her son has brought a token from his true love (c) her son refuses to answer her questions (d) he has a wound in his side.

4. In *The Graduate,* the role of Lochinvar is taken by (a) Kevin Costner (b) Mel Gibson (c) Dustin Hoffman (d) Brad Pitt.

5. As part of his escape plan, Lochinvar uses (a) a fight with the prospective groom (b) the dance (c) the groom's protectiveness (d) a friend.

6. The Assyrians were defeated by (a) the Babylonians (b) the Israelites (c) a terrible change of weather (d) an angel.

Inferences

7. "The Nymph's Reply to the Shepherd" (462) is an example of (a) wide-eyed innocence (b) bitter, bitter denunciation (c) logical argument (d) limited agreement.

8. When the Duke says (line 11, page 464), "If they durst," (a) he is revealing his own cruelty (b) the emissary from the Count is favorably impressed (c) he is stopping the emissary from drawing the curtain (d) he is demonstrating a sly sense of humor.

9. Lord Randal (a) is showing his independence in his relationship with his mother (b) cannot understand why he feels so ill (c) realizes his true love has poisoned him (d) seeks vengeance.

10. The bride-to-be in "Lochinvar" (a) openly defied her father (b) was happy to join Lochinvar's plan (c) hated to lose her groom (d) had the same personality as her mother.

11. The setting of "Lochinvar" is (a) Scotland (b) Canada (c) southern England (d) not suggested.

Tone of the Selection

12. The tone of the "Nymph's Reply" (462) is one of (a)indignation (b) passionate disagreement (c) gentle humor (d) unreasonable demand.

Author's Attitude

13. The poet's attitude toward the Duke of Ferrara (464) is one of (a) affection (b) cheerful acceptance (c) amazement (d) intense dislike.

Outcomes

14. As a result of the emissary's visit to the Duke (464), (a) the emissary will report a murder (b) the Duke will imprison the emissary (d) the Duke will lower his demand for a dowry (d) the Count's daughter will be delivered to the Duke.

Fact or Opinion

Tell whether the following is a fact or an opinion.

15. John Suckling (463) offers "Advice to the Lovelorn."

Words in Context

1. "The story of the Duke of Ferrara and his 'Last Duchess' has a plot, motivation, conflict, and *resolution*." **Resolution** (460) means (a) solving of the problem (b) determination to act (c) humorous commentary (d) subtle humor.

2. "There are no *extraneous* elements, no opinions, no interpretations." **Extraneous** (460) means (a) not essential (b) expert (c) unestablished (d) meager.

3. "The three poems suggest that love and *infatuation* haven't changed in those 400 years." **Infatuation** (462) means (a) jealousy (b) happiness (c) envy (d) foolish attachment.

4. "The bough of cherries some *officious* fool broke in the orchard for her." **Officious** (465) means (a) vigorous (b) official (c) meddlesome (d) efficient.

5., 6. "The Count your master's known *munificence* is ample *warrant* that no just pretense of mine for dowry will be disallowed." **Munifi-**

cence (465) means (a) good nature (b) generosity (c) intelligence (d) friendliness. **Warrant** (465) means (a) release (b) guarantee (c) search (d) prize.

7. "These wonderful little poems have come down to us from the past without*ascribed* authorship." **Ascribed** (466) means (a) the usual (b) written down (c) satisfactory (d) credited.

8. "'Lochinvar' is a true love story, complete with a young couple in love about to be *thwarted* by the young lady's father." **Thwarted** (467) means (a) defeated (b) supported (c) misunderstood (d) examined.

9. "A laggard in love and a *dastard* in war was to wed the fair Ellen of brave Lochinvar." **Dastard** (468) means (a) respected leader (b) fearless knight (c) nasty coward (d) unfriendly comrade.

10. "He *quaffed* off the wine, and he threw down the cup." **Quaffed** (468) means drank (a) proudly (b) casually (c) deeply (d) noisily.

11. "So daring in love, and so *dauntless* in war, have you e'er heard of gallant like young Lochinvar?" **Dauntless** (469) means (a) inventive (b) fearless (c) respected (d) beloved.

12. Sennacherib was a powerful king of Assyria, conqueror of Babylon, *scourge* of his neighbors." **Scourge** (470) means (a) destructive enemy (b) envy (c) constant protector (d) persistent observer.

13. "The *sheen* of their spears was like stars on the sea." **Sheen** (471) means (a) appearance (b) great number (c) threat (d) brightness.

Thinking Critically about the Selections

1. In the pair of "Shepherd" poems, the stanzas are balanced. Stanza 1 in the Marlowe poem is matched by stanza 1 in the Raleigh poem. Reread the poems and point out how Raleigh answers Marlowe point by devastating point.

2. The newspapers are filled with stories of jilted lovers who resort to stalking or even violence. How does Sir John Suckling's poem seek to avoid such obsession?

3. What question has the emissary asked the Duke that brings forth the response in lines 5–13, page 464? How does the Duke's response show his evil arrogance? Point to lines to prove your point.

4. What has so enraged the Duke? His wife was faithful, lovely, pleasant, appreciative, friendly to all. What "fault" did she have that so enraged the Duke?

5. Although we don't know for certain what happened to the Duchess, we can make a reasonable guess. Why is the poem more effective if the Duchess's fate is not spelled out in detail?

6. How does the Duke's obvious love of art contrast with his character?

7. How does the rollicking rhythm of "Lochinvar" complement the romantic story?

8. "The Destruction of Sennacherib" begins with a vivid image. The Assyrian assault is compared with the attack of a wolf on a sheepfold. What points of similarity make this comparison effective?

Language in Action

Poetic Rhythms

Even if you were unaware of the technique, you could feel the powerful rhythms of "Lochinvar" and "The Destruction of Sennacherib." That feeling of being swept along is no accident. The poets cleverly devised their sentences to sweep the reader or, preferably, listener along. If you read the poems aloud, you'll appreciate the poet's mastery of his medium. *Meter*, as it is called, is a repeated basic pattern. The elements of meter are called *feet*. These are the four most common metrical feet.

Name of Foot	Number of Syllables	Syllable Accented	Example
iamb	two	second	Marié
trochee	two	first	Máry
anapest	three	third	Gabriellé
dactyl	three	first	Gábriel

A poetic line is sometimes identified by the number of metrical feet. The most common are *trimeter* (three feet), *tetrameter* (four feet), *pentameter* (five feet) and *hexameter* (six feet). Both "Lochinvar" and "Sennacherib" have four feet and can be identified as *anapestic tetrameter.* Both "Shepherd" poems are written in *iambic tetrameter.* "My Last Duchess" is written in *iambic pentameter,* as are the great works of Shakespeare. The Suckling poem is written in alternating trochaic tetrameter and trochaic trimeter. The poet allows variations in the rhythm, but usually one of the types predominates.

These may seem at first like forbidding terms, but an awareness of the poet's technique can add a measure of enjoyment to the reading of a poem. The marching rhythm of the iamb is quite different from the galloping rhythm of the anapest. Appreciating the technical skills of the poet adds a grace note to contacts with poetry.

Lyric Poetry

> I believe a leaf of grass is no less than the journeywork of the stars.
>
> Add the running blackberry would adorn the parlors of heaven,
> And the narrowest hinge in my hand puts to scorn all machinery,
> And the cow crunching with depress'd head surpasses any statue,
> And a mouse is miracle enough to stagger sextillions of infidels.
>
> —From "Song of Myself"

These lines by Walt Whitman suggest the power of poetry to open doors to new experiences and new ways of thinking.

> The sea is calm tonight,
> The tide is full, the moon lies fair
> Upon the straits;—on the French coast the light
> Gleams and is gone: the cliffs of England stand,
> Glimmering and vast, out in the tranquil bay.
>
> —From "Dover Beach"

These lines by Matthew Arnold suggest the power of poetry to transport the reader or listener to another place, both emotionally and physically. Both of these selections belong to that type of poetry often called **lyric**. The dictionary definition of **lyric** suggests a means of identifying it: "expressing direct, usually intense, personal emotion, especially in a manner suggestive of song."

The selections in this chapter display a variety of emotions and style, from the delicate, introspective, sensitive lyrics of Emily Dickinson to the more objective observations of the haiku poets. Yet even in the latter, a certain personal style comes through, in varying degrees. The haiku of Issa, for example, tend to be more personal than those of Basho.

The lyrics of country music tend to be deeply personal. They often sing of heartbreak and loss, yearning and joy, even as do the lyrics of an earlier day.

Four Representative Short Lyrics

The following four selections are a good introduction to the lyric. They're quite brief; yet each one presents a mood, a picture, a philosophical idea. Each is a complete poem. Little more can be said.

The Eagle

He clasps the crag with crooked hands;
Close to the sun in lonely lands,
Ringed with the azure world, he stands.

The wrinkled sea beneath him crawls;
He watches from his mountain walls,
And like a thunderbolt he falls.

—Lord Tennyson
British

Heaven-Haven

I have desired to go
   Where springs not fail,
To fields where flies no sharp and sided hail
   And a few lilies blow.

And I have asked to be
   Where no storms come,
Where the green swell is in the havens dumb,
   Out of the swing of the sea.

—Gerard Manley Hopkins
British

Memory

My mind lets go a thousand things,
Like dates of wars and deaths of kings,

And yet recalls the very hour—
'Twas noon by yonder village tower,
And on the last blue moon in May—
The wind came briskly up this way,
Crisping the brook beside the road;
Then, pausing here, set down its load
Of pine-scents, and shook listlessly
Two petals from that wild-rose tree.

—Thomas Bailey Aldrich
American

Outwitted

He drew a circle that shut me out—
Heretic, rebel, a thing to flout.
But Love and I had the wit to win:
We drew a circle that took him in.

—Edwin Markham
American

Poetic impulses are universal. The next selections come, respectively, from Africa and from China. The former poems suggest the writer's love for Africa. The latter poems provide a bitterly ironic pair. The poet almost resents having a daughter, not a son. He thinks of the problems ahead, but the problems are removed in a way he deeply regrets.

Up-Country

Then I came back
Sailing down the Guinea coast,
Loving the sophistication
Of your brave new cities:
Dakar, Accra, Cotonou,
Lagos, Bathurst, and Bissau,
Freetown, Libreville.
Freedom is really in the mind.

Go up-country, they said,
To see the real Africa.
For whomsoever you may be,
That is where you come from.
Go for bush—inside the bush

You will find your hidden heart,
Your mute ancestral spirit.

And so I went,
Dancing on my way.

—Abioseh Nicol
African

On An African Beach

Here I stand
On the white-fringed edge of the world:
Its limits are my mind.
Let your white sun
Wash my strong brown body.

I feel the crinkle of your golden sands
Under the yellow soles of my feet.
If I lose this certain grip,
If this blue sea washes all of you away,
I will have been widowed
By the moon's rising tide.

I have taken you for better or for worse,
Yet between the thick and the thin
Of this ebbing flow I cannot form a whole.

But if with love again
I turn my face towards you, Africa,
Turning away from the faithless horizon,
Your green mountains will give me
My fulfillment.

—Abioseh Nicol
African

Golden Bells

When I was almost forty
I had a daughter whose name was Golden Bells.
Now it is just a year since she was born;
She is learning to sit and cannot yet talk.
Ashamed—to find that I have not a sage's heart:
I cannot resist vulgar thoughts and feelings.
Henceforward I am tied to things outside myself:
My only reward—the pleasure I am getting now.
If I am spared the grief of her dying young,

Then I shall have the trouble of getting her married.
My plan for retiring and going back to the hills
Must now be postponed for fifteen years!

—Po Chü-I
Chinese

Remembering Golden Bells

Ruined and ill—a man of two score;
  Pretty and guileless—a girl of three.
Not a boy—but still better than nothing:
To soothe one's feeling—from time to time a kiss!
There came a day—they suddenly took her from me;
Her soul's shadow wandered I know not where.

And when I remember how just at the time she died
She lisped strange sounds, beginning to learn to talk,
Then I know that the ties of flesh and blood
Only bind us to a load of grief and sorrow.
At last, by thinking of the time before she was born,
By thought and reason I drove the pain away.
Since my heart forgot her, many days have passed
And three times winter has changed to spring.
This morning, for a little, the old grief came back,
Because, in the road, I met her foster-nurse.

—Po Chü-I
Chinese

Poetry has been used effectively for social protest. The following
two poems, written by black women poets, have a central core of social
concern, but they are vastly different, especially in tone. The first, written more than two centuries ago by a slave, is a gentle prayer for the
spread of freedom. The second, by Alice Walker, is a powerful and
loving tribute to the black mothers of a previous generation. Strong,
loving, undaunted, and unselfish, these women kept their strong convictions and self-respect—and never yielded.

from *To the Right Honorable William, Earl of Dartmouth*

Should you, my lord, while you pursue my song,
Wonder from whence my love of *Freedom* sprung,

Whence flow these wishes for the common good,
By feeling hearts alone best understood,
I, young in life, by seeming cruel fate
Was snatch'd from *Afric's* fancy'd happy seat:
What pangs excruciating must molest,
What sorrows labour in my parent's breast?
Steel'd was the soul and by no misery mov'd
That from a father seiz'd his babe belov'd.
Such, such my case. And can I then but pray
Others may never feel tyrannic sway?

—Phillis Wheatley
American

Women

They were women then
My mama's generation
Husky of voice—Stout of
Step
With fists as well as
Hands
How they battered down
Doors
And ironed
Starched white
Shirts
How they led
Armies
Headragged Generals
Across mined
Fields
Booby-trapped
Ditches
To discover books
Desks
A place for us
How they knew what we
Must know
Without knowing a page
Of it
Themselves.

—Alice Walker
American

A Gathering of Haiku

The haiku is not confined to Japan. Many persons write haiku for personal enjoyment. Some writers in English restrict themselves to 17 syllables, as in Japanese. They find that writing a haiku sharpens perceptions and challenges ingenuity to work within the space limitations. The first three haiku that follow are by Buson, who was born in 1716, 22 years after the death of Basho. The second three are by Issa. Issa was born in 1763, 20 years before Buson's death, so that the two were contemporaries for a while. They flourished two centuries or more ago; yet their haiku seem contemporary. The third three are by Stewart W. Holmes, a contemporary American writer of haiku.

Butterfly
   sleeping—
      on the temple bell.

   Sudden shower—
a flock of sparrows
   clinging to the grasses

   Before the white Chrysanthemums
the scissors hesitate
   a moment.

                                             —Buson
                                             Japanese

   Under my house
an inchworm
   measuring the joists

   That wren—
looking here, looking there,
   You lose something?

   Don't kill that fly!
Look—it's wringing its hands,
   Wringing its feet

                                             —Issa
                                             Japanese

   In the chill spring air
clouds white with the full moon's light
   move slowly, slowly.

The moon, the mountains, the leaves
are silent,
        The churr of a katydid.

        Chickadees come to the feeder
in vain this morning.
        A hungry squirrel?

—Stewart W. Holmes
American

An Indian Prayer

Though written as prose, the following selection has all the qualities of great lyric poetry.

An Indian Prayer

Oh Father whose voice I hear in the wind and whose breath gives
    life to all the world, hear me. I am a man before you, one of
    your many children. I am small and weak, I need your strength
    and wisdom.
Let me walk in beauty and make my eyes ever behold the red
    and purple sunset. Make my hands respect the things you
    have made, my ears sharp to hear your voice. Make me
    wise, so that I may know the things you have taught my
    people, the lessons you have hidden in every leaf and rock.
I seek strength, Father .. not to be superior to my brothers,
    but to be able to fight my greatest enemy . . . myself.
    Make me ever ready to come to you with clean hands and
    straight eyes so that when life fades as the fading sunset,
    my spirit may come to you without shame.

—Tom Whitecloud
Native American

Nine by Emily Dickinson

The American poet with perhaps the greatest lyric voice was a recluse who seldom left her Amherst home. In secret, she wrote over a thou-

sand poems, but her reputation had to wait until many of the poems were published after her death. Her physical world was narrow, but her spiritual world was wide and deep. You may find these poems a little strange at first. You may, for example, expect rhyme, but Emily doesn't always worry about exact rhymes. Sometimes the end words don't seem to rhyme at all, like *whole* and *tell* in Poem 6. No matter. The poems deserve quiet reading and rereading. There are no finer examples of lyric poetry in all of literature.

1

For Emily, Nature is intoxicating.

I TASTE a liquor never brewed,
From tankards scooped in pearl;
Not all the vats upon the Rhine
Yield such an alcohol!

Inebriate of air am I,
And debauchee of dew,
Reeling, through endless summer days,
From inns of molten blue.

When landlords turn the drunken bee
Out of the foxglove's door,
When butterflies renounce their drams,
I shall but drink the more!

Till seraphs* swing their snowy hats,
And saints to windows run,
To see the little tippler
Leaning against the sun!

2

Emily pays tribute to a book.

HE ate and drank the precious words,
His spirit grew robust;
He knew no more that he was poor,
Nor that his frame was dust.
He danced along the dingy days,
And this bequest of wings
Was but a book. What liberty
A loosened spirit brings!

---

*angels

3

The earliest light of spring is special.

A LIGHT exists in spring
  Not present on the year
At any other period.
  When March is scarcely here

A color stands abroad
  On solitary hills
That science cannot overtake,
  But human nature *feels*.

It waits upon the lawn;
  It shows the furthest tree
Upon the furthest slope we know;
  It almost speaks to me.

Then, as horizons step,
  Or noons report away,
Without the formula of sound,
  It passes, and we stay:

A quality of loss
  Affecting our content,
As trade had suddenly encroached
  Upon a sacrament.

4

Emily welcomes the return of March.

DEAR March, come in!
How glad I am!
I looked for you before.
Put down your hat—
You must have walked—
How out of breath you are!
Dear March, how are you?
And the rest?
Did you leave Nature well?
Oh, March, come right upstairs with me,
I have so much to tell!

5

Emily compares her inner life with a brook.

HAVE you got a brook in your little heart,
Where bashful flowers blow,
And blushing birds go down to drink,
And shadows tremble so?

And nobody knows, so still it flows,
That any brook is there;
And yet your little draught of life
Is daily drunken there.

Then look out for the little brook in March,
When the rivers overflow,
And the snows come hurrying from the hills,
And the bridges often go.

And later, in August it may be,
When the meadows parching lie,
Beware, lest this little brook of life
Some burning noon go dry!

6

Perhaps the mysteries of Nature are best left unsolved.

THE skies can't keep their secret!
They tell it to the hills—
The hills just tell the orchards—
And they the daffodils!

A bird, by chance, that goes that way
Soft overheard the whole.
If I should bribe the little bird,
Who knows but she would tell?

I think I won't, however,
It's finer not to know;
If summer were an axiom,
What sorcery had snow?

So keep your secret, Father!
I would not, if I could,
Know what the sapphire fellows do,
In your new-fashioned world!

7

Emily fantasizes about the flight of two butterflies.

TWO butterflies went out at noon
And waltzed above a stream,
Then stepped straight through the firmament
And rested on a beam;

And then together bore away
Upon a shining sea,—
Though never yet, in any port,
Their coming mentioned be.

If spoken by the distant bird,
If met in ether sea
By frigate or by merchantman,
Report was not to me.

8

Emily visits the seashore and experiences the sea.

I STARTED early, took my dog,
And visited the sea;
The mermaids in the basement
Came out to look at me,

And frigates in the upper floor
Extended hempen hands,
Presuming me to be a mouse
Aground, upon the sands.

But no man moved me till the tide
Went past my simple shoe,
And past my apron and my belt,
And past my bodice too,

And made as he would eat me up
As wholly as a dew
Upon a dandelion's sleeve—
And then I started too.

And he—he followed close behind;
I felt his silver heel
Upon my ankle,—then my shoes
Would overflow with pearl.

Until we met the solid town,
No man he seemed to know;
And bowing with a mighty look
At me, the sea withdrew.

9

Emily wonders whether science has gone too far.

ARCTURUS is his other name,—
I'd rather call him star!
It's so unkind of science
To go and interfere!

I pull a flower from the woods,—
A monster with a glass
Computes the stamens in a breath,
And has her in a class.

Whereas I took the butterfly
Aforetime in my hat,
He sits erect in cabinets,
The clover-bells forgot.

What once was heaven, is zenith now.
Where I proposed to go
When time's brief masquerade was done,
Is mapped, and charted too!

What if the poles should frisk about
And stand upon their heads!
I hope I'm ready for the worst,
Whatever prank betides!*

Perhaps the kingdom of Heaven's changed!
I hope the children there
Won't be new-fashioned when I come,
And laugh at me, and stare!

I hope the father in the skies
Will lift his little girl,—
Old-fashioned, naughty, everything,—
Over the stile of pearl!

---

*happens

Reading for Understanding

Main Idea

1. In general, lyric poetry is characterized by (a) personal emotion (b) narrative skill (c) understated humor (d) dramatic monologues.

Details

2. The poem about miracles was written by (a) Lord Tennyson (b) Emily Dickinson (c) Walt Whitman (d) Matthew Arnold.
3. Modern examples of lyric poetry can be found in (a) opera (b) rock (c) musical comedy (d) country music.
4. The two writers who were partial contemporaries are (a) Basho and Holmes (b) Buson and Issa (c) Basho and Issa (d) Issa and Holmes.
5. In "Memory," Thomas Bailey Aldrich especially remembers (a) dates of wars (b) deaths of kings (c) an early snow (d) rose petals.
6. *Golden Bells* is the name of (a) a young girl (b) temple bells (c) a house in the country (d) a love song.

Inferences

7. The poem that calls for release from the problems of life is (a) "Outwitted" (b) "Heaven-Haven (c) "Memory" (d) "An Indian Prayer."
8. Edwin Markham's poem (477) displays (a) a sneaky spirit (b) a great soul (c) revenge (d) intense curiosity.
9. The poem "Up-Country" (479) suggests the author's (a) search for roots (b) despair over his past (c) disillusion with the up-country (d) desire to settle in one of the cities mentioned.
10. In "Remembering Golden Bells" (481), the poet meets a foster nurse and (a) greets the woman coldly (b) may feel some regret (c) decides to adopt another child (d) is elated by the experience.

Poet's Attitude

11. The poet's attitude in the two "Golden Bells" poems (480–481) may be characterized as (a) joyous (b) charitable (c) carefree (d) selfish.

Tone of the Selection

12. The tone of "An Indian Prayer" (484) can be characterized as one of (a) despair (b) self-pity (c) reverence (d) relief.

Author's Language

13. The extended image in Emily Dickinson's first poem is one of pretended (a) intoxication (b) hunger (c) story-telling (d) indifference.

Author's Attitude

14. Emily Dickinson's attitude toward the "light in spring," Poem 3 (486), is one of (a) happiness at the extent of that light (b) obvious irritation at its arrival (c) sadness and a sense of loss (d) curiosity about its nature.

Fact or Opinion

Tell whether the following is a fact or an opinion.

15. Japanese haiku are superior to those of any other culture.

Words in Context

1. The selections in this chapter display a variety of emotions and style, from the delicate, *introspective,* sensitive lyrics of Emily Dickinson to the more objective observations of the haiku poets. **Introspective** (477) means (a) colorful (b) thoughtful (c) critical (d) rebellious.

2.,3. "He drew a circle that shut me out—*heretic,* rebel, a thing to *flout.*" A major characteristic of a **heretic** (479) is (a) insincerity (b) weakness (c) cooperation (d) doubt. **Flout** (479) means treat with (a) contempt (b) respect (c) disbelief (d) kindness.

4. "Ashamed—to find that I have not a *sage's* heart: I cannot resist vulgar thoughts and feelings." A **sage** (480) is a (a) merchant (b) writer (c) wise man (d) wistful clown.

5. "They find that writing a haiku sharpens *perceptions* and challenges ingenuity to work within the space limitations." **Perceptions** (483) suggests (a) awareness (b) critical feelings (c) dramatic incidents (d) wittiness.

6. "The American poet with perhaps the greatest lyric voice was a *recluse* who seldom left her Amherst home." A **recluse** (484) is a kind of (a) poet (b) actor (c) hermit (d) social climber.

7.,8. "*Inebriate* of air am I, and *debauchee* of dew." **Inebriate** (485) suggests (a) inspiration (b) drunkenness (c) keenness of inspiration (d) vigor. By using **debauchee** (485) humorously, Emily Dickinson is suggesting (a) evil motives (b) antagonism (c) immobility (d) loss of control.

9. "When butterflies *renounce* their drams, I shall but drink the more!" **Renounce** (485) means (a) consume (b) refuse (c) discover (d) decorate.

10. "This *bequest* of wings was but a book." **Bequest** (485) means (a) matched pair (b) inheritance (c) library (d) foretelling.

11. "Trade had suddenly encroached upon a sacrament." **Encroached** (486) means (a) entered (b) happened (c) relied (d) trespassed.

12. "If summer were an *axiom*, what sorcery had snow?" An **axiom** (487) is a (a) self-evident truth (b) false principle (c) legal agreement (d) brief moment.

13. "The butterflies . . . stepped straight through the *firmament* and rested on a beam." **Firmament** (488) refers to (a) a meadow (b) a weeded area (c) the sky (d) a garden.

Thinking Critically about the Selections

1. Lord Tennyson chooses an unusual adjective to describe the sea (478): *wrinkled*. Is this an appropriate word? How can water be wrinkled? Did the description appeal to you? Why?

2. Thomas Bailey Aldrich describes a common mystery: the inconsistency of memory. Are there incidents in your own life that remain with you even though they seemed insignificant at the time? Suggest an example.

3. How much time elapses between the first and second poems in the Golden Bells poems? What clues tell you exactly? What has happened in the intervening time? How do the poems reveal that father's character?

4. What requests does Tom Whitecloud make of his God (484)? How do these requests reveal something about the author?

5. In Poem 1 (485) what is Emily Dickinson drinking that causes her giddy

state? Note that she keeps the image of exhilaration and intoxication throughout. How can anyone "lean against the sun"? Is this a vivid image for you?

6. Which three poems mention March, a month that usually has few champions? What special qualities does March have, at least in the eyes of Emily Dickinson?

7. In Poem 9, the poet takes sides against the preciseness and labeling of science. Why?

8. Lyric poetry often selects some insignificant object or incident and makes it beautiful. Select a poem from this chapter. Tell why you think it successfully brings to life an image we might otherwise overlook.

Language in Action

Rhyme

Rhyme depends upon a similarity in sound. Young lovers have been rhyming *June* and *moon* for centuries. Shakespeare sometimes ends a scene with a rhyme, as in these lines from *Hamlet:*

> The play's the thing
> Wherein I'll catch the conscience of the king.

Letters are often used to indicate a rhyme scheme. The rhyme scheme in "The Eagle" (478), for example, can be designated aaa bbb; in "Heaven-Haven," (478), abba cddc; in "Memory," aa bb cc dd ee; in "Outwitted" (479), aa bb. By contrast, Walt Whitman's poetry (477), called *free verse,* has neither a set rhythm nor rhyme. Except for an occasional song or scene ending as above, Shakespeare's plays have a recognizable rhythm but not rhyme. This form of poetry is called *iambic pentameter* (475), or blank verse.

Most amateur writers tend to use rhyme in their poetry. There is something satisfying in the recognition of a familiar sound at the end of a line.

Note that "The Destruction of Sennacherib" (471) has not only a galloping rhythm but a recognizable rhyme scheme. The rhyme scheme of the first stanza is aa bb. How would you designate the rhymes of the remaining stanzas? And "Lochinvar" (467)?

Humorous Poetry

Stick close to your desks and never go to sea,
And you all may be rulers of the Queen's Navee.

—W. S. Gilbert

Poetry seems especially able to handle absurdity. The songs of Gilbert and Sullivan are prime examples of that skill, but other writers, too, have tried their hand at fun in verse.

Humor seems to be as difficult to define as poetry. "I know what it is, but I can't tell you" is a typical response to a question about humor. Understatement, exaggeration, incongruity all contribute to a sense of fun, and poets use all three. Incongruity depends upon absurdity, on contrast, on something out of place. A powerfully built athlete leading a tiny dog on a chain is incongruous, likely to provoke laughter. See also pages 357–358.

The poems in this section rely on a variety of methods to bring forth a smile. The unexpected plays a role in "Twins," and "Elegy on the Death of a Mad Dog." Exaggeration is used in "The Height of the Ridiculous." Sheer nonsense is the appeal of "Jabberwocky." The joy of recognizing humorous human failings in others is the appeal of "Get Up and Bar the Door." "Sir Joseph Porter's Song" from **H.M.S. Pinafore** is, of course, sung in the operetta, but the humor comes through in the verse itself. Two haiku also demonstrate that this simple poetic form can contain humor along with keen observation.

494

Elegy on the Death of a Mad Dog

Oliver Goldsmith
British

The Twins

Henry S. Leigh
British

These two poems make an interesting pair. They show similar approaches to humorous poetry, but with several differences. Both pretend to be quite serious, a frequent device in humorous poetry. Both present a reasonable situation and then turn it topsy-turvy. Oliver Goldsmith makes the poem seem more serious than it otherwise might be by using the formal word *elegy,* a song of sorrow or lamentation. To tell the story, he uses a simple ballad stanza, with alternating rhyming lines. Henry S. Leigh addresses the reader directly and thus emphasizes the absurdity of the last line. He seems to have written ballad stanzas (466) and then joined two together to make the longer stanzas of the poems.

Elegy on the Death of a Mad Dog

Good people all, of every sort,
  Give ear unto my song;
And if you find it wondrous short—
  It cannot hold you long.

In Islington there was a man,   5
  Of whom the world might say,
That still a godly race he ran—
  Whene'er he went to pray.

A kind and gentle heart he had,
  To comfort friends and foes;   10
The naked every day he clad—

When he put on his clothes.

And in that town a dog was found,
    As many dogs there be,
Both mongrel, puppy, whelp, and hound,   15
    And cur of low degree.

This dog and man at first were friends;
    But when a pique began,
The dog, to gain some private ends,
    Went mad, and bit the man.   20

Around from all the neighboring streets,
    The wondering neighbors ran,
And swore the dog had lost his wits,
    To bite so good a man.

The wound it seemed both sore and sad   25
    To every Christian eye;
And while they swore the dog was mad,
    They swore the man would die.

But soon a wonder came to light,
    That showed the rogues they lied;   30
The man recovered of the bite,
    The dog it was that died.

The Twins

IN form and feature, face and limb,
    I grew so like my brother
That folks got taking me for him,
    And each for one another.
It puzzled all our kith and kin,
    It reached an awful pitch;
For one of us was born a twin,
    Yet not a soul knew which.

One day (to make the matter worse),
    Before our names were fixed,
As we were being washed by nurse
    We got completely mixed;
And thus, you see, by Fate's decree,
    (Or rather nurse's whim),
My brother John got christened *me*,
    And I got christened *him*.

This fatal likeness even dogged
  My footsteps when at school,
And I was always getting flogged,
  For John turned out a fool.
I put this question hopelessly
  To every one I knew—
What *would* you do, if you were me,
  To prove that you were *you?*

Our close resemblance turned the tide
  Of my domestic life;
For somehow my intended bride
  Became my brother's wife.
In short, year after year the same
  Absurd mistakes went on;
And when I died—the neighbors came
  And buried Brother John!

The Height of the Ridiculous

Oliver Wendell Holmes
American

In many collections of light verse, "The Height of the Ridiculous" has an honored place. Understatement is a form of humor, when someone says, "I had a bit of trouble" after running into gridlock traffic and missing an important appointment, he is using understatement. Mark Twain's famous "Journalism in Tennessee" is an example of sustained humorous understatement. Exaggeration, the other side of the coin, is often used for humorous effect, as here.

The Height of the Ridiculous

I wrote some lines once on a time
  In wondrous merry mood,
And thought, as usual, men would say
  They were exceeding good.
They were so queer, so very queer,
  I laughed as I would die;

5

Albeit, in the general way,
  A sober man am I.

I called my servant, and he came;
  How kind it was of him   10
To mind a slender man like me,
  He of the mighty limb!

"These to the printer," I exclaimed,
  And, in my humorous way,
I added, (as a trifling jest,)   15
  "There'll be the devil* to pay."

He took the paper, and I watched,
  And saw him peep within;
At the first line he read, his face
  Was all upon the grin.   20

He read the next; the grin grew broad,
  And shot from ear to ear;
He read the third; a chuckling noise
  I now began to hear.

The fourth; he broke into a roar;   25
  The fifth; his waistband split;
The sixth; he burst five buttons off,
  And tumbled in a fit.

Ten days and nights, with sleepless eye,
  I watched that wretched man,   30
And since, I never dare to write
  As funny as I can.

Get Up and Bar the Door

Although most old English and Scottish ballads are grim tales of
heartbreak and tragedy, a few are bright, filled with humorous observation.
Here's an all-too-human situation. Husband and wife get into a disagreement about who is to bar the cottage door. Neither one will give in: two
supposedly mature persons who let stubborn pride get them into a situation that could have been avoided. Who will outlast the other and who will
"get up and bar the door"?

---

*devil: a pun; a "printer's devil" is an apprentice printer

It fell about the Martinmas time,
 And a gay time it was then,
When our goodwife got puddings to make,
 And she's boiled them in the pan.

The wind so cold blew south and north,
 And blew into the floor;
Quoth our goodman to our goodwife,
 "Go out and bar the door."

"My hand is in my hussyfskap,*
 Goodman, as you may see;
If it should not be barred this hundred year,
 It's no be barred for me."

They made a pact between the two,
 They made it firm and sure,
That the first word whoe'er should speak
 Should rise and bar the door.

Then by there came two gentlemen,
 At twelve o'clock at night,
And they could neither see house nor hall,
 Nor coal nor candle-light.

"Now whether is this a rich man's house,
 Or whether is it a poor?"
But ne'er a word would one of them speak,
 For barring of the door.

And first they ate the white puddings,
 And then they ate the black;
Though much thought the goodwife to herself,
 Yet ne'er a word she spake.

Then said the one unto the other,
 "Here, man, take you my knife;
Do you take off the old man's beard,
 And I'll kiss the goodwife."

"But there's no water in the house,
 And what shall we do than?"
"What ails thee at the pudding-broo,
 That boils into the pan?"

*kneading-trough

O up then started our goodman,
  An angry man was he:
"Will you kiss my wife before my eyes,
  And scald me with pudding-bree?"

Then up and started our goodwife,
  Gave three skips on the floor:
"Goodman, you've spoken the foremost word.
  Get up and bar the door."

Sir Joseph Porter's Song

W. S. Gilbert
British

The operettas of W. S. Gilbert and Arthur Sullivan were out-
standingly successful when they first appeared over a century ago. They
have retained a solid popularity ever since. For his efforts, Sullivan was
knighted in 1883 by Queen Victoria. Gilbert was also knighted—by
Edward VII in 1907, 24 years later. Gilbert was not happy at the slight,
and his verse showed his annoyance.

Gilbert was not one of the Queen's favorites. Time and again, in his
operettas he poked fun at her government. In *Iolanthe*, for example, he
poked fun at the House of Lords. The verse that may have irritated the
Queen most is the song in *H.M.S. Pinafore* by Sir Joseph, the First Lord of
the Admiralty. Though the Lord's position may not actually require nautical
skills, the tone of the song is mocking . . . and the Queen "was not amused."

Sir Joseph Porter's Song from H.M.S. Pinafore

When I was a lad I served a term
As office boy to an Attorney's firm.
I cleaned the windows and I swept the floor,
And I polished up the handle of the big front door,
  I polished up that handle so carefullee
  That now I am the Ruler of the Queen's Navee!

As office boy I made such a mark
That they gave me the post of a junior clerk.

I served the writs with a smile so bland,
And I copied all the letters in a big round hand—
    I copied all the letters in a hand so free,
    That now I am the Ruler of the Queen's Navee.

In serving writs I made such a name
That an articled clerk I soon became;
I wore clean collars and a brand-new suit
For the pass examination at the Institute,
    And that pass examination did so well for me,
    That now I am the Ruler of the Queen's Navee.

Of legal knowledge I acquired such a grip
That they took me into the partnership,
And that partnership, I ween,
Was the only ship that I ever had seen.
    But that kind of ship so suited me,
    That now I am the Ruler of the Queen's Navee.

I grew so rich that I was soon sent
By a pocket borough into Parliament
I always voted at my party's call,
And I never thought of thinking for myself at all.
    I thought so little, they rewarded me
    By making me the Ruler of the Queen's Navee.

Now Landsmen all, whoever you may be,
If you want to rise to the top of the tree,
If your soul isn't fettered to an office stool.
Be careful to be guided by this golden rule—
    Stick close to your desks and never go to sea,
    And you all may be Rulers of the Queen's Navee.

Jabberwocky

Lewis Carroll
British

Lewis Carroll is immortal because of the Alice books: *Alice in Wonderland* and *Through the Looking-Glass*. However, he also wrote much humorous verse, as well as some serious books in mathematics. You may already have met "The Walrus and the Carpenter" and "Father William." Of all the humorous verse, perhaps the most unusual is "Jabberwocky."

This is obviously the tale of a heroic young man who set out to slay a fearsome monster and succeeded. This is a hackneyed plot, found in old English tales of heroism, in stories of King Arthur, and in legends and fairy tales everywhere. The plot is used in science fiction, too, though the monster is often not of this world. Think of the Alien movies. What makes "Jabberwocky" so special is the language. Carroll has invented a great many nonsense words. Some of these have entered the language as blends (507). Who knows what borogoves are or what a frumious Bandersnatch might do! Some words have recognizable parts. *Slithy* is a blend (507) of *lithe* and *slimy*. No matter where the words came from, the poem makes a kind of sense. Each reader or listener sees a different Jabberwock, but nobody fails to see the hero galumphing back home.

Jabberwocky

'Twas brillig, and the slithy toves
  Did gyre and gimble in the wabe:
All mimsy were the borogoves,
  And the mome raths outgrabe.

"Beware the Jabberwock, my son!
  The jaws that bite, the claws that catch!
Beware the Jubjub bird, and shun
  The frumious Bandersnatch!"

He took his vorpal sword in hand;
  Long time the manxome foe he sought—
So rested he by the Tumtum tree,
  And stood awhile in thought.

And, as in uffish thought he stood,
  The Jabberwock, with eyes of flame,
Came whiffling through the tulgey wood,
  And burbled as it came!

One, two! One, two! And through and through
  The vorpal blade went snicker-snack!
He left it dead, and with its head
  He went galumphing back.

"And hast thou slain the Jabberwock?
  Come to my arms, my beamish boy!
O frabjous day! Callooh! Callay!"
  He chortled in his joy.

'Twas brillig, and the slithy toves
  Did gyre and gimble in the wabe:
All mimsy were the borogoves,
  And the mome raths outgrabe.

Anon

R. J. Lowenherz
American

In Budapest there is a statue of an early Hungarian hero. No one knows much about him. There is no record of his appearance. As a result, the statue has a hood over the face, concealing those unknown features.

There are unknown elements in literature, too. Literary works whose authors are unknown are always attributed to *Anonymous,* or *Anon* as it is usually abbreviated. The author of the following poem playfully imagines that Anon is a person who has been cruelly blamed for all those inferior works ascribed to him.

Of all the bards of song and verse,
What Jennifer or John
Right from the first has suffered worse
Than he they call *Anon?*

The feeble fable, murky myth,
Or legendary lay
Lies never with a Jones or Smith:
"It's by *Anon,*" they say.

If minstrels drone a dreary tale,
Disclaiming they first said it,
Whose name goes on that weary wail?
Anon gets all the credit.

No vulgar verse, low limerick,

Or witticism lame
Is left to stick a Tom or Dick:
Anon gets all the blame.

Of all the bards of song and verse,
None lives so put upon
As that poor lad whose cruel curse
Was to be named *Anon.*

Two Haiku

The haiku, so impressive in capturing a moment in a few syllables, is sometimes used for humor. The first, by a contemporary writer of haiku, uses a colloquial pun. The second, by a fourth-grade elementary school student, contrasts beauty and work.

Waiting in the darkness
I hear nothing.
Owl, why don't you give a hoot?

—Stewart W. Holmes

The leaves are falling,
They look like a new rainbow.
Aw! Where is the rake?

—Thomas F. Christ

Reading for Understanding

Main Idea

1. A major idea of the chapter is contained in which of the following sentences?
   (a) The greatest humorous poems contain nonsense words.
   (b) Three major ingredients of humorous poetry are under-statement, exaggeration, absurdity.
   (c) The greatest humorous poets are happy in their own lives, secure in their accomplishments.

(d) Old English ballads often have tragic themes unrelieved by humor.

Details

2. Exaggeration is mentioned as a major appeal of (a) "Get Up and Bar the Door" (b) the Owl haiku (c) "The Height of the Ridiculous" (d) "Elegy on the Death of a Mad Dog."
3. In "The Twins," the fool is (a) John (b) the speaker (c) the wife (d) the doctor.
4. In "The Height of the Ridiculous," the poor victim is (a) the printer (b) a stranger (c) a relative (d) a servant.
5. In "Get Up and Bar the Door," the husband was finally prompted to action by (a) the threatened kiss (b) the loss of the puddings (c) the arrival of strangers (d) his wife's surrender.
6. Sir Joseph Porter started out in life as (a) a junior clerk (b) an articled clerk (c) a junior partner (d) an office boy.

Inferences

7. When the husband said, "Go out and bar the door," (a) he didn't expect his wife to do it (b) his wife resented the order (c) he expected visitors (d) the door was closed but not barred.
8. *Manxome* (502, line 10) probably means something like (a) "sluggish" (b) "invisible" (c) "terrifying" (d) "cowardly."

Author's Attitude

9. The author's attitude toward political appointees in "Sir Joseph Porter's Song" is one of (a) ridicule (b) awe (c) approval (d) hatred.

Fact or Opinion

Tell whether the following is a fact or an opinion.

10. "Get Up and Bar the Door" is the finest humorous ballad in existence.

Words in Context

1. "A powerfully built athlete leading a tiny dog on a chain is *incongruous,* likely to provoke laughter." **Incongruous** (494) means (a) insulting (b) out of place (c) charming (d) not understandable.

2. "The Lord's position may not actually require *nautical* skills." **Nautical** (500) pertains to (a) magic (b) artisans (c) puzzles (d) ships.

3. "If your soul isn't *fettered to* an office stool, be careful to be guided by this golden rule." **Fettered to** (501) means (a) associated with (b) chained to (c) dissatisfied with (d) separated from.

4. "This is a *hackneyed* plot." **Hackneyed** (502) means (a) sparkling (b) original (c) shopworn (d) ancient.

Thinking Critically about the Selections

1. In "Elegy on the Death of a Mad Dog," is the poet making a sly, unexpected comment about the character of the man? Explain.

2. In "The Twins," how does the poet pile absurdity on absurdity? How does he cap the list at the end?

3. In "The Height of the Ridiculous," the poet writes completely objectively about the servant's comical disintegration. Point out the specific observations that convince the poet that his verses are dangerous.

4. Why are untested, inexperienced, unready persons often appointed to positions for which they are unsuited?

5. In "Get Up and Bar the Door," stubbornness almost turns into disaster. Why do people sometimes stubbornly refuse to take actions obviously beneficial, preferring instead to embark on a self-destructive course?

6. Which of the poems in this section seem to you most humorous? Can you tell why?

Language in Action

Blends

When Lewis Carroll joined *lithe* and *slimy* to make *slithy,* he was using a process that has given us many words in English. The results of such coinages are often called *portmanteau words,* or *blends.* Also in "Jabberwocky," Carroll combined *snort* and *chuckle* to produce *chortle,* a word found in most dictionaries. When Carroll wanted to create a name for another monster, he took two words that were unpleasant to him: *snake* and *shark.* He created *snark* and a masterpiece to go with it: "The Hunting of the Snark."

Lewis Carroll was only one source of blends. *Motor* plus *hotel* provides *motel. Agriculture* plus *business* equals *agribusiness.* The hybrid offspring of a lion and tiger is called a *ligon. Information* plus *commercial* provides *infomercial.* A *port* for a *helicopter* is a *heliport. Breakfast* plus *lunch* equals *brunch. Electric* and *execute* blend to form *electrocute.* The *World Almanac* published a visual encyclopedia for students and titled it *infopedia (information* plus *encyclopedia).*

Science and technology provide many blends. The common computer word *modem* is actually a blend of *modulator* and *demodulator.* A *pixel* is *pix* plus *element. Electronic* plus *mail* equals *e-mail.* The years ahead will see a flood of new blends entering the language.

The Power of Poetry

ACTIVITIES

Thinking Critically about the Selections

1. After reading the poems and the various definitions of poetry, how has your understanding of poetry been changed? Which poem or poems seem closest to your own feelings about poetry?

2. Does poetry tend to strike deeper into your inner feelings than prose? Explain.

3. Now that you've read many poems, return to the Issa haiku on page 453. Why has this poem been put with the other two? How is it different? Similar? Why does Issa make *dew* the key word? What is characteristic of dew?

4. "Ozymandias" on page 454 is analyzed in some detail. How can the analysis of a poem deepen appreciation and understanding?

5. Who is the most villainous person presented in the poems? Why did you choose this person?

6. Now that you've experienced a variety of poetic types, do you still prefer your poems with a set rhythm and rhyme? Explain.

7. What are the special appeals of the haiku?

8. W. S. Gilbert (500) was a master of satire, a literary form characterized by scorn and ridicule. Satire need not be in the form of poetry. *Gulliver's Travels* is one of the world's greatest satirical works, poking fun at mankind's stupidities. But satire does appear in poetry too, as in "Sir Joseph Porter's Song." Gilbert is being fairly good-humored here, but satire can be deadly. Some television comics rely on satire for their humor. Mark Russell is a good example. Can you think of others? Is their satire good natured or bitter? The characters

in sitcoms are often portrayed satirically. Can you suggest one or more examples?

The Writing Portfolio

Writing Original Poetry

Poetry is sometimes unfairly criticized. Many young people think that poetry is only for the few. Yet, throughout history, poetry has been for the many. Bards and storytellers often recited in poetry. Perhaps the greatest epics ever created, the *Iliad* and the *Odyssey*, were created in poetic form.

Even today, popular songs create poetic verse. The ballads of country music are modern equivalents of the poems the troubadours sang to their lady loves. Poetry is not dead. The impulses are all around us. Writing an original poem can be fun—and sometimes good therapy. Try your hand at one or more of the following. If you wish, start with the deceptively simple haiku and then attempt slightly longer poems.

1. A number of haiku have been included in this unit because they are deceptively simple, yet powerful in their impact. Even if longer poems intimidate you, you'll enjoy creating a haiku. The following haiku were all written by high school students.

> A wet spider web
> sagging from weight of raindrops
> sparkles in the sun.
>
> —Gigi Garrido

> Gazing at the sky,
> so bright is the rising moon
> above the mountains.
>
> —Frances DiGioia

> All is quiet now,
> The night is like a heavy curtain.
> The day's act is done.
>
> —Priscilla George

> The house I live in . . .
> the house, the grass, and the street
> all belong to me.
>
> —Nelson Jenkins

Try your hand. For an extra challenge, keep the haiku to 17 syllables, in lines of 5, 7, and 5 syllables. Nature, school, the city, people, travel . . . the possibilities are everywhere. Don't be "profound" or philosophical. For the haiku, just capture what you see.

2. One of the simplest poetic forms is the couplet: two rhyming lines. Couplets appear on commercial greeting cards, occasionally on radio and television commercials, now and then in letters between good friends. The couplet has been used for many purposes: Satire, social commentary, philosophy of life, humor, and character description. Shakespeare often used a couplet to conclude a scene in his plays. At the end of Act One, Hamlet cries,

> The time is out of joint; O cursed spite,
> That ever I was born to set it right.

The following samples suggest the range of the simple couplet.

> Oh, what a tangled web we weave,
> When first we practice to deceive.
>
> —Sir Walter Scott

> Hope springs eternal in the human breast;
> Man never is, but always to be blest.
>
> —Alexander Pope

> Swans sing before they die; 'twere no bad thing
> Should certain persons die before they sing.
>
> —Samuel Taylor Coleridge

> Seven wealthy towns contend for Homer dead,
> Through which the living Homer begged his bread.
>
> —John Dryden

> Slowly, silently, now the moon
> Walks the night in her silver shoon.
>
> —Walter de la Mare

Now try your hand at writing a couplet. Use any subject that comes to mind. Perhaps you'll create a humorous couplet like the following by Dorothy Parker.

Four be the things I'd been better without:
Love, curiosity, freckles, and doubt.

3. A quatrain is a stanza of four lines, with many varieties of rhyme scheme. A representative quatrain is "Outwitted" by Edwin Markham (479). The ballad stanza is a special form of the quatrain. The first and third rhymes are typically in unrhymed iambic tetrameter (475). The second and fourth lines are in rhymed iambic trimeter (475).

There lived a wife at Usher's Well,
    And a wealthy wife was she;
She had three stout and stalwart sons,
    And sent them o'er the sea.

—Early English Ballad

For other examples, see "The Height of the Ridiculous" (497) and "Get Up and Bar the Door" (498). Create a quatrain of your own

4. The limerick is an old favorite. This five-line form tends to be humorous, often with a surprising last line. One of the masters of the limerick was Edward Lear, who lived a century and a half ago:

There was an old man with a beard,
Who said, "It is just as I feared;
    Two owls and a hen
    Four larks and a wren.
Have all built their nests in my beard."

Write a humorous limerick, in good taste, and share it with your classmates.

5. If you wish, try a longer poem, either in traditional form or free verse. Use the suggestions in this chapter for guidance.

Other Areas of Communication

1. Try your hand at analyzing a short poem. With a student selected as class leader, prepare to discuss what the poet is suggesting. What does the puddle symbolize? What are those black pearls? Warm ooze of mud? What is the poet talking about?

Poetry

Yes, you can
talk about it
as you could
walk in dry boots
circumspectly
around a justfound puddle.

But what is that
to the joyful splash,
black pearls flying
in the startled air,
and the warm ooze of mud
between your bare toes?

—R. J. Lowenherz

2. Several poems are ideal for choral reading: "The Twins," The Destruction of Sennacherib," "Lochinvar," among others. With your teacher's guidance, break these poems into parts for a narrator and one or more choruses.

3. If you can borrow *H.M.S. Pinafore* from the library, bring it to school and play "Sir Joseph Porter's Song." If you have facilities for video, so much the better.

4. In the library, find "The Hunting of the Snark" by Lewis Carroll and prepare to read it aloud to the class.

5. A poet who resembles Emily Dickinson in some ways is A.E. Housman. Take a Housman volume from the library and prepare to read aloud to the class a lyric or two.

6. There are many fine collections of lyric poetry. Palgrave's *Golden Treasury* is one of the most famous. Select a volume from the poetry shelf in the school library and select a poem to present to the class. Read it and tell why you chose it.

7. The interaction of students and teacher of poetry is the central theme of *The Dead Poets Society* with Robin Williams. It is available on video. If you have access to it, view it and report on it. Does the story seem plausible to you? Explain.

8. For the next week, keep a notebook of all the metaphors you hear, then share them with classmates. Be aware of metaphors so common you may tend to overlook them, like *drop a hint, hit a blank wall,* and *frosty reception.*

9. Keep an eye out for blends (507), words formed by cementing two other words together. List them.

10. From country music, select a song that has strong narrative elements. If possible, bring to class the song's verses. Are these poetry?

Language in Action—a Review

You may refer to the preceding pages to answer these questions.

1. *Eye of the hurricane* is an example of (a) a simile (b) literal language (c) metonymy (d) metaphor.

2. Which of the following is an example of personification?
   (a) The district attorney took strong action.
   (b) Duty whispers low, but we must listen.
   (c) The fullback took the ball and rushed for three yards over tackle.
   (d) Our mother and father are coming for Thanksgiving.

3. The pattern of poetic feet is called (a) rhythm (b) rhyme (c) meter (d) free verse.

4. The name *Marie* is given as an example of a(n) (a) iambic foot (b) trochaic foot (c) anapestic foot (d) dactylic foot.

5. Shakespeare's poetry was written in (a) trochaic trimeter (b) iambic pentameter (c) the ballad form (d) none of these.

6. The poetry of Emily Dickinson often (a) deals with political topics (b) follows a standard stanza length (c) avoids metaphor (d) uses imperfect rhymes.

7. Shakespeare sometimes uses rhyming lines (a) to end a scene (b) to reveal character (c) for purely decorative reasons (d) to speed the action.

8. *Motel* is an example of a (a) metaphor (b) personification (c) blend (d) synecdoche.

9. One pleasure of rhyme is the feeling of (a) recognition (b) sympathy (c) excitement (d) contemplation.

10. The poet who wrote free verse is (a) Thomas Bailey Aldrich (b) Lord Tennyson (c) Walt Whitman (d) Oliver Wendell Holmes.

UNIT SEVEN

Actions and Motivations

I have always thought the actions of men the best interpreters of their thoughts.

John Locke

Have you ever done something that surprised you? Afterwards you may have said, "Did I say that?" Or "Did I do that?" If our own motivation is often so confusing to us, how much more complex and puzzling is the motivation of others. Human beings are complicated creatures. Novelists, playwrights, poets all try to reveal to us the motivations of a cross-section of people.

This unit provides a treasure trove of interesting actions and sometimes baffling motivations. "A Quarter's Worth of Fireworks" reaches into the heart of a troubled teenager while studying the interplay of a teenager and his peers, a teenager and his parents. "The Lottery Ticket" could be played out in a modern living room.

The remaining selections reveal a variety of motivations. "A Story Told to the Dark" carries an inspirational message and reveals positive motivation. It is balanced by "The Mysterious Mansion" and "Mateo Falcone," both of which dig into dark recesses of the human heart. In contrast to the violent action of these two, "Never" is a depiction of passivity and indecision. The seven selections provide a cross-section of humanity and human actions.

A Quarter's Worth of Fireworks

Norman Katkov
American

**Will I ever forget the feeling of desperate doom falling
upon us as Sid dropped to the ground and the bag slipped out
of my hands? Will I ever forget—can I forget—the panic as the
light blazed suddenly in the house and we heard her hobbling
across the bare floor of the sleeping porch upstairs?**

Peer pressure. Few words hold as much meaning, heartache,
and often disaster as these. Peer pressure suggests an overpowering
yearning to be part of a group, to be accepted, to be like the rest of
the crowd. Though peer pressure wields its influence throughout life,
it is especially strong during the teen years when young people are
trying to find out who they are. Smoking is a sad example. Many young
people who know the deadly results of smoking begin because others
in the crowd are smoking. Motivation has many sources.

"A Quarter's Worth of Fireworks" follows a young man through
an escapade that grew out of peer pressure. Though unpleasant, the
experience has an unexpected result, helping him toward greater
maturity. It proves a turning point in the relationship of a father and a
son.

A Quarter's Worth of Fireworks

In those days in our house we each got a dime for the Fourth of July: a nickel for ice cream and a nickel for the afternoon movie on Concord Street: Tom Mix in one feature and Hoot Gibson in the other. Louie would have his dime in his back pocket because there wasn't room for anything more in the front pocket. Joey, the baby, would have ten pennies in his handkerchief in his fist because he liked money. I, Danny, the eldest, would have mine in my stash pocket as I walked between them, holding a hand of each, because that was orders from pa. We were the three Lombardi kids from Colorado Street whose ma sewed for money and whose pa worked in the Great Northern yards, walking back and forth every day to save trolley fare.

In those days everything was orders in our house. It was orders to go to the movies to celebrate the Fourth of July. It was orders to come straight home, with me responsible. It was orders to cross the street before coming to the house with the high black fence where Harry Connery's mother lived. They said he had something to do with moonshine. They said he was bad. When he came to visit his mother, the men from Colorado Street would stand on the corner and guess how much his long touring car cost.

For me it was also orders to keep clear of the bluff where the other guys were shooting off the Minnesota Salutes: three- and five-inch firecrackers as big around as a penny. They were against the law to sell in the city limits, so the guys bought them up on Dodd Road in Dakota County.

Everything was an order from pa, who called us into the living room that one night before the Fourth, the evening paper spread on the couch and the citizenship certificates, his and ma's, hanging on the wall above his head in the double frame she had bought on Robert Street.

He sat like a kid—I can see him yet, with one leg under him. We could hear the money in his fist as he smiled at us.

"Dan, how you feel, eh?" he asked, as though we hadn't been eating supper together in the kitchen half an hour ago.

"I feel fine, pa," I said, because you had to do it this way, like he had done for his pa in Sicily.

Pa said, "Louie, everything O.K. with you?"

"Sure, pa," Louie said, and I had the idea then. As I heard the coins, I thought of it. My heart caught so that for an instant it hurt when I breathed.

I watched pa, who said, "Hey, you, Joey," as I stood there feeling all the danger of what I was going to say before I even knew if I was going to say it. I waited, biting my lip for guts as pa pulled Joey forward, bending to kiss the uncombed black hair. "How is my baby?" he asked. Joey nodded, waiting patiently for his due.

"All right," pa said. "So. Tomorrow is Fourth of July. Larry Ho says please make safe-and-sane holiday. Newspaper says all should be careful."

Larry Ho was the nickname of our mayor, whom pa had never seen, but never called anything else because he had voted for the man.

"Movies is safe and sane," pa said. "Movies, and for each ice cream and, later, when night comes, sparklers."

Sparklers again!

Sitting on the front-porch steps below ma and pa, as I had last year, watching the sparklers he had stuck in the ground, waiting for them to burn out, so I could go up to the corner where the guys were. I almost said it then, because I had said it three times to myself, but only stood quiet as pa counted pennies aloud, dropping each one into Joey's cupped hands.

When pa got to ten, he said, "Louie," and handed over a dime.

"Thanks," Louie said, as pa looked up at me. He smiled at me and I saw the dime in his hand.

He said, "Danny," and I couldn't hold it back.

"No," I said, instead of the speech I had repeated to myself three times.

"Take your dime," pa said. He hadn't even heard me. "For movies tomorrow."

"No," I said. He heard me that time. "I don't want——"

"Take, mister," pa said.

"I don't want a dime," I announced, stepping back from the couch. "I don't want to go to the movies," I said. "I don't want to watch sparklers. I want a quarter."

"A quarter?" he repeated, moving on the couch so both legs were swung over the side now, the stockinged feet touching the floor. "Why a quarter?" he asked. "You tell me, please," he said.

"Why a quarter?"

I could feel my fingernails all the way into my palms, but I said it. "Minnesota Salutes," I said. "I want to buy two packs like the rest of the——"

"——guys in block," pa finished for me. "And if they smoke, mister? Then will you smoke? And if they will hitch a ride to a truck to go——"

"Peter," ma said, but he didn't even look up at her.

"——downtown and be bums on the streets?"

"I'm no bum," I said. I was in it now, I guess, talking to him as I had never talked to him before. "I don't smoke," I continued. "You know that. Do you think I smoke?" I demanded, and he reached out on the couch for the newspaper.

"You heard Larry Ho of this safe-and-sane holiday," he declared. "You know of this terrible burn and explosion from big firecrackers, eh? You know I like if you take Louie and Joey to the movies?"

"How about what I like?" I asked.

"Daniel," ma said.

I turned my head, but she said no with her lips.

"Here, you," pa said. He was holding the dime out. I turned to ma again, but she said no again without saying anything, and then I didn't care.

I grabbed the dime and threw with all my might, and then I ran. I banged the swinging door into the kitchen so that it slammed the sink, and the dishes in the dryer rattled, but I kept going, down the back steps, over our yard, through Morgan's yard and Dwyer's yard. When I reached the sidewalk I turned right, and slowed down a little.

Robert Street was a shopping street. A shopping street was trouble where pa was concerned, so it was against orders. He didn't want his kids there. I was never going back home, so I didn't care. Five minutes later I was on it, with all the lights in the world burning at once, and enough people to fill the ball park just walking along.

I walked with them, my hands in my pockets and wondering where I would sleep. I wondered where I would eat and what kind of a job I should look for. I wondered if pa and ma would go to the cops. There was a cop on the corner ahead of me. Behind him, leaning against the windows of a fruit-and-vegetable store, I saw Sid Glotter and Gutless Wonder, whose real name was Tommy Richards. I turned quick, taking big steps to the curb. I was waiting for the traffic light to change when I heard Sid.

"Hey, Dan!" he said. "Get home before I tell your old man."

I walked back slow, wanting to see Sid's nose splattered over his face, my hands loose at my sides and the fingers curled just a little.

"Tell him," I said.

Sid sneered at me. "Does he know you're out, baby boy?"

"Yeh," Gutless put in, "ain't mamma gonna spank when mamma gets you home?"

I wasn't afraid of him. I looked right at him. "What's it to you, Gutless?" I asked. "What business is it of yours?"

Sid put his hand on my arm. "Take it easy, Dan," he said.

I pushed his hand off me. "Just mind your business," I said. I was mad and I was afraid. I had seen Sid give it to Joe Grabowski, and Joe was bigger too. But I couldn't back away. Gutless Wonder would never let me forget it.

"Beat it," Gutless said. "Go on, beat it."

"When I'm ready," I said. By busting in, Gutless had stopped anything happening between Sid and me. I could get away now, but I had to wait a minute, so it wouldn't look like they were chasing me. I opened my belt and pulled it tight, looking down to get it right, taking as much time as a pitcher.

"I'll see you guys," I said, and felt Sid's hand on my arm again.

"Where you headed for, Dan?" he said.

"To get some Minnesota Salutes," I told him. I moved his hand off me, turning away from them, my hands in my pockets lifting my pants high off my shoes, swearing at myself for saying what I did. I don't know why I said it. Tomorrow they would be waiting on the bluff. I'd be the bum of the street.

I crossed with the light, walking with my head down. I'd never been so alone in my life. I guess I'd never really felt hopeless. I would just have to keep going and hitch a ride on a truck. I headed out toward the Flats, where Robert Street ended and the highway began. I was down near the license-plate factory when they caught up with me. They ran around in front of me, walking backward.

"There ain't no Salutes out here," Sid said. "There's nothing but potato farms out here. You ain't got money, Dan."

"I'll get it," I said. "I'll get it." Why had I stopped to talk with them in the first place?

"Where?" Sid asked.

"Don't worry."

"Where?"

"Don't worry!"

That's when Sid stopped walking backward. He stopped—boom, like that—putting his hands against my chest and pushing. "I know where," he said. He was pushing backward, not hard, but the way a friend pushes. Now I was walking backward while they were going forward until we were all in the dark, against the wall of the license-plate factory. "Do you want to know where?" Sid asked.

"Maybe," I said.

He put his face right up to mine. "Harry Connery's mother is where," he said, and I shivered.

I felt it cold all across my back. I felt it hurt in my chest. "You're crazy," I whispered.

"Unh-uh," he said. He shook his head real slow. "I'm smart, Dan."

"Yeh," Tommy said, giggling. He was nervous. I could tell he was nervous. "Yeh, Sid's smart," Gutless said.

"Ah, you shut up," Sid said. He looked at me again. "There's a tree in the alley behind Harry Connery's house," he whispered. "We go up the tree, swing out over the fence, drop down into the yard. We got three empty bags here. We fill them full of tomatoes out of old lady Connery's garden. We take them up on Robert Street to the fruit-and-vegetable store. We get a quarter a box. We send Gutless Wonder up on Dodd Road. He comes back with two packs each of Minnesota Salutes."

"You're crazy," I said. "What about Harry Connery?"

"He's not there," Sid assured me.

"How do you know there's tomatoes?" I asked.

"Quit stalling," Sid said. "I need somebody to——"

"I got to be home," I said.

"——come into the yard with me. Gutless Wonder will stand watch outside. That's the most you can expect from Gutless Wonder. What are you, Dan, another one?"

"I got to be——"

"Gutless," Sid said, and took his hands from my chest. "I knew it." He started walking toward the lighted end of Robert Street. I ran ahead of him and turned. I said, "I never stole before. Nothing."

"This ain't stealing, for Pete's sake," he said. "Old lady Connery all alone. Nutty as a hoot owl. What's she going to do with all those tomatoes?"

It was pa's fault. One stinking quarter! He could have done that. He didn't have to order my whole life!

"O.K.," I said. I put my hands in my pockets, lifting my pants high above my shoes. "Come on."

"Yeh, that's the stuff," Gutless said. He started to come up beside me. Sid didn't even look. He just reached over and pushed Gutless. "Behind us," he said. "You can't walk with the men."

That was all he or any of us said until we were in the alley behind the block old lady Connery lived in.

There he whispered, "Give me the bags, Gutless." He got the bags. "We'll fill 'em together, Dan. We'll stack 'em against the tree. I'll go up. You hand 'em to me. I'll go over with 'em, one at a time. Gutless will run 'em up here." He pointed at the grassy slope behind Eli Watkins' house. "When you hand me the third bag, follow me out. O.K.?"

I wanted to say no, but I nodded. I was in it, nodding at Sid Glotter, whom I didn't even like. Whom I was afraid of, really.

I can never remember all of it. I remember going up in the tree. I don't remember coming down into the garden. I can remember the ground smell still, and on a clear summer night, wherever I am, I can still see the tomato vines in the moonlight, yet I can't remember picking the tomatoes. I can't remember filling the bags, or carrying the bags, or handing the bags up to Sid, but I remember the tree groaning with his weight. I remember Sid leaning forward for the third bag, and will I ever forget the terrifying moment when the branch broke?

Will I ever forget the feeling of desperate doom falling upon us as Sid dropped to the ground and the bag slipped out of my hands? Will I ever forget—can I forget—the panic as the light blazed suddenly in the house and we heard her hobbling across the bare floor of the sleeping porch upstairs?

"Sid?" I said. I couldn't find him. I tried to whisper. "Sid, are you all right? Where are you, Sid?"

"Shut up and come on," he whispered. "Come on," he whispered, reaching for a branch, swinging with his legs free like a man on a trapeze.

For a crazy second I was paralyzed until another light flashed on in the house, and a third. I jumped and grabbed and was kicked in the ribs as Sid struggled upward. I saw the lights going on in the house and twisted like a monkey from side to side moving up, up, up until I was even with the fence, reaching, holding, climbing higher than the fence and then pushing away from the tree with all my might, falling over and down.

Over the fence with palms out into the dry, rocky, hard-as-cement alley, feeling the rocks cut, feeling my pants rip at the knees, feeling my ribs hurt, crawling forward as I moved, even while I tried to straighten up, like a sprinter after the starting gun sounds.

I passed Sid. I was running with all my might, but I couldn't pass Gutless, who was waiting for us when we got to the grass behind Eli Watkins' house.

"Get the two bags," Sid said, but he was through bossing me. He took one. I got Gutless Wonder by the shoulder, shoving him so he almost fell.

"Go on," I said. I was shaking. I was sick from what had happened. "Go on, Gutless. Running Gutless. Worrying about yourself. Go on, take——"

"Watch yourself, Dan," Sid said.

"And you," I said, turning to him. "Thief," I called him. "What are you going to do, thief? I'm a thief, so what do you think you'll do? Come on, then," I said. "Come on," as Gutless backed off, cradling his bag of tomatoes.

"I'll see you later," Sid warned me.

"Now," I said. "Now if you want it, or tomorrow, or whenever you think you're big enough." I was ready. I didn't care if he beat me up. I just wanted to be clean of him. He made me sick, and what I had done made me more sick.

"O.K.," Sid said. He was hurrying off, carrying the tomatoes. "O.K., Dan, I'll remember."

I watched them go. Then I turned toward home.

Don't you see? It was like I wanted a licking. I wanted pa to beat me up. It would be kind of payment for what I did.

He didn't even say hello. He looked at me over the rim of the glass of soda water he was drinking, sitting across the kitchen table from ma. I got one look before he went back to the newspaper.

"Good morning," ma said. I saw it was five minutes to ten.

"Hi," I said, starting for my bedroom.

Ma dropped her sewing. "Dan!" she cried. I had forgotten my hands. My hands, my knees, the ripped pants, and the ribs she couldn't see.

"Daniel Lombardi, you hurt!"

"No, I'm not, ma." I was looking at him, but he kept reading the newspaper.

"Hitched a ride by a truck," ma decided, "and fell."

I wanted to tell him then. I wanted him to share it with me, I guess, and take some of the sickness away, but as ma grabbed me my knees hurt so much I almost cried out.

"Look, Peter; from truck," she said.

"I didn't fall off no truck, ma," I said. "We were scaling the fire-barn wall. I fell off."

"Peter, look here on Dan," ma said.

He folded the newspaper real slow. He got up. He put the newspaper under his arm. He looked at me. Looked through me. Then he walked out.

"Come on, come on," ma said, pulling me to the sink.

"I'm no baby," I said. "I can wash myself." He had never done anything like that: just walked out when one of us was hurt. While I was washing and ma was bandaging, I waited for him to come into the kitchen. All I heard was the turning of the newspaper pages. When I was finished, when ma had poured me milk and given me three cookies, I said, "Pa never did that."

"What?" She was busy with the needle once more.

"Paid no attention if someone was hurt."

"Pa hurts, too, Dan."

"What are you talking about?" I demanded.

"Hurts here," she said, pressing her heart.

"What if I don't want to go to the movies?" I asked. "Is that so wrong?"

"Wrong for pa," she said. "Dan, you don't know hows pa feel about Fourth of July? Pa feels like go to church on Fourth of July. Pa feels this is the most important day, Independence Day."

I got up, leaving the milk and cookies. I ran into the living room, stopping in front of him. I moved the papers with my hand so he could see me, and I said, "I'm sorry, pa."

"M'm'm'm'm," he said.

"I didn't mean it."

"M'm'm'm'm'm."

"Pa, please."

"All right, mister. Now maybe I finish this newspaper."

I almost ripped the paper. I almost kicked it like you would punt a football. I wanted to do something, anything, to get rid of all the feelings inside of me, but I could only walk back into the kitchen to dunk my cookies.

"What's the matter with him?" I asked ma.

"He hurts," ma announced again.

"I hurt, too," I said. "Haven't I got feelings?"

Ma smiled, shaking her head. "Someday you be a papa, Danny. Someday you have a oldest son. Oldest son can hurt like nothing can hurt."

"Is that a reason to——"

"Listen, you," ma said. She wasn't sewing now. "Finish milk and go to bedroom."

On my way to bed I went into the living room for a book I didn't want. After I was in my pajamas, I came back and got another book I didn't want, but he didn't even look up. I waited about five minutes and went back.

"Can I have the funnies?" I asked.

Pa went through the paper like each sheet was a thousand dollars. When he gave me the funnies, I said, "Thanks."

"M'm'm'm'm," he said. I went to sleep with that. That's what my pa gave me for good night. Long afterward, when the lights were out in the house, when I could hear the floor boards creaking and I seemed all alone in the world, I got to sleep by telling myself he would make up in the morning. He would grab my neck, cup my neck in his hand like he always had done, pulling me forward to knock my head against his head so lightly it was like a leaf falling to the ground.

I was wrong. I couldn't have been wronger. Pa was gone.

He came in while I was finishing my toast. He carried a bag under his arm. I said, "Hi, pa. Is it hot out?" but he only turned to ma.

"Where are the boys?" he asked. "I don't see Louie or Joey."

"I can't tell," she said. "My nurse is off today."

Pa went through the kitchen as she shook her head. "Sicilians," ma said. "Stay 'way from him, Danny."

"Yes," I said. "I can do it now," I said. I slid out from behind the kitchen table. I got my cap from the peg as I went out into the sun. I guess I was just tired of begging. Of begging, of being kicked around, of being brushed off. I went down Colorado Street to the playgrounds to shag flies for an hour. Afterward I watched a scrub game between two teams of older guys. Then Herman Simon wanted to see some planes take off, so we walked to the airport. The sun was almost straight over us, so we sat alongside the hangar in the shade for a while. Coming back, we cut across the old city dump before returning over the State Street Bridge. I left Herman there to walk to the top of the Ohio Street hill, which looked down on half of the city. That's where Louie found me—sitting on the ground and leaning against a tree.

"Dan?"

"What?"

"Can I sit with you?" he asked, sitting with me.

"All right."

"The movies were terrible," Louie said.

"All right."

"You would have hated them, Dan."

"O.K."

"Do you want my ice-cream nickel?" he asked.

"No," I said. "Thanks."

"You can have it."

"No!"

"Dan," Louie said, "I'm supposed to bring you home for supper. Ma said to find you."

"You didn't find me," I said.

"Yes, I did." He was worried. "Here you are."

"I'm not hungry," I said. "Go on home."

"Come with me, Dan." He was standing now. "Please, Dan."

"I'm not hungry! Can't you understand English?" I asked, and saw he was going to cry. I got to my feet, brushing my pants. "Come on, I'll walk with you, but I'm not going home."

We came down the hill without talking. We went past the playground so we could come into Colorado Street from the near side. I said, "I'm going down to the bluff."

"Please, Dan," Louie said. He took my hand. "I'm supposed to bring you home."

"No," I said. Pa wouldn't even look at me. "No, I'm not hungry." I shook myself free, walking toward the bluff.

He walked beside me, half running to keep up with me. I could hear the Salutes going a block away. When I got there, Gutless Wonder was touching a long piece of smoking punk to a firecracker Sid Glotter held. As the wick smoldered, Sid lunged forward. Gutless Wonder said, "Sid, don't!" There was real fear in his voice as he jumped away. Sid saw me and said, "Here, Dan," motioning with the Salute. Louie jumped. Eli Watkins, on the other side of me, jumped while I stood there.

"Guts," said Sid, throwing it over the bluff. "You got guts, ain't you, Dan?"

"Enough for you."

He took a Salute from a pack. "Here," he said.

Louie tugged at my sleeve. I pushed him away as Sid came forward. "Take it," Sid insisted, holding the firecracker in front of him. "Let's be divvies. Partners."

I said, "Beat it," and behind me, a man said, "Hi, Sid."

I turned to see Harry Connery. I knew it was Harry. He was looking at me. He was big. He was taller than anybody I had ever seen. He was wearing brown-and-white shoes, and my chest hurt. I wanted a drink of water as he said, "How are you, Sid?" talking to me.

I knew then. His mother had heard me calling Sid in the darkness in the garden last night.

"I'm not Sid," I said, while Louie started to run. Louie, who couldn't look at anyone who was in trouble. I was alone now, all right. All of them around me had spread out, stepping back or to either side until there were only Harry Connery and me.

"You're not, eh? What do they call you, kid?"

"I'm Dan. Dan Lombardi." My whole back was wet. I could feel my shirt sticking to me. Then a breeze came, blowing his pants back. His legs were as big around as lampposts.

"Who's Sid?" Harry Connery asked me. He reached down to take my arm in his hand. He held my arm until it began to hurt. He said, "Come on, kid, which one? If he isn't here, where does he live? What's his last name? I'm telling you, kid, don't make me——"

"That's him!"

Harry Connery released me and I turned to see Gutless Wonder. He was already over the side of the bluff, pointing at Sid.

"There he is, mister," said Gutless Wonder. "That's the guy, Sid Glotter," and he disappeared.

Harry Connery moved, but Sid was too fast. He leaped like a broad jumper going after Gutless Wonder, and as Harry Connery stood with his back to me, I said, "Me too. I was with them, Mr. Connery."

He stopped dead, boom, like he had run against a wall. He had his back to me. I wasn't running, that's all. I had to get it over with, that's all. I didn't care what he did or what happened, I had to get it out of my head.

I had my hand to my face, feeling his five fingers on my cheek like five whips before I believed it. He had turned and come ahead and grabbed me, holding my shirt with one hand, slapping me with the other.

"Lousy little punk," he said, holding me. My face hurt so I could hardly see. "No-good, thieving punk," he said, hitting me again, on the same side again. I had to bite my lips or I would have cried. I would have just screamed, it hurt so. He had his hand up and I was trying to hide my face when Pa grabbed his arm.

"My boy," he said. "That's my boy you hit," he said, holding Harry Connery's arm in both his hands, his undershirt over his pants and his bedroom slippers on his bare feet. "You stop now," pa said.

Harry Connery stopped. He let me go and turned to pa. He looked pa up and down. He said, "Your kid?"

"Bet my life," pa said, and Harry Connery hit pa with his fist. He got him on the side of the face below the eye, and pa went on his back on the ground. His bedroom slipper fell off. I was crying then, all right. I couldn't stand it to see him on the ground. He was on his back, and he turned and pushed himself. He was on his hands and knees then, shaking his head, and when he saw me, he said, "Don't cry here," he said. "This is America. Don't have to be afraid here!"

"I stole tomatoes," I said. "Pa, I stole." And I told him.

"Will be all right," he said, and got to his feet then. He stood before Harry Connery, and he said, "Is just a boy, mister. I 'pologize for my boy. I pay hows much you say," and as he reached for his coin purse, with his hand in his pocket, Harry Connery hit him again, right under the same eye.

When he fell—when pa fell this time, he didn't lie on the ground. He got up and backed away, and he said, "You don't do nice, mister." He shook his head. "If my boy do wrong, he's a boy. I teach him," and Harry Connery swung.

But pa swung. Pa had closed his right hand, which all week used a sledge and a crowbar in the Great Northern Railroad shops, and as pa got hit, his fist found Harry Connery. Pa closed his left fist, swinging with that, and that found Harry Connery. Harry Connery went back against the big round disk on the fence that lit up to show drivers it was a dead end. He was hanging there a minute with pa in front of him and both bedroom slippers were off.

"Now you stop, mister," pa said in his bare feet. "Now you finish. I don't care if you real tough guy; you don't hit boys. Not kids. My kid. My Dan," pa said, and I could see him beginning to shake. I saw him shake, which was the real sign he was mad. I had only seen him like that once, when an uncle of ma's in Naples wrote a letter and sent a picture of Benito Mussolini.

"I don't care who you bootleg, you hear me, mister," pa said. "You don't touch kids. I go tomorrow. I 'pologize to your mamma. Sweet woman, your mamma; always say hello with my wife. I bring him," pa said, gesturing at me, "and he 'pologize. And whatever she say, he do: plant tomato, sweep sidewalk, shovel snow all winter, whatever. But you don't hit, mister. Not in America. . . . Dan, bring slippers," pa said. He turned to Harry Connery again. "Not in America," pa repeated.

I dropped the slippers on the ground, because he would yell if I bent to help him. He said that nobody had to bend. He got his slippers on and he turned to me.

"You stay, Dan?" he asked. "Stay or come home?" he asked.

I wanted to grab his hand. I wanted to swing on his arm and jump on his back, like I used to, but I was too old now. I just wanted to hold him, but I said, "I'll go home."

That's all I said and that's all he said. We walked in the street. His eye was beginning to puff. He was going to have some shiner. We passed Clinton Avenue without talking, and Greenwood Street, and there, half-way down the block, when I could see the chairs on our front porch, pa stopped. He turned to me in the street, reaching into his pocket.

He had his hand in his pocket and he said, "Dan, you listen." He said, "Dan, I am——You too old——I do——" He took a deep breath. "No," he said. "Start over." I saw the quarter in his hand. "Here, Dan," he said. "You buy Minnesota Salutes," and I shook my head.

Shook my head and stepped back, turning away, or I would cry and he couldn't stop me.

"Here, take," pa said.

He stepped toward me with the quarter out, and I said, "I don't want it, pa."

"Take, son," he said, and I grabbed it. I wanted only to end this.

"I want to go home with you," I said, and pulled back my arm. I couldn't stand it about the money any longer. As I started to throw, pa grabbed me.

He was laughing and holding me, and he said, "Whoa! Whoa, Dan, I don't make these quarters." He held me to him, with my head in his chest, rubbing my hair until, in a minute, he said, "All right?" He nodded at me. "Are you all right, my son?"

"Yes," I said. "Yes, I'm all right, pa," and he took the quarter. He put the quarter in my stash pocket and he cupped my neck. He was bending forward and he moved me forward until our heads touched.

"Come on, Dan," he said. "We go light our sparklers for safe-and-sane Fourth."

Reading for Understanding

Main Idea

1. The central problem of the story is (a) Sid's lack of responsibility (b) the danger in playing with fireworks (c) the value of friendship (d) Dan's self-image.

Details

2. Harry Connery's mother (a) was a criminal (b) lived near the movie theater (c) grew tomatoes (d) disowned her son.
3. Gutless Wonder is (a) Sid's brother (b) Harry Connery (c) Louie (d) Tommy Richards.
4. The lights went on in the house because (a) Sid cried out (b) a branch broke (c) Harry arrived home (d) Gutless hurt himself.
5. Larry Ho was (a) a seller of firecrackers (b) an owner of a restaurant in town (c) the mayor (d) chief of police.

Inferences

6. Pa acted as he did because he (a) was deeply concerned about his children (b) had a streak of cruelty in him (c) was indifferent about the younger children (d) had lost the respect of his wife.
7. Harry Connery (a) was probably engaged in a shady business (b) enjoyed meeting with the young people of the community (c) made Danny's father run away from him (d) had little respect for his mother.

Author's Attitude

8. The author's attitude toward pa was one of (a) coldness (b) respect (c) disapproval (d) bafflement.

Order of Events

9. Arrange the items in the order in which they occurred. Use letters only.
   A. Pa strikes Connery.
   B. Danny runs away from home.
   C. The boys steal tomatoes.
   D. Pa and Danny walk off together.
   E. Connery hurts Danny.

Outcomes

10. At the end of the story, (a) Sid gets Danny to go on another tomato raid (b) Danny refuses to apologize to Mrs. Connery (c) Danny and

his father get along better together (d) Danny is punished severely by his father.

Thinking Critically about the Story

1. Why did the author choose the title "A Quarter's Worth of Fireworks"? Why not choose a title more directly associated with the robbery?

2. Why was Dan led to do something he basically disapproved of?

3. Was Danny's father a good father? Explain.

4. How did Sid's attitude toward Dan change when Dan began to challenge him?

5. A story may have what is often called a *turning point* or a *defining moment*. What episode in "A Quarter's Worth of Fireworks" proved to be the turning point of the story?

6. What is the strength of peer pressure, a power that makes people do what they really don't want to do? Do people respect those who don't always run with the crowd? Explain.

7. Why did Dan say, "Me, too. I was with them, Mr. Connery"? At that point, Dan seemed to be safe from Connery. Why did he jeopardize himself?

8. How does the author contrast Harry Connery and Dan's father?

9. Motivations are a major consideration in this unit. What makes Gutless act the way he does?

10. *Gutless* is a cruel nickname. Why do people often commit little acts of cruelty in dealing with each other?

Language in Action

Levels of Usage

Sid put his hand on my arm. "Take is easy, Dan," he said.

"Beat it," Gutless said. "Go on, beat it."

"This ain't stealing, for Pete's sake," he said.

You wouldn't wear a tuxedo or evening dress to a picnic, nor would you wear dungarees or sports dress at a formal wedding reception. There's a time and place for everything—including words.

The three statements above have a slightly different flavor. The first is colloquial English, the language of conversation. This is the language we use nearly all the time. If you listen to the conversations at a party, you'll notice that they tend to use colloquial English.

The second example is also colloquial, but it uses the slang expression *beat it,* meaning "go away." Slang expressions dominate some conversations, with expressions like *neat, cool, far out.* Slang has been called "the poetry of the streets." It can be colorful, but slang expressions often die out when the fad has passed. Some slang words like *fun* and *stingy* do eventually make it into the language.

The third expression, with its use of *ain't,* is considered substandard English. Though a long resident in the English language, *ain't* has still not gained acceptance as a respectable word of choice. When Dan says, "I didn't fall off no truck, ma," he is using the double negative, another unacceptable usage in situations where language counts—as in a job interview.

Formal English, or literary English, is reserved for more serious occasions: a scholarly book, a funeral oration, a wedding ceremony. Some words that appear in literary English—like *confront, relegate,* and *compliance*—seldom find their way into colloquial English. The Declaration of Independence and the Constitution of the United States are written in formal English.

> Formal: "We hold these truths to be self-evident, that all men are created equal, that they are endowed by their Creator with certain unalienable rights . . ."

> Colloquial: "It's pretty clear to us that people are really equal and have some rights that can't be taken away from them."

The seriousness of the Declaration of Independence calls for impressive, formal language. The colloquial counterpart lacks grandeur and is inappropriate for the occasion. As a paraphrase on another occasion though, it's good. It avoids the now-disapproved use of *men* for *humankind.* The Declaration was written in a much earlier time.

A good rule is to use language that doesn't call attention to itself. Don't use formal English in a friendly conversation. Don't use slang in a formal situation. Avoid substandard English in any situation that affects your future.

The Lottery Ticket

Anton Chekhov
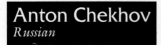
Russian

> "Masha, 9,499 is there!" he said in a hollow voice.
> His wife looked at his astonished and panic-stricken face,
> and realized that he was not joking.
> "9,499?" she asked, turning pale and dropping the folded
> tablecloth on the table.
> "Yes, yes . . . it really is there!"

Whatever you may think of lotteries, they are a fact of life in many states. Millions of people check television and newspaper reports, hoping that their special numbers will turn up. Heavy advertising promotions add fuel to the fire by picturing what life would be like for a lottery winner. "The Lottery Ticket" was written a century or more ago, but the plot is timeless. The characters' actions and motivations are recognizable.

Ivan and Masha may have a ticket to luxury. The first part of the problem has been solved. They have a ticket with the first four numbers, but what of the remaining two? Why does Ivan delay checking the remaining two numbers? How does this delay reveal character and sum up two lives?

The Lottery Ticket

Ivan Dmitritch, a middle-class man who lived with his family on an income of twelve hundred a year and was very well satisfied with his lot, sat down on the sofa after supper and began reading the newspaper.

"I forgot to look at the newspaper today," his wife said to him as she cleared the table. "Look and see whether the list of drawings is there."

"Yes, it is," said Ivan Dmitritch; "but hasn't your ticket lapsed?"

"No; I took the interest on Tuesday."

"What is the number?"

"Series 9,499, number 26."

"All right . . . we will look . . . 9,499 and 26."

Ivan Dmitritch had no faith in lottery luck, and would not, as a rule, have consented to look at the lists of winning numbers, but now, as he had nothing else to do and as the newspaper was before his eyes, he passed his finger downwards along the column of numbers. And immediately, as though in mockery of his skepticism, no further than the second line from the top, his eye was caught by the figure 9,499! Unable to believe his eyes, he hurriedly dropped the paper on his knees without looking to see the number of the ticket, and, just as though some one had given him a douche of cold water, he felt an agreeable chill in the pit of the stomach; tingling and terrible and sweet!

"Masha, 9,499 is there!" he said in a hollow voice.

His wife looked at his astonished and panic-stricken face, and realized that he was not joking.

"9,499?" she asked, turning pale and dropping the folded table-cloth on the table.

"Yes, yes . . . it really is there!"

"And the number of the ticket?"

"Oh, yes! There's the number of the ticket too. But stay . . . wait! No, I say! Anyway, the number of our series is there! Anyway, you understand . . . ."

Looking at his wife, Ivan Dmitritch gave a broad, senseless smile, like a baby when a bright object is shown it. His wife smiled too; it was as pleasant to her as to him that he only mentioned the series, and did not try to find out the number of the winning ticket. To torment and tantalize oneself with hopes of possible fortune is so sweet, so thrilling!

"It is our series," said Ivan Dmitritch, after a long silence. "So there is a probability that we have won. It's only a probability, but there it is!"

"Well, now look!"

"Wait a little. We have plenty of time to be disappointed. It's on the second line from the top, so the prize is seventy-five thousand. That's not money, but power, capital! And in a minute I shall look at the list, and there—26! Eh? I say, what if we really have won?"

The husband and wife began laughing and staring at one another in silence. The possibility of winning bewildered them; they could not have said, could not have dreamed, what they both needed that seventy-five thousand for, what they would buy, where they would go. They thought only of the figures 9,499 and 75,000 and pictured them in their imagination, while somehow they could not think of the happiness itself which was so possible.

Ivan Dmitritch, holding the paper in his hand, walked several times from corner to corner, and only when he had recovered from the first impression began dreaming a little.

"And if we have won," he said—"why, it will be a new life, it will be a transformation! The ticket is yours, but if it were mine I should, first of all, of course, spend twenty-five thousand on real property in the shape of an estate; ten thousand on immediate expenses, new furnishing . . . travelling . . . paying debts, and so on. . . . The other forty thousand I would put in the bank and get interest on it."

"Yes, an estate, that would be nice," said his wife, sitting down and dropping her hands in her lap.

"Somewhere in the Tula or Oryol provinces. . . . In the first place we shouldn't need a summer villa, and besides, it would always bring in an income."

And pictures came crowding on his imagination, each more gracious and poetical than the last. And in all these pictures he saw himself well-fed, serene, healthy, felt warm, even hot! Here, after eating a summer soup, cold as ice, he lay on his back on the burning sand close to a stream or in the garden under a lime-tree. . . . It is hot. . . . His little boy and girl are crawling about near him, digging in the sand or catching ladybirds in the grass. He dozes sweetly, thinking of nothing, and feeling all over that he need not go to the office today, tomorrow, or the day after. Or, tired of lying still, he goes to the hayfield, or to the forest for mushrooms, or watches the peasants catching fish with a net. When the sun sets he takes a towel and soap and saunters to the bathing-shed, where he undresses at his leisure, slowly rubs his bare chest with his hands, and goes into the water. And in the water, near the opaque soapy circles, little fish flit to and fro and green water-weeds nod their heads. After bathing there is tea with cream and milk rolls. . . . In the evening a walk or *vint* with the neighbours.

"Yes, it would be nice to buy an estate," said his wife, also dreaming, and from her face it was evident that she was enchanted by her thoughts.

Ivan Dmitritch pictured to himself autumn with its rains, its cold evenings, and its St. Martin's summer.* At that season he would have to take longer walks about the garden and beside the river, so as to get thoroughly chilled, and then drink a big glass of vodka and eat a salted mushroom or a soused cucumber, and then—drink another. . . . The children would come running from the kitchen-garden, bringing a carrot and a radish smelling of fresh earth. . . . And then, he would lie stretched full length on the sofa, and in leisurely fashion turn over the pages of some illustrated magazine, or, covering his face with it and unbuttoning his waistcoat, give himself up to slumber.

The St. Martin's summer is followed by cloudy, gloomy weather. It rains day and night, the bare trees weep, the wind is damp and cold. The dogs, the horses, the fowls—all are wet, depressed, downcast. There is nowhere to walk; one can't go out for days together; one has to pace up and down the room, looking despondently at the grey window. It is dreary!

Ivan Dmitritch stopped and looked at his wife.

"I should go abroad, you know, Masha," he said.

And he began thinking how nice it would be in late autumn to go abroad somewhere to the South of France . . . to Italy . . . to India!

"I should certainly go abroad too," his wife said. "But look at the number of the ticket!"

"Wait, wait! . . ."

He walked about the room and went on thinking. It occurred to him: what if his wife really did go abroad? It is pleasant to travel alone, or in the society of light, careless women who live in the present, and not such as think and talk all the journey about nothing but their children, sigh, and tremble with dismay over every farthing. Ivan Dmitritch imagined his wife in the train with a multitude of parcels, baskets, and bags; she would be sighing over something, complaining that the train made her head ache, that she had spent so much money. . . . At the stations he would continually be having to run for boiling water, bread and butter. . . . She wouldn't have dinner because of its being too dear . . . .

"She would begrudge me every farthing," he thought, with a glance at his wife. "The lottery ticket is hers, not mine! Besides, what is the use of her going abroad? What does she want there? She would shut herself up in the hotel, and not let me out of her sight. . . . I know!"

And for the first time in his life his mind dwelt on the fact that his wife had grown elderly and plain, and that she was saturated through and through with the smell of cooking, while he was still young, fresh, and healthy, and might well have got married again.

---

*Usually around November 11, St. Martin's Day. It is a European term for our *Indian Summer.*

"Of course, all that is silly nonsense," he thought; "but . . . why should she go abroad? What would she make of it? And yet she would go, of course. . . . I can fancy . . . In reality it is all one to her, whether it is Naples or Klin. She would only be in my way. I should be dependent upon her. I can fancy how, like a regular woman, she will lock the money up as soon as she gets it. . . . She will hide it from me. . . . She will look after her relations and grudge me every farthing."

Ivan Dmitritch thought of her relations. All those wretched brothers and sisters and aunts and uncles would come crawling about as soon as they heard of the winning ticket, would begin whining like beggars, and fawning upon them with oily, hypocritical smiles. Wretched, detestable people! If they were given anything, they would ask for more; while if they were refused, they would swear at them, slander them, and wish them every kind of misfortune.

Ivan Dmitritch remembered his own relations, and their faces, at which he had looked impartially in the past, struck him now as repulsive and hateful.

"They are such reptiles!" he thought.

And his wife's face, too, struck him as repulsive and hateful. Anger surged up in his heart against her, and he thought malignantly:

"She knows nothing about money, and so she is stingy. If she won it she would give me a hundred roubles, and put the rest away under lock and key."

And he looked at his wife, not with a smile now, but with hatred. She glanced at him too, and also with hatred and anger. She had her own daydreams, her own plans, her own reflections; she understood perfectly well what her husband's dreams were. She knew who would be the first to try and grab her winnings.

"It's very nice making daydreams at other people's expense!" is what her eyes expressed. "No, don't you dare!"

Her husband understood her look; hatred began stirring again in his breast, and in order to annoy his wife he glanced quickly, to spite her at the fourth page on the newspaper and read out triumphantly:

"Series 9,499, number 46! Not 26!"

Hatred and hope both disappeared at once, and it began immediately to seem to Ivan Dmitritch and his wife that their rooms were dark and small and low-pitched, that the supper they had been eating was not doing them good, but lying heavy on their stomachs, that the evenings were long and wearisome. . . .

"What the devil's the meaning of it?" said Ivan Dmitritch, beginning to be ill-humoured. "Wherever one steps there are bits of paper under one's feet, crumbs, husks. The rooms are never swept! One is simply forced to go out. Damnation takes my soul entirely! I shall go and hang myself on the first aspen-tree!"

Reading for Understanding

Main Idea

1. The central point of the story can best be expressed by the phrase (a) What if? (b) A penny saved (c) Time and tide (d) Not worth a farthing.

Details

2. The prize was for (a) 9,499 (b) 10,000 (c) 25,000 (d) 75,000.

3. All the following are Ivan's daydreams EXCEPT (a) watching peasants fishing (b) going into the water (c) buying an expensive colt (d) traveling abroad.

4. The remaining winning number was (a) 16 (b) 26 (c) 36 (d) 46.

5. The ticket actually belonged to (a) Masha (b) Ivan (c) the oldest daughter (d) a favorite aunt.

Inferences

6. The one who would be most affected by a winning lottery ticket is probably (a) Masha (b) Ivan (c) the son (d) the daughter.

7. A possible misfortune of a winning lottery ticket is (a) extra money (b) bothersome relatives (c) cruelty to the children (d) giving up a job.

Outcomes

8. At the conclusion of the story, Masha and Ivan probably (a) were closer than ever (b) went abroad (c) continued as before (d) divorced.

Author's Attitude

9. The author's attitude toward Ivan is probably one of (a) restrained enthusiasm (b) awed admiration (c) mild dislike (d) envy.

Fact or Opinion

Tell whether the following is a fact or an opinion.

10. Ivan and Masha would have been better off winning the lottery.

Words in Context

1. "In all these pictures he saw himself well-fed, *serene,* healthy, felt warm, even hot!" **Serene** (534) means (a) unhurt (b) bold (c) wealthy (d) peaceful.

2. "In the water, near the *opaque* soapy circles, little fish flit to and fro and green water-weeds nod their heads." **Opaque** (534) is the opposite of (a) transparent (b) dark (c) filmy (d) swiftly running

3. "'She would *begrudge* me every farthing.'" **Begrudge** (535) means (a) allot (b) give reluctantly (c) take away (d) count.

4. "All those wretched brothers and sisters and aunts and uncles would come crawling about as soon as they heard of the winning ticket, would begin whining like beggars, and *fawning* upon them with oily, hypocritical smiles." **Fawning** (536) upon means (a) addressing openly (b) commenting critically to (c) bowing to (d) asking opinions of.

5. "Anger surged up in his heart against her, and he thought *malignantly.*" **Malignantly** (536) means (a) hatefully (b) thoughtlessly (c) quickly (d) wearily.

Thinking Critically about the Story

1. The opening sentences tell us that Ivan "was very well satisfied with his lot." In the last paragraph, Ivan is "beginning to be ill-humoured." Why? Nothing has really happened. Ivan is no richer and no poorer than at the beginning. What has changed Ivan's mood?

2. Would Ivan and Masha have been better off if their ticket hadn't come close? Explain.

3. Why does Ivan delay so long in looking for the winning number in the lottery series 9,499?

4. How does Chekhov reveal the lifestyle of Masha and Ivan? Is it a purely materialistic way of life? Explain.

5. We learn more of Ivan's innermost feelings than of Masha's. Why doesn't the author give them "equal time"?

6. How do *you* personally feel about state-run lotteries? What are the arguments usually used in favor? Against?

7. What is the significance of the statement "Hatred and hope both disappeared at once"?

8. How does the lottery experience focus a lifetime of little irritations and hatreds ordinarily buried in the business of living?

Language in Action

Tracing Word Origins

She would begrudge me every farthing.

Every word has a story to tell, and *farthing* is no exception. A farthing is a former British coin worth a fourth of a penny. It took on the meaning *of little value*. The expression *not worth a farthing* expressed scorn for this forgotten coin. When you pronounce *farthing* and *fourthing* in turn, you can guess the origin: *fourth*. Language scholars, however, don't jump to conclusions. They know that explanations that seem obvious are often wrong.

Sometimes a colorful guess is correct. *Caterpillar* is indeed derived from *cat*. A caterpillar is a hairy cat. Sometimes though, the guess is incorrect. A *pantry* is not connected to the word *pan* but ultimately to the Latin *panis, bread*. Such a mistake is often called *folk etymology*.

Scholars have traced *farthing* back to Old English *feortha*, meaning a *fourth*. The Middle English form was *ferthing*. The word is related to *vierdunc (fourth part)* in Middle High German. For most purposes, that information is enough, but for scholars, the road extends farther back. There are related words in Gothic, Old Norse, Latin, Greek, and even Sanskrit. These languages are all part of the great Indo-European family.

Some students collect interesting word origins, or etymologies, as others collect stamps. Following the trail of word's history opens doors to many exciting new areas.

A Story Told to the Dark

Rainer Maria Rilke
German

In the night, unable to sleep in the overcrowded train, it became clear to him that he was really going for the sake of his childhood, hoping to rediscover something in those old streets: a doorway, a tower, a fountain, anything to induce some joy or some sorrow by which he might recognize himself again.

In Thomas Wolfe's novel **You Can't Go Home Again**, the title suggests the theme of the book. In this story, Dr. Lassmann can't exactly go home again, either, but he finds something more precious than he could ever have anticipated.

In search of Klara, a childhood friend, Dr. Lassmann learns what seems to be a sordid story of abandonment and possible betrayal. Expecting to find his friend miserable, beaten down, pessimistic, he is amazed to find the opposite.

Klara is radiantly happy. She has had a spiritual awakening that has changed her life. The explanation of that experience will challenge you.

The word **dark** in the title has rich connotations discussed in the last paragraph of the story.

A Story Told to the Dark

I WANTED to put on my coat and go to my lame friend Ewald. But I had lingered over a book, an old book at that, and evening had come, as in Russia spring comes. A moment ago the room had been distinct, even to its remotest corners, and now all the things in it were as though they had never known anything but twilight; everywhere large dark blossoms opened, and luminous gleams slipped about their velvet calyxes as on dragonfly wings.

The lame man would surely no longer be at his window. So I stayed at home. What was it I had wanted to tell him? I no longer knew. But after a while I felt that someone was entreating me for this lost story—some lonely soul, perhaps, standing far away at the window of his dusky chamber, or perhaps this very darkness itself, that surrounded me and him and all things. So it happened that I told my story to the dark. And it leaned ever closer to me so that I could speak more and more softly, quite as befits my story. It takes place in the present and begins:

After a long absence Doctor Georg Lassmann was returning to the home of his birth. He had never possessed much there, and now he had only two sisters left in his native city, both married, apparently well married; to see them again after twelve years was the purpose of his visit. So he himself believed. But in the night, unable to sleep in the over-crowded train, it became clear to him that he was really going for the sake of his childhood, hoping to rediscover something in those old streets: a doorway, a tower, a fountain, anything to induce some joy or some sorrow by which he might recognize himself again. One gets so lost in life. And then he remembered many things: the little apartment in the Heinrichsgasse with the shiny door-latch and the dark-coated tiles, the well-cared-for furniture and his parents, those two threadbare beings, standing almost awed beside it; the swift and harassed week-days and the Sundays that were like emptied rooms, the rare visitors whom one received laughing and embarrassed, the out-of-tune piano, the old canary, the heirloom armchair in which one might not sit, a birthday, an uncle who came from Hamburg, a puppet-show, a barrel-organ, a children's party, and someone calling: "Klara." The doctor had almost dropped off. They were in a station, lights went by and the listening hammer went ringing along the wheels. And that was like: Klara, Klara "Klara," the doctor reflected, now wide awake, "who was Klara anyway?" And immediately he became aware of a face, a child's face with blond, straight hair. Not that he could have described it, but he had a sense of something

541

quiet, helpless, resigned, and of a pair of narrow childish shoulders drawn still more together by a washed-out little dress, and he began to imagine a face to go with them—but then he knew that he need not imagine it. It was there—or rather, it had been there, then. So the doctor recalled his single playfellow Klara, not without effort. Until the day he went to boarding-school, at the age of about ten, he had shared with her everything that happened to him, little that it was (or was it much?). Klara had no sisters or brothers, and he had as good as none; for his older sisters did not concern themselves with him. But since then he had never asked anyone about her. How had that been possible?—He leaned back. She had been a pious child, he still remembered, and then he asked himself: "What can have become of her?" For a time the thought frightened him that she might have died. An immeasurable dread overcame him in the closely packed compartment; everything seemed to confirm this assumption: she had been a sickly child, she hadn't been very well off at home, she had often cried; undoubtedly, she was dead. The doctor could not stand it any longer; he disturbed certain of the sleepers, shoving his way between them into the corridor of the car. There he opened a window and gazed out into the blackness with the dancing sparks. That quieted him. And when he returned to the compartment later, despite the uncomfortable position, he soon went to sleep.

The reunion with his two married sisters passed off not without embarrassment. The three had forgotten how far apart, notwithstanding their close relationship, they had always remained, and endeavored for a while to act like brother and sisters. But they soon silently agreed to take refuge behind that polite mediate tone which social intercourse has invented for all occasions.

He dined at his younger sister's, whose husband was in particularly comfortable circumstances, a manufacturer with the title of Imperial Councilor; and it was after the fourth course that the doctor asked:

"Tell me, Sophie, what's become of Klara?"

"Klara who?"

"I don't remember her name. The little one, you know, a neighbor's daughter, with whom I played as a child."

"Oh, you mean Klara Söllner?"

"Söllner, that's it, Söllner. Now I remember: old Söllner was that awful old man—but what of Klara?"

His sister hesitated. "She married—and now she lives altogether in retirement."

"Yes," went on the Imperial Councilor, and his knife slid rasping across his plate, "quite retired."

"You know her too?" The doctor turned to his brother-in-law.

"Y-ye-es—just slightly; she's pretty well known here, of course."

Husband and wife exchanged a look of understanding. The

doctor noticed that for some reason they did not care to say more on the subject, and he let it drop.

The more eagerness to pursue it did the Councilor show when the lady of the house had left them to their coffee.

"This Klara," he asked with a sly smile, watching the ash that fell from his cigar into a silver bowl, "wasn't she supposed to be a quiet child and homely too?"

The doctor said nothing. The Councilor moved confidentially closer.

"That was a story!—Did you never hear of it?"

"But I haven't seen anybody to talk to."

"Talk to?" the Councilor laughed cunningly. "You could have read it in the papers."

"What?" asked the doctor nervously.

"Why, she ran off and left him—" From behind a cloud of smoke the manufacturer discharged this astonishing sentence and waited in unconfined well-being for the effect. But the effect did not seem to please him. He took on a businesslike manner, sat up straight and began to report in another, an injured tone, as it were: "Well, they had married her to Lehr, of the building council. You wouldn't have known him. Not an old man—my age. Rich, thoroughly respectable, you know, thoroughly respectable. She hadn't a penny and in addition she had no looks, no bringing-up, etc. Still, Lehr didn't want a great lady, just a modest housekeeping wife. But Klara—she was taken into society all over, everybody was kindly disposed towards her—really, they acted—well, you know, she could easily have made a position for herself—when one day, hardly two years after the wedding, off goes Klara. Can you imagine it: gone. Where? To Italy. A little pleasure-trip, not alone, naturally. All that last year we hadn't invited them—as though we had suspected! Lehr, a good friend of mine, a man of honor, a man—"

"And Klara?" the doctor broke in, rising.

"Oh, yes—well, the chastisement of heaven fell upon her. You see, the man in question—an artist, they say, you know—a casual sort of bird, naturally, just—well, when they got back from Italy, to Munich: goodbye, and she saw him no more. Now she's sitting there with her child!"

Doctor Lassmann strode excitedly up and down: "In Munich?"

"Yes, in Munich," replied the Councilor and also rose. "They say she's having a pretty miserable time—"

"How miserable?"

"Well," the Councilor gazed at his cigar, "peculiarly, and then anyhow—God, what an existence—"

Suddenly he laid his well-groomed hand on his brother-in-law's shoulder and clucked with pleasure: "You know they also used to say that she lived on—"

The doctor turned short about and walked out of the door. The Councilor, whose hand had fallen from the other's shoulder, needed ten minutes to recover from his astonishment. Then he went in to his wife and said angrily:

"I've always said so, your brother is decidedly strange."

And she, having just dozed off, yawned lazily: "Oh, Lord yes."

A fortnight later the doctor departed. He knew all at once that he must seek his childhood elsewhere. In the Munich directory he found: Klara Söllner, the name of a suburb, the street and number. He announced his coming and drove out. A slender woman greeted him in a room full of light and kindliness.

"Georg, and you remember me?"

The doctor stood still in amazement. At last he said: "So this is you, Klara."

She held her calm face with its clear brow quite still, as though to give him time to recognize her. It took long. Finally the doctor seemed to have found something that proved to him that his old playfellow really stood before him. He sought her hand again and pressed it; then slowly let it go and looked about the room. It seemed to contain nothing superfluous. At the window a desk with papers and books, at which Klara must just have been sitting. The chair had been pushed back.

"You were writing?" . . . and the doctor felt how silly the question was.

But Klara answered, unconcernedly: "Yes, I'm doing some translating."

"For publication?"

"Yes," Klara said simply, "for a publishing house."

Georg noticed some Italian photographs on the walls. Among them Giorgione's "Concert."

"You are fond of this?" He stepped nearer to the picture.

"And you?"

"I have never seen the original; it's in Florence, isn't it?"

"In the Pitti. You must go there."

"For the purpose?"

"For the purpose." There was a free and simple serenity about her. The doctor looked up thoughtfully.

"What's the matter, Georg? Won't you sit down?"

"I'm upset," he faltered. "I thought—but you aren't in the least miserable—!" he suddenly exclaimed.

Klara smiled. "You have heard my story?"

"Yes, that is—"

"Oh," she interrupted quickly, as she saw his brow darken, "it's not people's fault if they speak differently of it. The things we experience are often inexpressible, and any one who insists on telling them nevertheless, necessarily makes mistakes—" A pause.

And the doctor: "What has made you so kind?"

"Everything," she said softly and warmly. "But why do you say: kind?"

"Because—because you really ought to have grown hard. You were such a weak, helpless child; children of that sort later either grow hard or—"

"Or they die, you mean. Well, I died too. I died for many years. From the time I last saw you at home, until—" She took up something from the table. "See, this is his picture. It flatters him a little. His face is not so clear-cut, but—nicer, simpler. I'll show you our child in a moment, it's asleep in the next room. It's a boy. Called Angelo, like him. He is away now, traveling, far away."

"And you are all alone?" asked the doctor absently, still absorbed in the photograph.

"Yes, I and the child. Isn't that enough? I will tell you how it is. Angelo is a painter. His name is little known; you would never have heard it. Until lately he had been struggling with the world, with his plans, with himself and with me. Yes, with me too; because for a year I've been begging him to travel. I felt how much he needed it. Once he asked jokingly: 'Me or a child?' 'A child,' said I, and then he went."

"And when will he come back?"

"When the child can say his name, that's how we arranged it." The doctor was about to say something, but Klara laughed: "And as it's a difficult name, it will take a while yet. Angelino won't be two till summer."

"Extraordinary," said the doctor.

"What, Georg?"

"How well you understand life. How big you have grown, how young! What have you done with your childhood? We were both such—such helpless children. But that can't be altered or made never to have happened."

"You mean, we ought to have suffered from our childhood, by rights?"

"Yes, I mean just that. From that heavy darkness behind us with which we preserve such feeble, vague relations. There comes a time when we deposit in it all our firstlings, all beginning, all confidence, the seeds of all that which might perhaps some day come to be. And suddenly we realize that the whole thing has sunk in a deep sea, and we don't even know just when. We never noticed it. As though some one were to gather in all his money and buy with it a feather to stick in his hat: whish!—the first breeze carries it away. Naturally he arrives home without his feather, and nothing remains for him but to look back and think when it could have flown off."

"You are thinking of that, Georg?"

"Not any more. I've given it up. I begin somewhere behind my tenth year, at the point where I stopped praying. The rest doesn't belong to me."

"And how is it, then, that you remember me?"

"That is just why I have come to you. You are the only witness to that time. I believed I could find again in you—that which I cannot find in myself. Some gesture, some word, some name, that has significance—some enlightenment—" The doctor's head sank into his cold, uneasy hands.

Frau Klara pondered. "I remember so little of my childhood, as though there were a thousand lives between. But now that you remind me of it so, something comes back to me. One evening. You came to us, unexpectedly; your parents had gone out, to the theater or something of the sort. Our house was all lit up. My father was expecting a guest, a relative, a distant wealthy relative, if I remember rightly. He was coming from, from—I don't know where, but in any case from some distance. We had already been awaiting him for two hours. The doors were open, the lamps were burning, my mother went over from time to time and smoothed an antimacassar* on the sofa, father stood at the window. Nobody dared sit down for fear of displacing a chair. As you happened to come, you waited with us. We children listened at the door. And the later it grew, the more marvelous a guest did we expect. Yes, we even trembled lest he come before he should have attained that last degree of gloriousness to which with every minute of his not-coming he drew nearer. We were not afraid that he might not appear at all; we knew for certain he would come, but we wanted to leave him time to grow great and mighty."

Suddenly the doctor raised his hand and said sadly: "So we both know that—that he didn't come. I had not forgotten it either."

"No," Klara corroborated, "he didn't come—" And after a pause: "But it was lovely all the same!"

"What?"

"Oh, well—the waiting, the many lamps—the stillness—the festive spirit."

Something stirred in the next room. Frau Klara excused herself for a moment; and as she came brightly and serenely back, she said: "We can go in now. He's awake and smiling.—But what was it you wanted to say just now?"

"I was just wondering what could have helped you to—to yourself, to this calm possession of yourself. Life certainly hasn't made it easy for you. Evidently something helped you that I haven't got?"

"What might that be, Georg?" Klara sat down beside him.

---

*chair-back cover

"It is strange; when I first remembered you again, one night, three weeks ago, on the train, I thought: She was a pious child. And now, since I have seen you, although you are so entirely different from what I had expected—in spite of that, and yet, I would like to say, only the more surely, I believe I feel that what led you through all dangers was—your piety."

"What do you call piety?"

"Well, your relation to God; your love of God, your belief."

Frau Klara closed her eyes. "Love of God? Let me think." The doctor watched her tensely. She seemed to speak her thoughts slowly, as they came to her: "As a child—did I love God? I don't believe so. Why, I never even—it would have seemed to me insane presumption—that isn't the right word—like the worst sin, to think: *he is*. As though I had thereby compelled him to be in me, in that weak child with the absurdly long arms, in our poor apartment where everything was imitation and false, from the bronze wall-plaques of papier mâché to the wine in the bottles that bore such expensive labels. And later—" Klara made a defensive gesture with her hands, and her eyes closed tighter, as though she feared to see something dreadful through the lids—"why, I would have had to drive him out of me if he had been living in me then. But I knew nothing about him. I had quite forgotten him. I had forgotten everything.—It was in Florence, when for the first time in my life I saw, heard, felt, realized and simultaneously learned to be thankful for all those things, that I first thought of him again. There were traces of him everywhere. In all the pictures I found bits of his smile, the bells were still alive with his voice, and on the statues I saw the imprints of his hands."

"And you found him there?"

Klara looked at the doctor with large, happy eyes: "I felt that he had been—somewhere, once, had been . . . why should I have felt more? That was already more than enough."

The doctor got up and went to the window. From it one could see a stretch of field and the little old village church, and above it sky, no longer quite untouched by evening. Suddenly Doctor Lassmann asked, without turning round:

"And now?"

Receiving no answer, he came softly back again.

"Now—" Klara faltered as he stood before her, and then raised her eyes full to his face, "now I sometimes think: he will be."

The doctor took her hand and kept it a moment. He seemed to gaze into the unknown.

"What are you thinking of, Georg?"

"I'm thinking that it's like that evening once more: you are again waiting for the wonderful guest, for God, and know that he will come. And I have joined you by chance—"

Klara rose, calm and happy. She looked very young. "Well, this time we'll really wait until it happens." She said it so joyfully and so simply that the doctor had to smile. And so she led him into the adjoining room, to her child—

In this story there is nothing that children may not know. Still, the children haven't heard it. I have told it only to the dark, to no one else. And the children are afraid of the dark, and run away from it, and if some time they have to stay in it, they press their eyes shut and put their fingers in their ears. But for them also the time will come when they love the dark. From it they will learn my story, and then they will understand it better, too.

Reading for Understanding

Main Idea

1. A principal idea of the story is that (a) train travel is irritating (b) hardships may lead to spiritual awakenings (c) the more life changes, the more it remains the same (d) art is eternal.

Details

2. Dr. Lassmann hadn't seen his sisters (a) since he first met Klara (b) since his graduation (c) after a disagreement (d) in 12 years.
3. The Imperial Councilor was (a) Klara's father (b) the village schoolteacher (c) the doctor's brother-in-law (d) an artist.
4. The doctor found Klara (a) in Florence (b) in Munich (c) in his hometown (d) on the train.

Inferences

5. Which of the following best symbolizes Klara's personality.
   (a) "A room full of light and kindliness."
   (b) "Goodbye and she saw him no more."
   (c) "She had been a sickly child."
   (d) "Rich, thoroughly respectable, you know, thoroughly respectable."
6. A major quality displayed by Klara was (a) a witty tongue (b) a sensitivity to criticism (c) a love of life (d) an artistic talent.

7. When the expected guest didn't arrive, Klara felt (a) it didn't matter (b) her life was shattered (c) Georg should have gone for him (d) something crucial was missing.

8. The doctor's trip to see Klara was really (a) a rest from his family (b) to find material for a book (c) to repay a loan from long ago (d) a spiritual quest.

9. When the Imperial Councilor says (542) that Klara is "quite retired," he is being (a) kindly (b) sarcastic (c) neighborly (d) curious.

Fact or Opinion

Tell whether the following is a fact or an opinion.

10. The doctor left the Councilor's presence without waiting for him to finish his conversation.

Words in Context

1. "Luminous gleams slipped about their velvet *calyxes* as on dragonfly wings." **Calyxes** (541) are (a) dragonflies (b) cushions (c) flower parts (d) kinds of sewing material.

2. "There was a free and simple *serenity* about her." **Serenity** (544) means (a) inquisitiveness (b) shyness (c) contentment (d) tactlessness.

Thinking Critically about the Story

1. This story could have omitted the first two paragraphs and the last. The story itself is complete without them. Why did the author provide this framework? Are the three paragraphs essential to the story, helping to emphasize the author's point? Explain.

2. Was the child Klara different from the woman she became, or were the bases of her personality already evident in childhood? Explain.

3. What is Georg looking for in his return to his hometown? Does he find it?

4. The expected guest at the childhood party did not come, but Klara

says, "It was lovely all the same." What did Klara mention to support her statement that "it was lovely all the same"?

5. "It was in Florence, when for the first time in my life I saw, heard, felt, realized, and simultaneously learned to be thankful for all those things, that I first thought of him again. There were traces of him everywhere. In all the pictures I found bits of his smile, the bells were still alive with his voice, and on the statues I saw the imprints of his hands."

Here Klara seems to be expressing her philosophy of life. What does that self-revelation mean to you?

6. Klara says, "I felt that he had been—somewhere, once, had been . . . why should I have felt more? That was already more than enough."

How does this statement reflect Klara's reactions to the failure of the visitor to appear (question 4)?

7. How is Georg affected by the expression of Klara's philosophy?

8. "Live in the moment and accept all our blessings with gratitude and humility." Would Klara agree with this statement? Why or why not?

9. What does the author mean by saying, "The time will come when they (the children) love the dark"? What does the dark symbolize for the author?

10. Trying to put matters of the spirit into words, into a story, is a difficult feat. Do you think the author has successfully suggested a spiritual quest and a possible solution? Explain.

11. In a painting in the Boston Museum of Fine Arts, the artist Paul Gauguin wrote three basic questions asked by people since ancient times:

Whence do we come?

Who are we?

Whither are we going?

Does "A Story Told to the Dark" ask similar questions?

Language in Action

Punctuation: the Semicolon

The doctor could not stand it any longer; he disturbed certain of the sleepers, shoving his way between them into the corridor of the car.

This is a good example of the way in which a semicolon (;) is used. There are two independent clauses that have to be connected in some way. A comma after *longer* would produce an unacceptable run-on sentence. A conjunction, *and,* might be used.

> The doctor could not stand it any longer, and so he disturbed certain of the sleepers, shoving his way between them into the corridor of the car.

The author chose to use a semicolon, often used between two independent clauses that are closely related in meaning. Sometimes the semicolon joins two short clauses.

> Prentice voted for the resolution; Fazio voted against it.

Sometimes the conjunction is used in a sentence with more than two independent clauses. The following long sentence contains four independent clauses. The semicolon links the first two independent clauses with the second two.

> A moment ago the room had been distinct, even to its remotest corners, and now all the things in it were as though they had never known anything but twilight; everywhere large dark blossoms opened, and luminous gleams slipped about their velvet calyxes as on dragonfly wings.

The author might have used a period after *twilight,* but he preferred the semicolon.

The colon, a related punctuation mark, is discussed on page 558.

Never

H. E. Bates
British

"No one will believe I've gone. But it's true—I'm going at last."

Are we architects of our own destinies? Or, like prisoners, do we sometimes fall in love with our chains? "Never" is a deceptively simple story, with a single character and shadowy figure in the background. Yet in the space of a few pages, it sums up a life, lays bare a character, and raises questions about human motivation.

For a long time, Nellie has planned to break away from a stifling routine, freeing herself from the boring restraints of everyday life. The solution, she thinks, is simple: taking the train to London and freedom. Or so she has daydreamed. At last, the time is right. The clothes are packed. The timetable has been checked. Nellie starts out on the first step to a new life. How does she fare? What happens? Why? The answers probe the depths of a human personality.

Never

It was afternoon: great clouds stumbled across the sky. In the drowsy, half-dark room the young girl sat in a heap near the window, scarcely moving herself, as if she expected a certain timed happening, such as a visit, sunset, a command. Slowly she would draw the fingers of one hand across the back of the other, in the little hollows between the guides, and move her lips in the same sad, vexed way in which her brows came

552

together. And like this too, her eyes would shift about, from the near, shadowed fields, to the west hills, where the sun had dropped a strip of light, and to the woods between, looking like black scars one minute, and like friendly sanctuaries the next. It was all confused. There was the room, too. The white keys of the piano would now and then exercise a fascination over her which would keep her whole body perfectly still for perhaps a minute. But when this passed, full of hesitation, her fingers would recommence the slow exploration of her hands, and the restlessness took her again.

It was all confused. She was going away: already she had said a hundred times during the afternoon—'I am going away, I am going away. I can't stand it any longer.' But she had made no attempt to go. In this same position, hour after hour had passed her and all she could think was: 'Today I'm going away. I'm tired here. I never do anything. It's dead, rotten.'

She said, or thought it all without the slightest trace of exultation and was sometimes even methodical when she began to consider: 'What shall I take? The blue dress with the rosette? Yes. What else? what else?' And then it would all begin again: 'Today I'm going away. I never do anything.'

It was true: she never did anything. In the mornings she got up late, was slow over her breakfast, over everything—her reading, her mending, her eating, her playing the piano, cards in the evening, going to bed. It was all slow—purposely done, to fill up the day. And it was true, day succeeded day and she never did anything different.

But today something was about to happen: no more cards in the evening, every evening the same, with her father declaring: 'I never have a decent hand, I thought the ace of trumps had gone! It's too bad!!' and no more: 'Nellie, it's ten o'clock—Bed!' and the slow unimaginative climb of the stairs. Today she was going away: no one knew, but it was so. She was catching the evening train to London.

'I'm going away. What shall I take? The blue dress with the rosette? What else?'

She crept upstairs with difficulty, her body stiff after sitting. The years she must have sat, figuratively speaking, and grown stiff! And as if in order to secure some violent reaction against it all she threw herself into the packing of her things with a nervous vigour, throwing in the blue dress first and after it a score of things she had just remembered. She fastened her bag: it was not heavy. She counted her money a dozen times. It was all right! It was all right. She was going away!

She descended into the now dark room for the last time. In the dining-room someone was rattling tea-cups, an unbearable, horribly domestic sound! She wasn't hungry: she would be in London by eight—eating now meant making her sick. It was easy to wait. The train went at 6.18. She looked it up again: 'Elden 6.13, Olde 6.18, London 7.53.'

She began to play a waltz. It was a slow, dreamy tune, ta-tum, tum, ta-tum, tum, ta-tum, tum, of which the notes slipped out in mournful, sentimental succession. The room was quite dark, she could scarcely see the keys, and into the tune itself kept insinuating: 'Elden 6.13, Olde 6.18,' impossible to mistake or forget.

As she played on she thought: 'I'll never play this waltz again. It has the atmosphere of this room. It's the last time!' The waltz slid dreamily to an end: for a minute she sat in utter silence, the room dark and mysterious, the air of the waltz quite dead, then the teacups rattled again and the thought came back to her: 'I'm going away!'

She rose and went out quietly. The grass on the roadside moved under the evening wind, sounding like many pairs of hands rubbed softly together. But there was no other sound, her feet were light, no one heard her, and as she went down the road she told herself: 'It's going to happen! It's come at last!'

'Elden 6.13. Olde 6.18.'

Should she go to Elden or Olde? At the crossroads she stood to consider, thinking that if she went to Elden no one would know her. But at Olde someone would doubtless notice her and prattle about it. To Elden, then, not that it mattered. Nothing mattered now. She was going, was as good as gone!

Her breast, tremulously warm, began to rise and fall as her excitement increased. She tried to run over the things in her bag and could remember only 'the blue dress with the rosette,' which she had thrown in first and had since covered over. But it didn't matter. Her money was safe, everything was safe, and with that thought she dropped into a strange quietness, deepening as she went on, in which she had a hundred emotions and convictions. She was never going to strum that waltz again, she had played cards for the last, horrible time, the loneliness, the slowness, the oppression were ended, all ended.

'I'm going away!'

She felt warm, her body tingled with a light delicious thrill that was like the caress of a soft night-wind. There were no fears now. A certain indignation, approaching fury even, sprang up instead, as she thought: 'No one will believe I've gone. But it's true—I'm going at last.'

Her bag grew heavy. Setting it down in the grass she sat on it for a brief while, in something like her attitude in the dark room during the afternoon, and indeed actually began to rub her gloved fingers over the backs of her hands. A phrase or two of the waltz came back to her. . . . That silly piano! Its bottom G was flat, had always been flat! How ridiculous! She tried to conjure up some sort of vision of London, but it was difficult and in the end she gave way again to the old cry: 'I'm going away.' And she was pleased more than ever deeply.

On the station a single lamp burned, radiating a fitful yellowness that only increased the gloom. And worse, she saw no one and in the cold emptiness traced and retraced her footsteps without the friendly assurance of another sound. In the black distance all the signals showed hard circles of red, looking as if they could never change. But she nevertheless told herself over and over again: 'I'm going away—I'm going away.' And later: 'I hate everyone. I've changed until I hardly know myself.'

Impatiently she looked for the train. It was strange. For the first time it occurred to her to know the time and she pulled back the sleeve of her coat. Nearly six-thirty! She felt cold. Up the line every signal displayed its red ring, mocking her. 'Six-thirty, of course, of course.' She tried to be careless. 'Of course, it's late, the train is late,' but the coldness, in reality her fear, increased rapidly, until she could no longer believe those words. . . .

Great clouds, lower and more than ever depressing, floated above her head as she walked back. The wind had a deep note that was sad too. These things had not troubled her before, now they, also, spoke failure and foretold misery and dejection. She had no spirit, it was cold, and she was too tired even to shudder.

In the absolutely dark, drowsy room she sat down, telling herself: 'This isn't the only day. Some day I shall go. Some day.'

She was silent. In the next room they were playing cards and her father suddenly moaned: 'I thought the ace had gone.' Somebody laughed. Her father's voice came again: 'I never have a decent hand! I never have a decent hand! Never!'

It was too horrible! She couldn't stand it! She must do something to stop it! It was too much. She began to play the waltz again and the dreamy, sentimental arrangement made her cry.

'This isn't the only day,' she reassured herself. 'I shall go. Some day!'

And again and again as she played the waltz, bent her head and cried, she would tell herself that same thing:

'Some day! Some day!'

Reading for Understanding

Main Idea

1. The main idea of the story is best expressed in (a) the opening three sentences (b) the second paragraph (c) the title (d) the father's comments about cards.

Details

2. The central character, Nellie, emphasized packing (a) cards (b) the blue dress (c) the waltz (d) the London address.
3. Elden and Olde are (a) train stations (b) German cities (c) London contacts (d) helpful relatives.
4. One train left the station at (a) 6:13 (b) 6:30 (c) 7:53 (d) 8:07.

Inferences

5. The "hard circles of red" (555) indicated that (a) the trains were delayed (b) the train had already left (c) there was an accident down the road (d) the London trains had been detoured.
6. The father's attitude seemed (a) vicious (b) insane (c) loving (d) dictatorial.
7. The timetables suggest that London was about (a) a half hour away (b) an hour away (c) an hour and a half away (d) three hours away.

Tone of the Story

8. The tone of the story is (a) cheerful (b) angry (c) confused (d) melancholy.

Outcomes

9. Probably a year later, Nellie would be saying, (a) "Happy at last." (b) "Events are for the best." (c) "I owe my father a debt of gratitude." (d) "Some day! Some day!"

Fact or Opinion

Tell whether the following is a fact or an opinion.

10. Nellie missed her train.

Words in Context

1. "Slowly she would draw the fingers of one hand across the back of the other in the little hollows between the guides, and move her lips in the same, sad, *vexed* way in which her brows came together." **Vexed** (552) means (a) inquisitive (b) ugly (c) picturesque (d) irritated.

2. "She said, or thought it all without the slightest trace of *exultation*." **Exultation** (553) means (a) blame (b) rejoicing (c) gloom (d) interference.

Thinking Critically about the Story

1. What kind of person is Nellie? How is her character revealed?

2. What kind of person is the father? How do his few comments provide a clue to Nellie's unhappiness?

3. What does playing the waltz symbolize in the development of the story?

4. Why did Nellie miss the train?

5. Nellie is called "the young girl." How young do you think she is?

10? 12? 16? 20? How does her age affect the impact of the story? If she were 50, would the impact be different? How?

6. Define *habit*. Has Nellie fallen into a bad habit? Explain.

7. Is it more difficult to break a perennial lateness habit than a smoking habit? Explain.

8. Are some habits good and desirable? Mention several examples.

Language in Action

Punctuation: the Colon

And then it would all begin again: "Today I'm going away. I never do anything."

One of the most useful—and neglected—punctuation marks is the colon. It appears in certain formal situations, like the salutation of a business letter.

Dear Mr. Hopkins:

It separates hours and minutes in expressing time.

6:37 P.M.

It separates numbers of a Biblical chapter and verse.

Genesis 1:17

Perhaps its most useful rule, though, is in compound sentences. The semicolon (551) helps to join together two independent clauses without a conjunction. The colon goes further: it does link the two clauses together, like a semicolon. It also introduces the clause or statement that explains, restates, or proves the statement in the first clause. (Did you notice the use of a colon in the third sentence of this paragraph?) In the example at the head of this section, the colon is used to introduce a quotation that explains the pronoun *it* in the main clause.

Unlike many other authors, H. E. Bates seems especially fond of the colon. Point out another example from the story and decide whether that colon is justified, or whether a semicolon or comma might have served as well.

The Rising of the Moon

Lady Gregory
Irish

One word more, for signal token,
Whistle up the marching tune,
With your pike upon your shoulder,
At the Rising of the Moon.

In 1907, when this play was written, Ireland was still an unhappy part of the United Kingdom. For 700 years, the Anglo-Irish struggle had continued, with bitter rebellions and equally bitter countermeasures. The Easter Monday Rebellion in 1916 failed but was followed by guerrilla warfare and harsh British reprisals. A succession of events led to the formation of the Irish Free State as part of the British Commonwealth. In 1937, the name changed to **Eire**, with a new constitution. In 1948, Eire became a republic and withdrew from the British Commonwealth.

Six northern counties, however, remained part of the United Kingdom. Peace did not come to Northern Ireland at that time, and peace has remained elusive ever since.

As noted above, "The Rising of the Moon" was written in 1907, during the troubles. Irish policemen, still part of the British structure, are being asked to capture a member of the Irish underground. The sergeant, in particular, is torn by opposing motivations. Where will he be at "the rising of the moon"?

The Rising of the Moon

Scene: Side of a quay in a seaport town. Some posts and chains. A large barrel. Enter three policemen. Moonlight.

SERGEANT, *who is older than the others, crosses the stage to right and looks down steps. The others put down a pastepot and unroll a bundle of placards.*

POLICEMAN B. I think this would be a good place to put up a notice. (*He points to barrel.*)

POLICEMAN X. Better ask him. (*Calls to* SERGEANT) Will this be a good place for a placard? (*No answer.*)

POLICEMAN B. Will we put up a notice here on the barrel? (*No answer.*)

SERGEANT. There's a flight of steps here that leads to the water. This is a place that should be minded well. If he got down here, his friends might have a boat to meet him; they might send it in here from outside.

POLICEMAN B. Would the barrel be a good place to put a notice up?

SERGEANT. It might; you can put it there. (*They paste the notice up.*)

SERGEANT (*reading it*). Dark hair—dark eyes, smooth face, height five feet five—there's not much to take hold of in that—It's a pity I had no chance of seeing him before he broke out of gaol.* They say he's a wonder, that it's he makes all the plans for the whole organization. There isn't another man in Ireland would have broken gaol the way he did. He must have some friends among the gaolers.

POLICEMAN B. A hundred pounds is little enough for the Government to offer for him. You may be sure any man in the force that takes him will get promotion.

SERGEANT. I'll mind this place myself. I wouldn't wonder at all if he came this way. He might come slipping along there (*points to side of quay*), and his friends might be waiting for him there (*points down steps*), and once he got away it's little chance we'd have of finding him; it's maybe under a load of kelp he'd be in a fishing boat, and not one to help a married man that wants it to the reward.

POLICEMAN X. And if we get him itself, nothing but abuse on our heads for it from the people, and maybe from our own relations.

---

*jail

SERGEANT. Well, we have to do our duty in the force. Haven't we the whole country depending on us to keep law and order? It's those that are down would be up and those that are up would be down, if it wasn't for us. Well, hurry on, you have plenty of other places to placard yet, and come back here then to me. You can take the lantern. Don't be too long now. It's very lonesome here with nothing but the moon.

POLICEMAN B. It's a pity we can't stop with you. The Government should have brought more police into the town, with *him* in gaol, and at assize* time too. Well, good luck to your watch. (*They go out.*)

SERGEANT (*walks up and down once or twice and looks at placard*). A hundred pounds and promotion sure. There must be a great deal of spending in a hundred pounds. It's a pity some honest man not to be the better of that.

(*A ragged man appears at left and tries to slip past.* SERGEANT *suddenly turns.*)

SERGEANT. Where are you going?

MAN. I'm a poor ballad-singer, your honor. I thought to sell some of these (*holds out bundle of ballads*) to the sailors. (*He goes on.*)

SERGEANT. Stop! Didn't I tell you to stop? You can't go on there.

MAN. Oh, very well. It's a hard thing to be poor. All the world's against the poor!

SERGEANT. Who are you?

MAN. You'd be as wise as myself if I told you, but I don't mind. I'm one Jimmy Walsh, a ballad-singer.

SERGEANT. Jimmy Walsh? I don't know that name.

MAN. Ah, sure, they know it well enough in Ennis. Were you ever in Ennis, Sergeant?

SERGEANT. What brought you here?

MAN. Sure, it's to the assizes I came, thinking I might make a few shillings here or there. It's in the one train with the judges I came.

SERGEANT. Well, if you came so far, you may as well go farther, for you'll walk out of this.

MAN. I will, I will; I'll just go on where I was going. (*Goes toward steps.*)

SERGEANT. Come back from those steps; no one has leave to pass down them tonight.

---

*court proceeding

MAN. I'll just sit on the top of the steps till I see will some sailor buy a ballad off me that would give me my supper. They do be late going back to the ship. It's often I saw them in Cork carried down the quay in a hand-cart.

SERGEANT. Move on, I tell you. I won't have any one lingering about the quay tonight.

MAN. Well, I'll go. It's the poor have the hard life! Maybe yourself might like one, Sergeant. Here's a good sheet now. (*Turns one over.*) "Content and a pipe"—that's not much. "The Peeler and the Goat"—you wouldn't like that. "Johnny Hart"—that's a lovely song.

SERGEANT. Move on.

MAN. Ah, wait till you hear it. (*Sings.*)

> *There was a rich farmer's daughter*
> *lived near the town of Ross;*
> *She courted a Highland soldier,*
> *his name was Johnny Hart;*
> *Says the mother to her daughter,*
> *"I'll go distracted mad*
> *If you marry that Highland soldier*
> *dressed up in Highland plaid."*

SERGEANT. Stop that noise.

(MAN *wraps up his ballads and shuffles toward the steps.*)

SERGEANT. Where are you going?

MAN. Sure you told me to be going, and I am going.

SERGEANT. Don't be a fool. I didn't tell you to go that way; I told you to go back to the town.

MAN. Back to the town, is it?

SERGEANT (*taking him by the shoulder and shoving him before him*). Here, I'll show you the way. Be off with you. What are you stopping for?

MAN (*who has been keeping his eye on the notice, points to it*). I think I know what you're waiting for, Sergeant.

SERGEANT. What's that to you?

MAN. And I know well the man you're waiting for—I know him well—I'll be going. (*He shuffles on.*)

SERGEANT. You know him? Come back here. What sort is he?

MAN. Come back is it, Sergeant? Do you want to have me killed?

SERGEANT. Why do you say that?

MAN. Never mind. I'm going. I wouldn't be in your shoes if the reward was ten times as much. (*Goes on off stage to left.*) Not if it was ten times as much.

SERGEANT (*rushing after him*). Come back here, come back. (*Drags him back.*) What sort is he? Where did you see him?

MAN. I saw him in my own place, in the County Clare. I tell you you wouldn't like to be looking at him. You'd be afraid to be in the one place with him. There isn't a weapon he doesn't know the use of, and as to strength, his muscles are as hard as that board. (*Slaps barrel.*)

SERGEANT. Is he as bad as that?

MAN. He is then.

SERGEANT. Do you tell me so?

MAN. There was a poor man in our place, a sergeant from Bally-vaughan.—It was with a lump of stone he did it.

SERGEANT. I never heard of that.

MAN. And you wouldn't, Sergeant. It's not everything that happens gets into the papers. And there was a policeman in plain clothes, too . . . It is in Limerick he was. . . . It was after the time of the attack on the police barrack at Kilmallock. . . . Moonlight . . . just like this . . . waterside. . . . Nothing was known for certain.

SERGEANT. Do you say so? It's a terrible county to belong to.

MAN. That's so, indeed! You might be standing there, looking out that way, thinking you saw him coming up this side of the quay (*points*), and he might be coming up this other side (*points*), and he'd be on you before you knew where you were.

SERGEANT. It's a whole troop of police they ought to put here to stop a man like that.

MAN. But if you'd like me to stop with you, I could be looking down this side. I could be sitting up here on this barrel.

SERGEANT. And you know him well, too?

MAN. I'd know him a mile off, Sergeant.

SERGEANT. But you wouldn't want to share the reward?

MAN. Is it a poor man like me, that has to be going the roads and singing in fairs, to have the name on him that he took a reward? But you don't want me. I'll be safer in the town.

SERGEANT. Well, you can stop.

MAN (*getting up on barrel*). All right, Sergeant. I wonder, now, you're not tired out, Sergeant, walking up and down the way you are.

SERGEANT. If I'm tired I'm used to it.

MAN. You might have hard work before you tonight yet. Take it easy while you can. There's plenty of room up here on the barrel, and you see farther when you're higher up.

SERGEANT. Maybe so. (*Gets up beside him on barrel, facing right. They sit back to back, looking different ways.*) You made me feel a bit queer with the way you talked.

MAN. Give me a match, Sergeant (*he gives it and* MAN *lights pipe*); take a draw yourself? It'll quiet you. Wait now till I give you a light, but you needn't turn around. Don't take your eye off the quay for the life of you.

SERGEANT. Never fear, I won't. (*Lights pipe. They both smoke.*) Indeed it's a hard thing to be in the force, out at night and no thanks for it, for all the danger we're in. And it's little we get but abuse from the people, and no choice but to obey our orders, and never asked when a man is sent into danger, if you are a married man with a family.
MAN (*sings*).

> As through the hills I walked to view the hills and shamrock plain,
> I stood awhile where nature smiles to view the rocks and streams,
> On a matron fair I fixed my eyes beneath a fertile vale,
> As she sang her song it was on the wrong of poor old Granuaile.

SERGEANT. Stop that; that's no song to be singing in these times.

MAN. Ah, Sergeant, I was only singing to keep my heart up. It sinks when I think of him. To think of us two sitting here, and he creeping up the quay, maybe, to get to us.

SERGEANT. Are you keeping a good lookout?

MAN. I am; and for no reward too. Amn't I the foolish man? But when I saw a man in trouble, I never could help trying to get him out of it. What's that? Did something hit me? (*Rubs his heart.*)

SERGEANT (*patting him on the shoulder*). You will get your reward in heaven.

MAN. I know that, I know that, Sergeant, but life is precious.

SERGEANT. Well, you can sing if it gives you more courage.

MAN (*sings*).

> *Her head was bare, her hands and feet with iron bands were bound,*
> *Her pensive strain and plaintive wail mingles with the evening gale,*
> *And the song she sang with mournful air, I am old Granuaile.*
> *Her lips so sweet that monarchs kissed . . .*

SERGEANT. That's not it. . . . "Her gown she wore was stained with gore." . . . That's it—you missed that.

MAN. You're right, Sergeant, so it is; I missed it. (*Repeats line*) But to think of a man like you knowing a song like that.

SERGEANT. There's many a thing a man might know and might not have any wish for.

MAN. Now, I daresay, Sergeant, in your youth, you used to be sitting up on a wall, the way you are sitting up on this barrel now, and the other lads beside you, and you singing "Granuaile"? . . .

SERGEANT. I did then.

MAN. And the "Shan Bhean Bhocht"? . . .

SERGEANT. I did then.

MAN. And the "Green on the Cape"?

SERGEANT. That was one of them.

MAN. And maybe the man you are watching for tonight used to be sitting on the wall, when he was young, and singing those same songs. . . . It's a queer world.

SERGEANT. Whisht! . . . I think I see something coming. . . . It's only a dog.

MAN. And isn't it a queer world? . . . Maybe it's one of the boys you used to be singing with that time you will be arresting today or tomorrow, and sending into the dock.

SERGEANT. That's true inded.

MAN. And maybe one night, after you had been singing, if the other boys had told you some plan they had, some plan to free the country, you might have joined with them . . . and maybe it is you might be in trouble now.

SERGEANT. Well, who knows but I might? I had a great spirit in those days.

MAN. It's a queer world, Sergeant, and it's little any mother knows when she sees her child creeping on the floor what might happen to it before it has gone through its life, or who will be who in the end.

SERGEANT. That's a queer thought now, and a true thought. Wait now till I think it out. . . . If it wasn't for the sense I have, and for my wife and family, and for me joining the force the time I did, it might be myself now would be after breaking gaol and hiding in the dark, and it might be him that's hiding in the dark and that got out of gaol would be sitting up where I am on this barrel. . . . And it might be myself would be creeping up trying to make my escape from himself, and it might be himself would be keeping the law, and myself would be breaking it, and myself would be trying maybe to put a bullet in his head, or to take up a lump of a stone the way you said he did . . . no, that myself did. . . . Oh! (*Gasps. After a pause*) What's that! (*Grasps* MAN'S *arm*.)

MAN (*jumps off barrel and listens, looking out over water*). It's nothing, Sergeant.

SERGEANT. I thought it might be a boat. I had a notion there might be friends of his coming about the quays with a boat.

MAN. Sergeant, I am thinking it was with the people you were, and not with the law you were, when you were a young man.

SERGEANT. Well, if I was foolish then, that time's gone.

MAN. Maybe, Sergeant, it comes into your head sometimes, in spite of your belt and your tunic, that it might have been as well for you to have followed Granuaile.

SERGEANT. It's no business of yours what I think.

MAN. Maybe, Sergeant, you'll be on the side of the country yet.

SERGEANT (*gets off barrel*). Don't talk to me like that. I have my duties and I know them. (*Looks round.*) That was a boat; I hear the oars. (*Goes to the steps and looks down.*)
MAN (*sings*).

> O, then, tell me, Shawn O'Farrell,
> Where the gathering is to be.
> In the old spot by the river
> Right well known to you and me!

SERGEANT. Stop that! Stop that, I tell you!

MAN (*sings louder*).

> One word more, for signal token,
> Whistle up the marching tune,

> *With your pike upon your shoulder,*
> *At the Rising of the Moon.*

SERGEANT. If you don't stop that, I'll arrest you.

(*A whistle from below answers, repeating the air.*)

SERGEANT. That's a signal. (*Stands between him and steps*) You must not pass this way. . . . Step farther back. . . . Who are you? You are no ballad-singer.

MAN. You needn't ask who I am; that placard will tell you. (*Points to placard.*)

SERGEANT. You are the man I am looking for.

MAN (*takes off hat and wig.* SERGEANT *seizes them*). I am. There's a hundred pounds on my head. There is a friend of mine below in a boat. He knows a safe place to bring me to.

SERGEANT (*looking still at hat and wig*). It's a pity! It's a pity. You deceived me. You deceived me well.

MAN. I am a friend of Granuaile. There is a hundred pounds on my head.

SERGEANT. It's a pity, it's a pity!

MAN. Will you let me pass, or must I make you let me?

SERGEANT. I am in the force. I will not let you pass.

MAN. I thought to do it with my tongue. (*Puts hand in breast.*) What is that?

(*Voice of* POLICEMAN X *outside.*) Here, this is where we left him.

SERGEANT. It's my comrades coming.

MAN. You won't betray me . . . the friend of Granuaile. (*Slips behind barrel.*)

(*Voice of* POLICEMAN B.) That was the last of the placards.

POLICEMAN X (*as they come in*). If he makes his escape it won't be unknown he'll make it.

(SERGEANT *puts hat and wig behind his back.*)

POLICEMAN B. Did any one come this way?

SERGEANT (*after a pause*). No one.

POLICEMAN B. No one at all?

SERGEANT. No one at all.

POLICEMAN B. We had no orders to go back to the station; we can stop along with you.

SERGEANT. I don't want you. There is nothing for you to do here.

POLICEMAN B. You bade us to come back here and keep watch with you.

SERGEANT. I'd sooner be alone. Would any man come this way and you making all that talk? It is better the place to be quiet.

POLICEMAN B. Well, we'll leave you the lantern anyhow. (*Hands it to him.*)

SERGEANT. I don't want it. Bring it with you.

POLICEMAN B. You might want it. There are clouds coming up and you have the darkness of the night before you yet. I'll leave it over here on the barrel. (*Goes to barrel.*)

SERGEANT. Bring it with you I tell you. No more talk.

POLICEMAN B. Well, I thought it might be a comfort to you. I often think when I have it in my hand and can be flashing it about into every dark corner (*doing so*) that it's the same as being beside the fire at home, and the bits of bogwood blazing up now and again. (*Flashes it about, now on the barrel, now on* SERGEANT.)

SERGEANT (*furious*). Be off the two of you, yourselves and your lantern!

(*They go out.* MAN *comes from behind barrel. He and* SERGEANT *stand looking at one another.*)

SERGEANT. What are you waiting for?

MAN. For my hat, of course, and my wig. You wouldn't wish me to get my death of cold?

(SERGEANT *gives them.*)

MAN (*going toward steps*). Well, good night, comrade, and thank you. You did me a good turn tonight, and I'm obliged to you. Maybe I'll be able to do as much for you when the small rise up and the big fall down . . . when we all change places at the Rising (*waves his hand and disappears*) of the Moon.

SERGEANT (*turning his back to audience and reading placard*). A hundred pounds reward! A hundred pounds! (*Turns toward audience*) I wonder, now, am I as great a fool as I think I am?

CURTAIN

Reading for Understanding

Central Theme

1. The central theme of this play is (a) man's inhumanity to man (b) police brutality (c) conflicting loyalties (d) Irish humor.

Details

2. The ragged man says he is there (a) to help the Sergeant (b) to sell ballads (c) as a representative of local government (d) to fish.
3. "Johnny Hart" is (a) the balladeer's brother (b) Policeman B (c) a British folk hero (d) a song title.
4. The reward has been set at (a) 25 pounds (b) 50 pounds (c) 75 pounds (d) 100 pounds.

Inferences

5. When the ragged man tells what a fiend the wanted man is, he is (a) talking about himself (b) understating the truth (c) hoping to make the Sergeant laugh (d) frightening the other two policemen.
6. The Sergeant's mood throughout is one of (a) nervousness (b) great joy (c) assurance (d) indifference.
7. "The Rising of the Moon" is a symbol of (a) peace and contentment (b) rebellion (c) a renewed interest in the drama (d) the brotherhood of man.
8. The ragged man is a (a) coward (b) good psychologist (c) vicious killer (d) secret member of the British police.

Outcomes

9. The ragged man will (a) charge the Sergeant with treason (b) give himself up (c) flee to safety (d) be captured soon after leaving the wharf.

Author's Attitude

10. The author's attitude toward the Sergeant and the ragged man is one of (a) stunned disbelief (b) antagonism (c) misplaced sentiment (d) sympathetic understanding.

Words in Context

1. "Will this be a good place for a *placard*?" A **placard** (560) is a (a) barrel (b) guard post (c) poster (d) meeting.
2. "Points to side of *quay*." A **quay** (560) is (a) a stairway (b) an entrance to a shack (c) a houseboat (d) a wharf.

Thinking Critically about the Play

1. At the very beginning, the Sergeant doesn't answer two of his assistants' questions. What does this lack of attention suggest about the Sergeant's thoughts?
2. How does the Sergeant differ from the two policemen? How would the policemen have handled the meeting with the ragged man?
3. How significant is the fact that the Sergeant seems to know a revolutionary ballad better than the ragged man does? Was the man trying to test the Sergeant? How?
4. What does the Sergeant mean when he says (565), "There's many a thing a man might know and might not have any wish for"?
5. Why does the ragged man say, "You needn't ask who I am; that placard will tell you"? Why is the man willing to take the risk at that point?
6. When the Sergeant answers, "No one," he has made a decision. What was it?
7. How great a sacrifice did the Sergeant make in letting the wanted man escape? What does this sacrifice tell us about the character of the Sergeant?
8. At what point did you realize that the ragged man was also the wanted man? What clues helped you?
9. Why has the Sergeant changed over the years from a potential young revolutionary to a representative of the hated government? Is the change complete? Explain.
10. Could this play have been written today, in a different setting, but with the same impact? Explain.

Language in Action

Dialogue in a Play

POLICEMAN B. I think this would be a good place to put up a notice. (*He points to barrel.*)

POLICEMAN X. Better ask him. (*Calls to* SERGEANT.) Will this be a good place for a placard? (*No answer.*)

How do you indicate dialogue in a printed play? It would obviously be inconvenient to keep using quotation marks. Over the years, certain conventions have prevailed. Notice the two bits of dialogue above. The speaker is indicated by capital letters followed by a period. Then the words follow. If there are any stage directions, they are included in parentheses, usually in *italics*. Nothing could be simpler. You will have an opportunity to try your hand at some dialogue or a short play at the end of this unit.

In addition to providing dialogue, the playwright may also set the scene, using italics for this helpful information. In our play, italics are used for the stage directions at the beginning. Italics are also used, here, as they would be in any written material, for the quotations from patriotic Irish songs.

Some playwrights use extended stage directions, providing an almost novel-style presentation . . . subjective rather than objective (239). When Eugene O'Neill set the scene for the opening pages of *Strange Interlude,* he used a page and a half. George Bernard Shaw used his plays to express his personal philosophy, some of which found its way into extended stage directions. Shaw visualized his plays being read as well as acted. At times he introduced humor into these stage directions, obviously never to be used in the play itself. In the opening stage directions for *Saint Joan,* Shaw describes one of the characters, a handsome military squire, as "the sort of man whom age cannot wither because he has never bloomed."

The dramatis personae (cast of characters listed at the beginning of the play) may have identifying labels, as in this from Oscar Wilde's *The Importance of Being Earnest:*

MERRIMAN, *butler to Mr. Worthing*

The Mysterious Mansion

Honore de Balzac
French

**All three then saw a man's face; it was dark and gloomy
with black hair and eyes of flame. Before her husband turned,
the poor woman had time to make a sign to the stranger that
signified: Hope!**

Robert Louis Stevenson once wrote, "Some places speak
distinctly. Certain dark gardens cry aloud for a murder; certain old
houses demand to be haunted; certain coasts are set apart for ship-
wrecks." The mysterious mansion in our story is just such a place. The
author takes great pains in setting the scene. The old house is in bad
shape. Why has such a magnificent old house been allowed to fall into
such a state of disrepair?

The story told is an old one. Greek and Roman playwrights
used the theme in both comedies and tragedies. Medieval folktales
concerned themselves with plots akin to this. But there is a great
difference, with a conclusion inevitable but still shocking.

A young Spanish prisoner of war, captured during Napoleon's
Peninsular War, is allowed the freedom of the French village. He finds
himself in church near the chapel of the beautiful young Madame de
Merret. The ingredients are present for tragedy. The author cleverly
builds suspense and then a sense of horror when the Monsieur's
intentions become apparent. What kind of twisted motivation impels
the husband toward such an action? The last sentence in the story has
a terrifying finality.

572

The Mysterious Mansion

ABOUT a hundred yards from the town of Vendôme, on the borders of the Loire, there is an old gray house, surmounted by very high gables, and so completely isolated that neither tanyard nor shabby hostelry, such as you may find at the entrance to all small towns, exists in its immediate neighborhood.

In front of this building, overlooking the river, is a garden, where the once well-trimmed box borders that used to define the walks now grow wild as they list. Several willows that spring from the Loire have grown as rapidly as the hedge that encloses it, and half conceal the house. The rich vegetation of those weeds that we call foul adorns the sloping shore. Fruit trees, neglected for the last ten years, no longer yield their harvest, and their shoots form coppices.* The wall-fruit grows like hedges against the walls. Paths once graveled are overgrown with moss, but, to tell the truth, there is no trace of a path. From the height of the hill, to which cling the ruins of the old castle of the Dukes of Vendôme, the only spot whence the eye can plunge into this enclosure, it strikes you that, at a time not easy to determine, this plot of land was the delight of a country gentleman, who cultivated roses and tulips and horticulture in general, and who was besides a lover of fine fruit. An arbor is still visible, or rather the débris of an arbor, where there is a table that time has not quite destroyed. The aspect of this garden of bygone days suggests the negative joys of peaceful, provincial life, as one might reconstruct the life of a worthy tradesman by reading the epitaph on his tombstone. As if to complete the sweetness and sadness of the ideas that possess one's soul, one of the walls displays a sun-dial decorated with the following commonplace Christian inscription: "Ultimam cogita!" The roof of this house is horribly dilapidated, the shutters are always closed, the balconies are covered with swallows' nests, the doors are perpetually shut, weeds have drawn green lines in the cracks of the flights of steps, the locks and bolts are rusty. Sun, moon, winter, summer, and snow have worn the paneling, warped the boards, gnawed the paint. The lugubrious silence which reigns there is only broken by birds, cats, martins, rats and mice, free to course to and fro, to fight and to eat each other. Everywhere an invisible hand has graven the word *mystery*.

Should your curiosity lead you to glance at this house from the side that points to the road, you would perceive a great door which the

---

*thickets

children of the place have riddled with holes. I afterward heard that this door had been closed for the last ten years. Through the holes broken by the boys you would have observed the perfect harmony that existed between the façades of both garden and courtyard. In both the same disorder prevails. Tufts of weed encircle the paving-stones. Enormous cracks furrow the walls, round whose blackened crests twine a thousand garlands. The steps are out of joint, the wire of the bell is rusted, the spouts are cracked. What fire from heaven has fallen here? What tribunal has decreed that salt should be strewn on this dwelling? Has God been blasphemed, has France been here betrayed? These are the questions we ask ourselves, but get no answer from the crawling things that haunt the place. The empty and deserted house is a gigantic enigma, of which the key is lost. In bygone times it was a small fief,* and bears the name of the Grande Bretèche.

I inferred that I was not the only person to whom my good landlady had communicated the secret of which I was to be the sole recipient, and I prepared to listen.

"Sir," she said, "when the Emperor sent the Spanish prisoners of war and others here, the Government quartered on me a young Spaniard who had been sent to Vendôme on parole. Parole notwithstanding he went out every day to show himself to the official. He was a Spanish grandee! Nothing less! His name ended in *os* and *dia,* something like Burgos de Férédia. I have his name on my books; you can read it if you like. Oh! but he was a handsome young man. He was only five feet and a few inches high, but he was well-grown; he had small hands that he took such care of; ah! you should have seen! He had as many brushes for his hands as a woman for her whole dressing apparatus! He had thick black hair, a fiery eye, his skin was rather bronzed, but I liked the look of it. He wore the finest linen I have ever seen on any one, although I have had princesses staying here, and, among others, General Bertrand, the Duke and Duchess d'Abrantès, Monsieur Decazes, and the King of Spain. He didn't eat much; but his manners were so polite, so amiable, that one could not owe him a grudge. Oh! I was very fond of him, although he didn't open his lips four times in the day, and it was impossible to keep up a conversation with him. For if you spoke to him, he did not answer. It was a fad, a mania with them all, I heard say. He read his prayer book like a priest, he went to Mass and to all the services regularly. Where did he sit? Two steps from the chapel of Madame de Merret. As he took his place there the first time he went to church, nobody suspected him of any intention in so doing. Besides, he never raised his eyes from his prayer-book, poor young man! After that, sir, in the evening he would walk on the mountains, among the castle ruins. It was the poor man's only

---

*a lord's estate

amusement, it reminded him of his country. They say that Spain is all
mountains! From the commencement of his imprisonment he stayed out
late. I was anxious when I found that he did not come home before
midnight; but we got accustomed to this fancy of his. He took the key of
the door, and we left off sitting up for him. He lodged in a house of ours
in the Rue des Casernes. After that, one of our stable-men told us that in
the evening when he led the horses to the water, he thought he had seen
the Spanish grandee swimming far down the river like a live fish. When
he returned, I told him to take care of the rushes; he appeared vexed to
have been seen in the water. At last, one day, or rather one morning, we
did not find him in his room; he had not returned. After searching
everywhere, I found some writing in the drawer of a table, where there
were fifty gold pieces of Spain that are called doubloons and were worth
about five thousand francs; and ten thousand francs' worth of diamonds
in a small sealed box. The writing said, that in case he did not return, he
left us the money and the diamonds, on condition of paying for Masses
to thank God for his escape, and for his salvation. In those days my
husband had not been taken from me; he hastened to seek him everywhere.

"And now for the strange part of the story. He brought home
the Spaniard's clothes, that he had discovered under a big stone, in a sort
of pilework by the river-side near the castle, nearly opposite to the Grande
Bretêche. My husband had gone there so early that no one had seen him.
After reading the letter, he burned the clothes, and according to Count
Férédia's desire we declared that he had escaped. The sous-préfet sent all
the gendarmerie in pursuit of him; but they never caught him. Lepas
believed that the Spaniard had drowned himself. I, sir, don't think so; I
am more inclined to believe that he had something to do with the affair
of Madame de Merret, seeing that Rosalie told me that the crucifix that
her mistress thought so much of, that she had it buried with her, was of
ebony and silver. Now in the beginning of his stay here, Monsieur de
Férédia had one in ebony and silver, that I never saw him with later. Now,
sir, don't you consider that I need have no scruples about the Spaniard's
fifteen thousand francs, and that I have a right to them?"

"Certainly; but you haven't tried to question Rosalie?" I said.

"Oh, yes, indeed, sir; but to no purpose! the girl's like a wall. She
knows something, but it is impossible to get her to talk."

After exchanging a few more words with me, my landlady left me
a prey to vague and gloomy thoughts, to a romantic curiosity, and a
religious terror not unlike the profound impression produced on us when
by night, on entering a dark church, we perceive a faint light under high
arches; a vague figure glides by—the rustle of a robe or cassock is heard,
and we shudder.

Suddenly the Grande Bretêche and its tall weeds, its barred

windows, its rusty ironwork, its closed doors, its deserted apartments, appeared like a fantastic apparition before me. I essayed to penetrate the mysterious dwelling, and to find the knot of its dark story—the drama that had killed three persons. In my eyes Rosalie became the most interesting person in Vendôme. As I studied her, I discovered the traces of secret care, despite the radiant health that shone in her plump countenance. There was in her the germ of remorse or hope; her attitude revealed a secret, like the attitude of a bigot who prays to excess, or of the infanticide* who ever hears the last cry of her child. Yet her manners were rough and ingenuous—her silly smile was not that of a criminal, and could you but have seen the great kerchief that encompassed her portly bust, framed and laced in by a lilac and blue cotton gown, you would have dubbed her innocent. No, I thought, I will not leave Vendôme without learning the history of the Grande Bretêche. To gain my ends I will strike up a friendship with Rosalie, if needs be.

"Rosalie," said I, one evening.

"Sir?"

"You are not married?"

She started slightly.

"Oh, I can find plenty of men, when the fancy takes me to be made miserable," she said, laughing.

She soon recovered from the effects of her emotion, for all women, from the great lady to the maid of the inn, possess a composure that is peculiar to them.

"You are too good-looking and well favored to be short of lovers. But tell me, Rosalie, why did you take service in an inn after leaving Madame de Merret? Did she leave you nothing to live on?"

"Oh, yes! But, sir, my place is the best in all Vendôme."

The reply was one of those that judges and lawyers would call evasive. Rosalie appeared to me to be situated in this romantic history like the square in the midst of a chessboard. She was at the heart of the truth and chief interest; she seemed to me to be bound in the very knot of it. The conquest of Rosalie was no longer to be an ordinary siege—in this girl was centered the last chapter of a novel, therefore from this moment Rosalie became the object of my preference.

One morning I said to Rosalie: "Tell me all you know about Madame de Merret."

"Oh!" she replied in terror, "do not ask that of me, Monsieur Horace."

Her pretty face fell—her clear, bright color faded—and her eyes lost their innocent brightness.

---

*child killer

"Well, then," she said, at last, "if you must have it so, I will tell you about it; but promise to keep my secret!"

"Done! my dear girl, I must keep your secret with the honor of a thief, which is the most loyal in the world."

Were I to transcribe Rosalie's diffuse eloquence faithfully, an entire volume would scarcely contain it; so I shall abridge.

The room occupied by Madame de Merret at the Bretêche was on the ground floor. A little closet about four feet deep, built in the thickness of the wall, served as her wardrobe. Three months before the eventful evening of which I am about to speak, Madame de Merret had been so seriously indisposed that her husband had left her to herself in her own apartment, while he occupied another on the first floor. By one of those chances that it is impossible to foresee, he returned home from the club (where he was accustomed to read the papers and discuss politics with the inhabitants of the place) two hours later than usual. His wife supposed him to be at home, in bed and asleep. But the invasion of France had been the subject of a most animated discussion; the billiard-match had been exciting, he had lost forty francs, an enormous sum for Vendôme, where every one hoards, and where manners are restricted within the limits of a praiseworthy modesty, which perhaps is the source of the true happiness that no Parisian covets. For some time past Monsieur de Merret had been satisfied to ask Rosalie if his wife had gone to bed; and on her reply, which was always in the affirmative, had immediately gained his own room with the good temper engendered by habit and confidence. On entering his house, he took it into his head to go and tell his wife of his misadventure, perhaps by way of consolation. At dinner he found Madame de Merret most coquettishly attired. On his way to the club it had occurred to him that his wife was restored to health, and that her convalescence had added to her beauty. He was, as husbands are wont to be, somewhat slow in making this discovery. Instead of calling Rosalie, who was occupied just then in watching the cook and coachman play a difficult hand at cards, Monsieur de Merret went to his wife's room by the light of a lantern that he deposited on the first step of the staircase. His unmistakable step resounded under the vaulted corridor. At the moment that the Count turned the handle of his wife's door, he fancied he could hear the door of the closet I spoke of close; but when he entered Madame de Merret was alone before the fireplace. The husband thought ingenuously that Rosalie was in the closet, yet a suspicion that jangled in his ear put him on his guard. He looked at his wife and saw in her eyes I know not what wild and hunted expression.

"You are very late," she said. Her habitually pure, sweet voice seemed changed to him.

Monsieur de Merret did not reply, for at that moment Rosalie entered. It was a thunderbolt for him. He strode about the room, passing from one window to the other, with mechanical motion and folded arms.

"Have you heard bad news, or are you unwell?" inquired his wife timidly, while Rosalie undressed her.

He kept silent.

"You can leave me," said Madame de Merret to her maid; "I will put my hair in curl papers myself."

From the expression of her husband's face she foresaw trouble, and wished to be alone with him. When Rosalie had gone, or was supposed to have gone (for she stayed in the corridor for a few minutes), Monsieur de Merret came and stood in front of his wife, and said coldly to her:

"Madame, there is someone in your closet!" She looked calmly at her husband and replied simply:

"No, sir."

This answer was heartrending to Monsieur de Merret; he did not believe in it. Yet his wife had never appeared to him purer or more saintly than at that moment. He rose to open the closet door; Madame de Merret took his hand, looked at him with an expression of melancholy, and said in a voice that betrayed singular emotion:

"If you find no one there, remember this, all will be over between us!" The extraordinary dignity of his wife's manner restored the Count's profound esteem for her, and inspired him with one of those resolutions that only lack a vaster stage to become immortal.

"No," said he, "Josephine, I will not go there. In either case it would separate us forever. Hear me, I know how pure you are at heart, and that your life is a holy one. You would not commit a mortal sin to save your life."

At these words Madame de Merret turned a haggard gaze upon her husband.

"Here, take your crucifix," he added. "Swear to me before God that there is no one in there; I will believe you, I will never open that door."

Madame de Merret took the crucifix and said:

"I swear."

"Louder," said the husband, "and repeat 'I swear before God that there is no one in that closet.' "

She repeated the sentence calmly.

"That will do," said Monsieur de Merret, coldly.

After a moment of silence:

"I never saw this pretty toy before," he said, examining the ebony crucifix inlaid with silver, and most artistically chiseled.

"I found it at Duvivier's, who bought it of a Spanish monk when the prisoners passed through Vendôme last year."

"Ah!" said Monsieur de Merret, as he replaced the crucifix on the nail, and he rang. Rosalie did not keep him waiting. Monsieur de Merret went quickly to meet her, led her to the bay window that opened on to the garden and whispered to her:

"Listen! I know that Gorenflot wishes to marry you, poverty is the only drawback, and you told him that you would be his wife if he found the means to establish himself as a master mason. Well! go and fetch him, tell him to come here with his trowel and tools. Manage not to awaken any one in his house but himself; his fortune will be more than your desires. Above all, leave this room without babbling, otherwise—" He frowned. Rosalie went away, he recalled her.

"Here, take my latchkey," he said. "Jean!" then cried Monsieur de Merret, in tones of thunder in the corridor. Jean, who was at the same time his coachman and his confidential servant, left his game of cards and came.

"Go to bed, all of you," said his master, signing to him to approach; and the Count added, under his breath: "When they are all asleep—*asleep*, d'ye hear?—you will come down and tell me." Monsieur de Merret, who had not lost sight of his wife all the time he was giving his orders, returned quietly to her at the fireside and began to tell her of the game of billiards and the talk of the club. When Rosalie returned she found Monsieur and Madame de Merret conversing very amicably.

The Count had lately had all the ceilings of his reception rooms on the ground floor repaired. Plaster of Paris is difficult to obtain in Vendôme; the carriage raises its price. The Count had therefore bought a good deal, being well aware that he could find plenty of purchasers for whatever might remain over. This circumstance inspired him with the design he was about to execute.

"Sir, Gorenflot has arrived," said Rosalie in low tones.

"Show him in," replied the Count in loud tones.

Madame de Merret turned rather pale when she saw the mason.

"Gorenflot," said her husband, "go and fetch bricks from the coach-house, and bring sufficient to wall up the door of this closet; you will use the plaster I have over to coat the wall with." Then calling Rosalie and the workman aside:

"Listen, Gorenflot," he said in an undertone, "you will sleep here to-night. But to-morrow you will have a passport to a foreign country, to a town to which I will direct you. I shall give you six thousand francs for your journey. You will stay ten years in that town; if you do not like it, you may establish yourself in another, provided it be in the same country. You will pass through Paris, where you will await me. There I will insure you an additional six thousand francs by contract, which will be paid to you on your return, provided you have fulfilled the conditions of our bargain. This is the price for your absolute silence as to what you are about to do to-night. As to you, Rosalie, I will give you ten thousand francs on the day of your wedding, on condition of your marrying Gorenflot; but if you wish to marry, you must hold your tongues; or—no dowry."

"Rosalie," said Madame de Merret, "do my hair."

The husband walked calmly up and down, watching the door, the mason, and his wife, but without betraying any insulting doubts. Madame de Merret chose a moment when the workman was unloading bricks and her husband was at the other end of the room to say to Rosalie: "A thousand francs a year for you, my child, if you can tell Gorenflot to leave a chink at the bottom." Then out loud, she added coolly:

"Go and help him!"

Monsieur and Madame de Merret were silent all the time that Gorenflot took to brick up the door. This silence, on the part of the husband, who did not choose to furnish his wife with a pretext for saying things of a double meaning, had its purpose; on the part of Madame de Merret it was either pride or prudence. When the wall was about half-way up, the sly workman took advantage of a moment when the Count's back was turned, to strike a blow with his trowel in one of the glass panes of the closet-door. This act informed Madame de Merret that Rosalie had spoken to Gorenflot.

All three then saw a man's face; it was dark and gloomy with black hair and eyes of flame. Before her husband turned, the poor woman had time to make a sign to the stranger that signified: Hope!

At four o'clock, toward dawn, for it was the month of September, the construction was finished. The mason was handed over to the care of Jean, and Monsieur de Merret went to bed in his wife's room.

On rising the following morning, he said carelessly:

"The deuce! I must go to the Mairie for the passport." He put his hat on his head, advanced three steps toward the door, altered his mind and took the crucifix.

His wife trembled for joy. "He is going to Duvivier," she thought. As soon as the Count had left, Madame de Merret rang for Rosalie; then in a terrible voice:

"The trowel, the trowel!" she cried, "and quick to work! I saw how Gorenflot did it; we shall have time to make a hole and to mend it again."

In the twinkling of an eye, Rosalie brought a sort of axe to her mistress, who with unparalleled ardor set about demolishing the wall. She had already knocked out several bricks and was preparing to strike a more decisive blow when she perceived Monsieur de Merret behind her. She fainted.

"Lay Madame on her bed," said the Count coldly. He had foreseen what would happen in his absence and had set a trap for his wife;

he had simply written to the mayor, and had sent for Duvivier. The jeweler arrived just as the room had been put in order.

"Duvivier," inquired the Count, "did you buy crucifixes of the Spaniards who passed through here?"

"No, sir."

"That will do, thank you," he said, looking at his wife like a tiger. "Jean," he added, "you will see that my meals are served in the Countess's room; she is ill, and I shall not leave her until she has recovered."

The cruel gentleman stayed with his wife for twenty days. In the beginning, when there were sounds in the walled closet, and Josephine attempted to implore his pity for the dying stranger, he replied, without permitting her to say a word:

"You have sworn on the cross that there is no one there."

Reading for Understanding

Main Idea

1. Which of the Biblical commandments serves as the central point of the story?
   (a) You shall not steal.
   (b) You shall not bear false witness against your neighbor.
   (c) You shall not commit adultery.
   (d) Honor your father and your mother.

Details

2. The background of the story was told to the narrator by (a) the Spaniard's landlady (b) the Duke of Vendôme (c) Duvivier (d) Rosalie.

3. A crucial element in the story is a (a) wardrobe (b) high window (c) horse and carriage (d) hand of cards.

4. The plaster of Paris was available because the Count had (a) done some repair work (b) anticipated the problem with his wife (c) been advised by Jean to stockpile the scarce material (d) planned to sell the useful substance.

Inferences

5. Which of the following commandments is broken by the husband?

   (a) You shall not worship false gods.
   (b) Remember the sabbath day.
   (c) You shall not covet your neighbor's wife.
   (d) You shall not kill.

6. Madame was unable to save her lover because (a) the Count was indifferent to the problem (b) the Count didn't leave her side (c) Rosalie confessed to the Count (d) Gorenflot had lied.

7. Gorenflot (a) tried to help the Madame (b) sold Madame a crucifix (c) refused to build the wall (d) was the coachman.

8. Rosalie's "germ of remorse or hope" (576) arose from (a) a desire to make a good impression (b) a naturial shiftiness (c) her unhappiness with her job at the inn (d) the memory of her part in the tragedy.

9. The Madame's convalescence and radiant beauty can be attributed to (a) a good dinner (b) her love for the Count (c) her new love (d) the prospects of a trip to Paris.

Outcome

10. As a result of the events in this story, (a) the Madame and her husband were reconciled (b) Duvivier and Rosalie were married (c) the Count relented (d) three people died.

Words in Context

1. "There is an old gray house, *surmounted* by very high gables. **Surmounted** (573) means (a) improved (b) topped (c) decorated (d) marred.

2. "The empty and deserted house is a gigantic *enigma*, of which the key is lost." An **enigma** (574) is a (a) puzzle (b) household (c) place (d) challenge.

3. "He didn't eat much, but his manners were so polite, so *amiable*, that no one could owe him a grudge." **Amiable** (574) means (a) unusual (b) obedient (c) shy (d) agreeable.

4. "Suddenly the Grande Bretêche . . . appeared like a fantastic *appari-*

tion before me." **Apparition** (576) means (a) jigsaw (b) temple (c) ghost (d) meeting place.

5. "She soon recovered from the effects of her emotion, for all women, from the great lady to the maid of the inn, possess a *composure* that is peculiar to them." **Composure** (576) means (a) self-assurance (b) irritability (c) reliability (d) secret.

6., 7. "Were I to describe Rosalie's *diffuse* eloquence faithfully, an entire volume would scarcely contain it; so I shall *abridge*." **Diffuse** (577) means (a) keen (b) unappreciated (c) wordy (d) admirable. **Abridge** (577) means (a) shorten (b) join together (c) comment (d) expand.

8. "A praiseworthy modesty, which perhaps is the source of the true happiness that no Parisian *covets*." **Covets** (577) means (a) imitates (b) desires (c) talks about (d) rejects.

9. "At dinner he found Madame de Merret most *coquettishly* attired." **Coquettishly** (577) means (a) simply (b) richly (c) surprisingly (d) flirtatiously.

10. "On his way to the club it had occurred to him that his wife was restored to health, and that her *convalescence* had added to her beauty." **Convalescence** (577) means (a) new plan of action (b) dogged determination (c) expression of love (d) recovery of health.

11. "The husband thought *ingenuously* that Rosalie was in the closet; yet suspicion that jangled in his ear put him on his guard." **Ingenuously** (577) means (a) erroneously (b) quickly (c) angrily (d) innocently.

12. "At these words Madame de Merret turned a *haggard* gaze upon her husband." **Haggard** (578) means (a) interesting (b) gaunt (c) slightly amused (d) unblinking.

13. "When Rosalie returned she found Monsieur and Madame de Merret conversing very *amicably*." **Amicably** (579) means (a) in a friendly fashion (b) heatedly (c) without listening to each other (d) in a tense manner.

14., 15. "This silence, on the part of the husband, who did not choose to furnish his wife with a *pretext* for saying things of double meaning, had its purpose; on the part of Madame de Merret it was either pride or *prudence*." A **pretext** (580) is (a) special skill (b) an excuse (c) a slander (d) a kind of summary. **Prudence** (580) means (a) error (b) lack of morality (c) prejudice (d) good judgment.

16. "In the twinkling of an eye, Rosalie brought a sort of axe to her mistress, who with unparalleled *ardor* set about demolishing the wall." **Ardor** (580) means (a) ability (b) intensity (c) weeping (d) curiosity.

17. "When . . . Josephine attempted to *implore* his pity for the dying

stranger, he replied, 'You have sworn on the cross that there is no one there.' " **Implore** (581) means (a) awaken (b) undo (c) beg (d) recover.

Thinking Critically about the Story

1. La Rochefoucauld wrote, "There is more self-love than love in jealousy." That is one of those simple sentences that contain a profound truth. What does it mean to you? How can you apply it to the Monsieur?

2. The wife's infidelity is clearly wrong; yet the author provides some clues to explain, though not forgive, her unfaithfulness to her husband.

3. To whom did Rosalie owe first loyalty? How did this backfire and speed the eventual tragedy?

4. How does the setting of the tragedy add to the mood of the story?

5. In the Spaniard's will (575), he left money "for masses to thank God for his escape." Technically a prisoner of France, he may have hoped to flee the country. Then something happened, and escape became an ironic impossibility. Why?

6. The Madame was buried with the Spaniard's crucifix. What information does this provide about her feelings toward the Spaniard?

7. The Count says, "Take your crucifix. Swear to me before God that there is no on in there; I will believe you, I will never open that door." Which part of his statement is true? Which false?

8. Is the husband's action understandable? Forgivable? Inexcusable? Is his punishment of his wife excessive, even if we consider the provocation?

9. We know the wife died. She was buried with the crucifix. What indication do we have that the husband died soon after? What destroyed him, his wife's infidelity or his own blasted pride? What do you think?

10. We can assume that the wife was religious. Most ladies of that period were. She prayed. She treasured a crucifix. Why was she willing to commit perjury before God when her husband asked her to swear on the crucifix? How does this provide a clue to her character?

Language in Action

Tricky Word Pairs

I **inferred** that I was not the only person to whom my good landlady had communicated the secret of which I was to be the sole recipient, and I prepared to listen.

Inferred is used here in the best traditional sense. *Infer* means *draw a conclusion.* It is sometimes confused with *imply: hint* or *insinuate.*

"What are you *inferring* by that remark?"

Implying would be the more traditional preferred word. The writer implies; the reader infers. The *imply-infer* distinction is a careful distinction gradually breaking down in general use.

Other pairs also provide useful distinctions of meaning:

1. **Deprecate** means **disapprove. Depreciate** means **lessen in value.**
2. A **dilemma** is a **problem** with two possible solutions: **both bad.**
3. **Enviable** means **arousing envy. Envious** means **feeling envy.**
4. **Flaunt** suggests **show off. Flout** suggests **scorn, disregard.**
5. **Learn** is to **acquire knowledge. Teach** is to **impart it.**
6. **Legible** refers to the **clarity** of handwriting or printing. **Readable** includes the **meaning of legible** and adds the **quality of interest.**
7. A **majority** is more than half the votes. A **plurality** is more than anyone else's.
8. **Reputation** is what people think you are. **Character** is what you are.
9. When **sentiment** becomes **excessive,** it becomes **sentimentality.**
10. **Taunt** means **reproach. Taut** means **tight, tense.**

Mateo Falcone

Prosper Mérimée
French

Giuseppa drew near. She had just discovered the watch-chain, the end of which was hanging out of Fortunato's pocket.

"Who gave you that watch?" she demanded in a severe tone.

"My cousin, the Adjutant."

Falcone seized the watch and smashed it into a thousand pieces against a rock.

"Wife," said he, "is this my child?"

The parent-child bond is one of the strongest in human relationships, but it can be tested and even broken when the provocation is severe enough. "Mateo Falcone" is the story of such a bond, but it is even more. It describes a rigid code of behavior that puts "honor" above love.

Young Fortunato Falcone, only son of the dangerous Mateo Falcone, finds himself facing a temptation that is difficult to resist. Only ten years old, he lacks the insight and judgment of maturity. The story agonizes over his actions. Will he make a mistake? Will his mistake have unpleasant consequences later. In 19th-century Corsica, law is sometimes far away, but a twisted kind of justice may be right at hand.

It may be difficult to find a more incredible person than Mateo Falcone. Is his action the very depth of evil?

Mateo Falcone

ON leaving Porto-Vecchio from the northwest and directing his steps towards the interior of the island, the traveler will notice that the land rises rapidly, and after three hours' walking over tortuous paths obstructed by great masses of rock and sometimes cut by ravines, he will find himself on the border of a great mâquis*. The mâquis is the domain of the Corsican shepherds and of those who are at variance with justice. It must be known that, in order to save himself the trouble of manuring his field, the Corsican husbandman sets fire to a piece of woodland. If the flame spread farther than is necessary, so much the worse! In any case he is certain of a good crop from the land fertilized by the ashes of the trees which grow upon it. He gathers only the heads of his grain, leaving the straw, which it would be unnecessary labor to cut. In the following spring the roots that have remained in the earth without being destroyed send up their tufts of sprouts, which in a few years reach a height of seven or eight feet. It is this kind of tangled thicket that is called a mâquis. They are made up of different kinds of trees and shrubs, so crowded and mingled together at the caprice of nature that only with an ax in hand can a man open a passage through them, and mâquis are frequently seen so thick and bushy that the wild sheep themselves cannot penetrate them.

If you have killed a man, go into the mâquis of Porto-Vecchio. With a good gun and plenty of powder and balls, you can live there in safety. Do not forget a brown cloak furnished with a hood, which will serve you for both cover and mattress. The shepherds will give you chestnuts, milk and cheese, and you will have nothing to fear from justice nor the relatives of the dead except when it is necessary for you to descend to the city to replenish your ammunition.

When I was in Corsica in 18—, Mateo Falcone had his house half a league from this mâquis. He was rich enough for that country, living in noble style—that is to say, doing nothing—on the income from his flocks, which the shepherds, who are a kind of nomads, lead to pasture here and there on the mountains. When I saw him, two years after the event that I am about to relate, he appeared to me to be about fifty years old or more. Picture to yourself a man, small but robust, with curly hair, black as jet, an aquiline nose, thin lips, large, restless eyes, and a complexion the color of tanned leather. His skill as a marksman was considered extraordinary even in his country, where good shots are so common. For

---

*pronounced "ma-KEE"

example, Mateo would never fire at a sheep with buck-shot; but at a hundred and twenty paces, he would drop it with a ball in the head or shoulder, as he chose. He used his arms as easily at night as during the day. I was told this feat of his skill, which will, perhaps, seem impossible to those who have not traveled in Corsica. A lighted candle was placed at eighty paces, behind a paper transparency about the size of a plate. He would take aim, then the candle would be extinguished, and, at the end of a moment, in the most complete darkness, he would fire and hit the paper three times out of four.

With such a transcendent accomplishment, Mateo Falcone had acquired a great reputation. He was said to be as good a friend as he was a dangerous enemy; accommodating and charitable, he lived at peace with all the world in the district of Porto-Vecchio. But it is said of him that in Corte, where he had married his wife, he had ridded himself very vigorously of a rival who was considered as redoubtable in war as in love; at least, a certain gun-shot which surprised this rival as he was shaving before a little mirror hung in his window was attributed to Mateo. The affair was smoothed over and Mateo was married. His wife Giuseppa had given him at first three daughters (which infuriated him), and finally a son, whom he named Fortunato, and who became the hope of his family, the inheritor of the name. The daughters were well married: their father could count at need on the poniards* and carbines of his sons-in-law. The son was only ten years old, but he already gave promise of fine attributes.

On a certain day in autumn, Mateo set out at an early hour with his wife to visit one of his flocks in a clearing of the mâquis. The little Fortunato wanted to go with them, but the clearing was too far away; moreover, it was necessary someone should stay to watch the house; therefore the father refused: it will be seen whether or not he had reason to repent.

He had been gone some hours, and the little Fortunato was tranquilly stretched out in the sun, looking at the blue mountains, and thinking that the next Sunday he was going to dine in the city with his uncle, the Caporal, when he was suddenly interrupted in his meditations by the firing of a musket. He got up and turned to that side of the plain whence the noise came. Other shots followed, fired at irregular intervals, and each time nearer; at last, in the path which led from the plain to Mateo's house, appeared a man wearing the pointed hat of the mountaineers, bearded, covered with rags, and dragging himself along with difficulty by the support of his gun. He had just received a wound in his thigh.

This man was an outlaw, who, having gone to the town by night to buy powder, had fallen on the way into an ambush of Corsican light-infantry. After a vigorous defense he was fortunate in making his

---
*daggers

retreat, closely followed and firing from rock to rock. But he was only a little in advance of the soldiers, and his wound prevented him from gaining the mâquis before being overtaken.

He approached Fortunato and said: "You are the son of Mateo Falcone?"—"Yes."

"I am Gianetto Saupiero. I am followed by the yellow-collars. Hide me, for I can go no farther."

"And what will my father say if I hide you without his permission?"

"He will say that you have done well."

"How do you know?"

"Hide me quickly; they are coming."

"Wait till my father gets back."

"How can I wait? Malediction! They will be here in five minutes. Come, hide me, or I will kill you."

Fortunato answered him with the utmost coolness:

"Your gun is empty, and there are no more cartridges in your belt."

"I have my stiletto."

"But can you run as fast as I can?"

He gave a leap and put himself out of reach.

"You are not the son of Mateo Falcone! Will you then let me be captured before your house?"

The child appeared moved.

"What will you give me if I hide you?" said he, coming nearer.

The outlaw felt in a leather pocket that hung from his belt, and took out a five-franc piece, which he had doubtless saved to buy ammunition with. Fortunato smiled at the sight of the silver piece; he snatched it, and said to Gianetto:

"Fear nothing."

Immediately he made a great hole in a pile of hay that was near the house. Gianetto crouched down in it and the child covered him in such a way that he could breathe without it being possible to suspect that the hay concealed a man. He bethought himself further, and, with the subtlety of a tolerably ingenious savage, placed a cat and her kittens on the pile, that it might not appear to have been recently disturbed. Then, noticing the traces of blood on the path near the house, he covered them carefully with dust, and, that done, he again stretched himself out in the sun with the greatest tranquillity.

A few moments afterwards, six men in brown uniforms with yellow collars, and commanded by an Adjutant, were before Mateo's door. This Adjutant was a distant relative of Falcone's. (In Corsica the degrees of relationship are followed much further than elsewhere.) His name was Tiodoro Gamba; he was an active man, much dreaded by the outlaws, several of whom he had already entrapped.

"Good day, little cousin," said he, approaching Fortunato; "how tall you have grown. Have you seen a man go past here just now?"

"Oh! I am not yet so tall as you, my cousin," replied the child with a simple air.

"You soon will be. But haven't you seen a man go by here, tell me?"

"If I have seen a man go by?"

"Yes, a man with a pointed hat of black velvet, and a vest embroidered with red and yellow."

"A man with a pointed hat, and a vest embroidered with red and yellow?"

"Yes, answer quickly, and don't repeat my questions!"

"This morning the curé passed before our door on his horse, Piero. He asked me how papa was, and I answered him—"

"Ah, you little scoundrel, you are playing sly! Tell me quickly which way Gianetto went? We are looking for him, and I am sure he took this path."

"Who knows?"

"Who knows? It is I know that you have seen him."

"Can any one see who passes when they are asleep?"

"You were not asleep, rascal; the shooting woke you up."

"Then you believe, cousin, that your guns make so much noise? My father's carbine has the advantage of them."

"The devil take you, you cursed little scapegrace! I am certain that you have seen Gianetto. Perhaps, even, you have hidden him. Come, comrades, go into the house and see if our man is there. He could only go on one foot, and the knave has too much good sense to try to reach the mâquis limping like that. Moreover, the bloody tracks stop here."

"And what will papa say?" asked Fortunato with a sneer. "What will he say if he knows that his house has been entered while he was away?"

"You rascal," said the Adjutant, taking him by the ear, "do you know that it only remains for me to make you change your tone? Perhaps you will speak differently after I have given you twenty blows with the flat of my sword."

Fortunato continued to sneer.

"My father is Mateo Falcone," said he with emphasis.

"You little scamp, you know very well that I can carry you off to Corte or to Bastia. I will make you lie in a dungeon, on straw, with your feet in shackles, and I will have you guillotined if you don't tell me where Gianetto is."

The child burst out laughing at this ridiculous menace. He repeated:

"My father is Mateo Falcone."

"Adjutant," said one of the soldiers in a low voice, "let us have no quarrels with Mateo."

Gamba appeared evidently embarrassed. He spoke in an undertone with the soldiers who had already visited the house. This was not a very long operation, for the cabin of a Corsican consists only of a single square room, furnished with a table, some benches, chests, housekeeping utensils and those of the chase. In the meantime, little Fortunato petted his cat and seemed to take a wicked enjoyment in the confusion of the soldiers and of his cousin.

One of the men approached the pile of hay. He saw the cat, and gave the pile a careless thrust with his bayonet, shrugging his shoulders as if he felt that his precaution was ridiculous. Nothing moved; the boy's face betrayed not the slightest emotion.

The Adjutant and his troop were cursing their luck. Already they were looking in the direction of the plain, as if disposed to return by the way they had come, when their chief, convinced that menaces would produce no impression on Falcone's son, determined to make a last effort, and try the effect of caresses and presents.

"My little cousin," said he, "you are a very wide-awake little fellow. You will get along. But you are playing a naughty game with me; and if I wasn't afraid of making trouble for my cousin, Mateo, the devil take me, but I would carry you off with me."

"Bah!"

"But when my cousin comes back I shall tell him about this, and he will whip you till the blood comes for having told such lies."

"You don't say so!"

"You will see. But hold on!—be a good boy and I will give you something."

"Cousin, let me give you some advice: if you wait much longer Gianetto will be in the mâquis and it will take a smarter man than you to follow him."

The Adjutant took from his pocket a silver watch worth about ten crowns, and noticing that Fortunato's eyes sparkled at the sight of it, said, holding the watch by the end of its steel chain:

"Rascal! you would like to have such a watch as that hung around your neck, wouldn't you, and to walk in the streets of Porto-Vecchio proud as a peacock? People would ask you what time it was, and you would say: 'Look at my watch.' "

"When I am grown up, my uncle, the Caporal, will give me a watch."

"Yes; but your uncle's little boy has one already; not so fine as this either. But then, he is younger than you."

The child sighed.

"Well! Would you like this watch, little cousin?"

Fortunato, casting sidelong glances at the watch, resembled a cat that has been given a whole chicken. It feels that it is being made sport of, and does not dare to use its claws; from time to time it turns its eyes away so as not to be tempted, licking its jaws all the while, and has the appearance of saying to its master, "How cruel your joke is!"

However, the Adjutant seemed in earnest in offering his watch. Fortunato did not reach out his hand for it, but said with a bitter smile:

"Why do you make fun of me?"

"Good God! I am not making fun of you. Only tell me where Gianetto is and the watch is yours."

Fortunato smiled incredulously, and fixing his black eyes on those of the Adjutant tried to read there the faith he ought to have had in his words.

"May I lose my epaulettes,"* cried the Adjutant, "if I do not give you the watch on this condition. These comrades are witnesses; I cannot deny it."

While speaking he gradually held the watch nearer till it almost touched the child's pale face, which plainly showed the struggle that was going on in his soul between covetousness and respect for hospitality. His breast swelled with emotion; he seemed about to suffocate. Meanwhile the watch was slowly swaying and turning, sometimes brushing against his cheek. Finally, his right hand was gradually stretched toward it; the ends of his fingers touched it; then its whole weight was in his hand, the Adjutant still keeping hold of the chain. The face was light blue; the cases newly burnished. In the sunlight it seemed to be all on fire. The temptation was too great. Fortunato raised his left hand and pointed over his shoulder with his thumb at the hay against which he was reclining. The Adjutant understood him at once. He dropped the end of the chain and Fortunato felt himself the sole possessor of the watch. He sprang up with the agility of a deer and stood ten feet from the pile, which the soldiers began at once to overturn.

There was a movement in the hay, and a bloody man with a poniard in his hand appeared. He tried to rise to his feet, but his stiffened leg would not permit it and he fell. The Adjutant at once grappled with him and took away his stiletto. He was immediately secured, notwithstanding his resistance.

Gianetto, lying on the earth and bound like a fagot,** turned his head towards Fortunato, who had approached.

"Son of—!" said he, with more contempt than anger.

The child threw him the silver piece which he had received, feeling that he no longer deserved it; but the outlaw paid no attention to the movement, and with great coolness said to the Adjutant:

---

*indications of rank
**bundle of sticks

"My dear Gamba, I cannot walk; you will be obliged to carry me to the city."

"Just now you could run faster than a buck," answered the cruel captor; "but be at rest. I am so pleased to have you that I would carry you a league on my back without fatigue. Besides, comrade, we are going to make a litter for you with your cloak and some branches, and at the Crespoli farm we shall find horses."

"Good," said the prisoner. "You will also put a little straw on your litter that I may be more comfortable."

While some of the soldiers were occupied in making a kind of stretcher out of some chestnut boughs and the rest were dressing Gianetto's wound, Mateo Falcone and his wife suddenly appeared at a turn in the path that led to the mâquis. The woman was staggering under the weight of an enormous sack of chestnuts, while her husband was sauntering along, carrying one gun in his hands, while another was slung across his shoulders, for it is unworthy of a man to carry other burdens than his arms.

At the sight of the soldiers Mateo's first thought was that they had come to arrest him. But why this thought? Had he then some quarrels with justice? No. He enjoyed a good reputation. He was said to have a particularly good name, but he was a Corsican and a highlander, and there are few Corsican highlanders who, in scrutinizing their memory, cannot find some peccadillo, such as a gun-shot, dagger-thrust, or similar trifles. Mateo more than others had a clear conscience; for more than ten years he had not pointed his carbine at a man, but he was always prudent, and put himself into a position to make a good defense if necessary. "Wife," said he to Giuseppa, "put down the sack and hold yourself ready."

She obeyed at once. He gave her the gun that was slung across his shoulders, which would have bothered him, and, cocking the one he held in his hands, advanced slowly towards the house, walking among the trees that bordered the road, ready at the least hostile demonstration, to hide behind the largest, whence he could fire from under cover. His wife followed closely behind, holding his reserve weapon and his cartridge-box. The duty of a good housekeeper, in case of a fight, is to load her husband's carbines.

On the other side the Adjutant was greatly troubled to see Mateo advance in this manner, with cautious steps, his carbine raised, and his finger on the trigger.

"If by chance," thought he, "Mateo should be related to Gianetto, or if he should be his friend and wish to defend him, the contents of his two guns would arrive amongst us as certainly as a letter in the post; and if he should see me, notwithstanding the relationship!"

In this perplexity he took a bold step. It was to advance alone towards Mateo and tell him of the affair while accosting him as an old acquaintance, but the short space that separated him from Mateo seemed terribly long.

"Hello! old comrade," cried he. "How do you do, my good fellow? It is I, Gamba, your cousin."

Without answering a word, Mateo stopped, and in proportion as the other spoke, slowly raised the muzzle of his gun so that it was pointing upward when the Adjutant joined him.

"Good-day, brother," said the Adjutant, holding out his hand. "It is a long time since I have seen you."

"Good-day, brother."

"I stopped while passing, to say good-day to you and to cousin Pepa here. We have had a long journey to-day, but have no reason to complain, for we have captured a famous prize. We have just seized Gianetto Saupiero."

"God be praised!" cried Giuseppa. "He stole a milch goat from us last week."

These words reassured Gamba.

"Poor devil!" said Mateo. "He was hungry."

"The villain fought like a lion," continued the Adjutant, a little mortified. "He killed one of my soldiers, and not content with that, broke Caporal Chardon's arm; but that matters little, he is only a Frenchman. Then, too, he was so well hidden that the devil couldn't have found him. Without my little cousin, Fortunato, I should never have discovered him."

"Fortunato!" cried Mateo.

"Fortunato!" repeated Giuseppa.

"Yes, Gianetto was hidden under the hay-pile yonder, but my little cousin showed me the trick. I shall tell his uncle, the Caporal, that he may send him a fine present for his trouble. Both his name and yours will be in the report that I shall send to the Attorney-general."

"Malediction!" said Mateo in a low voice.

They had rejoined the detachment. Gianetto was already lying on the litter ready to set out. When he saw Mateo and Gamba in company he smiled a strange smile, then, turning his head towards the door of the house, he spat on the sill, saying:

"House of a traitor."

Only a man determined to die would dare pronounce the word traitor to Falcone. A good blow with the stiletto, which there would be no need of repeating, would have immediately paid the insult. However, Mateo made no other movement than to place his hand on his forehead like a man who is dazed.

Fortunato had gone into the house when his father arrived, but now he reappeared with a bowl of milk which he handed with downcast eyes to Gianetto.

"Get away from me!" cried the outlaw, in a loud voice. Then, turning to one of the soldiers, he said:

"Comrade, give me a drink."

The soldier placed his gourd in his hands, and the prisoner drank the water handed to him by a man with whom he had just exchanged bullets. He then asked them to tie his hands across his breast instead of behind his back.

"I like," said he, "to lie at my ease."

They hastened to satisfy him; then the Adjutant gave the signal to start, said adieu to Mateo, who did not respond, and descended with rapid steps towards the plain.

Nearly ten minutes elapsed before Mateo spoke. The child looked with restless eyes, now at his mother, now at his father, who was leaning on his gun and gazing at him with an expression of concentrated rage.

"You begin well," said Mateo at last with a calm voice, but frightful to one who knew the man.

"Oh, father!" cried the boy, bursting into tears, and making a forward movement as if to throw himself on his knees. But Mateo cried, "Away from me!"

The little fellow stopped and sobbed, immovable, a few feet from his father.

Giuseppa drew near. She had just discovered the watch-chain, the end of which was hanging out of Fortunato's jacket.

"Who gave you that watch?" demanded she in a severe tone.

"My cousin, the Adjutant."

Falcone seized the watch and smashed it in a thousand pieces against a rock.

"Wife," said he, "is this my child?"

Giuseppa's cheeks turned a brick-red.

"What are you saying, Mateo? Do you know to whom you speak?"

"Very well, this child is the first of his race to commit treason."

Fortunato's sobs and gasps redoubled as Falcone kept his lynx-eyes upon him. Then he struck the earth with his gun-stock, shouldered the weapon, and turned in the direction of the mâquis, calling to Fortunato to follow. The boy obeyed. Giuseppa hastened after Mateo and seized his arm.

"He is your son," said she with a trembling voice, fastening her black eyes on those of her husband to read what was going on in his heart.

"Leave me alone," said Mateo. "I am his father."

Giuseppa embraced her son, and bursting into tears entered the house. She threw herself on her knees before an image of the Virgin and prayed ardently. In the meanwhile Falcone walked some two hundred paces along the path and only stopped when he reached a little ravine which he descended. He tried the earth with the butt-end of his carbine, and found it soft and easy to dig. The place seemed to be convenient for his design.

"Fortunato, go close to that big rock there."

The child did as he was commanded, then he kneeled.

"Say your prayers."

"Oh, father, father, do not kill me!"

"Say your prayers!" repeated Mateo in a terrible voice.

The boy, stammering and sobbing, recited the Pater and the Credo. At the end of each prayer the father loudly answered, "Amen!"

"Are those all the prayers you know?"

"Oh! father, I know the Ave Maria and the litany that my aunt taught me."

"It is very long, but no matter."

The child finished the litany in a scarcely audible tone.

"Are you finished?"

"Oh! my father, have mercy! Pardon me! I will never do so again. I will beg my cousin, the Caporal, to pardon Gianetto."

He was still speaking. Mateo raised his gun, and, taking aim, said: "May God pardon you!"

The boy made a desperate effort to rise and grasp his father's knees, but there was not time. Mateo fired and Fortunato fell dead.

Without casting a glance on the body, Mateo returned to the house for a spade with which to bury his son. He had gone but a few steps when he met Giuseppa, who, alarmed by the shot, was hastening hither.

"What have you done?" cried she.

"Justice."

"Where is he?"

"In the ravine. I am going to bury him. He died a Christian. I shall have a mass said for him. Have my son-in-law, Tiodoro Bianchi, sent for to come and live with us."

Reading for Understanding

Main Idea

1. A central idea in the story is (a) the place of women in 19th-century Corsica (b) the influence of thick-growing vegetation in Corsican

society (c) superb marksmanship among the shepherds of Corsica (d) the conflict between a father's love and a code of honor.

Details

2. The mâquis is defined as a (a) fertile pasture (b) forest of pine trees (c) dense thicket of shrubs and trees (d) kind of vegetable garden.
3. Mateo Falcone had once been suspected of (a) murder (b) sheep stealing (c) treason (d) wife abuse.
4. Gianetto was (a) the Adjutant (b) Fortunato's brother (c) Giuseppa's father (d) none of these.
5. Fortunato was first tempted by (a) a stiletto (b) a watch (c) a carbine (d) a five-franc piece.

Inferences

6. Fortunato was led into his fatal action by (a) kindness (b) greed (c) reason (d) unselfishness.
7. Upon being discovered, the prisoner took his fate (a) with weeping (b) with disbelief (c) calmly (d) happily.
8. When the Adjutant saw Mateo Falcone advancing, he was (a) nervous (b) ready to pounce upon Fortunato (c) belligerent (d) joking.
9. Mateo smashed the watch because he considered it (a) of no real value (b) a symbol of Fortunato's treachery (c) too small a reward for Fortunato's actions (d) too much desired by Giuseppa.

Order of Events

10. Arrange the items in the order in which they occurred. Use letters only.
    A. Mateo returns to find soldiers at his home.
    B. The outlaw first speaks to Fortunato.
    C. Mateo exacts his own kind of justice.
    D. Fortunato accepts the silver watch.
    E. Fortunato conceals the outlaw.

Words in Context

1. "They are made up of different kinds of trees and shrubs, so crowded and mingled together at the *caprice* of nature that only with an ax in hand can a man open a passage through them" **Caprice** (587) means (a) expense (b) assistance (c) whim (d) control.

2. "Picture to yourself a man, small but robust, with curly hair, black as jet, an *aquiline* nose, thin lips, large, restless eyes, and a complexion the color of tanned leather." **Aquiline** (587) means (a) unusually large (b) curved (c) watery (d) smooth.

3. "With such a *transcendent* accomplishment, Mateo Falcone had acquired a great reputation." **Transcendent** (588) means (a) extraordinary (b) modest (c) much envied (d) momentary.

4. "He had rid himself very vigorously of a rival who was considered as *redoubtable* in love as in war." **Redoubtable** (588) means (a) fortunate (b) technically competent (c) dubious (d) terrifying.

5. "How can I wait? *Malediction!*" A **malediction** (589) is a (a) cry of hope (b) curse (c) distress signal (d) problem with no solution.

6. "I have my *stiletto*." A **stiletto** (589) is a kind of (a) musket (b) broadsword (c) lance (d) dagger.

7. "He bethought himself further, and, with the *subtlety* of a tolerably ingenious savage, placed a cat and her kittens on the pile, that it might not appear to have been recently disturbed." **Subtlety** (589) means (a) slyness (b) anxiety (c) boldness (d) proud display.

8. While speaking, he gradually held the watch nearer till it almost touched the child's pale face, which plainly showed the struggle that was going on in his soul between *covetousness* and respect for hospitality." **Covetousness** (592) is (a) anger (b) deception (c) greed (d) thoughtlessness.

9. "The face was light blue; the cases newly *burnished*." **Burnished** (592) means (a) intact (b) pressed together (c) sandpapered (d) made shiny.

10., 11. "There are few Corsican highlanders who, in *scrutinizing* their memory, cannot find some *peccadillo*, such as a gun-shot, dagger-thrust, or similar trifles." **Scrutinizing** (593) means (a) announcing (b) examining (c) retelling (d) arousing. A **peccadillo** (593) is (a) deed of note (b) crime (c) upset (d) slight sin.

12. "It was to advance alone toward Mateo and tell him of the affair while *accosting* him as an old acquaintance." **Accosting** (594) means (a) addressing (b) scolding (c) discovering (d) celebrating.

13. "She threw herself on her knees before an image of the Virgin and prayed *ardently*." **Ardently** (595) means (a) steadily (b) passionately (c) slowly and thoughtfully (d) hopelessly.

Thinking Critically about the Story

1. If Giuseppa's life was typical, what was the lot of peasant women at the time of "Mateo Falcone"?

2. Is Mateo a victim of his times or is he truly an evil man? Give your point of view.

3. What personality weaknesses did Fortunato display? How did they play a part in his downfall?

4. Mateo says of Gianetto's theft of a goat (594), "Poor devil! He was hungry." What strange set of principles allows him to forgive a theft and then exact the most terrible vengeance for a young child's weakness?

5. How did Gianetto react to the betrayal by Fortunato?

6. In talking about Gianetto's crimes, the Adjutant says, "He killed one of my soldiers, and not content with that, broke Caporal Chardon's arm; but that matters little, he is only a Frenchman." What does that suggest about a Corsican's attitude toward non-Corsicans?

7. The Adjutant also says, "Both his name and yours will be in the report that I shall send to the Attorney-general." What is Mateo's reaction to this news? Why is he so affected?

8. The author talks about a gun-shot or a dagger-thrust as a "trifle." Is the author being ironic (264) here? Explain.

Language in Action

Doublets

"Good-day, brother," said the Adjutant.

Some languages, like French, bewail the adoption of new words into the language. Other languages, like English, welcome newcomers with enthusiasm. English is so adept at borrowing from other languages that it will often borrow the same word twice, three times, or even more.

In the sentence above, *brother* has traveled a long route from Greek through Latin, through Old High German, and Old English. It is now one of our commonest words. But English has also adopted the word *friar* from the French *frère* and ultimately from the same roots as *brother.* We call such words that borrow the same root twice *doublets.* *Royal* and *regal, loyal* and *legal* are common doublets. In our story, *devil* comes from the same root as *diabolic.* Doublets provide additional words with varied shades of meaning.

Some other common doublets include *eatable, edible; word, verb; shriek, screech; eat, etch; influence, influenza; musket, mosquito; papyrus, paper.* Some word roots appear in three, four, or even five different forms. *Debit, debt,* and *due* come from one root. *Gentle, genteel, gentile,* and *jaunty* come from a single root, as do *discus, disk, dish, desk,* and *dais.*

How do the following doublets differ in meaning?

abridge, abbreviate	frail, fragile
amiable, amicable	human, humane
aptitude, attitude	hotel, hospital
chieftain, captain	pale, pallid
coy, quiet	poor, pauper
estate, state	reason, ration

Actions and Motivations

ACTIVITIES

Thinking Critically about the Selections

1. Which story had the greatest emotional impact on you? Why?

2. Was your choice in #1 your favorite story? Why or why not?

3. Do you agree with John Locke's statement at the beginning of the unit (515)? Why or why not?

4. In the "The Black Cat," Edgar Allan Poe wrote, "Who has not, a hundred times, found himself committing a vile or a stupid action, for no other reason than because he knows he should *not?*" Is this rather pessimistic view of human nature true, perhaps in part? Does starting to smoke as a teenager qualify as an example of such an action? Explain.

5. In contrast to #4, La Rochefoucauld wrote, "There are countless actions which appear ridiculous, whose hidden motives are very wise and weighty." What does this mean? Do you agree? Are both #4 and #5 accurate? Explain.

6. In Shakespeare's *Henry IV, Part 2,* Prince Hal knows his father is dying. He tries on the crown and later says to his father, "I never thought to hear you speak again." The King, thinking Hal couldn't wait to be king, replies, "Thy wish was father to that thought." Is the King's statement accurate? Do our wishes influence our thoughts? Do our thoughts influence our wishes? Can they be separated?

7. Here's a real-life problem for you, one that is very much involved with actions and motivations. In the 1996 Olympic Games at Atlanta, the great athlete Carl Lewis won his ninth career gold medal in the broadjump, tying the achievement of several other athletes. Then he began campaigning for a place on the 400-meter relay team, thus giving him a chance for a unique tenth gold medal. The problem was that the relay team had already been set after qualifying and practicing together. A substantial number of people said, "Put Carl in; he's the best." An equal number of people said, "Don't take away another runner's dream unfairly by replacing him at the last moment. The team members earned their places." If you were the coach, what

would be your decision? Why? What are the two ideals being balanced and contrasted here?

After you have made your decision and discussed the possibilities, turn to page 605 to find out what actually happened. Then tell whether the actual result made you change your opinion.

8. Select two selections in this unit and provide for each an adjective that you think best describes the tone. Here are some suggestions to start you thinking. You may prefer others. Justify your choices.

angry	haunting	reflective
anguished	humorous	romantic
bittersweet	inspiring	satirical
depressing	ironical	scholarly
despairing	jittery	solemn
gloomy	joyous	upbeat
grim	menacing	uneasy

The Writing Portfolio

Types of Writing

You have undoubtedly had experience with a variety of writing types: business and friendly letters, narratives, descriptions, explanations, essays, articles, various kinds of persuasion and argumentation, research papers. Many of these will be duplicated in the college and business years ahead.

This section is a continuation of the activities in Unit 5 (441–442). As you look over the following suggestions, choose those that you are most interested in.

1. Write a short one-act play based on a school experience. Follow the suggestions for "Dialogue in a Play," (571). Perhaps it was a lunchroom episode, a conversation just before health ed, dialogue in the school bus, or some other situation. If you can add a touch of humor, so much the better.

2. Try your hand at a short story, using "A Quarter's Worth of Fireworks" (517) as a model. Provide these six elements: situation,

complication, conflict, development, climax, and outcome. Preferably, take an episode from your own experience, but if your interests run to fantasy or science fiction, why not!

3. Write a character sketch of someone you know. These are ways of revealing character: by dialogue, by actions, by the person's thoughts, by the reactions of other persons, by others' opinions, and by your own direct statements.

4. In a letter to a friend, review one of the selections in this unit. Among possible areas of comment are these: general effect, setting, plot, an effective scene, use of dialogue, central idea, effectiveness of beginning and ending, clarity, progress of the plot.

5. Select a television movie, watch it, and then write a review. Some of the elements mentioned in #4 apply here, as well.

6. Write a summary of one of the selections in this unit. Condense the plot to a page or two. Try to use your own words rather than the words of the original.

Other Areas of Communication

1. The horror of being buried alive provides the major shock in "The Mysterious Mansion." That dread occupied the imagination of Edgar Allan Poe, great American master of the short story. In at least four stories, premature burial is the central theme. Indeed, one of the stories is called "The Premature Burial." These are the other three: "The Fall of the House of Usher," "The Cask of Amontillado," and "The Black Cat." If your taste runs to old-fashioned horror stories, read one of these and report to the class.

2. Two of the stories in this unit especially suggest the inferior position of women in the past. Which stories? How do they make that point clear? Be ready to set up a panel discussion considering these points and any others that seem relevant:

(a) The Position of Women Throughout History
(b) Major Gains in Recent Years
(c) Current Inequities That Need Correction
(d) The Portrayal of Women on Television Sitcoms
(e) Strategies for Further Improvement

3. "The Rising of the Moon" makes a suitable class play. With the help of your teacher, cast the play and choose a student director. Present

it with the book as a script. An unusually energetic cast might prefer to memorize the parts.

4. Writers weave their stories from life experiences and a keen imagination. Many writers get story ideas from the newspapers. Find a newspaper article that resembles, in one or more respects, one of the selections in this unit. Perhaps it's the experience of a lottery winner or a boy saved from a gang. Bring the article to class and prepare to tell about it.

5. Choose a partner in the class. Prepare to present an interview originating from a selection in this unit. For example, a reporter interviews the Sergeant of "The Rising of the Moon" after it's discovered that the wanted man has escaped. Or the Adjutant tells about his uneasiness during the episode at the cottage of Mateo Falcone.

6. A major legal problem is what to do with preteen and teenage criminals, often perpetrators of major crimes like assault, theft, arson, and murder. Debate the following resolution in class. Divide the class into two groups, one taking the positive and one the negative:

> Resolved; That teenagers who are major offenders should be treated in court as adults.

Language in Action—a Review

You may refer to the preceding pages to answer these questions.

1. In talking about levels of usage, to replace the word *colloquial,* we might choose (a) *slang* (b) *substandard* (c) *informal* (d) *formal.*

2. As a general rule, the best language to use (a) is standard formal English (b) doesn't call attention to itself (c) is colloquial with a touch of slang (d) is slang that is lively, colorful, and striking.

3. The word *farthing* is related to (a) four (b) far (c) fear (d) fire.

4. All the following are listed as part of the Indo-European family EXCEPT (a) Gothic (b) Old Norse (c) Sanskrit (d) Finnish.

5. Both the colon and the semicolon are used to (a) introduce quotation marks (b) join together adjectives in a series (c) replace the exclamation point (d) join independent clauses together.

6. A person who loved to introduce long stage directions to help a play's readers is (a) William Shakespeare (b) Lady Gregory (c) George Bernard Shaw (d) Moss Hart.

7. In a printed play, the parentheses include words that (a) are not actually said in the play itself (b) often distract from an understanding of the play (c) contradict what the character has just said (d) provide an opportunity for the principal actor to present the theme of the play.

8. "Attempting to arouse envy, Harris _____ his wealth for all to see." The missing word is (a) *depreciated* (b) *flaunted* (c) *flouted* (d) *deprecated*.

9. All the following pairs are doublets EXCEPT (a) *frail, fragile* (b) *common, comma* (c) *amiable, amicable* (d) *hotel, hospital*.

10. A language that is mentioned as receptive to new words is (a) French (b) Spanish (c) English (d) German.

Atlanta Olympics problem, page 602:

The coach did not put Carl Lewis into the relay.

The team did not win the gold medal, won by Canada.

The team did win the silver medal, however.

UNIT EIGHT

The World Over

If civilization is to survive, we must cultivate the science of human relationships—the ability of all peoples, of all kinds, to live together, in the same world at peace.

Franklin Delano Roosevelt

A major purpose of this book has been to provide a cross-section of writing around the world. If we are ever to live safely in one world, we need to recognize the things we all have in common. There are obvious cultural differences, and these can make for a varied and colorful world. But the similarities are profound, more important than the superficial differences.

In addition to selections by American authors, you have already met Chinese, Irish, English, French, German, Hungarian, Norwegian, Japanese, African, Philippine and Russian writers. This unit will add selections by Chilean, Egyptian, Indian, Polish, Chinese, and Syrian writers. The settings are different, but they all reveal a common humanity.

Throughout the book we have met stories that brought tears and those that stimulated laughter. In this final unit, we again provide extremes. The sadness of "My Lord, the Baby" is matched by the gentle humor of "Bontshe the Silent." The two young people in "Hillbred" will seem familiar and recognizable to young lovers anywhere in the world. Politically, we are far from living in "One World," but emotionally we are all kin.

My Lord, the Baby

Rabindranath Tagore
Indian

The baby saw the river rushing by, splashing and gurgling as it went. . . . At the sight, the heart of the human child grew excited and restless. He got down stealthily from the go-cart and toddled off toward the river. On his way he picked up a small stick and leaned over the bank of the stream, pretending to fish.

World travelers are always impressed when they hear children laughing and playing in a schoolyard or park. Differences in language disappear. The cries and shouts sound the same in Bombay and Nairobi as they do in Nashville and Seattle. Children are children around the world. They tend to play together without awareness of religion or the political backgrounds of their parents. For a while, they are citizens of the world. As they grow older, differences and prejudices begin to appear.

The child in "My Lord, the Baby" is a typical child, recognizable by anyone who has been with a baby for a time. He is happy, demanding, willful, and utterly defenseless. The person assigned to take care of him is loving, careful, thoughtful . . . and unlucky. Though the setting is India, the mother's grief knows no national boundaries.

My Lord, the Baby

I

RAICHARAN was twelve years old when he came as a servant to his master's house. He belonged to the same caste as his master and was given his master's little son to nurse. As time went on the boy left Raicharan's arms to go to school. From school he went on to college, and after college he entered the judicial service. Always, until he married, Raicharan was his sole attendant.

But, when a mistress came into the house, Raicharan found two masters instead of one. All his former influence passed to the new mistress. This was compensated for by a fresh arrival. Anukul had a son born to him, and Raicharan by his unsparing attentions soon got a complete hold over the child. He used to toss him up in his arms, call to him in absurd baby language, put his face close to the baby's, and draw it away again with a grin.

Presently the child was able to crawl and cross the doorway. When Raicharan went to catch him, he would scream with mischievous laughter and make for safety. Raicharan was amazed at the profound skill and exact judgment the baby showed when pursued. He would say to his mistress with a look of awe and mystery: "Your son will be a judge someday."

New wonders came in their turn. When the baby began to toddle, that was to Raicharan an epoch in human history. When he called his father Ba-ba and his mother Ma-ma and Raicharan Chan-na, then Raicharan's ecstasy knew no bounds. He went out to tell the news to all the world.

After a while Raicharan was asked to show his ingenuity in other ways. He had, for instance, to play the part of a horse, holding the reins between his teeth and prancing with his feet. He had also to wrestle with his little charge, and if he could not, by a wrestler's trick, fall on his back defeated at the end, a great outcry was certain.

About this time Anukul was transferred to a district on the banks of the Padma. On his way through Calcutta he bought his son a little go-cart. He bought him also a yellow satin waistcoat, a gold-laced cap, and some gold bracelets and anklets. Raicharan was wont to take these out and put them on his little charge with ceremonial pride whenever they went for a walk.

Then came the rainy season, and day after day the rain poured down in torrents. The hungry river, like an enormous serpent, swallowed down terraces, villages, cornfields, and covered with its flood the tall grasses and wild casuarinas on the sandbanks. From time to time there was a deep thud, as the riverbanks crumbled. The unceasing roar of the main current could be heard from far away. Masses of foam, carried swiftly past, proved to the eye the swiftness of the stream.

One afternoon the rain cleared. It was cloudy, but cool and bright. Raicharan's little despot did not want to stay in on such a fine afternoon. His lordship climbed into the go-cart. Raicharan, between the shafts, dragged him slowly along till he reached the rice fields on the banks of the river. There was no one in the fields, and no boat on the stream. Across the water, on the farther side, the clouds were rifted in the west. The silent ceremonial of the setting sun was revealed in all its glowing splendor. In the midst of that stillness the child, all of a sudden, pointed with his finger in front of him and cried: "Chan-na! Pitty fow."

Close by on a mud flat stood a large *Kadamba* tree in full flower. My lord, the baby, looked at it with greedy eyes, and Raicharan knew his meaning. Only a short time before he had made, out of these very flower balls, a small go-cart; and the child had been so entirely happy dragging it about with a string, that for the whole day Raicharan was not made to put on the reins at all. He was promoted from a horse into a groom.

But Raicharan had no wish that evening to go splashing, knee-deep through the mud to reach the flowers. So he quickly pointed his finger in the opposite direction, calling out: "Oh, look, baby, look! Look at the bird." And with all sorts of curious noises he pushed the go-cart rapidly away from the tree.

But a child destined to be a judge cannot be put off so easily. And besides, there was at the time nothing to attract his eyes. And you cannot keep up forever the pretense of an imaginary bird.

The little Master's mind was made up, and Raicharan was at his wits' end. "Very well, baby," he said at last, "you sit still in the cart, and I'll go and get you the pretty flower. Only mind you don't go near the water."

As he said this, he made his legs bare to the knee and waded through the oozing mud toward the tree.

The moment Raicharan had gone, his little Master went off at racing speed to the forbidden water. The baby saw the river rushing by, splashing and gurgling as it went. It seemed as though the disobedient wavelets themselves were running away from some greater Raicharan with the laughter of a thousand children. At the sight of their mischief, the heart of the human child grew excited and restless. He got down stealthily from the go-cart and toddled off toward the river. On his way he picked up a small stick and leaned over the bank of the stream pretending to fish. The mischievous fairies of the river with their mysterious voices seemed to be inviting him into their playhouse.

Raicharan had plucked a handful of flowers from the tree and was carrying them back in the end of his cloth, with his face wreathed in smiles. But when he reached the go-cart, there was no one there. He looked on all sides and there was no one there. He looked back at the cart and there was no one there.

In that first terrible moment his blood froze within him. Before his eyes the whole universe swam round like a dark mist. From the depth of his broken heart he gave one piercing cry: "Master, Master, little Master!"

But no voice answered "Chan-na." No child laughed mischievously back; no scream of baby delight welcomed his return. Only the river ran on, with its splashing, gurgling noise as before—as though it knew nothing at all and had no time to attend to such a tiny human event as the death of a child.

As the evening passed by, Raicharan's mistress became very anxious. She sent men out on all sides to search. They went with lanterns in their hands and reached at last the banks of the Padma. There they found Raicharan rushing up and down the fields, like a stormy wind, shouting the cry of despair: "Master, Master, little Master!"

When they got Raicharan home at last, he fell prostrate at his mistress' feet. They shook him, and questioned him, and asked him repeatedly where he had left the child; but all he could say was that he knew nothing.

Though everyone held the opinion that the Padma had swallowed the child, there was a lurking doubt left in the mind. For a band of gypsies had been noticed outside the village that afternoon, and some suspicion rested on them. The mother went so far in her wild grief as to think it possible that Raicharan himself had stolen the child. She called him aside with piteous entreaty and said: "Raicharan, give me back my baby. Oh! give me back my child. Take from me any money you ask, but give me back my child!"

Anukul tried to reason his wife out of this wholly unjust suspicion: "Why on earth," he said, "should he commit such a crime as that?"

The mother only replied: "The baby had gold ornaments on his body. Who knows?"

It was impossible to reason with her after that.

II

Raicharan went back to his own village. Up to this time he had had no son, and there was no hope that any child would now be born to him. But it came about before the end of a year that his wife gave birth to a son and died.

An overwhelming resentment at first grew up in Raicharan's heart at the sight of this new baby. At the back of his mind was resentful suspicion that it had come as a usurper in place of the little Master. He also thought it would be a grave offense to be happy with a son of his own after what had happened to his master's little child. Indeed, if it had not been for a widowed sister, who mothered the new baby, it would not have lived long.

But a change gradually came over Raicharan's mind. A wonderful thing happened. This new baby began to crawl about and cross the doorway with mischief in its face. It also showed an amusing cleverness in making its escape to safety. Its voice, its sounds of laughter and tears, its gestures, were those of the little Master. On some days, when Raicharan listened to its crying, his heart suddenly began thumping wildly against his ribs, and it seemed to him that his former little Master was crying somewhere in the unknown land of death because he had lost his Chan-na.

Phailna (for that was the name Raicharan's sister gave to the new baby) soon began to talk. It learned to say Ba-ba and Ma-ma with a baby accent. When Raicharan heard those familiar sounds the mystery suddenly became clear. The little Master could not cast off the spell of his Chan-na, and therefore he had been reborn in his own house.

The arguments in favor of this were, to Raicharan, altogether beyond dispute:

> (i) The new baby was born soon after his little Master's death.
> (ii) His wife could never have accumulated such merit as to give birth to a son in middle age.
> (iii) The new baby walked with a toddle and called out Ba-ba and Ma-ma. There was no sign lacking which marked out the future judge.

Then suddenly Raicharan remembered that terrible accusation of the mother. "Ah," he said to himself with amazement, "the mother's heart was right. She knew I had stolen her child." When once he had come to this conclusion, he was filled with remorse for his past neglect. He now gave himself over, body and soul, to the new baby, and became its devoted attendant. He began to bring it up as if it were the son of a rich man. He bought a go-cart, a yellow satin waistcoat, and a gold-embroidered cap. He melted down the ornaments of his dead wife and made gold bangles and anklets. He refused to let the little child play with anyone of the neighborhood and became himself its sole companion day and night. As the baby grew up to boyhood, he was so petted and spoiled and clad in such finery that the village children would call him "Your Lordship," and jeer at him; and older people regarded Raicharan as unaccountably crazy about the child.

At last the time came for the boy to go to school. Raicharan sold his small piece of land and went to Calcutta. There he got employment with great difficulty as a servant and sent Phailna to school. He spared no pains to give him the best education, the best clothes, the best food. Meanwhile he lived himself on a mere handful of rice and would say in secret: "Ah! my little Master, my dear little Master, you loved me so much that you came back to my house. You shall never suffer from any neglect of mine."

Twelve years passed away in this manner. The boy was able to read and write well. He was bright and healthy and good-looking. He paid a great deal of attention to his personal appearance and was specially careful in parting his hair. He was inclined to extravagance and finery, and spent money freely. He could never quite look on Raicharan as a father, because, though fatherly in affection, he had the manner of a servant. A further fault was this, that Raicharan kept secret from everyone that he himself was the father of the child.

The students of the hostel, where Phailna was a boarder, were greatly amused by Raicharan's country manners, and I have to confess that behind his father's back Phailna joined in their fun. But, in the bottom of their hearts, all the students loved the innocent and tender-hearted old man, and Phailna was very fond of him also. But, as I have said before, he loved him with a kind of condescension.

Raicharan grew older and older, and his employer was continually finding fault with him for his incompetent work. He had been starving himself for the boy's sake. So he had grown physically weak and was no longer up to his work. He would forget things, and his mind became dull and stupid. But his employer expected a full servant's work out of him and would not brook excuses. The money that Raicharan had brought with him from the sale of his land was exhausted. The boy was continually grumbling about his clothes and asking for more money.

III

Raicharan made up his mind. He gave up the situation where he was working as a servant, and left some money with Phailna and said: "I have some business to do at home in my village and shall be back soon."

He went off at once to Baraset, where Anukul was magistrate. Anukul's wife was still broken down with grief. She had had no other child.

One day Anukul was resting after a long weary day in court. His wife was buying, at an exorbitant price, an herb from a mendicant quack, which was said to ensure the birth of a child. A voice of greeting was heard in the courtyard. Anukul went out to see who was there. It was Raicharan. Anukul's heart was softened when he saw his old servant. He asked him many questions and offered to take him back into service.

Raicharan smiled faintly and said in reply: "I want to make obeisance to my mistress."

Anukul went with Raicharan into the house, where the mistress did not receive him as warmly as his old master. Raicharan took no notice of this, but folded his hands, and said: "It was not the Padma that stole your baby. It was I."

Anukul exclaimed: "Great God! Eh! What! Where is he?"

Raicharan replied: "He is with me. I will bring him the day after tomorrow."

It was Sunday. There was no magistrate's court sitting. Both husband and wife were looking expectantly along the road, waiting from early morning for Raicharan's appearance. At ten o'clock he came, leading Phailna by the hand.

Anukul's wife, without question, took the boy into her lap, and was wild with excitement, sometimes laughing, sometimes weeping, touching him, kissing his hair and his forehead, and gazing into his face with hungry, eager eyes. The boy was very good-looking and dressed like a gentleman's son. The heart of Anukul brimmed over with a sudden rush of affection.

Nevertheless, the magistrate in him asked: "Have you any proofs?"

Raicharan said: "How could there be any proof of such a deed? God alone knows that I stole your boy, and no one else in the world."

When Anukul saw how eagerly his wife was clinging to the boy, he realized the futility of asking for proofs. It would be wiser to believe. And then—where could an old man like Raicharan get such a boy from? And why should his faithful servant deceive him for nothing?

"But," he added severely, "Raicharan, you must not stay here."

"Where shall I go, Master?" said Raicharan, in a choking voice, folding his hands. "I am old. Who will take an old man as a servant?"

The mistress said: "Let him stay. My child will be pleased. I forgive him."

But Anukul's magisterial conscience would not allow him. "No," he said, "he cannot be forgiven for what he has done."

Raicharan bowed to the ground and clasped Anukul's feet. "Master," he cried, "let me stay. It was not I who did it. It was God."

Anukul's conscience was worse stricken than ever, when Raicharan tried to put the blame on God's shoulders.

"No," he said, "I could not allow it. I cannot trust you anymore. You have done an act of treachery."

Raicharan rose to his feet and said: "It was not I who did it."

"Who was it then?" asked Anukul.

Raicharan replied: "It was my fate."

But no educated man could take this for an excuse. Anukul remained obdurate.

When Phailna saw that he was the wealthy magistrate's son, and not Raicharan's, he was angry at first, thinking that he had been cheated all this time of his birthright. But seeing Raicharan in distress, he generously said to his father: "Father, forgive him. Even if you don't let him live with us, let him have a small monthly pension."

After hearing this, Raicharan did not utter another word. He looked for the last time on the face of his son; he made obeisance to his old master and mistress. Then he went out and was mingled with the numberless people of the world.

At the end of the month Anukul sent him some money to his village. But the money came back. There was no one there of the name of Raicharan.

Reading for Understanding

Main Idea

1. The best word to describe the central theme of the story is (a) oppression (b) devotion (c) absurdity (d) selfishness.

Details

2. Raicharan became a servant at (a) 10 (b) 12 (c) 14 (d) 16.
3. Ba-ba was another name for (a) Raicharan (b) Chan-na (c) Anukul (d) Phailna.
4. Tragedy was caused by (a) Raicharan's complaints (b) a loss of the Master's fortune (c) the mother's indifference (d) carelessness at the swollen river.

Inferences

5. The "playhouse" mentioned on page 610 is really (a) the depths of the river (b) a treehouse (c) a spot at the foot of the rainbow (d) a glen in the forest.
6. Raicharan repeatedly said that he knew nothing about the disappearance because (a) he had secretly kidnaped the boy (b) he was in league with gypsies (c) he wanted to punish the Master's wife (d) it was true.
7. It seems safe to assume that the baby (a) had indeed been kidnaped (b) was taken to Calcutta (c) had drowned (d) disliked Raicharan.

8. At story's end, Raicharan's son was (a) forgiving (b) actually Anukul's child (c) proud of Raicharan (d) a servant.

9. At first, when Raicharan said that Phailna was really the couple's son, (a) the mother refused to believe it (b) Phailna himself objected (c) Anukul was not convinced (d) Raicharan withdrew the claim.

Outcomes

10. At the end of the story, Phailna (a) went back with Raicharan (b) was raised as a wealthy boy (c) actually struck his father (d) proved to be the baby lost earlier.

Words in Context

1. "When the baby began to toddle, that was to Raicharan an *epoch* in human history." An **epoch** (609) is (a) a setback (b) an important period of time (c) a period of turmoil (d) a paradise.

2. "Raicharan's little *despot* did not want to stay in on such a fine afternoon." A **despot** (610) is a (a) child (b) neighbor (c) responsibility (d) tyrant.

3. "When they got Raicharan home at last, he fell *prostrate* at his mistress' feet." **Prostrate** (611) means (a) stretched out (b) weeping (c) protesting (d) rapidly.

4. "At the back of his mind was a resentful suspicion that it had come as a *usurper* in place of the little Master." A **usurper** (612) is one who (a) claims special privileges (b) is constantly dictatorial (c) takes on a demon's form (d) takes the place of another.

5. "But, as I have said before, he loved him with a kind of *condescension*." **Condescension** (613) arises from (a) kindness (b) a feeling of superiority (c) bitterness and dread (d) awe and mystery.

6., 7. "His wife was buying, at an *exorbitant* price, an herb from a *mendicant* quack, which was said to ensure the birth of a child." **Exorbitant** (613) means (a) advertised (b) excessive (c) bartered (d) honest. A **mendicant** (613) is a (a) medical expert (b) qualified salesperson (c) beggar (d) circus performer.

8. "I want to make *obeisance* to my mistress." **Obeisance** (613) is (a) a communication (b) a mark of respect (c) payment (d) discovery.

9. "Anukul remained *obdurate*." **Obdurate** (614) means (a) stubborn (b) interested (c) agreeable (d) violent.

Thinking Critically about the Story

1. What little touches does Tagore include to show that he has observed babies?
2. "He belonged to the same caste as his master." What does that mean? Does the caste system survive in modern India?
3. Some people have an uncanny ability to relate to children, to meet them on their level, and provide enlightened companionship. Was Raicharan such a person? Point out examples.
4. Why did Anukul finally decide to accept Phailna as his son despite his early misgivings?
5. How was Raicharan's act in giving up his own son characteristic of him throughout the story?
6. What happened to Raicharan? Why?

Language in Action

Nonverbal Communication

> When they got Raicharan home at last, he fell prostrate at his mistress' feet. They shook him, and questioned him, and asked him repeatedly where he had left the child; but all he could say was that he knew nothing.

The essential element in communication is the word. As we write and speak, we use these marvelous tools that have been given to us. But communication is more than words. In the quotation above, Raicharan's actions display his grief more than any words could do.

Facial expressions are rich with meaning. "Allison is a great tennis player" can be destroyed with a wink. "I'm happy to see you" can be reversed with a pained expression. A smile can take the sting out of a gentle criticism. It's difficult to suppress an expression of surprise if the news is unexpected. Lady Macbeth says to her husband, "Your face, my thane, is as a book where men may read strange matters."

Bodily attitude is as revealing as the face. When two tennis players leave the court, their bodily attitudes usually tell which won and which lost. The loser's shoulders may slump. His eyes may be downcast. The very picture tells a story.

Gestures are rich elements in communication. Sign languages are obvious examples. Even though we have a rich store of words at our command, we cannot refrain from *pointing* when giving directions. Ask someone to describe a spiral staircase without using hands. In some cultures, gestures play a stronger part than in our culture. A traveler abroad should refrain from gestures. He or she may be using an apparently innocent gesture that is insulting in the foreign culture.

Silence can also convey a message. "How did you enjoy the new Thursday sitcom?" No reply may speak volumes. Silence can also signal to a friend, "I'd like to have some quiet time."

Signs and graphic symbols are also effective nonverbal communicators. Street signs, traffic signs, protesters' placards, parking spaces with pictures of a wheelchair—all convey a message without a word.

Taken altogether, you have a vast array of elements to use in communicating.

Hillbred

Arreph El-Khoury
Syrian

The Clerk went inside his office and faced them across a wide desk. He sat on a chair.

"Now," he said, business-like, "what can we do for you?"

"We want a marriage license," announced Kasid, his face flushing darkly. Hind giggled.

Young love is the theme of Shakespeare's **Romeo and Juliet**, as well as well as stories derived from it—like the musical **West Side Story**. Older adults sometimes fail to understand the depth of feeling that even puppy love can inspire. This lack of sympathy is the core of many stories, novels, and films.

Kasid and Hind are in love. They travel down from their native hills to secure a marriage license. They are intimidated by the strangeness of their surroundings but are finally taken to his office by a gentle clerk. The clerk is eager to help these frightened lovers, but he has bad news for them.

Another time, another place, other lovers, but this story by a Syrian author has an immediacy that will put you into the story, wishing you could help.

Hillbred

HASBAYA IS A NICE little city—"The Biggest Little City Between Mount Hermon and the Mediterranean," as it is called by its inhabitants. Squatting on its two slopes around the banks of its river, its gray and white stone houses with their flat or pyramidal roofs among the trees give the appearance of bas-relief on emerald-green, deep-sea majolica.* The most noticeable building in Hasbaya, next to the ancient crusaders' castle, is the courthouse, which was built by the Turks, to be inherited by the Arabs when His Majesty King Faisal was the head of the Syrian government after the World War, and most recently by the Lebanese government after the French had added Hasbaya to Mount Lebanon.

On a warm and sunny spring day in which the glorious Syrian sun was bathing in a sea of jade and the warm wind was racing over the purple and blue hills, a young man by the name of Kasid and a girl by the name of Hind were seen entering the high archway gate of the courthouse, in front of which a Lebanese soldier with a fixed bayonet stood motionless as if carved of rock.

They were dressed in homespun clothes and wore native shoes, black and hobnailed. A black *ighal* of coiled goat's hair encircled Kasid's white muslin headkerchief. Under the tight-fitting red *aba* which reached to his knees, he wore an embroidered jacket and vest of black cloth and a shirt of effulgent white. A peach-colored silk sash around his waist held a curved dagger. His trousers were voluminous and indigo-dyed. As for Hind, her gentle, brown eyes were heavily loaded with kohl and her fingertips dyed red with henna. The white muslin *mandil* over her head fell in folds to her ankles, partially obscuring her blue dress and black coat.

The eyes of this young pair were scrutinizing every object around them as they proceeded forward. Silently they advanced toward the inner courtyard where a number of soldiers were basking in the sun. They turned their eyes away from the soldiers as if these were gray *jin* of evil and looked to the left, knowing not what to do. On the wall they saw a number of bulletins on blackboards. Kasid advanced toward the bulletins, read a while, turned his head away from them and came back to Hind. He motioned her to follow him. She obeyed, and they walked to the end of the corridor, glanced to the left and right. Kasid, seeing a few doors at their right, motioned Hind to follow him a second time, walked toward these doors and began to read the signs on them. He read the sign on the first, the second, the third, and, seeing that none of these doors was that of the office he sought, he advanced to the foot of a winding stairway which led to the second story.

Kasid looked at the grim, ghastly walls and the disconsolate steps and paused for a moment. Finally he told Hind to follow him and began to climb the stairs with the uncertain, suspicious step of the hillbred who reckons with the inequalities of the land. Hind followed him in silence. Sometimes he was looking at the walls, at other times glancing over his shoulder

---

*a kind of earthenware

at Hind behind him, and with added mistrust at the higher steps. Finally they reached a door at their left with the Clerk's sign on it. Here they stood firm—their eyes like those of a cat confronted by a mastiff.

"Enter," Kasid ordered Hind with a motion of his head.

"You enter—you who are armed with a dagger!" retorted Hind.

Kasid stood his ground. Hind looked at him. He grinned childishly. She turned her head away from him and stared at the wall. Kasid drew his head close to her. She turned facing him. She was the first to speak. "What shall we do?"

"I do not know, by Allah!" replied Kasid with an awkward shrug of his broad shoulders. They looked at each other helplessly. Kasid ventured a step forward toward the door of the Clerk's office. Hind followed him with her eyes as her red lips opened with a sardonic smile. Suddenly he stopped, pondered a while and as suddenly sat down on the steps. Hind came and sat beside him as if they were on the steps of their respective houses.

"Why don't you enter?" asked Kasid.

"Why don't you enter first and bring it?" she snapped at him.

Kasid shook his head disapprovingly.

At that moment they heard footsteps coming toward them from the higher part of the steps and in unison they looked over their shoulders. A man, dressed in European clothes, came down toward them. They turned their heads away from him. The man continued to descend until he was two steps from them.

"What are you doing here?" the man asked. They did not answer but smiled. "What are you doing here—what do you want?" he asked impatiently.

They stood up. "We want to enter this room," Kasid said, pointing to the door of the Clerk's office.

"Come on," said the man, smiling, "I am the Clerk." He walked to the door and pushed it open. He entered. Kasid and Hind followed him inside with a shambling gait.

The Clerk went inside his office and faced them across a wide desk. He sat on a chair. "Now," he said, business-like, "what can we do for you?"

"We want a marriage license," announced Kasid, his face flushing darkly. Hind giggled.

The Clerk smiled broadly, opened a drawer and produced a sheet of paper which he handed to Kasid across the table, saying, "Fill it in."

Kasid took the sheet of paper with a shaky hand, looked at Hind, motioned her to follow him and went to another desk in the room and sat down on a chair. There were penholders, inkwells and blotters on the desk. Kasid began to read and write without asking Hind a question. She stood looking at him and smiling sarcastically. Finally, he stood up, breathed contentedly, motioned Hind to follow him and came toward the

Clerk. He handed him the sheet of paper. The Clerk began to read what Kasid had written in an exceptionally poor penmanship; he read their names, ages, conditions, birthplaces, the names of their parents, their occupations, their addresses and the date. Glancing at the sheet of paper for a second time, the Clerk smiled and shook his head.

"My lad," said the Clerk sympathetically, "you are not old enough nor is she!"

"*Allahu Akbar!* (God is Greater)" Kasid and Hind exclaimed in unison. "How old do we have to be?" asked Kasid with a dark frown on his highly hawkish face.

The Clerk told him the age required by the law.

"But we are not that and we want to marry each other," argued Kasid, vehemently.

"It is necessary, then, to have your parents sign this sheet of paper before we can issue a license for you," the Clerk informed him as he handed him the sheet of paper.

"We are orphans. Our parents were killed by the French in the last uprising against them," pronounced Kasid with a pain in his heart.

"It is regrettable; you have to wait until you are old enough!" said the Clerk.

Kasid made a wry face. He looked at Hind beside him and suddenly his face became haggard, passionate and tragic. Quickly he returned the sheet of paper to the Clerk, and, with his right hand on the haft of his dagger and his left grasping Hind by the arm, he went out of the room, whispering in her ears, "Allah did not say so in the Book!"

Reading for Understanding

Main Idea

1. The main theme of the story is (a) military cruelty (b) the stupidity of children (c) frustrated love (d) devouring distrust.

Details

2. The original disagreement between Kasid and Hind was over (a) clothes to be worn (b) who was to enter first (c) the actual date (d) Hind's parents.

3. The act of kindness was shown to them by (a) a soldier (b) a relative of Kasid's (c) a court judge (d) the Clerk.

4. Besides their age, the barrier to the marriage of Kasid and Hind was (a) the lack of parents to approve (b) the Clerk's hidden attraction to Hind (c) Kasid's timid behavior (d) the closeness of the holiday season.

Inferences

5. When Kasid and Hind entered the courthouse, they were exceptionally (a) shy (b) confident (c) rude to an old man (d) well prepared.

6. The Clerk's behavior toward the pair was (a) mean (b) indifferent (c) irritating (d) sympathetic.

7. Kasid's temperament could be characterized as (a) calm (b) hotheaded (c) stable (d) mature.

8. The clothing of the two lovers could be described as (a) ugly (b) unfashionable (c) oppressively hot (d) stylish.

9. The word *Hillbred* is meant to convey (a) sense of long-held superiority (b) stability, like the rock-ribbed peaks (d) a slightly negative suggestion (d) a source of revolutionary zeal.

Fact or Opinion

Tell whether the following is a fact or an opinion.

10. The marriage license regulations were unfair.

Words in Context

1. "He wore an embroidered jacket and vest of black cloth and a shirt of *effulgent* white." **Effulgent** (620) means (a) brilliant (b) subdued (c) eggshell (d) threadbare.

2. "The eyes of this young pair were *scrutinizing* every object around them as they proceeded forward." **Scrutinizing** (620) means (a) envying (b) pricing (c) touching (d) examining.

3. "Kasid looked at the grim, ghastly walls and the *disconsolate* steps and paused for a moment." **Disconsolate** (620) means (a) steep (b) colorful (c) cheerless (d) partly broken.

4. "At that moment they heard footsteps coming toward them from the higher part of the steps and *in unison* they looked over their shoul-

ders." **In unison** (621) means (a) at the same time (b) with fear (c) smiling with relief (d) in succession.

5. Kasid and Hind followed him inside with a *shambling* gait." **Shambling** (621) means (a) rushing (b) walking awkwardly (c) tiptoeing carefully (d) stately.

6. " 'But we are not that and we want to marry each other,' argued Kasid *vehemently*." **Vehemently** (622) means (a) reasonably (b) quietly (c) forcefully (d) breathlessly.

7. "Kasid made a *wry* face." **Wry** (622) means (a) sour (b) funny (c) teary (d) twisted.

8. "He looked at Hind beside him and suddenly his face became *haggard*, passionate and tragic." **Haggard** (622) means (a) alert (b) angry (c) careworn (d) animated.

Thinking Critically about the Story

1. What is the significance of the title of the story?
2. Do Kasid and Hind show signs of maturity sufficient to make a successful marriage?
3. At what age should young people be allowed to marry without parental consent?
4. Why were Kasid and Hind particularly unfortunate?
5. Most areas of the world have regulations for issuing marriage licenses. Why should the state control the issuance of licenses? What stake do nations have in the control of marriages?
6. Could this story be set in the United States without losing credibility? Explain.

Language in Action

Synonyms: No Two Alike

Kasid looked at the grim, ghastly walls and the disconsolate steps and paused for a moment.

In one sense *grim* and *ghastly* are synonyms. They both suggest the dreadful appearance of the walls. They also suggest a basic truth about synonyms. Though synonyms are words that mean approximately the same, no two words are interchangeable in any and all situations. A beautiful woman's facial expression may be grim . . . but not ghastly.

In addition to their commonly accepted meanings, words also have connotations (323) that help to distinguish them. *Abode, house, dwelling, habitation, domicile* and *home* can be interchanged in some situations but not all.

"The dwelling on 108 Maple Drive is for sale." *House* and perhaps even *home*—can be substituted for *dwelling* without a problem.

When I've been away for a week or more, I can't wait to go home again."

Not a single synonym can be substituted for *home* here without destroying the feel of the sentence.

Home is an emotional word, rich with connotations. *House* is rather neutral and colorless. *Dwelling* is a bland word used in real estate. *Habitation* carries no warmth. *Abode* might be used in a scientific article:

The *abode* of the cliff dwellers seems cold and cheerless to us today.

How do the following synonyms for a "country retreat" suggest different qualities: *shack, shanty, ranch, hut, cabin, hunting lodge?*

from The Stream of Days

Taha Hussein
Egyptian

He hurried along nervously at his companion's side, breathing the nauseous smells, and half-deafened by the medley of sounds that came from all sides at once, left and right, above and below, to meet in midair, where they seemed to unite above the boy's head, layer upon layer, into a single fine mist.

Many young people of the industrial nations take education for granted. It's there. It's free. It's nearly universal. In the United States, education through the secondary school is provided for everyone to take advantage of. Even college is available for most motivated students. Sometimes those things made available are not appreciated.

In Third World countries, education is a precious and often limited commodity. An education is a ticket to a better life, but it is not easily obtainable universally. Students who attend the schools and colleges realize how precious the gift is.

In this story, a young man comes in from the countryside to the overpopulated capital of Egypt: Cairo. He is overwhelmed by the sights, sounds, and smells of the poverty-stricken area he must live in, but it's all worthwhile when he reaches the lecture halls and hears messages that sometimes bewilder him but always excite him.

Nothing dramatic happens in this story, by an Egyptian author, but it gives the flavor of life in a poor nation. Visualize the scenes: the crowded streets, alleys, and stairways near his lodgings; the more spacious rooms of the lecture halls. Share the experiences of the young student . . . and get a renewed appreciation of your own school setting.

from The Stream of Days

FOR the first two or three weeks of his stay in Cairo he was lost in bewilderment. All he knew was that he had left the country behind him and settled in the capital as a student attending lectures at the Azhar. It was more by imagination than by sense that he distinguished the three phases of his day.

Both the house he lived in and the path that led to it were strange and unfamiliar. When he came back from the Azhar he turned to the right through a gateway which was open during the daytime and shut at night; after evening prayer there was only a narrow opening left in the middle of the door. Once through it, he became aware of a gentle heat playing on his right cheek, and a fine smoke teasing his nostrils; while on the left he heard an odd gurgling sound which at once puzzled and delighted him.

For several days, morning and evening, he listened curiously to this sound, but lacked the courage to inquire what it might be. Then one day he gathered from a chance remark that it came from the bubbling of a *narghile** smoked by tradesmen of the district. It was provided for them by the proprietor of the café from which the gentle heat and the fine smoke cloud issued.

He walked straight on for a few steps before crossing a damp, roofed-in space in which it was impossible to stand firmly because of the slops thrown there by the café proprietor. Then he came out into an open passageway; but this was narrow and filthy and full of strange, elusive smells, which were only moderately unpleasant early in the day and at nightfall, but as the day advanced and the heat of the sun grew stronger, became utterly intolerable.

He walked straight on through this narrow passage; but rarely did he find it smooth or easy. More often than not his friend would have to push him either this way or that so as to avoid some obstacle or other. Then he would continue in the new direction, feeling his way toward a house either to left or right, until he had passed the obstacle and taken the old direction again. He hurried along nervously at his companion's side, breathing the nauseous smells, and half-deafened by the medley of sounds that came from all sides at once, left and right, above and below, to meet in midair, where they seemed to unite above the boy's head, layer upon layer, into a single fine mist.

---

*a water pipe, similar to a hookah

There was in fact a remarkable variety of sounds. Voices of women raised in dispute, of men shouting in anger or peaceably talking together; the noise of loads being set down or picked up; the song of the water carrier crying his wares; the curse of a carter to his horse or mule or donkey; the grating sound of cart wheels; and from time to time this confused whirl of sounds was torn by the braying of a donkey or the whinnying of a horse.

As he passed through this babel,* his thoughts were far away, and he was scarcely conscious of himself or of what he was doing; but at a certain point on the road he caught the confused sound of conversation through a half-open door on the left; then he knew that a pace or two further on he must turn to the left up a staircase which would bring him to his lodging.

It was an ordinary sort of staircase, neither wide nor narrow, and its steps were of stone; but since it was used very frequently in both directions, and no one troubled to wash or sweep it, the dirt piled up thickly and stuck together in a compact mass on the steps, so that the stone was completely covered up, and whether you were going up or coming down the staircase appeared to be made of mud.

Now whenever the boy went up or down a staircase he was obliged to count the steps. But long as were the years he stayed in this place, and countless the times he negotiated this staircase, it never occurred to him to count the number of its steps. He learned at the second or third time of climbing it that after going up a few steps he had to turn a little to the left before continuing his ascent, leaving on his right an opening through which he never penetrated, though he knew that it led to the first floor of the building in which he lived for so many years.

This floor was not inhabited by students, but by workers and tradesmen. He left the entrance to it on his right, and went on up to the second floor. There his harassed spirit found rest and relief; lungfuls of fresh air drove away the sense of suffocation with which he had been oppressed on that filthy staircase, and then too there was the parrot, whistling on without a break, as if to testify before all the world to the tyranny of her Persian master, who had imprisoned her in an abominable cage, and would sell her tomorrow or the day after to another man who would treat her in exactly the same way. And when he was rid of her and had laid hands on the cash, he would buy a successor for her who would be cooped up in the same prison pouring forth the same curses on her master, and waiting as her sister had waited to be passed on from hand to hand, and from cage to cage, while everywhere she went that plaintive cry of hers would delight the hearts of men and women.

When our friend reached the top of the staircase he breathed in

---

*scene of confusion

the fresh air that blew on his face, and listened to the voice of the parrot calling him toward the right. He obeyed, turning through a narrow corridor, past two rooms in which two Persians lived. One of these was still a young man, while the other was already past middle age. The one was as morose and misanthropic as the other was genial and good-natured.

At last the boy was home. He entered a room like a hall, which provided for most of the practical needs of the house. This led on to another room, large but irregular in shape, which served for social and intellectual needs. It was bedroom and dining room, reading room and study, and a room for conversation by day or by night. Here were books and crockery and food; and here the boy had his own particular corner, as in every room he occupied or visited at all frequently.

This place of his was on the left inside the door. After advancing a pace or two he found a mat spread on the ground, and above that an old but quite serviceable carpet. Here he sat in the daytime, and here he slept at night, with a pillow for his head and a rug to cover him. On the opposite side of the room was his elder brother's pitch, a good deal higher than his own. He had a mat spread on the ground, and a decent carpet on top of that, then a felt mattress, and above that a long, wide piece of bedding stuffed with cotton, and finally, crowning all, a coverlet. Here the young sheikh* would sit with his close friends. They were not obliged to prop up their backs against the bare wall, as the boy did, having cushions to pile up on the rugs. At night this couch was transformed into a bed on which the young sheikh slept.

II

This was all the boy ever learned about his immediate surroundings. The second phase of his life consisted in the tumultuous journey between his home and the Azhar. He went out through the covered passage till he felt the heat of the café on his left cheek, and heard the bubbling of the *narghile* on his right. In front of him was a shop which played an important part in his life; it belonged to El-Hagg Firûz, who supplied the neighborhood with most of the necessities of life. In the morning he sold boiled beans, prepared in the usual variety of ways. But El-Hagg Firûz used to boast the special virtues of his beans—and raise their prices accordingly. He had plain beans, beans in fat, beans in butter, beans in every kind of oil; he added, if required, all sorts of spices. As for the students, they adored these beans, and often made far too large a meal of

---

*The word *sheikh* meant originally "old man" or "elder." In this translation it is used in two senses: (1) as more or less equivalent to *álim*, "doctor," and so teacher at the Azhar; (2) "scholar" or aspirant to learning, as here.

them. So by mid-morning they were already dull in the head, and at the noon lecture they slept.

When evening came El-Hagg Firûz sold his customers their supper: cheese, olives, milled sesame, or honey. To the more luxurious he supplied boxes of tuna or sardines. And to a few of them perhaps, as night approached, he sold things which have no name, and nothing to do with food, things spoken of in a whisper, yet passionately vied for.

The boy used to overhear these whisperings; sometimes he half understood, but as a rule the whole transaction was a mystery to him. As the days passed by and he grew older, he came to see through these subtle hints and ambiguities. What he learned then obliged him to overhaul his standards of judgment, and to revise his valuation both of people and of things.

El-Hagg Firûz held a unique position in the neighborhood and among the students especially. It was to him that they went when their money ran out toward the end of the month, or when their remittances were overdue. He it was who gave them food on credit, lent them a piaster or two from time to time, and helped them out in all kinds of emergencies. No wonder his name was as often on their lips as those of the most learned sheikhs of the Azhar.

But this was not all. El-Hagg Firûz was essential to the students in yet another way. It was to him that were addressed all the letters bringing them news of their families, or enclosing flimsy notes which they took to the post office with empty pockets, to return with the jingle of silver falling cheerily on their ears and into their very hearts.

Naturally not a single student missed an opportunity of passing the time of day morning and evening at El-Hagg Firûz' shop, or of casting a quick furtive glance at the spot where letters were waiting to be collected. How often one of them would go home grasping a sealed envelope which was spotted with oil and butter stains; yet despite its greasiness that envelope was more precious in his eyes than any composition or textbook on law, grammar or theology.

On leaving the covered passage, then, the boy found himself in front of El-Hagg Firûz' shop; his friend would take him a few paces in that direction to greet El-Hagg Firûz and to inquire if there was a letter for him or not; the reply would bring either smiles or frowns to his face. Then he turned away to the left, and walked straight forwards down the long narrow street crowded with passersby. It was full of students, merchants, tradesmen, laborers; carts drawn by donkeys, horses or mules; carters shouting out warnings or curses at the men, women or children blocking their path. Then on each side of the street were different kinds of shops, in many of which was prepared the meager diet of the poor. The smells that issued from them were abominable, but that did not prevent them from delighting most of the passersby, whether they were students, laborers or porters. Some of them turned aside to these shops and bought a scrap of food to gulp down on the spot, or take home and eat, either alone or with others. And some of them, assailed by this battery of smells, remained unmoved. They were tempted but did not yield. Their eyes saw, their nostrils smelled, their appetite was stirred; but, alas, their pockets were empty. They passed on with yearning in their souls and with bitterness and resentment in their hearts; yet at the same time they were content with their lot and accepted it with resignation.

In some other shops a quiet, unhurried trade was transacted, almost without any words passing at all. If anything was said, it was under the breath, so as scarcely to be heard. In spite of this—or perhaps for this very reason—the trade in question brought great wealth and prosperity to those who practiced it. To all appearances the majority of these shops dealt only in coffee and soap, though some of them also sold sugar and rice.

As he passed through all this a warm interest stirred in the boy. But he would have understood practically nothing had not his friend from time to time volunteered an explanation. He continued on his way, sometimes walking firmly forwards, sometimes swerving aside. When the road was clear he marched with a sure step, but stumbled and faltered on its edges when it was crowded or twisty. At last he came to a spot where he had to turn a little to the left and then plunge into a lane as narrow and crooked and filthy as could be. Its atmosphere was foul with an abominable medley of smells, and from time to time weak, hollow voices which reflected its misery and wrong echoed back cries for charity to the footfalls of passersby, begging at the sound of steps, as if life had only been perceptible through the ears. They were answered by other voices: the thin, harsh, strangled cries of those winged creatures which love darkness and desolation and ruins. Often enough these noises were accompanied by the flutter of wings, which sometimes, to his horror, shaved past his ear or his face. Instinctively his hand would fly up for protection, and for sometime afterwards his heart would be throbbing with apprehension.

On he walked with his friend along this narrow, dark, twisting alley, now rising, now descending, now going straight on, now turning to left or right. And all the time these loathsome sounds assailed him, sometimes from in front, and sometimes from behind, but never without dismaying him. After a time he felt his heart lighten and his lungs expand, and knew that the moment of release had come. He heaved one sigh of relief, loaded with all the weight of his anxiety and distress.

Now he breathed freely and easily, as if he were taking in great drafts of life from the fresh air which flowed over him as he left the bat-ridden alley. On he went along the road, which twisted treacherously under his feet for a few moments, then became firm again so that he could step forward easily and with confidence. His heart thrilled with joy at the strange harmony of sounds which came to his ears as he walked along the pleasant, peaceful street. On one side of him was the Mosque of Sayyidna-l-Hussein, and on the other a series of small shops. How often he would stop at one of these during the days that followed, and what good things he tasted there! Soaked figs and their juice in summertime, and in winter *bassbûssa,** which diffused a warm glow of well-being through the body. Sometimes he would stop at a Syrian retailer's to choose from a variety of foods, hot or cold, salt or sweet. Their taste gave him inexpressible pleasure, yet if they were offered him now he would be afraid they might make him ill, or even poison him.

He continued along this street until he came to a place where the voices grew louder and more numerous. He realized that the roads divided here and that he could branch right or left, go straight on, or turn about. "Here are the crossroads," said his companion. "If you go right you reach the Sikka El-Gadida, then the Musky, then 'Ataba El-Khadra. To the left you have Sharia El-Darrâssa. But we must go straight on into Sharia El-Halwagi, the street of learning and hard work. It is so narrow that if you stretched out your arms left and right you could almost touch both walls. Now you are walking between a number of small bookshops. There are books of every kind in them, new and old, good and bad, in print of manuscript."

How many a pleasant and rewarding halt did our friend make in that narrow street, which remained fixed in his memory later on, after his life had changed its course.

But this time he must hurry past. His guide had to be at the Azhar before the lecture began. Here they were, arrived at the Barbers' Gate. He took off his sandals, laid them one on top of the other, then picked them up in his hand as he followed his companion. A little further on he stepped over a shallow threshold into the quiet courtyard of the Azhar, and felt a cool morning breeze blow refreshingly upon his face. And so he entered the third phase of this new life of his.

III

This third phase of his existence was the one he loved best of all. In his own room he endured all the pains of exile. It was like a foreign country to him, and he never became familiar with its contents, except perhaps those nearest to him. He did not live in it in the same sense that he had lived in his country home or in other familiar rooms where nothing was unknown to him. He passed his days there in exile from people and things alike, and in such anguish of heart that the oppressive air he breathed there brought him no rest or refreshment, but only heaviness and pain.

---

*nut-cake of Syrian origin

Nor was there any doubt of his preferring these hours in the Azhar to the agitated journey back and forth, whose hazards drove him almost to despair. It was not only his steps that were confused and unsteady; his very heart was overwhelmed by that unnerving perplexity which perverts a man's purposes and drives him blindly onwards, not only along the material road which he needs must follow, but also along the free paths of the mind, feckless and without a plan. Not only was he distracted by the hubbub and tumult that eddied around him. He was distressed at the unsteadiness of his walk and the impossibility of harmonizing his own quiet, faltering steps with the firm and even brutal pace of his companion.

It was only in the third phase of his day that he found rest and security. The fresh breeze that blew across the court of the Azhar at the hour of morning prayer met him with a welcome and inspired him with a sense of security and hope. The touch of this breeze on his forehead, damp with sweat from that feverish journey, resembled nothing so much as the kisses his mother used to give him during his early years, when he chanted verses from the Koran to her or entertained her with a story he had heard at the village school; or when, as a pale, delicate infant, he abandoned the corner in which he had been reciting the litany from the *sura* Ya-Sin to go and carry out some household task or other.

Those kisses revived his heart and filled him not only with tenderness but with hope and confidence. The breeze which welcomed him in the court of the Azhar, no less, brought rest after weariness, calm after tumult, a smile after gloomy looks. However, he as yet knew nothing of the Azhar, and had not the least idea what he would find there. But it was enough for him to brush with his bare feet the ground of that court, to feel on his face the caress of its morning breeze, and to realize that around him the Azhar was preparing to awake from its drowsiness, that its inertia would soon give place to activity. He began to recover consciousness of himself, as life returned to him. He felt the conviction of being in his own country, among his own people, and lost all sense of isolation, all sadness. His soul blossomed forth, and with every fiber of his being he yearned to discover . . . well, what? Something he was a stranger to, though he loved it and felt irresistibly drawn toward it—knowledge. How many times had he heard this word, and longed to find out its hidden meaning! His impression of it was vague enough, to be sure; but of this he was convinced, that knowledge had no limits and that people might spend their whole lives in acquiring a few drops of it. He too wished to devote his whole life to it and to win as much of it as he could, however little that might be. His father and the learned friends who came to visit him had spoken of knowledge as a boundless ocean, and the child had never taken this expression for a figure of speech or a metaphor, but as the simple truth. He had come to Cairo and to the

Azhar with the intention of throwing himself into this ocean and drinking what he could of it, until the day he drowned. What finer end could there be for a man of spirit than to drown himself in knowledge? What a splendid plunge into the beyond!

All these thoughts suddenly thronged into his young spirit, filling it and taking possession of it, blotting out the memory of that desolate room, of the turbulent, twisty road, and even of the country and its delights. They convinced him that it was no mistake or exaggeration to be consumed with love for the Azhar as well as with regret for the country.

The boy paced on with his companion until he had crossed the court and mounted the shallow step which is the threshold of the Azhar itself. His heart was all modesty and humility, but his soul was filled with glory and pride. His feet stepped lightly over the worn-out mats that were laid out across the floor, leaving a bare patch here and there, as if on purpose to touch the feet which passed over them with something of the benediction attached to that holy ground. The boy used to love the Azhar at this moment, when worshipers were finishing their early-morning prayer and going away, with the marks of drowsiness still in their eyes, to make a circle round some column or other and wait for the teacher who was to give a lecture on tradition or exegesis, first principles or theology.*

At this moment the Azhar was quiet, and free from the strange intermingled murmurs that filled it from sunrise until evening prayer. You could only hear the whispered conversations of its inmates or the hushed but steady voice of some young man reciting the Koran. Or you might come upon a worshiper who had arrived too late for the common service, or had gone on to perform extra prayers after completing the statutory number. Or maybe you would hear a teacher beginning his lecture in the languid tone of a man who has awakened from sleep and said his prayers but has not yet eaten anything to give him strength and energy. He starts in a quiet, husky voice: "In the name of God, the merciful, the compassionate: Praise be to God, father of the worlds: May His peace and blessing be upon our lord Muhammad, the most noble of the prophets, upon his family and his companions. These are the words of the author of the Book, may God rest his soul and grant us the fruits of his learning. Amen!"

The students listened to the lecture with the same quiet languor in which it was given. There was a striking contrast between the different tones the sheikhs used at the early-morning and midday lectures. At dawn their voices were calm and gentle, with traces of drowsiness in them. At noon they were strong and harsh, but fraught too with a certain sluggishness induced by the lunch they had just eaten, the baked beans and pickles

---

* These are the four primary subjects of the traditional Azharite course.

and so on which made up the usual fare of an Azharite at this time. At dawn the voices seemed to beg humbly for favor from the great authorities of the past, while by noon they were attacking them almost as if they were adversaries. This contrast always astonished and delighted the boy.

On he went with his friend up the two steps leading into the *liwân.** There beside one of those sacred pillars, to which a chair was bound by a great chain, our friend was deposited by his companion, who left him with these words: "Wait there and you will hear a lecture on tradition; when mine is over I will return and fetch you." His companion's lecture was on the first principles of Islamic law, given by Sheikh Râdy, God rest his soul. The textbook was the *Tahrîr* of El-Kemal Ibn El-Humam. When the boy heard this sentence, every word filled him at once with awe and curiosity. First principles of law? What science was this? Sheikh Râdy? Who could he be? *Tahrîr?* What was the meaning of this word? El-Kemal Ibn El-Humam? Could there be a more wonderful pair of names? How true it was that knowledge is a boundless ocean, full of unimaginable benefit for any thoughtful being who is ready to plunge into it. The boy's admiration for this lecture especially grew deeper every day as he listened to his brother and his brother's friends studying their lesson beforehand. What they read sounded very strange, but there was no doubt of its fascination.

As he listened the boy used to burn with longing to grow six or seven years older, so that he might be able to understand it, to solve its riddles and ambiguities, to be master of the whole subject as those distinguished young men were, and to dispute with the teachers about it as they did. But for the present he was compelled to listen without understanding. Time and again he would turn over some sentence or other in his mind on the chance of finding some sense in it. But he achieved nothing by all this, except perhaps a greater respect for knowledge and a deeper reverence for his teachers, together with modesty as to his own powers and a determination to work harder.

There was one sentence in particular. How many sleepless nights it cost him! How many days of his life it overcast! Sometimes it tempted him to miss an elementary lecture—for he had understood his first lessons without difficulty—and so led him on to playing truant from the sheikh's lecture on tradition, in order to speculate on what he had heard from the lips of those older students.

The sentence which took possession of him in this way was certainly a remarkable one. It would fall echoing in his ears as he lay on the threshold of sleep, and drag him back to a wakefulness which lasted all night through. This was the sentence: "Right is the negation of negation." What could these words mean? How could negation be

---

* colonnade surrounding the central court of the mosque

negated? What might such negation be? And how could the negation of negation be right? The sentence began to whirl round in his head like the ravings of delirium in a sick man's brain, until one day it was driven out of his mind by one of El-Kafrawy's *Problems*. This problem he understood at once and was able to argue about. Thus he came at last to feel that he had begun to taste the water of the boundless ocean of knowledge.

The boy sat beside the pillar, toying with the chain and listening to the sheikh on tradition. He understood him perfectly, and found nothing to criticize in his lesson except the cascade of names which he poured forth on his listeners in giving the source and authorities for each tradition. It was always "so-and-so tells us" or "according to so-and-so." The boy could not see the point of these endless chains of names, or this tedious tracing of sources. He longed for the sheikh to have done with all this and come down to the tradition itself. As soon as he did so the boy listened with all his heart. He memorized the tradition and understood it, but showed not the slightest interest in the sheikh's analysis, which reminded him too well of the explanations given by the Imam of the mosque in his country village and the sheikh who used to teach him the elements of law.

While the sheikh proceeded with his lesson the Azhar began gradually to wake up, as if stirred out of its torpor by the voices of the teachers holding forth, and by the discussions which arose between them and the students, amounting sometimes almost to quarrels. The students came closer, the voices rose higher, the echoes intermingled and the sheikhs raised their voices again, so that the students might be able to hear them, ever higher and higher, up to the final climax of the words "God is all-wise." For meanwhile other students had come up to wait for a lecture on law by another sheikh, or maybe the same one; so he had no choice but to end the early-morning lecture and begin the next. Then the boy's companion would return, take him by the hand without a word and drag him off all ungently to another place, where he dumped him like a piece of luggage and abandoned him again.

The boy realized that he had been transferred to the law class. He would listen to this lecture until it came to an end and both sheikhs and students went off. Then he would stay rooted to the spot until his friend came back from Sayyidna-l-Hussein, where he had been attending a lecture on law given by Sheikh Bakhît, God rest his soul.

Now Sheikh Bakhît was prolix in the extreme, and his students used to harass him with objections. So he never finished the lesson until the middle of the morning. Then the boy's companion would return to where he was, take him by the hand without a word and lead him out of the Azhar. And so back he went through the second phase along the road between the Azhar and his lodgings into the third and final phase, where he was left alone in his place in the corner on the old carpet stretched out over a rotten worn-out mat.

Reading for Understanding

Main Idea

1. The main point of the story is (a) the sights and sounds of a crowded inner city (b) a boy's thirst for knowledge (c) a greedy tradesperson (d) a hopeless situation.

Details

2. The first portion of the story describes in detail the boy's (a) return to his lodgings (b) stay at the school (c) departure for the school (d) reactions to the lectures.

3. The smells in the narrow, filthy passageway (a) were strongest in the morning (b) were almost universally pleasant (c) reminded the boy of home (d) were most unpleasant in the heat.

4. The filthiest part of his dwelling was (a) the gateway (b) the study (c) the staircase (d) his own room.

5. The boy owed a special debt to (a) the two Persians (b) the owner of the parrot (c) the mayor of Cairo (d) his friend.

Inferences

6. The impression given by the neighborhood in which the boy lived was that of (a) intellectual curiosity (b) poverty (c) elegance (d) protest.

7. The story is being told (a) as a reminiscence in later years (b) to criticize the lecturers at the Azhar (c) to warn others of the problems of Egyptian education (d) in the form of an extended letter.

8. The boy disapproved of (a) his brother (b) his friend's interference in his life (c) teaching by just pouring forth names (d) the custom of removing shoes on entering the Azhar.

9. The style of the story is (a) indifferent and uninvolved (b) bitter and pessimistic (c) frivolous and rigid (d) calm and factual.

Fact or Opinion

Tell whether the following is a fact or an opinion.

10. Conditions in the boy's home area were unlivable.

Words in Context

1. "There was the parrot, whistling on without a break, as if to testify before all the world to the tyranny of her Persian master, who had imprisoned her in an *abominable* cage." **Abominable** (628) means (a) disgusting (b) narrow (c) strong metal (d) carelessly constructed.

2. "Everywhere she went that *plaintive* cry of hers would delight the hearts of men and women." **Plaintive** (628) means (a) loud (b) chattering (c) mournful (d) repeated.

3., 4. "The one was as *morose* and *misanthropic* as the other was genial and good-natured." **Morose** (629) means (a) cruel (b) ill-humored (c) nervous (d) thoughtful. **Misanthropic** (629) means (a) misunderstood (b) quiet and reserved (c) disbelieving (d) unsociable.

5. "The second phase of his life consisted in the *tumultuous* journey between his home and the Azhar." **Tumultuous** (629) means (a) turbulent (b) long and boring (c) daily (d) enjoyable.

6. "Naturally not a single student missed an opportunity . . . of casting a quick *furtive* glance at the spot where letters were waiting to be collected." **Furtive** (630) means (a) unashamed (b) secret (c) longing (d) conspicuous.

7. "They were content with their lot and accepted it with *resignation*." **Resignation** (631) means (a) despair (b) disapproval (c) surrender (d) high spirits.

8., 9. And all the time these *loathsome* sounds *assailed* him, sometimes from in front, and sometimes from behind, but never without dismaying him." **Loathsome** (631) means (a) loud and constant (b) unexpected (c) disgusting (d) harmonious. **Assailed** (631) means (a) amused (b) stimulated (c) wearied (d) attacked.

10. "He passed his days there in exile from people and things alike and in such *anguish* of heart that the oppressive air he breathed there brought him no rest or refreshment, but only heaviness and pain." **Anguish** (632) means (a) distress (b) tightness (c) alertness (d) death.

11. "This heart was all modesty and *humility,* but his soul was filled with glory and pride." **Humility** (634) means (a) fury (b) humbleness (c) wonder (d) mirth.

12. "Or maybe you would hear a teacher beginning his lecture in the *languid* tone of a man who has awakened from sleep and said his prayers but has not yet eaten anything to give him strength and energy." **Languid** (634) means (a) oppressive (b) unattractive (c) listless (d) curious.

13. "By noon they were attacking them almost as if they were *adversaries.*" **Adversaries** (635) are (a) unbelievers (b) criminals (c) monsters (d) enemies.

14. "The Azhar began gradually to wake up, as if stirred out of its *torpor* by the voices of the teachers holding forth." **Torpor** (636) means (a) debate (b) sluggishness (c) exercises (d) disagreements.

15. "Now Sheikh Bakhit was *prolix* in the extreme, and his students used to harass him with objections." **Prolix** (636) means (a) belligerent (b) unpleasant (c) inconsistent (d) wordy.

Thinking Critically about the Selection

1. This selection is a masterpiece of vivid description. The author captures the setting by appealing to the senses of smell, taste, sight, and sound. Point out some of the vivid descriptions that bring the setting to life.

2. Was El-Hagg Firûz a good influence, a friend of the students? Explain.

3. Did the boy love learning for learning's sake? Point to the story to prove your point.

4. How did the boy react to all the difficulties he faced in seeking to get an education?

5. The author talks about the three phases of the boy's life. What were they?

6. Does the method of lecture and challenge seem like a good one to you? Why or why not?

7. "How many a pleasant and rewarding halt did our friend make in that narrow street, which remained fixed in his memory later on, after his life had changed its course."

Do you think the author is talking about his own boyhood? If so, why would he choose the third person (000) instead of the first person to tell the story?

Language in Action

Antonyms

At dawn their voices were calm and gentle, with traces of drowsiness in them. At noon, they were strong and harsh.

Calm and *gentle* are here contrasted with *strong* and *harsh*. A pair like *gentle* and *harsh* are called *antonyms:* words opposed in meaning. The roots distinguish them:

anti—against   *onym*—name
syn—with, together   *onym*—name

Antonyms are extremely useful. They help us to define: for example, *discordant* means *not harmonious*. They enrich our speech by introducing contrasts: "India is a land of unbelievable *poverty* and *wealth*." They help us to build vocabularies; for example, we can remember easily what *humility* means if we recall it is the opposite of *pride*.

Many common expressions include pairs of opposites: *feast* or *famine, thick* or *thin, friend* or *foe, ups* and *downs, win* or *lose*. A word may have both a synonym and an antonym. *Banquet,* for example, is a synonym of *feast,* an antonym of *fasting*.

Since words have different meanings in different contexts, a single word may have many antonyms. *Clear* is such a word. We may talk about a *clear* day, a *clear* conscience, or a *clear* style of writing. Obviously one antonym will not do for all of these. The antonym of the first might be *overcast* or *cloudy*. Of the second it might be *troubled*. Of the third it might be *confused*.

Lucero

Oscar Castro Z.
Chilean

> In fact, this pass was one of the most impressive in the mountain chain. The path at that point was only eighty centimeters wide, just enough to let an animal get by between the stone wall and the abrupt drop. One false step . . . and that would be the end till Judgment Day.

Rarely does a setting play a more important role in a story than in "Lucero." The towering Andes mountains with their snow-clad peaks and awesome abysses, are at the very heart of the story, a tale of a mountain guide and his beloved horse Lucero.

Ruben must catch up with four companions, who left the ranch an hour before him. The trail is treacherous, as the quotation vividly makes clear, but Ruben has his old friend, his horse Lucero, who has traveled the mountains with him for many years. The two face Vulture's Pass, whose name suggests its soaring height. Then, the unexpected happens. Ruben and Lucero are not alone.

Few stories set the stage so briefly and skillfully for the shattering climax. Few people have had to make a decision so quickly and painfully as Ruben. You will not soon forget the gallant Lucero and his loving master in this tale by a Chilean author.

Lucero

OUTLINED ONE AGAINST THE OTHER, the crests of the mountain chain seemed shuffled like a deck of stony cards as far as Ruben Olmos' eyes could travel. Dazzling white peaks, bluish dips, upjutting points arose before his gaze, constantly shifting, more inaccessible as the traveler mounted. Before starting on an abrupt and tiring descent, he decided to give a rest to his mount panting like bellows. During the pause, he crossed his left leg over the saddle and let his eyes wander down toward the valley. The first thing that attracted his gaze was the mirror-like glitter of the river stretching with reluctance its capricious windings among pastures and filled fields. Then his view shifted over beyond some rectangular enclosures, and sought the village he had left that morning. There it was framed in the distance like the toys in a shop window with its tiny houses and the dim ravines of its streets. A few zinc plate roofs darted back the sun's brilliance, cutting the air with streaks of violent silvery radiance.

With a flutter of his eyelids Ruben Olmos rubbed out the picture of the valley and now examined his mount, whose damp flanks rose and fell in rhythmical movement.

"So you're getting old, Lucero?" he asked in an affectionate tone. And the animal, as if it understood, turned toward him its face, black with a white star on its forehead.

"Well, it's a sure thing that you have worked plenty, but you have many years of travel ahead of you yet. At least, while there are still some mountains around here."

He turned to gaze at the Andean massiveness, familiar and friendly to him and Lucero. They hadn't crossed and recrossed it for nothing during these eleven years. Ruben Olmos, a bit dazzled by the white blaze of the sun on the snow, thought of his travel comrades and of the lead they had over him. But he didn't pay much attention to this detail, for he was certain he would overtake them before nightfall.

"So long as you go along with me, we won't have to spend the night alone," he declared to his horse, finishing his thought.

Ruben Olmos was an experienced mountain guide. He had learned his difficult art from his father who had taken him along even as a child over these precipices and ravines in spite of his unwillingness and the mistrust that the mountains at first had roused in him. When the old man had died, peacefully in his bed, the ranch owner had appointed the young man as successor. He had crossed at least a hundred times this mountain barrier which, in his young days, had seemed to him impassible, and had led over numerous herds of cattle from Cuyó, always with good luck on his side.

He chose Lucero when the animal was still a frisking colt and had broken him in himself. After that the rider had never been willing to use another mount although his boss had presented him with two other horses apparently more powerful and from better breeds. Lucero had become for him a mascot to which he clung with a sort of superstition induced by a hazardous life.

The guide, accustomed to the epic struggle against the elements, loved danger more than women. With instinctive wisdom he centered his devotion on a beast, perhaps with the feeling that from it he need expect no rebuff or treason. If some day he were asked to choose between losing his brother or Lucero, he would hesitate before making up his mind, because this creature, more than a mere conveyance, inspired in him from the beginning the feeling of a friend. He was in a sense an extension of his own being, as if the push of his muscles flowed into the tendons of Lucero.

Ruben Olmos was born with flesh fashioned out of hard substance. He felt life in a rush of tides throbbing along the passages of his being. On horseback he was always the leader, not one to be led. And this energy needed space to exert itself; no place could seem more favorable or more adapted to his talents than the tumultuous heights of the Andes.

If observed superficially, the guide looked like an ordinary fellow. At the best, he gave the impression of self-confidence. His coppery skin and flattened nose evoked the Indian in his ancestry. His smile had no brightness, it was dimmed by his eyes, at most it gleamed momentarily at the edge of his teeth. A herdsman amidst solitudes, he had learned from them silence and penetration. He had a deeper tie with Lucero than with human beings. It must have been because the horse did not answer, or because he always said "yes" with his loving moist eyes. There was no telling.

"Fine, now we must be moving."

Setting his iron shoes into the cracks, the horse ascended toward heaven. The rider, bent forward, moved with the rhythmic sway of each step. Pebbles rolled down into the depths and the rings on the reins tinkled. And Lucero—toc, toc, toc—was finally there on the crest after toiling upwards for a quarter-hour.

Upon the heights the wind flowed more constant, bearing more cold moisture. It glided over the face of the guide. It sought some opening in his cloak, in order to grasp it with its teeth. However, long practice made this man safe from its attack, and although the blast persisted, it did not succeed in altering his course.

With several crests of mountains crossed, the valley was no longer visible. There were hills ahead, toward which the eye looked. And above stretched a thin sky, pure, more blue than the cold of the wind, hardly speckled by the flashing flight of an eagle, sole possessor of this unattainable space.

The loneliness of the heights was so immense, so clearly desolate, that the traveler sometimes had the swift impression of drowning in the wind, as if he were swirling in the depths of treacherous waters. But this man did not have time to admire the magnificent stretches of the landscape. The atmosphere, like a transparent bubble, the deep orchestral tones of the verdure,* the symphony of birds and insects which mounted upwards in delicate surges—none of these things found an echo in his spirit, formed as it was out of the dark substances of struggle and decision.

From a rise which gave a clear view of the near-by heights, Ruben Olmos scanned the path in the hope of seeing those who had gone ahead of him. But he perceived nothing but emptiness during this exploration. The man pursed his lips. The four companions who had left the ranch an hour ahead of him had gained quite a lead. He would have to press his horse.

On he went past the familiar landmarks, the Lion's Cave, the Condor's Perch, the Black Gap. "My comrades must be waiting for me in the Muleteer Shelter," he thought, and sank his spurs into Lucero's ribs.

The path was hardly more than a vague track from whose line other eyes less experienced than his might stray. But Ruben Olmos couldn't go wrong. This slight rut over which he was traveling was, for him, a wide and spacious thoroughfare leading to one goal: the pueblo of Cuyó.

As he reached higher land, vegetation became tougher and more twisted to resist the attacks of the storms. Hawthorn, rosemary, sharp-edged cactus loomed up like dark splashes of a painter's brush against the pale snow. The solitudes began to get whiter and deeper, clothed with a dignified serenity. Ruben Olmos imagined that it was five o'clock in the afternoon. The sun, already slipping into the West, was struggling to sift its warmth through the wind.

The setting suddenly changed as the horse of the guide emerged into an immense stadium of stone. Two enormous mountains framed it, each with its half parenthesis circling a crevice whose depths could not be plumbed. It seemed as if an immense cataclysm had severed the mountain chain at a blow.

The rider stopped Lucero. The Vulture Pass exerted a strange fascination on his mind. When he was fifteen and had crossed it for the first time, he had had a whim to look down into it in spite of his father's

---

*green vegetation

warning, and after a moment he had noticed that the ravine began to whirl around like a blue funnel. Something like an invisible claw was pulling him into the abyss and he was letting himself go. Fortunately his father had observed the danger and shouted, "Turn your head around, you fool!" From that time on, in spite of all his calm control, he had not dared to let his gaze wander down that unfathomable depth.

Moreover, the Vulture's Pass had its legends. No herd of cattle could cross it on Good Friday, without some terrible misfortune. It was his father who had given him this information, illustrating with stories of various incidents when cattle or horses had been swallowed up in some mysterious way by this chasm.

In fact, this pass was one of the most impressive in the mountain chain. The path at that point was only eighty centimeters* wide, just enough to let an animal get by between the stone wall and the abrupt drop. One false step . . . and that would be the end till Judgment Day.

Before venturing along that shelf suspended who knew how many feet above the depth, Ruben Olmos complied scrupulously with the agreement established among those who crossed the mountains: he took his pistol out of his holster and fired two shots into the air to give warning to any possible traveler that the route was being used and that he was to wait. The explosions sent their waves into the clear air. They rebounded against the rocks and returned multiplied to the ears of the guide. After a little pause, the rider decided to resume his journey. Lucero, carefully setting his iron shoes on the rocky road was apparently unaware of any change in the aspect of the route. "Splendid horse!" mused the rider, summing up in these words all his affection for the animal.

Ruben Olmos will never be able to forget what was about to happen. Upon emerging from an abrupt turn, his heart gave one wild leap in his breast. From the opposite direction, less than twenty paces away, appeared a man mounted on a dark sorrel-colored nag. Amazement, frustration, and anger flashed across the faces of the travelers. Both, with an instinctive pull, reined in their horses. The first to break the anguished silence was the rider on the sorrel. After a growling curse, he shouted, "And how did you ever presume to start on this way without giving warning?"

Ruben Olmos knew that mere words would not help. He kept on advancing till the heads of the two horses almost touched. Then in a quiet firm voice that seemed to come from way down in his chest, he said, "It was you, my friend, who didn't give the signal shots."

The other drew his revolver and Ruben did likewise, with a promptness unsuspected in him. They looked at each other fixedly for a moment, with a spark of defiance in their eyes. The stranger had steely

---

*a little over 30 inches

cold eyes and features that betrayed will-power and decisiveness. In his aspect, his assurance, he revealed that he was a mountaineer accustomed to danger. Both realized that they were worthy adversaries.

Ruben Olmos finally decided to prove that he was in the right. Grasping his weapon with the barrel pointed to the abyss so as not to arouse distrust, he drew out the bullets, presenting a pair of empty cartridges.

"Here are my two shots," he declared.

The stranger imitated him, likewise offering as proof two leadless shells.

"Tough luck, my friend; we fired at the same time," declared the guide.

"That's how it was, comrade. And now what are we going to do?"

"As for going back, it just can't be done."

"Well then, one of us will have to get along on foot."

"Yes, that's so, but which one of us?"

"Luck will have to decide that."

And without any other comment the sorrel rider took a coin out of his pocket, and put it between his two hands without looking.

"You say which," he said.

There was a terrible hesitation in Ruben's mind. Those two clamped hands which he beheld hid the secret of an unalterable verdict. They represented more power than all the laws written by men. Fate would speak through them in its inexorable, impartial voice. And, as Ruben Olmos never defied the decrees of uncertain Fate, he pronounced the word that someone whispered in his brain.

"Heads!"

The other then slowly uncovered the coin and the oblique afternoon sun lit up a laurel wreath circling a sickle and hammer: Ruben had lost. He did not betray by the slightest gesture his inner dismay. His eyes turned softly and slowly toward the head and neck of Lucero. Presently, his hand gestured the caress that burst from his heart. And finally, as if to free himself from the fatality bearing down on him, he let himself drop to the path over the shining croup of his horse. He untied the gun and the provision-bag attached to the saddle. Then he slipped off the blanket roll resting on the animal's haunch. And all this slowly created between the two men a silence more dreadful than the Andean solitude.

During these preparations, the stranger seemed to suffer as much as the loser. Pretending to see nothing, he was busy braiding and unbraiding the thongs of his whip. Ruben Olmos was deeply grateful to him for this feigned indifference. When his painful work was done, he said to the other in a voice which preserved an inexpressibly desperate firmness, "Did you happen to meet four herdsmen with two mules on the way?"

"Yes, they're resting at the Refuge. Are they your companions?"

"Yes, it happens they are."

Lucero, perhaps surprised to be freed from the saddle in such an inappropriate spot, turned his head, and Ruben gazed for a moment upon his eyes, gentle as dark pools. The star on his forehead. His ears erect. His nostrils quivering. To gather his determination, Ruben uttered into the air in a voice laden with secret sorrow, "Keep a close rein on your beast, friend."

The other pulled in the reins, turning the head of his sorrel toward the rocky wall.

Only then Ruben Olmos, his heart dissolved in agony, lightly patted Lucero's neck once more, and with an immense shove sent him rolling into the abyss.

Reading for Understanding

Main Idea

1. The main idea of the story can best be summed up in the phrase (a) mountain problems (b) a faithful friend lost (c) careless planning (d) an act of evil.

Details

2. Ruben and Lucero had worked together (a) since the previous spring (b) six years (c) eleven years (d) for half of Ruben's lifetime.

3. Ruben (a) was trying to reach four companions (b) planned to return to the ranch the next day (c) dreaded crossing the Andes (d) took Lucero along as a last thought.

4. All the following are mentioned as part of the Andes mountains EXCEPT (a) Lion's Cave (b) Eagle's Nest (c) Black Gap (d) Condor's Perch.

5. Ruben fired two shots to (a) prove his manhood (b) try to bring down a deer (c) warn that he was crossing the Pass (d) break the boredom.

Inferences

6. If Ruben were asked to choose between Lucero and his brother, he'd (a) be almost persuaded by his love for Lucero (b) immediately

choose his brother as his closest friend (c) refuse to answer such a
foolish question (d) choose Lucero without another thought.

7. Apparently, the two men (a) were convinced the other was dishonest
(b) hadn't heard the others' shots (c) decided to return the way they
had come (d) fought hand to hand.

8. The laurel wreath on the coin indicated that (a) there was still glory
in Ruben's decision (b) the coin was not a perfect one (c) Ruben had
made a lucky decision (d) the coin was tails.

9. Ruben felt that the outcome (a) proved his own manhood (b) was
fate (c) left the other traveler untouched (d) was somehow dishonest.

Fact or Opinion

Tell whether the following is a fact or an opinion.

10. One of the animals had to die.

Words in Context

1. "Dazzling white peaks, bluish dips, upjutting points arose before his
gaze, constantly shifting, more *inaccessible* as the traveler mounted."
Inaccessible (642) means (a) unreachable (b) invisible (c) unsettling
(d) uninviting.

2. "The first thing that attracted his gaze was the mirror-like glitter of
the river stretching with reluctance its *capricious* windings among
pastures and tilled fields." **Capricious** (642) means (a) gradual (b)
striking (c) erratic (d) picturesque.

3. "With instinctive wisdom he centered his devotion on a beast, perhaps with the feeling that from it he need expect no *rebuff* or
treason." **Rebuff** (643) means (a) repetition (b) disagreement (c)
illness (d) rejection.

4. "The solitudes began to get whiter and deeper, clothed with a
dignified *serenity*." **Serenity** (644) means (a) intensity (b) vividness
(c) tranquility (d) abundance of color.

5. "It seemed as if an immense *cataclysm* had severed the mountain
chain at a blow." A **cataclysm** (644) is a (a) violent upheaval (b)
strong thunderstorm (c) blizzard with hail (d) giant.

6. "Ruben Olmos complied *scrupulously* with the agreement established

among those who crossed the mountains." **Scrupulously** (645) means (a) reluctantly (b) precisely (c) willingly (d) undoubtfully.

7. "The first to break the *anguished* silence was the rider on the sorrel." **Anguished** (645) means (a) embarrassed (b) hostile (c) long (d) tortured.

8. "Grasping his weapon with the barrel pointed to the *abyss* so as not to arouse distrust, he drew out the bullets, presenting a pair of empty cartridges." An **abyss** (646) is a (a) pleasant valley (b) deep gorge (c) gentle slope (d) lofty peak.

Thinking Critically about the Story

1. How does the author emphasize the closeness between Ruben and Lucero? How does this make the final tragedy stronger?

2. Show how the author suggests that the other traveler keenly feels the tragedy that is about to unfold.

3. How does the author build suspense, leading to the final event?

4. Why was Ruben grateful to the other traveler for his "feigned indifference"?

5. What descriptive touches suggest that the author himself loved the mountains?

6. How does the following sentence show irony (264–265)?

    "Well, it's a sure thing that you have worked plenty, but you have many years of travel ahead of you yet."

7. What incredible coincidence necessitated the tragic decision?

Language in Action

E-Prime

The loneliness of the heights was so immense, so clearly desolate, that the traveler sometimes had the swift impression of drowning in the wind.

The word *is* in all its forms has come in for criticism from students of language, especially when it passes subjective judgments (118) as in "Adrienne is too vain." A form of writing, called *E-Prime,* has been devised to eliminate *is* in its many forms.

If the quoted text sentence had been written in E-Prime, it might have looked like this: "The immense and desolate loneliness of the heights sometimes gave the traveler the swift impression of drowning in the wind." Because the original sentence communicated the picture effectively, the E-Prime sentence may not strike you as a great improvement. Sometimes, though, the recast sentence makes a point directly, clearly, and more objectively:

With *is:* The ant is an excellent preacher because she is not talkative.

Without *is:* None preaches better than the ant, and she says nothing.

Convenience will probably not eliminate *is* and other linking verbs from the language. But occasionally trying to write and speak in E-Prime sharpens perceptions and gives users additional awareness of the ways in which language may mislead us.

Except for quoted passages and the word *is* used as an example, this section has been written in E-Prime. Did you notice?

Benediction

"I was truly stupid, truly," she would repeat. "I only knew
that when the snow lies on the mountains the wild animals
will sometimes venture into the valleys and will even come
into the villages in search of food. I did not know that they
could be fierce long after the coming of spring."

Story plots are sometimes simplified as "Boy meets girl. Boy
loses girl. Boy wins girl." In a more helpful analysis, plots are sometimes divided into six sections: situation, complication, conflict, development, climax, and outcome. Let's see how the division works in
Shakespeare's famous play, **Romeo and Juliet**.

Romeo sees Juliet at a ball and falls instantly in love with her.
(Situation) Unfortunately, the two lovers belong to rival families.
(Complication) The warring families continue to feud. (Conflict) Romeo
and Juliet profess their love. (Development) In a duel, Romeo kills
Juliet's kinsman. (Climax) Romeo and Juliet try to be together but die as
a result of a breakdown in communication. (Outcome)

The plot of "Benediction" can also be considered to fall into
six sections. The climax is the turning point, the point at which the
outcome seems inevitable. In this powerful tale by a Chinese author,
the fortunes of Hsiang-lin Sao, the central character, are never bright,
but the quotation above suggests the turning point.

Hsiang-lin Sao is a tragic figure, a victim of other people's
disregard for her well-being. Happily hardworking at first in the
household of Fourth Uncle and Fourth Aunt, she is suddenly caught
up in a series of events that ultimately break her valiant spirit. The
setting is Chinese; some of the customs seem strange to us, but similar
stories can be found in literature around the world.

I

The end of the year according to the lunar calendar is, after all, the right time for a year to end. A strange almost-new-year sort of atmosphere seems to overlay everything; pale grey clouds at evening, against which flash the hot little fires of crackers giving a thunderous boost to the kitchen god's ascent into heaven. And as one draws into it the scene grows noisier, and scattered on the air is the sting of gunpowder.

On such a night I return to Long Ching—my 'home town' as I call it, but in reality I have no home there at all. I stay with Lo Shih Lao-yeh, a relative one generation older than myself, a fellow who ought to be called 'Fourth Uncle,' according to the Chinese family way of reckoning. He is a *chien-sheng,** and talks all the time about the old virtues and the old ethics.

I find him not much changed; a little aged of course, but still without a whisker. We exchange salutations. After the "How are you?" he tells me I've grown fat. With that done, he at once commences a tirade against the 'new party.' But I know that the phrase to him still means poor Kang Yu-wei, and not the Renaissance, of which he probably has not even heard. We have at any rate nothing in common, and before long I am left alone in the study.

Next day I get up very late, and after lunching go out to call on some relatives and friends. The day after is the same, and the day after that. None of them has changed much, each is a little older, and everywhere they are busily preparing for New Year prayers-of-blessing. It is a great thing in Lo Ching: every one exerts himself to show reverence, exhausts himself in performing rites, and falls down before the god of benediction to ask favours for the year ahead. There is much chicken-killing, geese-slaughtering, and pork-buying; women go round with their arms raw and red from soaking in hot water preparing such fowl. When they are thoroughly cooked they are placed on the altar, with chopsticks punched into them at all angles, and offered up as sacrifices at the sixth watch. Incense sticks and red candles are lighted, and the men (no women allowed) make obeisance and piously invite the blessing-spirits to eat away. And after this, of course, the crackers.

Every year it is that way, and the same in every home—except those of the miserable poor who cannot buy either sacrifices or candles or crackers—and this year is like any other. The sky is dark and gloomy, and in the afternoon snow falls—flakes like plum blossoms darting and dancing across a screen of smoke and bustle, and making everything more confused. By the time I return home the roof-tiles are already washed white, and inside my room seems brighter. The reflection from the snow

---

*A *chien-sheng* is an honorary degree equivalent to the *hsiu-ts'ai,* but is purchased, whereas the latter is given only to scholars.

also touches up the large crimson character. LONGEVITY,* which hangs on a board against the wall. It is said to be the work of the legendary Chen Tuan Lao-tso. One of the scrolls has fallen down and is rolled up loosely and lying on the long table, but the other still admonishes me: "Understand deeply the reason of things, be moderate, and be gentle in heart and manner." On the desk under the window are incomplete volumes of the *K'ang Hsi Dictionary,* a set of *Recent Thoughts,* with collected commentaries, and the *Four Books.* How depressing!

I decided to return tomorrow, at the very latest, to the city.

The incident with Hsiang-lin Sao also has very much disturbed me. This afternoon I went to the eastern end of the town to visit a friend, and while returning I encountered her at the edge of the canal. The look in her staring eyes showed clearly enough that she was coming after me, so I waited. Although other folk I used to know in Lo Ching have apparently changed little, Hsiang-lin Sao was no longer the same. Her hair was all white, her face was alarmingly lean, hollow, and burnt a dark yellow. She looked completely exhausted, not at all like a woman not yet forty, but like a wooden thing with an expression of tragic sadness carved into it. Only the movement of her lustreless eyes showed that she still lived. In one hand she carried a bamboo basket: inside it was an empty broken bowl; and she held herself up by leaning on a bamboo pole. She had apparently become a beggar.

I stood waiting to be asked for money.

"So—you've come back?"

"Yes."

"That's good—and very timely. Tell me, you are a scholar, a man who has seen the world, a man of knowledge and experience"—her faded eyes very faintly glowed—"tell me, I just want to ask you one thing."

I could not, in ten thousand tries, have guessed what she would ask. I waited, shocked and puzzled, saying nothing.

She moved nearer, lowered her voice, and spoke with great secrecy and earnestness.

"It is this: after a person dies is there indeed such a thing as the *soul?*"

Involuntarily I shuddered. Her eyes stuck into me like thorns. Here was a fine thing! I felt more embarrassed than a schoolboy given a surprise examination, with the teacher standing right beside him. Whether there was such a thing as the 'soul' had never bothered me, and I had speculated little about it. How could I reply? In that brief moment I remembered that many people in Lo Ching believed in some kind of spirits, and probably she did too. Perhaps I should just say it was rather

---

*long life

doubtful—but no, it was better to let her go on hoping. Why should I burden a person obviously on the 'last road' with even more pain? Better for her sake say yes.

"Perhaps," I stammered. "Yes, I suppose there is."

"Then there is also a *hell?*"

"Ah—hell?" She had trapped me, and I could only continue placatingly, "Hell? Well, to be logical, I dare say there ought to be. But, then, again—there may not be. What does it matter?"

"Then in this hell do all deceased members of a family come together again, face to face?"

"H'mm? Seeing face to face, eh?" I felt like a fool. Whatever knowledge I possessed, whatever mental dexterity, was utterly useless; here I had been confounded by three simple questions. I made up my mind to extricate myself from the mess, and wanted to repudiate everything I had said. But somehow I could not do so in the gaze of her intensely earnest and tragic eyes.

"That is to say . . . in fact, I cannot definitely say. Whether there is a soul or not in the end I am in no position to deny or affirm."

With that she did not persist, and, taking advantage of her silence, I strode away with long steps and hastened back to Fourth Uncle's home, feeling very depressed. I could not help thinking that perhaps my replies would have an evil effect on her. No doubt her loneliness and distress had become all the more unbearable at this time, when every one else seemed to be praying for benediction—but perhaps there was something else on her mind. Perhaps something that had recently happened to her. If so, then my answers might be responsible . . . for what? I soon laughed about the whole thing, and at my absurd habit of exaggerating the importance of casual happenings. Educators unquestionably would pronounce me mentally unbalanced. Hadn't I, after all, made it clear that all I could say was, "Cannot definitely say"? Even should all my replies be refuted, even if something happened to the woman, it could in no way concern me.

"Cannot definitely say" is a very convenient phrase. Bold and reckless youths often venture so far as to offer a positive opinion on critical questions for others, but responsible people, like officials and doctors,* have to choose their words carefully, for if events belie their opinion then it becomes a serious affair. It is much more advisable to say, "Cannot definitely say"; obviously it solves everything. This encounter with the woman mendicant impresses upon me the importance of that practice, for even in such cases the deepest wisdom lies in ambiguity.

Nevertheless, I continue to feel troubled, and when the night is

---

*The author was formerly a doctor, having studied medicine in Japan.

gone I wake up with the incident still on my mind. It is like an unlucky presentiment of a movement of fate. Outside the day is still gloomy, with flurrying snow, and in the dull study my uneasiness gradually increases. Certainly I must go back to the city to-morrow. . . . To be sure, there is still unsampled the celebrated pure-cooked fish-fins at Fu Shing Lou—excellent eating and very cheap at only a dollar a big tray. Has the price by now increased? Although many of my boyhood friends have melted away like clouds in the sky, there must remain, at least, the incomparable fish-fins of Lo Ching, and these I must eat, even though I eat alone. . . . All the same, I am returning to-morrow. . . .

Because I have so often seen things happen exactly as I predicted—but hoped against, and tried to believe improbable—so I am not unprepared for this occasion to provide no exception. Towards evening some of the family gather in an inner room, and from fragments of their talk I gather they are discussing some event with no little annoyance. Presently all the voices cease except one, that of Fourth Uncle, who thunders out above the thud of his own pacing feet:

"Not a day earlier nor a day later, but just at this season she decided upon it. From this alone we can see that she belongs to a species utterly devoid of human sense!"

My curiosity is soon followed by a vague discomfort, as if these words have some special meaning for me. I go out and look into the room, but every one has vanished. Suppressing my increasing impatience, I wait till the servant comes to fill my teapot with hot water. Not until then am I able to confirm my suspicions.

"Who was it Fourth Uncle was blowing up about a while ago?"

"Could it after all have been any other than Hsiang-lin Sao?" he replies in the brief and positive manner of our language.

"What has happened to her?" I demand in an anxious voice.

"Aged."*

"Dead?" My heart twinges and seems to jump back; my face burns. But he doesn't notice my emotion at all, doesn't even lift his head, so that I control myself to the end of further questioning.

"When did she die then?"

"When? Last night—or possibly to-day. I cannot definitely say."

"What did she die of?"

"What did she die of? Could it indeed be anything else than that she has been strangled to death by poverty?" His words are absolutely colourless, and without even looking at me he goes out.

My terror at first is great, but I reason that this is a thing which was bound to happen very soon, and it is merely an accident that I even

---

*The word 'die' and its synonyms are forbidden at this season, and 'aged' is commonly used to describe death. Ordinarily Chinese refer to the dead as 'not here,' or 'outside.'

know about it. I further reassure my conscience by recalling my non-committal "Cannot definitely say," and the servant's report that it was simply a case of "strangled to death by poverty." Still, now and then I feel a prick of guilt, I don't know exactly why, and when I sit down beside the dignified old Fourth Uncle I am continually thinking of opening a discussion about Hsiang-lin Sao. But how to do it? He still lives in a world of religious taboos, and at this time of year these are like an impenetrable forest. You cannot, of course, mention anything connected with death, illness, crime, and so on, unless it is absolutely imperative. Even then such references must be disguised in a queer riddle-language in order not to offend the hovering ancestral spirits. I torture my brain to remember the necessary formula, but, alas, I cannot recall the right phrases, and at length have to give it up.

Fourth Uncle throughout the meal wears an austere look on his face. At last I suspect that he regards me also as "belonging to a species utterly devoid of human sense," since "neither a day earlier, nor a day later, but just at this season" I have put in an appearance. To loosen his heart and save him further anxiety I tell him that I have determined to return to-morrow. He doesn't urge me to stay very enthusiastically, and I conclude that my surmise was correct. And thus in a cheerless mood I finish my meal.

The short day is ended, the curtain of snow dropping over it earlier than usual even in this month, and the black night falls like a shroud over the whole town. People still busy themselves under the lamplight, but just beyond my window there is the quiet of death. Snow lies like a down mattress over the earth, and the still falling flakes make a faint *suh-suh* sound that adds to the intense loneliness and the unbearable melancholy. Sitting alone under the yellow rays of the rape-oil lamp, my mind goes back again to that blown-out flicker, Hsiang-lin Sao.

This woman who once stood among us in this house, thrown now, like an old toy, discarded by a child, on to the dustheap. For those who find the world amusing, for the kind for whom she is created, no doubt if they think about her at all it is simply to wonder why the devil she should so long have had the effrontery to continue to exist. Well, she has obliged them by disappearing at last, swept away thoroughly by Wu Chang,* and a very tidy job. I don't know whether there is such a thing as the 'soul' that lives on after death, but it would be a great improvement if people like Hsiang-lin Sao were never born, would it not? Then nobody would be troubled, neither the despised nor those who despise them.

Listening to the *suh-suh* of the leafy autumnal snow I go on musing, and gradually find some comfort in my reflections. It is like

---

*A sheriff-spirit who 'sweeps up' the soul at the last breath of life.

putting together an intricate puzzle, but in the end the incidents of her life fit together into a single whole.

II

Hsiang-lin Sao was not a native of Lo Ching. She arrived in early winter one year with Old Woman Wei, who bargained in the labour of others. Fourth Uncle had decided to change the servant, and Hsiang-lin Sao was Old Woman Wei's candidate for the job.

She wore a white scarf wrapped round her head, a blue jacket, a pale green vest, and a black skirt. She was perhaps twenty-six or twenty-seven, still quite young and rather pretty, with ruddy cheeks and a bronzed face. Old Woman Wei said that she was a neighbor of her mother's. Her husband had died, she explained, and so she had to seek work outside.

Fourth Uncle wrinkled up his brow, and his wife, looking at him, knew what he meant. He didn't like hiring a widow. But Fourth Aunt scrutinized her carefully, noting that her hands and feet looked strong and capable, and that she had honest, direct eyes. She impressed her as a woman who would be content with her lot, and not likely to complain about hard work; and so in spite of her husband's wrinkled brow Fourth Aunt agreed to give her a trial. For three days she worked as if leisure of any kind bored her; she proved very energetic and as strong as a man. Fourth Aunt then definitely hired her, the wage being five hundred cash* per month.

Everybody called her simply Hsiang-lin Sao, without asking for her surname. The Old Woman Wei was, however, a native of Wei Chia Shan (Wei Family Mountain), and since she claimed that Hsiang-lin Sao came from that village no doubt her surname also was Wei. Like most mountaineers, she talked little, and only answered others' questions in monosyllables, and so it took more than ten days to pry out of her the bare facts that there was still a severe mother-in-law in her home; that her young brother-in-law cut wood for a living; that she had lost her husband, ten years her junior, in the previous spring; and that he also had lived by cutting firewood. This was about all people could get out of her.

Day followed day, and Hsiang-lin Sao's work was just as regular. She never slackened up, she never complained about the food, she never seemed to tire. People agreed that Old Lord Lo Shih had found a worthy worker, quick and diligent, more so in fact than a man. Even at New Year she did all the sweeping, dusting, washing, and other household duties, besides preparing geese and chickens and all the sacrifices, without any other help. She seemed to thrive on it. Her skin became whiter, and she fattened a little.

---

*This is about 50 cents. Wages for similar work would be from $2 to $6 per month.

New Year had just passed when one day she came hurrying up from the canal, where she had been washing rice. She was much agitated. She said she had seen, on the opposite bank, a man who looked very much like her late husband's first cousin, and she was afraid he had come to take her away. Fourth Aunt was alarmed and suspicious. Why should he be coming for her? Asked for details, Hsiang-lin Sao could give none. Fourth Uncle, when he heard the story, wrinkled his brow and announced:

"This is very bad. It looks as though she has run away, instead of being ordered."

And, as it turned out, he was correct. She was a runaway widow.

Some ten days later, when everybody was gradually forgetting the incident, Old Woman Wei suddenly appeared, accompanied by a woman who, she claimed, was Hsiang-lin Sao's mother-in-law. The latter seemed not at all like a tongue-bound mountaineer, but knew how to talk, and after a few courtesy words got to the subject of her business at once. She said she had come to take her daughter-in-law back home. It was spring, there was much to be done at home, and in the house at present were none but the very old and the very young. Hsiang-lin Sao was needed.

"Since it is her own mother-in-law who requests it, how can we deny the justice of it?" said Fourth Uncle.

Hsiang-lin Sao's wage, therefore, was figured out. It was discovered that altogether one thousand seven hundred and fifty cash were due. She had let the sum accumulate with her master, not taking out even a single cash for use. Without any more words, this amount was handed over to the mother-in-law, although Hsiang-lin Sao was not present. The woman also took Hsiang-lin Sao's clothes, thanked Fourth Uncle and left. It was then past noon. . . .

"*Ai-ya!* the rice? Didn't Hsiang-lin Sao go out to scour the rice?"

Fourth Aunt, some time later, cried out this question in a startled way. She had forgotten all about Hsiang-lin Sao until her hunger reminded her of rice, and the rice reminded her of the former servant.

Everybody scattered and began searching for the rice basket. Fourth Aunt herself went first to the kitchen, next to the front hall, and then into the bedroom, but she didn't see a shadow of the object of her search. Fourth Uncle wandered outside, but he saw nothing of it either till he came near the canal. There, upright on the bank, with a cabbage near by, lay the missing basket.

Apparently not until then had anyone thought to inquire in what manner Hsiang-lin Sao had departed with her mother-in-law. Now eye-witnesses appeared who reported that early in the morning a boat, carrying a white canopy, anchored in the canal, and lay there idly for some time. The awning hid the occupants, and no one knew who was in it. Presently Hsiang-lin Sao came to the bank, and just as she was about to kneel down for water two men quickly jumped out, grabbed her, and forcibly put her inside the boat. They seemed to be mountain people, but they certainly took her against her will; she cried and shouted for help several times. Afterwards she was hushed up, evidently with some kind of gag. Nothing more happened until the arrival of two women, one of whom was Old Woman Wei. Nobody saw very clearly what had happened to Hsiang-lin Sao, but those who peered in declared that she seemed to have been bound and thrown on the deck of the cabin.

"Outrageous!" exclaimed Fourth Uncle. On reflection, however, he simply ended impotently, "But after all . . . "

Fourth Aunt herself had to prepare the food that day, and her son Ah Niu made the fire.

In the afternoon Old Woman Wei reappeared.

"Outrageous!" Fourth Uncle greeted her.

"What is this? How wonderful! You have honoured us once more with your presence!" Fourth Aunt, washing dishes, angrily shouted at the old bargain-maker. "You yourself recommend her to us, then you come with companions to abduct her from the household. This affair is a veritable volcanic eruption. How do you suppose it will look to outsiders? Are you playing a joke at our expense, or what is it?"

"*Ai-ya! Ai-ya!* I have surely been fooled and tricked. I came here to explain to you. Now how was I to know she was a rebel? She came to me, begged me to get her work, and I took her for genuine. Who would have known that she was doing it behind her mother-in-law's back, without in fact even asking for permission? I'm unable to look in your face, my lord and my lady. It's all my fault, the fault of a careless old fool. I can't look you in the face. . . . Fortunately, your home is generous and forgiving, and will not punish insignificant people like myself too strictly, eh? And next time the person I recommend must be doubly good to make up for this sin—"

"But—" interjected Fourth Uncle, who, however, could get no farther.

And so the affair of Hsiang-lin Sao came to an end, and indeed she herself would have been entirely forgotten were it not that the Fourth Aunt had such difficulty with subsequent servants. They were too lazy, or they were gluttonous, or in extreme cases they were both lazy and gluttonous, and in truth were totally undesirable, "from the extreme left to the extreme right." In her distress, Fourth Aunt always mentioned the exemplary Hsiang-lin Sao. "I wonder how she is living?" she would say, inwardly wishing that some misfortune would oblige her to return to work. By the time the next New Year rolled round, however, she had given up hope of ever seeing her again.

Towards the end of the holidays Old Woman Wei called one day to *k'ou-t'-ou* and offer felicitations. She had already drunk herself into semi-intoxication, and was in a garrulous mood. She explained that because of a visit to her mother's home in Wei Village, where she had stayed for several days, she was late this year in paying her courtesy calls. During the course of the conversation their talk naturally touched upon Hsiang-lin Sao.

"She?" the old woman cried shrilly and with alcoholic enthusiasm. "There's a lucky woman! You know, when her mother-in-law came after her here she had at that time already been promised to a certain Hu Lao-liu, of Hu Village. After staying in her home only a few days she was loaded again into the Flowery Sedan Chair and borne away!"

"*Ai-ya,* what a mother!" Fourth Aunt exclaimed.

"*Ai-ya,* my lady! You speak from behind a lofty door.* We mountaineers, of the small-doored families, for us what does it matter? You see, she had a young brother-in-law, and he had to be married. If Hsiang-lin Sao was not married off first, where would the family get money enough for the brother-in-law's presents to his betrothed? So you understand the mother-in-law is by no means a stupid woman, but keen and calculating. Moreover, she married the daughter-in-law to an inner mountain dweller. Why? Don't you see? Marrying her to a local man, she would have got only a small betrothal gift, but, since few women want to marry deep into the mountains, the price is higher. Hence the husband actually paid eighty thousand cash for Hsiang-lin Sao. Now the son of the family has also been married, and he gave his bride presents costing but five thousand cash. After deducting the cost of the wedding there still remained over ten thousand cash profit. Is she clever or not? Good figuring, eh?"

"And Hsiang-lin Sao—she obeyed all right?"

"Well, it wasn't a question of obedience with her. Anybody in such a situation has to make a protest, of course. They simply tie her up, lift her into the Flowery Sedan Chair, bear her away to the groom's home, forcibly put the Flowery Hat on her head, forcibly make her *k'ou-t'ou* in the ancestral hall, forcibly 'lock her up' with the man—and the thing is done."

"*Ai-ya!*"

"But Hsiang-lin Sao was unusually rebellious. I heard people say that she made a terrific struggle. In fact, it was said that she was different from most women, probably because she had worked in your home—the home of a scholar. My lady, I have seen much in these years. Among widows who remarry I have seen the kind who cry and shout. I have seen those who threaten suicide. There is in addition the kind who, after being taken to the groom's home, refuse to make the *k'ou-t'ou* to Heaven and

---

*That is, an upper-class family. It is not against the mother-in-law's tyranny that Fourth Aunt protests, but her lack of virtue in remarrying her widowed daughter-in-law.

Earth, and even go so far as to smash the Flowery Candles used to light the bridal chamber! But Hsiang-lin Sao was like none of those demonstrators.

"From the beginning she fought like a tigress. She screamed and she cursed, and by the time she reached Hu Village her throat was so raw that she had almost lost her voice. She had to be dragged out of the sedan chair. It took two men to get her into the ancestral hall, and still she would not *k'ou-t'ou*. Only for one moment they carelessly loosened their grip on her, and, *ai-ya!* by Buddha's name! she knocked her head a sound whack on the incense altar, and cut a deep gash from which blood spurted out thickly! They used two handfuls of incense ash on the wound, and bound it up with two thicknesses of red cloth, and still it bled. Actually, she struggled till the very last, when they locked her with her husband in the bridal room, and even then she cursed! This was indeed a *protest*. *Ai-ya,* it really was!"

She shook her gnarled head, bent her gaze on the floor, and was silent.

"How was it afterwards?"

"They say she did not get up the first day, nor the second."

"Afterwards?"

"After that? Oh, she finally got up. At the end of the year she bore him a child, a boy. While I was at my mother's home I saw some people who had returned from Hu Village, and they had seen her. Mother and son were both fat. Above their heads was fortunately no mother-in-law. Her husband, it seems, is strong and a good worker. He owns his house. *Ai-ya,* she is a lucky one indeed."

From that time on Fourth Aunt gave up any thought of Hsiang-lin Sao's excellent work, or at any rate she ceased to mention her name.

III

In the autumn, two years after Old Woman Wei had brought news of Hsiang-lin Sao's extraordinary good luck, our old servant stood once more in person before the hall of Fourth Uncle's home. On the table she laid a round chestnut-shaped basket and a small bedding-roll. She still wore a white scarf on her head, a black skirt, a blue jacket, and 'moon-white' vest. Her complexion was about the same, except that her cheeks had lost at all their colour. Traces of tears lay at the corners of her eyes, from which all the old brightness and lustre seemed washed away. Moreover, with her once more appeared Old Woman Wei, wearing on her face an expression of commiseration. She babbled to Fourth Aunt:

"So it is truly said, 'Heaven holds many an unpredictable wind and cloud.' Her husband was a strong and healthy man. Who would have guessed that at a green age he would be cut down by fever? He had actually recovered from the illness, but ate a bowl of cold rice, and it attacked him again. Fortunately she had the son. By cutting wood, plucking tea-leaves, raising silkworms—and she is skilled at each of these jobs—she could make a living. Could anyone have preducted that the child itself would be carried off by a wolf? A fact! By a wolf!

"It was already late spring, long after the time when anyone fears a wolf. Who could have anticipated this one's boldness? *Ai-ya!* And now she is left only her one bare body. Her late husband's elder brother-in-law took possession of the house, and everything in it, and he drove her out without a cash. She is, in fact, in the 'no-road no-destination' predicament, and can but return to beg you to take her in once more. She no longer has any connections (such as a mother-in-law) whatever. Knowing you want to change servants, I brought her along. Since she already knows your ways, it's certain she'll be more satisfactory than a raw hand."

"I was truly stupid, truly," said Hsiang-lin Sao in a piteous voice, and lifting up her faded eyes for a moment. "I knew that when the snow lies on the mountains the wild animals will sometimes venture into the valleys and will even come into the villages in search of food. I did not know that they could be so fierce long after the coming of spring. I got up early one morning, took a small basket of beans, and told little Ah Mao to sit in the doorway and string the beans. He was very bright, and he was obedient. He always listened to every word, and this morning he did so, and I left him in the door. I myself went behind the house to chop kindling and to scour rice. I had just put the rice in the boiler and was ready to cook the beans, so I called to Ah Mao. He didn't answer. I went round to the door, but there was no Ah Mao; only beans scattered on the ground. He never wandered to play, but I hurried to each door to ask for him. Nobody had seen him. I was terror-stricken! I begged people to help me hunt for him. All the morning and into the afternoon we moved back and forth, looking into every corner. Finally we found one of his little shoes hanging on a thorn bush. From that moment every one said that he be had been seized by a wolf, but I would not believe it. After a little while, going farther into the mountains, we . . . found . . . him. Lying in a grassy lair was his partly devoured body. But the bean basket was still tightly clutched in his little hand." Here she broke down, and could only make incoherent sounds, without stringing a sentence together.

Fourth Aunt had at first hesitated, but after hearing this story her eyes reddened, and she instantly told the widow to take her things to the servants' quarters. Old Woman Wei sighed with relief, as if she had just put down a heavy bundle. Hsiang-lin Sao quieted somewhat, and without waiting for a second invitation she took her bedding-roll into the familiar room.

Thus she once more became a worker in Lo Ching, and everybody still called her Hsiang-lin Sao, after her first husband.

But she was no longer the same woman. After a few days her mistress and master noticed that she was heavy of hand and foot, that she was listless at her work, that her memory was bad, and over her corpse-like face all day there never crossed the shadow of a smile. One could tell by Fourth Aunt's tone of voice that she was already dissatisfied, and with Fourth Uncle it was the same. He had, as usual, wrinkled his brow in disapproval when she had first arrived, but since they had been having endless difficulties with servants he had raised no serious objection to the re-employment of Hsiang-lin Sao. Now, however, he informed Fourth Aunt that, though the woman's case seemed indeed very lamentable, and it was permissible because of that to give her work, still she was obviously out of tune with Heaven and Earth. She must not, therefore, be allowed to pollute precious vessels with her soiled hands, and especially on ceremonial occasions Fourth Aunt herself must prepare all food. Otherwise the ancestral spirits would be offended and, likely as not, refuse to touch a crumb.

These ancestral sacrifices were, in fact, the most important affairs in Fourth Uncle's home, for he still rigidly adhered to the old beliefs. Formerly they had been busy times for Hsiang-lin Sao also, and so the next time the altar was placed in the centre of the hall and covered with a fine cloth she began to arrange the wine cups and bowls and chopsticks on it exactly as before.

"Hsiang-lin Sao," Fourth Aunt cried, rushing in, "never mind that. I'll fix the things."

Puzzled, she withdrew and proceeded to take out the candlesticks. "Never mind that, either. I'll get the sticks," Fourth Aunt said again.

Hsiang-lin Sao walked about several times in a rather dazed manner, and ended up by finding nothing to do, for Fourth Aunt was always ahead of her. She went away suspiciously. She found the only use they had for her that day was to sit in the kitchen and keep the fire burning.

People in Lo Ching continued to call her Hsiang-lin Sao, but there was a different tone in their voices. They still talked with her, but smiled in a cool way, and with faint contempt. She did not seem to notice, or perhaps did not care. She only stared beyond them, and talked always about the thing that day and night clung to her mind.

"I was truly stupid, truly," she would repeat. "I only knew that when the snow lies on the mountains the wild animals will sometimes venture into the valleys and will even come into the villages in search of food. I did not know that they could be fierce long after the coming of spring. . . ."

Retelling her story in the same words, she would end up sobbing and striking her breast.

Every one who heard it was moved, and even the sneering men, listening, would loosen their smiles and go off in depressed spirits. The women not only forgot all their contempt for her, but at the moment forgave her entirely for her black sins—remarrying and causing the death not only of a second husband but also of his child—and in many cases ended by joining with her in weeping at the end of the tragic narrative. She talked of nothing else, only this incident that had become the central fact of her life, and she told it again and again.

Before long, however, the entire population of Lo Ching had heard her story not once but several times, and the most generous old women, even the Buddha-chanters, could not muster up a tear when she spoke of it. Nearly everybody in the town could recite the story word for word, and it bored them excessively to hear it repeated.

"I was truly stupid, truly," she would begin.

"Yes, you only knew that when the snow lies on the mountains the wild animals will sometimes venture into the valleys and will even come into the villages in search of food. . . . " Her audience would recite the next lines, cruelly cutting her short, and walk away.

With her mouth hanging open, Hsiang-lin Sao would stand stupefied for a while, stare as if seeing some one for the first time, and then drag away slowly as if weary of her continued existence. But her obsession gave her no rest, and she ingenuously tried to interest others in it by indirect approaches. Seeing a bean, a small basket, or other people's children, she would innocently lead up to the tragedy of Ah Mao. Looking at a child three or four years old, for instance, she would say:

"If Ah Mao were still here, he would be just about that size."

Frightened by the wild light in Hsiang-lin Sao's eyes, the children signalled for a retreat by pulling on their mother's skirts. She would therefore soon find herself alone again, and falter off until the next time. Pretty soon every one understood these tactics too, and made fun of her. When they saw her staring morosely at an infant they would look at her mockingly.

"Hsiang-lin Sao, if our Ah Mao were still here, wouldn't he be just about that big?"

Probably she had not suspected that her misery had long since ceased to afford any vicarious enjoyment for anyone, and that the whole episode had now become loathsome to her former sympathizers, but the meaning of this kind of mockery pierced her armour of preoccupation at last, and she understood. She glanced at the jester, but did not utter a word of response.

IV

Lo Ching never loses its enthusiasm for the celebration of New Year. Promptly after the twentieth of the Twelfth Moon the festivities begin.

Next year at this time Fourth Uncle hired an extra male worker, and in addition a certain Liu Ma, to prepare the chickens and geese. This Liu Ma was a 'good woman,' a Buddhist vegetarian who really kept her

vow not to kill living creatures. Hsiang-lin Sao, whose hands were polluted, could only feed the fire and sit watching Liu Ma working over the
sacred vessels. Outside a fine snow was matting the earth.

"*Ai-ya*, I was truly stupid," sighed Hsiang-Lin Sao, staring despondently at the sky.

"Hsiang-lin Sao, you are back on the same trail!" Liu Ma interrupted, with some exasperation. "Listen to me, is it true you got the scar
by knocking your forehead against the altar in protest?"

"Um-huh."

"I ask you this: If you hated it that much, how was it that later
on you actually submitted?"

"I?"

"Ah, you! It seems to me you must have been half-willing,
otherwise—"

"Ha, Ha! You don't understand how great were his muscles."

"No, I don't. I don't believe that strength such as your own was
not enough to resist him. It is clear to me that you must have been ready
for it yourself."

"Ah—*you!* I'd like to see you try it yourself, and see how long
you could struggle."

Liu Ma's old face crinkled into a laugh, so that it looked like a
polished walnut. Her dry eyes rested on Hsiang-lin Sao's scar for a
moment, and then sought out her eyes. She spoke again.

"You are really not very clever. One more effort that time to
really kill yourself would have been better for you. As it is, you lived with
your second man less than two years, and that is all you got for your great
crime. Just think about it: when you go into the next world you will be
held in dispute between the spirits of your two husbands. How can the
matter be settled? Only one way: Yen Lu-t'a, the Emperor of Hell, can
do nothing else but saw you in half and divide you equally between the
two men. That, I think, is a fact."

An expression of mingled fear and astonishment crept over
Hsiang-lin Sao's face. This was something she had not considered before,
had never even heard in her mountain village.

"My advice is that you'd better make amends before it is too late.
Go to the Tu-ti Temple and contribute money for a threshold. This
threshold, stepped on by a thousand, stepped over by ten thousand,* can
suffer for you and perhaps atone for the crime. Thus you may avoid
suffering after death."

Hsiang-lin Sao did not say a word, but felt intolerably crushed
with pain. Next day dark shadows encircled her eyes. Right after breakfast

---

*It is believed that the stone threshold acts as a kind of proxy body for the sinner, and every step
on it is a blow subtracted from the total punishment awaiting him in Hell.

she went off to the Tu-ti Temple to beg the priest to let her buy a new threshold. He stubbornly refused at first, and only when she released a flood of tears would he consider it. Then, unwillingly, he admitted that it might be arranged for twelve thousand cash.

She had long since stopped talking with the villagers, who shunned her and the tiresome narrative of Ah Mao's death, but news soon spread that there was a development in her case. Many people came now and inquisitively referred to the scar on her forehead.

"Hsiang-lin Sao, I ask you this: Why was it that you submitted to the man?"

"Regrettable, regrettable," sighed another, "that the knock was not deep enough."

She understood well enough the mockery and irony of their words, and she did not reply. She simply continued to perform her duties in silence. Near the end of next year's service she drew the money due to her from Fourth Aunt, exchanged it for twelve silver dollars, and asked permission to visit in the west end of the town. Before the next meal she returned, much altered. Her face no longer seemed troubled, her eyes held some life in them for the first time in months, and she was in a cheerful mood. She told Fourth Aunt that she had bought a threshold for the temple.

During the Coming-of-Winter Festival she worked tirelessly, and on the day of making sacrifices she was simply bursting with energy. Fourth Aunt brought out the holy utensils, and Ah Niu carried the altar to the centre of the room. Hsiang-lin Sao promptly went over to bring out the wine cups and chopsticks.

"Never mind," Fourth Aunt cried out. "Don't touch them."

She withdrew her hand as if it had been burned, her face turned ashen, and she did not move, but stood as if transfixed. She remained standing there, in fact, until Fourth Uncle came in to light the offertory incense, and ordered her away.

From that day she declined rapidly. It was not merely a physical impoverishment that ensued, but the spark of life in her was dimmed almost to extinction. She became extremely nervous, and developed a morbid fear of darkness or the sight of anyone, even her master or mistress. She became altogether as timid and frightened as a little mouse that has wandered from its hole to blink for a moment in the glaring light of day. In half a year her hair lost all its colour. Her memory became so clouded that she sometimes forgot even to scour the rice.

"What has got into her? How has she become like that? It's better not to have her around," Fourth Aunt began saying in her presence.

But "become like that" she had, and there did not seem to be any possibility of improving her. They talked of sending her away, or of returning her to the management of Old Woman Wei. Nothing came of it while I was still in Lo Ching, but the plan was soon afterwards carried out.

Whether Old Woman Wei actually took charge of her for a while after she left Fourth Uncle's home or whether she at once became a beggar I never learned.

I am awakened by giant crackers, and see yellow tongues of flame, and then immediately afterwards hear the sharp *pipipapao* of exploding gunpowder. It is near the Fifth Hour, and time for the prayers and blessings. Still only drowsily aware of the world, I hear far away the steady explosive notes, one after another, and then more rapidly and thickly, until the whole sky is echoing, and the whirling snowflakes, eddying out of little white balls themselves like something shot from above, hover everywhere. Within the compass of the medley of sound and gentle storm I feel somehow a nostalgic contentment, and all the brooding of the dead day and the early night is forgotten in the stir around me, lost in the air of expectancy that pervades these homes about to receive benediction.* What a satisfaction it is to understand that the Holy Spirits of Heaven and Earth, having bountifully inhaled their fill of the offertory meat and wine and incense, now limp about drunkenly in the wide air. In such a mood they are certain to dispense boundless prosperity on the good people of Lo Ching!

Reading for Understanding

Main Idea

1. Another title for this story might be (a) strange Chinese customs (b) the tyranny of mothers-in-law (c) an ill-starred life (d) a story of unrelieved cruelty.

Details

2. Hsiang-lin Sao asks the narrator questions about (a) her former employer (b) her missing child (c) her first husband (d) the soul and an afterlife.

3. In this story, the word *aged* means (a) remarried (b) dead (c) deathly ill (d) widowed.

4. The narrator uses the expression "that blown-out flicker" to refer to (a) Hsiang-lin Sao (b) Lo Shih (c) Lao-yeh (d) Fu Shing Lou.

*blessing

5. The first festival described is (a) the lunar New Year (b) the birthday of Fourth Uncle (c) the day of the spring planting (d) midsummer eve.

6. Lo Ching is the name of a (a) local magistrate (b) store proprietor (c) magician (d) community.

7. Hsiang-lin Sao was taken away by (a) the narrator (b) her mother-in-law (c) her first husband (d) Lo Shin.

8. Ah Mao was the name of (a) the narrator (b) Fourth Aunt (c) the son (d) Old Woman Wei.

9. The immediate cause of death of her second husband was (a) eating cold rice (b) a woodcutting accident (c) a heart attack (d) not mentioned.

10. Cruelly discouraging words were visited upon Hsiang-lin Sao by (a) the narrator (b) Fourth Aunt (c) Liu Ma (d) Ah Mao.

Inferences

11. Fourth Uncle (a) abused his wife (b) will be glad to see his younger relative, the narrator, leave (c) grieves deeply over the death of his former faithful servant (d) is annoyed by the fuss of cooking.

12. Upon first arriving at Lo Shih's household, Hsiang-lin Sao was (a) a poor worker (b) a disappointment to Fourth Aunt (c) a troublemaker (d) shy.

13. Hsiang-lin Sao was not allowed to participate in the rituals on her return because (a) she was a disbeliever (b) she was considered polluted (c) Fourth Aunt wanted to do the work herself (d) she was too old.

Author's Attitude

14. The author's attitude toward Hsiang-lin Sao was one of (a) discreet indifference (b) undisguised hostility (c) tender sympathy (d) reluctant disapproval.

Order of Events

15. Arrange the items in the order in which they occurred. Use letters only.
    A. Hsiang-lin Sao joins the household of Fourth Uncle for the first time.
    B. Hsiang-lin Sao dies.
    C. Fourth Aunt rehires her former servant.
    D. Hsiang-lin is taken away from the household of Fourth Uncle.
    E. Hsiang-lin Sao's second husband dies.

Words in Context

1. "The men make *obeisance* and piously invite the blessing-spirits to eat away." An **obeisance** (652) is (a) an expression of respect (b) solemn conversation (c) cooked delicacies (d) polite objections.

2. "She had trapped me, and I could only continue *placatingly*." **Placatingly** (654) means (a) sarcastically (b) soothingly (c) firmly (d) uninterruptedly.

3., 4. "I made up my mind to *extricate* myself from the mess, and wanted to *repudiate* everything I had said." **Extricate** (654) means (a) illuminate (b) insulate (c) disentangle (d) complicate. **Repudiate** (654) means (a) deny (b) confirm (c) repeat (d) recall.

5. "Even should all my replies be *refuted*, even if something happened to the woman, it could in no way concern me." **Refuted** (654) means (a) verified (b) weighed seriously (c) broadcast (d) disproved.

6. "The encounter with the woman *mendicant* impresses upon me the importance of that practice, for even in such cases the deepest wisdom lies in ambiguity." A **mendicant** (654) is a (a) marriage broker (b) unlicensed physician (c) priest (d) beggar.

7. "It is like an unlucky *presentiment* of a movement of fate." A **presentiment** (655) is (a) an appearance (b) a premonition (c) an announcement (d) a preparation.

8. "From this alone we can see that she belongs to a species utterly *devoid of* human sense!" **Devoid of** (655) means (a) blessed with (b) lacking in (c) unhappy with (d) forcibly stripped of.

9. "*Suppressing* my increasing impatience, I wait till the servant comes to fill my teapot with hot water." **Suppressing** (655) means (a) strenghtening (b) observing (c) restraining (d) baffled by.

10. "You cannot, of course, mention anything connected with death, illness, crime, and so on, unless it is absolutely *imperative*." **Imperative** (656) means (a) approved by the master (b) unexpected (c) necessary (d) in keeping with the occasion.

11. "Fourth Uncle throughout the meal wears an *austere* look on his face." **Austere** (656) means (a) stern (b) jovial (c) expectant (d) puzzled.

12. "He doesn't urge me to stay very enthusiastically, and I conclude that my *surmise* was correct." A **surmise** (656) is (a) an answer (b) a question (c) behavior (d) a guess.

13. "If they think about her at all it is simply to wonder why the devil

she should so long have had the *effrontery* to continue to exist."
Effrontery (656) is (a) nerve (b) means (c) false beliefs (d) strength.

14. "On reflection, however, he simply ended *impotently*, 'But after all
    . . .' " **Impotently** (659) means (a) suddenly (b) powerlessly (c)
    confidingly (d) confidently.

15. "In her distress, Fourth Aunt always mentioned the *exemplary*
    Hsiang-lin Sao." **Exemplary** (659) means (a) undependable (b)
    sought after (c) praiseworthy (d) powerfully built.

16. "Towards the end of the holidays Old Woman Wei called one day
    to . . . offer *felicitations*." **Felicitations** (659) are (a) festival foods
    (b) messages from relatives (c) unsought advice (d) good wishes.

17. "She had already drunk herself into semi-intoxication and was in a
    garrulous mood." **Garrulous** (660) means (a) talkative (b) mournful
    (b) quiet (d) lighthearted.

18. "The woman's case seemed indeed very *lamentable* . . . still she was
    obviously out of tune with Heaven and Earth." **Lamentable** (663)
    means (a) unusual (b) distressing (c) corrupt (d) mysterious.

19., 20. "But her *obsession* gave her no rest, and she *ingenuously* tried to
    interest others in it by indirect approaches." An **obsession** (664) (a)
    adds spice to life (b) opens doors to new interests (c) seeks to control
    its victims (d) is an attitude that wins new friends. **Ingenuously** (664)
    means (a) cleverly (b) insistently (c) occasionally (d) innocently.

21. "When they saw her staring *morosely* at an infant they would look at
    her mockingly." **Morosely** (664) means (a) gloomily (b) gleefully (c)
    wildly (d) sleepily.

22. " 'Ai-ya, I truly stupid,' sighed Hsiang-lin Sao, staring *despondently*
    at the sky." **Despondently** (665) means (a) intently (b) now and
    then (c) hopelessly (d) calmly.

Thinking Critically about the Story

1. Isn't *Benediction,* or "blessing," an odd title for such a tragic story?
   How can the narrator feel a benediction after the heartbreaking
   death of the unfortunate Hsiang-lin Sao? How has the joyous atmosphere lifted his spirits, but perhaps clouded his vision?

2. Hsiang-lin Sao has appeared in Lo Ching three times: on her first
   acceptance as a servant in Fourth Uncle's household; on her return

after the death of her child and second husband; on her reappearance ultimately to die. How does Fourth Uncle show a callous annoyance at her death? What other clues are there to portray the character of Fourth Uncle?

3. Why does the author contrast the happy activities of the coming of winter festival with the miserable situation of Hsiang-lin Sao? How does this contrast deepen the sense of tragedy?

4. How does Liu Ma, the "good woman," show a streak of cruelty in talking with Hsiang-lin Sao (665)?

5. How does Hsiang-lin Sao finally lose the good will of people who formerly pitied her? Was the change in people's attitude justifiable?

6. What specific incident involving Fourth Aunt changed Hsiang-lin Sao's personality and led to her tragic decline and death?

7. The message on the scroll (653) says, "Understand deeply the reason of things, be moderate, and be gentle in heart and manner." What does this mean to you? Do you agree with it?

8. How does the narrator ease his conscience about his own contact with Hsiang-lin Sao?

9. What is your impression of Hsiang-lin Sao through all her hardships? Was anyone in the story fair to her?

10. The six elements listed below are often considered essential parts of a typical plot (651). Though not all narratives fit into such a convenient structure, many do. Does "Benediction" qualify? Below the six elements are six events from the story, events that might be matched with the plot elements listed. Try matching them to see whether "Benediction," though long and complicated, does contain the usual structure.

    A. Situation   D. Development

    B. Complication   E. Climax

    C. Conflict   F. Outcome

(a) Hsiang-lin Sao is forcibly abducted from the household of Fourth Uncle.
(b) Hsiang-lin Sao is "strangled to death by poverty."
(c) Hsiang-lin Sao is married a second time, against her will.
(d) Haiang-lin Sao is happily working in the household of Fourth Uncle.
(e) Hsiang-lin Sao lives two years with her second husband.
(f) Hsiang-lin Sao loses her son and incessantly talks about the tragedy.

Language in Action

The Problem of Translation

> "What has happened to her?" I demand in an anxious voice.
> "Aged."
> "Dead?" My heart twinges and seems to jump back; my face burns.

This brief segment reflects some of the difficulties of translation. The best translation cannot quite capture all the subtleties of the original. No translation can be 100 percent faithful to the original text. Though two languages may be similar in origin and vocabulary, words develop different literal meanings (denotation) and associated meanings (connotation).

Sometimes even simple, seemingly obvious words do not have exact equivalents in other languages. In *Explorations in Awareness*, J. Samuel Bois tells of an experience he had in translating a word into another language. He is a Canadian whose native language is French. When he tried to translate the French word *fleuve* into English, he found the word *river* in the dictionary. But the translation for *riviere* was also *river*. French has two distinct words: *fleuve* and *riviere*; yet both words have only one English equivalent.

He found a problem in reverse when he had to translate English into French. The English *giggle* has the corresponding French word *ricaner*. Then he found a number of other, related English words all translated by the one French word *ricaner*. Each language makes distinctions that the other doesn't.

In our own sample above, the unusual Chinese word for *aged* instead of *dead* is so puzzling it requires a footnote. Fourth Uncle is another phrase unique to the Chinese. Most of the time the translation is quite adequate, capturing the spirit and sense of the original. In *Casablanca*, Rick says, "Here's looking at you, kid." The French subtitle in the movie had "Bonne chance," *good luck!* Idioms (430) are translated literally, but the spirit can sometimes be captured in words seemingly unrelated.

Bontshe the Silent

Isaac Peretz
Polish

**"Gentlemen judges," begins a strident, incisive, and sting-
ing voice—but stops short.**

**"Gentlemen," he begins again, this time more softly but
once more he interrupts himself.**

**And at last, very soft, a voice issues from the throat of the
accuser:**

"Gentlemen judges! He was silent! I shall be silent too."

"Bontshe the Silent" is a fitting story to end a book. The story
begins in tears and ends in joy and laughter. In his lifetime, Bontshe
was a lost soul. Few knew and no one cared that he existed. He lived
a simple life as a poor man—not a giant of intellect or a powerful leader
of others. He was merely "Bontshe the Silent."

On his death, Bontshe appears before the heavenly tribunal for
judging. What does this poor soul have to offer in his own behalf? By
most of the standards of the world, Bontshe is a failure. What can he
expect from the tribunal where there can be no delusion, no deception, no pretense, no self-promotion?

This lovely fanciful tale was written in Yiddish by the Polish
author Isaac Peretz. It raises questions about what is "most worth,"
how a person should be judged. It uses a trial to determine whether
Bontshe will receive in heaven the kind of mistreatment and negative
evaluation he suffered on earth.

The story has been cited for its perfect example of a "characteristic last act." Even in heaven, it seems, Bontshe is still Bontshe.

Bontshe the Silent

HERE, in this world below, the death of Bontshe produced no impression whatever. In vain you will ask: "Who was Bontshe? How did he live? What did he die of? Was it his heart that burst, his strength that gave out, or his dorsal spine that broke under a burden too heavy for his shoulders?" No one knows. Maybe it was hunger that killed him.

Had a dray horse fallen dead in the street, people would have displayed much more interest than they did in this case of a poor man. The newspapers would have reported the incident, and some of us would have hurried to the spot to look at the carcass and examine the place where the accident had occurred. But were there as many horses as there were men—a thousand millions—then even a horse would not have received such distinction.

Bontshe had lived quietly, and quietly died; like a shadow he passed over the face of the earth. When he celebrated his confirmation he made no brilliant speech. He lived, a grain of sand on the sea shore, among the millions of its kind. And when the wind at last carried him off to the other side, no one noticed it. In his life-time the dust of the roads kept no impression of his footsteps, and after his death the wind swept away the small board over his grave. The grave-digger's wife found it at some distance from the grave and made a fire with it to boil a pot of potatoes. Three days after Bontshe's death you would ask the grave-digger in vain to show you the spot where he had buried him.

Had there been a tombstone over Bontshe's grave, a learned archaeologist might have discovered it after a century, and once more the name of Bontshe would have been heard among us. He was only a shadow. No head or heart preserved his image, and no trace remained of his memory.

He left behind neither child nor property. He had lived miserably, and miserably he died. Had it not been for the noise of the crowd, someone might, by accident, have heard how Bontshe's vertebral column was snapping under a too heavy burden. Had the world had more time, someone might have noticed that during his life Bontshe's eyes were already dim and his cheeks terribly hollow. He might have noticed that even when he was not carrying loads on his shoulders his head was always bent to the ground, as if he were looking for his grave. Had there been as few poor people as there are horses someone might, perhaps, have asked: "What has become of Bontshe?"

When they took him to the hospital, Bontshe's corner in his

basement hovel did not for long remain unoccupied; ten people of his kind were already waiting for it, and they knocked it down among themselves to the highest bidder. When they carried him from his hospital bed to the mortuary chamber, twenty poor patients were already waiting for the place vacated. And scarcely had Bontshe left the morgue, when twenty corpses extricated from underneath the ruins of a fallen house were brought in.

Who knows how long he will remain undisturbed in his grave? Who knows how many corpses are already waiting for the piece of ground he is buried in? Born quietly, he lived in silence, died in silence, and was buried in a silence even greater.

But it was not thus that things happened in the *other* world. There, the death of Bontshe produced a deep impression, a veritable sensation. The bugle-call of the Messiah, the sound of the ram's horn, was heard throughout the seven heavens: "Bontshe the Silent has died." Broad-winged archangels were flying about, announcing to each other that Bontshe had been summoned to appear before the Supreme Judgment Seat. In Paradise there was a noise, an excitement, and one could hear the joyful shout: "Bontshe the Silent! Just think of it! Bontshe the Silent!"

Very young angels, with eyes of diamond, gold-threaded wings, wearing silver slippers, were rushing out, full of joy, to meet Bontshe. The buzzing of their wings, the clatter of their small slippers, and the merry laughter of those dainty, fresh, and rosy little mouths, filled the heavens and reached the throne of the Most High. God himself knew that Bontshe was coming—

The Patriarch Abraham stationed himself at the gate of heaven, stretching out his right hand to Bontshe in cordial welcome: "Peace be with you," a sweet smile illuminating his delighted old countenance.

What means this rumbling and rolling here in heaven? Two angels were rolling an armchair of pure gold for Bontshe. Whence this luminous flash of light? It was a golden crown, set with the most precious stones, that they were carrying—for Bontshe!

"But the Supreme Court has not yet pronounced judgment?" ask the astonished saints, not without a tinge of jealousy.

"Bah!" reply the angels, "that will only be a formality. Against Bontshe, even the attorney for the prosecution himself will not find a word to say. The case will not last five minutes. Don't you know who Bontshe is? He is of some importance, this Bontshe."

When the little angels seized Bontshe in mid-air and played a sweet tune to him; when the Patriarch Abraham shook hands with him as if he had been an old comrade; when he learned that his chair was ready for him in Paradise and that a crown was waiting for his head, that before the Celestial Tribunal not one superfluous word would be spoken in his

case, Bontshe, as once upon earth, was frightened into silence. He was
sure that it could only be a dream from which he would soon awake, or
simply a mistake.

He was used to both. More than once, when he was still on earth,
he had dreamed of picking up money from the ground. Veritable treasures were lying there!—and yet—when he awoke in the morning, he was
more miserable and poorer than ever. More than once it had happened
to him that someone in the street had smiled at him and spoken a kind
word to him. But when he found out his mistake, the stranger turned and
spat out in disgust, full of contempt. "Just my luck," thought Bontshe,
scarcely daring to raise his eyes, afraid lest the dream should disappear.
He trembles at the thought of suddenly waking up in some horrible
cavern full of serpents and lizards. He is careful not to let the slightest
sound escape his mouth, to stir or move a limb for fear of being recognized and hurled into the abyss. He trembles violently, and does not hear
the compliments paid him by the angels, nor does he notice how they are
dancing around him. He pays no heed to the Patriarch's cordial "Peace
be with you," nor does he even wish good-morning to the celestial court
when he is at last brought in. He is simply beside himself with fear.

His fear increased greatly when his eyes involuntarily fell upon
the flooring of the Supreme Court of Justice. It was of pure alabaster,
inset with diamonds. "And my feet," thought Bontshe, "are treading
such a floor!" He grew quite rigid. "Who knows," he thought, "what rich
man, what Rabbi, what saint they are expecting? He will soon arrive and
mine will be a sad end!"

Terror-stricken, he did not even hear the President of the Court
call out in a loud voice: "The case of Bontshe the Silent!" He did not
hear how, handing over a dossier to the counsel for the defence, he
commanded: "Read, but briefly." All around Bontshe the whole hall
seemed to be turning. A muffled noise reached his ears, but in the midst
of the din he began to distinguish more clearly and sharply the voice of
the angelic advocate—a voice as sweet as a violin:

"His name," the voice was saying, "suited him even as a gown
made by an artist's hand suits a graceful body."

"What is he talking about?" Bontshe asks himself. And then he
heard an impatient voice interrupting the speaker:

"No metaphors, please."

"Never," continues the advocate, "never has he uttered a complaint against God or men. Never has a spark of hatred flamed up in his
eyes, never has he lifted his eyes with pretensions to heaven."

Again Bontshe fails to understand what it is all about, but once
more the stern voice interrupts the speaker:

"No rhetoric, please."

"Job succumbed, but Bontshe has suffered more than Job."

"Facts, bare facts, please," the President emphatically calls again.

"He was always silent," the advocate proceeds, "even when his mother died and at the age of thirteen there came a stepmother, a serpent, a wicked woman."

"Perhaps after all he means me," thinks Bontshe to himself.

"No insinuations, please, against third persons," angrily says the President.

"She used to begrudge him a piece of bread; throw him a few musty crusts three days old and a mouthful of gristle for meat, whilst she herself drank coffee with cream."

"Come to business!" cries the President.

"She never spared him her fingernails, blows, or cuffs, and through the holes of his miserable musty rags there peeped out the blue and black body of the child. Barefooted he used to chop wood for her in winter, in the biting frost. His hands were too young and too weak to wield the dull ax, and the blocks were too big. More than once did he sprain his wrists, more than once were his feet frozen, but he remained silent. He was silent even before his father—"

"Oh, yes, the drunkard," laughs the accusing attorney, and Bontshe feels cold all over.

"Even to his father he never complained," the advocate concludes.

"He was always miserable and alone, had no friends, no schooling, no religious instruction, no decent clothes and not a minute of respite."

"Facts, facts," the President once more interrupts.

"He was silent even later, when his own father, the worse for drink, seized him by the hair and threw him out of the house on a bitterly cold and snowy winter night. He picked himself up from the snow, without weeping, and ran whither his eyes carried him. He was silent during his lonely walk, and when the pangs of hunger began to torture him, he begged only with his eyes.

"On a wet and foggy spring night he reached a large town. He entered it like some drop of water that is falling into the ocean, but he nevertheless passed his first night in the police jail. He was silent, without asking the why or wherefore. Set free, he started to look for work, for the hardest work possible; but he was silent. What was even harder than work itself, was the finding of it, and he was silent. He was always silent. Splashed by the mud thrown at him by strangers, spat upon by strangers, driven with his heavy load from the sidewalk into the midst of the road, among cabs, cars, coaches, and vehicles of every sort—at every instant looking death in the face, he remained silent. Bathed in a cold sweat, crushed under the heavy loads he was carrying, his stomach empty and tortured, he was silent.

"He never calculated how many pounds he was carrying for a farthing, how often he stumbled for a penny and how many errands he had to run, how many times he almost breathed his last when going to collect his pay. He was always silent. He never dared to raise his voice when asking for his pay, but like a beggar or a dog he stood at the door and his dumb and humble request could only be read in his eyes. 'Come later,' he was told, and he disappeared like a shadow until later, when he would ask even more quietly, nay *beg* for his due. He was silent even when people haggled over his pay, knocked off something from it, or slipped a counterfeit coin into his hand. He was always silent!"

"Then after all it is me that they mean," Bontshe consoles himself.

"One wonderful day Bontshe's fortune changed," proceeded the advocate, after taking a drink of water. "Two spirited, frightened, runaway horses were rushing by, dragging a rich coach with rubber wheels. With a broken skull the driver lay way back on the pavement. Foam was spurting from the mouths of the animals, sparks flew from their hoofs, and their eyes shone like glowing coals on a dark night. In the coach, there sat a man, more dead than alive. Bontshe stopped the runaway horses. The man whose life he had thus saved was a Jew; he proved to be of a charitable disposition and was grateful to Bontshe. He handed over to him the whip of his dead coachman, and Bontshe became a coachman. The charitable man even found him a wife. He did more: he provided Bontshe with a child. And Bontshe always kept silent."

"They mean me; they mean me!" thought Bontshe, strengthening himself in his belief; but nevertheless he dared not raise his eyes on the august tribunal. Still he listened to his angelic advocate.

"Bontshe was silent," continued the latter, "even when his benefactor became bankrupt and neglected to pay Bontshe his wages. He was silent when his wife ran away from him, leaving him alone with an infant in arms. He was silent even fifteen years later, when the same child grew up till he was strong enough to throw the father out of his own house."

"They mean me, they mean me!" Bontshe thinks joyfully.

"He was silent," continued the defending angel, as his voice grew still softer and more sad, "when his former benefactor paid all his creditors except Bontshe, to whom he did not give a penny. And when, riding again in his coach with rubber tires and with horses like lions, the benefactor one day ran over him, Bontshe still kept silent. He did not even tell the police. Even in the hospital where one is allowed to cry, he kept silent! He was silent even when the house physician refused to approach his bed unless he had paid him fifteen coppers, or when the attendant refused to change his bed linen unless he gave him five coppers.

"He was silent in his death agony, he was silent in his last hour.

Never did he utter a word against God, never a word against man. . . . I have spoken!"

Bontshe began to tremble in his whole body. He knew that after the speech for the defence it was the turn of the prosecution. "What will the prosecuting counsel say now?" Bontshe did not remember his life. Down *below* he used to forget everything the moment it occurred. The angel advocate had recalled to his mind all his past. Who knows what the prosecuting angel will recall to his memory?

"Gentlemen judges," begins a strident, incisive, and stinging voice—but stops short.

"Gentlemen," he begins again, this time more softly but once more he interrupts himself.

And at last, very soft, a voice issues from the throat of the accuser:

"Gentlemen judges! He was silent! I shall be silent too."

Profound silence fell over the assembly. Then from above a new soft, sweet, and trembling voice is heard:

"Bontshe, my child, Bontshe," said the voice, and it sounded like a harp. "Bontshe, my well-beloved child."

And Bontshe's heart begins to weep for joy. He would like to raise his eyes, but they are dimmed by tears. Never in his life had he felt such joy in weeping.

"My child, my well-beloved!" Since his mother's death he had never heard such a voice or such words.

"My child," continues the President of the Celestial Tribunal, "you have suffered everything in silence. There is not a limb in your body that is whole, not a bone that is intact, not a corner in your soul that is not bleeding—and you have always kept silent.

"Down below upon the earth they never understood such things. You yourself were not aware of your power; you did not know that you could cry and that your cries would have caused the very walls of Jericho to tremble and tumble down. You yourself did not know what strength lay hidden in you. Down below your silence was not rewarded, but down below is the world of delusion, whilst here in heaven is the world of truth, here you will reap your reward.

"The Supreme Tribunal will never pass sentence against you; it will never judge and condemn you, nor will it mete out to you such and such a reward. Everything here belongs to you; take whatever your heart desires."

For the first time Bontshe ventures to lift his eyes. He is dazzled by so much light and splendor. Everything is sparkling, everything around him is flashing, beams are issuing from all sides, and he droops his weary eyes once more.

"Really?" he asks, still doubting and embarrassed.

"Yes, really," replies the President of the Celestial Tribunal; "verily I tell you that it is so indeed, and that everything here is yours; everything in heaven belongs to you. All the brightness and the splendor you perceive is only the reflection of your own silent goodness of heart, the reflection of your own pure soul. You will only be drawing from your own source."

"Really?" Bontshe asks again, but this time his voice sounds more firm and assured.

"Certainly, certainly, certainly," he is assured on all sides.

"Then, if such is the case," says Bontshe with a happy smile, "I should like to have every morning a hot roll with fresh butter."

Abashed, angels and judges drooped their heads; while the accuser burst out into loud laughter.

Reading for Understanding

Main Idea

1. This is the story of (a) a truly good man (b) a life of no accomplishment (c) revenge (d) misunderstandings.

Details

2. "Serpent, wicked woman" is used to describe Bontshe's (a) wife (b) ungrateful son (c) stepmother (d) benefactor.

3. For saving the life of a wealthy man, Bontshe was at first (a) sent to Warsaw (b) made a coachman (c) given no reward (d) given half the man's fortune.

4. Bontshe was owed money by his (a) father (b) son (c) runaway wife (d) benefactor.

Inferences

5. Bontshe's death caused a stir in heaven because of his (a) blameless life (b) forgiveness of his wife (c) heroic death (d) confidence in his own saintliness.

6. Which of the following is an example of irony (264–265)?

   (a) Barefooted he used to chop wood for her in winter, in the biting frost.

(b) He was always miserable and alone.

(c) He was silent, without asking the why or wherefore.

(d) "Who knows what rich man, what Rabbi, what saint they are expecting?"

7. The prosecuting angel (a) disapproved of Bontshe (b) had no evil deeds to report (c) used trickery in his attack (d) was shouted down by other angels.

8. Bontshe's request was (a) expected by the angels (b) excessive (c) ridiculously modest (d) never made orally.

9. The best adjective to apply to Bontshe is (a) grasping (b) uncomplaining (c) proud (d) dissatisfied.

Fact or Opinion

Tell whether the following is a fact or an opinion.

10. Bontshe should have stood up for himself when he was poorly treated.

Words in Context

1. "And scarcely had Bontshe left the morgue, when twenty corpses *extricated* from underneath the ruins of a fallen house were brought in." **Extricated** (675) means (a) discovered (b) abandoned (c) toppled (d) freed.

2. "There, the death of Bontshe produced a deep impression, a *veritable* sensation." **Veritable** (675) means (a) true (b) uncommon (c) understated (d) brief.

3. "He did not hear how, handing over a *dossier* to the counsel for the defense, he commanded: 'Read, but briefly.'" A **dossier** (676) is a (a) legal complaint (b) kind of fiction (c) challenge (d) bundle of documents.

4. "'Never has he lifted his eyes with *pretensions* to heaven.'" **Pretensions** (676) means (a) pleadings (b) complaints (c) cries of rage (d) claims.

5. "'Job *succumbed,* but Bontshe has suffered more than Job.'" **Suc-**

cumbed (676) means (a) prevailed (b) rejoiced (c) was defeated (d) relayed.

6. "She used to *begrudge* him a piece of bread; throw him a few musty crusts." **Begrudge** (677) means (a) allot (b) dislike giving (c) give with ceremony (d) share fairly.

7., 8. " 'Gentlemen judges,' begins a *strident, incisive,* and stinging voice—but stops short." **Strident** (679) means (a) harsh-sounding (b) low key (c) repressed (d) colorless. **Incisive** (679) means (a) pleasant (b) penetrating (c) thoughtful (d) unfriendly.

9. " 'There is not a limb in your body that is whole, not a bone that is *intact.*' " **Intact** (679) means (a) reinforced (b) unharmed (c) useful (d) stressed.

10. "The Supreme Tribunal will never pass sentence against you; it will never judge and condemn you, nor will it *mete* out to you such and such a reward." **Mete** (679) means (a) measure (b) transfer (c) confirm (d) reserve.

11. " 'Yes, really,' replies the President of the Celestrial Tribunal; '*verily* I tell you that it is so indeed, and that everything here is yours; everything in heaven belongs to you.'" **Verily** (679) means (a) hesitantly (b) loudly (c) carefully (d) truly.

12. "*Abashed,* angels and judges drooped their heads; while the accuser burst out into loud laughter." **Abashed** (680) means (a) amazed (b) pleased (c) embarrassed (d) momentarily angry.

Thinking Critically about the Story

1. Of the following world leaders, which one most closely accepted a philosophy similar to Bontshe's: Winston Churchill, Mahatma Gandhi, Franklin D. Roosevelt, Josef Stalin? Justify your choice.

2. What do you think the author's purpose was in writing "Bontshe the Silent"?

3. Why do good people suffer? In the Bible, Job is a symbol of suffering virtue. He becomes a test of righteousness in the face of despair. Because of a debate between God and Satan, Job's family and possessions are taken from him. He is covered with sores and suffers physical torment. Though Job eventually comes through his troubles and finds wealth and happiness, there were times when he bewailed

his fate. Why does the story mention Job (676)? How does Bontshe differ from Job?

4. At what point does Bontshe begin to realize that the trial is going his way?

5. Some plays and stories end with a "characteristic last act," an action typical of the central character. Episodes of *Murder, She Wrote*, for example, ended with Angela Lansbury's gentle laughter after the resolution of the problem. What is Bontshe's last action? Is it typical?

6. In the face of life's problems, does your own philosophy lean toward acceptance and pacifism or struggle and activism? Which seems to you a better course? Is a blend sometimes best?

Language in Action

Homonyms and Related Words

"The Supreme Tribunal will never pass sentence against you; it will never judge and condemn you, nor will it mete out to you such and such a reward."

Mete belongs to a common class of words in English: words that are spelled differently but pronounced alike: *mete, meet, meat.* The word *homonym* has won wide acceptance to mean "one of two or more words pronounced alike but having different spellings and meanings." Such words are also sometimes called *homophones.* Words that are spelled and pronounced alike but with different meanings are also called *homonyms:* bear—carry; bear—animal. Pairs like lead (metal)—lead (guide) and tear (drop)—tear (rip), which are spelled alike but differ in meaning and pronunciation, are called heteronyms or homographs.

The Greek roots help you to remember the meanings:

homonym = *homo,* same + *onym,* name

homophone = *homo,* same + *phon,* sound

homograph = *homo,* same + *graph,* writing (spelling)

heteronym = *hetero,* other + *onym,* name

Can you distinguish the meaning of each word in the following pairs?

ascent, assent
capital, capitol
coarse, course
fair, fare
groan, grown
hail, hale
hear, here
hew, hue
it's, its
main, mane

muscle, mussel
ode, owed
plain, plane
profit, prophet
rap, wrap
read, reed
stationary, stationery
steal, steel
thyme, time
yolk, yoke

The World Over

Thinking Critically about the Stories

1. Select a story that could be transferred to an American setting without loss of effectiveness. Justify your choice.

2. In the movie *Independence Day,* all nations join against the common enemy, the alien invaders. Is not the common enemy of all nations hunger, poverty, hatred? How far should the United States go in assuming world leadership against the common enemies?

3. Hsiang-lin Sao in "Benediction" and Raicharan in "My Lord, the Baby" suffered far beyond the normal allotment of misfortune. Which life seems to you more tragic? Why?

4. "They shall beat their swords into plowshares and their spears into pruning-hooks; nation shall not lift up sword against nation, neither shall they learn war any more."

   —Isaiah 2:4

   How does this statement compare with Franklin Delano Roosevelt's (607)? Is the goal attainable? What are some of the obstacles to overcome?

5. "If there is righteousness in the heart there will be beauty in the character. If there be beauty in the character, there will be harmony in the home. If there is harmony in the home, there will be order in the nation. When there is order in the nation, there will be peace in the world"

   —Chinese proverb

   Is the proverb a realistic blueprint for world peace? Present your own viewpoint.

6. "It is better to be a dog in peaceful times than a man in times of unrest."

   —Chinese proverb

   Another proverb says, "May you live in uninteresting times!" What do these two mean? Would you prefer to live in "uninteresting times"?

7. Which story could best be expanded into a novel? Justify your choice.

685

Other Areas of Communication

1. The trial scene of "Bontshe the Silent" lends itself to dramatization. Cast the little play and perform it in class. One character will be needed for the nonspeaking part.

2. The name *Job* appears in certain expressions like *poor as Job* and *the patience of Job. Job's tears* are seeds sometimes used as beads. The most interesting allusion is *Job's comforter.* Your dictionary will provide a simple definition, but for a more complete and helpful description, consult *The Encyclopedia of Word and Phrase Origins,* by Robert Hendrickson, published by Facts on File, or another book of allusions.

3. Which story is the one you'll be likely to remember for some time to come? Why? Hold a class discussion on enduring elements in fiction.

4. "The Stream of Days" could be the basis of a television documentary on life as a student in Cairo, Egypt. If you were filming the documentary, how would you go about it? What features would you emphasize? Present your plan to the class.

5. If you have tapes of music from other lands, prepare to bring one to class. Point out elements you consider different from those the class is familiar with.

The Writing Portfolio

A Look Back and a Look Ahead

If you have followed the units in this anthology in sequence, you now have a considerable body of writing in your portfolio. Even if you have skipped here and there, you will have valuable samples of your writing prowess. Do not discard your work. You will find yourself referring to the portfolio from time to time. Whatever you have learned can be kept fresh by looking back now and then at this important achievement.

For this final unit, suggestions will help you review all your writing and all your reading. The following ideas for follow-up should provide a fitting climax to the book.

1. Complete three of the following sentences, keeping in mind the suggestions on pages 81–83. Give reasons. Be specific.
   (a) For me, the most memorable character in this anthology was . . .
   (b) The story, in the book, that surprised me most was . . .
   (c) In general, the type of story I prefer is . . .
   (d) In poetry, I was surprised to learn that . . .
   (e) The unit that most appealed to me was . . .

2. Complete the paragraph (152) of which the following is the topic sentence:

   The computer and the Internet will (or will not) ultimately destroy the effectiveness and value of the written word.

3. Can you suggest a better title for this book? Give your views in three or four well developed paragraphs. Demonstrate your acquaintance with several selections.

4. Recall the setting of each selection in this unit. Which seemed to you most exotic, least like the world you live in? Develop your point in three or four well-structured paragraphs.

5. Did something you learned in another school subject deepen your appreciation and understanding of a selection in this book? For example, a knowledge of Corsican life and history would deepen appreciation of "Matteo Falcone."

6. How do you picture yourself five or ten years in the future? Write a description of that future scenario.

7. Write a theme listing your present goals. Save this paper and read it again years hence to see how well you achieved those goals.

SAVE THIS PORTFOLIO!

Language in Action—a Review

You may refer to the preceding pages to answer these questions.

1. All these are examples of nonverbal communication EXCEPT (a) gestures (b) facial expressions (c) exclamations (d) silence.

2. In traveling abroad, tourists should be particularly careful in using (a) questions (b) foreign road maps (c) clothing (d) gestures.

3. Of the following, the word that usually holds the warmest feelings is (a) *abode* (b) *home* (c) *dwelling* (d) *house*.

4. It may truthfully be said about synonyms that (a) no two are inter-changeable in all contexts (b) every word has a dozen synonyms in English (c) *grim* and *ghastly* are exact synonyms (d) the wealth of synonyms in English can be a disadvantage for writers.

5. *Troubled* is (a) a possible antonym of *clear* (b) a synonym of *humble* (c) a word without an antonym (d) rarely used outside medical situations.

6. E-Prime (a) is a term used in mathematics (b) recommends a flowery style of writing (c) avoids the use of *is* (d) is desirable but impossible to use.

7. A problem of translation is that (a) foreign languages: have more words than English (b) few words in different languages are exactly alike (c) translators use imperfect reference books (d) it's impossible to give the sense of a statement in a different language.

8. All the following are homonyms EXCEPT (a) *hear—here* (b) *bass* (voice)—*bass* (fish) (c) *eight—ate* (d) *pine* (tree)—*pine* (long for).

9. *Stationery* means *letter paper; stationary* means (a) not movable (b) cardboard envelope (c) pertaining to a train (d) faithful to a cause.

10. Two words often paired are (a) *heteronym* and *homonym* (b) *homo-phone* and *homograph* (c) *homonym* and *homophone* (d) *heteronym* and *homophone*.

Index to
Language in Action

Language in Action

G

generalizations, 136
Germanic basis,
   397–398, 539, 639

gestures, 618

Greek contribution,
   368, 412–413

H

haiku, 453, 483–484
heteronyms, 683
homographs, 683

homonyms, 683–684
homophones, 683
humor, 357–358, 494

hyphen, 421

I

iamb, 475, 493
idioms, 430–431, 672

imagery, 450
intonation, 126–127

irony, 264–265, 455

J

judgment words,
   108–109, 118, 239

L

labeling, 118–119, 239
Latin contribution,

209, 369, 390–391,
539

Latin phrases in Eng-
   lish, 245
levels of usage, 530–531

M

malapropisms, 438–439
metaphor, 22, 150,
   350, 450, 459

meter, 475
metonymy, 459

mythology, 223, 458

N

new words, 332, 413,
   507

nonverbal communica-
   tion, 617–618

Norman Conquest,
   397–398

O

objective writing,
   239–240, 571

Old English, 368–369,
   390, 539, 560

omniscient point of
   view, 174
onomatopoeia, 201, 450

Glossary

Glossary

The best way to build a vocabulary is to meet new words in helpful contexts. A word's context is the setting it appears in, all the other words around it. The following list contains a great many new words that are worth adding to your word store.

All the words in the list appear in the stories you have read. Here you will find helpful definitions. In addition, you will meet the words in new contexts, sentences designed to suggest the meaning of the listed words. These sentences, together with the contexts in which the words originally appeared, will help you add the words to your use vocabulary.

A

abashed (680) embarrassed, ashamed, dismayed.
> Though he tripped on the steps to the stage, Fred was not abashed and proceeded on with a firm step to receive his diploma.

abominable (628) repulsive, hateful, horrible.
> Conditions in the Rwandan refugee camp were abominable until international agencies stepped in.

abridge (577) shorten, abbreviate, condense.
> A desk-top dictionary tends to abridge the contents of a larger dictionary.

abstracted (271) inattentive, thoughtful, absentminded.
> Lil may seem abstracted at times, but she is rarely unaware of the conversations around her.

abyss (36, 647) gulf, gorge, ravine, void.
> The cable car hung limply over the abyss until the power was restored.

acclaimed (91) applauded, approved, praised.
> *Casablanca* has been acclaimed as one of the ten best pictures of all times.

accosting (594) addressing, approaching, encountering.
> After accosting the dignified gentleman on the steps of the Capitol, Dan realized he had made a mistake.

acumen (418) keenness, shrewdness, cleverness.
> Acumen is extremely important in business success, but a bit of luck doesn't hurt.

adversaries (635) foes, enemies, opponents.
> Florida and Florida State have been football adversaries for many years.

adversity (384) misfortune, hardship, suffering.

David Copperfield showed great courage during periods of mistreatment and adversity.

affable (229, 275) agreeable, gracious, friendly.

Underneath his hypocritically affable manner, Uriah Heep was a hard and vicious person.

altruistic (296) unselfish, kind-hearted, humanitarian.

Naomi's actions were entirely altruistic, without thought of any benefit to herself.

ambiance (214) atmosphere, environment, mood.

There is a certain ambiance in the gathering of a happy family at Thanksgiving.

ambivalent (216) uncertain, conflicting, unsure.

Sinbad was ambivalent about leaving his home again, but the lure of the sea sent him forth on another voyage.

ambrosia (163) food of the gods, something very pleasing.

The root beer at the end of a long and difficult tennis match was like ambrosia to him.

amenities (214) pleasantries, contributions to social gatherings.

The buyer and seller of the house exchanged amenities before beginning the hard bargaining.

amiable (274, 574) pleasant, good-natured, agreeable.

In the short story "The Most Dangerous Game," the outwardly amiable manner of General Zaroff concealed a killer instinct.

amiabilities (215) pleasantnesses, friendlinesses.

The amiabilities of the Palmer family have won them a legion of friends.

amicably (579) agreeably, in a friendly fashion.

Through the efforts of a third neighbor, the dispute between the Carters and the Adamsons was settled amicably.

anarchists (408) rebels against all authority.

In Russia before World War I, the Anarchists helped pave the way for revolution.

anarchy (216) lawlessness, disorder, chaos.

For a brief period during every civil riot, anarchy reigns and shows what can happen when lawlessness rules.

anguish (632) agony, misery, distress.

The disappearance of the cat Muffy caused the family as much anguish as losing a close friend.

anguished (645) distressed, tormented.

When Angela came upon the smoldering ruins of her house, she gave an anguished cry.

anodyne (212) painkiller, relief, balm.

When Jeremy is troubled by his many problems, he uses detective stories as an anodyne.

apoplexy (416) stroke.

When the news of his financial ruin reached him, the fatigued industrialist suffered apoplexy and died.

apparition (576) ghost, shade, hallucination.

When Dr. Manette appeared after hearing the tragic news from France, he seemed more like an apparition than a flesh-and-blood person.

appendages (400) branches, arms, attachments.
> In some science-fiction movies, the aliens sport all kinds of weird appendages.

apprehension (214, 326) worry, dread, concern.
> When Jason heard the doorbell ring, a shiver of apprehension went through him.

apprehensive (167) uneasy, anxious, nervous.
> In *Les Miserables,* Jean Valjean is apprehensive about the pitiless pursuit by the policeman Javert.

apprehensively (229) uneasily, fearfully, anxiously.
> During the blitz, Londoners waited apprehensively for the next wave of Nazi bombers.

aquiline (587) hooked, curved, like an eagle's beak.
> On the coins of the Roman Empire, the emperors are shown realistically, with their jutting chins and aquiline noses.

arbitrarily (448) high-handedly, obstinately, willfully.
> Josef Stalin arbitrarily decided to eliminate millions of peasant farmers.

ardently (595) passionately, fervently, emotionally.
> Supreme Court Justice Felix Frankfurter ardently supported the cause of minorities.

ardor (291, 580) warmth, intensity, enthusiasm.
> The ardor of football fans has provided a twelfth player for the home team.

arduous (53) strenuous, exhausting, difficult.
> Replacing the roof timbers blown off by the hurricane was a long and arduous task.

aria (404) air, melody, especially as sung in opera by a single voice.
> The arias of Tosca in Puccini's opera are haunting and powerful.

ascribed (466) credited, assigned, attributed.
> Poems ascribed to the Celtic poet Ossian were later shown to have been written by an 18th-century poet, James MacPherson.

askance (34) with a side glance, scornfully.
> The drill sergeant looked askance at the green recruits as they filed out of the barracks.

assailed (631) attacked, assaulted, charged.
> The judge assailed Charles Darnay for his lineage, not for any evil actions.

assuage (25) relieve, moderate, lessen.
> Ice on a just-sprained ankle can assuage the pain.

atrocious (75) horrible, shocking, dreadful.
> News of the atrocious events at the Nazi extermination camps began to leak to the outside world.

audacious (311) bold, daring, courageous.
> In the Battle of the Bulge, the Germans made one last audacious move to roll back the allied advance.

aura (402) atmosphere, character, tone.
> There was an aura of greatness about George Washington that deeply impressed his fellow Americans.

austere (656) stern, severe, strict.

> The austere demeanor of the cold Mr. Murdstone frightened David Copperfield.

autocrat (271) dictator, absolute ruler.

> In his own household, Father Clarence Day was an autocrat, but a kindly one.

avariciously (65) greedily, selfishly, stingily.

> At first, Silas Marner avariciously guarded his wealth, but the physical wealth was replaced for him by the child Eppie.

aversion to (363) dislike of, hatred for, prejudice against.

> Larry loves sweet pickles but has an aversion to dill.

axiom (487) self-evident truth.

> The American Constitutional system of checks and balances demonstrates an axiom of good government.

B

begrudge (535, 677) resent, grudge, envy.

> Scrooge was so greedy, he would begrudge his employees the slightest pleasure.

belied (271) contradicted, misrepresented, denied.

> The modest car driven by John Shubert belied his great wealth and power.

bellicose (58) aggressive, hostile, warlike.

> Adolf Hitler's bellicose attacks upon the Czechs preceded his invasion of their homeland.

benighted (344) unenlightened, overtaken by darkness or night.

> At times, Father Clarence Day considered his sons benighted idiots, but he never lost his great love for them.

bequest (485) inheritance, legacy.

> Part of the philanthropist's bequest was a substantial grant to our town library.

bizarre (401) strange, odd, weird.

> Prizes were awarded for the most bizarre costumes on Halloween night.

blight (343) disease, affliction, sickness.

> A blight destroyed most of America's elm trees.

bludgeon (91) club, cudgel, heavy stick.

> The victim had obviously been struck by a bludgeon wielded with great force.

brevity (453) briefness, shortness, conciseness.

> President Calvin Coolidge was famous for the brevity of his speech . . . in conversation or on public occasions.

burly (243) heavily built, husky.

> The team of burly players was ready to fight.

burnished (217, 592) made shiny, polished.

> The burnished shields dazzled the Gauls as the Roman army advanced in disciplined formation.

C

cache (52) hiding place, vault, repository.

> When discovered, the nest of the pack rat included many lost household items.

calyxes (541) flower parts.

The calyxes of the poinsettia were a beautiful green.

cantankerous (242) unfriendly, ill-natured, quarrelsome.

A stock figure in fiction is the cantankerous old man who really has a heart of gold.

caprice (587) whim, impulse, notion.

As a logical, unemotional person, Lou never acts from caprice alone.

capricious (642) fanciful, erratic, fickle.

The building of the Taj Mahal was considered a capricious whim by Shah Jahan's subjects.

carnage (383) slaughter, destruction, extermination.

The carnage at the Battle of the Somme in World War I destroyed the flower of the Allied and German armies.

cataclysm (644) a sudden upheaval that destroys or changes drastically.

The 1908 earthquake was a cataclysm that destroyed much of San Francisco.

cavil (140) faultfinding, objection.

Marylou's cavil about the place chosen for the picnic was disregarded by the other members.

clarion (25) clear, loud, shrill.

The clarion call of the ambulance sent cars scattering to the sides of roads.

commendably (434) admirably, in a manner worthy of praise.

The teacher was commendably generous in the extra time she put in to help students.

complacent (51) smug, self-satisfied, at ease.

Despite the early returns from urban areas, the senatorial candidate remained complacent, certain that the rural vote would turn the tide.

composure (165, 206, 576) poise, level-headedness, self-control.

The witness lost his composure on the witness stand and forfeited the sympathy of the previously well-disposed jurors.

conceits (58) fanciful ideas, concepts, imagination.

The conceits of television's *X-Files* have stirred the imagination of millions.

condescension (613) patronizing attitude or behavior, snobbery.

The aristocracy looked with condescension on the laboring classes that made their luxuries possible.

congenital (139) existing at birth, inborn, innate.

Congenital deafness may not be noticed in children until they are old enough to respond.

connoisseurs (405) experts, authorities, persons with good taste.

Connoisseurs of modern art enjoyed the exhibit of the works of Mark Rothko and Jackson Pollock.

consternation (407) dismay, confusion, bewilderment.

To the astronauts' consternation, a hatch on the Shuttle was stuck, forcing NASA to cancel the space walk.

consummate (345) complete, total, perfect.

Though some people criticize Pablo Picasso's subject matter, all agree that he was a consummate craftsman.

contentions (408) struggles, conflicts, debating points.

  The defense attorneys disputed the contentions of the plaintiffs that their client was on the scene of the crime at the critical times.

contrived (337) planned, schemed, designed.

  Nedra cleverly contrived to bring the hostile former partners together again.

convalescence (577) recovery of health, recuperation.

  After a long period of convalescence, with spirit unbroken, Peg Delaney slowly returned to health.

convulsive (361) agitated, unsettled, agonized.

  With a convulsive movement, Leona grasped her prepared speech and ran off the stage.

coquettishly (577) flirtatiously.

  In *Gone with the Wind,* Scarlett O'Hara acts coquettishly in the presence of Ashley Wilkes.

covetousness (592) greed, craving, desire.

  The covetousness of those already wealthy is a source of amazement to me.

covets (577) desires, craves, hungers for.

  One of the Ten Commandments warns, "Thou shalt not covet thy neighbor's house."

crannies (450) cracks, grooves, clefts, gaps.

  Mountain laurel somehow grows out of crannies in a rock face in the Appalachian Mountains.

D

dappled (7) spotted, mottled, variegated.

  The colt's hide was a dappled pattern of brown and white.

dastard (468) coward, weakling.

  Though Shakespeare's John Falstaff was a dastard in war, his sense of humor makes audiences love him.

dastardly (315, 336) cowardly, underhanded, deceitful.

  Mussolini's dastardly attack on Ethiopia aroused the world's conscience, but nothing was done to stop him.

dauntless (469) fearless, courageous, daring.

  Marcia's dauntless scaling of the cliff at El Capitan aroused the admiration of her fellow climbers.

debauchee (485) ne'er-do-well, one who is corrupted.

  In *Dr. Jekyll and Mr. Hyde,* the principal character turns from a respected physician to a debauchee of the worse kind.

deferential (145) respectful, obedient, subordinate.

  Uriah Heep was deferential to those he considered his social superiors.

demeanor (297) conduct, behavior, outward manner.

  Though she was but a simple girl, Cinderella's demeanor at the ball was that of a princess.

demoralized (24) disheartened, depressed, downcast.

  After two touchdowns had been scored against them, the home team seemed demoralized.

deprecated (168) played down, reproached, deplored.

After passing for the winning touchdown, John Elway deprecated his own achievement, giving credit to his offensive line.

deprecatory (229) apologetic, disapproving, belittling.

Whenever he was praised for his heroic act, Carl always made a deprecatory gesture as though the incident were really trivial.

deputation (102) committee, delegation.

A deputation from the striking workers met with the employers in the hope of finding a mutually satisfactory settlement.

desolate (301) barren, deserted, cheerless.

In the Greek myth, Andromeda was chained to a desolate crag until Perseus came to rescue her.

despondence (162) dejection, depression, melancholy.

The failure of his efforts for a peaceful world led President Woodrow Wilson into a state of deep despondence.

despondent (433) depressed, dejected, downhearted.

Ophelia became despondent over the death of her father at the hands of Hamlet.

despondently (665) hopelessly, dejectedly, sadly.

After receiving the failure notice for the bar exam, Matthew despondently called his parents.

despot (610) dictator, tyrant, ruler with absolute authority.

The president of Singapore has been called a despot by some, an enlightened leader by others.

desultory (142, 256) aimless, erratic, sluggish.

Frank made a few desultory comments to start the conversation, but when no one picked up the threads, he gave up altogether.

deteriorates (402) declines, goes downhill, worsens.

The quality of eggs deteriorates if kept in storage too long.

devastation (76) destruction, desolation, ruin.

During the blitz, the devastation in the inner city of London was extensive.

deviation (56) swerve, departure, turning.

Because of irregularities in the earth's magnetic field, the compass direction of north is a deviation from true north.

devoid (655) lacking, wanting, deficient.

At first, Ebenezer Scrooge seemed to be devoid of any human quality.

devotees (404) followers, adherents, disciples.

There are magazines published for the devotees of just about every sport or hobby.

diabolical (301) devilish, fiendish, evil.

Richard the Third's diabolical planning resulted in the murder of his brother Clarence.

diffuse (577) wordy, long-winded, rambling.

By the time Jim has finished his diffuse explanation, we listeners have forgotten what the topic is.

dire (140) dreadful, terrible, frightful.

Despite the dire warnings of a possible storm, the small boat sailed out of the harbor.

discerned (382) seen, observed, recognized.

>From the valley, two climbers could be discerned, scaling the steep walls of Looking Glass Ledges.

discernible (61) recognizable, apparent, visible.

> With no discernible reason or explanation, Charlotte broke off the conversation and stormed out of the house.

disconsolate (168, 620) heartbroken, dejected, despondent.

> Romeo was disconsolate when he came upon the apparently lifeless body of Juliet.

discreet (99) cautious, sensible, prudent.

> The Scarlet Pimpernel was too discreet to allow his true identity to be known.

dispersed (383) scattered, spattered.

> The Million-Man March on Washington dispersed after the program had been completed.

dissipated (293) self-indulgent, free-living, wasted.

> Though Dorian Gray led a dissipated life, it wasn't he but the painting that grew old.

dissonant (212) out of tune, discordant, grating.

> The heckler's insistent interruptions of the candidate's speech provided a dissonant note in an otherwise happy occasion.

distractedly (188) confusedly, absent-mindedly, excitedly.

> When Hamlet spoke distractedly, Polonius thought the Prince had gone mad over love of his daughter Ophelia.

docile (72, 315) passive, gentle, easily led.

> In the story of Androcles and the lion, the lion is docile so that Androcles can remove a thorn from his forepaw.

dossier (676) bundle of documents, detailed records.

> Before exposing the spy, the CIA had built a dossier of treasonous actions.

dote on (344) love excessively, adore, pamper.

> How can Angela dote on that ill-tempered, mangy, ugly mongrel?

dumbfounded (341) confused, astonished, bewildered.

> When I saw some pictures by the Hubble telescope, I was dumbfounded to see galaxies billions of light years away.

E

eddied (415) swirled, ran counter to the main stream.

> The wave eddied around the feet of the nervous bather.

effrontery (656) nerve, impertinence, impudence.

> Hitler had the effrontery to blame the Poles for starting World War II.

effulgent (620) radiant, brilliant, shining.

> Joseph, in his coat of many colors, was effulgent, the envy of his brothers.

effusively (260) generously, enthusiastically, exuberantly.

> Mrs. Bennet effusively greeted the young guests in the hope of finding a husband for one of her daughters.

elated (161) overjoyed, jubilant, thrilled.

> Marie was elated upon hearing the news of her acceptance at Swarthmore.

emaciated (145) gaunt, shriveled, haggard.
> The emaciated survivors of the Nazi death camps looked like living skeletons.

emanation (141) outflow, discharge, outpouring.
> An emanation from a radioactive substance can fog a photographic plate.

emancipated (99) freed, liberated, released.
> In 1833, all slaves throughout the British Empire were emancipated.

embellished (215) adorned, decorated, enriched.
> The medieval Books of Hours were embellished with fine decorations in gold and lapis lazuli.

encroached (486) intruded, moved in on, trespassed.
> The airport runways illegally encroached upon the wildlife preserve and had to be rerouted.

engrossed in (164,364) absorbed in, preoccupied with, involved with.
> When Daphne becomes engrossed in her trips on the Internet, the house could almost burn down around her with scarcely any notice.

enigma (574) puzzle, mystery, riddle.
> The motives of Fox Mulder in the *X-Files* often remain an enigma.

ennobled (24) honored, glorified, exalted.
> The human race is ennobled by the presence of men like Martin Luther King.

enormity (75) wickedness, cruelty, dreadfulness.
> In *Hamlet,* Queen Gertrude seems unaware of the enormity of Claudius's crime.

enshrouding (141) concealing, enveloping, enclosing.
> The cloud enshrouding Mt. Shasta lifted long enough for us to get a superb picture.

entente (101) understanding, agreement, treaty.
> By the end of the first day in college, the three girls had already established a kind of entente.

ephemeral (163) short-lived, temporary, fleeting.
> An athlete must realize that the roar of the crowd is an ephemeral blessing.

epoch (609) era, important period of time.
> The epoch of westward expansion in the United States ended with the 19th century.

equanimity (217) calmness, coolness, poise.
> Debbie Reynolds took the loss of her fortune with equanimity and decided to try again.

evade (337) avoided, shunned.
> In *Much Ado about Nothing,* the villains couldn't evade capture by the silliest, most inept constable in all of Shakespeare.

evasion (345) avoidance, escape.
> The fox used many evasion tactics to throw the hounds off the scent.

evasions (365) avoidances, bypasses, escapes.
> Most tax evasions are quickly uncovered by the IRS.

evoked (161) brought out, summoned, called forth.
> Falstaff's antics evoked as much laughter in Shakespeare's day as in our own.

exalted (233) uplifted, inspired, jubilant.

> After working with the Habitat crew for a week, Sharon felt both proud and exalted.

exemplary (659) praiseworthy, outstanding, admirable.

> Raoul Wallenberg led an exemplary life, devoting his energies to rescuing the Jews in Hitler's Europe.

exhilaration (195) high spirits, light-heartedness, elation.

> When the roller coaster begins its breathtaking drop, Bev and Stan feel a special sense of exhilaration.

exorbitant (613) excessive, unreasonable, too expensive.

> Some companies charge young customers exorbitant prices for common stamps.

expatriate (214) exile, one who lives outside his native country.

> An expatriate in Venice for many years, George felt a sudden yearning to be back on his native soil.

expatriates (402) those not living in their native countries, exiles.

> After World War I, Ernest Hemingway joined a group of American expatriates living in Paris.

explicate (242) explain, interpret, analyze logically.

> The detective had to explicate the meaning of the coded message in Edgar Allan Poe's "The Gold Bug."

extraneous (460) nonessential, irrelevant, inappropriate.

> Solving a crime requires eliminating all extraneous clues and focusing on those that seem relevant.

extricate (654, 675) disentangle, free, unbind.

> An addicted gambler usually falls deeper into debt while trying to extricate himself from losses already incurred.

exultation (553) rejoicing, gladness, joy.

> After crossing the goal line, the running back lifted his arms in a gesture of wild exultation.

F

facetious (384) humorous, comical, witty.

> Some stand-up comics pride themselves on being able to make a facetious remark on any political occasion.

fanaticism (296) single-mindedness, infatuation, excessive enthusiasm.

> Extremists in every group are characterized by closed minds and fanaticism.

fastidious (139) critical, finicky.

> The fastidious Carl Butler didn't notice the tomato stain on his own necktie.

fawning (288, 536) flattering, insincere.

> A strong, confident leader does not like to be surrounded by fawning assistants who never provide contradictory insights.

felicitations (659) good wishes, congratulations, greetings.

> The entire community joined in offering felicitations to the mayor and his bride.

fettered (501) chained, shackled, bound, hampered.
>   When the defendant entered the courtroom, he was fettered, hands and feet.

firmament (488) the sky.
>   At sunset, the entire firmament was aglow with a radiance that brightened the landscape.

floridly (417) radiantly, fussily, showily.
>   Chet speaks too floridly for me, using ten words where one would do.

flout (479) disdain, scorn, denounce.
>   Terence's tendency to flout rules of sensitive behavior has lost him most of his friends.

forbore (62) ceased, gave up, refrained.
>   After five useless attempts at solving the puzzle, Dick finally sighed and forbore.

formidable (270) feared, menacing, powerful.
>   The Dallas Cowboys were formidable opponents, but the Packers managed to eke out a victory.

fretful (270) irritable, ill-tempered, sulky.
>   Maurya was fretful because she hadn't heard from Tim in over a month.

furtive (143, 630) secret, sly, stealthy.
>   Elizabeth Bennet stole furtive glances at the proud but handsome Mr. Darcy.

furtively (164) secretly, cunningly, stealthily.
>   Our cat furtively eyed Samson's bowl before grabbing a piece of meat and running.

futile (145) useless, vain, ineffective.
>   Trying to disprove the four-color map theory seems to be a futile exercise. Four colors will be enough for any map.

G

garner (418) gather, store, collect.
>   We saw Danny Wuerffel, Florida quarterback, garner more and more trophies for his football skills.

garrulous (660) talkative, long-winded, prattling.
>   The garrulous old man told anyone who would listen how he sank the winning basket in the Ohio State game fifty years before!

genial (242) pleasant, cordial, cheerful.
>   The unexpected Thanksgiving guests proved to be genial and helpful.

germane (59) closely related, relevant, allied.
>   Unless the matter was proved germane to the trial, the judge did not allow the evidence to be used.

girth (163) size, dimension, body measure.
>   As the man of huge girth headed for the narrow airplane seat next to mine, I wondered if we'd have room.

gist (189) substance, essence, core.
>   Edward Everett spoke at length, but Abraham Lincoln in his brief Gettysburg Address better summed up the spirit of the occasion.

grotesque (25) weird, abnormal, repulsive.

> In the Disney version, the grotesque image of the Hunchback of Notre Dame was modified by the character's warmth.

gusto (99) enthusiasm, zest, delight.

> The family attacked the pumpkin pie with gusto and soon disposed of it.

H

hackneyed (502) overdone, commonplace, shopworn.

> The humorous poet Ogden Nash poked fun at hackneyed experiences and expressions.

haggard (578,622) gaunt, emaciated, exhausted.

> After a week wandering around the forest, the two boys emerged looking gaunt and weary.

havoc (381) destruction, ruin, devastation.

> The tornado played havoc with the new trailers in Golden Crest Park.

heinousness (269) nastiness, viciousness, sinfulness.

> The heinousness of Macbeth's crimes eventually turned former friends against him.

heretic (479) nonbeliever, skeptic, freethinker.

> Joan of Arc, who was burnt at the stake as a heretic, was canonized in 1920.

homogeneous (300) of one nature, similar, of uniform structure.

> In their zeal for new observations, bird-watchers are a homogeneous group.

hue (129) color.

> The dominant hue of the wild rose is red, but the color is not pure.

humility (453, 634) humbleness, meekness, mildness.

> Mahatma Gandhi showed true humility of spirit in all his actions.

I

ignominy (425) dishonor, disgrace, shame.

> The so-called ignominy of defeat is often a harmful and needless emotion.

illusory (166) misleading, deceptive, fanciful.

> Though Columbus's dreams of reaching Asia were illusory, the magnitude of his achievement was proved by later events.

imminent (364) approaching, impending, threatening.

> The imminent arrival of the French ambassador had the entire White House staff on red alert.

impact (427) shock, clash, collision.

> Scientists around the world watched the impact of the comet's crash into the surface of Jupiter.

imperative (656) necessary, unavoidable, required.

> The Allies felt it imperative to establish a beachhead in Normandy before the ultimate destruction of the German army could begin.

imperceptible (36) slight, unnoticeable, subtle.

> By almost imperceptible motion at first, the tide began to inch slowly up the beach.

implore (581) appeal to, beg, plead.

> Desdemona tried to implore Othello for mercy, but he was unyielding.

impotently (34, 659) powerlessly, helplessly, weakly.

> Mussolini's armies attacked Ethiopia while the rest of the world looked on impotently.

impoverished (406) poor, poverty-stricken, strained.

> Sir Walter Scott's efforts to earn enough money to get out of bankruptcy almost impoverished him.

impudence (318) insolence, impertinence, rudeness.

> The impudence of an undisciplined six-year-old may evolve into the alarming and uncontrollable revolt of the teenager.

impunity (339) lack of punishment, immunity, reprieve.

> In India, Mother Teresa can walk into the most dangerous areas with impunity.

inaccessible (642) unapproachable, impassable, unreachable.

> The Spanish parador near Cadiz was perched on a seemingly inaccessible mountain crag.

inanimate (37) lifeless, sluggish, dead.

> To the astronauts, the surface of the moon, though inanimate, glowed with exotic beauty.

inarticulate (145) unclear, soundless, indistinct.

> Some of the greatest thinkers have been relatively inarticulate in ordinary conversation.

incipient (211) beginning, becoming apparent.

> An incipient sore throat often warns of a cold to come.

incisive (679) penetrating, sharp, piercing.

> The reviewer's incisive criticism of the play helped the performer to improve.

incoherently (64) in a wild, rambling disconnected way.

> In *Treasure Island,* Ben Gunn's voice rambled incoherently, but throughout could be heard the word *cheese.*

incongruous (494) inappropriate, out of place, conflicting.

> At the White House, Woody Allen's sneakers seemed incongruous with his formal attire.

incredulity (313) disbelief, mistrust, doubt.

> The unprovoked attack on Pearl Harbor was at first greeted with incredulity by the American public.

indignity (99) insult, mistreatment, discourtesy.

> The snobbish socialite considered it an indignity to be seated at a side table rather than on the dais.

indulgent (231) tolerant, pampering, permissive.

> The children of parents who are too indulgent often cry out for help and discipline.

inebriate (485) drunken, intoxicated.

> In "Arthur," Dudley Moore plays a character who is inebriate through a good part of the film.

ineffectually (62) ineffectively, useless, fruitlessly.

> After trying the front door lock ineffectually for several minutes, Alice realized that she had been using the wrong key.

706

ineptitude (165) awkwardness, incompetence, unfitness.

   The prosecutor's ineptitude in handling the case practically guaranteed an
   acquittal.

inexorable (145) inescapable, fated, destined.

   Credit-card users often forget that there is an inexorable law that discour-
   ages unresolved debt.

inexplicable (217, 426) unexplainable, baffling, bewildering.

   The inexplicable outbreak of certain diseases presents an unending challenge for research scientists.

infatuation (462) loss of sound judgment, foolish attachment, unwise passion.

   What seemed at first, to friends of Romeo, like a mere infatuation with
   Juliet proved to be a profound love.

infusion (194) saturation, immersion, injection.

   An infusion of new blood into South Florida revitalized many older quiet areas.

ingenuously (577, 664) openly and sincerely, innocently.

   Othello ingenuously believed Iago's deceitful insinuations about Desdemona.

inimical (164) harmful, dangerous, hostile.

   Democracy is always threatened by the inimical forces of racism, intolerance, and bigotry.

intact (679) unbroken, perfect, whole.

   If the package is returned intact, you will be entitled to a full refund.

interloper (214) intruder, interferer, trespasser.

   In Cinderella's family, she felt alone, an interloper.

interpolated (405) inserted, injected.

   Scholars try to separate the original words of William Shakespeare from
   the interpolated lines of other playwrights or even actors.

introspective (477) thoughtful, meditative, reflective.

   Geraldine is an outgoing extrovert; Beth is more introspective.

intrusive (164) meddlesome, bothersome, prying.

   "Pardon me for being intrusive," interrupted Jonathan, "but your coat is
   dragging in the mud."

intuitively (434) instinctively, spontaneously, involuntarily.

   In general, animals seem to select intuitively the foods that are best for them.

invalidate (292) make void, revoke, disprove.

   A missing punctuation mark may sometimes invalidate a will or other
   document.

invincible (74) unconquerable, invulnerable.

   The invincible armies of the invading Tartars swept across Europe to the
   gates of Vienna.

iridescent (215) shimmering, glittering, lustrous.

   A drop of rain on a window pane can cast an iridescent glow when the
   sun appears.

J

jettisoned (218) discarded, tossed out, expelled.

   When Jack heard the previous speaker's talk, he jettisoned his prepared
   speech and decided to talk without notes.

L

lacerated (64) torn, mangled, wounded.

> An examination after the accident showed that Larry's forearm was lacerated, but no bones had been broken.

laconic (341) concise, brief, to the point.

> When asked by the press for particulars about the crime, the detectives remained laconic and noncommittal.

lamentable (663) distressing, regrettable, unfortunate.

> Carson's lamentable pre-election commercials actually lost more potential voters than they won.

languid (204, 634) listless, inactive, sluggish.

> Wealthy young ladies in Jane Austen's novels often struck a languid pose around potential suitors.

languor (312) weakness, faintness, listlessness.

> During the filming of *The African Queen,* the humid, tropical atmosphere often induced a feeling of languor in the stars.

legacy (296, 406) inheritance, heirloom, bequest.

> The conspirators' assassination of Julius Caesar left a legacy of hate that eventually proved their undoing.

limpid (216) clear, transparent, straightforward.

> The limpid turquoise waters of Lake Louise have provided inspiration for photographers for a century.

loathsome (63, 631) disgusting, offensive, vile.

> Certain special effects in horror movies are loathsome but impressive.

lowering (271) gloomy, dismal, threatening.

> The lowering clouds on the western horizon were motivation enough to turn the sailboat around and head for the dock.

ludicrous (63) ridiculous, amusing, laughable.

> Some of Garry's solutions for the budget deficit were ludicrous to the members of the Camera Club.

lugubriously (62) mournfully, gloomily, sadly.

> Spots howled lugubriously at being put out into the cold, if only for a little while.

lurching (51, 364) staggering, swerving, tottering.

> The sudden turn on the narrow-gauge railway to Skagway had us all lurching and grabbing for something to hold onto.

luxuriant (288) abundant, overflowing.

> The tropical greenhouse showed a luxuriant growth of flowering shrubs and trees.

M

maelstrom (242) whirlpool, disorder.

> The water running down a bathtub drain forms a miniature maelstrom as it disappears.

malediction (589) curse.

> The prisoner's last words were a malediction on those who first led him into crime.

malignant (143) hostile, deadly.

> The malignant curse of drugs is threatening the stability of the American family.

malignantly (536) evilly, hatefully.

> When Hitler wrote malignantly about the Jews in *Mein Kampf,* he foretold his actions upon coming into power.

mandate (99) command, decree, order.

> The new Congress believed that it had received a mandate for change.

manifest (371) apparent, evident, obvious.

> The true intentions of Benito Mussolini were made manifest when he invaded Ethiopia.

mendicant (65, 613, 654) beggar, member of a certain religious order.

> In oriental society, a mendicant is often a holy man, not an outcast.

mete (679) allot, distribute, apportion.

> In his decisions, King Arthur tried to mete out justice to his petitioners.

meticulous (141) precise, exact, conscientious.

> His meticulous calculations convinced Clyde Tombaugh that the new planet Pluto would be found just about where he looked.

misanthropic (639) cynical, unsociable, antisocial.

> The misanthropic ways of Ebenezer Scrooge were altered when the ghosts of Christmas appeared to him.

misconception (24) misunderstanding, misjudgment.

> The belief that doubling a medicine's dosage will double the benefits is a common misconception.

monologue (286) a speech by one person.

> When Dan talks about his glory days in football, we are subjected to a long and exhausting monologue.

morose (424, 629) gloomy, somber, melancholy.

> Tad's morose disposition made him an unpopular member of the bird-watching expedition.

morosely (664) gloomily, somberly, glumly.

> After losing the crucial game, the coach morosely faced the media for the post-game show.

munificence (465) generosity, extravagance.

> In Shakespeare's play *Timon of Athens,* the central character showers his munificence upon his friends, only to be scorned by them in his later hour of need.

murky (76) gloomy, dismal, bleak, hazy.

> The murky interior of the cafe was heavy with smoke.

N

nautical (500) naval, maritime, pertaining to the sea.

> A nautical mile is slightly longer than the unit used on land.

nocturnal (217) pertaining to night.

> Though the raccoon is generally a nocturnal animal, a family of raccoons struts in our backyard in the late afternoon.

nostalgia (162) longing for the past, homesickness.

In *Citizen Kane,* the word *Rosebud* reveals a deep nostalgia for a childhood experience.

novice (374) beginner, learner, apprentice.

When Tiger Woods joined the professional ranks of golfers he was already a seasoned veteran, not a novice.

O

obdurate (613) obstinate, stubborn, unbending.

King Claudius urged Hamlet to look upon him as a father, but Hamlet remained obdurate in his rejection.

obeisance (613, 652) mark of respect or submission.

The curtsy that ladies give before Queen Elizabeth is a form of obeisance.

oblivious (214) unaware, unmindful, distracted.

When Norma works at her computer, she is oblivious to outside noises.

obscene (168) indecent, immodest, vile.

Certain lines from the movie were considered obscene and cut.

obscure (189) conceal, hide, cloak.

To obscure the real purpose of his aggression, Adolf Hitler pretended to invade Czechoslovakia to protect a German minority.

obscured (51) concealed, hidden, overshadowed.

When, during the total solar eclipse, the moon had completely obscured the disk of the sun, an eerie twilight awed the previously noisy crowd.

obsession (328, 664) control, mastery, fixed idea.

Charles Babbage's obsession with mechanical calculating machines foreshadowed the rise of electronic computers a century after his death.

officious (465) interfering.

An officious clerk at a public agency like the motor vehicle bureau can be a source of irritation to those waiting on line.

opaque (534) nontransparent, impervious to light.

The neighboring chimneys had poured forth so much soot, the house windows were almost opaque.

ornate (407) showily decorated, elaborate, luxurious.

The ornate details of New Orleans houses never fail to charm tourists.

ostentatious (163) showy, flashy, flamboyant.

An ostentatious lifestyle does not characterize the actions of many wealthy Americans.

P

pallet (112) small, hard, temporary bed.

When the family arrives for Thanksgiving, someone has to sleep on a pallet in the TV room.

pandemonium (91) confusion, turmoil, uproar.

Pandemonium broke loose when a cage with snakes accidentally fell to the floor and opened.

paradoxical (300) apparently contradictory.

> Mild Aunt Grace's love of football seems paradoxical until you know her better.

peccadillo (593) petty offense, slight sin, minor shortcoming.

> Terry's most obvious peccadillo is his listening only to his own half of a conversation.

pelt (73) bombard, beat steadily, assail.

> From the window, we watched the hailstorm pelt the land with golfball-sized stones.

perceptible (166) recognizable, noticeable, unconcealed.

> When the villain was revealed in Act Two, a perceptible murmur ran through the audience.

perceptions (483) sensations, impressions, insight.

> False perceptions of Adolf Hitler's motives gave Hitler a head start in rebuilding his powerful army.

peremptorily (337) dictatorily, arrogantly, autocratically.

> James Bond's voice rang out peremptorily, "Stand where you are!"

peremptory (299) compelling, commanding, decisive.

> Our beagle is a free spirit who responds only to peremptory commands.

perspicacity (418) sharpness, insight, awareness.

> Todd's perspicacity and keen eye for good art helped him discover a forgotten Wyeth in an attic.

perturbation (139) restlessness, alarm, turmoil.

> There was perturbation in the locker room when it was announced that the star player would be suspended for the next two games.

pinnacle (400) high point, summit, top.

> For a professional football player, to win the Super Bowl is to reach the pinnacle of success.

placard (560) poster, notice posted in a public place.

> After election, candidates are supposed to remove all placards from public buildings.

placatingly (654) soothingly, moderately, calmly.

> After Timmy's outburst over the broken toy, his mother spoke placatingly, attempting to calm him down.

placid (25, 376) peaceful, calm, tranquil.

> The placid surface of the lake in early morning was unruffled by any breeze.

plaintive (628) sad, melancholy, sorrowful.

> The plaintive call of the mourning dove has given the bird its name.

polytheism (302) a religion with many gods.

> The Greek pharaoh Akhenaton replaced the polytheism of ancient Egypt with the worship of one god: the sun.

ponderous (141) bulky, massive, weighty.

> Despite his ponderous bulk, the detective moved lightly across the room.

portly (25) stout, plump, stocky.

> After many years, I found my once-slender friend quite portly.

prepossessing (338) attractive, pleasing, charming.

The famous architect Frank Lloyd Wright made a prepossessing appearance with his high collar, porkpie hat, and dramatic cape.

presentiment (655) premonition, foreboding, misgiving.
> When the visitor entered the House of Usher, he had a presentiment of tragedy to come.

pretensions (676) claims.
> The pretensions of Bonnie Prince Charlie to the British throne eventually came to nothing.

pretext (580) excuse.
> On the pretext of showing her the latest stamps he had received, Bob managed to see Marie nearly every night.

prolix (636) wordy, long-winded, rambling.
> The prolix report of the membership committee soon had the other members nodding.

propitiate (272) soothe, conciliate, appease.
> When the god Thor sent his thunderbolts crashing over the land, the Norse sought to propitiate him.

propitiating (371) appeasing, soothing, satisfying.
> Propitiating possibly angry gods is a major element in primitive religions.

prostrate (611) stretched out, lying flat, completely overcome.
> The nervous councillor fell prostrate at the feet of the shogun and began to speak.

protean (218) changeable, variable, flexible.
> Marilyn Monroe was noted for her protean moods, some negative, others leading to some of her finest acting moments.

provocation (293) something that arouses, stimulates, moves to action.
> For his attack upon Poland in 1939, Hitler used a manufactured provocation.

prudence (580) good judgment, practical wisdom.
> By managing affairs with prudence, the executors of Elvis Presley's estate increased its value many times over.

psychic (141) spiritual, mystical, extrasensory.
> So-called psychic givers-of-advice solicit gullible customers in many cheap magazines.

pulsating (57) throbbing, beating, palpitating.
> Doctors studied the pulsating of the man's heart on the electrocardiograph.

Q

quaffed (468) drank deeply.
> John Falstaff quaffed a pint of ale before setting out to war.

quay (560) wharf, landing place.
> The high tides associated with the hurricane caused beach erosion and damaged the quay.

R

ravaged (381) ruined, plundered, sacked.
> Europe was ravaged by the Black Plague on several terrible visitations.

rebuff (643) rejection, refusal, snub.

> Despite many rebuffs, Margaret Mitchell persisted and finally sold the manuscript of *Gone With the Wind*.

rebuke (232) scold, reprimand, reproach.

> King Arthur had to rebuke Sir Bedivere for not tossing the sword Excalibur back into the lake as he had been ordered.

recapitulated (342) summarized, reviewed, restated.

> After discussing all safety precautions for the hike, the leader recapitulated what he had said just to make sure.

recluse (484) hermit, loner, solitary person.

> Until the arrival of the little girl Eppie, Silas Marner was a recluse, avoiding other people.

redoubtable (588) awesome, causing fear of alarm.

> In *Auntie Mame,* the main character is a redoubtable lady who lives life to the full on her own terms.

refuted (408, 654) disproved, discredited, denied.

> Galileo refuted the popular belief that the sun revolves around the earth.

relentlessly (130) strictly, harshly, ruthlessly.

> For three days, the northeast wind relentlessly attacked the sand dunes and caused considerable beach erosion.

renounce (485) give up claim or right to, give up, refuse.

> Edward VIII renounced the throne of England because of his love for an American divorcée.

rent (377) hole, tear, rip.

> The rent in the new jacket showed where Sybil had caught it on a protruding nail.

repercussions (17) reactions, recoils, rebounds.

> The repercussions from the assassination of John F. Kennedy were felt around the world.

repudiate (654) reject, cancel, disapprove.

> During the English Wars of the Roses, both sides were quick to repudiate treaties, no matter how recently made.

repugnance (328) disgust, queasiness, revulsion.

> It took a full week for Caroline to overcome her repugnance at dissecting a frog in the biology lab.

repugnant (63) repulsive, disagreeable, offensive.

> At first, the thought of leaving home for college was repugnant to Marianne, but she gradually warmed to the idea.

resignation (631) surrender, submission, yielding.

> Charles Darnay accepted with resignation his condemnation to death.

resolution (460) solving of the problem.

> Some of the situations on television's *X-files* have no clearcut resolution, allowing the listener to provide his own solution.

resonant (73) resounding, echoing, full-bodied.

> James Earl Jones' resonant voice can reach the top seats in any theater without amplification.

resumé (342) summary, synopsis, digest.

> Sheila presented her resumé to the personal director and waited for her first question.

reticent (142) close-mouthed, quiet, reserved.

> Though somewhat reticent with adults, young Norma was a chatterbox when with her friends.

retorted (292) replied, answered, responded.

> "Did you know," the young lady commented to George Bernard Shaw, "that there are only two English words beginning with *su* and pronounced *sh:* sugar, and sumac?" Shaw retorted, "Surely!"

retributive (145) deserved.

> Greek tragedies are tales of retributive justice on a vast scale.

revel (130) celebrate, enjoy, carouse.

> Romeo and Juliet reveled in their love, though they feared for the future.

rigorous (337) strict, relentless, severe.

> In reality more crimes are solved by rigorous police work than by intuition.

ritualist (299) someone excessively devoted to set forms.

> Even eating a simple meal, Drew is a ritualist, selecting only one vegetable at a time.

S

sadistic (242) cruel, taking pleasure in the pain of others.

> In Dickens' *David Copperfield,* Mr. Murdstone seems to take a sadistic delight in making David unhappy.

sagacity (377) shrewdness, clear thinking.

> The steadiness and sagacity of the football commissioner was demonstrated by his strict enforcement of the anti-drug code.

sage (480) wise man, master, authority.

> Lao-tzu, a possibly legendary sage of ancient China, is the father of Taoism.

sallow (339) sickly, pale, unhealthy-looking.

> The liberated prisoners emerged into the sunlight, sallow, and wasted in frame.

scourge (470) affliction, misfortune, someone or something to inflict pain.

> The nomadic Mongols rode west, becoming the scourge of eastern and central Europe.

scrupulously (645) precisely, extremely carefully.

> The referee followed the rule book scrupulously.

scrutinizing (593) examining, inspecting, studying.

> After scrutinizing the stamp with the inverted center, the experts pronounced it a fake.

scuttled (204) hurried, scurried, shuffled.

> The cattle egrets scuttled through the field, looking for insects.

sedate (415) serene, self-posssessed, calm.

> My grandmother is a sedate old lady with a mischievous sense of humor.

sediment (55) deposit, dregs, grounds.

> The sediment at the bottom of the water boiler proved to be mostly iron.

seething (25) rushing, boiling, furious.

> Though Jeremy was seething inside, he managed a forced smile and a greeting when his old enemy appeared.

self-indulgence (455) pursuit of pleasure, dissipation, selfishness.

   The self-indulgence of Roman Emperors like Caligula finally destroyed them.

sensibility (56) sensitivity, acuteness, awareness.

   Jane Austen's *Sense and Sensibility* contrasts the common elements: reason and emotion.

sensuous (139) luxurious, sumptuous, relating to the senses.

   The Hawaiian surf, with its sensuous warmth, filled Diane with pleasure.

sepulchral (360) mournful, woeful, gloomy.

   In his black clothes and hat and with his sallow complexion, Mr. Dolby gave a sepulchral appearance.

serene (215, 534) peaceful, calm, at peace.

   Our cat Tammy rules the entire family with serene self-assurance.

serenity (544, 644) peacefulness, calmness, stillness.

   Though Terry's business world was hectic, his own home provided the serenity that refreshed his spirit.

shambling (621) shuffling, tottering, walking awkwardly.

   Shambling footsteps outside the door announced the arrival of the hunchback of Notre Dame.

sheen (471) brilliance, glow, luster.

   The metallic automobile paints have a sheen that ordinary paints cannot produce.

siblings (427) children having a common parent.

   Elizabeth Bennet lives with her siblings in a house they are destined to lose upon their father's death.

singularly (344) exceptionally, uniquely, remarkably.

   With his height and great reflexes, Michael Jordan was singularly adept in the game of basketball.

sorrel (7) light chestnut horse.

   Among the pure-white Arabians was a lively sorrel, conspicuous by his color.

spewing (243) spurting, gushing.

   The volcano was spewing hot lava.

steadfast (42) steady, direct, constant.

   Columbus remained steadfast in his belief that he had reached the shores of Asia.

stereotyped (181) overdone, shopworn, lacking originality.

   Seinfeld's Kramer was stereotyped as an acrobatic comic, but he wanted to break out of that rigid perception.

stiletto (589) kind of dagger.

   The stiletto has a blade thick in proportion to its length.

stodgy (336) dull, boring, tiresome.

   On first meeting, Dan seemed a stodgy, uninteresting fellow, but once on the topic of minerals, he became a spellbinder.

strident (679) harsh-sounding, shrill, rasping.

   The strident voice of the speaker reached every corner of the huge auditorium.

stringent (407) strict, severe, demanding.

   In an effort to curb drunk driving, the state issued new stringent regulations involving the amount of alcohol in the blood.

sublimity (215) nobility, grandeur, loftiness.

  The sublimity of the message in the Twenty-third Psalm chokes me with emotion.

subtlety (589) slyness, cleverness, artfulness.

  Iago's devilish insinuations about Desdemona were given with a subtlety that completely tricked Othello.

succinct (374) brief and to the point, concise, condensed.

  Jerry's telegram to his parents couldn't be more succinct: "We won!"

succumbed (676) surrendered, admitted defeat, died.

  In about 1670 B.C., the Egyptian forces succumbed to the Hyksos, who are known as the "shepherd kings."

sundry (407) miscellaneous, assorted, diversified.

  Shopping with Leo means coming home with chocolates, hard candies, and sundry other sweets.

superficial (454) shallow, trivial, without substance.

  The superficial charm of a cheat often tricks trusting homeowners.

suppressing (655) restraining, curbing, blocking.

  Suppressing any natural animosity they may have felt toward each other, the cat and the pet rabbit became fast friends.

surmise (656) conjecture, guess.

  My surmise that Holly won a scholarship proved to be correct.

surmounted (573) topped, towered above, overcome.

  The house, nestled against the hillside, was surmounted by towering cliffs.

surreptitiously (101) secretly, stealthily, slyly.

  Before being taken from the room, Charles surreptitiously left a message under the telephone for his brother.

swaggered (226) walked in an arrogant, pompous manner.

  When Jason swaggered into the room, all conversation momentarily ceased.

swarthy (269, 312) dark-complexioned, dark-skinned.

  Years under the desert sun had turned her blond brother into a swarthy stranger.

T

taciturn (317) shy, reserved, close-mouthed.

  When Brett is bored, he becomes taciturn and distant.

taunting (72) mocking, ridiculing, insulting.

  After taunting Romeo and Mercutio, Tybalt kills Mercutio in a duel and is then slain by Romeo.

thwarted (467) frustrated, foiled, checked.

  In England, Guy Fawkes Day celebrates the day the authorities thwarted the Gunpowder Plot to blow up the Houses of Parliament.

torpor (636) inactivity, sluggishness, lethargy.

  During the rain and heat of the monsoon season, travelers to India experience an overwhelming torpor.

tractability (365) obedience, willingness, submissiveness.

  Many mustangs when treated gently and calmly become models of tractability.

transcendent (588) extraordinary, surpassing, beyond comprehension.

When Sylvia glimpsed the Taj Mahal by moonlight, it was a transcendent moment, never to be forgotten.

transience (211) impermanence, briefness, brevity.

Great art is often concerned with the brevity of life and the transcience of beauty.

transitory (217) temporary, short-lived, fleeting.

Some celebrities discover too late that fame can be transitory.

truisms (298) self-evident truths.

In our democracy we accept as truisms the rights so often lacking elsewhere in the world.

tryst (293) lovers' meeting, rendezvous.

The arranged tryst in the tomb of the Capulets turned into tragedy for Romeo and Juliet.

tumultuous (216, 629) agitated, wild, boisterous.

The tumultuous crowd decided to storm the Bastille and set the prisoners free.

tumultuously (18) wildly, turbulently, fiercely.

The soccer fans celebrated tumultuously when England defeated Italy.

U

unabated (243) undiminished, continuing.

The barking of the neighbor's dog continued unabated throughout the night.

unassuming (423) modest, humble, low-key.

In the *Star Trek* series, Dr. Spock's generally unassuming manner underplayed his technical skill and profound understanding of his fellow staff members.

unfathomable (75) past understanding, unknowable, profound.

The best literature gives readers a glimpse into the unfathomable depths of the human soul.

unhinged (339) unbalanced, unnerved, confused.

Ophelia thought that Hamlet's mind had become unhinged because of unrequited love for her.

unison (621) at the same time, in perfect agreement.

When Mark entered, the guests lit the lights and shouted "Surprise!" in unison.

unobtrusive (271) inconspicuous, modest, shy.

The journalist's unobtrusive manner won over the interviewer's confidence and produced a lively dialogue.

unrequited (159) not returned or reciprocated.

The unrequited love of Cyrano de Bergerac for the beautiful Roxanne is one of the world's bittersweet stories.

unwarranted (365) uncalled for, not justified, inappropriate.

To his loyal soldiers, any attack on their leader Robert E. Lee was unwarranted.

urchin (276) mischievous youngster.

Whenever Sherlock Holmes had a special assignment in London, he called upon a streetwise urchin.

usurper (612) one who takes the place of another, often without right.

> The defeated Yorkist factions in England after Bosworth Field considered Henry VII a usurper.

V

veered (343) turned, swerved, changed direction.

> Just when the forest fires seemed out of control, the wind veered and eased the threat.

vehemently (622) earnestly, keenly, eagerly.

> Though the suspect vehmently protested his innocence, he was taken to the station house for questioning.

verily (679) certainly, truly in fact.

> Harold chuckled: "Verily I say unto you that we'll win tonight's hockey game."

veritable (675) real, genuine.

> Before the battle of Agincourt, King Henry V was a veritable tower of strength for his men.

vexed (552) irritated, angered, annoyed.

> The witness was vexed by the probing questions the plaintiff's lawyer kept asking him.

vigilance (407) watchfulness, wariness, caution.

> Every scholar of history knows that eternal vigilance is the price of liberty.

voluble (273) talkative, fluent, glib.

> The suspect was voluble in his protestations of innocence.

volubly (407) talkatively, wordily, fluently.

> Though eyewitnesses put the suspect at the crime scene, he volubly protested his innocence.

vortex (76) whirlpool, eddy.

> The threatening vortex of the approaching tornado sent everyone scurrying to the safest places to wait out the storm.

vouchsafed (50) granted, bestowed, allowed.

> The authorities vouchsafed Anderson's return to America.

W

warily (372) carefully, cautiously, prudently.

> Travis warily approached the plover's nest, hoping for a clear picture.

warrant (465) guarantee, authorization, approval.

> Hamlet gave gifts to Ophelia as a warrant of his affections.

whimsicalities (58) fanciful ideas, absurdities.

> The whimsicalities of Ogden Nash's mind are displayed in the humorous verse he created.

wince (424) flinch, draw back, shrink.

> The long-suffering members of the Cotter family wince when Dan begins to practice his violin.

wincing (51) flinching, recoiling, cringing.

> Though wincing with pain from a foot blister, Sampras played out the match.

wistful (62) melancholy, sorrowful, forlorn.

>With a wistful look back at his native land, Robert Louis Stevenson set out for the South Seas.

wry (622) twisted, lopsided, witty.

>Samantha's wry expression suggested that she disagreed with Meg's comments.